MAKING THE MOST OF

OFFICE 97

FOR IBT III

ANGELA BESSANT

Heinemann Educational Publishers,
Halley Court, Jordan Hill, Oxford OX2 8EJ
A division of Reed Educational & Professional Publishing Ltd

Heinemann is a registered trademark of Reed Educational & Professional Publishing Limited

OXFORD MELBOURNE AUCKLAND JOHANNESBURG BLANTYRE GABORONE
IBADAN PORTSMOUTH NH (USA) CHICAGO

First published 1999
2002 2001 2000 99
10 9 8 7 6 5 4 3 2 1

A catalogue record for this book is available from the British Library on request.

ISBN 0 435 45543 5

Designed by Wendi Watson

Typeset by TechType, Abingdon, Oxon

Printed and bound in Great Britain by Thomson Litho Ltd, East Kilbride, Scotland

Screenshots reprinted with permission from Microsoft Corporation

Contents

Introduction

This book covers the syllabus for the OCR/RSA Integrated Business Technology (IBT) Level III qualification, but it would be equally useful for anyone wanting to advance their skills in Microsoft Office 97. It assumes competence in Microsoft Office 97 to OCR/RSA IBT Level II (this includes word processing, spreadsheet, database, graphical representation and integration skills) and is the natural progression from the book *Learning to Use Office 97 for CLAIT and IBT II.* The quick reference guides at the end of chapters will serve to refresh topics that were covered in detail in the aforementioned book.

The disk accompanying this book contains files for practice exercises and assignments that will be used to demonstrate skills step by step, together with files for the Full Practice Assignment given in Part 2.

Part 1 covers and revises skills required for success in this qualification.

Part 2 contains a Full Practice Assignment.

Also included are the syllabus for IBT III, specimen answers to the exercises and an appendix containing hints and tips and forms for you to complete as you work through the assignments.

The RSA IBT III scheme

For the RSA IBT III qualification candidates need to demonstrate competence in the following areas (applications used in this book are given in brackets).

- Electronic communications (Outlook Express)
- File management (Windows Explorer)
- Source data processing (Access and Excel)
- Automated presentation production (PowerPoint)
- Publication production (Word)

You are given a scenario together with accompanying files and tasks that need to be completed in a certain time limit.

This book covers all the skills necessary to gain competence at this level. Part 1 is broken down into chapters which concentrate on each application program in detail, giving step-by-step guidance, practice and quick reference guides. The examples and exercises are based around the scenario, 'Naturetrail Holidays' (see below). The same scenario is the basis for the Full Practice Assignment in Part 2. Here you are able to consolidate your skills as you work through the exercises. At this stage the emphasis is on dealing with information (in hard copy and electronic format) and on following and carrying out instructions accurately to produce the required results. There are further hints and tips on achieving these goals.

Specimen answers to exercises are given at the end of the book. At this level, you have a considerable amount of freedom over layout, etc and so you may notice that the answers do not always look exactly like yours. However, you must check that all criteria have been met. Your tutor will be able to advise you.

The syllabus and assessment details are provided on page 160 and other useful information including changing default settings, file management, document layout and forms for completion while undertaking the assignments, etc is to be found in the appendix.

Scenario

You work for a company called Naturetrail Holidays. This organisation has properties for rent during the spring and summer months. The annual presentation to regional offices is about to take place.

The Publicity Officer will be doing the presentation and will need help in preparing materials that will be presented to regional office staff. You have been asked to help by extracting information stored in the database and spreadsheet files and to include this information in a publication and an automated presentation.

The publication will consist of a four-page leaflet (which will be used in conjunction with the annual brochure). The automated presentation will be on display in the foyer from the presentation day onwards.

You will need to access files from the accompanying disk in order to carry out some of the assignments. *So that you always have access to the original files, it is* ***essential*** *to make a copy of the disk before starting on any of the exercises.*

Note: During an actual assignment the scenario files are e-mailed to you. As you work through the exercises, you will need to note down details on a File Store Record Sheet. This can be found in the appendix.

INFO

There are many ways of performing a task in Windows 95 and Office 97 applications – for example, via the keyboard, using the mouse or using the menus. For simplicity, the practical exercises usually show one method. There will, however, be instructions for other methods in the quick reference guides or in the appendix. You will then be able to decide which is the best method for you.

Note: In this book the terms **click on**, **select** and **press** are used to distinguish between mouse, menu and keyboard actions. For example:

Click on: the **Save** button
From the **File** menu, select: **Save**
Press: **Ctrl + S**

Getting help

There are quick reference guides at the end of chapters and useful information in the appendix. In addition, in all Office 97 applications there is a **Help** menu, or pressing **F1** will activate the **Help Topics** dialogue box. There is also the Office Assistant. Throughout the book, I have hidden this facility so as not to be distracted from the main objectives. More details on the Office Assistant can be found in the appendix.

PART 1

Explanation and exercises

Chapter 1

Electronic communications using Outlook Express

1 Getting started

In this section you will learn how to:

- understand electronic mail (e-mail) basics
- load Outlook Express
- understand the Outlook Express window
- create messages
- transmit messages
- route/address messages
- exit Outlook Express.

1.1 Understanding electronic mail (e-mail) basics

Electronic mail (e-mail) is a method of sending information from one computer to another. You can send and receive the electronic equivalent of letters, faxes, pictures and sound. Some organisations have their own internal e-mail systems for communications between colleagues. Others are connected to the Internet in order to send and receive e-mail locally and internationally. It is a quick and efficient means of communication. It has the advantage that you can send and receive your messages when you choose (unlike telephone communication). Due to its flexibility and cost effectiveness, it is being adopted at an ever-increasing rate.

This chapter focuses on sending and receiving e-mail using Microsoft Outlook Express 4. In demonstrating the methods used by Outlook Express you will gain an insight into the procedures involved even though you may be using a different e-mail system. It should be relatively easy to apply what you learn here to your own e-mail system.

Note: Since Outlook Express can be configured to suit your needs, the Outlook Express settings used in this chapter may differ slightly from your settings. This could result in some of the methods given not conforming exactly to those you may see on your computer.

1.2 Loading Outlook Express

Load Outlook Express.

METHOD 1 **1** In the Windows 95 desktop, click on: the **Start** button – a menu appears.
2 Select **Programs** by moving the mouse over it – another menu appears.
3 Select: **Internet Explorer** – another menu appears.
Click on: **Outlook Express** (Figure 1.1).

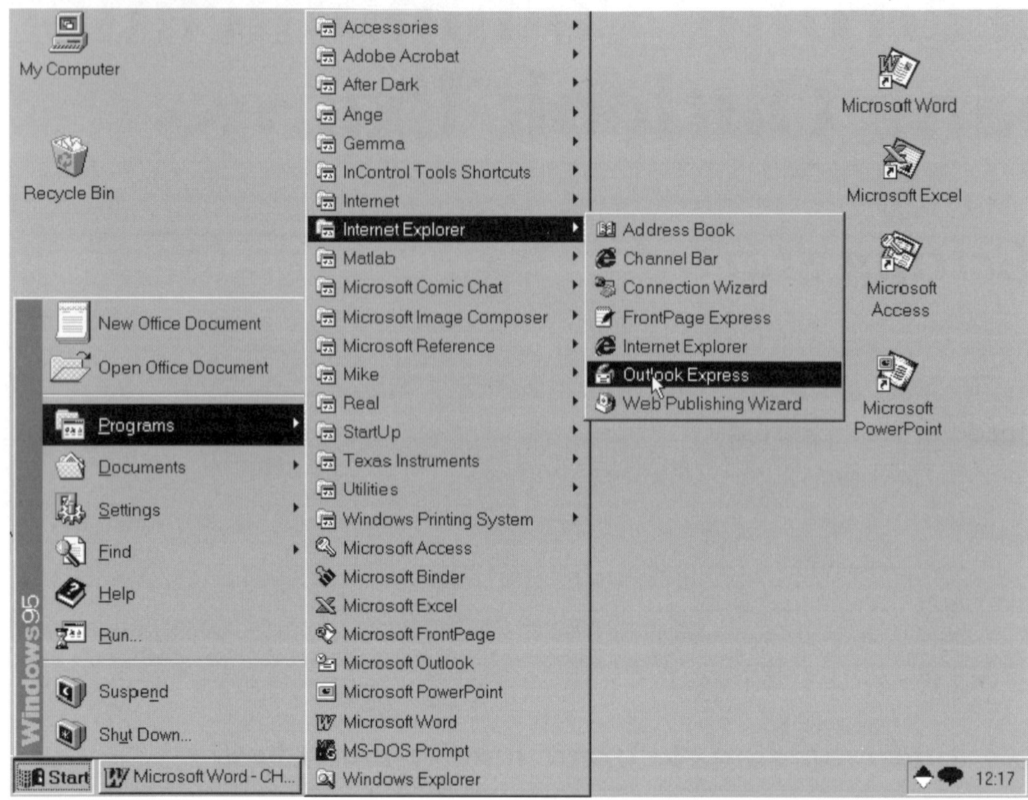

Figure 1.1 Loading Outlook Express from the Start menu

METHOD 2 *(Use this method if you have a shortcut icon to Outlook Express on your desktop.)*
1 In the Windows 95 desktop, click on: the **Outlook Express** shortcut icon:

Either method will result in the Outlook Express window being displayed on screen (Figure 1.2).

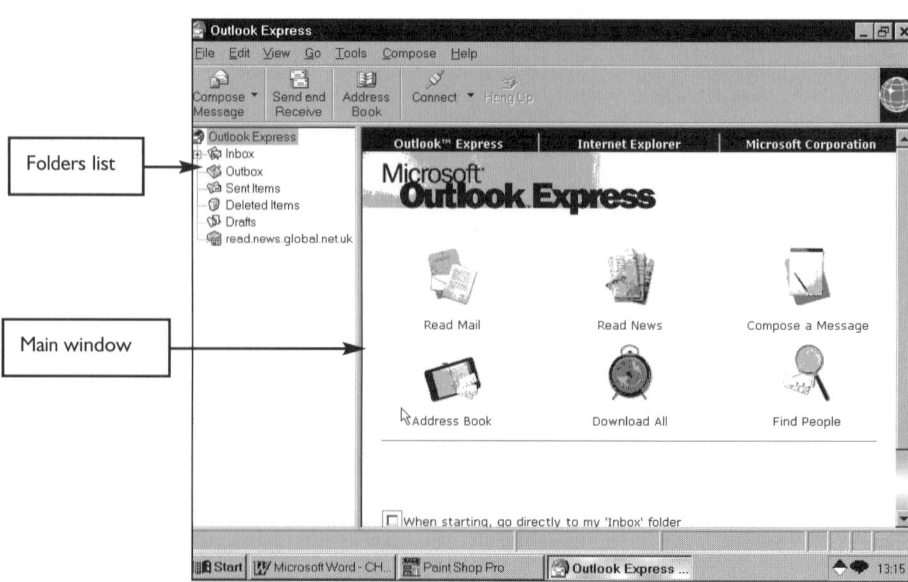

Figure 1.2 Outlook Express window

The Folders list contains:

- Inbox folder – where incoming messages are stored
- Outbox folder – where outgoing messages are stored
- Sent Items folder – where sent messages are stored
- Deleted Items folder – where deleted messages are stored
- Drafts folder – where draft messages are stored.

The main window displays shortcuts for commonly used activities.

1.3 Creating messages

Create the message shown below and send it to someone you know who has an e-mail address.

Note: If you do not have anyone to send it to, then send it to your own e-mail address.

Hi there [insert person's name]

I am learning how to use e-mail. Please let me know if you have received this message.

Thanks.

[Insert your name.]

METHOD

1 Click on: the **Compose Message** button (see Figure 1.2):

The New Message window appears (Figure 1.3).

2 Click in the **To**: box and enter the e-mail address of the person you are sending the message to. Check that you have keyed in the address correctly.

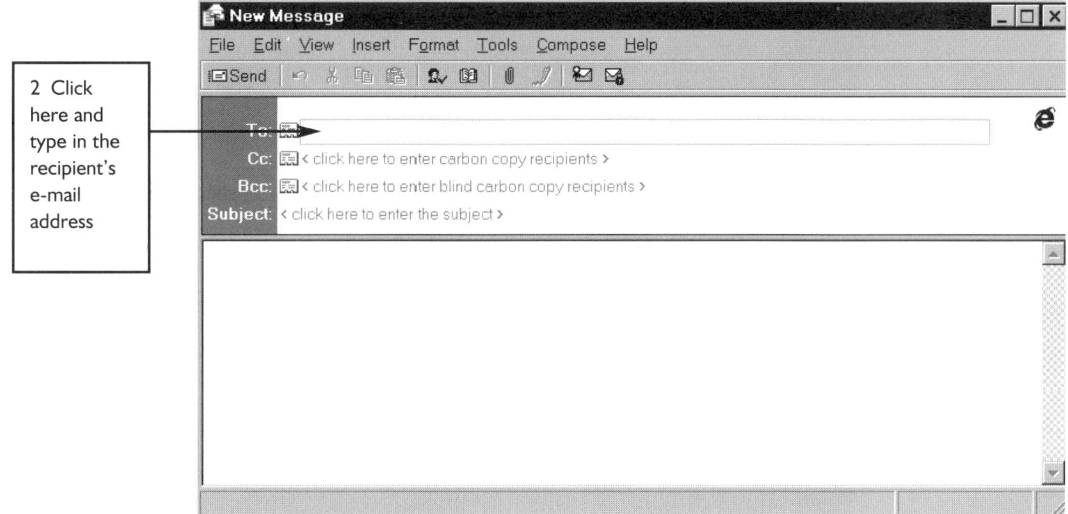

Figure 1.3 New Message window

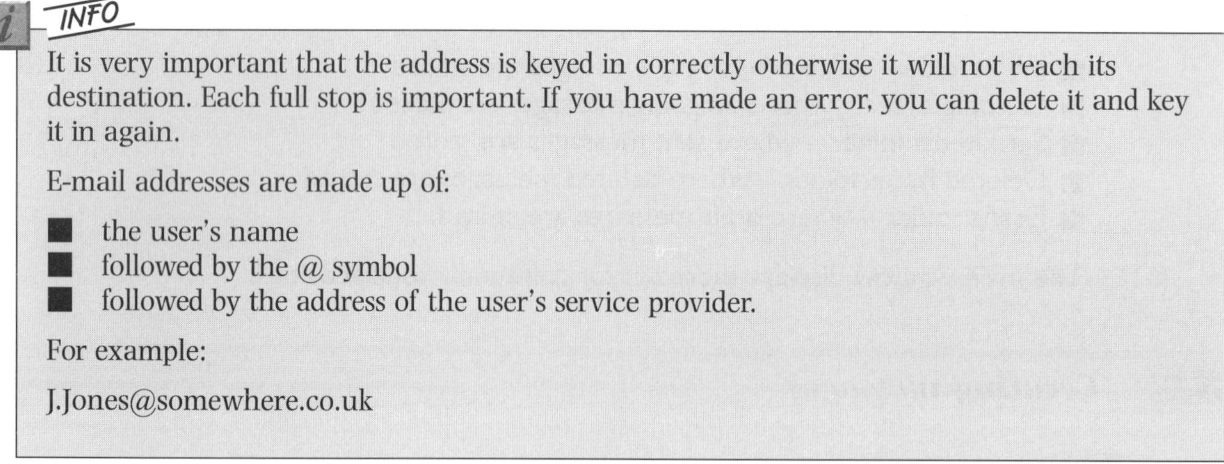

INFO

It is very important that the address is keyed in correctly otherwise it will not reach its destination. Each full stop is important. If you have made an error, you can delete it and key it in again.

E-mail addresses are made up of:

- the user's name
- followed by the @ symbol
- followed by the address of the user's service provider.

For example:

J.Jones@somewhere.co.uk

3 Click in the subject line, and key in: **Just testing**.
4 Click in the space underneath and key in the message, as shown in Figure 1.4.

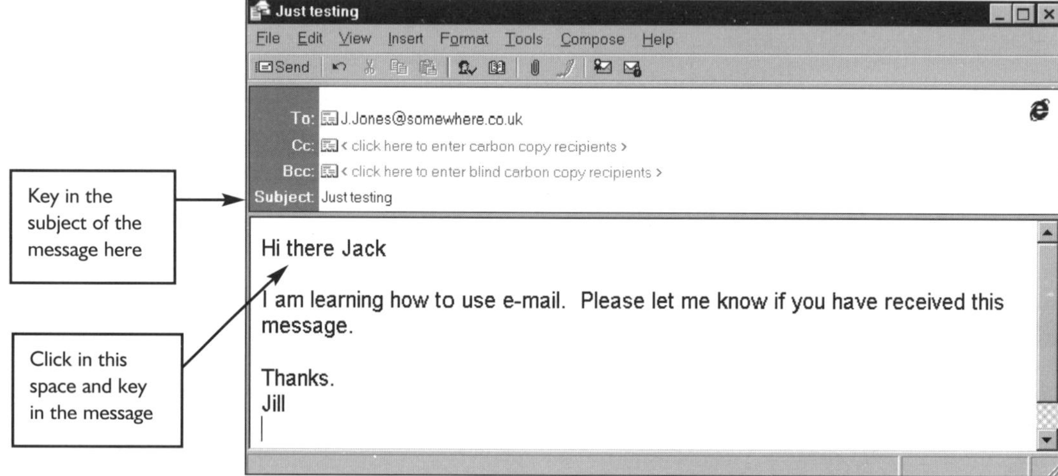

Figure 1.4 Creating a message

Note: The subject of your message **Just testing** has replaced **New Message** on the Title bar.

5 Click on: the **Send** button

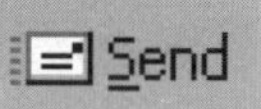

Note: This will not send the message at this stage but will transfer it to your Outbox folder. The message in Figure 1.5 may appear (depending on your settings).

Figure 1.5 Send mail

Click on: **OK**

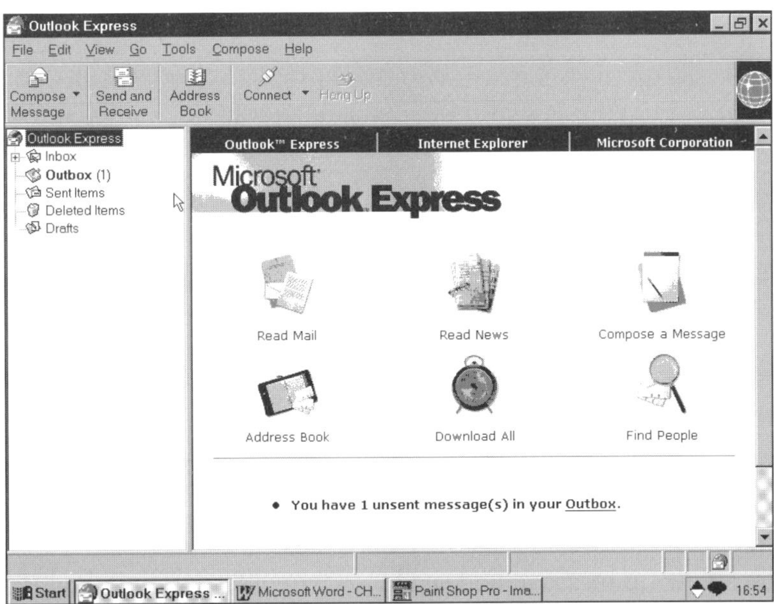

Figure 1.6 Outlook Express main window

6 You are returned to the original Outlook Express window (Figure 1.6). You can see that your Outbox now has a (1) next to it and there is a message in the main window:

You have 1 unsent message(s) in your <u>Outbox</u>.

(You may need to use the scroll bar to scroll down in order to see the above message.)

i INFO

You have composed your message 'offline' – ie not connected to the phone line and therefore not incurring phone costs. When you have learnt how to use e-mail, it is a good idea to compose several messages and then send them all at the same time since there is a minimum phone call charge. They will be stored in your Outbox folder until you are ready to send them but in this example we are sending just one message. Outlook Express will automatically check if there are any incoming messages at the same time as sending messages.

1.4 *Transmitting messages*

Transmit the message you have prepared.

METHOD

1 Click on: the **Send and Receive** button:

2 Outlook Express will send the message automatically and will display that it is sending the message.

3 When it has been transmitted, it is placed in the **Sent Items** folder. Click on: the folder to check.

Outlook Express can be set up to connect/disconnect automatically from the phone line. If this is not set you will need to do this manually and you should be prompted to do so. When you are connected to the phone line, the following icon will be visible on the Taskbar:

Right-click on this icon for a menu with the option to disconnect.

1.5 *Routing/addressing messages*

The same message can be sent to more than one address at a time.

Compose the following message and send it to two different e-mail addresses:

Just to remind you that due to the weather the annual barbecue has been postponed and will now take place next Wednesday. Please e-mail me to confirm that you can still come.

Thanks

[Your name]

There are several ways to send the same message to more than one person. Two methods are shown below. Method 1 sends the messages on equal terms to both recipients. In Method 2 the main recipient is the person in the **To**: box, with a 'carbon copy' sent to the second addressee. Use this method only if you are asked to 'cc' the message to the second recipient.

METHOD 1

1 In the **To**: box, key in in the e-mail addresses and separate them with semi-colons. For example:

J.Jones@somewhere.co.uk;A.Smith@somewhereelse.co.uk

Note: You don't need a space after the semi-colon.

METHOD 2

1 In the **To**: box, key in the first person's e-mail address.
2 In the **Cc**: box, key in the second person's e-mail address.

Create the message (as in Section 1.3) and transmit the message (as in Section 1.4) to the two addresses.

Note: The message is again placed in your **Sent** folder and is still treated as one message, even though it has been transmitted to two different addresses.

1.6 *Exiting Outlook Express*

Exit Outlook Express.

METHOD

From the **File** menu, select: **Exit**.

2 Receiving and printing attachments

In this section you will learn how to:

- access received messages
- print messages including records of transactions
- attach files to messages
- view attached files.

2.1 Accessing received messages

Exercise 1

Access messages received.

Note: If you have not yet received a reply to your e-mails then you will need to send an e-mail to your own e-mail address as a demonstration, so that you have a received message.

METHOD

1 Load Outlook Express as in Section 1.2 (if not already loaded).

2 You will notice that there is a number next to your Inbox folder (Figure 1.7).

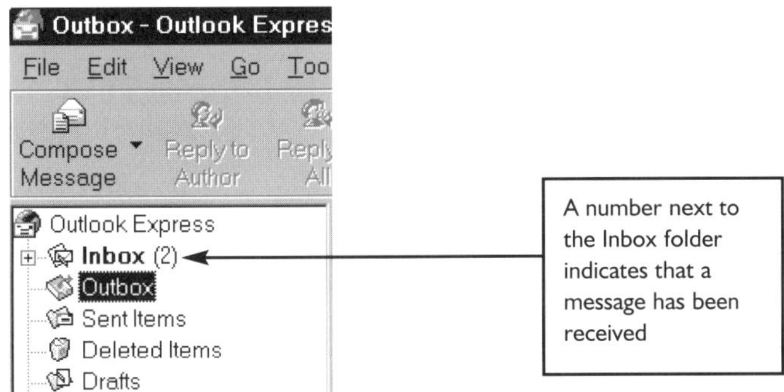

Figure 1.7 Inbox folder

3 Click on: **Inbox**. The message(s) will be displayed in the right-hand window.

4 Click once on the message to see it in the Preview window – bottom right – (Figure 1.8), or double-click on it to see it in a separate window.

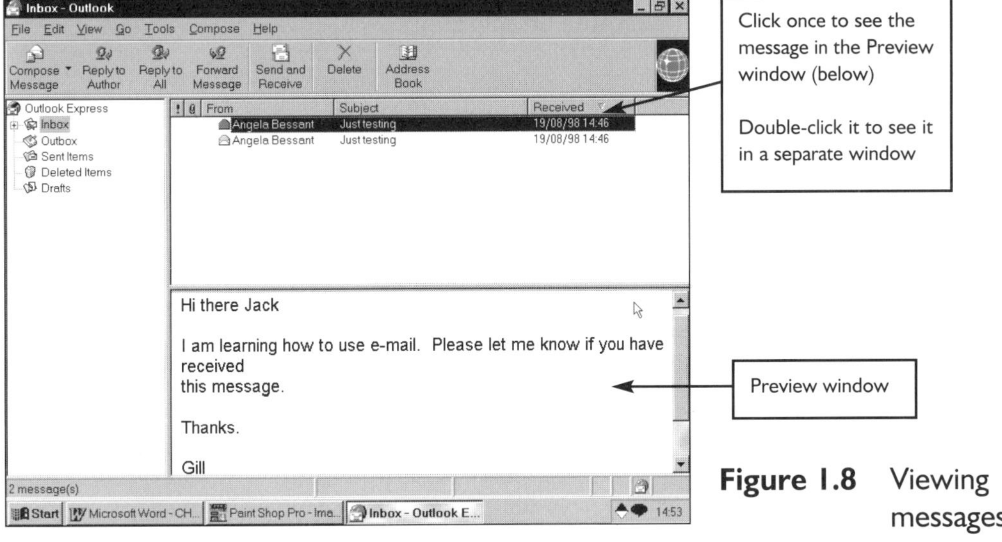

Figure 1.8 Viewing messages

2.2 Printing messages including records of transactions

Sometimes you may want to print an e-mail message (this is a requirement for IBT III).

Exercise 2 Print a copy of a message you have received.

METHOD

1 Ensure the message is visible in its own window (see Section 2.1.4 above).
2 From the **File** menu, select: **Print**; the Print dialogue box appears.
3 Check that the printer is ready and loaded with paper.
4 Click on: **OK**.

INFO

You will notice that your printed copy includes transaction details. This is required for IBT III.

2.3 Attaching files to messages

Sometimes you may want to enclose something with your message, eg a picture or a different type of file. In such cases you can add a file to your message. This is called an attachment. You can add more than one file. These are then called attachments.

Exercise 3 Create a simple Excel or Word file. Save the file with the filename **TEST**. Send a message, together with the file **TEST** (the attachment), to an e-mail address. Ask the recipient to send you an attachment back.

METHOD

1 Create a simple file and save it with the name **TEST** in a place where you will know where to find it (eg on a floppy disk in drive A).
2 Load Outlook Express and key in the following message:

> Hi [name of recipient]
>
> I am practising sending and receiving attachments to e-mail messages. Please find the attached file TEST.
>
> Please could you let me know that you have received this and also please could you send me an example attachment?
>
> Thanks.
>
> [Your name]

Note: Do not click send yet.

3 Click on: the **Attach File** toolbar button:

4 The Insert Attachment dialogue box appears.
5 Select the drive where the file is located, eg Drive A.
Click on: the file so that it appears in the **File name:** box (or key in the filename).
6 Click on: **Attach** (Figure 1.9).

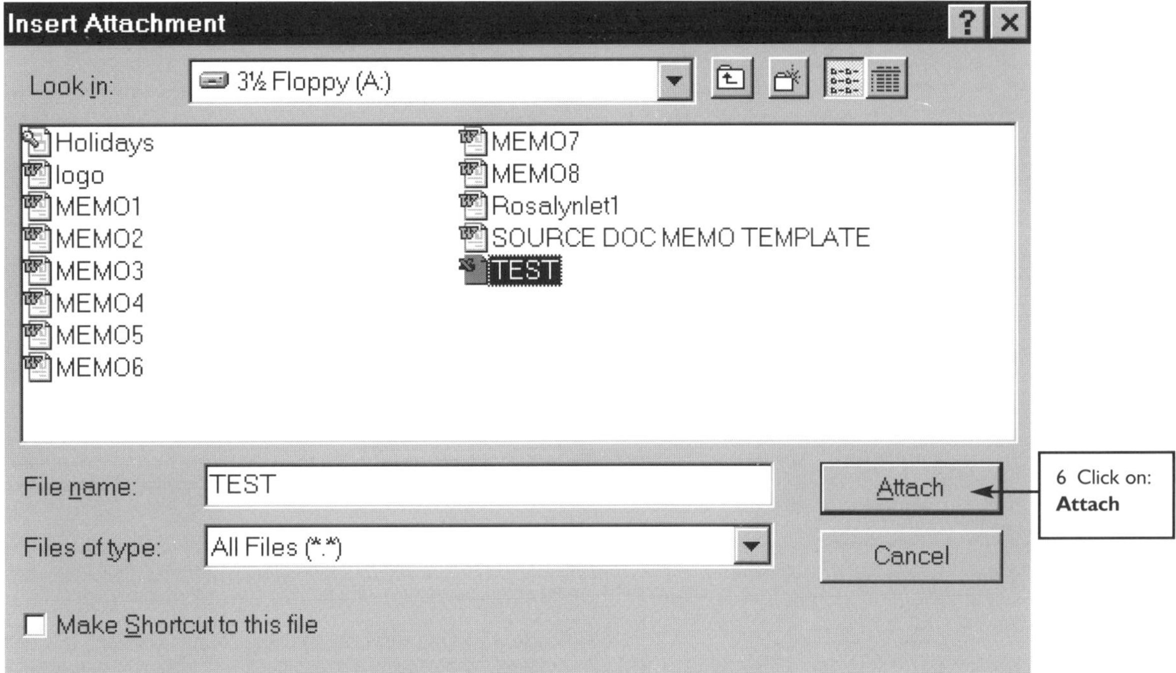

Figure 1.9 Insert Attachment dialogue box

7 You will notice that your attachment is now shown below your message (Figure 1.10).

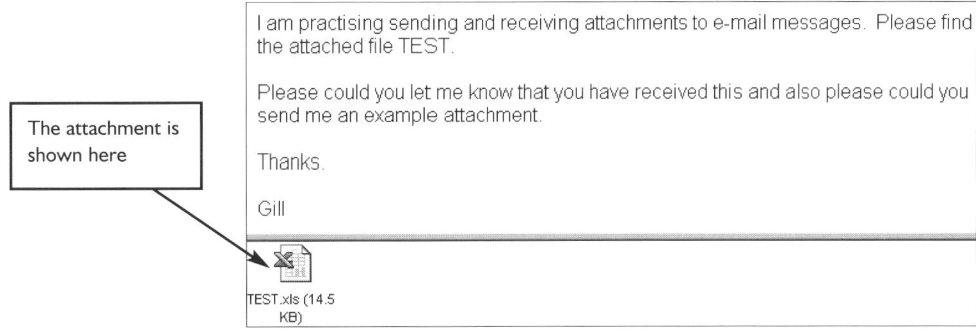

Figure 1.10 Attachment icon

8 You can now send the file in the normal way.

INFO

You can attach more than one file to a message by repeating steps 3–6 for each extra file.

2.4 *Viewing attachments*

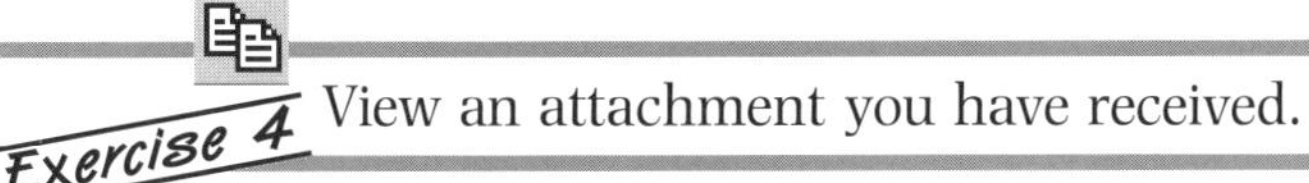

View an attachment you have received.

METHOD

When you receive a message with an attachment, the message has a paperclip icon next to it, as shown in Figure 1.11.

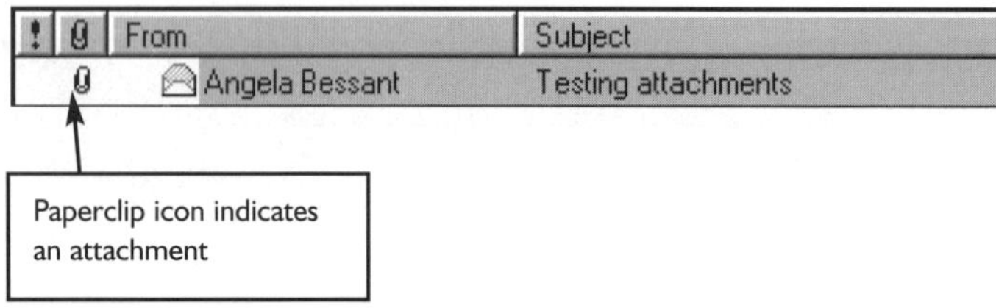

Figure 1.11 Attachment received icon

1. Double-click on: the message to view it in a separate window.
2. Double-click on: the attached file (Figure 1.12). The file will appear in its own program window.

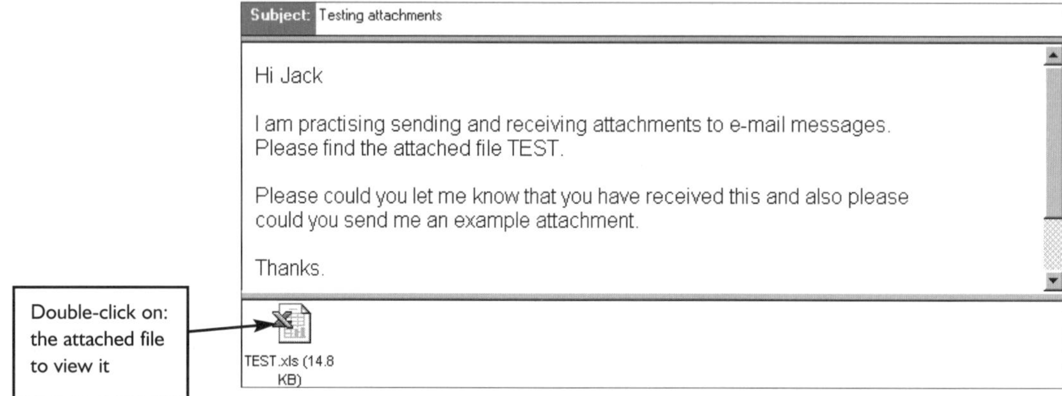

Figure 1.12 Opening an attachment

3. When you have finished viewing the file, close its window in the normal way. You are returned to Outlook Express.

For IBT III you need to print e-mail messages showing attachments. With some e-mail applications, this is simply a matter of using the **File** menu and selecting the **Print** option. In this case you will need to have the message, in its entirety, on screen together with the attachments in the window below. Press the **Print Scrn** key on the keyboard. Open Word and click on: the **Paste** button. The message and attachments (screen shot) will be pasted into the Word document. From the **File** menu, select: **Print** and print in the usual way.

2.5 *Exit*

Exit Outlook Express as shown in Section 1.6.

Outlook Express quick reference for IBT III

Action	Keyboard	Mouse	Right-mouse menu	Menu
Access received messages		Click: **Inbox** in left-hand window Click: the message (to view in Preview) *or* Double-click: the message (to view in own window)		
Attach files to messages		Click: the **Attach File** button		**Insert**, **File Attachment**
Create messages		Click: the **Compose Message** button		
Exit Outlook Express		Click: the Close window button		**File**, **Exit**
Load Outlook Express	In Windows 95 desktop			
		Double-click: the **Outlook Express** shortcut icon		**Start**, **Programs**, **Internet Explorer**, **Outlook Express**
Print messages	(With transaction details and message visible in its own window)			
	Ctrl + P	Click: the **Print** button		**File**, **Print**
Print messages with attachments	(With transaction details, message and attachments visible) Press: **Print Scrn** Open Word			
	Ctrl + V **Ctrl + P**	Click: the **Paste** button Click: the **Print** button	Select: **Paste**	**Edit**, **Paste** **File**, **Print**
Route/address messages *Multiple recipients*	Key in the address in the **To**: box Separate addresses with semicolons (;) Use **Cc** box to send a 'carbon copy'			
Transmit messages	**Ctrl + Enter**	Click: the **Send and Receive** button		**File**, **Send**
View attachments	(With message in its own window – attachment visible)			
		Double-click: the attachment		

Hints and tips

Common errors made when completing IBT III assignments:

- Double-check that you have keyed in the *exact* e-mail address.
- Have you attached the correct file(s), and only the correct file(s), to the e-mail message?
- Have you printed out a message and transaction details when requested?
- Ensure you have disconnected after sending/receiving messages.

There are many more features to Outlook Express which are beyond the scope of this book. Experiment with the menus and toolbar buttons. Use the online Help to find out more about topics you are particularly interested in.

Chapter 2

File management using Windows Explorer

1 Getting started

In this section you will learn how to:

- start Explorer
- create directories/folders
- create subdirectories/subfolders
- manage files
  - save/name
  - retrieve
  - copy/move
  - delete
- record file storage details
- exit Explorer.

This chapter concentrates on Windows Explorer to demonstrate file management, although some file management can be carried out within programs like Word and Excel (see the appendix).

Note: Much of this chapter was covered for the IBT II qualification, but is repeated here for revision purposes.

Windows Explorer allows you to view all the folders and files on your computer. It can be used for disk and file management.

Windows 95 uses the word 'folder' and not 'directory'. Older versions of Windows refer to folders as directories.

When carrying out the following exercises, if you suspect things have gone wrong, pressing the **Esc** key will usually cancel a command in progress.

1.1 Starting Explorer

From the **Start** menu, select: **Programs**, then **Windows Explorer**. The Explorer window appears. Figure 2.1 shows the $3\frac{1}{2}$ Floppy (A:) drive selected in the left window; the contents of the disk in drive A are displayed in the window on the right.

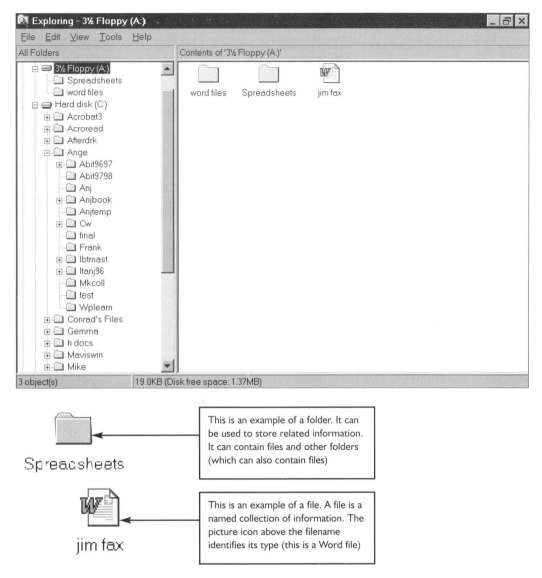

This is an example of a folder. It can be used to store related information. It can contain files and other folders (which can also contain files)

This is an example of a file. A file is a named collection of information. The picture icon above the filename identifies its type (this is a Word file)

Figure 2.1 Folders and files

Displaying the contents of a folder

Double-click on: the folder.

It is better to double-click on the icon rather than the text as, sometimes, you will not get the action you expect (if you have not double-clicked properly). Instead a box may appear around the text, waiting for your input. If this happens, press the **Esc** key and try again.

1.2 *Creating a new folder*

You can create new folders in which to store related documents. This is always good practice as it makes for easier location of files. Always give folders and files meaningful names that you will be able to remember at a later date.

Create a folder on the floppy disk in drive A. Name the folder **Practice**.

METHOD

1 With a disk in drive A, in the left-hand (All Folders) window, click on: **3½ Floppy (A:)**.
2 The contents of the floppy disk in drive A are displayed in the right-hand (Contents) window.
3 Right-click in the white space of this window: a menu appears (Figure 2.2).

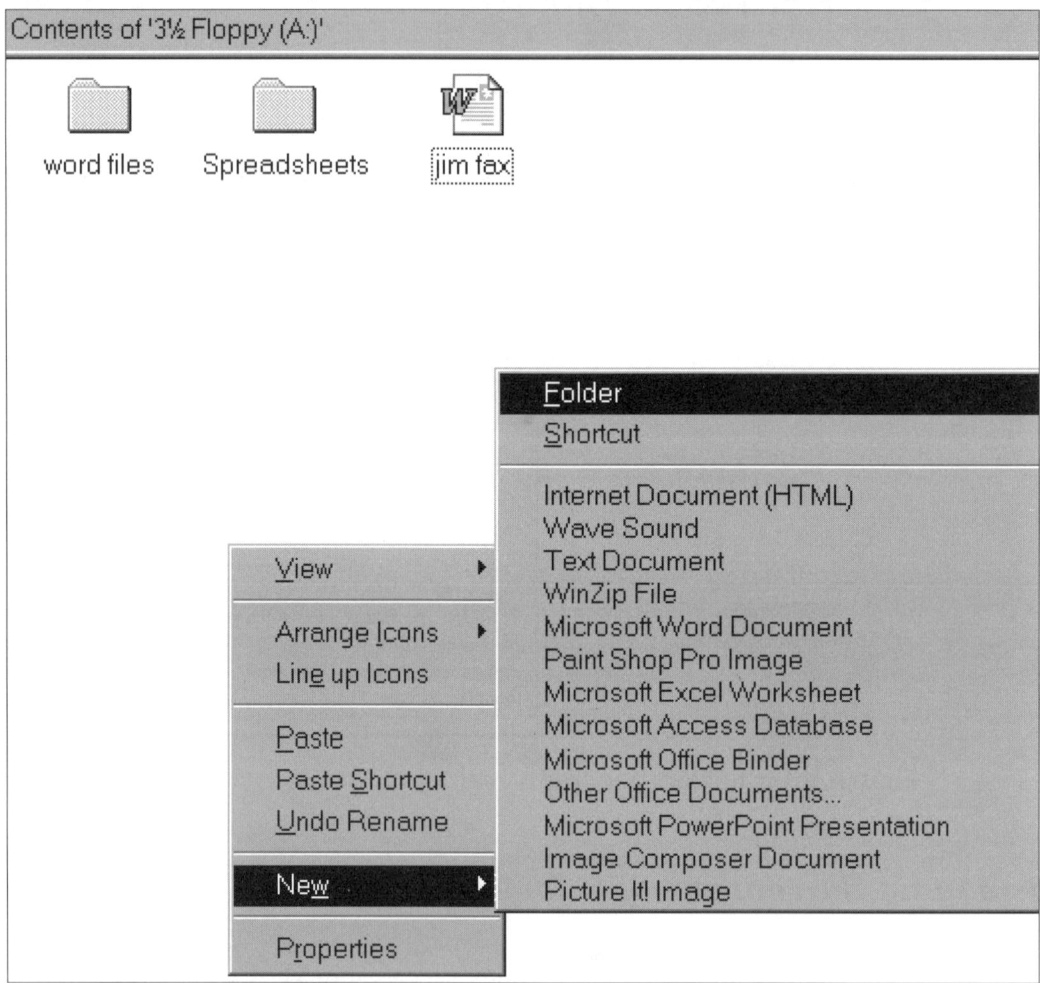

Figure 2.2 Contents window

4 Select: **New** and then **Folder**.
5 Key in a name, **Practice** for the new folder and press **Enter** (Figure 2.3).

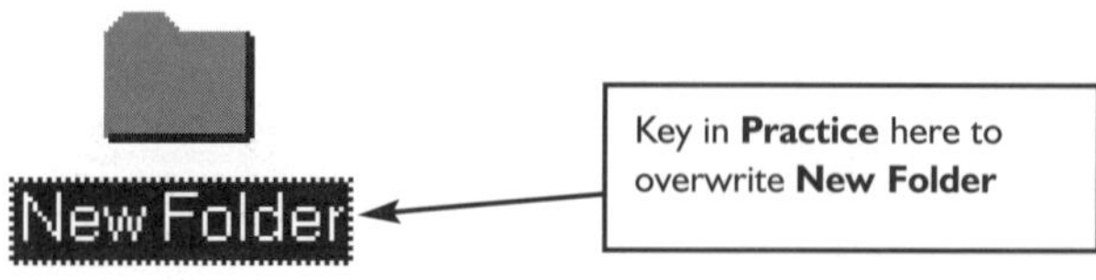

Figure 2.3 New folder

1.3 Creating a subfolder

A subfolder is a folder within a folder.

Create a subfolder named **wp** within the folder **Practice**.

METHOD

1 In the **All Folders** window, double-click on: **3½ Floppy (A:)**. The folder **Practice** is now listed.
Click on: the **Practice** folder to select it. It opens and **Exploring – Practice** is displayed on the Title bar (Figure 2.4).

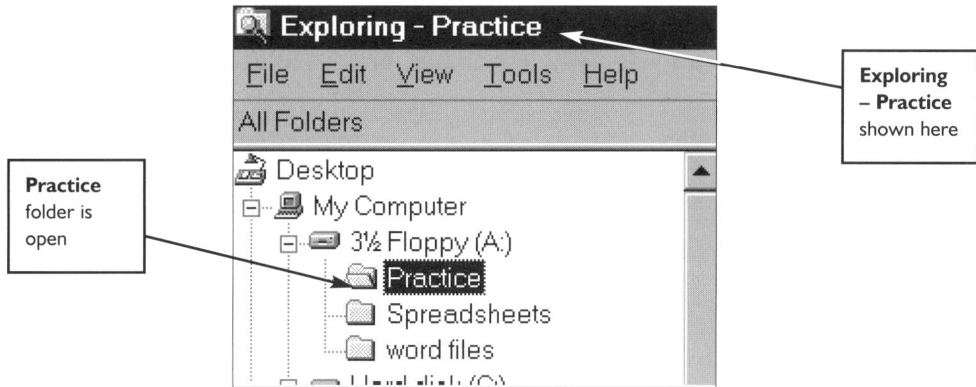

Figure 2.4 Exploring – Practice

2 From the **File** menu, select: **New** and then **Folder** (Figure 2.5).

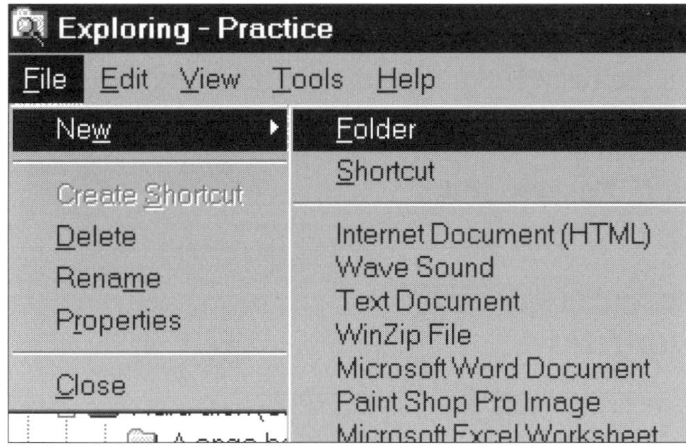

Figure 2.5 New Folder

3 A new folder appears in the right-hand window and you will notice that a + sign has appeared next to the folder **Practice** in the left-hand window. This denotes that the folder **Practice** has a subfolder.
Key in a name, **wp** for the folder. Press: **Enter** (Figure 2.6).

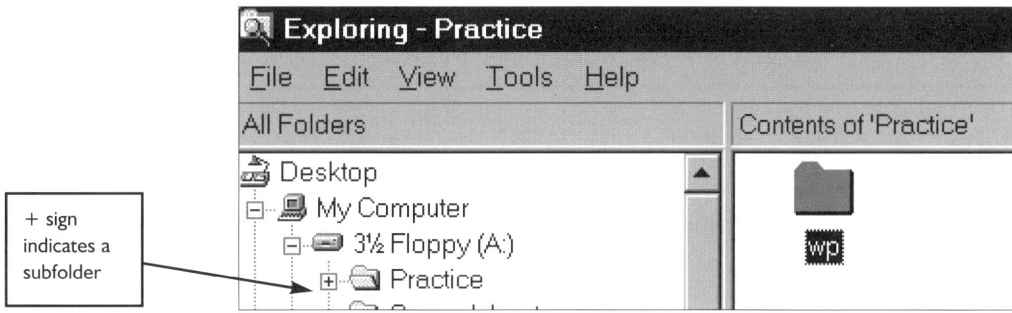

Figure 2.6 Creating a subfolder

Note: If you double-click on the folder **Practice** in the **All Folders** window, the subfolder **wp** will be displayed:

INFO

You can create numerous subfolders within a folder, following the method above. You can also create subfolders within subfolders if you wish.

1.4 Deleting a folder/file

Select the folder/file you want to delete by clicking it. Press: **Delete**. You will be asked to confirm the delete.
Click on: **Yes**.

Note: When you delete a folder, its contents are also deleted including all subfolders and files.

The Recycle Bin

You can restore a deleted file (**not one deleted from a floppy disk**) from the Recycle Bin by clicking on the **Recycle Bin**, selecting the file you want to restore and selecting **Restore** from the **File** menu.

Emptying the Recycle Bin

It is a good idea to remove files from the Recycle Bin from time to time. To do this:

1 Click on: the **Recycle Bin** to select it.
2 From the **File** menu, select: **Empty Recycle Bin**.

1.5 Saving and naming files

Files are normally saved and named within their applications, eg word processing files are saved and named when using Word.

1.6 Copying files

Create a short file in Word. Save the file with the name **Short File** on a floppy disk in drive A. Copy this file to the folder **Practice**, which you created earlier.

METHOD

1 Create and save the Word file on the A drive. Close the Word file.
2 Start Explorer and select: **Floppy (A:)** if it is not already selected. The file you have saved is displayed in the Contents window (Figure 2.7).

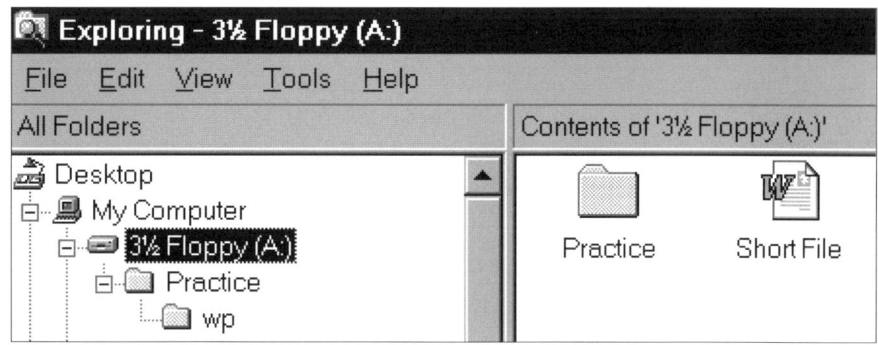

Figure 2.7 Contents window displaying file

3 There are three main ways to copy the file:

METHOD 1 Select the file **Short File**, hold down the left mouse button and, at the same time, hold down the **Ctrl** key. Drag the file to the folder **Practice**. Release the **Ctrl** key and the mouse button.

METHOD 2
a Select the file **Short File**, hold down the right mouse button and drag the file to the folder **Practice**.
b Release the mouse button – a menu appears.
c Select: **Copy Here**.

METHOD 3
a Right-click on: the file **Short File** – a menu appears:

b Select: **Copy**.
c Right-click where you want to copy to.
d Select: **Paste**.

The third method is sometimes easier when you have numerous files and folders, as they may scroll out of view when you try to drag them.

You can check that the file is in the **Practice** folder by clicking on it to reveal its contents.

Note: Folders can be copied in the same way.

1.7 *Moving files*

Files/folders can be moved following the methods above, except:

METHOD 1 Do not hold down the **Ctrl** key when moving files/folders.

METHOD 3 At stage **b** select: **Cut** and at stage **d** select: **Paste**.

Selecting multiple files

You can select more than one file to delete, copy or move.

Selecting a group of files:

1 Select the first file in the group.
2 Hold down the **Shift** key on the keyboard and select the last file you want.

Selecting any files (not grouped together):

1 Select the first file.
2 Hold down the **Ctrl** key on the keyboard and select each file in the group.

1.8 *Recording file storage details*

For the IBT III assessment you will be asked to record file storage details on a File Store Record Sheet so that tutors can confirm they are able to recall your work. For the purposes of this book, there is a practice File Store Record Sheet in the appendix. (*Note*: This is not exactly the same as the OCR/RSA document.)

Ensure you have entered all the details requested:

- Your name.
- The name of the directory (folder) for the IBT III project.
- Step number, subdirectory (subfolder), filename or reference, query/report name.
- Also ensure you have ticked the end box if the file is to be used later in the assignment.

Note: Practise using a File Record Sheet throughout the Naturetrail Holidays scenario exercises.

1.9 *Exiting Explorer*

From the **File** menu, select: **Close**.

2 Copying attachments

In this section you will learn how to:

- copy attachments to folders and subfolders.

2.1 Copying attachments to folders and subfolders

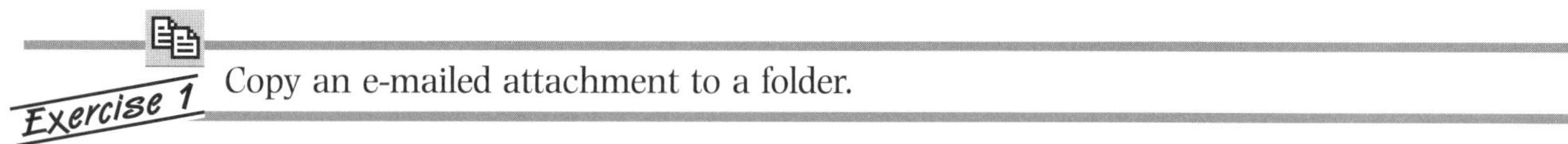

Copy an e-mailed attachment to a folder.

METHOD

1 Load Outlook Express in order to access your mailbox.

If you do not have a received message with an attachment, then send one to your own e-mail address. Also ensure you have a folder where you can store the attachment. For the purposes of this exercise, use the **TEST** file, created in Chapter 1, Section 2.3, and put it into the folder **Practice** also created earlier in Chapter 2, Section 1.2.

2 Double-click on the message so that it appears in its own window (Figure 2.8).

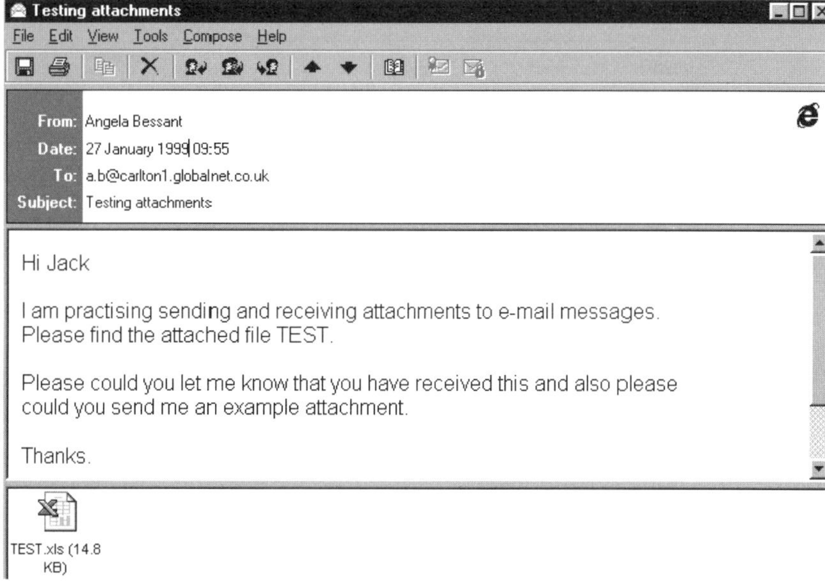

Figure 2.8 Testing attachments window

3 From the **File** menu, select: **Save Attachments**, and click on: the attached file (Figure 2.9).

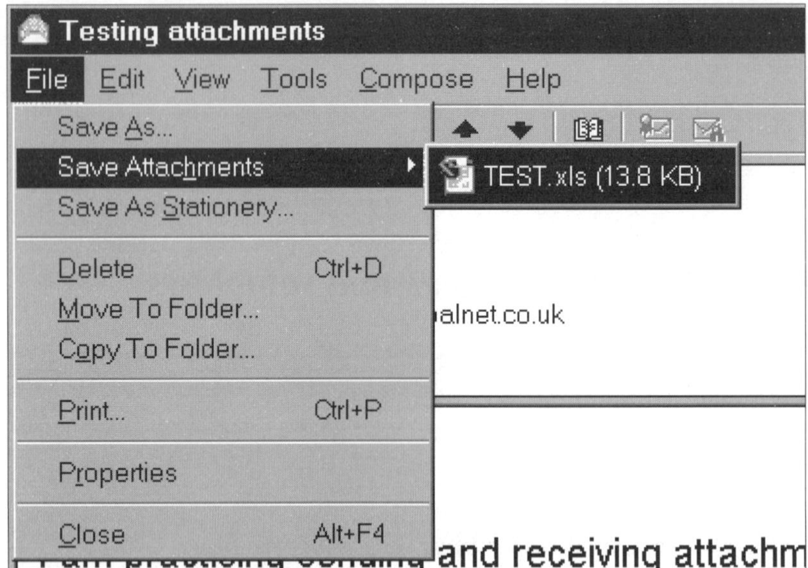

Figure 2.9 Saving attachment

4 The Save Attachment As dialogue box appears (Figure 2.10).

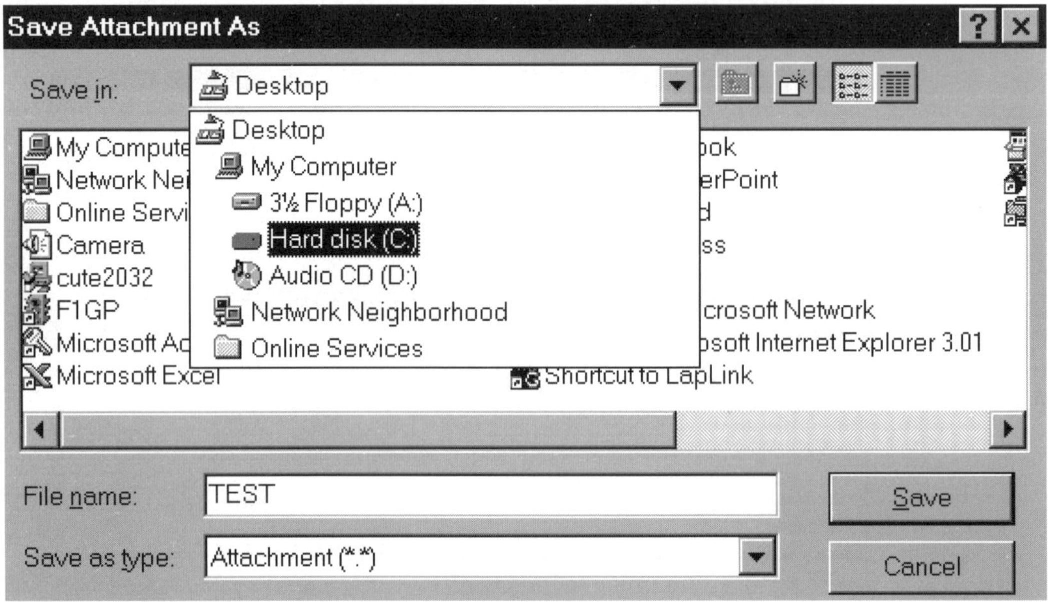

Figure 2.10 Save Attachment As dialogue box

5 Select the location and click on: **Save**. You are returned to Outlook Express.

Note: The procedure is the same for multiple attachments, except that there is an **All** option (Figure 2.11).

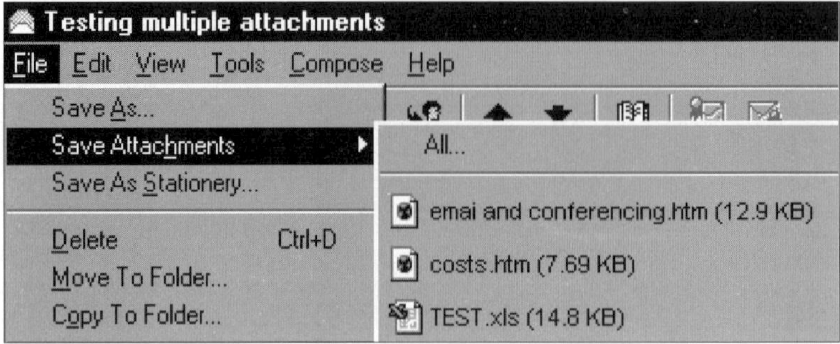

Figure 2.11 Save Attachments, All …

File management quick reference for IBT III

Action	Keyboard	Mouse	Right-mouse menu	Menu
Copy e-mail attachments	With Outlook Express loaded and message in its own window			
				File, **Save Attachments**
Copy file/folder	Select the file			
	Ctrl + C	Click: the **Copy** button	**Copy**	**Edit**, **Copy**
	Click where you want to copy the file			
	Ctrl + V	Click: the **Paste** button	**Paste**	**Edit**, **Paste**
Create a new folder	Select where you want the new folder to be			
			New, **Folder**	**File**, **New**, **Folder**
Create a subfolder	Select the folder in which you want the subfolder to be and follow the steps for creating a new folder.			
Delete a file/folder	Select the file/folder			
	Delete			**File**, **Delete**
Display contents of folder		Double-click: the folder		
Exit Explorer		Click: the Close window button		**File**, **Close**
Load Explorer	In Windows 95 desktop			
		Double-click: the **Windows Explorer** shortcut icon		**Start**, **Programs**, **Windows Explorer**
Restore files	Select the Recycle Bin Select the file you want to restore			
			Right-click Select: **Restore**	**File, Restore**
Select files *files grouped together* *any files*	Click: the first file Holding down: **Shift**, click: the last file Click: the first file Holding down: **Ctrl**, click: each file in turn			

Hints and tips

- For easier location, always give your files and folders/subfolders meaningful names.
- Use the File Store Record Sheet when requested to record details.
- Sometimes files are embedded in other files, eg charts in spreadsheet files, queries in database files. Ensure you note down where any embedded files are stored.

Practice exercise

This exercise is to help you practise the skills learnt in Chapter 2. Throughout the rest of this part of the book, you will be working through exercises and saving files in folders and subfolders.

Please create folders and subfolders for storage and retrieval of files as follows:

1 Create a folder for the project.

2 Record the folder name on your File Store Record Sheet.

3 Within this folder create and name two subfolders:

- one is for working copies
- one is for backup copies.

4 Record the names on your File Store Record Sheet.

Note: Use these folders and subfolders when saving files throughout Part 1 of this book. Record file details on the File Store Record Sheet.

Chapter 3

Databases using Access

1 Getting started

In this section you will revise and learn how to:

- access existing database files
- process existing database files
- insert data
  - records
  - fields
- edit data
  - text
  - numeric
- delete data
  - records
  - fields
- find and replace data
- format data.

INFO

If you have achieved competence at IBT Stage II, you will already be familiar with most of the database procedures above.

You will see (from the example Full Practice Assignment in Part 2) that at IBT Stage III you are given various tasks to perform with different delivery methods for the tasks, eg memos, data request forms. In this regard the assignments are meant to resemble actual office procedures. Therefore the skills required are analysis of the task and selection and processing of the relevant data. Some of the tasks are appropriate for, and require action for, *both* the database and the spreadsheet assignments.

Spreadsheet skills are covered in the next chapter. In this chapter we will concentrate only on the database skills. You are not expected to create a database file, but you will notice that the database files at this level are considerably larger than at IBT II level.

In order to aid understanding of these skills, the tasks are broken down in these chapters. You will be able to consolidate these skills by completing tasks in the context of the example Full Practice Assignment in Part 2. Detailed instructions for skills that were covered for IBT II will not be given here. However, the quick reference guide at the end of this chapter should help you to remember any topics you may have forgotten.

Important

Before starting on the exercises, ensure you make a backup copy of the database files so that you have an original file to use with the example Full Practice Assignment given in Part 2.

1.1 *Accessing the appropriate file and adding a record*

Load the appropriate database file and add the following property to it. Ensure you follow the existing upper- and lower-case conventions.

PROPERTY NAME	HEADLANDS
CODE	R691
LOCATION	RIVERS
OCCUPANTS	4
BEDROOMS	2
PARKING	YES
BOOKED(A)	7
BOOKED(B)	12
PRICE CODE	B
CHANGE DAY	SAT
DATE BOOKED	18 SEP 1999
AGENT	PAUL

METHOD

1 Load the database file and the appropriate table.

The database filename is not given. When carrying out the IBT III assessment, there will be a choice of database files. They may look quite similar. Ensure you are working with the correct one by looking at the database in Table View and Table Design View, and matching the fields with the record to add to the database. If the fields are not the same or are not all there, you most likely are not working with the correct database file. Examine the other database files to see which one *exactly* matches the new record.

2 To insert a new record in a large database, use one of the following methods:

- **a** From the **Insert** menu, select: **New Record** and enter the record in the normal way.
- **b** Click on: the **Insert New Record** ▶* button and enter the record in the normal way.
- **c** Go directly to the last record by clicking on: the ▶* button at the bottom of the table window.

Note: For each of the methods above, the cursor automatically moves to locate itself after the last record.

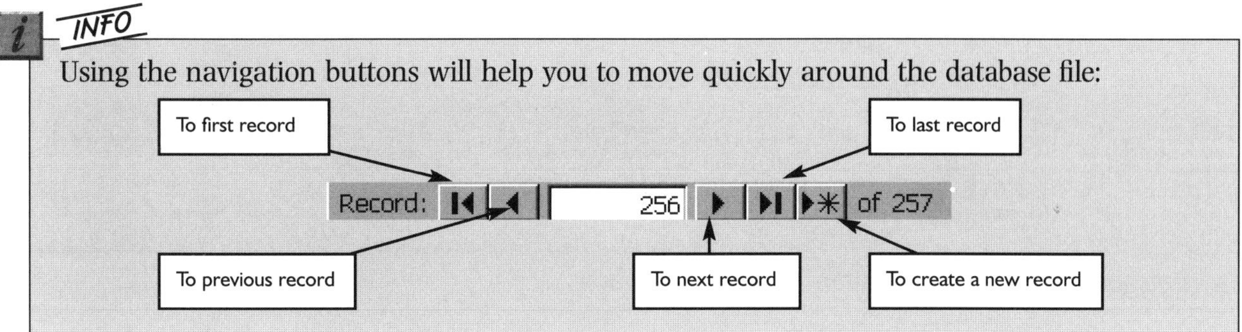

3 Follow any conventions that have already been set, eg upper case for text.
4 When you close, the changes are saved automatically and the records will be placed in the existing sort order.

1.2 *Deleting a record*

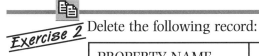

Delete the following record:

PROPERTY NAME	GREEN
CODE	F642
LOCATION	FOREST

METHOD

INFO

With a large database file it is not sensible to scroll through all the records to find the one you are looking for. Instead use the following method.

1 With the table displayed, position the cursor in the field you want to search – in this case we have been given details that are unique to this record ie PROPERTY NAME or CODE. In this example choose **PROPERTY NAME**:

PROPERTY NAME	CODE	LOCAT
LARKS	C123	COUNT
MINT	C181	COUNT
GINGER	C207	COUNT

2 Click on: the **Find** button.

3 The **Find in field:** dialogue box appears. In the **Find What** box, key in the word **GREEN**. You will note that there are several options you may want to explore. Click to select (and place a tick in) the **Search Only Current** Field box and click on: **Find First** (Figure 3.1).

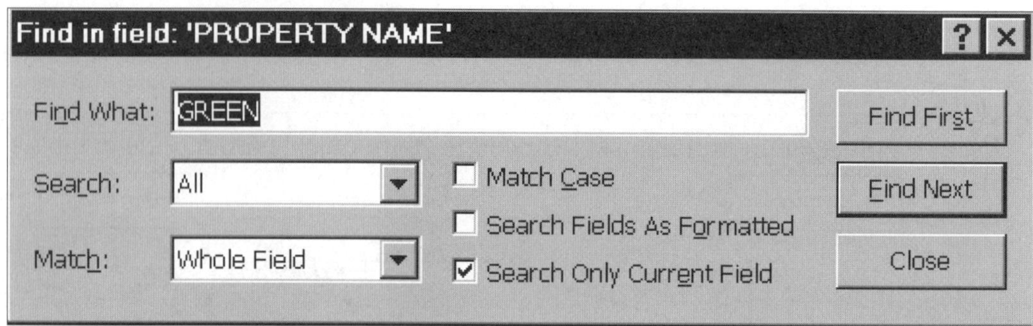

Figure 3.1 Find in field: dialogue box

4 The PROPERTY NAME **GREEN** has been highlighted. Click on: **Close** (Figure 3.2).

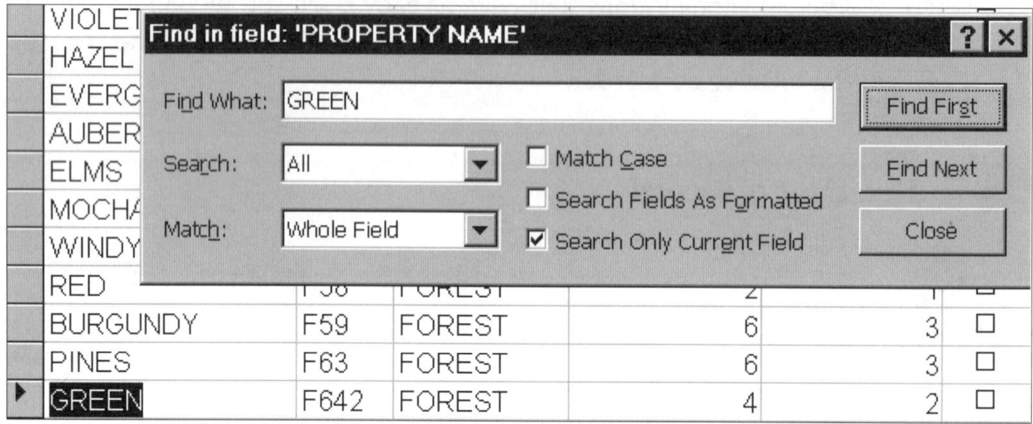

Figure 3.2 Find in field – **GREEN**

5 Delete the record in the normal way.

1.3 *Deleting a field*

Exercise 3 Delete the field **PARKING** from the database file.

1 In Table Design View, select the field to be deleted by clicking to the left of it as shown. The entire field is highlighted (Figure 3.3).

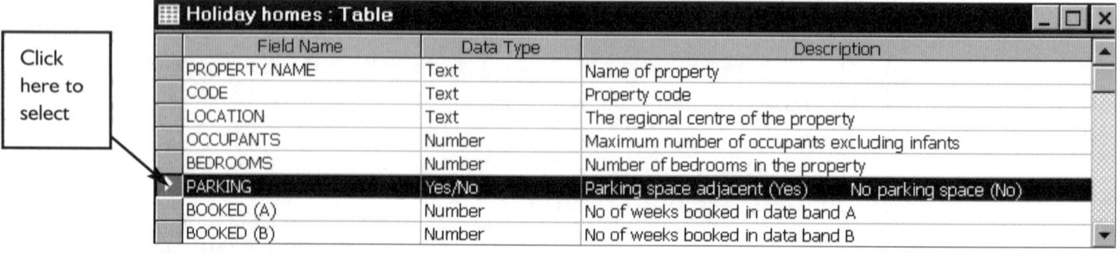

Figure 3.3 **PARKING** field

2 Press: **Delete**. A box appears. Click on: **Yes** (Figure 3.4).

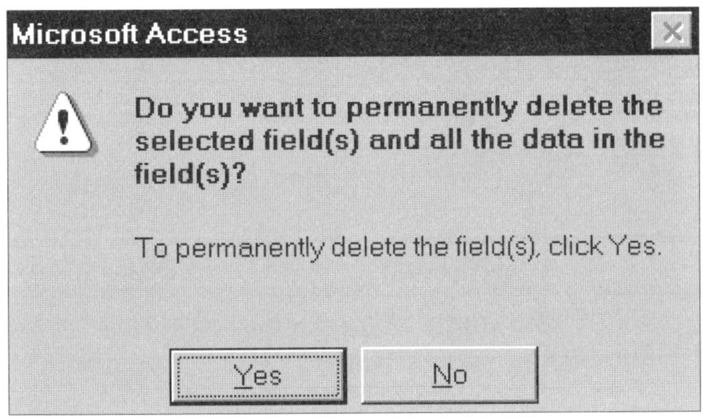

Figure 3.4 Deleting a field

3 Close Table Design View. You are prompted to save changes. Click on: **Yes**.

1.4 *Adding a field*

Exercise 4

It has been decided to add TVs to all COUNTRY properties. Add a new field **TV** to the database file. This field will show those properties that have a TV and those that do not. Set up the field accordingly between the PRICE CODE field and the CHANGE DAY field.

METHOD

1 In Table Design View, position the cursor in the field below where the new field is to be, ie in the CHANGE DAY field.
2 Right-click – a menu appears.
3 Select: **Insert Rows**. A new row appears above the CHANGE DAY field (Figure 3.5).
4 Enter the details for the new field in the normal way. *Hint:* The Data Type will be Yes/No.
5 Save changes.
6 In Table (Datasheet) View, click in the boxes in the TV field to add TV to the records of COUNTRY properties only. *Hint:* Change the sort order to LOCATION so all the records to amend are grouped together.

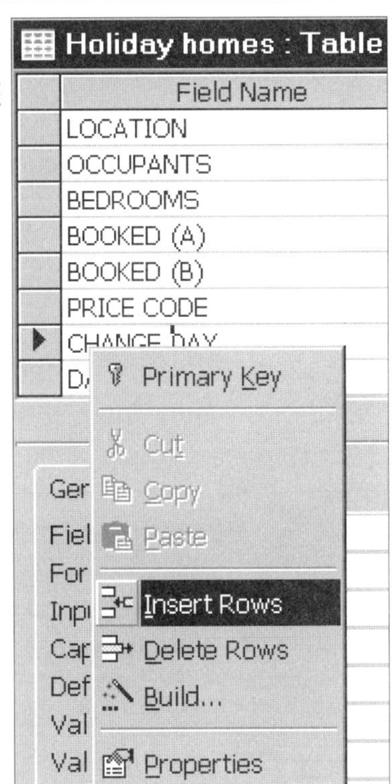

Figure 3.5 Insert Rows

1.5 Editing data

Exercise 5 It has been noticed that one of the properties has been entered incorrectly. Please amend as follows:

	ENTERED AS	SHOULD READ
CODE	M342	M340
BOOKED(A)	8	7
BOOKED(B)	14	10

METHOD

1 Find the record by clicking on: the **Find** button and following the method shown in Section 1.2, this time ensuring the cursor is in the CODE field.
2 Edit the record in the normal way.

Exercise 6 Please amend all properties BOOKED(A) from 6 weeks to 7 weeks.

INFO

This time you will be looking for multiple entries since there is likely to be more than one.

METHOD

1 Move the cursor to the top of the database file (**Ctrl** + **Home**).
2 Position the cursor in the BOOKED(A) field and then from the **Edit** menu, select: **Replace**.
3 Enter 6 in the **Find What** box and 7 in the **Replace With** box. Ensure that **Search Only Current Field** is ticked.
4 Click on: **Replace All**.

Note: There should be seven records to change.

1.6 Formatting data

Ensure you have conformed to the formatting that is already on the database file (or, in an IBT III assignment, any instructions that you may be given) and that you do not have lower-case entries in those fields where upper case is already entered.

INFO

You may find it helpful to print out the database file at this stage and check that you have correctly completed all the exercises in this section. The amended database file is used in the next section.

Ensure all fields fit to one page for easier reading and to save wasting paper. Do this by changing column widths (ensure that headings and contents are still fully visible) and using **Page Setup** to alter margins.

2 *Creating queries and reports, printing and transferring data*

In this section you will revise and learn how to:

- create and run queries containing up to five specified criteria
- print data as specified
- create reports and display data as specified
- transfer data between files/applications.

INFO

The following practice exercises are based on the amended (in the last section) database file. Answers to the exercises are given at the end of the book, including the designs for the queries. Please note that, at this level, some aspects of layout are at your discretion so your answer may not look exactly the same as the one given. However, you should check you have met all the criteria requested.

2.1 *Creating, running and printing queries*

Exercise 1

Load the database file, which was amended in the previous section, and create, run and print the following query:

QUERY

Fields/headings to print	All (in the existing order)
Sort order	Ascending order of CODE
Search criteria	BOOKED(A) 7 or less; PRICE CODE B; DATE BOOKED 18 September 1999 or later
Other details (please specify)	Field headings must be shown

Printout required Yes ✓ No ☐ Fit one page 

METHOD

1 Carry out the query in the normal way. See the Working with Queries info box overleaf for guidance on designing your query. Save your query as **Query1**.

Working with queries

Queries can seem quite complicated at this level and may have as many as five specified criteria. Take each criterion in turn and remember to check (in Design View) that you have done everything you have been asked. In Datasheet View, check again that the results match up with what has been requested and that the search order is correct.

Use the following as a guide:

In the Criteria row you can enter any of the following:

- ❑ An exact match, eg SMITHSON
- ❑ The wildcard *

The * wildcard stands for any number and type of character, eg if you were unsure how to spell the name you could enter SM*THSON or SM*SON. You can place the * wildcard before, after and between characters and you can use it more than once in a single field, eg SM*TH*.

- ❑ The wildcard ?

The ? wildcard acts as a placeholder for one character, eg SM?THSON.

- ❑ LIKE

This tells Access not to look for an exact match, eg LIKE SMYTHSON.

- ❑ NOT

If you want to find all the records but not SMITHSON you could enter NOT SMITHSON.

- ❑ NULL

If you have records with no value in the field, you can type NULL to find these records, eg if you were looking for all properties without central heating and the database design had allowed no value in the central heating field for properties without central heating but a YES value for those with central heating.

- ❑ Mathematical operators

>	more than	>=	more than or equal to
<	less than	<=	less than or equal to
=	equal to	<>	not equal to

- ❑ AND and OR

You can use AND when you need to restrict results, eg for all employees aged over 20 and under 30 use >20 AND <30. You can use OR when you want a combination of results: GREEN OR RED OR BLUE.

- ❑ Fields containing YES/NO data. If YES the data will show as a ticked box. Use YES if you want to find the ticked box data and NO if not.

- ❑ Working with dates:

Before 12 September 1999	<12 September 1999 (note: You can use an abbreviated version of the date and it will change to the correct format, eg 12/9/99)
After 12 September 1999	>12 September 1999
12 September 1999 or after	>=12 September 1999
12 September 1999 or before	<=12 September 1999
12 September 1999 to 18 September 1999 inclusive	>11 September 1999 and <19 September 1999

2 When printing the query, use Print Preview to ensure it fits on one page. If it does not fit, you can alter the following:
   a From the **File** menu, select: **Page Setup**:
      – with the **Margins** tab selected, you can alter the left and right margins
      – with the **Page** tab selected, you can set the printout to landscape.
   b If it still does not fit, you could reduce the width of the columns. (*Note*: Headings **must** be shown in full unless requested otherwise.)
   c You could **select all** and reduce the font size.

Create, run and print out the following query:

QUERY

Fields/headings to print	PROPERTY NAME LOCATION, BOOKED(A), PRICE CODE
Sort order	Descending order of PROPERTY NAME
Search criteria	PROPERTY NAME beginning with the letter S, the letter G or the letter M; LOCATION Sea or Forest; OCCUPANTS 4 or more; CHANGE DAY Saturday; BOOKED(B) more than 8 weeks
Other details (please specify)	Show only required fields in specified order, including field headings.

Printout required Yes ✓ No ☐ Fit one page 

METHOD

1 Carry out the query in the normal way.

Notes:

a You will need to use the wildcard for the PROPERTY NAME search.

b You will need to widen the PROPERTY NAME column in Design View to accommodate all the criteria on the same row.
Note: Do not enter criteria on a separate row.

c Some of the fields in the search criteria should not be shown.
Hint: It is a good idea to run the query with these fields showing so that you can check it has achieved the required results. Remember to switch back to Design View, to remove the ticks from the boxes in the Show row and to resave the query.

2 Save the query as **Query 2**.

3 Print the query in the normal way.

Exercise 3 Create, run and print out the following query:

QUERY

Fields/headings to print	PROPERTY NAME LOCATION, BOOKED(A), CHANGE DAY, AGENT
Sort order	Ascending BOOKED(A)
Search criteria	Weeks BOOKED(A) 7 to 14 inclusive; Weeks BOOKED(B) 12 or more; AGENT Paul or Gail
Other details (please specify)	Show only required fields in specified order, including field headings.

Printout required — Yes ✓ No ☐ Fit one page ✓

METHOD

1 Create and run the query in the normal way.
2 Save this query as **Query3**.
3 Print the query.

2.2 *Creating reports and displaying data as specified*

Exercise 4 Create a report as specified below:

REPORT/EXTRACT

Report format — Group ☐ Column ✓ Tabular ☐

Title	LOW BOOKINGS PERIOD A
Fields/headings to print	PROPERTY NAME and BOOKED(A) only in this order
Sort order	PROPERTY NAME ascending
Other details (please specify)	Using Query1 (saved in Exercise 1) produce a report to be used where specified in the publication.

Printout required — Yes ✓ No ☐ To be dated — Yes ☐ No ✓

Fit one page — Yes ✓ No ☐ Page numbered — Yes ☐ No ✓

Important! This report will be used in the publication assignment in Chapter 6.

METHOD Create the report using the **Report Wizard**.

Notes:

a When working through the Report Wizard, remember to base the report on **Query1** (Figure 3.6).

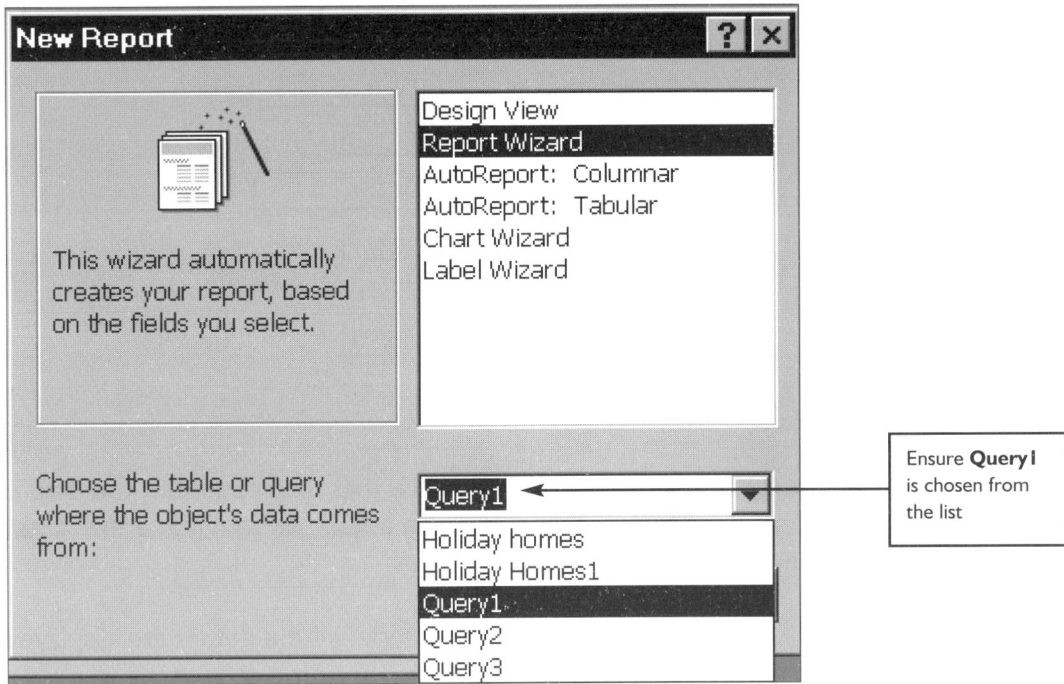

Figure 3.6 New Report

b Ensure **Columnar** is chosen at the stage shown in Figure 3.7.

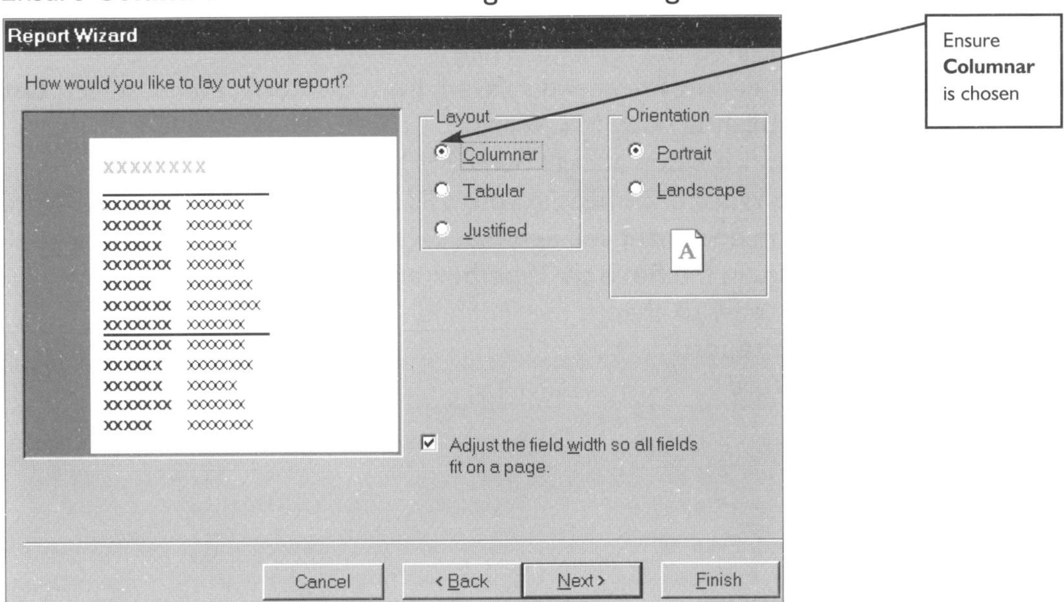

Figure 3.7 Report Wizard

c When choosing the style for the report, **Compact** works best as it requires fewer changes in Design View to fit in all the entries in their entirety.

d The Report Preview should look similar to the one shown in Figure 3.8.

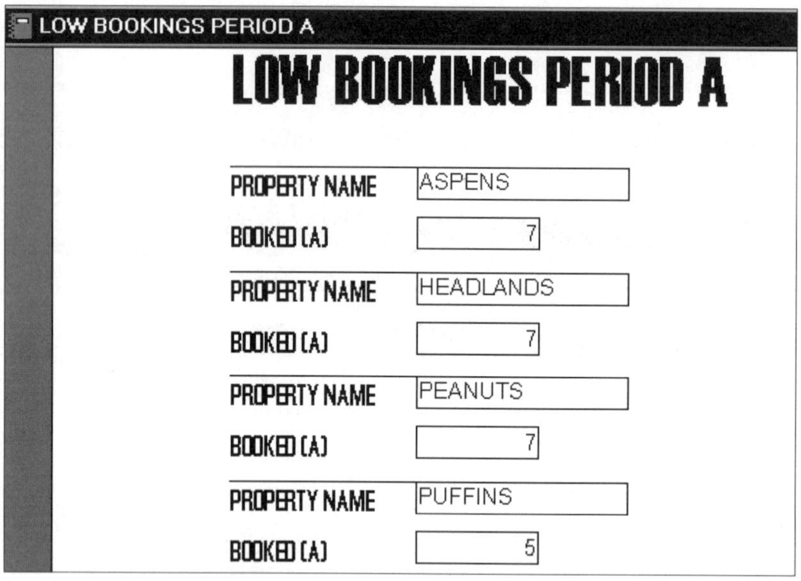

LOW BOOKINGS PERIOD A

LOW BOOKINGS PERIOD A

PROPERTY NAME	ASPENS
BOOKED (A)	7
PROPERTY NAME	HEADLANDS
BOOKED (A)	7
PROPERTY NAME	PEANUTS
BOOKED (A)	7
PROPERTY NAME	PUFFINS
BOOKED (A)	5

Figure 3.8 Report Preview

Note: If you scroll down you will notice that the report has the date and page number at the bottom. You have been asked not to include this. Change to Design View and delete these items.

This is sufficient as a printout for this task. All the details are displayed in full. Sometimes this is not the case and it is very time consuming to alter it in Report Design View. It is also difficult to manipulate at a later stage. Therefore, it is easier if the report is output and saved in Word where it can be formatted more easily. The instructions for this are given below.

To output an Access report to Word:

1. With the Report Preview displayed, from the **Tools** menu, select: **Office Links** and then **Publish It with MS Word**.
2. The report is automatically output to Word.
3. Save the Word document in your folder. Ensure you save it as a Word document. *Note:* The document will automatically save in RTF format. Change this to a Word document in the **Save as Type** box in the **Save As** dialogue box.
   It is now easy to change the font and font size.
4. Print the report.
5. Close Word.

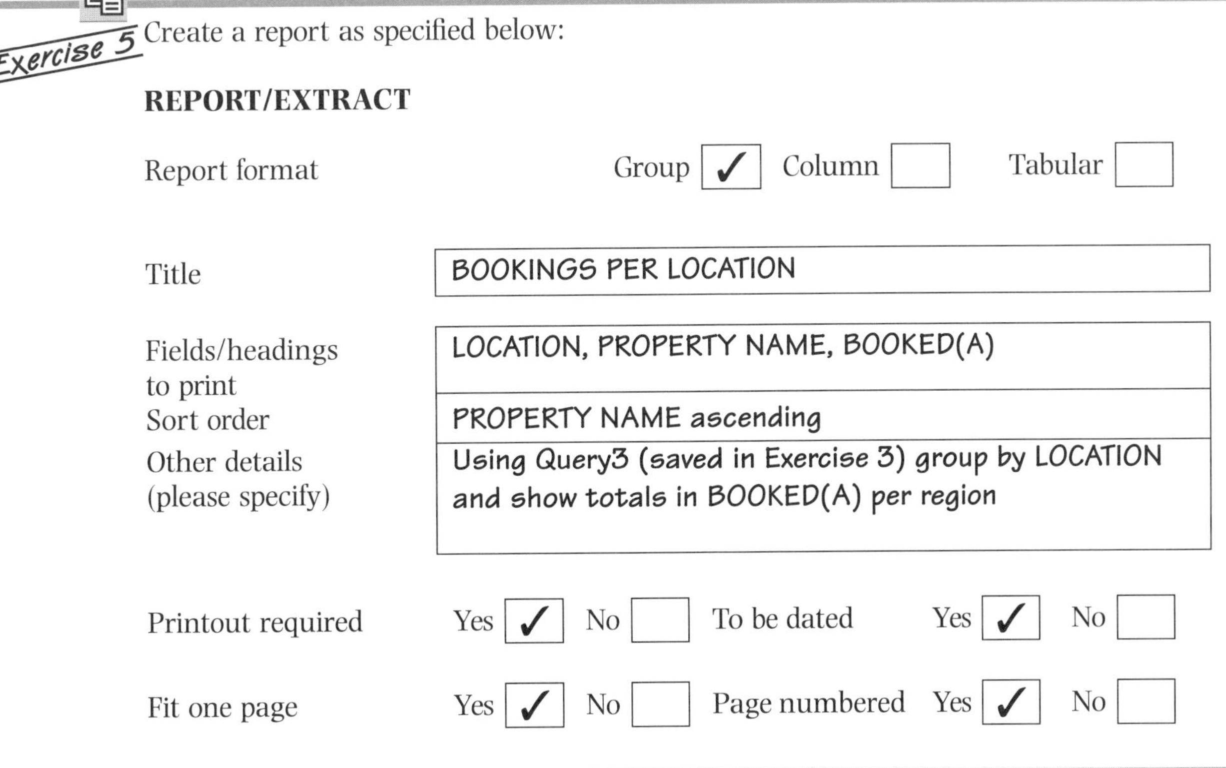

Exercise 5 Create a report as specified below:

REPORT/EXTRACT

Report format	Group ✓ Column ☐ Tabular ☐
Title	BOOKINGS PER LOCATION
Fields/headings to print	LOCATION, PROPERTY NAME, BOOKED(A)
Sort order	PROPERTY NAME ascending
Other details (please specify)	Using Query3 (saved in Exercise 3) group by LOCATION and show totals in BOOKED(A) per region
Printout required	Yes ✓ No ☐ To be dated Yes ✓ No ☐
Fit one page	Yes ✓ No ☐ Page numbered Yes ✓ No ☐

METHOD

1 Create the report using the **Report Wizard**, this time basing the report on **Query3**.

2 Select **LOCATION** when asked if you want to add any grouping levels as shown in Figure 3.9.

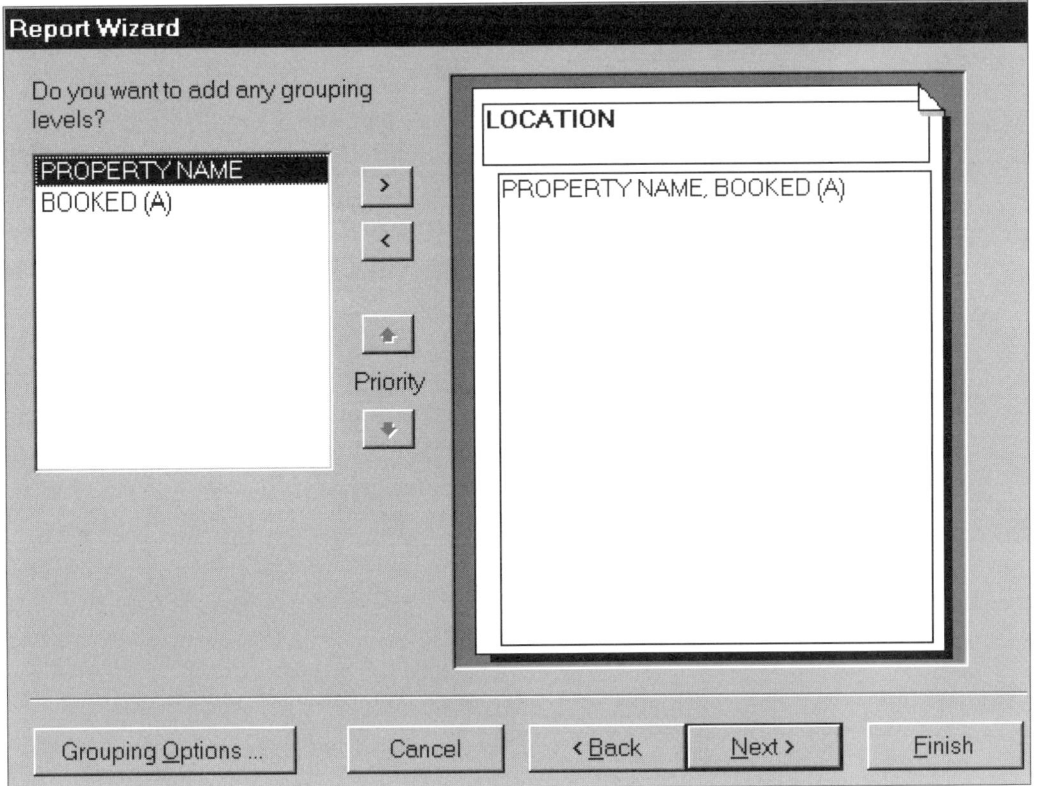

Figure 3.9 Grouping level location

3 Experiment with different layouts at the stage in Figure 3.10. Stepped will work well for this report, as it leaves space to add the totals for BOOKED(A).

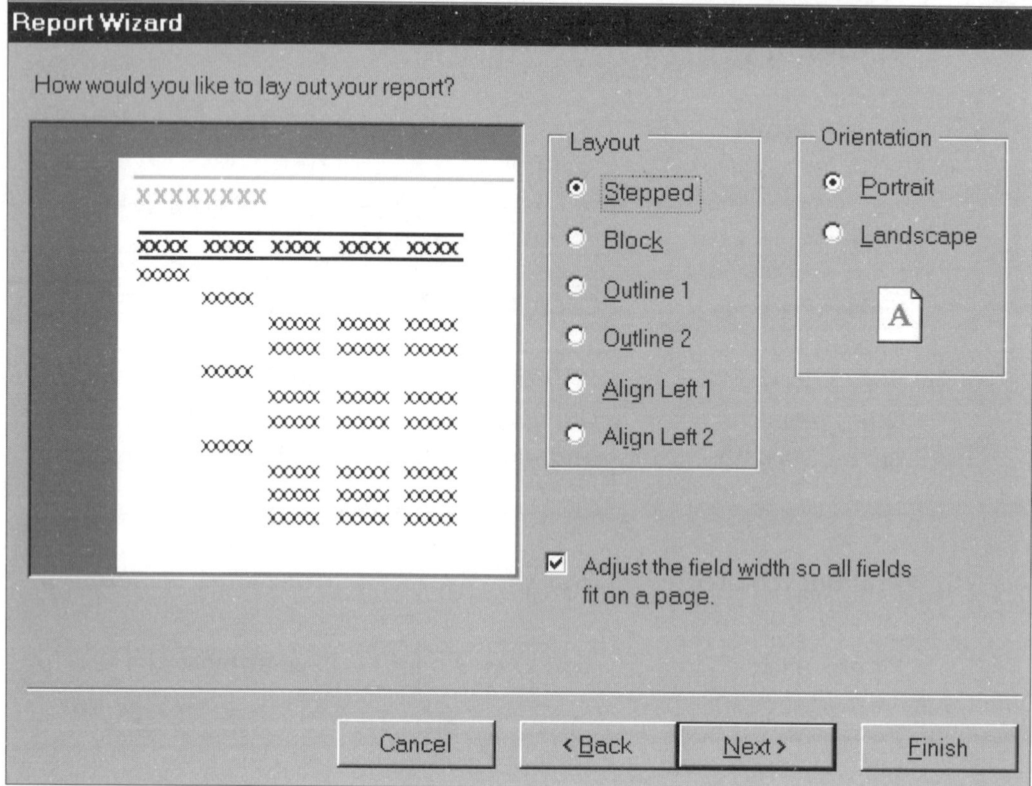

Figure 3.10 Report Wizard – Layout

4 The report is grouped by LOCATION as requested, but there are no totals per location in the BOOKED(A) column. In this case the report can be output to Excel, where it can be manipulated with ease.

To output an Access report to Excel:

a With the Report Preview displayed, from the **Tools** menu, select: **Office Links** and then **Analyse It with MS Excel**.

b The report is automatically output to Excel.

c Here you can add any details you need, eg the totals BOOKED(A) per LOCATION, and format the spreadsheet as you like.
Note: You will notice that the report title has not been carried across. Insert a new row at the top of the spreadsheet and type in the report title.

d Add the other details requested, eg page number and date, to the spreadsheet (**View** menu, **Header and Footer**).

e Save the spreadsheet in your folder and print it.

Access quick reference for IBT III

Action	Keyboard	Mouse	Right-mouse menu	Menu
Add a field	In Design View: Click in the field below where you want to insert a new field			
		Click: the **Insert Rows** button	**Insert Rows**	**Insert**, **Rows**
	Add the field details Re-save the table design			
Add a record		Click: the **New Record** button *OR* Click: in the blank cell immediately after the last record	(Right-click to the left of any record) **New Record**	**Insert**, **New Record**
Change Data Type	(see separate table for Data Types) Click: in the **Data Type** box next to the field name you wish to change Click: the arrow Click: the Data Type you require eg Number Select the field properties (see separate table for Field Properties) from the box below Close the Table window, saving the table design			
Close a database	**Ctrl + W**	Click: the **Close** icon on the database window		**File**, **Close**
Close the Table window		Click: the **Close Window** icon		**File**, **Save As/Export** Select: **Within current database**
	Click: **Yes** to save the table design Key in: a name for the table You will be asked if you want to create a primary key: Click: **No** The table will save automatically			
Create a columnar report	Follow the method for creating a tabular report (see page 40) – except select **Columnar** instead of **Tabular**			
Create a database	Load Access Click: **Blank Database**, **OK** Select: the location Enter: the filename Click: **Create** Click: **Tables** tab, **New**, **Design View**, **OK** Enter the field names (these will all appear (by default) as text entries under Data Type)			
Create a query	In the Database window ensure the **Queries** tab is selected Click: **New** Click: **Design View**, **OK** Click: **Add**, **Close**			
	The fields of the table are now displayed in a list box in the Query window. Place the fields that you want to see in your query in the field row of the query grid by double-clicking or dragging them. *Note:* Place the fields in the order that you want them to appear.			

<table>
<tr><th>Action</th><th>Keyboard</th><th>Mouse</th><th>Right-mouse menu</th><th>Menu</th></tr>
<tr><td>Create a tabular report</td><td colspan="4">Ensure the database is open and that the Reports tab is selected
Click: New
Click: Report Wizard
Select: the name of the object – eg query, table – that the report is to be generated from
Click: OK
Select the fields to include in the report using the >> or > buttons
Click: Next
(If you want to group the report – select the field(s) you want to group by here)
Click: Next
(If you want to change the sort order select the field you want to sort by and the sort order here)
Click: Next
Select: Tabular
Select the orientation you want – ie Landscape or Portrait
Click: Next
Select a style (Compact is good)
Click: Next.
Key in: the report title
Click: Finish</td></tr>
<tr><td rowspan="2">Delete a field</td><td colspan="4">In Table Design View
Select the field to be deleted by clicking to the left of it</td></tr>
<tr><td>Delete, Y</td><td>Click: the Delete Rows button
Click: Yes</td><td>Delete Rows</td><td>Edit, Delete Rows</td></tr>
<tr><td rowspan="3">Delete a record</td><td colspan="4">Select the record by clicking to the left of the first field of that record</td></tr>
<tr><td>Delete, Y</td><td>Click: the Delete Record button
Click: Yes</td><td>Delete Record
Yes</td><td>Edit, Delete Record</td></tr>
<tr><td colspan="4">Select: Yes to save the change</td></tr>
<tr><td>Edit data</td><td colspan="4">Open the table (if it is not already open)
Click: in the entry you want to edit
Delete the old data
Key in the new data</td></tr>
<tr><td>Enter data</td><td colspan="4">In the Database window
Click: Open
Enter the data required in the correct fields. Widen the field columns as necessary.
Close the Table window. The data is saved automatically.</td></tr>
<tr><td rowspan="3">Find a record</td><td colspan="4">With the Table displayed, position the cursor in the field you want to search.</td></tr>
<tr><td>Ctrl + F</td><td>Click: the Find button</td><td></td><td>Edit, Find</td></tr>
<tr><td colspan="4">In the Find What box, key in what you want to find
Click: Find First.
Click: Find Next
Continue until all records have been found
Note: You may need to choose a field that has a unique entry to ensure you find the correct record.</td></tr>
</table>

Action	Keyboard	Mouse	Right-mouse menu	Menu
Load Access	In the Windows 95 desktop			
		Double-click: the **Microsoft Access** shortcut icon		**Start**, **Programs**, **MS Office**, **Microsoft Access**
Open a table	In the Database window, make sure the **Tables** tab is selected			
in Datasheet View *in Design View*		Double-click: the table Click: the table Click: **Design**		
Output a report	Ensure you are in the **Report Preview** view			
to Word		Click: the **Publish It with MS Word** button *OR* Click the next to the **Analyze It with MS Excel** button and select **Publish It with MS Word**		**Tools**, **Office Links**, **Publish it with MS Word**
to Excel		Click: the **Analyze It with MS Excel** button *OR* Click the next to the **Publish It with MS Word** button and select **Analyze It with Excel**		**Tools**, **Office Links**, **Analyze it with MS Excel**
Print a query	In **Datasheet View**			
	Ctrl + P	Click: the **Print** button		**File**, **Print**
Print a report	**Ctrl + P**	Click: the **Print** button	**Print**	**File**, **Print**
Print, quick		Click: the **Print** button Access will automatically print the whole table.		
Print specific fields	Use the **Show** row in the grid to choose whether or not to display a particular field in the query. A tick in the **Show** box means that the field will show, no tick means that it will not show. Click to toggle between them.			

Action	Keyboard	Mouse	Right-mouse menu	Menu
Print a table	Open the table you want to print.			
	Ctrl + P			**File**, **Print**
	Make the necessary selections Choose Setup if you want to print Landscape Make the necessary selections from the Setup dialogue box Click: **OK**, **OK**			
Replace field entries	**Ctrl + H**			**Edit**, **Replace**
Save a query	**Ctrl + S**	Click: the **Save** button		**File**, **Save**
	To see the results of your query			
		Click: the **Run** button		**Query**, **Run**
Sort a query	Click: in the **Sort** box of the appropriate field Click: the arrow Select: **Ascending** or **Descending**.			
Sort records (quick sort)	Open the Table if it is not already open. Select the field that you want to sort by clicking on the Field Name at the top of the field column			
ascending order		Click: the **Sort Ascending** button	**Sort Ascending**	
descending order		Click the **Sort Descending** button	**Sort Descending**	
Specify criteria	Use the **Criteria** row in the grid to specify the conditions in a specific field – eg **RED** in the **Colour** field. (See *Working with Queries* page 32)			

Important: Always close the database file properly.

DATA TYPE	PROPERTIES
Text (the default)	No need to set, unless short of storage space.
Number	*Field Size* Long Integer is the default – this is OK for whole numbers. Double – for numbers with decimal places *Format* Choose **Fixed** for 2 decimal places to show (even if the last is a zero) Choose **Decimal Places** and enter the number required (Leave the Format blank for other numbers.)
Date/Time	Choose the most appropriate format for the task. (You can key in the date in any format and it will convert to the format you have set.)
Currency	Choose **Format Fixed** to display 2 decimal places with no commas or £ symbol.
Yes/No	No need to set

Hints and tips

- At this level, you are not expected to create a database file. However, you will need to choose which database file to work with from those given. Examine the database files very carefully in order to establish which one is appropriate.
- The files are quite large and it will not be immediately obvious, for example, if your query results are correct. It is therefore essential to carry out the work thoroughly in order to produce the required output.
- Always check query criteria in Design View and remember to show only the requested fields in printouts.
- Check that all the database-specified data is shown in full.
- Proofread and double-check at all stages to ensure accuracy.

Chapter 4

Spreadsheets using Excel

1 Getting started

In this section you will revise and learn how to:

- access existing spreadsheet files
- process existing spreadsheet files
- insert data
  - columns
  - rows
- edit data
  - text
  - numeric
- delete data
  - columns
  - rows
- format data
  - case.

Important

Before starting on the exercises below, ensure you make a backup copy of the spreadsheet file so you have an original file to use with the example Full Practice Assignment in Part 2.

1.1 *Accessing the appropriate file and inserting data*

Load the appropriate spreadsheet file and add the following data to it (where it applies). Ensure you follow the existing upper- and lower-case conventions. Ensure the existing order of LOCATION is maintained and any necessary formulae replicated.

PROPERTY NAME	HEADLANDS
CODE	R691
LOCATION	RIVERS
OCCUPANTS	4
BEDROOMS	2
PARKING	YES
BOOKED(A)	7
BOOKED(B)	12
PRICE CODE	B
CHANGE DAY	SAT
DATE BOOKED	18 SEP 1999
AGENT	PAUL

METHOD 1 Load the appropriate spreadsheet file.

INFO

It is important you take time to study the spreadsheet carefully. This will ensure you choose the appropriate one and enable you to work with it more effectively.

2 Enter *only* the relevant details into the spreadsheet following the instructions.

INFO

When asked to maintain the existing order, check carefully to see what that order is before inserting data. In this case, the sort order is ascending and, since the codes start with an alphabetic character, the numerical digits are taken in turn and not as their overall numeric value.

All properties which have BOOKED(A) as 6 should be amended to 7.

METHOD This is simply a matter of locating the appropriate cells and overwriting them.

The entry for the Mountain property M342 has been entered incorrectly. Please amend it to M341. The BOOKED(A) column for this entry should read 7, not 8, and the BOOKED(B) column for this entry should read 13, not 14.

METHOD Again, this is a matter of locating the appropriate cells and overwriting them.

Exercise 4 The Rivers property, property code R401, should not be entered on this spreadsheet. Please delete all reference to this property.

METHOD Delete the row containing this entry.

Exercise 5

1 Save the spreadsheet and record the details on the File Store Record Sheet.
2 Print the spreadsheet. Ensure it fits on one page.

Note: For the quickest way to ensure it fits on one page, use **Fit to Page** in **Page Setup**.

2 Cell addresses, functions, replicating formulae, formatting data

In this section you will revise and learn:

- absolute cell addresses
- relative cell addresses
- named ranges/cells
- functions
  - sum
  - average
  - count
  - lookup
  - if
- how to replicate formulae
- how to format data
  - decimal places
  - integer
  - currency
  - alignment.

Omissions have been identified in the spreadsheet. Please check all sections and insert the relevant formulae and functions.

Use the following functions where appropriate:

SUM
AVERAGE
COUNT
LOOKUP

INFO

Excel can work out common tasks such as the ones above. These functions (and others) are built into Excel to make formulae easier and quicker to enter. You are already familiar with the SUM function. Other functions work in a similar way. The exact way of entering the formulae using functions is demonstrated as you work through the exercises.

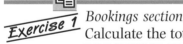

Bookings section
Calculate the total number of BOOKED(A) and BOOKED(B) for each of the six LOCATIONS. Display the figures as whole numbers without decimal places.

METHOD Check on the printout where these should appear. Use the **Autosum** button. Syntax is =SUM(cell ref:cell ref).

Note: You will not be able to replicate the formulae for the BOOKED(A) column but you will be able to replicate from BOOKED(A) to BOOKED(B) since you will already have the correct cell ranges.

Properties per location section

Calculate the number of properties per location.

METHOD

Use the COUNT function for this. Syntax is =COUNT(cell ref:cell ref).

1 Select the cell where the answer is to appear and key in **=COUNT(** (Figure 4.1).

PROPERTIES PER LOCATION		
LOCATION	NO OF PROPERTIES	
COUNTRY	=COUNT(	
FOREST		
LAKES		
MOUNTAIN		
RIVERS		
SEA		

Figure 4.1 Properties per location

2 Drag the mouse across the cells to count, ie the Country properties. A dotted line appears.
Note: The COUNT function will only work with numeric data, so we cannot use the PROPERTY CODE column – Figure 4.2.

	LOCATION AND PROPERTY CODE	BOOKED(A)	BO(
16			
17	COUNTRY		
18	C181	12	
19	C34	14	
20	C66	14	
21	C670	11	
22	C777	9	
23	C91	14	
24	C997	14	
25	FOREST		

Figure 4.2 Country properties

3 Press: **Enter**:

LOCATION	NO OF PROPERTIES
COUNTRY	=COUNT(B18:B24)

4 The result 7 appears in the cell.

5 Carry out the same process for each of the other locations.

Properties per location section

Calculate the average number of properties per location. Display the result as a whole number with no decimal places.

METHOD Use the AVERAGE function. Syntax is =AVERAGE(cell ref:cell ref).

Note: In some spreadsheet applications you can shorten the word AVERAGE. Excel does not allow this.

1 In the LOCATION column, select the cell below SEA and key in **AVERAGE** (Figure 4.3).

64	**PROPERTIES PER LOCATION**	
65	**LOCATION**	**NO OF PROPERTIES**
66	COUNTRY	7
67	FOREST	3
68	LAKES	8
69	MOUNTAIN	9
70	RIVERS	5
71	SEA	8
72	AVERAGE	

Figure 4.3 Properties per location – average

2 Enter the formula in cell B72:

=AVERAGE(B66:B71)

Press: **Enter**

3 The answer appears:

70	RIVERS	5
71	SEA	8
72	AVERAGE	6.666666667

4 To display this with no decimal places, click nine times on the Decrease Decimal button until the whole number 7 appears.

INFO

You can also use the **Format** menu, selecting **Cells**, to format cells in a particular way.

Exercise 4

Price code details section

Name the range of cells containing the price code and cost per week.

INFO

Excel allows you to give a meaningful name to a cell or to a range of cells. You can then use the name as part of a formula, since Excel will be able to look things up for you in this range. This makes your formulae shorter and easier to understand. It is particularly useful for large spreadsheets or for spreadsheets that are not often used, as it reminds you what the formulae are about.

METHOD

1 Select the range of cells you want to name. In this case A7–G8.
2 From the **Insert** menu, select: **Name**. Click: **Define**.
3 The Define Name dialogue box appears (Figure 4.4).

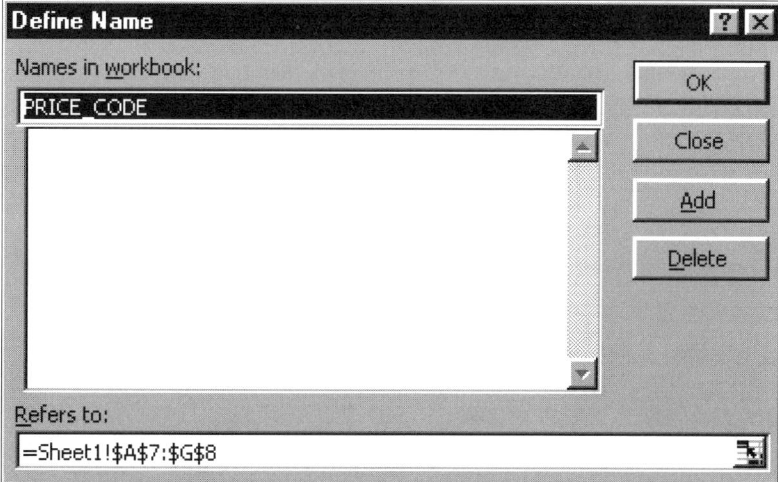

Figure 4.4 Define Name dialogue box

4 Excel suggests a name for the range, in this case PRICE_CODE. At this stage you can change the name if you wish. In this case shorten it to CODE by overwriting it and clicking on: **OK**.
5 You will notice that the name CODE appears in the Name Box (Figure 4.5).

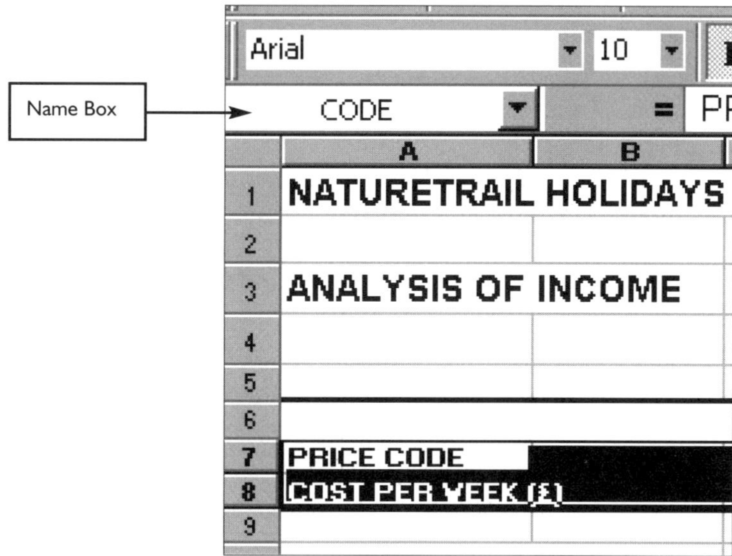

Figure 4.5 Name Box

INFO

Note: We will use this in a formula later.

Exercise 5

Property details section

Calculate the total weeks booked and replicate the formula for each property.

METHOD

Use the SUM function to do this.

Property details section

Please calculate the income and replicate the formula for each property. Use the TOTAL WEEKS BOOKED, the PRICE CODE and the FIXED CHARGE. Please note that the FIXED CHARGE should only be applied once per property and not per week booked. The formula must contain the use of the named range together with a LOOKUP function and an absolute cell reference for the FIXED CHARGE. Format this data to two decimal places *without* a £ sign.

METHOD This is quite a complicated formula, so we need to take each part in turn. Explanations and definitions will be given as they occur.

1 We need to start with the = sign to show it is a formula and follow this by the cell reference for the first property in the TOTAL WEEKS BOOKED column, ie **E18**, so the formula so far is:

=E18

2 We then need to multiply this by the price per week. This is shown in the PRICE CODE DETAILS section of the spreadsheet (the range that we named CODE). Since we have named this range, we can use Excel's LOOKUP function to find the PRICE CODE's corresponding price in £ sterling.

The syntax for the LOOKUP function is =LOOKUP(Cell that holds the compare value, range).

In this case, the cell that holds the compare value is in the PRICE CODE column, cell D18. The range that holds the value in £ sterling is the one we named CODE. Therefore this part of the formula is:

=LOOKUP(D18,CODE)

3 This needs to be multiplied by the first part of the formula, so we now have:

=E18*LOOKUP(D18,CODE)

Note: We only need one = sign in the formula.

4 We now need to add on the FIXED CHARGE. We have been asked that this should be an absolute cell reference. The cell that contains the fixed charge is C10. In order to make this cell address absolute in our formula, we must add a **$** sign in front of the column letter and in front of the row number, so that it becomes: **$C$10**.

An absolute cell reference will not change even if it is replicated or moved to another part of the spreadsheet. By contrast, a relative cell reference will change relatively to its position on the spreadsheet. This happens when you replicate formulae – the cell references change to reflect their new position.

5 Our complete formula now reads:

=E18*LOOKUP(D18,CODE)+$C$10

This gives an INCOME figure for the first property of 4850.

6 Replicate this formula for the other properties.

7 To format these values to two decimal places without a £ sign:

Highlight the cells to format
Click on: the **Increase Decimal** button twice.

Please calculate the total of the INCOME column and format to currency, showing the £ sign and two decimal places.

METHOD Use the SUM function. Format the cell using the **Currency** button.

In the TOTAL WEEKS NOT BOOKED column, calculate the total for the first property and replicate the formula for each property. (The maximum number of bookable weeks is 28.)

METHOD This is straightforward.

Add a column after the TOTAL WEEKS NOT BOOKED column, with the heading LOW(A). You must use this column to indicate whether the bookings are fewer in the BOOKED(A) column than in BOOKED(B) column.

Note: You will need to use the IF function to give the correct message for each property.

If BOOKED(A) is less than BOOKED(B) then LOW(A) will read 'YES'; otherwise it will read 'NO'. Right align the new column heading.

METHOD

1. Enter the column heading in the usual way. Remember to format it as requested, ie right align.
2. You have been asked to use the IF function.

INFO

Using the IF function

Syntax is =IF(test, "value if true", "value if false"). The IF function tests the condition specified and returns a verdict.

In this case, if BOOKED(A) is less than BOOKED(B) then LOW(A) will read 'YES'; otherwise it will read 'NO'. The formula for this is:

=IF(B18<C18,"YES","NO")

Replicate this formula for the other properties.

INFO

The syntax used to test the condition is the same as that used in Access query criteria. See Access (Chapter 3) for more details.

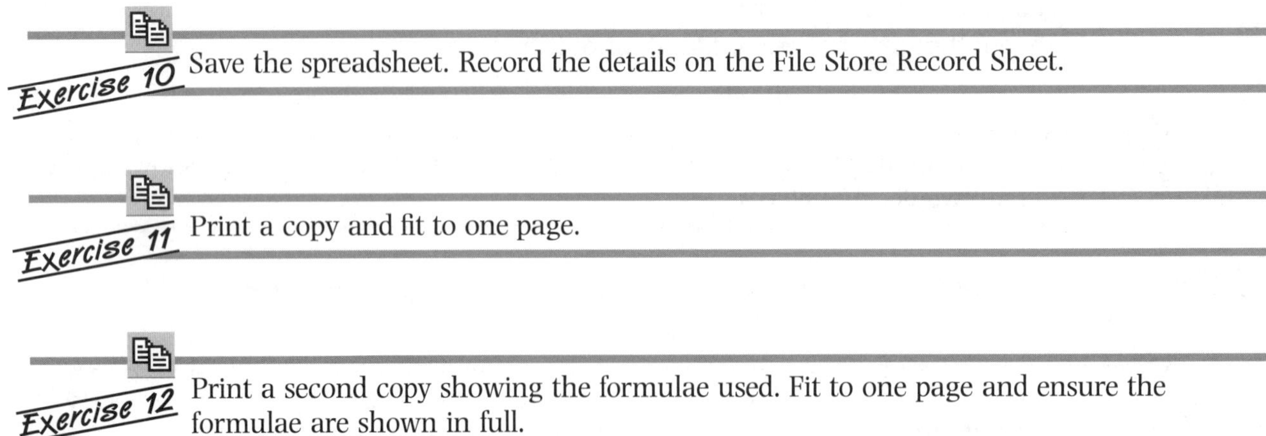
Exercise 10
Save the spreadsheet. Record the details on the File Store Record Sheet.
Exercise 11
Print a copy and fit to one page.
Exercise 12
Print a second copy showing the formulae used. Fit to one page and ensure the formulae are shown in full.

3 Printing, graphs

In this section you will revise and learn:

- printing spreadsheet extracts
- creating and printing graphs.

3.1 Printing spreadsheet extracts

Load the spreadsheet file saved in Section 2. In the PROPERTY DETAILS section, hide only the three columns containing the following headings:

BOOKED(A)
BOOKED(B)
PRICE CODE

Hiding columns

METHOD

1 Select the three columns to hide.
2 From the **Format** menu, select: **Column**, **Hide**.
Note: The same columns in other parts of the spreadsheet are also hidden (Figure 4.6).

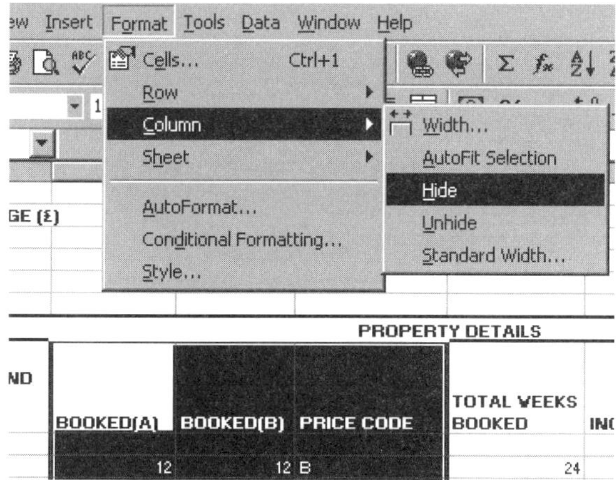

Figure 4.6 Hide

3 You will notice that a thick line appears in place of the hidden columns and the column references are also hidden (Figure 4.7).

	PROPERTY	
LOCATION AND PROPERTY CODE	TOTAL WEEKS BOOKED	INCOM
COUNTRY		
C181	24	48
C34	26	52
C66	23	46
C670	25	50
C777	21	42

Thick line denotes hidden columns

Figure 4.7 Hiding columns

Print the PROPERTY DETAILS section with the columns still hidden.

1 Select the area to print.
2 From the **File** menu, select: **Print**.
3 The Print dialogue box appears. In the **Print what** section, click on: **Selection**. Click on: **OK** (Figure 4.8).

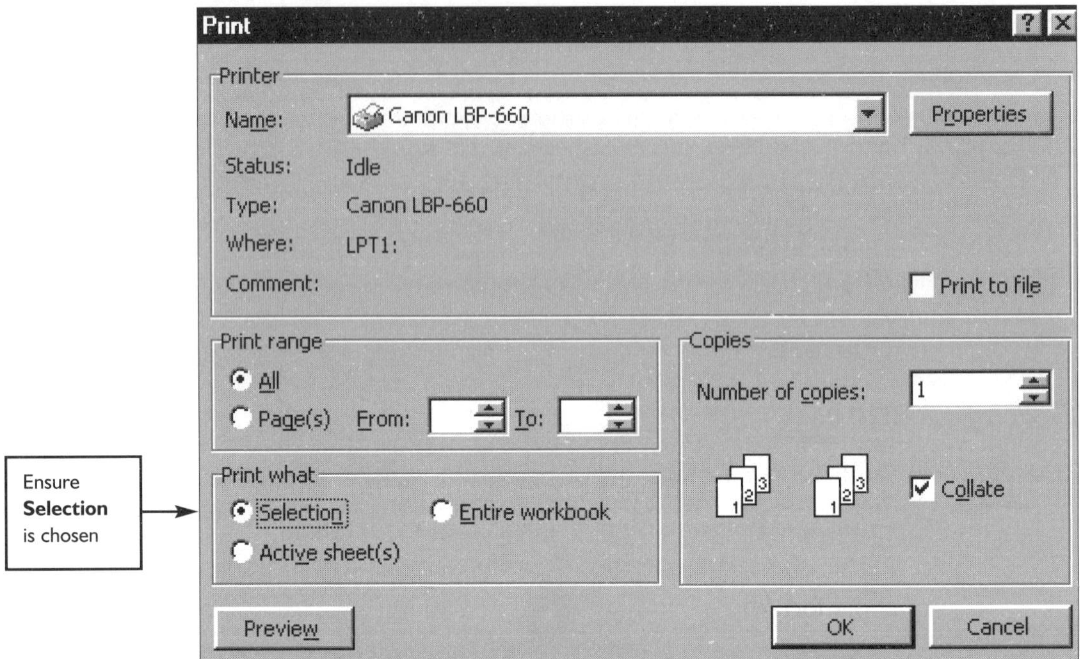

Figure 4.8 Print dialogue box

Note: You may need to check the Print Preview to ensure it fits one page. If not, adjust the size in **Page Setup**.

Change the display to show formulae. Produce a printout of the same section (as above) with the same columns still hidden. Ensure all formulae are shown in full.

METHOD

1 Press: **Ctrl** + ` (to the left of the number 1 key) to show the formulae.
2 Follow the method shown in the previous exercise.

Note: You will need to change the column widths to show the formulae in full.

Change the spreadsheet display from formulae back to values and display the previously hidden columns.

METHOD

1 Press: **Ctrl** + ` keys to return the formulae back to values.
2 Adjust column widths as necessary.

Unhiding columns

3 To unhide the columns, select the columns on each side of the hidden columns, ie LOCATION AND PROPERTY CODE and TOTAL WEEKS BOOKED.

4 From the **Format** menu, select: **Column**, **Unhide** (Figure 4.9).

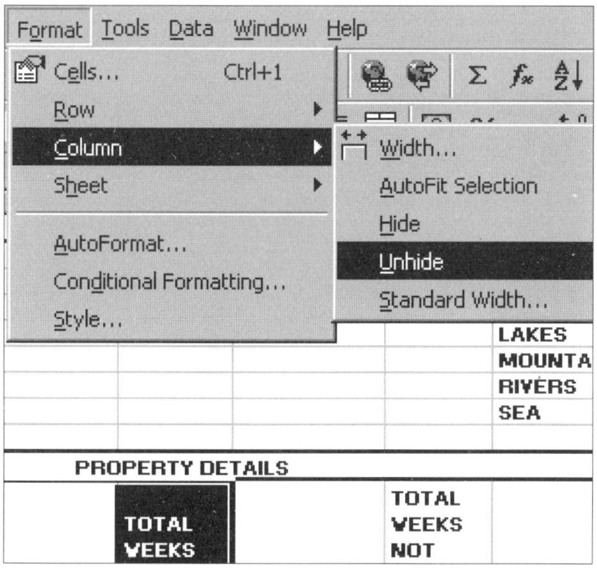

Figure 4.9 Unhide

Exercise 5

Produce the following:

REPORT/EXTRACT

Report format	Group ☐ Column ☐ Tabular ☐
Spreadsheet section	**PROPERTIES PER LOCATION**
Fields/headings to print	**LOCATION, NO OF PROPERTIES**
Sort order	
Other details (please specify)	**Produce and save separately an extract showing the column headings and the detail in these columns for all 6 locations (including AVERAGE row). To be used later where specified in publication. Do not include the section title in the extract.**
Printout required	Yes ✓ No ☐ To be dated Yes ☐ No ✓
Fit one page	Yes ✓ No ☐ Page numbered Yes ☐ No ✓

METHOD

1 Select the area to be printed.
2 From the **Edit** menu, select: **Copy** (Figure 4.10).

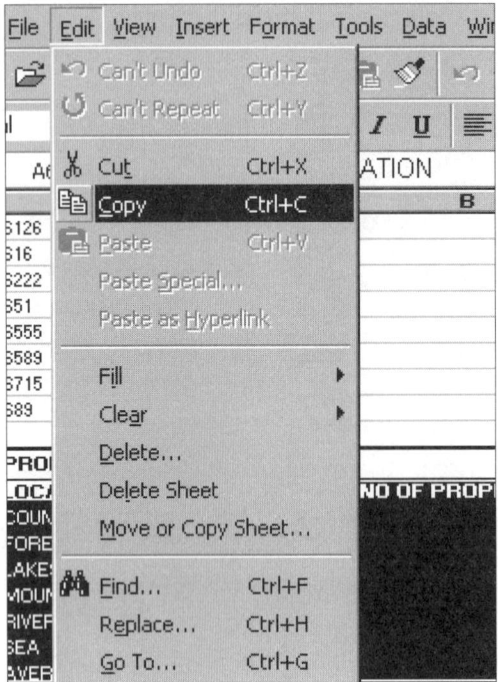

Figure 4.10 Copy

3 Click on: the **New** button to create a new spreadsheet where the extract can be pasted:

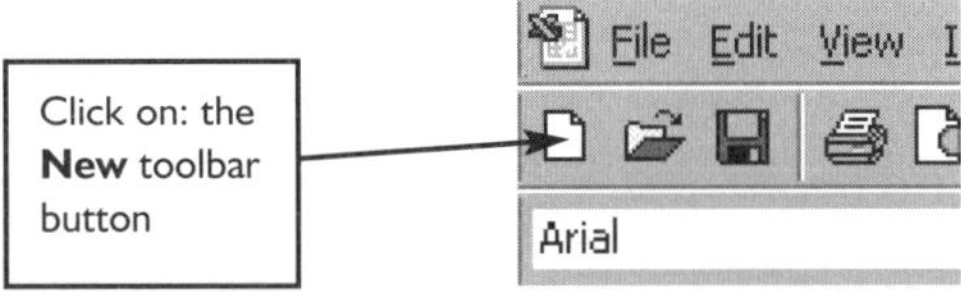

4 From the **Edit** menu, select: **Paste Special...**, the Paste Special dialogue box appears. Ensure **Values** is selected so that the values and not the formulas are copied. Click on: **OK** (Figure 4.11).

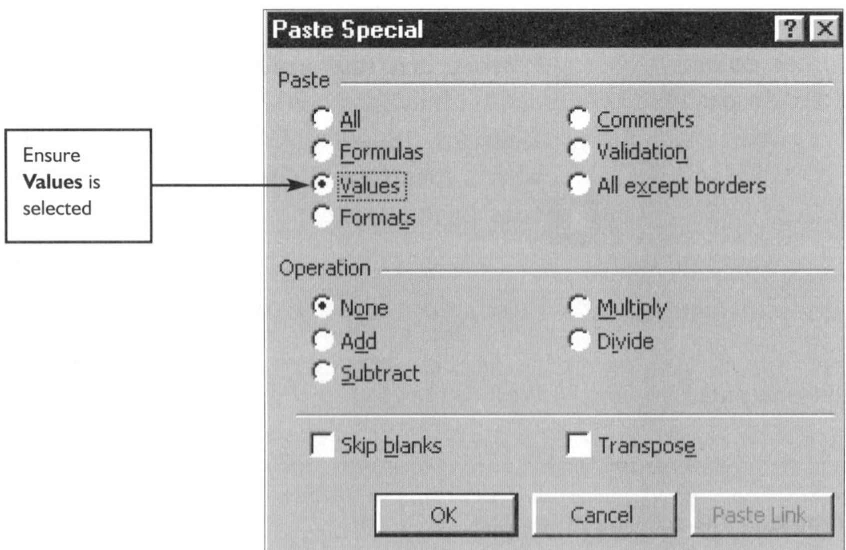

Figure 4.11 Paste Special box

INFO

Paste Special is used when copying cells that have formulae related to them. When they are copied to the new location, they will be unable to access the cells required to produce the formulae results.

5 You will notice that the Average cell has lost its formatting. To rectify this, from the **Edit** menu, select: **Paste Special...**; this time ensure **Formats** is selected. Click on: **OK**.
6 Adjust the cell widths as necessary and save the file with a unique name. Record the details on the File Store Record Sheet.
7 Print the spreadsheet.

Exercise 6 Produce the following:

REPORT/EXTRACT

Report format		Group	☐	Column	☐	Tabular	☐
Spreadsheet section	PROPERTY DETAILS						
Fields/headings to print	LOCATION AND PROPERTY CODE and PRICE CODE						
Sort order							
Other details (please specify)	Produce an extract showing the details for all properties, in these columns, that have LOW(A) bookings. Do not include the section title in the extract						
Printout required	Yes ✓	No ☐		To be dated		Yes ✓	No ☐
Fit one page	Yes ✓	No ☐		Page numbered		Yes ✓	No ☐

METHOD

1 Hide all the columns in this section except those to print. Hide all the rows that have a NO entry in the LOW(A) column. (Use the same method to hide rows as to hide columns, except from the **Format** menu, select: **Row** *not* Column.)
2 Add a page number and date to the spreadsheet. (Use **Page Setup**, **Header and Footer** – see the appendix.)

INFO

To save having to unhide all the columns and rows, you can save the spreadsheet before hiding them and then revert back to the saved spreadsheet after printing.

If you do want to unhide the rows/columns, remember you can see where the hidden ones are by looking at the row/column references. The column letters will be missing where there are hidden columns. Similarly, the row numbers will be missing where there are hidden rows.

3.2 *Creating and printing graphs*

Exercise 7

Create a graph from the spreadsheet following the instructions below:

GRAPH

Title	**COMPARISON OF BOOKED(A) AND BOOKED(B)**
Other details (please specify)	**Based on Bookings. Compare BOOKED(A) and BOOKED(B) for each location**

Printout required Yes ✓ No ☐ Legend required Yes ✓ No ☐

Axes labels required Yes ✓ No ☐ Type: bar/column ☐ Line ✓ Pie ☐

METHOD This is a straightforward graph and will provide useful revision. Ensure you follow the instructions carefully. (Refer to the quick reference guide on page 00 if you cannot remember hot to produce a graph).

Exercise 8

Follow the instructions below:

GRAPH

Title	**COMPARISON OF BOOKED(A) AND BOOKED(B)**
Other details (please specify)	**The wrong type of graph was requested, please change it. Retain the Y axis minimum value of 0 and increase the maximum to 150. Set intermediate values to intervals of 30. To be used where specified in the presentation.**

Printout required Yes ✓ No ☐ Legend required Yes ✓ No ☐

Axes labels required Yes ✓ No ☐ Type: bar/column ✓ Line ☐ Pie ☐

METHOD

1 With the line graph displayed, right-click on the graph; a menu appears. Click on: **Chart Type...** (Figure 4.12).

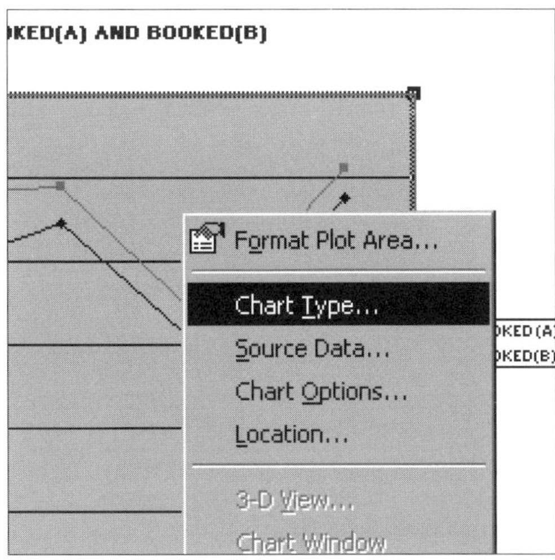

Figure 4.12 Chart Type ...

2 The Chart Type dialogue box appears. Click on: **Column** and then **OK** (Figure 4.13).

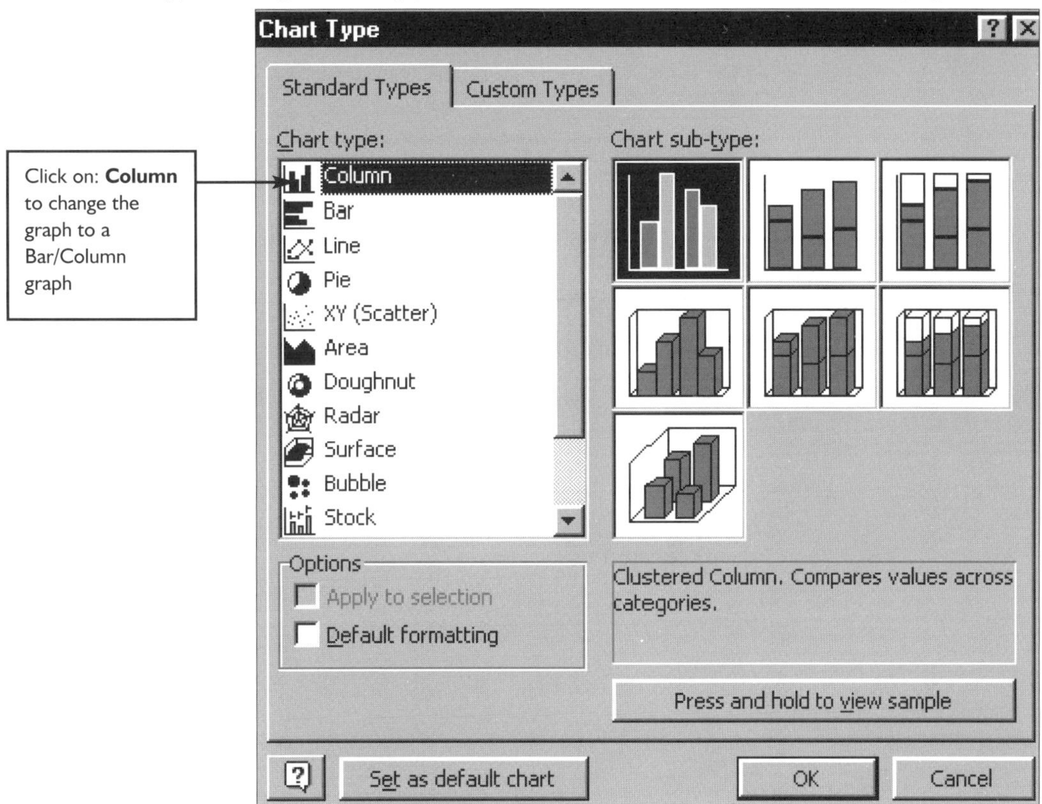

Figure 4.13 Chart Type dialogue box

3 To change the Y-axis values, double-click on: the **Value Axis** (Figure 4.14).

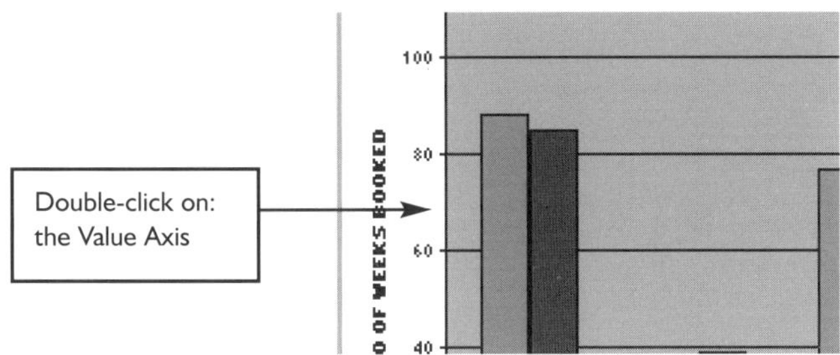

Figure 4.14 Value Axis

4 The Format Axis dialogue box appears.
5 With the **Scale** tab selected, change the Maximum value to 150 and the Major unit to 30. Click: **OK** (Figure 4.15).

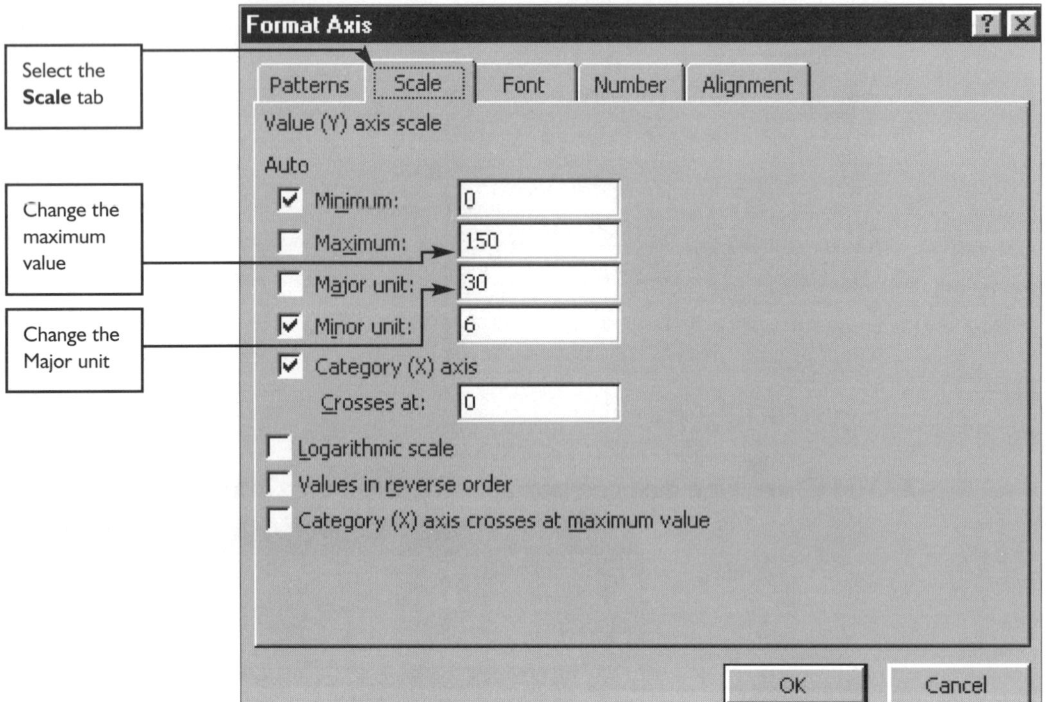

Figure 4.15 Format Axis dialogue box

6 Record the details on the File Store Record Sheet, making a note that this graph will be used in the presentation.

Excel quick reference for IBT III

Action	Keyboard	Mouse	Right-mouse menu	Menu
Align cell entries	Select cells to align			
		Click: the relevant button:	**Format Cells**	**Format, Cells**
			Select the **Alignment** tab Select from the **Horizontal:** drop-down menu as appropriate	
Absolute cell reference	Add **$** sign in front of the cell reference column letter and in front of the cell reference row number			
Bold text	Select cells to embolden			
	Ctrl + B	Click: the **B** **Bold** button	**Format Cells**	**Format, Cells**
			Select the **Font** tab Select **Bold** from the **Font style:** menu	
Capitals (blocked)	**Caps Lock** (Press again to remove)			
Close a file	**Ctrl + W**	Click: the **Close window** icon		**File, Close**
Columns, adding	Select the column following the one where you want the new column to appear – by clicking on the column ref box (at top of column)			
			Insert	**Insert, Columns**
Columns, changing width of		Drag the column border C D to fit the widest entry	Select the column(s) by clicking (and dragging) on the column ref box (at top of column)	
			Column Width Key in the width you want	**Format, Column, Width** Key in the width you want *OR* **Format, Column, AutoFit Selection**
Columns, deleting	Select the column you want to delete by clicking on the column ref box (at top of column)			
	Delete		**Delete**	**Edit, Delete**
Copy (replicate) formulae	Select cell with formula to be copied Drag the mouse from bottom right corner of cell over cells to copy to, release mouse			
Create a new file	**Ctrl + N**	Click: the **New** button		**File, New**
Date, adding	From the **View** menu, select: **Header and Footer** Click: **Custom Header** Click: where you want the date to appear Click: the **Date** button			

Action	Keyboard	Mouse	Right-mouse menu	Menu
Decimal places		Click: the **Increase Decimal** button to increase the number of decimal places Click: the **Decrease Decimal** button to decrease the number of decimal places	**Format Cells** Select the **Number** tab Click: **Number** in the **Category:** menu Select the number of decimal places you need	**Format, Cells**
Enter formulae	Click: in the cell where you want the result to appear Key in: = followed by the formula Press: **Enter**			
Enter numeric data	Click: in the cell where you want the number to appear Key in: the data Press: **Enter**			
Enter text	Click: in the cell where you want text to appear Key in: the text Press: **Enter**			
Exit the program		Click: the **Close Window** icon		**File, Exit**
Fit to page				**File, Page Setup, Fit to (1) Page**
Formulae, functions	Click on the cell where the result is required Use: **=SUM(cell ref:cell ref)** for adding a range of cells *OR* Click the: **AutoSum** button Click and drag over the cell range Press: **Enter** Use: **=AVERAGE(cell ref:cell ref)** to find the average value in a range of cells Use: **=COUNT(cell ref:cell ref)** to count the number of cells in range Use: **=LOOKUP(cell that holds the compare value, range)** to find the cell that contains the value specified Use: **=IF(test,"value if true", "value if false")** to return a value for the given test			
Formulae, operators	+ add - subtract * multiply / divide			
Formulae, printing	Ensure the formulae are showing in full			
				File, Page Setup, Page tab, **Landscape** *OR* **File, Page Setup, Page** tab Under **Scaling**, select **Fit to 1 page wide** and **1 page tall**
Formulae, showing	**Ctrl** + `			**Tools, Options, View** Under **Window options**, select **Formulas** so that a tick appears

Action	Keyboard	Mouse	Right-mouse menu	Menu
Help	**F1** **Shift + F1**			**Help** **Contents and Index** **What's This?**
Hide columns			**Hide**	**Format**, **Column**, **Hide**
Hide rows			**Hide**	**Format**, **Row**, **Hide**
Integers (whole numbers)		Click: the **Decrease Decimal** button until you have reduced the number of decimal places to zero	**Format Cells**	**Format**, **Cells**
			Select the **Number** tab Click: **Number** in the **Category:** menu Change the number of decimal places to zero	
Move to end of document	**Ctrl + End**	Use scroll bars		
Move to top of document	**Ctrl + Home**	Use scroll bars		
Moving around	Use the cursor keys	Click: where you want to move to		
Naming cells	From the **Insert** menu, select: **Name**, **Define** Key in: the name Click: **OK**			
Open an existing file	**Ctrl + O**	Click: the **Open** button		**File**, **Open**
	Select: the drive required Select: the filename Click: **OK**			
Page number, adding	From the **View** menu, select: **Header and Footer** Click: **Custom Header** Click: where you want the date to appear Click: the **Page** button			
Page Setup	From the **File** menu, select: **Page Setup** Choose from **Margins**, **Paper size**, **Paper Source**, **Layout**			
Print file	**Ctrl + P** Select the options you need Press: **Enter**	Click: the **Print** button		**File**, **Print** Select the options you need and click **OK**
Print preview		Click: the **Print Preview** button		**File**, **Print Preview**
Printing in Landscape	From the **File** menu, select: **Page Setup** Click: the **Page** tab Select: **Landscape** Click: **OK**			
Printing selected cells only	Select the cells to print			
	Ctrl + P Select: **Selection** Click: **OK**			**File**, **Print**

<table>
<tr><th>Action</th><th>Keyboard</th><th>Mouse</th><th>Right-mouse menu</th><th>Menu</th></tr>
<tr><td rowspan="3">Remove text emphasis</td><td colspan="4">Select text to be changed</td></tr>
<tr><td rowspan="2">Ctrl + B (remove bold)
Ctrl + I (remove italics)
Ctrl + U (remove underline)</td><td rowspan="2">Click: the appropriate button: B I U</td><td>Format Cells</td><td>Format, Cells</td></tr>
<tr><td colspan="2">Select the Font tab
Click: Regular in the Font Style: menu</td></tr>
<tr><td>Replicate (copy) formulae</td><td colspan="4">Select: the cell with the formula to be copied
Drag the mouse from the bottom right corner of the cell over the cells to copy to
Release mouse</td></tr>
<tr><td>Restore deleted input</td><td>Ctrl + Z</td><td>Click: the Undo button</td><td></td><td>Edit, Undo</td></tr>
<tr><td rowspan="2">Rows, adding</td><td colspan="4">Select the row by clicking in the row ref box (at side of row) below the one where you want the new row to appear</td></tr>
<tr><td colspan="2"></td><td>Insert</td><td>Insert, Rows</td></tr>
<tr><td rowspan="2">Rows, deleting</td><td colspan="4">Select the row by clicking in the row ref box (at side of row) below the one where you want the new row to appear</td></tr>
<tr><td></td><td></td><td>Delete</td><td>Edit, Delete</td></tr>
<tr><td rowspan="2">Save</td><td>Ctrl + S</td><td>Click: the Save button</td><td></td><td>File, Save</td></tr>
<tr><td colspan="4">If you have not already saved the file you will be prompted to specify the directory and to name the file.
If you have already done this, then Excel will automatically save it.</td></tr>
<tr><td rowspan="2">Save using a different name or to a different directory</td><td></td><td></td><td></td><td>File, Save As</td></tr>
<tr><td colspan="4">Select the appropriate drive and change the filename if relevant.
Click: Save</td></tr>
<tr><td>Selecting cells</td><td colspan="4">Click and drag across cells</td></tr>
<tr><td>Remove selection</td><td colspan="4">Click in any white space</td></tr>
<tr><td rowspan="2">Spell check</td><td colspan="4">Move cursor to top of document</td></tr>
<tr><td>F7</td><td>Click: the Spelling button</td><td></td><td>Tools, Spelling</td></tr>
<tr><td rowspan="2">Unhide columns</td><td colspan="4">Select the columns on either side of the hidden ones</td></tr>
<tr><td>Ctrl + Shift + 0</td><td></td><td>Unhide</td><td>Format, Column, Unhide</td></tr>
<tr><td rowspan="2">Unhide rows</td><td colspan="4">Select the rows on either side of the hidden ones</td></tr>
<tr><td></td><td></td><td>Unhide</td><td>Format, Row, Unhide</td></tr>
</table>

Hints and tips

- *Using Autofill:* If the cell contains a number, date or time period that can extend in a series, by dragging the fill handle of a cell you can copy that cell to other cells in the same row or column. The values are incremented. For example, if the cell contains MONDAY, you can quickly fill in other cells in a row or column with TUESDAY, WEDNESDAY and so on.

  METHOD

  1. Type and enter the first label or if numbers type and enter the first two numbers.
  2. Select the cell(s) containing the label or numbers you entered.
  3. Move the mouse over the bottom right corner of the selected cell(s).
  4. Press and hold down the left mouse and drag over the cells you want to include in the series.
  5. Release the mouse.

  You must not have a cell active whilst trying to format it.

- *Using Fit to Page:* Having problems printing on one page, even with a landscape setting (this may happen when printing formulae)? Use Fit to Page.

  From the **File** menu, select: **Page Setup**, **Page tab**, **Scaling** section – **Fit to 1 page**.

- Check the formulae you have used – are they generating the correct results? It is a good idea to check the first formula, in a range, with a calculator (or longhand). (*Note*: There may be a small discrepancy between the results due to rounding by the spreadsheet.)
- Ensure you have followed the alignment and formatting instructions.
- After replicating formulae, delete any zero or erroneous values in cells where they should not be.

Important! Check your work carefully. All numeric data must be 100% correct in spreadsheet assignments.

Charts using Excel quick reference for IBT III

<table>
<tr><th>Action</th><th>Keyboard</th><th>Mouse</th><th>Right-mouse menu</th><th>Menu</th></tr>
<tr><td rowspan="3">Create a chart</td><td colspan="4">Select the data to chart</td></tr>
<tr><td></td><td>Click: the Chart Wizard button</td><td></td><td>Insert, Chart</td></tr>
<tr><td colspan="4">STEP 1 Select: the chart type
Click: Next
STEP 2 Check that the source data is correct, if not change it
Click: Next
STEP 3 Select: the Titles tab
Key in the title
Select: the Legend tab
Click: in the Show legend box to add/remove tick as appropriate
(For pie charts only)
Select: the Data Labels tab
Click: Show label if appropriate
Click: Next
STEP 4 Click: As new sheet:
Key in: the chart name
Click: Finish</td></tr>
</table>

Action	Keyboard	Mouse	Right-mouse menu	Menu
Print a chart	With the chart displayed on screen			
	Ctrl + **P** Ensure **Active sheet** is selected. Click: **OK**	Click: the **Print** button (This will automatically print the sheet)		**File**, **Print** Ensure **Active sheet** is selected. Click: **OK**
Save a chart	**Ctrl** + **S**	Click: the **Save** button		**File**, **Save**
Change graphical display	*To change the scale ratios:* With the graph on screen Select: the **Plot Area** Drag the corner handles inwards (to reduce the scale) and outwards (to increase the scale) *To set upper and lower limits for Y (vertical) axis:* With the graph on screen Double-click: the **Value Axis** In the **Format Axis** dialogue box: Click: the **Scale** tab Key in: the new values in the **Maximum** and **Minimum** boxes Click: **OK** *To set intermediate values:* With the graph on screen Double-click: the **Value Axis** In the **Format Axis** dialogue box: Click: the **Scale** tab Change the **Major** unit to the required value Click: **Close** Change the Major unit to the required value. Click: **Close**.			

Hints and tips

- **Reloading a saved chart**: Reload the spreadsheet from which the chart was produced. Click on: the **Chart name** tab at the bottom of the sheet.
- When you change data in the spreadsheet, the data on the corresponding chart will change automatically to incorporate the amended data.
- Have you selected the required data to graph?
- Have you labelled it as requested?
- Have you controlled the Y axis as specified?

Automated presentation production using PowerPoint

1 Getting started

In this section you will learn how to:

- understand PowerPoint basics
- load PowerPoint
- create a new presentation
  - create slides
  - choose layouts
  - format and align text
  - save the presentation
  - insert, resize and reposition graphics
  - implement a colour scheme
  - spellcheck
- print a presentation
  - one slide per page
  - miniatures
  - notes
- exit PowerPoint.

1.1 Understanding PowerPoint basics

PowerPoint enables you to create, organise and design effective presentations. These can be used as handouts, overhead transparencies, 35 mm slides and automated presentations on a computer. We will be concentrating on automated presentations in this chapter but, as you work through the exercises, you will become aware of other options available through the menu systems.

PowerPoint is easy to learn and use if you know the basics of other Microsoft packages, eg Word, Excel. This section will enable you to gain a quick feel of PowerPoint basics before progressing to more IBT task-focused exercises.

1.2 Loading PowerPoint

Load PowerPoint.

METHOD 1

1 In the Windows 95 desktop, click on: the **Start** button – a menu appears.
2 Select: **Programs** by moving the mouse over it – another menu appears (Figure 5.1).
3 Select: **Microsoft PowerPoint** (Figure 5.1).

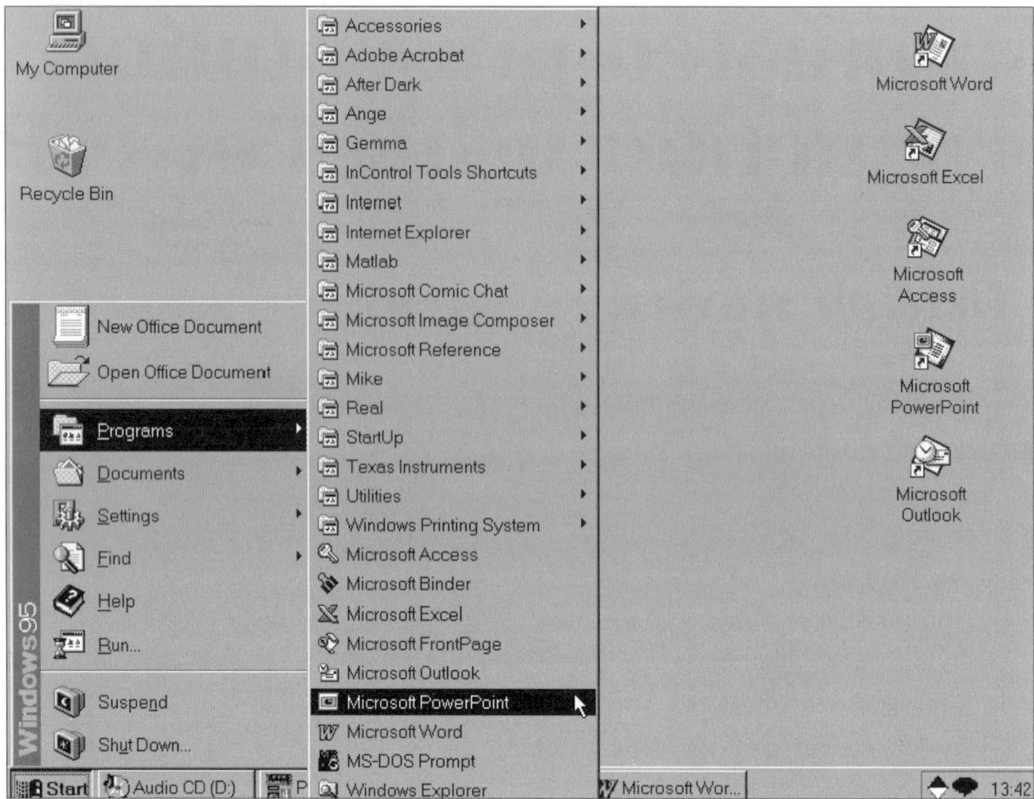

Figure 5.1 Programs – PowerPoint

METHOD 2

(Use if you have a shortcut icon to PowerPoint on your desktop.) In the Windows 95 desktop, click on: the **Microsoft PowerPoint** shortcut icon:

Either method results in the PowerPoint window being displayed on screen (Figure 5.2).

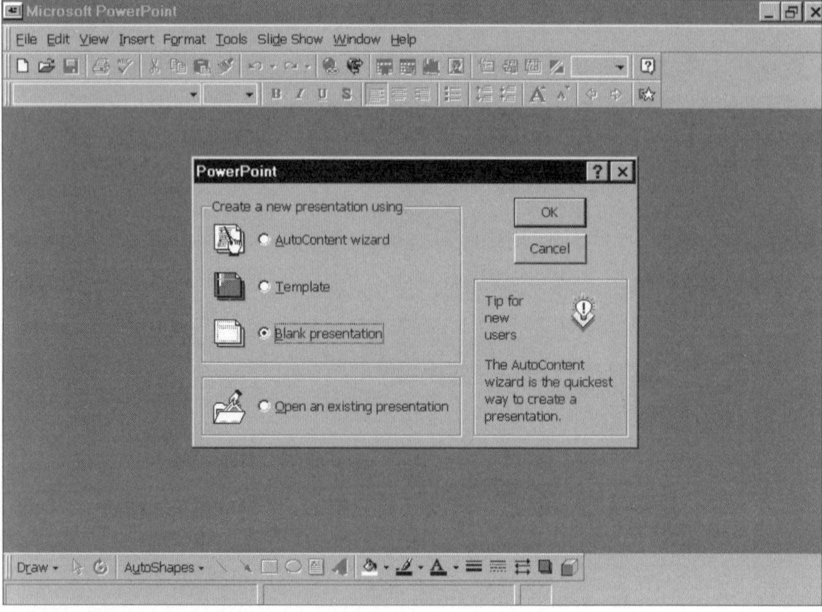

Figure 5.2 PowerPoint window

1.3 Creating a new presentation

Create slide 1.

Note: PowerPoint uses the word 'slide' for each page created, even for the production of paper printouts or overhead transparencies.

METHOD

1 Click on: **Blank Presentation** and **OK**. The New Slide dialogue box appears (Figure 5.3).

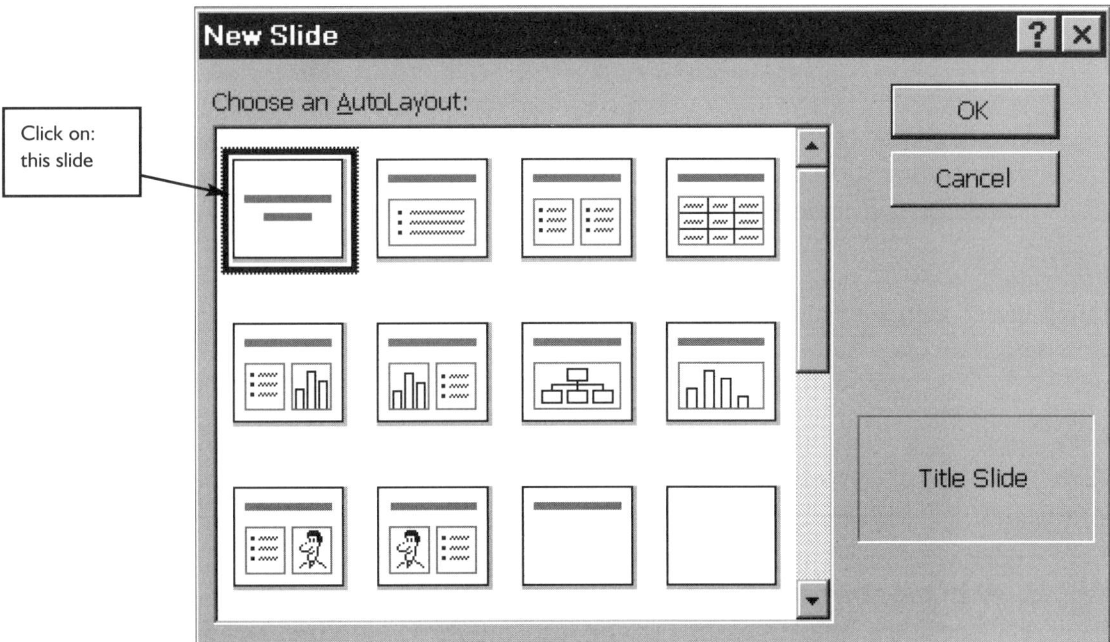

Figure 5.3 New Slide dialogue box

2 There are many different layouts to choose. In this case click the slide layout at the top left (it may already be chosen). Click on: **OK**.
3 This slide is now ready for your input (Figure 5.4).

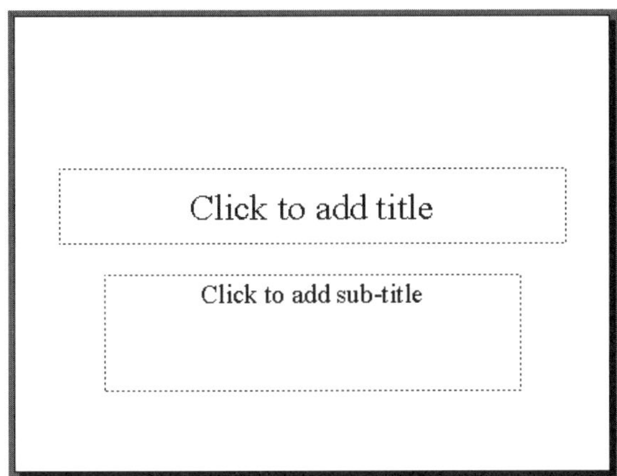

Figure 5.4 Slide ready for input

4 In the slide window, click on: the top box (click to add title) and key in **Learning PowerPoint**.
5 Click on: the bottom box (click to add sub-title) and key in your name.

Title and subtitle can also be referred to as heading and subheading. Body text is usually the text that follows the subheading.

Format the text on slide 1

METHOD

1 Ensure that the Formatting toolbar is visible (shown below). If not, from the **View** menu, select: **Toolbars** then **Formatting**.

2 As in Word, select the text you want to format and then use the Formatting toolbar buttons and drop-down menus to change the font type, point size, embolden, italicise and underline.

Serif and sans serif fonts

Serifs are small lines that stem from the upper and lower ends of characters. Serif fonts have such lines. Sans serif fonts do not have these lines. As a general rule, larger text in a sans serif font and body text in a serif font usually makes for easier reading. For example:

Times New Roman is a serif font
Arial is a sans serif font.

3 Align the text using the toolbar buttons.

4 Change the font colour by clicking the down arrow on the **Font Color** button on the **Drawing** toolbar. (By default this toolbar is at the bottom of the working area. If this is not visible, from the **View** menu, select: **Toolbars** and then **Drawing**.)

Saving the presentation

Save the presentation.

METHOD

From the **File** menu, select: **Save As**. Choose where you want to save the file and key in a filename. Click on: **Save**.

Creating slide 2

Create a second slide in the presentation.

METHOD

1 Click on: the **New Slide** button on the toolbar.

2 Choose the layout as shown. Click on: **OK** (Figure 5.5).

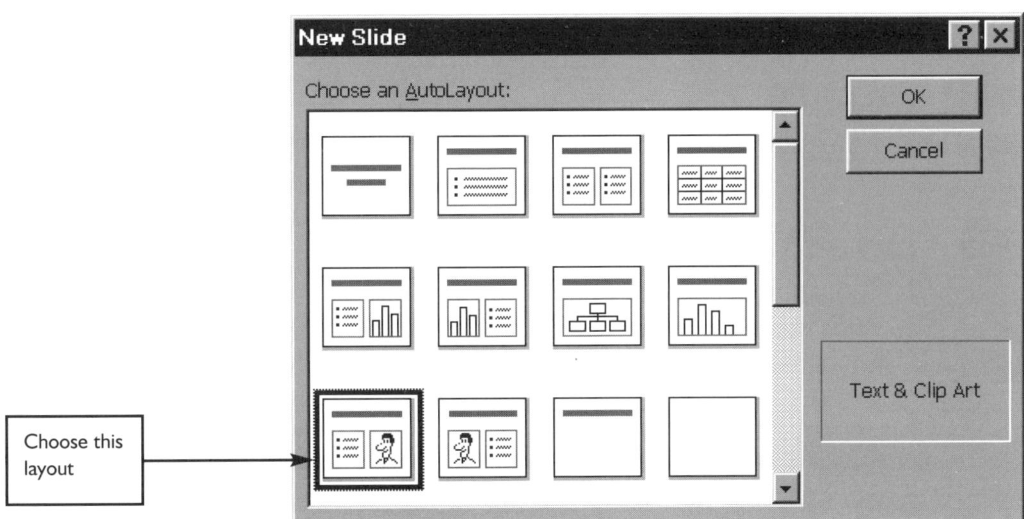

Figure 5.5 New Slide – layout

3 In the **Click to add title** box, key in **Bullets and Graphics**.
4 In the left-hand box, key in the numbers 1–7, pressing **Enter** after each number except 7 (the last one). Notice that a bulleted list has been created.
5 To insert a graphical image in the right-hand box, double-click in the box.
6 Scroll through **Clip Art** to decide which one to use.
7 Click on the chosen one and then click on: **Insert**.

Slide 2 will now look something like Figure 5.6.

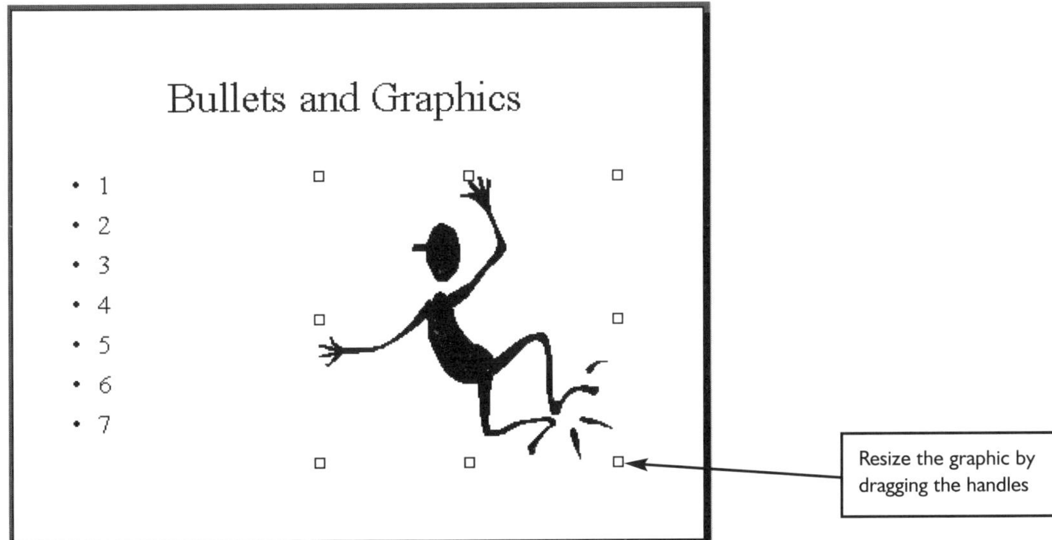

Figure 5.6 Slide 2

8 Resize the graphical image by dragging the handles.

INFO

If you want to preserve the proportions (aspect ratio) of the image always resize from a corner.

Moving the elements of the slide

Exercise 6 Reduce the size of the graphic and reposition it at the right-hand corner of the slide.

METHOD

1 Click on the graphic to select it.
2 Reduce the size as in **8** above.
3 With the graphic still selected, and holding down the left mouse button over it, drag it to the required position.

INFO

This repositioning can be carried out on any of the elements following the same method, but you will notice that you need to point the mouse at the border of some of the elements before the arrowhead cross appears. When this appears you can move the element.

Your slide will look something like Figure 5.7.

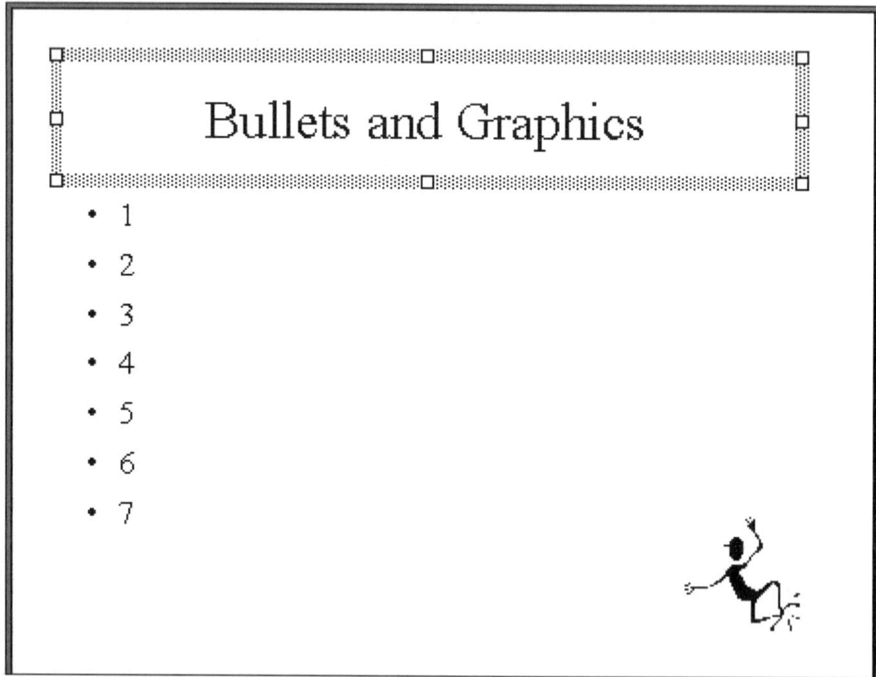

Figure 5.7 Slide – repositioning

4 Save your work using the toolbar button method.

Creating slide 3

Exercise 7 Create slide 3 for the presentation using the blank layout. Decide on your own text for this slide.

METHOD

1 Click on: the **New Slide** button.
2 Choose the **Blank** layout this time.
3 Experiment with adding your own text and graphics.

To add text

METHOD

1. Cick on: the **Text Box** button from the Drawing toolbar. (If this is not visible, from the **View** menu, select: **Toolbars** then **Drawing**.)
2. Click where you want the text to start.

   Note: You need not drag out a box, as the text will expand the box to fit.
3. Key in the text and format it as required.
4. Click in any white space on the slide when finished.

To add graphics

1. From the **Insert** menu, select: **Picture** then **Clip Art** (Figure 5.8).

Figure 5.8 Clip Art

Notice that the menu shows other types of picture you can insert. We will look at some of these later.

2. Choose the Clip Art you want to insert. Click on: **Insert**.

   Note: The graphic is placed in the centre of the slide. Resize and reposition it as necessary following the method given above. Be careful not to superimpose (overlap) any of the elements – resize and reposition them so that they do not overlap.

   Use your imagination and practise adding and changing elements on this slide. When you are happy with the result, save your work. You now have three slides in the presentation.

Viewing the slides

INFO

There are several ways to view your slides. The buttons at the bottom left of the window are for selecting the different options:

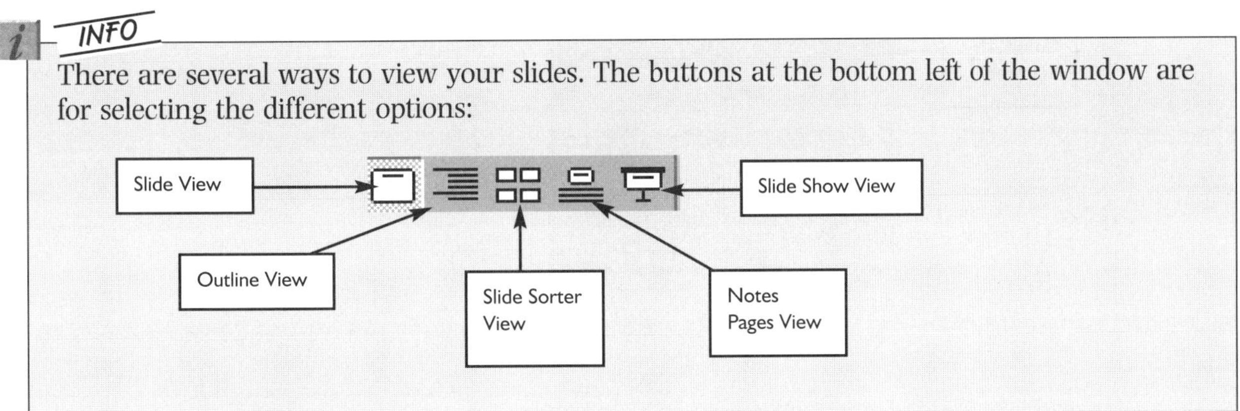

- *Slide View* – shows one slide at a time. Use this view to create/edit slides.
- *Outline View* – displays an outline of your presentation, ie the slide titles and any main text.
- *Slide Sorter* View:
  – you can view all your slides in this view as miniatures (small versions or thumbnails);
  – zoom in and out for more/less detail using **Zoom Control**;
  – sort slides into a different presentation order by clicking on the slide you want to move and dragging it to a new location;
  – add a new slide by placing the pointer between the slides where you want the new slide to appear and clicking on: the **New Slide** button;
  – delete a slide by selecting it and pressing the **Delete** key. Use the **Undo** button to reinstate the deleted slide.
- *Notes Pages View* – in this view you are able to see the slide together with a notes section where you can input any notes you want to make about the slide. This aids the speaker when making a presentation.
- *Slide Show View* – shows your slides on a full screen as they will appear when you set a slide show in motion. Select the first slide. Click on: the **Slide Show** button. To view the next slide, press the **Page Down** key. When all the slides have been viewed you will be returned to the previous view (this will be covered in more detail later).

Practise with the different views now.

Implementing a colour scheme

Change the background colour to light blue and the title text to red.

METHOD

1 In Slide View, from the **Format** menu, select: **Slide Color Scheme**. The Color Scheme dialogue box appears. The default here is Standard and you can experiment with the colour schemes provided. However, to create your own scheme, ensure **Custom** is selected, click on: **Background**, then **Change Color** (Figure 5.9).

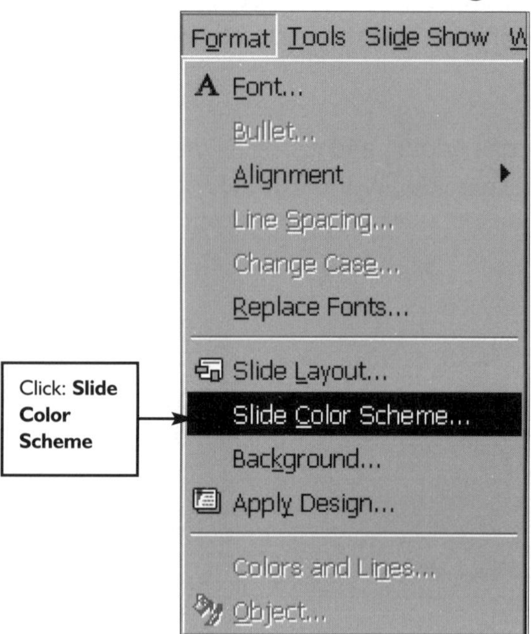

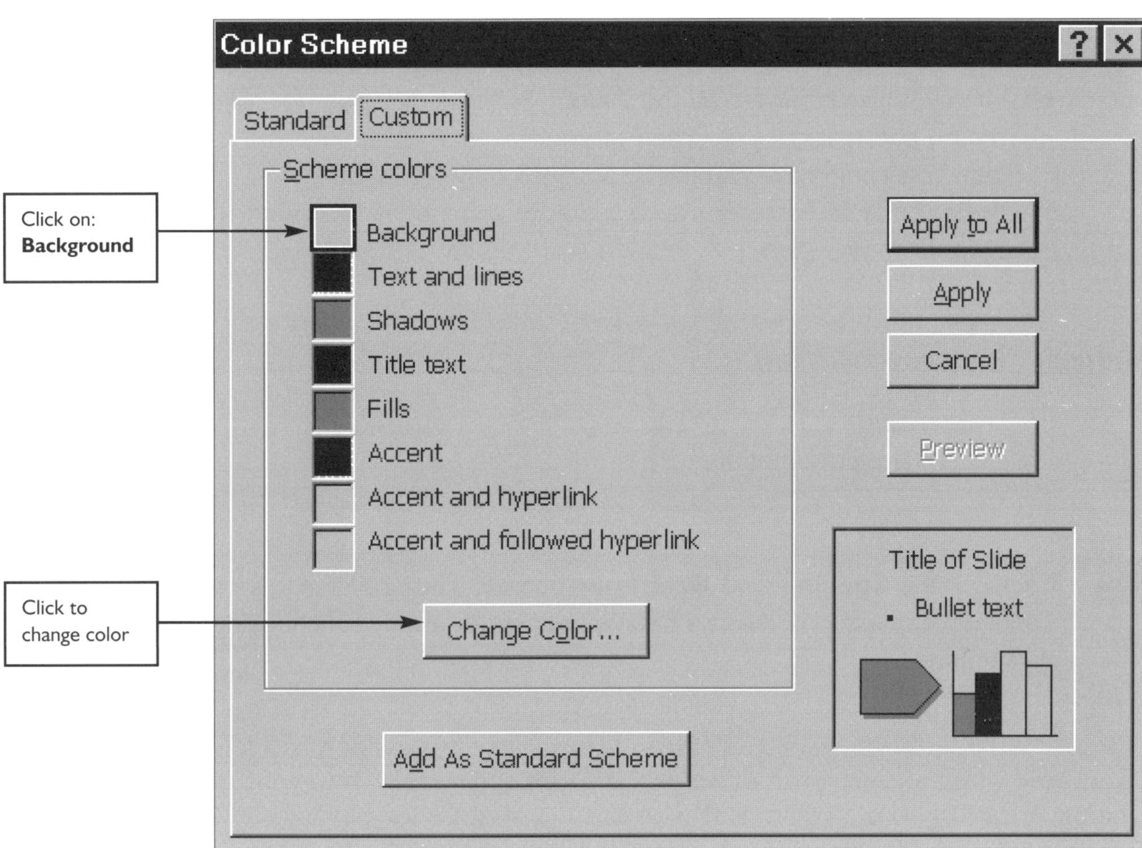

Figure 5.9 Color Scheme dialogue box

2 The Background Color dialogue box appears. With **Standard** selected, click on: a shade of light blue, then **OK** (Figure 5.10).

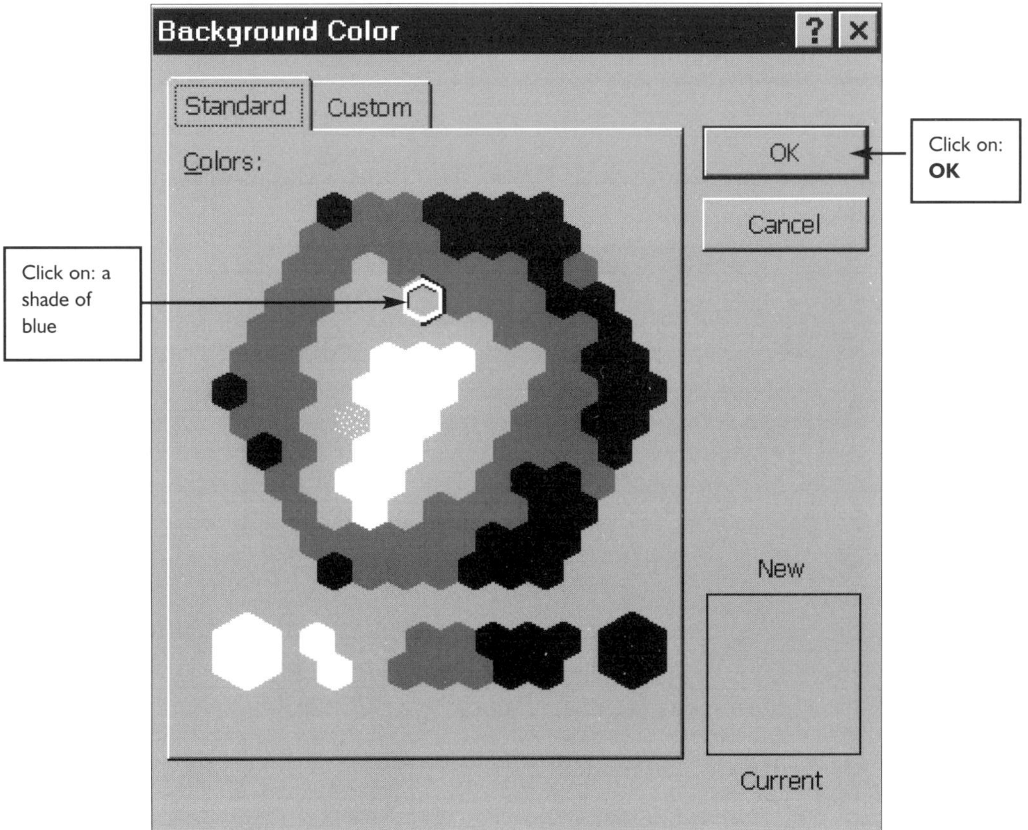

Figure 5.10 Background Color

3 You are returned to the Color Scheme dialogue box. This time select **Text** and **Lines** and follow the instructions above, choosing the colour red for the Title text.
4 When you are returned to the Colour Scheme dialogue box, click on: **Apply to All**. You are automatically returned to your slide.
Note: You could have chosen to apply to only one slide.
5 Change to Slide Sorter View to see how your slides look with this colour scheme. *Save your work.*

Spellcheck the presentation

Spellcheck the presentation.

METHOD Click on: the **Spelling and Grammar** button. The spellcheck is consistent with other Office 97 applications. Always resave your work after spellchecking to save any corrections.

Use a light background when you are printing a slide; it is easier to read. Dark backgrounds work well with an automated slide show. You can apply a design to your slide show (**Format** menu, **Apply Design**). Experiment with this later but for the purposes of IBT III, bearing in mind that the assignment must be completed in a set time, it is better to stick with the basics you can manipulate yourself.

1.4 *Printing your presentation*

Print the presentation of three slides, one slide per page.

METHOD From the **File** menu, select: **Print**. The Print – Basics dialogue box appears (Figure 5.11).

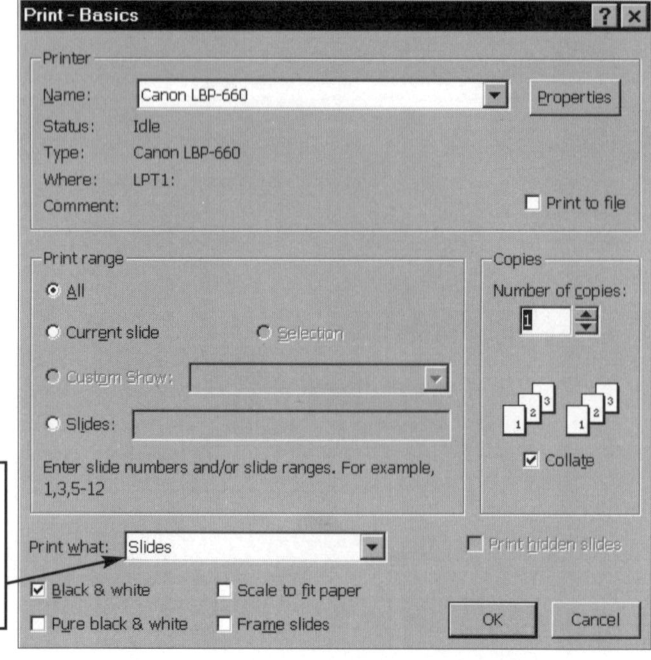

With the Slides option selected here, each slide will print on its own page

Figure 5.11 Print – Basics dialogue box

Exercise 11 Print the presentation as miniatures (thumbnails) on one page.

METHOD

1 From the **File** menu, select: **Print**. The Print – Basics dialogue box appears (as in Figure 5.11).
2 In the **Print what** box, click on: the **down arrow** and select: **Handouts** (six per page).
3 Click on: **OK**.

INFO

By choosing six slides per page (we only have three slides so far) the slides will print without leaving lines for notes.

You can also choose **Notes** pages from the **Print what** box.

1.5 *Exiting PowerPoint*

METHOD From the **File** menu, select: **Exit**.

2 Master slide, importing, copyfitting, slide order

In this section you will learn how to:

- set up a master slide
- import images and extracts
- copyfit material
- set up/change slide order.

2.1 *Setting up a master slide*

In order that your slides give a common feel to a presentation, it is a good idea to set up a master slide containing common elements that will appear on all the slides. These elements cannot then be deleted, except from the master slide. Setting up a master slide is essential for the IBT III assignment.

Set up a master slide with the following specifications:

To contain the graphic file **Logo** (this file is stored on the accompanying disk), the name of the organisation Naturetrail Holidays, the name of the designer (your name) and the date. Any text on the master slide should be between 12 and 16 pt and any typeface can be chosen.

METHOD

1. Load PowerPoint.
2. Select: **Blank presentation** and click on: **OK**.
3. Select: **Blank slide** and click on: **OK**.
4. From the View menu, select: **Master**, **Slide Master**. The Master slide appears (Figure 5.12).

You could work with some of the elements of this master slide but, as a personal preference, I find it easier to delete its contents and insert my own. You then have more control over the layout.

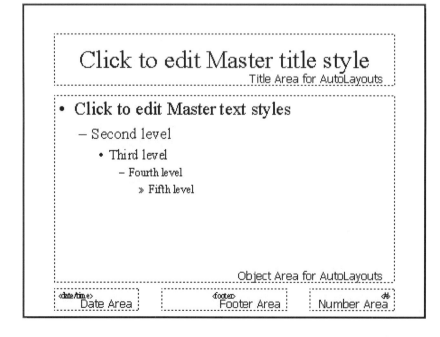

Click to edit Master title style
Title Area for AutoLayouts

- Click to edit Master text styles
  - Second level
    - Third level
      - Fourth level
        - » Fifth level

Object Area for AutoLayouts

<date/time> Date Area | <footer> Footer Area | <#> Number Area

Figure 5.12 Master slide

5 Delete all the elements on the master slide: select each one by clicking on the frame of an element and press: **Delete**.
6 Insert a text box for the name of the organisation **Naturetrail Holidays** (click on: the **Text Box** button on the **Drawing** toolbar and click on the slide where you want the text to appear). Ensure you have selected the requested point size of between 12 to 16, then key in the text.

You may not be able to read this size of text without zooming in. Using the **Toolbar Zoom**, change from 33% (the default) to a size which is comfortable for you. Change back to 33% zoom to view the whole slide.

7 Repeat for your name and for the date.
8 Rearrange these elements so they look pleasing to the eye. Remember that the main text for each slide will be placed in the centre, so it is a good idea to place them near the edges of the slide (Figure 5.13).

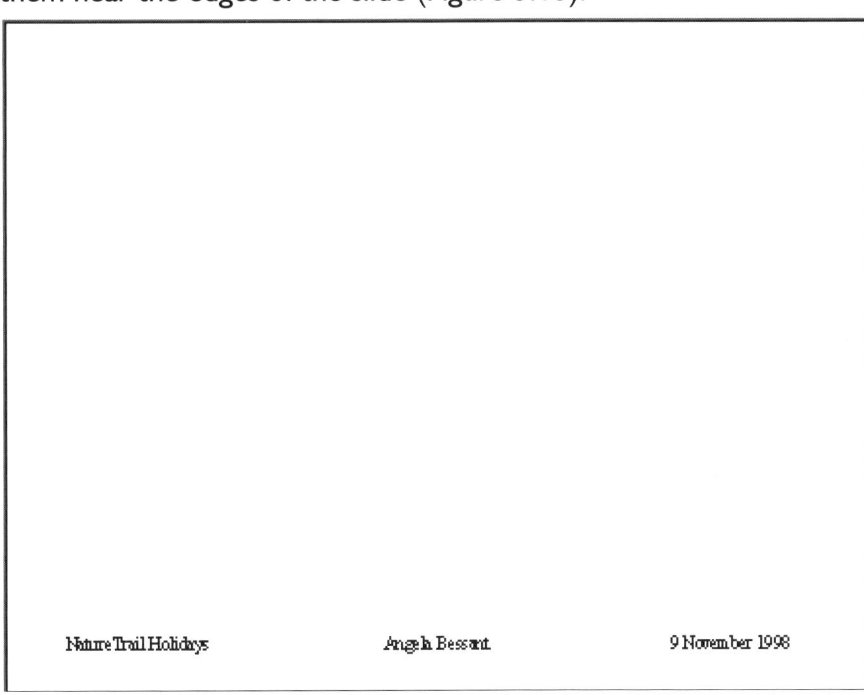

Figure 5.13 Rearranging the slide's elements

Inserting a graphic

METHOD

1 From the **Insert** menu, select: **Picture**, **From File...** (Figure 5.14).

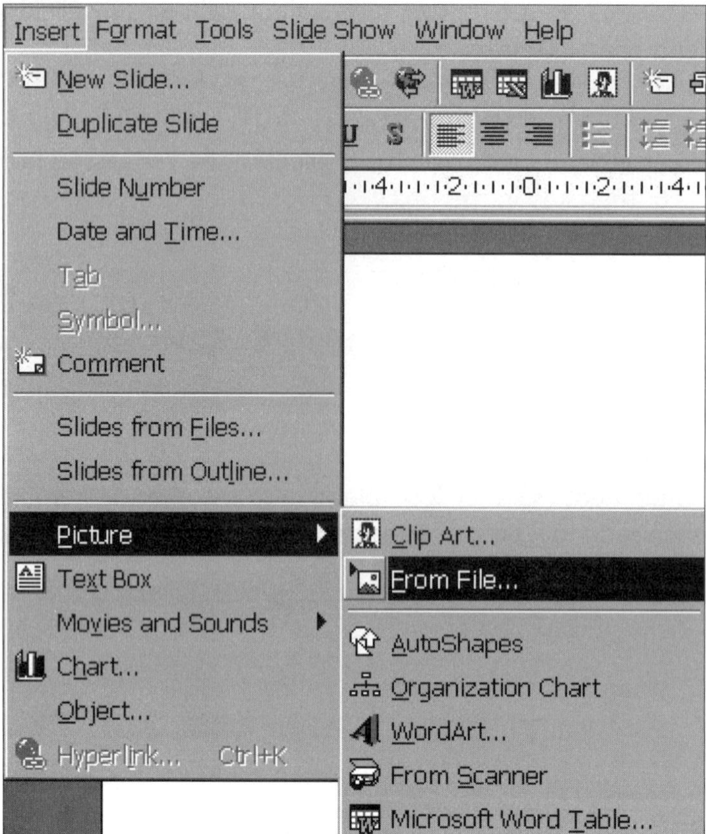

Figure 5.14 Picture, From File ...

2 The Insert Picture dialogue box appears. Select the drive and filename and click on: **Insert**.
3 Reduce the size of the graphic and position it on the slide.
4 The master slide is now complete and will look something like the one in Figure 5.15.

Figure 5.15 The completed slide

When you choose a new slide in the presentation it will be based on the master slide you have just created.

For IBT III you are given a specification for the presentation – you have two House Style Sheets and a Design Brief. Examples of these are given here and you should study them well before carrying out the following exercises. These exercises will take you through the necessary stages to complete the presentation.

Save the presentation ready for use in the next part of this section.

Design Brief: content of the presentation slides

Create a master slide. Please refer to the House Style Sheets to ensure this adheres to Naturetrail Holidays' conventions and for information on slide layout and effects. The text for the automated presentation is given below. You must retain case as shown.

Important! You must create a master slide to be used as a background for all five slides.

Text for automated presentation

Slide No.	Type of entry	Slide content	Slide duration
Master slide	Master slide text	Specified text and image – see House Style Sheet 2: Slide layout and effects, for details	
Slide 1	Heading Heading	WANT TO UNWIND? PUT US IN MIND!	5–10 secs
Slide 2	Heading Heading Subheading Subheading	NATURETRAIL HOLIDAYS TOTAL RELAXATION Tel: 01234 29786 Open 7 to 7	7–15 secs
Slide 3	Heading Body text Bullet text	DELIGHTFUL LOCATIONS Our holiday homes are situated in some of the most beautiful settings, for example: Mountains Lakes Sea	15–20 secs
Slide 4	Heading Body text Graph	BOOKINGS Why not take a holiday early in the year when there is usually more choice: *Insert graph here*	15–25 secs
Slide 5	Heading Heading Subheading Extract text	CONTACT US NOW ! WE'LL BE HAPPY TO HELP Loyalty Savings *Extract text from text file as specified in Design Brief*	15–20 secs

House Style Sheet 1: Presentation text styles

Style name	Typeface	Point size	Feature	Alignment	Additional
Master slide	Any	Between 12 and 16	Any	–	All master slide text must be the same style and consistent throughout the presentation
Heading	Sans serif	Between 40 and 60	Bold	Centre	Consistent throughout the presentation
Subheading	Sans serif	Between 26 and 36	Italic	Centre	Consistent throughout the presentation
Body text	Sans serif	Between 18 and 24	None	Left	Consistent throughout presentation
Bullet text	Sans serif	Between 18 and 24	Any	Left	No more than six bullet points per slide
Extract text	Sans serif	Between 18 and 24	Italic	Left	Consistent throughout the presentation. **Do not** apply to any text included in imported image or graph

Copyfitting

- Text and imported data are adjusted so that they are not superimposed on other text or data.
- Imported data must not be split across slides.

House Style Sheet 2: Presentation slide layout and effects

Feature	Colour	Style	Position	Max number	Additional
Background	Any	Any	–	One	Consistent use throughout the presentation
Data on master slide	Any – see Additional column	–	–	Two text colours	Consistent use throughout the presentation Ensure legibility against background colour/style To contain the organisation's logo, the name of the organisation, name of designer and the date
Text	Any – see Additional column	–	–	Two colours	Consistent use throughout the presentation Ensure legibility against background colour/style
Logo	Corporate colours or black-and-white	–	Master slide	–	Consistent use throughout the presentation and original proportions maintained
Images, diagrams or graphs	Any	–	As specified in Design Brief	As specified in Design Brief	Original proportions must be maintained at all times
Transitions	–	–	–	Four effects	At least two different effects must be used
Builds	–	–	–	Four effects	At least two different effects must be used

2.2 *Creating slides and copyfitting material*

Note: For the following exercises you will need to use the Design Brief and House Style Sheet 1 – Presentation text styles.

Create slide 1 as per specification.

METHOD

1 Click on: the **New Slide** button.
2 Refer to the Design Brief and House Style Sheet 1 and choose a slide that most resembles the slide you are producing.
Note: If there is not a slide format that resembles the one you want, choose: **Blank slide**.
3 Click on: **OK**.

The Design Brief requests that this slide is to contain two headings. House Style Sheet 1 gives details of the formatting of the text, ie typeface – sans serif point size – 40 to 60, feature – bold, alignment – centre.

4 Enter the text and format it as above.
Note: It is important that you match the case of the text.
Ensure you make a note of the point size and font you have chosen for the headings as this must be consistent throughout the presentation. I have chosen the sans serif font Arial, point size 44.
5 It will look something like Figure 5.16.

Figure 5.16 Slide 1

Ensure you make the spacing between lines consistent throughout the slides.

Exercise 4 Create slides **2** and 3 using the same steps as for slide 1. (They will look similar to Figure 5.17.)

Slide 2

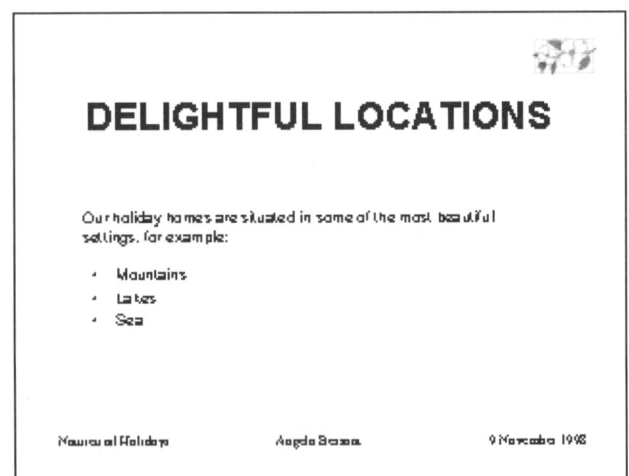

Slide 3

Figure 5.17 Slides 2 and 3

Importing a graph

Exercise 5 Create slide 4, inserting the graph saved in Chapter 4, Section 3.

METHOD

1 Using the Chart slide template as shown in Figure 5.18, enter the text for this slide.

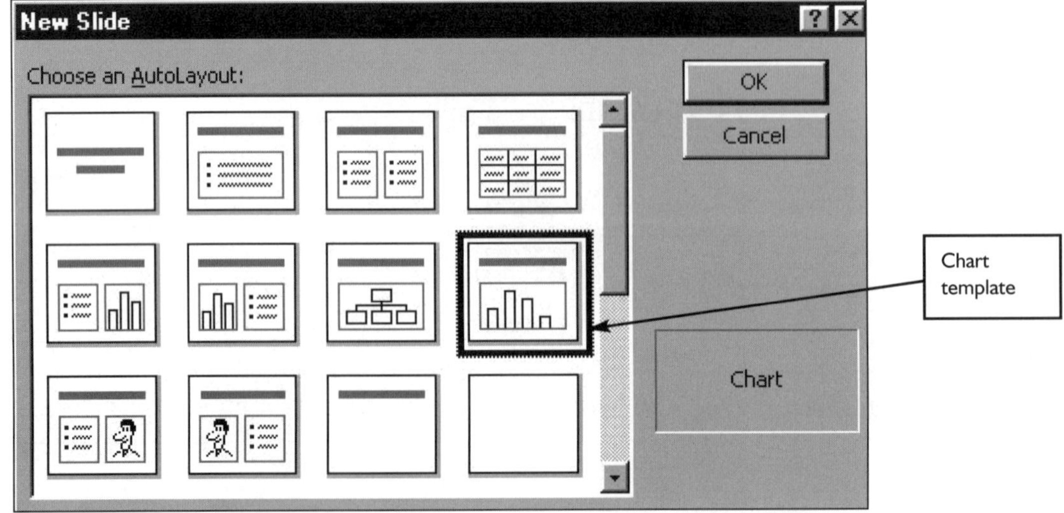

Figure 5.18 Chart slide template

2 Your slide will now look similar to the one in Figure 5.19.

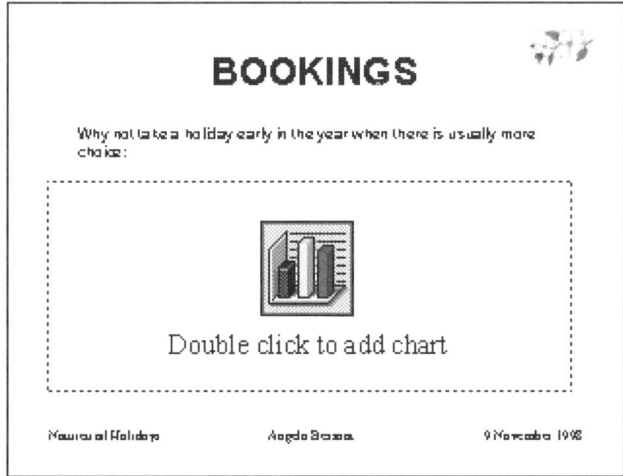

Figure 5.19 Slide 4 – text

3 Load Excel and load the saved graph to insert.
4 Ensure the graph is selected by clicking it (handles appear on the border of the chart area).
5 Click on: the **Copy** button.
6 Switch back to the PowerPoint window by clicking **PowerPoint** on the taskbar.
7 Click on: the **Paste** button. The graph appears on the slide.
8 Close Excel from the taskbar (right-click on Microsoft Excel and click on: **Close**).
9 Resize the graph so it does not overlap other elements on the slide.
10 Slide 4 will now look similar to the one shown in Figure 5.20.

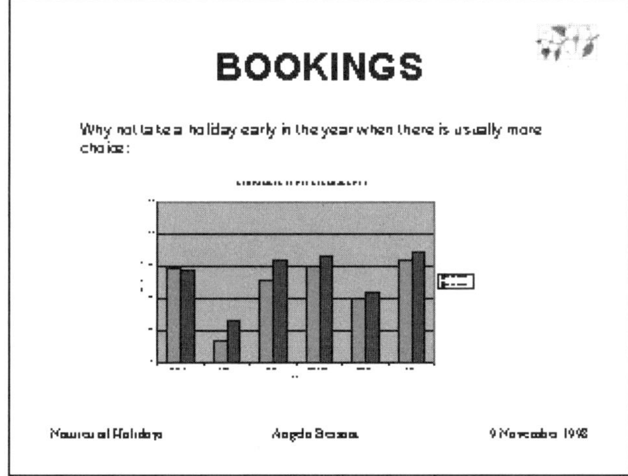

Figure 5.20 Slide 4 completed

Note: It is not essential that this slide template is used when importing a graph.

Create slide 5.
Note: This slide is to contain text that has been extracted from a text file – this file can be found on the accompanying disk.
The extract text is in the fourth paragraph. Use only the sentence beginning '**We will be continuing...**' and ending '**...super cash prizes**'.

Inserting extract text

METHOD

1. Create the slide in the usual way.
2. Load Word and load the file that contains the extract text.
3. Select the extract text and click on: the **Copy** button.
4. Switch back to the PowerPoint window by clicking **PowerPoint** on the taskbar.
5. Drag a text box big enough to accommodate the text on to the slide and click on: the **Paste** button.
6. Close Word from the taskbar.
7. Format the text as requested.
8. The slide will look similar to the one shown in Figure 5.21.

Figure 5.21 Slide 5 with extracted text

Note: You have now completed all the slides for the presentation. Save the presentation.

INFO

It is worth saving the file after each slide has been created just in case something goes wrong.

Changing slide order

Move slide 1 so that it becomes the last slide in the presentation.

METHOD

1. Change to **Slide Sorter** View.
2. Point and hold down the left mouse button on slide 1 and drag the slide to the required position.
3. Resave the presentation.

Spellcheck the presentation.

Exercise 9 Print a copy of each slide *and* an overview on one page containing a miniature (thumbnail) of each slide.

Exercise 10 Change the slides back to their original order, ie move the last slide so that it becomes slide 1 in the presentation.

Exercise 11 Resave the presentation.

METHOD Follow the method given above.

3 Transitional timings and effects, automated presentations, build effects

In this section you will learn how to:

- create transitional timings
- run an automated presentation
- create transitional effects
- create build effects.

3.1 Creating transitional timings

In Slide Show View you can see how the slides look on a full screen by moving to the next/previous slide using the **Page Up/Page Down** keys (other keys will also perform the same task. Pressing the **Home** key will take you to slide 1, and pressing the **End** key will take you to the last slide). The slides do not run automatically. In order for them to do this you need to set up transitional timings (slide durations) which automatically show the next slide after a set number of seconds.

Load PowerPoint and load the file saved at the end of Section 2. Create an automated presentation with slide durations shown on the design brief in Section 2 and reproduced below:

Slide no.	Slide duration (seconds)
Slide 1	5–10
Slide 2	7–15
Slide 3	15–20
Slide 4	15–25
Slide 5	15–20

METHOD

1 Click on: the **Slide Sorter** view.
2 Click on: **Slide 1** to select it.
3 Click on: the **Slide Transition** button:

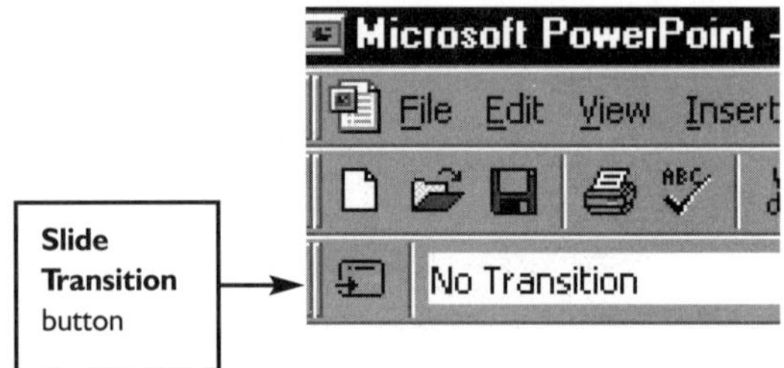

4 The Slide Transition dialogue box appears (Figure 5.22).

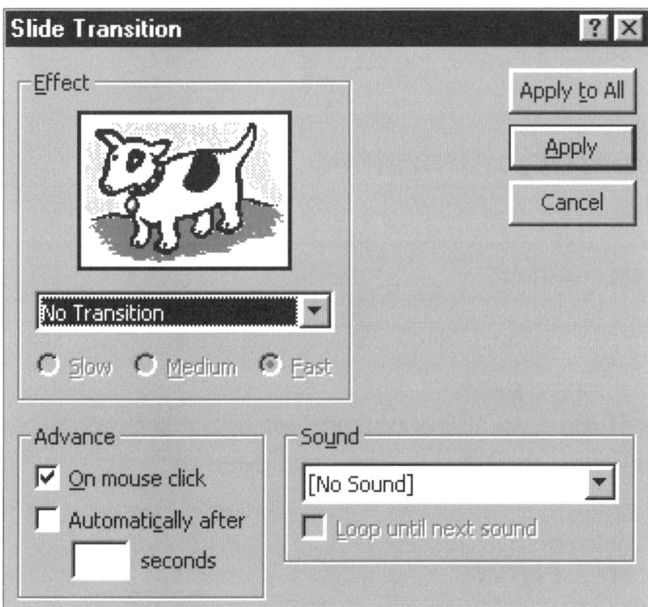

Figure 5.22 Slide Transition dialogue box

5 In the **Advance** section, click on: **On mouse click** so that there is no tick in the box. Click in **Automatically after** so that a tick is shown, and in the seconds box, key in the slide duration for slide 1 (in this example, it can be any number from 5 to 10).

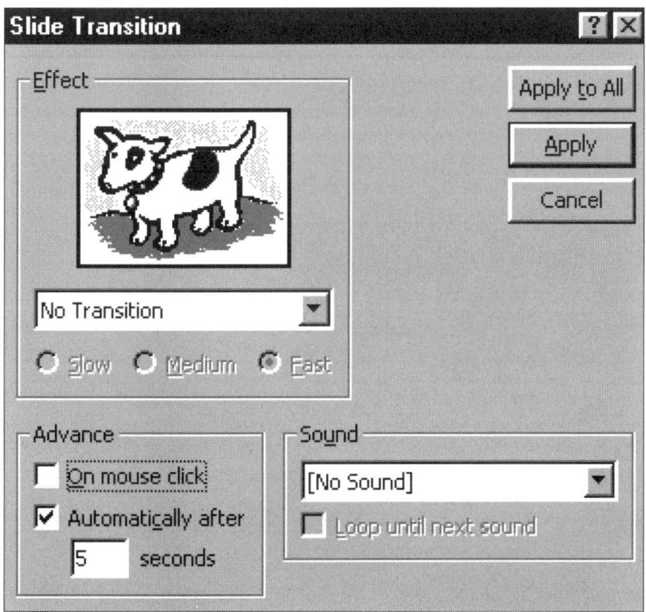

Figure 5.23 Slide Transition – 5 seconds

6 Click on: **Apply**. Slide 1 now has the duration (05) shown underneath at the left-hand side (Figure 5.24).

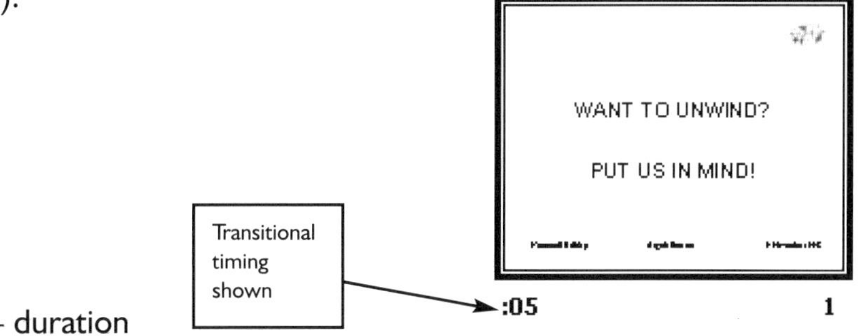

Figure 5.24 Slide 1 – duration

7 Repeat steps 2–6 for each of the other slides ensuring you have selected a timing in the range requested.
8 Save the presentation.

3.2 Running an automated presentation

Exercise 2 Run the automated presentation.

METHOD

1 Select slide 1 in Slide Sorter View.
2 Click on: the **Slide Show** icon at the bottom left of the screen and the presentation will run automatically with the timings that have been set.

3.3 Creating transitional effects

INFO

Transitional effects control how slides appear on the screen during a presentation. They are used to enhance the display and to ensure the audience of the presentation stay interested in it.

Exercise 3 Create different transition effects for each of the slides.

INFO

House Style Sheet 2 in Section 2 gives the maximum number of transition effects for the presentation as four, and at least two different effects must be used. For practice purposes, we will look at an effect for each slide.

METHOD

1 Click on: **Slide Sorter** view.
2 Click on: **Slide 1** to select it.
3 Click on: the **down arrow** on the **Slide Transition Effects** toolbar (Figure 5.25).

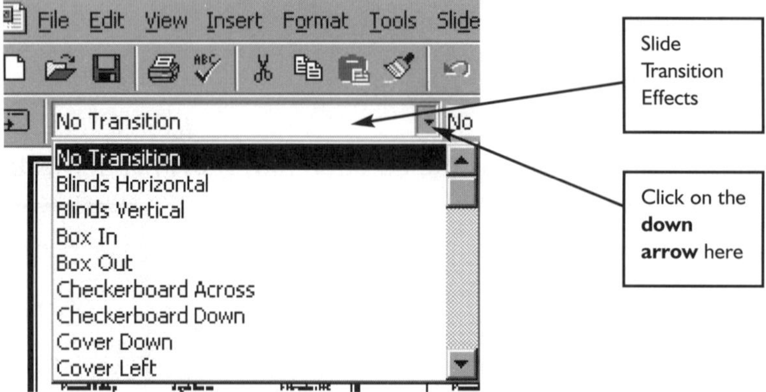

Figure 5.25 Slide Transition Effects toolbar box

4 A drop-down list appears. There are many transition effects to choose from – you can scroll down for more. Click on a transition effect – you will see a preview of the effect on slide 1. Experiment with the different effects. When you find one you like, click on that one so that it remains visible in the **Slide Transition Effects** box.

5 An icon appears beneath the slide to show it has a transition effect applied to it, as shown in Figure 5.26.

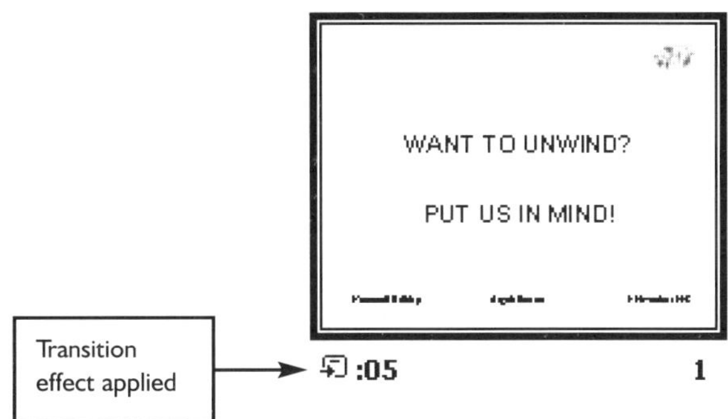

Figure 5.26 Applying a transitional effect

6 Repeat for the other slides, choosing a different transitional effect for each one.

7 Save the presentation.

8 You can now run the presentation so that you can view how the transitional effects look.

If you want to apply the same transition effect to more than one slide in the presentation, select more than one slide by holding down the **Shift** key while selecting them. It is best not to apply too many transition effects to an automated presentation. Stick to the ones you think work the best and ensure you follow the instructions on House Style Sheet 2 when working on an IBT III assignment.

You can define the transition effect further by clicking on: the **Slide Transition** button so that the Slide Transition dialogue box appears. Here you can choose the speed of the effect and add sound. Experiment with this if you have time. (*Note*: This is not required for IBT III.)

3.4 *Creating build effects*

Build effects determine the way text is revealed on a slide. They are usually very effective when applied to bulleted lists but can be applied to any slide.

Exercise 4 Add different build effects to all the slides except slide 4.

House Style Sheet 2 in Section 2 gives maximum number of build effects for the presentation as four, and at least two different effects must be used. For practice purposes, we will look at an effect for each slide except the slide with the graph.

METHOD

1 Click on: the **Slide Sorter** View button.
2 Click on: **Slide 1** to select it.
3 Click on: the **down arrow** on the **Text Preset Animation** box (Figure 5.27).

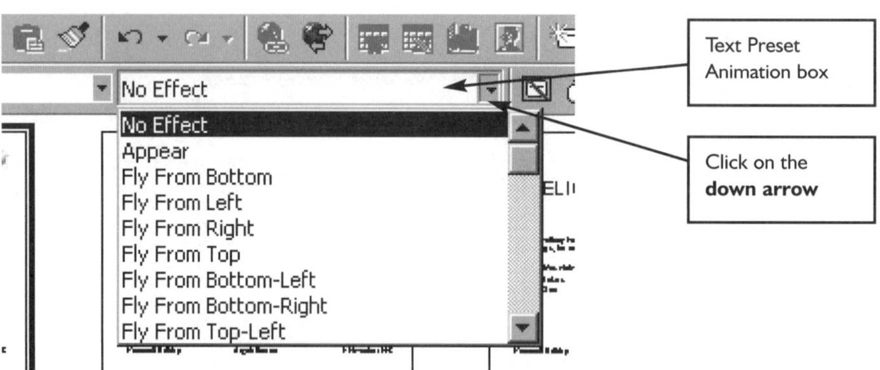

Figure 5.27 Text Preset Animation

4 A drop-down list appears. There are many effects to choose from – you can scroll down for more. Click on an effect. You will not see a preview, as is the case with transition effects.
5 An icon appears beneath the slide to show that a build effect has been applied to it (Figure 5.28).

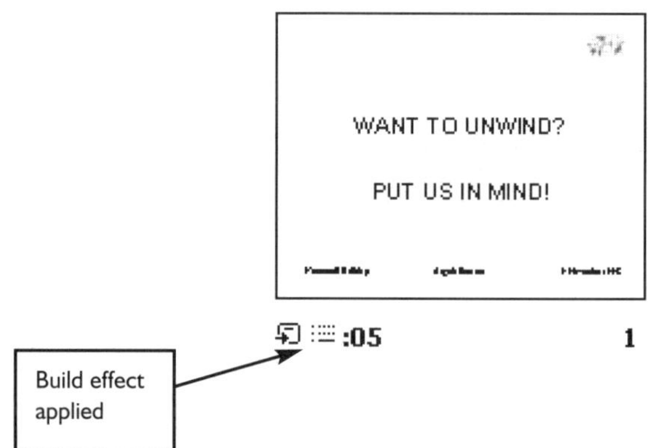

Figure 5.28 Build effect

6 To view the build effect, change to **Slide Show** View. The presentation will begin. To exit the slide show, press the **Esc** key.
7 Add build effects to the other slides as requested.
8 Save the presentation.
9 View the automated presentation.

PowerPoint quick reference for IBT III

Action	Keyboard	Mouse	Right-mouse menu	Menu
Bold text	**Ctrl + B**	Click: the **B** **Bold** button	**Font**	**Format**, **Font**
			Select: **Bold** from the **Font style:** menu	
Capitals (blocked)	**Caps Lock** Key in the text **Caps Lock** again to remove			Select text to be changed to capitals: **Format**, **Change Case**, **UPPERCASE**
Centre text	Select the text			
	Ctrl + E	Click: the **Center** button		**Format**, **Alignment**, **Center**
Change case	Select the text to be changed			
	From the **Format** menu, select: **Change Case** Select the appropriate case			
Close a file	**Ctrl + W**	Click: the **Close Window** icon		**File**, **Close**
Create a new file	**Ctrl + N**	Click: the **New** button		**File**, **New**
	Select the new slide template you want to use Click: **OK**			
Cut text	Select the text to be cut			
	Ctrl + X	Click: the **Cut** button	**Cut**	**Edit**, **Cut**
Delete a character	Press **Delete** to delete the character to the right of the cursor Press ← (Backspace) to delete the character to the left of the cursor			
Delete a word	Double-click: the word to select it Press: **Delete**			
Delete/cut a block of text	Select the text you want to delete			
	Delete *OR* **Ctrl + X**	Click: the **Cut** button	**Cut**	**Edit**, **Cut**
Effects, build effects	In **Slide Sorter** View			
		Click: the down arrow next to the **Text Preset Animation** box	**Slide Transition**	**Slide Show**, **Slide Transition**
			In the **Effects** section	
	Select: the effect you want from the drop-down menu			
Effects, transitional effects	In **Slide Sorter** View			
		Click: the down arrow next to the **Slide Transition Effects** box	**Slide Transition**	**Slide Show**, **Slide Transition**
			In the **Effects** section	
	Select: the effect you want from the drop-down menu			

Action	Keyboard	Mouse	Right-mouse menu	Menu
Effects, transitional timings	In **Slide Sorter** View			
		Click: the **Slide Transition** button	**Slide Transition**	**Slide Show, Slide Transition**
	In the **Advance** section Select: the timing you require			
Exit PowerPoint		Click: the **Close Window** icon		**File, Exit**
Font	Select the text you want to change			
		Click: the down arrow next to the **Font** box Select: the font you require	**Font**	**Format, Font**
			Select: the required font from the **Font:** menu	
Serif	Serif fonts have small lines at upper and lower ends of characters – eg Times New Roman			
Sans serif	Sans serif fonts do not have lines – eg Arial			
Font size	Select the text you want to change			
		Click: the down arrow next to the **Font Size** box Select: the font size you require	**Font**	**Format, Font**
			Select: the required size from the **Size:** menu	
Help	**F1**			**Help** **Contents and Index**
What's this?	**Shift + F1**			**What's This?**
Importing				
graphic	From the **Insert** menu, select: **Picture**			
extract text and Excel graph	Use copy (in the source application) and paste into PowerPoint			
Insert text	Position the cursor where you want the text to appear Key in the text			
Load PowerPoint	In Windows 95 desktop			
		Double-click: the **PowerPoint** shortcut icon		**Start, Programs, MS Office, Microsoft PowerPoint**
Master Slide setup				**View, Master, Slide Master**
New Slide	**Ctrl + M**	Click: the **New Slide** button		**Insert, New Slide**
Open an existing file	**Ctrl + O**	Click: the **Open** button		**File, Open**
	Select the appropriate directory and filename Click: **Open**			
Print – slides, thumbnails (miniatures), notes	**Ctrl + P**			**File, Print**
	Select from the **Print what:** drop-down menu			

Action	Keyboard	Mouse	Right-mouse menu	Menu
Remove text emphasis	Select text to be changed			
	Ctrl + B (remove bold) **Ctrl + I** (remove italics) **Ctrl + U** (remove underline)	Click: the appropriate button: **B** *I* U	**Font**	**Format, Font**
			Select **Regular** from the **Font Style:** menu	
Run automated presentation		Click: the **Slide Show** button at the bottom left of the screen		**View, Slide Show**
Save	**Ctrl + S**	Click: the **Save** button		**File, Save**
	If you have not already saved the file you will be prompted to specify the directory and to name the file. If you have already done this, then Excel will automatically save it.			
Save using a different name or to a different directory				**File, Save As**
	Select the appropriate drive and change the filename if relevant. Click: **Save**			
Slide order	In **Slide Sorter** View Click and drag: the slide to required position			
Spell check	**F7**	Click: the **Spelling** button		**Tools, Spelling**
Undo	**Ctrl + Z**	Click: the **Undo** button		**Edit, Undo**

Hints and tips

Check your work carefully:

Have you done everything asked? Have you:

- set up the master slide as requested?
- applied slide styles as requested?
- chosen font type (serif and sans serif) and size as specified and formatted it as requested? Does the imported text extract, graph or logo show in full? Is it the correct one?

Are text/images/lines superimposed?

Has the imported image retained its original proportions?

Have you sorted the slides as requested?

Have you applied the requested:

- build effects?
- transitional timings?
- transitional effects?

Have you printed the slides as requested?

Proofread carefully. Ensure you have not missed out exclamation marks, question marks, full stops or colons, etc where shown.

Publication production using Word

1 Getting started

In this section you will learn and practise how to:

- insert an image
- import a text file
- set up document layout
- apply styles.

In this chapter, you will be working with an existing text file and an image file (stored on the accompanying disk), together with files created in earlier sections. (The files you created earlier will have their names on your File Store Record Sheet.) Throughout the sections you will produce a publication to a set specification. This specification is found on House Style Sheet 1 – Publication page layout, and House Style Sheet 2 – Publication text style. You will need to study these carefully. In the IBT III assignment, you are able to exercise your own judgement over exact formatting of the publication. For practice purposes, this chapter will demonstrate a specific format. The Full Practice Assignment, in Part 2, will allow you to complete a similar task where you can decide on your own preferred format.

House Style Sheet 1: Publication page layout

Feature	Measurement	Position	Additional
Margins	1.5 cm left and right 2.5 cm top and bottom	–	Consistent throughout the publication
Spacing between columns	1.5 cm	–	Consistent between all columns
Page numbering	12 pt	At top of page	Not to be printed on front cover. To commence with number 2 on second page Align consistently throughout the publication
Headers/footers	12 pt	–	Footer should contain the name of the designer and the date of the publication
Pages	A4	–	Consistent orientation throughout the publication – either portrait or landscape
Columns	–	–	Two to four columns for all text except the headline Columns should be of equal size throughout the publication
Logo/image	On front cover – this should cover at least half of the width of the page When used elsewhere in the document it must be centred within the column	On front cover, centre horizontally, either within margins or page. It need not be centred vertically Elsewhere, position as specified in Text For Publication (pages 101–3)	When in colour only corporate colours may be used. Black-and-white image may be used if preferred

House Style Sheet 2: Publication text style

Style name	Typeface	Point size	Feature	Alignment	Additional
Headline	Sans serif	Between 36 and 60	Bold capitals	Centre	Position horizontally across the page or margins. Must be across full width of page spanning all columns
Subheading	Sans serif	Between 18 and 22	Italic	Left	Consistent throughout the publication **Do not** apply to text included within imported graphs, images or diagrams
Body text	Serif	Between 10 and 14	–	Left	Consistent throughout the publication. Set in two to four columns
Bullet text	Serif	Use same as body text (between 10 and 14)	To include a bullet character (eg •■○)	Left	Ensure the bullet text is indented from the bullet point (hanging indent) Consistent throughout
Extract text	Sans serif	Between 10 and 14	Bold	Any	Extract style applies to *all* extracted text, except text included within graphs, images or diagrams *Do not* exceed column width Consistent throughout the publication Place a box or border around the text

1.1 *Creating a front cover and inserting an image*

Create a front cover. This will be the first page of the four-page publication on A4-sized paper. Ensure it contains only the logo, as instructed in House Style Sheet 1.

METHOD

1 Open a new Word file. Decide what orientation to give the publication. In this example, I have chosen landscape. To do this, from the **File** menu, select: **Page Setup**, **Paper Size** tab. Ensure **Landscape** is chosen and **Apply to** whole document. Click on: **OK**.
(*Note*: Check that Paper Size A4 is chosen – it is the default.)

2 Import the image file. With the cursor at the top of the (blank) page you have just created, from the **Insert** menu, select: **Insert Picture**, **From File...** and choose the logo file to insert. Click on: **Insert**. Refer to House Style Sheet 1 for details on image positioning etc.

The logo should cover at least half of the width of the page. It must be centred horizontally. It must appear in full and original proportions must be maintained. It should not be given any extra colours.

You will need to reduce the zoom so that the whole page can be seen at once. To do this change the **Zoom** on the toolbar to **Whole Page**.

Alter the size of the image (from a corner to preserve proportions) so that it covers at least half the width of the page and centre it on the page. You can check that it is centred by looking at the ruler and examining the page in Print Preview.

Save the file with a different filename.

Saving the file with a different filename at regular intervals allows you to go back as many steps as you like if you are not happy with the result.

1.2 *Inserting a headline*

On the second page, insert the headline **Naturetrail Holidays**.

METHOD

1 Insert a page break after the logo. To do this, position the cursor under the logo, from the **Insert** menu, select: **Break...**, **Page Break**. Click on: **OK**.

2 Refer to House Style Sheet 2 for details of the heading (Headline) text.

INFO

It should be sans serif, between 36 and 60 pt size, bold, capitals and centred. It must be positioned horizontally across the page and must span all columns. Key in the text and format it as requested.

1.3 *Importing a text file*

Import the text file directly below the headline.

TEXT FOR PUBLICATION

If you are looking for a peaceful and relaxing holiday then look no further than Naturetrail Holidays. From small beginnings five years ago when the company had only one location we are now able to offer a choice of six completely different locations. Whatever your idea of the perfect place for a holiday we have the answer.

LOCATIONS

We have holiday cottages in the beautiful unspoit countryside of the Cotswolds. Here you are able to ramble along the picturesque footpaths and visit the charming villages and small towns that are dotted around this area. Our forest properties are situated in North Wales, close to Betws-y-Coed. There are endless outdoor activites in this area ranging from walking, canoeing or climing. In Cumbria you will find our lakes cottages - if you like sailing and fishing then this is the place for you. Again in North Wales, situated in the heart of Snowdonia, you will find our mountain complex. There are even trained mountaineers on hand to give you coaching in all aspects of climbing. So don't worry if you're a novice, there are activities ranging from those for beginers right through to the more experienced climber. Cornwall is the setting for our seaside properties. These are located between Boscastle and Newquay. The scenery in this area is second to none. There are wild coastal footpaths, fishing villages and sandy beaches. You will be spoilt for choice for your daily excursions! For those of you who enjoy the tranquillity of a riverside setting, you will find this at our site in Devon. Our properties are situated only 100 metres from the river Dart. Of course also in this area, in addition to riverside activities, there are beautiful moorland walks.

THE CHOICE IS YOURS. We beleve that you cannot fail to appreciate the natural beauty that abounds in all of these locations.

PROPERTIES AVAILABLE

Our properties vary in size and we have properties to suit most needs. You can choose from one to four bedrooms, with the maximum occupancy being eight people (there is the possibility that some of our properties can accommodate babies (cots and high chairs can be provided at no extra cost). Please ask the agent when booking.

PRICES

Prices vary depending on the size of the property. This year we have introduced a new system and now if you book for more than one week, any subsequent weeks are charged at a reduced rate.

The table below shows the prices relating to the different codes:

CODE	COST	EXTRA WEEK
A	£150	£135
B	£200	£185
C	£225	£210
D	£255	£240
E	£300	£285

Insert database report here

Why not reserve a property for our early booking period? The properties shown below are on special discount prices (deduct a further 10% from the price shown in the brochure) for this year only:

You can arrive on Friday or Saturday depending on which property you have chosen and at any time before 7 pm. Please let us know if you will be arriving later than this. Staggering arrivals in this way makes it easier to ensure that we have more staff available to give you a warm welcome. You may prefer to travel on a Friday, especially in summer when the roads are usually less congested. Whilst on the subject of transport, you will notice that most of our properties have parking adjacent to them. Where this is not the case your vehicle may be left in the parking areas which are never more than 50 metres away. For unloading purposes, parking outside the property is perfectly acceptable but please remember to move your vehicle as soon as you can since it will cause an obstruction.

Your property will have been fully cleaned and inspected beffore your arrival which can be anytime after 12 noon. All bed linen is provided but you will need to bring your own towels. All properties are self-catering but to help you settle in, we do provide a small grocery basket containing essentials, such as bread and milk. Should you find that things are not to your liking, please contact us straight away. WE PRIDE OURSELVES ON GIVING YOU THE BEST SERVICE AT ALL TIMES.

Insert logo here

LOYALTY SAVINGS

Naturetrail Holidays are pleased to to announce an important bonus for customers who have taken holidays with us in the past. We are now able to give substantial discounts on your holiday booking this year.

If you book your holiday before the end of January you will be entitled to a 20% discount on the standard cost of your chosen property (subject to its availability). If you book before the end of March you will be entitled to a 10% discount on the standard cost.

We feel that this is a very generous ofer and hope that you will be able to make your bookings early to benefit from the maximum savings.

Each 'loyalty' customer will be entered into our prize draw. We will be offering cash prizes ranging from £50 to £500 to those lucky ones picked out at random. If you are eligible for this discount, please have your previous booking reference to hand when you call. If you no longer have your booking reference, don't worry we will be able to look up your details on our database.

HOW TO BOOK

Our properties can be booked from our Head Office by telephoning 01234 29786. We are open from 7 am to 7 pm every day except Sunday. Our regional offices can also help you with any queries that you may have. They are each allocated several properties that are their major concern. Choosing the right accomodation to suit your needs can be difficult and we want to help you make an informed choice. You can rely on our staff giving informative and friendly advice. Our computerised booking system gives instant availability of our properties so that we can suggest an alternative should your first choice be taken. Shown below are the properties dealt with by our Bristol office:

Insert spreadsheet report here

As you can see each regional office deals with properties from all of the locations. Our staff training ensures that all staff have visited the six locations and are aware of the differences between them.

When booking please ensure that you have the following details to hand:

Bullet text

Reference of Property
Price Code
Date Required
Number in Party
Vehicle Registration Number
Credit Card Number
Former Booking Ref (if applicable)

Here at Naturetrail Holidays we pride ourselves in providing an excelent booking service and we hope that you feel that this level of excellence carries through to all of our operations. We know how important it is that everything runs smoothly so that you are able to relax and enjoy yourselves.

So what are you waiting for? Have another look through our brochure and imagiine the fun that you'll have with Naturetrail Holidays.

DON'T DELAY - BOOK TODAY.

METHOD

1. Position the cursor where you want the start of the text to appear.
2. From the **Insert** menu, select: **File....** Choose the file location and name.
3. Click on: **OK**.

1.4 *Spellchecking*

Perform a spellcheck and resave the file.

1.5 *Setting margins*

Set the margins as specified.

METHOD

1. Press: **Ctrl** + **Home** to take the cursor to the beginning of the file.
2. From the **File** menu, select: **Page Setup**. Select the **Margins** tab and set the margins as requested on House Style Sheet 1.

Margins should be 1.5 cm left and right, 2.5 cm top and bottom.

3. Ensure **Whole document** is selected in the **Apply to** section.

1.6 Setting styles and alignment

Exercise 6

Change the font typeface, point size and enhancement of the subheadings, body text and bullet text to those requested on House Style Sheet 2. Align the text as specified.

METHOD

1 Examine House Style Sheet 2 to determine the text style.
2 Select the text in turn and format, align and enhance it as requested.

Save your work.

INFO

Instead of using the manual method of changing text styles, the following method can be used.

METHOD

1 Apply the appropriate formatting to text that has been keyed in.
2 Select the text.
3 From the **Format** menu, select: **Style**.
4 The Style dialogue box appears. Click on: **New** (Figure 6.1).

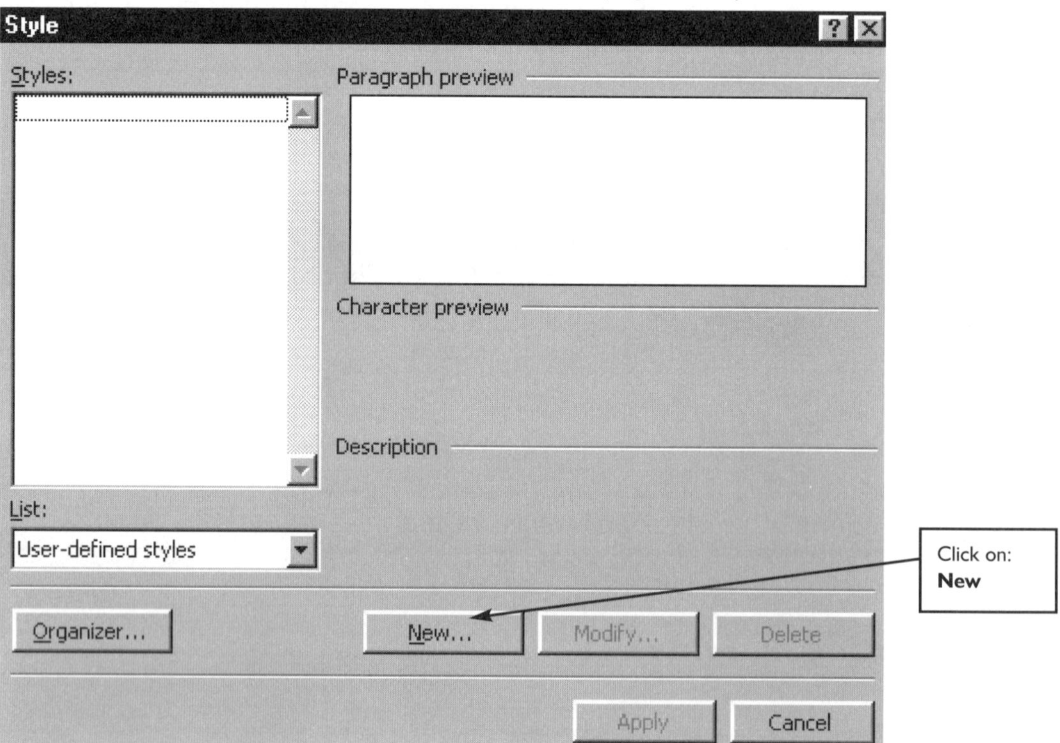

Figure 6.1 Style dialogue box

5 The New Style dialogue box appears (Figure 6.2).

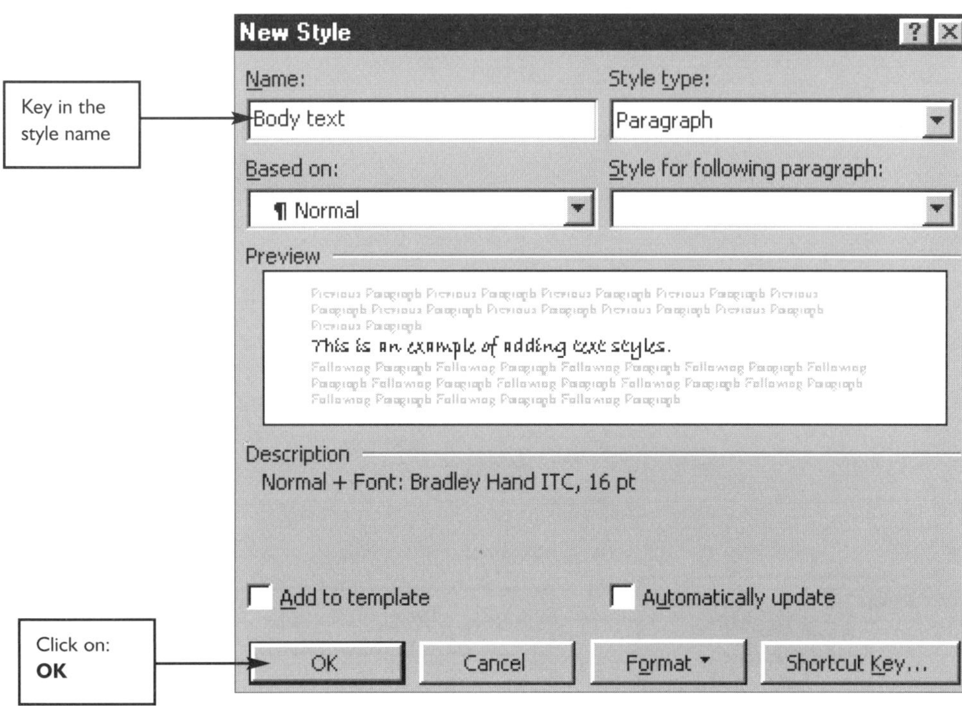

Figure 6.2 New Style dialogue box

6 In the **Name** box, key in the style name, eg Body text, Headline.
Note: A description of the text style is shown in the Description section.
7 Click on: **OK**.
8 You are returned to the Style dialogue box. The style you have chosen is now shown. Click on: **Apply** (Figure 6.3).

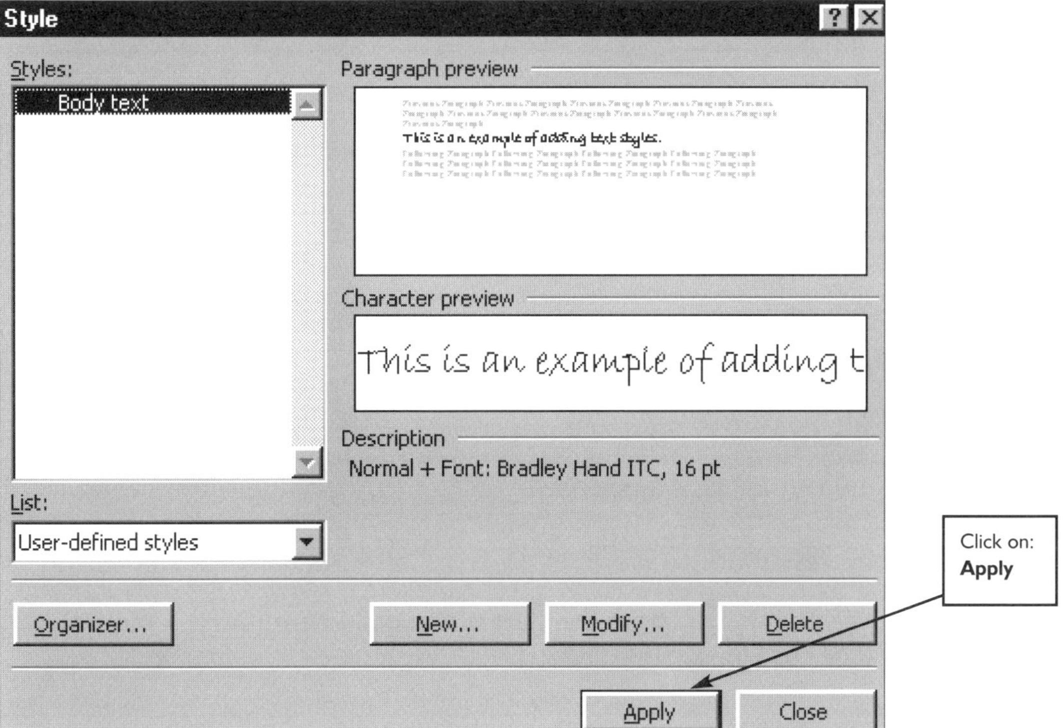

Figure 6.3 Applying a style

9 Repeat the above for each style of text you require.

To apply the text style to a block of text:

1 Select the text you want to apply the style to.
2 Choose the text style from the **Style** drop-down list (Figure 6.4).

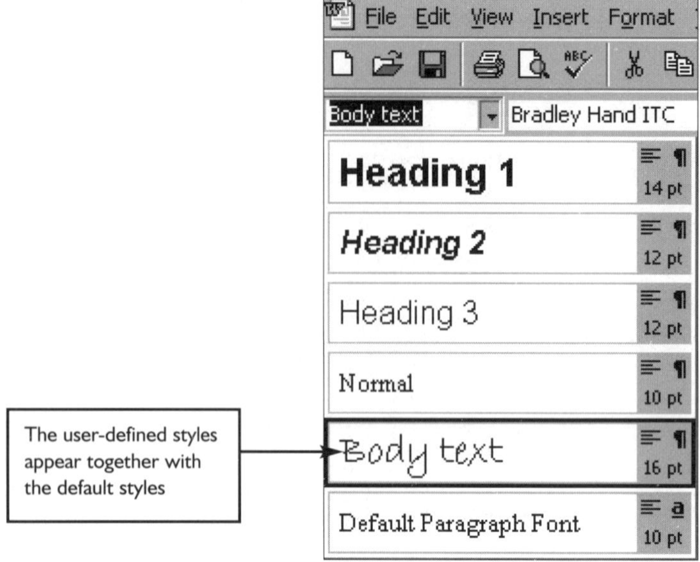

Figure 6.4 Style drop-down list

When carrying out IBT III assignments, you may want to change the style to ensure good layout. To amend a text style:

1 Format the text as required.
2 Select the text.
3 Click on: the **down arrow** so that the Style drop-down list is showing.
4 Click on: the style you want to amend. The Modify Style box appears.
5 Click to **Update** the style to reflect recent changes.
6 Click on: **OK**.

1.7 *Page numbering*

Number the pages as specified.

METHOD

1 Position the cursor at the start of the document (**Ctrl** + **Home**).
2 Refer to House Style Sheet 1.

Page numbers should be at top of page, 12 point size, not printed on front cover. To commence with number 2 on second page. Aligned consistently throughout the publication.

3 From the **Insert** menu, select: **Page Numbers...**; the Page Numbers dialogue box appears. Choose the **Position** for page numbers, choose the **Alignment** for page numbers and ensure that **Show number on first page** is not selected. Click on: **OK** (Figure 6.5).

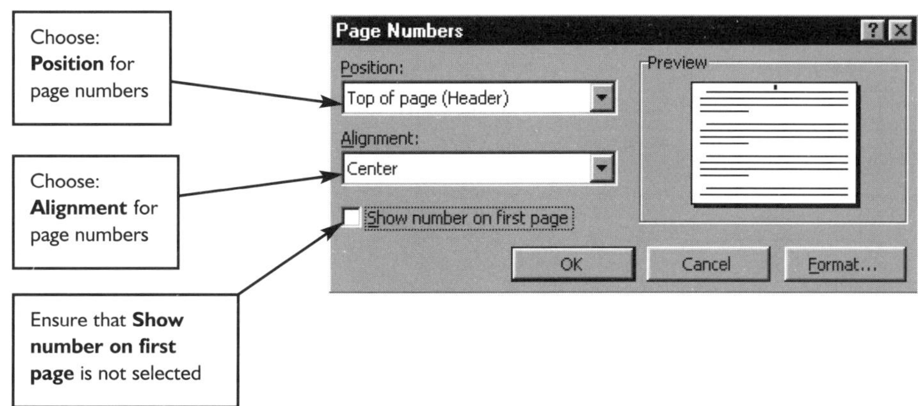

Figure 6.5 Page Numbers dialogue box

4 To set the point size for the page numbers, double-click on any page number. The **Header and Footer** dialogue box appears. Click once on the page number and then drag the mouse over it to select it. Change the font size using the drop-down Font Size list.
5 Click on: **Close**.

Use the **Format** option in the **Page Numbers** dialogue box if further formatting is

1.8 *Setting up columns*

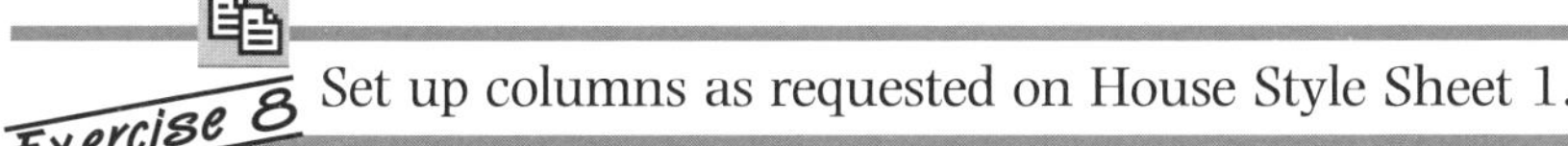

Set up columns as requested on House Style Sheet 1.

You can decide how many columns to have across the page (between two and four). In this instance I will choose three. When completing the Full Practice Assignment in Part 2, experiment with a different number of columns.

METHOD

1 Select the text that needs to be put into columns.
2 From the **Format** menu, select: **Columns...**; the Columns dialogue box appears (Figure 6.6).

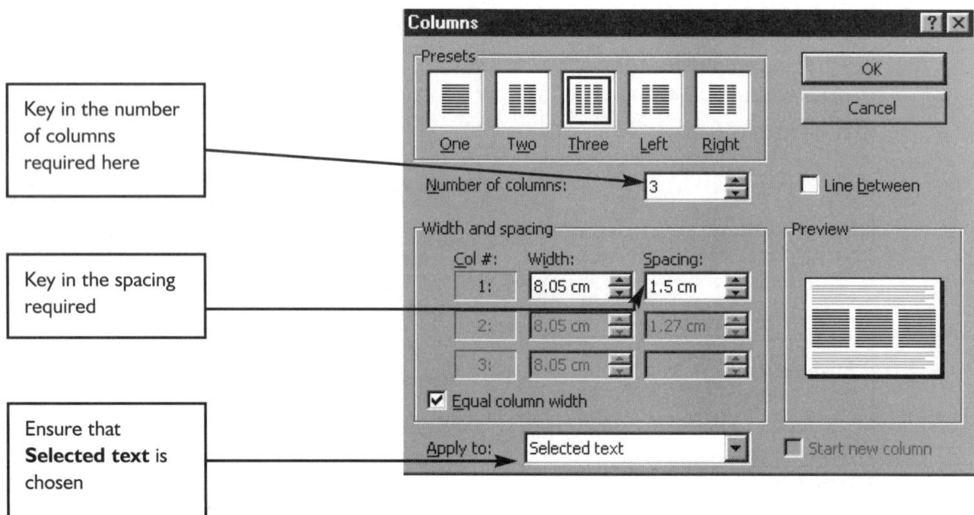

Figure 6.6 Columns dialogue box

3 Change the number of columns to 3 and the spacing to 1.5 cm. Ensure that **Apply to Selected text** is chosen.
Note: The columns will not show in Normal View. Switch to Page Layout view to see what the columns look like.

1.9 Adding bullets

Exercise 9 Add bullets to the list where requested.

METHOD

1 Select the list.
2 Click on: the **Bullet** button.
Note: The list may be divided between two columns. This can be altered later.

INFO

You can choose different styles of bullets. Select the bulleted list. From the **Format** menu, select: **Bullets and Numbering**... Select the bullet style and click on: **OK**.

1.10 Adding headers and footers

Exercise 10 Add a header/footer as requested.

METHOD

1 Move the cursor to the start of the document (**Ctrl** + **Home**).
2 Refer to House Style Sheet 1 for details.

INFO

The footer should contain the name of the designer and the date of publication. Font size 12 point.

3 From the **View** menu, select: **Header and Footer**. The Header and Footer dialogue box appears (Figure 6.7).

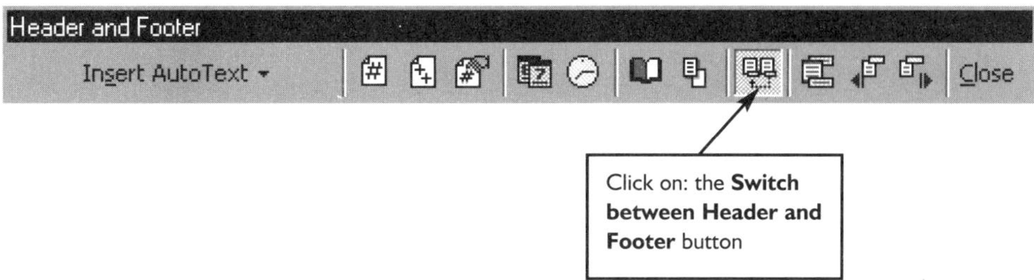

Figure 6.7 Header and Footer box

4 Click on: the **Switch between Header and Footer** button. The Footer section appears (Figure 6.8).

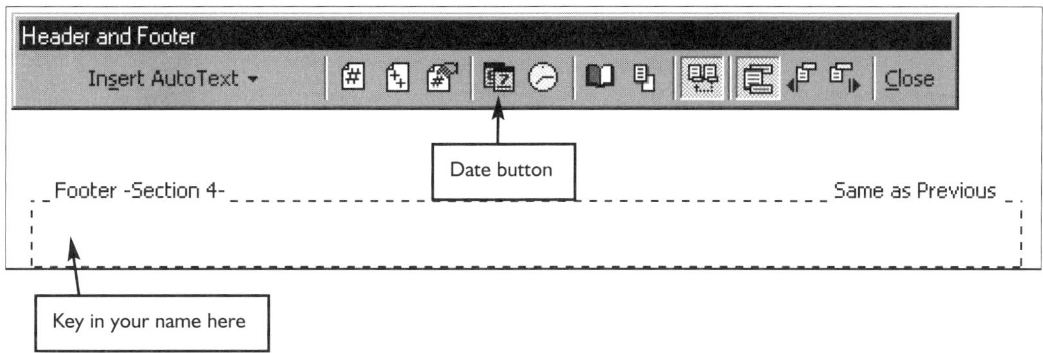

Figure 6.8 Footer section

5 Key in your name directly into the Footer section.
6 Press the **tab** key (or **spacebar**) several times to move the cursor across the page.
7 Click on the date toolbar button (see Figure 6.8) to insert today's date.
8 Select all the text in the footer and change the point size as requested on House Style Sheet 1.

INFO

Check the date is correct. The date may not be set up correctly on your computer. If it shows the wrong date, highlight it to select it, then press the **Delete** key. Key in the date.

Save your file.

2 *Adding extract text and borders, inserting from other applications, publication layout, printing*

In this section you will learn and practise how to:

- add extract text
- add borders
- insert a database report
- insert a spreadsheet report
- insert an image within the body of the document
- select optimum layout for the publication
- print your publication.

2.1 *Adding extract text*

Insert the following extract text at the end of the document you created in the last section. It begins:

We will be continuing...

and ends with:

...you may win one of ten super cash prizes.

This extract is the first sentence of the last paragraph in a Word file (which can be found on the accompanying disk). The file has the heading LOYALTY SAVINGS. Format the text as specified on House Style Sheet 2.

METHOD

1. Load the Word file created in Section 1. Position the cursor where you want the text to appear.
2. Open the Word file containing the extract text.
3. Select the text to be inserted. Click on: the **Copy** button.
4. Close the Word file.
5. Click on: the **Paste** button. The text is pasted into the publication.
6. Format and align the extract text as specified.

2.2 *Adding borders*

Add a border around the extract text.

METHOD

1. Select the text.
2. From the **Format** menu, select: **Borders and Shading.** The Borders and Shading dialogue box appears (Figure 6.9).

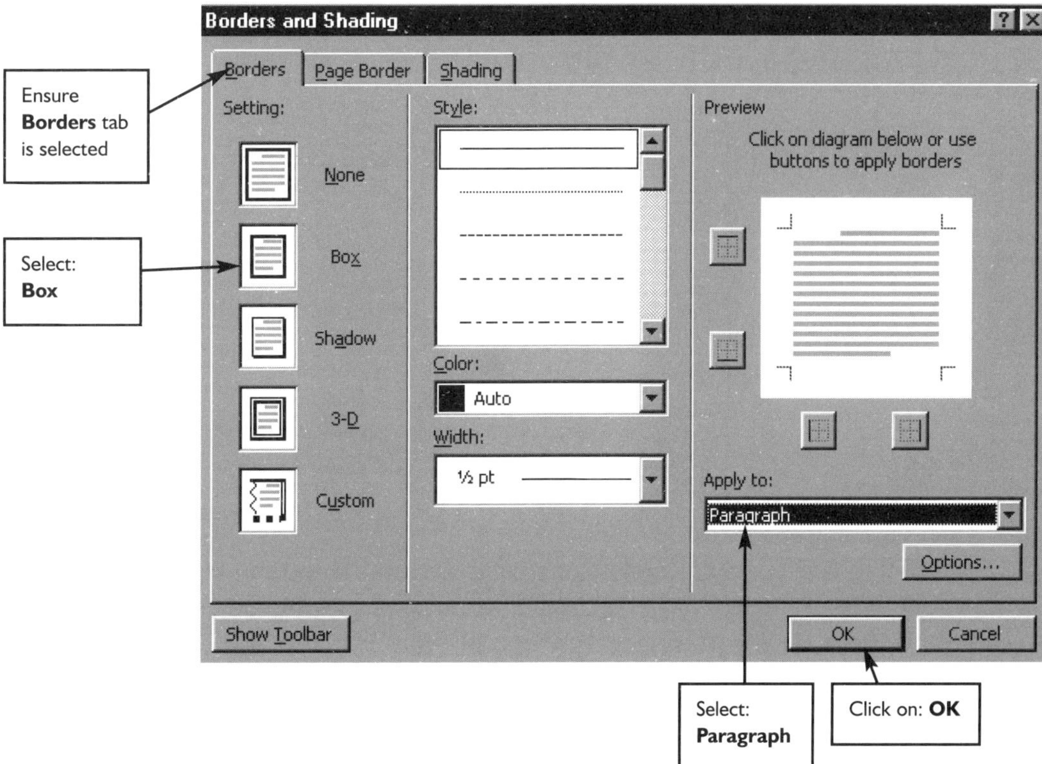

Figure 6.9 Borders and Shading dialogue box

3 Ensure the **Borders** tab is selected.
4 From the **Setting** section, select: **Box**.
5 In the **Apply to** section, select: **Paragraph**.
6 Click on: **OK**.

2.3 *Inserting a database report*

Insert the database report, saved in Chapter 3, Section 2, Exercise 4 where shown. (You should have entered details of this on your File Store Record Sheet.)

METHOD

1 Position the cursor where the database report is to appear.
2 Open the file containing the database report and select the report text.
3 Click on: the **Copy** button and close the file containing the database report.
4 Click on: the **Paste** button.

INFO

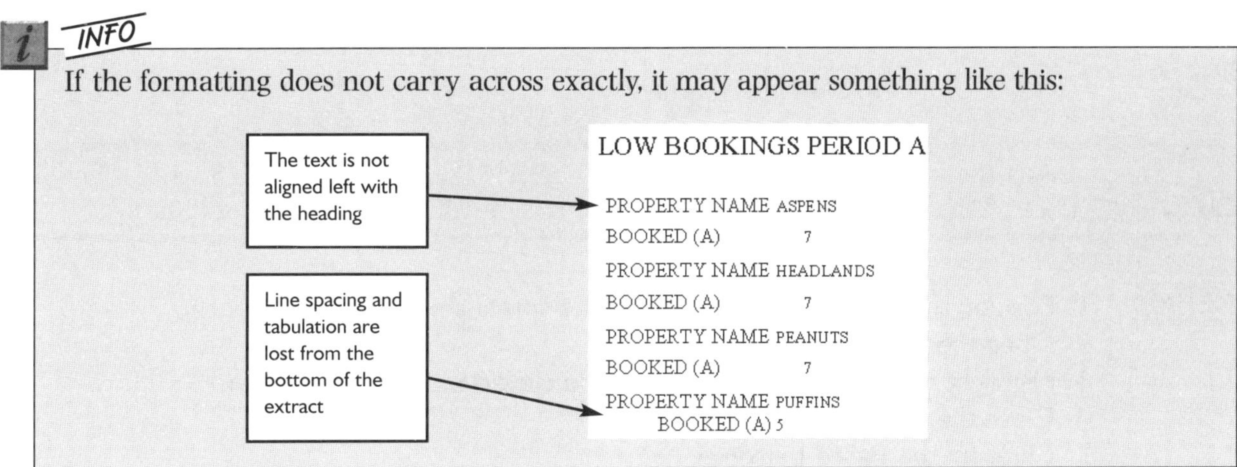
If the formatting does not carry across exactly, it may appear something like this:

5 Click on: the **Show/Hide** button to see the hidden formatting (Figure 6.10).

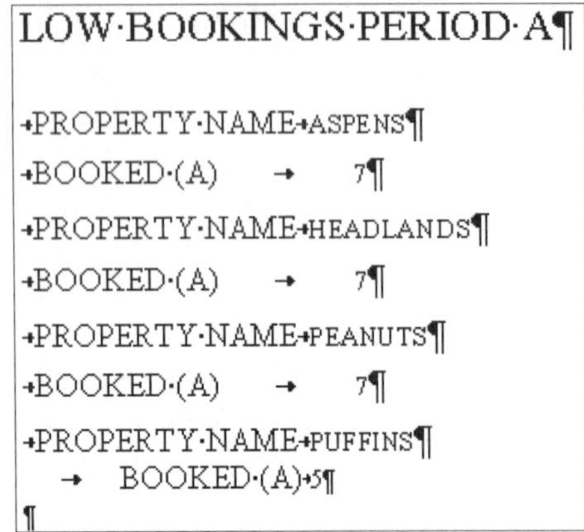

LOW·BOOKINGS·PERIOD·A¶

→PROPERTY·NAME→ASPENS¶
→BOOKED·(A) → 7¶
→PROPERTY·NAME→HEADLANDS¶
→BOOKED·(A) → 7¶
→PROPERTY·NAME→PEANUTS¶
→BOOKED·(A) → 7¶
→PROPERTY·NAME→PUFFINS¶
→ BOOKED·(A)→5¶
¶

Figure 6.10 Hidden formatting

6 To line up text: delete the characters on the left in front of the words.
7 The bottom two lines have different line spacing. Select them, then from the **Format** menu, select: **Paragraph**. Set the **Line Spacing** to 1.5. Click on: **OK**.
8 Your database report should now look like Figure 6.11.

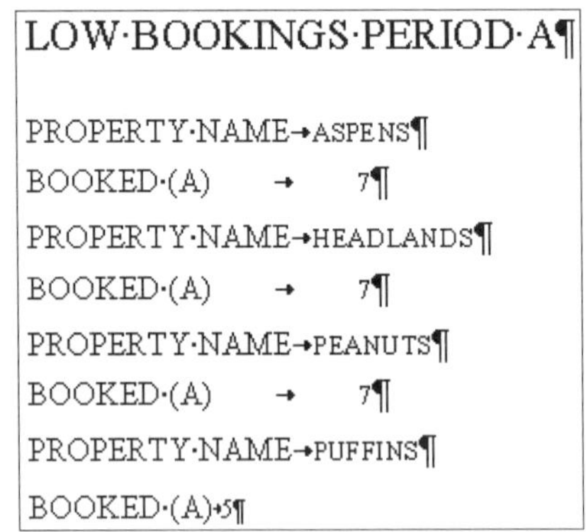

LOW·BOOKINGS·PERIOD·A¶

PROPERTY·NAME→ASPENS¶
BOOKED·(A) → 7¶
PROPERTY·NAME→HEADLANDS¶
BOOKED·(A) → 7¶
PROPERTY·NAME→PEANUTS¶
BOOKED·(A) → 7¶
PROPERTY·NAME→PUFFINS¶
BOOKED·(A)→5¶

Figure 6.11 Corrected database report

9 To correct the alignment of the 5 in the last line:

a Select all except the title of the report.
b On the ruler drag the **Left** tab marker so that it is in line with the numbers.
c Deselect the text by clicking in a white space.

10 Click on: the **Show/Hide** toolbar button to turn Show off.

2.4 *Inserting a spreadsheet report*

Insert the spreadsheet report, saved in Chapter 4, Section 3, Exercise 5 where shown. (*Note:* You should have entered details of this on your File Store Record Sheet.)

METHOD

1 Position the cursor where you want the spreadsheet report to appear.
2 Open the spreadsheet report.
3 Highlight the extract to be inserted and click on: the **Copy** button.
4 Close the spreadsheet file.
5 Click on: the **Paste** button.

2.5 Inserting the image within the document

Insert the logo image where specified.

Since you already have this image on the front cover of the publication, this is simply a matter of copying and pasting it to the requested place. You will need to resize and position it as specified on House Style Sheet 1.

2.6 Selecting optimum layout for the publication

Tidy up the publication so that it is copyfitted as follows:

- Headings/subheadings must not be split from the related text.
- Line spacing between subheadings, paragraphs and imported data must be applied consistently.
- One line or less of text is grouped with the rest of related text ('widows and orphans').
- No more than two clear lines of white space are left at the end of columns throughout the document, the only exception being at the end of the publication.
- Text and imported data are adjusted so that they are not superimposed on other text or data.
- Imported data must not be split across columns or pages.

There is no one optimum way to achieve the above. This will vary depending on what attributes you have chosen. It is important to save your work before commencing on this exercise so that you have access to your original file should things go wrong. You will need to experiment until you are sure all the points above have been addressed and incorporated.

2.7 Printing your publication

Print your publication.

METHOD

1. Check to see how the document looks using **Print Preview**.
2. Carry out any further adjustments.
3. Perform a final spellcheck in case any words have gone awry.
4. Print and proofread the printout carefully checking that it matches the House Style Sheets and conforms to the conditions set out in the previous exercise.

3 Using drawing features

In this section you will learn and practise how to:

- use drawing features
  - lines
  - circles
  - boxes
  - ellipses
  - fill/pattern.

INFO

You may be asked to use the drawing features of Word in the publication assignment. Only use them if requested. They are easy to use and also useful to know so that you can enhance any of your Word documents you work on outside IBT III work.

Exercise 1 Create a new Word document and add drawing features to it.

METHOD With a new Word document open, ensure the Drawing toolbar is visible. If not, from the **View** menu, select: **Toolbars**, click on: **Drawing** so that a tick appears next to it.

The Drawing toolbar buttons used in this section are shown in Figure 6.12.

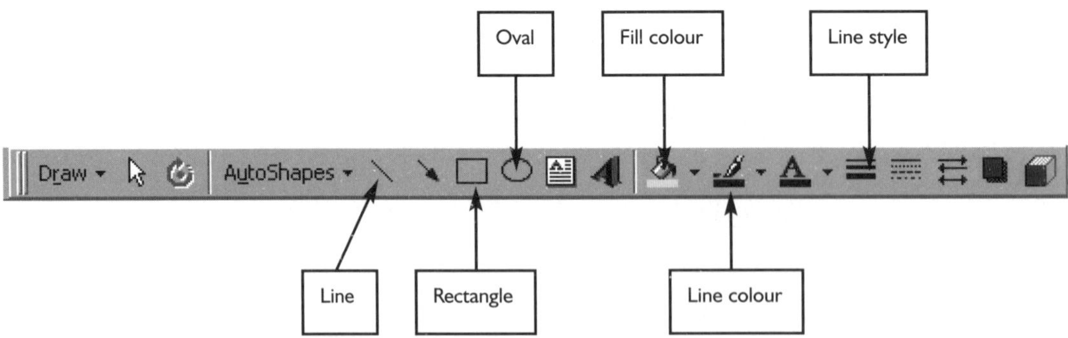

Figure 6.12 Drawing toolbar buttons

Adding a line

1 Click on: the **Line** toolbar button.
2 Position the crosshair where you want the line to start.
3 Hold down the left mouse button and drag the mouse to where you want the line to end. Release the mouse button.

Formatting the line

1 Select the line by clicking on it. When it is selected, handles appear at each end.
2 Click on: the **Line Style** toolbar button.
3 Click on: the line style you want.

Adding a circle or ellipse

1 Click on: the **Oval** button.
2 Hold down the left mouse button and drag out to the required shape.
3 Release the mouse button.

Adding a box

Follow the method for a circle/ellipse, shown above.

Filling a shape with colour

1 Select the shape to fill.
2 Click on: the **down arrow** next to the **Fill Color** button.
3 Click on: the chosen colour.

Filling a shape with a pattern

Follow steps 1 and 2 above.

1 Click on: **Fill Effects**. The Fill Effects dialogue box appears.
2 Click on: the **Pattern** tab.
3 Click on: the chosen pattern. Click on: **OK**.

Experiment with the other Drawing buttons to create some stunning effects.

Word quick reference for IBT III

Action	Keyboard	Mouse	Right-mouse menu	Menu
Bold text	Select text to embolden			
Bold text	**Ctrl + B**	Click: the **Bold** button	**Font**	**Format**, **Font**
			Select: **Bold** from the **Font style:** menu	
Borders			**Borders and Shading**	**Format**, **Borders and Shading**
	Select the border options you require			
Capitals (blocked)	**Caps Lock** Key in the text **Caps Lock** again to remove			Select text to be changed to capitals: **Format**, **Change Case**, **UPPERCASE**
Centre text	Select the text			
	Ctrl + E	Click: the **Center** button	**Paragraph**	**Format**, **Paragraph**
			Select **Center** from the **Alignment:** drop-down menu	
Change case	Select the text to be changed From the **Format** menu, select: **Change Case** Select the appropriate case			
Close a file	**Ctrl + W**	Click: the **Close Window** icon		**File**, **Close**
Columns		Click: the **Columns** button and drag the mouse until you have selected the number of columns		**Format**, **Columns** Select the number of columns and options you require
Create a new file	**Ctrl + N**	Click: the **New** button		**File**, **New**
	Select the new slide template you want to use Click: **OK**			
Cut text	Select the text to be cut			
	Ctrl + X	Click: the **Cut** button	**Cut**	**Edit**, **Cut**
Delete a character	Press **Delete** to delete the character to the right of the cursor Press ← (Backspace) to delete the character to the left of the cursor			
Delete a word	Double-click: the word to select it Press: **Delete**			
Delete/cut a block of text	Select the text you want to delete			
	Delete *OR* **Ctrl + X**	Click: the **Cut** button	**Cut**	**Edit**, **Cut**
Drawing features	To display the **Drawing** toolbar: From the **View** menu, select: **Toolbars**, **Drawing**			
	Select from the toolbar buttons (see Chapter 6, Section 3)			

Action	Keyboard	Mouse	Right-mouse menu	Menu
Exit Word		Click: the Close Window icon		**File**, **Exit**
Font	Select the text you want to change			
		Click: the down arrow next to the **Font** box Select: the font you require	**Font**	**Format**, **Font**
			Select: the required font from the **Font:** menu	
Font size	Select the text you want to change			
		Click: the down arrow next to the **Font Size** box Select: the font size you require	**Font**	**Format**, **Font**
			Select: the required size from the **Size:** menu	
Headers and Footers				**View**, **Header and Footer**
Help	**F1**			**Help** **Contents and Index**
What's this?	**Shift + F1**			**What's This?**
Indenting *To remove indent*		Click: the **Increase Indent** button Click: the **Decrease Indent** button	**Paragraph**	**Format**, **Paragraph**
			In the **Indentation** section, select your options as appropriate	
Insert text	Position the cursor where you want the text to appear Key in the text			
Justified margins	Select the text you want to change			
	Ctrl + J	Click: the **Justify** icon	**Paragraph**	**Format**, **Paragraph**
			Select **Justified** from the **Alignment:** drop-down menu	
Line length, changing		Use the ruler (see separate table)		**File**, **Page Setup**, **Margins** (see separate table)
Line spacing			**Paragraph**	**Format**, **Paragraph**, **Indents and Spacing**
			In the **Line Spacing** section, select the options you require	
Load Word	In Windows 95 desktop			
		Double-click: the **Word** shortcut icon		**Start**, **Programs**, **MS Office**, **Microsoft Word**
Margins				**File**, **Page Setup**, **Margins**

Action	Keyboard	Mouse	Right-mouse menu	Menu
Move a block of text	Select: the text to be moved Cut it and paste it where you want it moved to *OR* Select: the text to be moved Click and drag: it to the correct position Release the mouse button			
Moving around the document	Use the cursor keys (see separate table for more)	Click: in the required position		
Open an existing file	**Ctrl + O**	Click: the **Open** button		**File**, **Open**
	Select the appropriate directory and filename Click: **Open**			
Page break, adding	**Ctrl + Enter**			**Insert**, **Break**, **Page Break**, **OK**
Page break, deleting	Place the cursor on the page break Press: **Delete**			
Page numbering				**Insert**, **Page Numbers** Select the required options
Page Setup				**File**, **Page Setup** (Choose from **Margins**, **Paper size**, **Paper source**, **Layout**)
Paper size	(See Page Setup)			
Paragraphs - splitting/joining	*Splitting:* Move the cursor to the first letter of the new paragraph Press: **Enter** twice *Joining:* Move the cursor to the first character of the second paragraph Press ← (Backspace) twice (Press the spacebar to insert a space after a full stop)			
Print file	**Ctrl + P** Select the options you need Press: **Enter**	Click: the **Print** button		**File**, **Print** Select the options you need and click **OK**
Print preview		Click: the **Print Preview** button		**File**, **Print Preview**
Ragged right margin	Select text			
	Ctrl + L	Click: the **Align Left** button	**Paragraph**	**Format**, **Paragraph**
			Select **Left** from the **Alignment:** drop-down menu	

Action	Keyboard	Mouse	Right-mouse menu	Menu
Remove text emphasis	Select text to be changed			
	Ctrl + B (remove bold) **Ctrl + I** (remove italics) **Ctrl + U** (remove underline)	Click: the appropriate button: B I U	**Font**	**Format**, **Font**
			Select **Regular** from the **Font Style:** menu	
Replace text	**Ctrl + H**			**Edit**, **Replace**
Save	**Ctrl + S**	Click: the **Save** button		**File**, **Save**
	If you have not already saved the file you will be prompted to specify the directory and to name the file. If you have already done this, then Excel will automatically save it.			
Save using a different name or to a different directory				**File**, **Save As**
	Select the appropriate drive and change the filename if relevant. Click: **Save**			
Spellcheck	**F7**	Click: the **Spelling** button		**Tools**, **Spelling**
Styles	Select the text, from the **Format** menu, select **Style**			
Tables		Click: the **Insert Table** button		**Table**, **Insert Table**
	(See separate information below)			
Tabs	(See separate information below)			
Undo	**Ctrl + Z**	Click: the **Undo** button		**Edit**, **Undo**
Widows and Orphans				**Format**, **Paragraph**, **Line and Page Breaks** Select: **Widow/Orphan control**

Moving around the document

Move	Keyboard action
To top of document	**Ctrl + Home**
To end of document	**Ctrl + End**
Left word by word	**Ctrl + ←**
Right word by word	**Ctrl + →**
To end of line	**End**
To start of line	**Home**

Selecting text

Selecting what	Action
Whole document	**Ctrl + A**
One word	Double-click on the word
One paragraph	Double-click in the selection border
Any block of text	Click at the start of the text; press: **Shift**; click at the end of the text
Deselect text	Click in any white space

(*Note*: See appendix for keyboard shortcuts.)

Line lengths

Line lengths	Margin width
12,7 cm (5 in)	4.15 cm (1.63 in)
14 cm ($5\frac{1}{2}$ in)	3.5 cm (1.38 in)
15.3 cm (6 in)	2.85 cm (1.13 in)
16.5 cm ($6\frac{1}{2}$ in)	2.25 cm (0.88 in)

Indentation using the ruler

Select the text you want to indent.

Drag the respective markers (Figure 6.13) on the ruler to the location you want

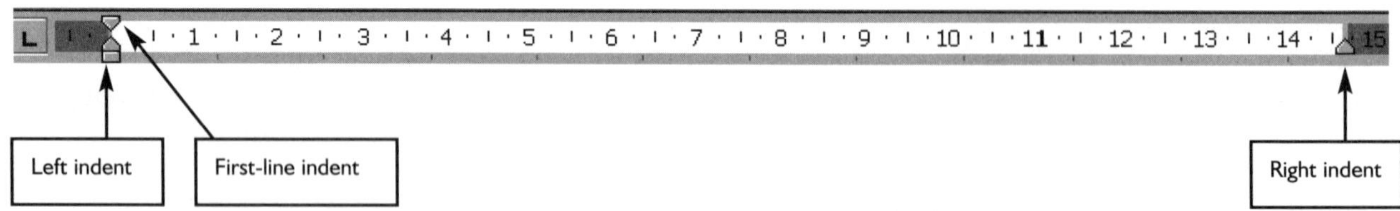

Figure 6.13 Ruler markers

First-line indents and hanging paragraphs using the Format menu

1. Select the text.
2. From the **Format** menu, select: **Paragraph**.
3. In the Paragraph dialog box, ensure the **Indents and Spacing** tab is selected.
4. In the Special box, click on the down arrow and select **Hanging** or **First line**, as appropriate.
5. Check the Preview box (Figure 6.14) to see what the text will look like.
6. Click on: **OK**.

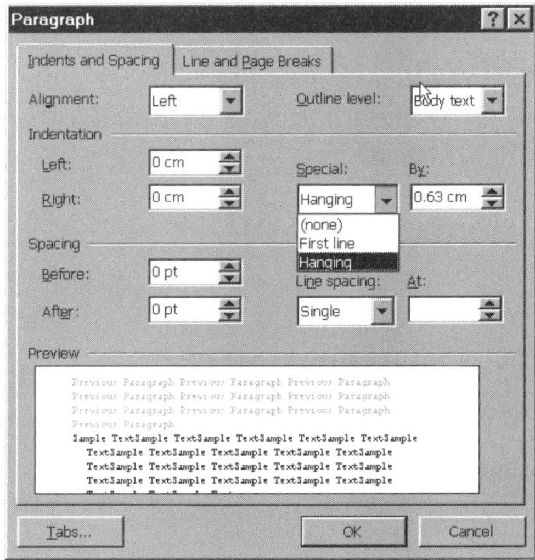

Figure 6.14 Paragraph Preview box

Working with tables

Inserting rows/columns: Select the row below where you want to insert new rows, or select the column to the right of where you want to insert new columns. Click the right mouse over the selection. From the pop-up menu, select: **Insert Rows** or **Insert Columns**.

Adding a row at the end of a table: Click in the last cell of the last row, and press the Tab key.

Adding a column to the right of the last column in a table: Click just outside the right-hand column. From the **Table** menu, select: **Select Column**, Right-click on the selection. Select **Insert Columns**.

Deleting a table and its contents: Select the table by clicking anywhere in it. From the **Table** menu, select: **Select Table**. Click on: the **Cut** button.

Deleting cells, rows or columns from a table: Select the cells, rows, or columns you want to delete. Right-click on the selection and select: **Delete Cells**.

Ensuring the contents fit the cells: Select the table (position the cursor in the table; from the **Table** menu, select: **Select Table**.) From the **Table** menu, select: **Cell Height and Width**. Select the **Column** tab, then **AutoFit** *or* select the column/row border to change and drag the column/row border to the required position.

Working with tabs

Tabs are used to line up columns and Word offers four types of tab.

By default, tabs are set every 1.27 cm ($\frac{1}{2}$ in) from the left margin. When a new tab is set, Word clears any default tabs set to the left of the new tab stop. The type of tab stop can be chosen by clicking on the tab button at the left-hand edge of the ruler (Figure 6.15).

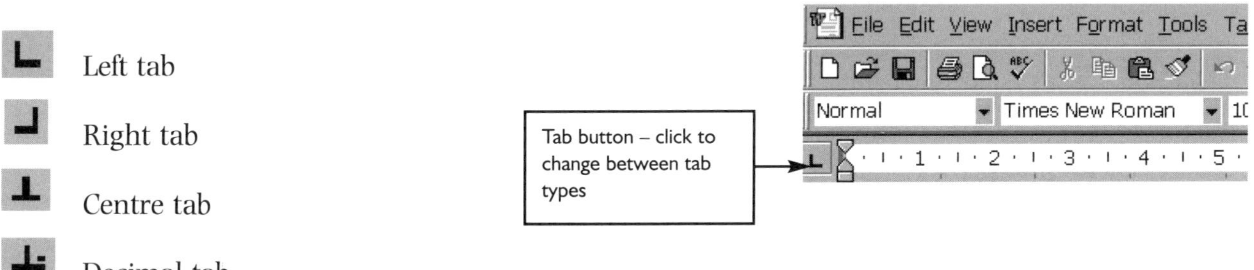

Hard spaces

It is better not to split some words at line ends eg Mr Brown – Mr and Brown should be on the same line. A hard space keeps the words on either side of it together. To insert a hard space: Instead of just pressing the spacebar between the words, press **Ctrl** + **Shift** + **Spacebar**.

Importing information using copy and paste method

1 Load the Word file.
2 Position the cursor where you want the import to appear.
3 Load the program that contains the import... **Start** button, **Programs**.
4 Load the file that contains the data to import.
5 Select the data that you want to copy.
6 Click on: the **Copy** button in the application with the selected data.
7 Click on: **Microsoft Word** on the taskbar.
8 Click on: the **Paste** button.
9 Close the application you have pasted from by clicking the right mouse over the application button on the taskbar, and clicking **Close**. (Do not save changes.)
10 Resize as necessary.

Importing a chart saved on the same sheet as a spreadsheet

Sometimes having a chart on the same sheet as the spreadsheet data can cause problems when importing as it can take some of the spreadsheet cells with it. To overcome this:

1 Carry out steps 1–5 above.
2 Hold down the **Shift** key while selecting the **Edit** menu.
3 Select: **Copy picture**.
4 Check that **As shown on screen** is selected. Click: OK.
5 Carry out Steps 7–9 above.

Using Office Links and importing using the Insert menu

You can also transfer data between applications using Office Links (you can import reports using this but you will still have to cut and paste into the Word document). You can import by selecting **Object** from the **Insert** menu. Check the **Help** menu for **Linked Objects and Importing Data** for more information.

An example of how to import an Access report into word follows:

METHOD

1 Move the cursor to where the database extract is to be inserted.
2 With Word still loaded, load Access and open the database file.
3 Open the report that you want to import.
4 Click on: the down arrow of the OfficeLinks button.
5 Click on: Publish It with MS Word (Figure 6.16).

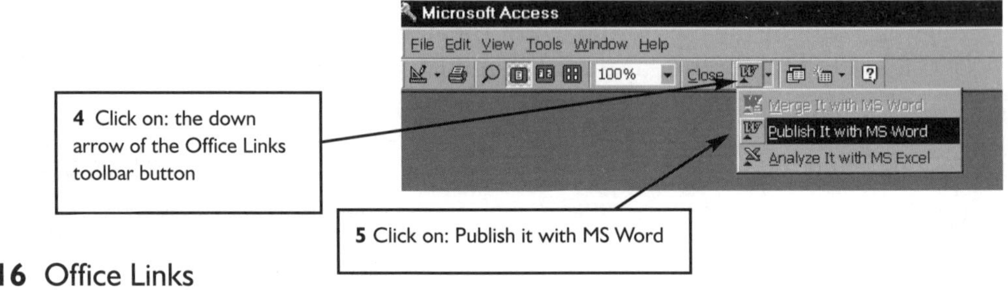

Figure 6.16 Office Links

6 The report will appear on screen as a Word document.

Hints and tips

Close down applications as soon as you have finished with them to ensure your computer is not slowed down unnecessarily.

Check spacing after importing. Keep it consistent throughout.

Common errors made when completing IBT III assignments:

- Not proofreading well enough – missing out words or longer portions of text.
- Inconsistency of spacing – between words, between paragraphs.

Have you carried out all the instructions?

Have you conformed to the House Style Sheets? Check carefully.

PART 2

Full Practice Assignment

Introduction

This part contains an example full practice assignment as it is presented for IBT III. All the skills have been covered in Part 1 and some of the exercises are repeated here for you to consolidate those skills. The assignment differs in places from that given in Part 1 resulting in the printouts varying in subtle ways. This allows you to approach this assignment without necessarily knowing exactly what to expect, making it much more worthwhile.

Study the format of the assignment in detail before you begin. You will soon notice the integrated approach of assignments at this level. Make notes before you begin and keep track of each piece of work as you go through by ticking off those tasks that you have completed. This will enable you to ensure that nothing is left out.

Read all the instructions very carefully so that you fully understand what you need to do and always check your work thoroughly at every stage.

The assignment consists of:

- a scenario
- Section A – File Management and E-mail
- Section B – Database
- Section C – Spreadsheet
- Section D – Presentation
- Section E – E-Mail
- Section F – Publication.

Source Documentation booklets are included within the set of material:

- Correspondence File
- Design Brief – Presentation
- Design Brief – Publication

A File Store Record Sheet should be completed throughout and a Time Log Sheet is included (in the appendix) and should also be completed. A total of 10 hours is allowed to complete the assignment.

Scenario

You work for a company called 'Naturetrail Holidays'. This organisation has properties for rent during the spring and summer months. The annual presentation to Regional Offices is about to take place.

The Publicity Officer will be doing the presentation and will need help in preparing materials that will be presented to the regional office staff. You have been asked to help by extracting information stored in the database and spreadsheet files and include this information in a publication and an automated presentation.

The publication will consist of a four-page leaflet (which will be used in conjunction with our brochure). The automated presentation will be on display in the foyer from the presentation day onwards.

You will need to access files from the accompanying disk in order to carry out some of the assignments. *So that you always have access to the original files, it is* ***essential*** *to make a copy of the disk before starting on any of the exercises.*

Note: During an actual assignment the scenario files are e-mailed to you.

To complete the project you will carry out the following tasks:

a) **Process source data** — You will examine and update a database, which contains information of all the company's properties.

You will examine and update a spreadsheet, which contains details of the holiday properties for rental. Use functions and formulae to complete the spreadsheet.

Data Request Forms are used to detail the data required for the project.

b) **File management** — You will create directories/folders and subdirectories/folders to contain the files used throughout the project. In addition you will be required to name, save and record details of new and amended files and ensure that copies are made for back-up purposes.

c) **Communications** — You will access an e-mail message, retrieve files sent electronically and respond on completion of the project, by sending your own message with an automated presentation as an attached file.

d) **Presentation** — You will be given a Design Brief to produce an automated promotional presentation incorporating text, an image and a graph.

e) **Publication** — You will be given a Design Brief incorporating text, an image and extracted information.

During the **Source Data Processing** section of the assignment you will be required to produce a number of printouts. You will submit these to the Publicity Officer (Tutor/Local Assessor) to be checked. Although you are ultimately responsible for the accuracy of the work, the Publicity Officer may point out errors that need to be corrected.

You will also be required to produce a number of printouts for the **Presentation** and **Publication** sections of the assignments. Once these have been submitted to the Tutor/Local assessor no amendments are allowed.

Project

Assignment Section A – File Management and E-Mail

On commencement of the project you will be sent a number of source files via e-mail, to enable you to carry out specified tasks. You are required to create directories/folders and sub-directories/subfolders for the storage and retrieval both of these files and the files you produce.

You will also be supplied with a hard copy of the Correspondence File, which is referred to in Section 3 of the project.

1 (a) Create a directory/folder for the project.

(b) Record the directory/folder name on your File Store Record Sheet.

(c) Within this directory/folder create and name two sub-directories/subfolders:

- one is for working copies
- one is for copy files.

(d) Record the names on your File Store Record Sheet.

2 You have been sent an e-mail message (these files are stored on disk):

(a) Open your mailbox and access this message.

(b) Follow the instructions contained in the e-mail message.

(c) Print a copy, including transaction details.

Assignment Section B – Database

Access the database containing details of holiday properties offered by the company.

3 Refer to the memos in your Correspondence File (Source Documentation) and carry out all the specified amendments to the database.

4 Ensure the updated database has been saved in the sub-directory/folder created for the working files. Use your File Store Record Sheet to record the full details, including the name of the sub-directory/folder.

5 Refer to the Data Request Forms in your Correspondence File (Source Documentation) which detail the information required from the database:

(a) Save the queries and reports using unique names.

Use your File Store Record Sheet to record the full details including the name of the sub-directory/folder. **Indicate which of the reports created will be used later in the publication.**

(b) Print the queries in table format, including the field headings. Ensure all data is displayed in full.

(c) Print the reports including the report title and field headings. Ensure all the data is displayed in full.

Submit these printouts to your Supervisor.

Assignment Section C – Spreadsheet

Access the spreadsheet containing an analysis of property income for 1999.

6 Refer to the memos in your Correspondence File (Source Documentation) and carry out all the specified amendments to the spreadsheet.

7 Using a unique filename – save the amended spreadsheet in the sub-directory/folder created for all the working files. Use your File Store Record Sheet to record the full details including the name of the sub-directory/folder.

8 (a) Print the entire spreadsheet. Ensure all the data is displayed in full.

(b) Change the display to show the formulae. Print the entire spreadsheet ensuring that the formulae are displayed in full.

9 (a) In the Property Details section, hide only the 3 columns containing the following headings:

- BOOKED(A)
- BOOKED(B)
- PRICE CODE

(b) Change the display to show values.

(c) Produce a printout of the PROPERTY DETAILS section only, displaying only those columns still visible. Ensure all the headings and data are displayed in full.

10 Submit these printouts to your Supervisor to check the data is correct.

11 After printing, change the spreadsheet to display the previously hidden columns.

12 In your Correspondence File (Source Documentation) refer to the Data Request Forms which detail the information required from the spreadsheet.

13 (a) Using a unique file reference – save the spreadsheet extract in the sub-directory/folder created for working files.

Use your File Store Record Sheet to record the full details including the name of the sub-directory/folder. **Indicate which extract and graph will be used later in the project, as specified in the Data Request Forms.**

(b) Produce the printouts as specified in the Data Request Forms.

14 Submit this printout to your Supervisor.

Do not proceed until authorised to do so.

Assignment Section D – Presentation

Do not begin this section until your Supervisor has authorised you to do so.

Delete all database and spreadsheet files **not** listed on your File Store Record Sheet form the working files sub-directory/folder.

15 Create an automated presentation to be used at the annual meeting for regional offices. Consult your Presentation Design Brief – (Source Documentation) for details and layout required for the regional presentation.

16 Access the supplied image and the text file used in a recent promotion. Extract the text to be included in the presentation.

17 Details for the positioning of the extracts are provided in the Presentation Design Brief – (Source Documentation). Refer to your File Store Record Sheet for the filename of the graph to be included in the presentation.

18 Run the presentation to check it meets all requirements.

19 (a) Using a unique filename, save the presentation in a format enabling it to be run at a later date.

(b) This file should be saved in the sub-directory/folder created for all the working files.

(c) Use your File Store Record Sheet to record the full details including the name of the sub-directory/folder.

20 Print one copy of each slide **and** an overview on one page containing a miniature (thumbnail) of each slide.

21 (a) It has been decided to change the order of the slides. Please move Slide 1 to become the last slide in the presentation.

(b) Print a copy as an overview on one page containing a miniature (thumbnail) of each slide.

(c) Re-save the amended presentation retaining the existing filename.

22 (a) Copy the presentation file you have saved to the sub-directory/folder created for copies.

(b) Use your File Store Record Sheet to record the full details, including the name of the sub-directory/folder.

Assignment Section E – E-Mail

23 Send an e-mail message confirming you have finished the presentation and are sending the presentation file for viewing.

Attach the presentation file to your e-mail message.

Address this message to your Supervisor and to one other person specified by your Supervisor.

Ensure your name is included as a reference.

24 Print a copy of your e-mail message, including transaction details.

Assignment Section F – Publication

Produce a publication containing information to be used in the NatureTrail catalogue. The publication will consist of supplied text, the NatureTrail logo and extracts taken from the database and spreadsheet.

25 Use the supplied text and image files.

26 Consult your File Store Record Sheet for the filenames of the database and spreadsheet extracts to be included ion the publication.

27 Consult your Publication Design Brief – (Source Documentation), for details of the layout required.

28 Review your document to ensure it is complete and perform a spellcheck, correcting any errors found.

29 (a) Using a unique filename, save the publication in the sub-directory/folder created for working files.

(b) Use your File Store Record Sheet to record the full details, including the name of the sub-directory/folder.

30 Print the entire promotional publication on A4 paper.

31 (a) Copy the publication file you have saved to the sub-directory/folder created for copies.

(b) Use your File Store Record Sheet to record the details, including the name of the sub-directory/folder.

SOURCE DOCUMENTATION

CORRESPONDENCE FILE

MEMORANDUM

TO: ALL REGIONAL AGENTS

FROM: HEAD OFFICE

DATE: 5 OCTOBER 1999

REF: PRESENTATION

Gemma Ambrose, our Publicity Officer, has been gathering information for a presentation to all regional agents.

We hope that you are able to attend the presentation on Friday 26 November at company headquarters.

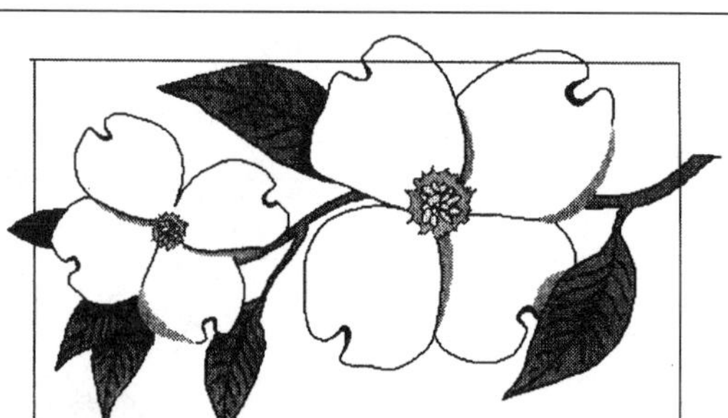

MEMORANDUM

TO: ALL STAFF

FROM: GEMMA AMBROSE

DATE: 15 OCTOBER 1999

REF: PRESENTATION TO REGIONAL AGENTS

The presentation date has been set for Friday 26 November.

I will require various reports and documents for this presentation and will be asking you to provide them in due course.

MEMORANDUM

TO: DATA PROCESSING SECTION

FROM: DATA PROCESSING MANAGER

DATE: 18 OCTOBER 1999

REF: UPDATING FILES

Please ensure that you follow existing upper and lower case conventions when updating spreadsheet and database files.

MEMORANDUM

TO: DATA PROCESSING MANAGER

FROM: PROPERTY MAINTENANCE OFFICE

DATE: 19 OCTOBER 1999

REF: REFURBISHED PROPERTY

The following property was inadvertently deleted from all files following flood damage in September. We are pleased to say that it has been completely refurbished. Please add the following details to the relevant database and spreadsheet files.

PROPERTY NAME	HEADLANDS
CODE	S122
LOCATION	SEA
OCCUPANTS	4
BEDROOMS	2
PETS	YES
TV	NO
BOOKED (A)	7
BOOKED (B)	10
PRICE CODE	B
CHANGE DAY	SAT
DATE BOOKED	18 SEP 1999
AGENT	PAUL

Also, please note that you should replicate all necessary formulae when adding new items to the spreadsheet.

When new details are added to the spreadsheet, they must be placed in the correct Location with the existing order of Property Code maintained.

MEMORANDUM

TO: DATA PROCESSING SECTION

FROM: ACCOUNTS SECTION

DATE: 21 OCTOBER 1999

REF: SPREADSHEET AMENDMENTS

Omissions have been identified in the property details spreadsheet. Please check all sections and insert the relevant formulae and functions.

Use the following formulae/functions where appropriate:

SUM
COUNT
LOOKUP

Bookings Section:

Calculate the total number of BOOKED(A) and BOOKED(B) for each of the 6 locations. Display the figures as whole numbers without decimal places.

Properties per Location Section:

Calculate the number of properties per location.

Price Code Details Section:

Name the range of cells containing the price code and cost per week.

Property Details Section:

Calculate the total weeks booked and replicate the formula for each property.

Please calculate the income and replicate the formula for each property. Use the total weeks booked, the price code and the fixed charge. Please note that the fixed charge should only be applied once per property and **NOT** per week booked. The formula must contain the use of the named range together with a lookup function and an absolute cell reference for the fixed charge. Format this data to 2 decimal places without a £ sign.

Calculate the total of the income column and format to currency, showing the £ sign and 2 decimal places.

MEMORANDUM

TO: DATA PROCESSING SECTION

FROM: SALES OFFICE

DATE: 26 OCTOBER 1999

REF: PROPERTY AMENDMENTS

All properties which have BOOKED(A) as 6 should be amended to 7.

MEMORANDUM

TO: DATA PROCESSING SECTION

FROM: SALES OFFICE

DATE: 27 OCTOBER 1999

REF: PROPERTY CHANGE

Details were entered incorrectly for the property below. Please amend the relevant database and spreadsheet files.

	ENTERED AS	SHOULD READ
CODE	**M342**	**M341**
BOOKED (A)	**8**	**7**
BOOKED (B)	**14**	**13**

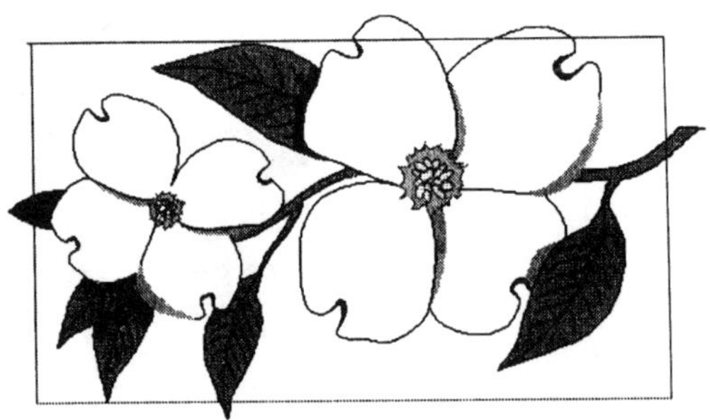

MEMORANDUM

TO: DATA PROCESSING SECTION

FROM: ACCOUNTS SECTION

DATE: 28 OCTOBER 1999

REF: SPREADSHEET AMENDMENTS

In the TOTAL WEEKS NOT BOOKED column, calculate the total for the first property and replicate the formula for each property. (The maximum number of bookable weeks is 28.)

Add a column after the TOTAL WEEKS NOT BOOKED column, with the heading LOW(A). You must use this column to indicate whether the bookings are less in the BOOKED(A) column than in the BOOKED(B) column.

You will need to use an IF function to give the correct message for each property in this column.

If BOOKED(A) is less than BOOKED(B), then LOW(A) will read 'Yes' otherwise it will read 'No'. Centre the new column heading and messages.

DATA REQUEST FORM

ORIGINATOR	Gemma Ambrose	**DATE**	1 Nov 1999
DEPARTMENT	Publicity		
DATA SOURCE	Spreadsheet [ ]	Database [✓]	
DATA SOURCE	Properties		

SEARCH INFORMATION (please complete the relevant boxes)

QUERY

Fields/Headings to Print	All
Sort Order	Ascending order of PROPERTY NAME
Search Criteria	BOOKED(A) 7 or less; PRICE CODE B; DATE BOOKED 18 September 1999 or later
Other Details (please specify)	Field headings must be shown

Printout Required Yes [✓] No [ ] Fit One Page [✓]

REPORT/EXTRACT

Report Format Group [ ] Column [✓] Tabular [ ]

Title	BOOKINGS PERIOD A
Spreadsheet Section	
Fields/Headings to Print	PROPERTY NAME and BOOKED(A) only in this order
Sort Order	PROPERTY NAME descending
Other Details (please specify)	Using the above query, produce a report to be used where specified in the publication

Printout Required Yes [✓] No [ ] To be dated Yes [ ] No [✓]

Fit One Page Yes [✓] No [ ] Page Numbered Yes [ ] No [✓]

GRAPH

Title	

Axes Labels Yes [ ] No [ ] Legend Required Yes [ ] No [ ]

Printout Required Yes [ ] No [ ] Type: Bar/Column [ ] Line [ ] Pie [ ]

Other Details (please specify)	

DATA REQUEST FORM

ORIGINATOR Gemma Ambrose **DATE** 2 Nov 1999

DEPARTMENT Publicity

DATA SOURCE Spreadsheet ☐ Database ☑

DATA SOURCE Properties

SEARCH INFORMATION (please complete the relevant boxes)

QUERY

Fields/Headings to Print	PROPERTY NAME, LOCATION, BOOKED(A), PRICE CODE
Sort Order	Ascending order of PROPERTY NAME
Search Criteria	PROPERTY NAME beginning with the letter S, the letter G or the letter M; LOCATION Sea or Forest; OCCUPANTS 4 or more; CHANGE DAY Saturday; BOOKED(B) more than 8 weeks
Other Details (please specify)	Show only required fields in specified order, including field headings

Printout Required Yes ☑ No ☐ Fit One Page ☑

REPORT/EXTRACT

Report Format Group ☑ Column ☐ Tabular ☐

Title	BOOKINGS PER LOCATION
Spreadsheet Section	
Fields/Headings to Print	LOCATION, PROPERTY NAME, BOOKED(A)
Sort Order	PROPERTY NAME descending
Other Details (please specify)	Use the above query - group by Location and show totals in BOOKED(A) per region

Printout Required Yes ☑ No ☐ To be dated Yes ☑ No ☐

Fit One Page Yes ☑ No ☐ Page Numbered Yes ☑ No ☐

GRAPH

Title

Axes Labels Yes ☐ No ☐ Legend Required Yes ☐ No ☐

Printout Required Yes ☐ No ☐ Type: Bar/Column ☐ Line ☐ Pie ☐

Other Details (please specify)

DATA REQUEST FORM

ORIGINATOR Gemma Ambrose **DATE** 2 Nov 1999

DEPARTMENT Publicity

DATA SOURCE Spreadsheet ✓ Database ☐

DATA SOURCE Properties Rental Income

SEARCH INFORMATION (please complete the relevant boxes)

QUERY

Fields/Headings to Print	
Sort Order	
Search Criteria	
Other Details (please specify)	

Printout Required Yes ☐ No ☐ Fit One Page ☐

REPORT/EXTRACT

Report Format Group ☐ Column ☐ Tabular ☐

Title	
Spreadsheet Section	PROPERTIES PER LOCATION
Fields/Headings to Print	LOCATION, NO OF PROPERTIES
Sort Order	
Other Details (please specify)	Produce and save separately an extract showing the column headings and the detail in these columns for all 6 locations. To be used later where specified in the publication. Do not include the section title in the extract.

Printout Required Yes ✓ No ☐ To be dated Yes ☐ No ✓

Fit One Page Yes ✓ No ☐ Page Numbered Yes ☐ No ✓

GRAPH

Title: BOOKED(A) AND BOOKED(B) COMPARED

Axes Labels Yes ✓ No ☐ Legend Required Yes ✓ No ☐

Printout Required Yes ✓ No ☐ Type: Bar/Column ☐ Line ✓ Pie ☐

Other Details (please specify): Based on Bookings. Compare BOOKED(A) and BOOKED(B) for each location

DATA REQUEST FORM

ORIGINATOR Gemma Ambrose **DATE** 3 Nov 1999

DEPARTMENT Publicity

DATA SOURCE Spreadsheet ✓ Database ☐

DATA SOURCE Properties Rental Income

SEARCH INFORMATION (please complete the relevant boxes)

QUERY

Fields/Headings to Print

Sort Order

Search Criteria

Other Details (please specify)

Printout Required Yes ☐ No ☐ Fit One Page ☐

REPORT/EXTRACT

Report Format Group ☐ Column ☐ Tabular ☐

Title

Spreadsheet Section

Fields/Headings to Print

Sort Order

Other Details (please specify)

Printout Required Yes ☐ No ☐ To be dated Yes ☐ No ☐

Fit One Page Yes ☐ No ☐ Page Numbered Yes ☐ No ☐

GRAPH

Title: BOOKED(A) AND BOOKED(B) COMPARED

Axes Labels Yes ✓ No ☐ Legend Required Yes ✓ No ☐

Printout Required Yes ✓ No ☐ Type: Bar/Column ✓ Line ☐ Pie ☐

Other Details (please specify): The wrong type of graph was requested on 2/11/99, please change it. Retain the Y axis minimum value of 0 and increase the maximum to 160. Set intermediate values to intervals of 40. To be used where specified in the presentation.

DATA REQUEST FORM

ORIGINATOR Gemma Ambrose **DATE** 5 Nov 1999

DEPARTMENT Publicity

DATA SOURCE Spreadsheet ✓ Database ☐

DATA SOURCE Properties Rental Income

SEARCH INFORMATION (please complete the relevant boxes)

QUERY

Fields/Headings to Print	
Sort Order	
Search Criteria	
Other Details (please specify)	

Printout Required Yes ☐ No ☐ Fit One Page ☐

REPORT/EXTRACT

Report Format Group ☐ Column ☐ Tabular ☐

Title	
Spreadsheet Section	PROPERTY DETAILS
Fields/Headings to Print	LOCATION AND PROPERTY CODE and PRICE CODE
Sort Order	
Other Details (please specify)	Produce an extract showing the details for all properties, in these columns, that have LOW(A) bookings. Do not include the section title in the extract

Filter

Printout Required Yes ✓ No ☐ To be dated Yes ✓ No ☐

Fit One Page Yes ✓ No ☐ Page Numbered Yes ✓ No ☐

GRAPH

Title	

Axes Labels Yes ☐ No ☐ Legend Required Yes ☐ No ☐

Printout Required Yes ☐ No ☐ Type: Bar/Column ☐ Line ☐ Pie ☐

Other Details (please specify)	

SOURCE DOCUMENTATION

PRESENTATION

DESIGN BRIEF

DESIGN BRIEF
PRESENTATION

The annual presentation to Regional Offices will take place during November. An automated presentation is to be produced and placed on display at this presentation and at various exhibitions after this date.

You have received, via e-mail, a promotional text file, an extract from which is to be used in the presentation.

You have also received the logo to be used in all promotional materials. This is supplied in corporate colours, but may also be used as a black-and-white or grey image.

Instructions have been given earlier to create a graph from the spreadsheet file, recording the details on your File Store Record Sheet. This graph is to be used in the presentation.

'NATURETRAIL' PROMOTIONAL PRESENTATION

Create a Master slide. Refer to the Presentation House Style Sheets for slide content and instructions on text styles, slide layout and effects. You must ensure that the content of the presentation adheres to Naturetrail's style conventions.

The text content of each slide is given in the Design Brief – Content of the Presentation Slides. Refer to the supplied promotional text file to obtain the extract to be used. The extract text is in the fourth paragraph. Use only the sentence beginning 'We will be continuing.....' and ending '...super cash prizes.'

Refer to your File Store Record Sheet to identify the previously saved graph, and refer to the Content of the Presentation Slides for the position of this graph.

You have discretion (artistic licence) on the final layout of the presentation but this must conform to Naturetrail's House Style Sheets. Select an appropriate point size from the range given in the House Style Sheets, to suit your design.

All presentation material must be checked for spelling before the final draft is approved. Naturetrail's convention is to use open punctuation (eg rather than e.g. and ie rather than i.e.).

DESIGN BRIEF

CONTENT OF THE PRESENTATION SLIDES

Create a Master slide. Please refer to the House Style Sheets to ensure that this adheres to Naturetrail Holidays conventions and for information on slide layout and effects. The text for the automated presentation is given below. You must retain case as shown.

You must create a Master Slide to be used as a background for all 5 slides.

SLIDE NO	TYPE OF ENTRY	SLIDE CONTENT	SLIDE DURATION
Master Slide	Master Slide Text	*Specified text and image – see House Style Sheet 2* Slide Layout and Effects for details	

Slide 1	Heading Heading	NATURETRAIL HOLIDAYS TOTAL RELAXATION	7 – 15 secs
Slide 2	Heading Heading Subheading Subheading	A PERFECT HOLIDAY PHONE NOW Tel: 01234 29786 Open 7 am to 7 pm	7 – 15 secs
Slide 3	Heading Body text (Bullet text)	BEAUTIFUL LOCATIONS Our holiday homes are situated in some of the most delightful settings, for example: Rivers Lakes Sea Mountains	15 – 20 secs
Slide 4	Heading Body text Graph	RESERVATIONS Why not take a holiday in the spring when there is usually more choice: *Insert graph here*	10 – 20 secs
Slide 5	Heading Heading Subheading Extract text	PREVIOUS CUSTOMER? EXTRA SAVINGS! Contact us now! *Extract text from text file as specified in Design Brief*	15 – 25 secs

HOUSE STYLE SHEET 1 PRESENTATION TEXT STYLES

STYLE NAME	TYPEFACE	POINT SIZE	FEATURE	ALIGNMENT	ADDITIONAL
Master Slide text	Any	Between 12 – 16 pt	Any	-	All Master slide text must be the same style and consistent throughout the presentation
Heading	Sans serif	Between 40 – 60 pt	Bold	Centre	Consistent throughout the presentation
Subheading	Sans serif	Between 26 – 36 pt	Italic	Centre	Consistent throughout the presentation
Body text	Serif	Between 18 – 24 pt	None	Left	Consistent throughout the presentation
Bullet text	Serif	Between 18 – 24 pt	Italic	Left	No more than 6 bullet points per slide
Extract text	Sans serif	Between 18 – 24 pt	Bold	Left	Consistent throughout the presentation. **DO NOT** apply to any text included in imported image or graph

COPYFITTING

- Text and imported data are adjusted so that they are not superimposed on other text or data
- Imported data must not be split across slides

HOUSE STYLE SHEET 2 PRESENTATION SLIDE LAYOUT AND EFFECTS

FEATURE	COLOUR	STYLE	POSITION	MAX NUMBER	ADDITIONAL
Background	Any	Any	-	1	Consistent use throughout the presentation
Data on Master Slide	Any – see ADDITIONAL column	-	-	2 text colours	Consistent use throughout the presentation Ensure legibility against background colour/style To contain the organisation's logo, the name of the organisation, name of designer and the date
Text	Any – see ADDITIONAL column	-	-	2 colours	Consistent use throughout the presentation Ensure legibility against background colour/style
Logo	Corporate colours or black and white	-	Master Slide	-	Consistent use throughout the presentation and original proportions maintained
Images, diagrams or graphs	Any	-	As specified in Design Brief	As specified in Design Brief	Original proportions must be maintained at all times
Transitions	-	-	-	4 effects	At least 2 different effects must be used
Builds	-	-	-	4 effects	At least 2 different effects must be used

SOURCE DOCUMENTATION

PUBLICATION

DESIGN BRIEF

DESIGN BRIEF

PUBLICATION

This year's annual presentation will address the issues of promotional literature. An A4 4-page publication is to be produced to send out to potential customers as a follow up to our annual brochure.

Included in your files you received via e-mail was a text file, which is to be used in the publication. A hard copy of this file is supplied in this Design Brief for reference.

You have also received the logo to be used in all promotional materials. This is supplied in corporate colours, but may also be used as a black and white or grey image.

You have been given instructions earlier to extract and save data from the database and spreadsheet files, recording these details on your File Store Record Sheet. These extracts are to be used in the publication.

'NATURETRAIL' PROMOTIONAL PUBLICATION

Create a front cover. This will be the first page of the 4-page publication. Ensure that it contains only the logo, as instructed in the Publication House Style Sheet 1.

On the second page use the headline **Naturetrail News**. Import the text file directly below the headline.

You have discretion (artistic licence) on the final layout of the publication but this must conform to Naturetrail's House Style Sheets.

Refer to the hard copy of the text file enclosed with this Brief, this shows the placement of the extracts from the database and spreadsheet files, the logo and the bulleted text.

GENERAL

All publication material must be checked for spelling before final draft is approved. Naturetrail's convention is to use open punctuation (eg rather than e.g. and ie rather than i.e.).

COPYFITTING

- Headings/subheadings must not be split from the related text
- Line spacing between subheadings, paragraphs and imported data must be applied consistently
- One line or less of text is grouped with the rest of related text ('widows and orphans')
- No more than two clear lines of white space are left at the end of columns throughout the document, the only exception is at the end of the publication.
- Text and imported data are adjusted so that they are not superimposed on other text or data
- Imported data must not be split across columns or pages

TEXT FOR PUBLICATION

If you are looking for a peaceful and relaxing holiday then look no further than Naturetrail Holidays. From small beginnings five years ago when the company had only one location we are now able to offer a choice of six completely different locations. Whatever your idea of the perfect place for a holiday we have the answer.

LOCATIONS

We have holiday cottages in the beautiful unspoit countryside of the Cotswolds. Here you are able to ramble along the picturesque footpaths and visit the charming villages and small towns that are dotted around this area. Our forest properties are situated in North Wales, close to Betws-y-Coed. There are endless outdoor activites in this area ranging from walking, canoeing or climing. In Cumbria you will find our lakes cottages – if you like sailing and fishing then this is the place for you. Again in North Wales, situated in the heart of Snowdonia, you will find our mountain complex. There are even trained mountaineers on hand to give you coaching in all aspects of climbing. So don't worry if you're a novice, there are activities ranging from those for beginers right through to the more experienced climber. Cornwall is the setting for our seaside properties. These are located between Boscastle and Newquay. The scenery in this area is second to none. There are wild coastal footpaths, fishing villages and sandy beaches. You will be spoilt for choice for your daily excursions! For those of you who enjoy the tranquillity of a riverside setting, you will find this at our site in Devon. Our properties are situated only 100 metres from the river Dart. Of course also in this area, in addition to riverside activities, there are beautiful moorland walks.

THE CHOICE IS YOURS. We beleve that you cannot fail to appreciate the natural beauty that abounds in all of these locations.

Insert logo here

PROPERTIES AVAILABLE

Our properties vary in size and we have properties to suit most needs. You can choose from one to four bedrooms, with the maximum occupancy being eight people (there is the possibility that some of our properties can accommodate babies – cots and high chairs can be provided at no extra cost). Please ask the agent when booking.

PRICES

Prices vary depending on the size of the property. This year we have introduced a new system and now if you book for more than one week, any subsequent weeks are charged at a reduced rate.

The table below shows the prices relating to the different codes:

CODE	COST	EXTRA WEEK
A	£150	£135
B	£200	£185
C	£225	£210
D	£255	£240
E	£300	£285

Insert database report here

Why not reserve a property for our early booking period? The properties shown below are on special discount prices (deduct a further 10% from the price shown in the brochure) for this year only:

You can arrive on Friday or Saturday depending on which property you have chosen and at any time before 7 pm. Please let us know if you will be arriving later than this. Staggering arrivals in this way makes it easier to ensure that we have more staff available to give you a warm welcome. You may prefer to travel on a Friday, especially in summer when the roads are usually less congested. Whilst on the subject of transport, you will notice that most of our properties have parking adjacent to them. Where this is not the case your vehicle may be left in the parking areas which are never more than 50 metres away. For unloading purposes, parking outside the property is perfectly acceptable but please remember to move your vehicle as soon as you can since it will cause an obstruction.

Your property will have been fully cleaned and inspected beffore your arrival which can be anytime after 12 noon. All bed linen is provided but you will need to bring your own towels. All properties are self-catering but to help you settle in, we do provide a small grocery basket containing essentials, such as bread and milk. Should you find that things are not to your liking, please contact us straight away. WE PRIDE OURSELVES ON GIVING YOU THE BEST SERVICE AT ALL TIMES.

LOYALTY SAVINGS

Naturetrail Holidays are pleased to to announce an important bonus for customers who have taken holidays with us in the past. We are now able to give substantial discounts on your holiday booking this year.

If you book your holiday before the end of January you will be entitled to a 20% discount on the standard cost of your chosen property (subject to its availability). If you book before the end of March you will be entitled to a 10% discount on the standard cost.

We feel that this is a very generous ofer and hope that you will be able to make your bookings early to benefit from the maximum savings.

Each 'loyalty' customer will be entered into our prize draw. We will be offering cash prizes ranging from £50 to £500 to those lucky ones picked out at random. If you are eligible for this discount please have your previous booking reference to hand when you call. If you no longer have your booking reference, don't worry we will be able to look up your details on our database.

HOW TO BOOK

Our properties can be booked from our Head Office by telephoning 01234 29786. We are open from 7 am to 7 pm every day except Sunday. Our regional offices can also help you with any queries that you may have. They are each allocated several properties that are their major concern. Choosing the right accomodation to suit your needs can be difficult and we want to help you make an informed choice. You can rely on our staff giving informative and friendly advice. Our computerised booking system gives instant availability of our properties so that we can suggest an alternative should your first choice be taken. Shown below are the properties dealt with by our Bristol office:

Insert spreadsheet report here

As you can see each regional office deals with properties from all of the locations. Our staff training ensures that all staff have visited the six locations and are aware of the differences between them.

When booking please ensure that you have the following details to hand:

Bullet text

Reference of Property
Price Code
Date Required
Number in Party
Vehicle Registration Number
Credit Card Number
Former Booking Ref (if applicable)

Here at Naturetrail Holidays we pride ourselves in providing an excelent booking service and we hope that you feel that this level of excellence carries through to all of our operations. We know how important it is that everything runs smoothly so that you are able to relax and enjoy yourselves.

So what are you waiting for? Have another look through our brochure and imagiine the fun that you'll have with Naturetrail Holidays.

DON'T DELAY – BOOK TODAY.

HOUSE STYLE SHEET 1 PUBLICATION PAGE LAYOUT

FEATURE	MEASUREMENT	POSITION	ADDITIONAL
Margins	1.5 cm left and right 1.5 cm top and bottom	-	Consistent throughout the publication
Spacing between Columns	1.5 cm	-	Consistent between all columns
Page Numbering	10 pt	At top of page	Not to be printed on front cover. To commence with number 2 on second page Align consistently throughout the publication
Headers/Footers	10 pt	-	Footer should contain the name of the designer and the date of the publication
Pages	A4	-	Consistent orientation throughout the publication – either portrait or landscape
Columns	-	-	2 – 4 columns for all text except the headline Columns should be of equal size throughout the publication
Logo/Image	On front cover – this should cover at least half of the width of the page When used elsewhere in the document it must be centred within the column	On front cover, centre horizontally, either within margins or page. It need not be centred vertically Elsewhere, position as specified in Text For Publication	Logo must always appear in full. Original proportions must be maintained at all times When in colour only corporate colours may be used. Black and white image may be used if preferred

HOUSE STYLE SHEET 2 PUBLICATION TEXT STYLE

STYLE NAME	TYPEFACE	POINT SIZE	FEATURE	ALIGNMENT	ADDITIONAL
Headline	Sans serif	Between 36-60 pt	Bold Capitals	Centre	Position horizontally across the page or margins. Must be across full width of page spanning all columns
Subheading	Sans serif	Between 16-22 pt	Italic	Centre	Consistent throughout the publication DO NOT apply to text included within imported graphs, images or diagrams
Body text	Serif	Between 10-14 pt	-	Left	Consistent throughout the publication. Set in 2 – 4 columns
Bullet text	Serif	Use same as body text (between 10-14 pt)	To include a bullet character (eg ● ◆ ▫)	Left	Ensure the bullet text is indented from the bullet point (hanging indent) Consistent throughout
Extract text	Sans serif	Between 10-14 pt	Bold	Any	Extract style applies to all extracted text, except text included within graphs, images or diagrams DO NOT exceed column width Consistent throughout the publication Place a box or border around the text

Syllabus for IBT III

1 Electronic communications

ASSESSMENT OBJECTIVES		SYLLABUS CONTENT
The Candidate must be able to:		❑ total coverage • selective coverage – selective coverage
1.1	**Communicate electronically**	
1.1a	Create and transmit e-mail message(s) attaching files as required	❑ use e-mail • access received message(s) and files • create message(s) • route/address message(s) • attach files to message(s) • transmit message(s) • print message(s) including records of transaction(s)
1.1b	Correctly route/address e-mail message(s)	
1.1c	Retrieve e-mail message(s) and access the attached files	
1.1d	Print e-mail message(s) including records of transaction(s) and evidence of attachments	

2 File management

ASSESSMENT OBJECTIVES	SYLLABUS CONTENT
The Candidate must be able to:	❑ total coverage ● selective coverage – selective coverage
2.1 Create, manage and maintain files	
2.1a Create and name directory/folder structures and files as required 2.1b Manage files and documents within directory/folder structures as specified 2.1c Record storage details	❑ access received message(s) and files ● create directory/folder structures ● create directories/folders ● create subdirectories/folders ❑ manage files/documents ● save/name – files – queries – reports – sheets – charts ● retrieve – files – queries – reports – sheets – charts ● copy/move – files – queries – reports – sheets – charts ● delete – files ● record storage details – files – queries – reports – sheets – charts

3 Source data processing

ASSESSMENT OBJECTIVES		SYLLABUS CONTENT
The Candidate must be able to:		❑ total coverage • selective coverage – selective coverage
3.1	**Analyse task(s), select and process the relevant data**	
3.1a	Select, locate and access correct data	❑ access existing files • text • database • spreadsheet ❑ process existing files • insert data – records – columns – fields – rows • edit data – text – numeric • delete data – records – columns – fields – rows • find and replace facility • format data – decimal places – integer – currency – case – alignment
3.1b	Process data as specified, to the required accuracy	

ASSESSMENT OBJECTIVES	SYLLABUS CONTENT
The Candidate must be able to: **3.2 Interrogate, manipulate and present data**	❑ total coverage ● selective coverage – selective coverage
3.2a Create and run queries containing up to five specified criteria 3.2b Use formulae and functions to provide the required solutions 3.2c Create graph(s) with the required accuracy, to display data as specified 3.2d Transfer data between files/applications 3.2e Create reports with the required accuracy, to display data as specified 3.2f Print required data as specified	❑ create and run queries ● search using: – logical operators – text – numeric or data range – wildcard ● sort – ascending – descending – alphabetically/numerically ❑ use formulae and functions ● absolute cell addresses ● relative cell addresses ● named cells/ranges ● functions – sum – average – count – lookup – if ● replicate formulae ❑ create graphs ● select type – line – area – bar – pie – comparative ● apply labels and legends ● control y-axis range ❑ transfer data between files/applications ● transfer data – copy – import – export – cut and paste – paste special (values) ❑ create and generate reports ● design/select layout ● display selected fields/cells ● group by categories ● total, count or average specified data ● format data – decimal places – interger – currency – case – alignment ● enter data ● hide data ❑ print data ● extracts ● formulae ● reports ● queries ● graphs

ASSESSMENT OBJECTIVES	SYLLABUS CONTENT
The Candidate must be able to: **4.1 Set up master slide in accordance with a specified house style**	❑ total coverage ● selective coverage – selective coverage
	❑ layout ● text – headings – sub-headings – body text – bulleted text ● graphics – images ❑ styles ● background ● text – headings – sub-headings – body text – bulleted text – extracts ● colours ● point size ● serif and sans serif fonts ● text alignment ● text enhancement – bold – italic – underline

ASSESSMENT OBJECTIVES		SYLLABUS CONTENT
4.2	**Insert, manipulate and produce a presentation**	
4.2a	Produce a presentation in accordance with a given design brief in a specified house style	❑ enter text ❑ transfer data between applications ● transfer data – copy – cut and paste – import ❑ manipulate and present data ● copyfit material – consistent spacing – group heading(s)/ sub-heading(s) with related data – text/images/lines not superimposed – imported images and/or extracts not split across slides ● control(s) of image(s) in proportion ● spellcheck ● slide order – set up – change ❑ effects ● transitional effects (up to four) ● transitional timings (various specified) ● build effects (up to four) ❑ provide specified output ● run automated presentation ● print – slides – thumbnails – notes
4.2b	Present required data as specified	

5 Publication production

ASSESSMENT OBJECTIVES	SYLLABUS CONTENT
The Candidate must be able to: **5.1 Set up document layout and styles**	❑ total coverage ● selective coverage – selective coverage
5.1a Set up document(s) in accordance with a specified house style	❑ layout ● margins – left – right – top – bottom ● columns – two to four columns – column spacing ● page – orientation – size ● multiple pages ● page numbering – position – first page excluded – start number (other than one) ● headers/footers ● indents/tabs ❑ styles ● categories – headline – headings -sub-headings – bullets – extracts – headers/footers ● borders/lines ● point sizes ● serif and sans serif fonts ● text alignment ● text enhancement – italic – bold

ASSESSMENT OBJECTIVES

5.2 Insert, manipulate and present data

5.2a Produce document(s) in accordance with a given design brief in a specified house style

5.2b Print required data as specified

SYLLABUS CONTENT

❑ enter text
❑ transfer data between files/applications
- transfer data
  – copy – cut and paste – import – export

❑ manipulate and present data
- copyfit material
  – widows/orphans – consistent spacing – group headings/sub-headings with related data – text/images/lines not superimposed – imported images and/or extracts not split across pages – control white space (ie no more than two blank lines at the bottom of any but the final column)
- control size(s) of image(s) in proportion
- spellcheck
- use drawing features
  – lines – circles – boxes – ellipses – shading/fill/pattern

❑ print

IBT III assessment procedures

The assessment consists of one practical assignment, similar to that given in Part 2. This takes place at the end of a course of study. Once candidates start the assignment, no further tuition can be given. No help, other than that for technical failure of equipment, can be given during the assessment. Candidates are allowed limited feedback on the source data processing action. This must be shown to your tutor before progressing.

The candidate is allowed a total of ten hours to complete all the components, spread over sessions to suit the centre and candidates. Ten hours is usually ample time for most candidates. The Time Log Sheet must be completed at the end of each session so that there is a running total. Printing can be done outside the ten hours.

The assessment must be supervised, as with CLAIT and IBT II assessments, but strict examination conditions are not necessary.

Your tutor will be able to advise you of the exact procedures for your situation.

Answers to exercises

Chapter 3, Section 2, Exercise 1

PROPERTY NAME	CODE	LOCATION	OCCUPANTS	BEDROOMS	BOOKED(A)	BOOKED(B)	PRICE CODE	TV	CHANGE DAY	DATE BOOKED	AGENT
PEANUTS	F919	FOREST	4	2	7	12	B	☐	SAT	18-Sep-99	PAUL
ASPENS	M340	MOUNTAIN	2	1	7	10	B	☐	FRI	24-Sep-99	JANE
HEADLANDS	R691	RIVERS	4	2	7	12	B	☐	SAT	18-Sep-99	PAUL
PUFFINS	S855	SEA	4	1	5	14	B	☐	SAT	25-Sep-99	MIKE

Chapter 3, Section 2, Exercise 2

PROPERTY NAME	LOCATION	BOOKED(A)	PRICE CODE
SURF	SEA	11	C
STARFISH	SEA	7	C
SHRIMPS	SEA	7	C
SHINGLE	SEA	11	C
SHELLFISH	SEA	11	C
SEASHORE	SEA	12	E
MUSSELS	SEA	10	C
MOLLUSCS	SEA	13	D
MISTY	SEA	12	D
MARBLE	FOREST	11	C

Chapter 3, Section 2, Exercise 3

PROPERTY NAME	LOCATION	BOOKED(A)	CHANGE DAY	AGENT
PEANUTS	FOREST	7	SAT	PAUL
SPARROWS	LAKES	7	SAT	PAUL
STARFISH	SEA	7	SAT	PAUL
OYSTERS	SEA	7	FRI	GAIL
BANANAS	MOUNTAIN	7	FRI	PAUL
HEADLANDS	RIVERS	7	SAT	PAUL
WATERFALLS	FOREST	7	SAT	PAUL
PARSLEY	LAKES	7	FRI	PAUL
WALNUTS	LAKES	7	FRI	PAUL
BEECHES	LAKES	8	FRI	PAUL
BEIGE	COUNTRY	8	SAT	GAIL
PRUNES	COUNTRY	9	FRI	PAUL
ULTRAMARINE	SEA	9	FRI	GAIL
BRONZE	MOUNTAIN	9	SAT	PAUL
LIMES	RIVERS	10	FRI	PAUL
PAWPAWS	SEA	10	FRI	PAUL
ISLANDS	SEA	11	SAT	PAUL
RAISINS	COUNTRY	11	FRI	PAUL
LIMPETS	SEA	12	FRI	GAIL
REDWINGS	RIVERS	12	FRI	PAUL
RIVERS	RIVERS	12	FRI	PAUL
MINT	COUNTRY	12	FRI	PAUL
SEA URCHINS	SEA	14	FRI	PAUL
BLACKCURRANTS	COUNTRY	14	SAT	PAUL
CINNABAR	LAKES	14	FRI	PAUL
CLIFFS	SEA	14	FRI	PAUL
THYME	COUNTRY	14	FRI	PAUL
PLUMS	COUNTRY	14	FRI	PAUL
BISCUIT	MOUNTAIN	14	FRI	PAUL

Chapter 3, Section 2

QUERY DESIGNS

NOTE: Only fields with sorting and a criteria search are shown.

Chapter 3 Section 2.2 QUERY 1

Field:	CODE	BOOKED(A)	PRICE CODE	DATE BOOKED
Table:	Holiday homes	Holiday homes	Holiday homes	Holiday homes
Sort:	Ascending			
Show:	☑	☑	☑	☑
Criteria:		<=7	"B"	>#17/09/99#

Chapter 3 Section 2.2 QUERY 2

PROPERTY NAME	LOCATION	OCCUPANTS	CHANGE DAY	BOOKED (B)
Holiday homes	Holiday homes	Holiday homes	Holiday homes	Holiday home
Descending				
☑	☑	☐	☐	☐
Like "S*" Or Like "G*" Or Like "M*"	"SEA" Or "FOREST"	> =4	"SAT"	>8

Chapter 3 Section 2.2 QUERY 3

Field:	BOOKED(A)	AGENT	BOOKED(B)
Table:	Holiday homes	Holiday homes	Holiday homes
Sort:	Ascending		
Show:	☑	☑	☐
Criteria:	>6 And <15	"PAUL" Or "GAIL"	>=12

Chapter 3, Section 2, Exercise 4

LOW BOOKINGS PERIOD A

PROPERTY NAME	ASPENS
BOOKED (A)	7
PROPERTY NAME	HEADLANDS
BOOKED (A)	7
PROPERTY NAME	PEANUTS
BOOKED (A)	7
PROPERTY NAME	PUFFINS
BOOKED (A)	5

Chapter 3, Section 2, Exercise 5

BOOKINGS PER LOCATION

LOCATION	PROPERTY NAME	BOOKED (A)
COUNTRY		
	BEIGE	8
	BLACKCURRANTS	14
	MINT	12
	PLUMS	14
	PRUNES	9
	RAISINS	11
	THYME	14
		82
FOREST		
	PEANUTS	7
	WATERFALLS	7
		14
LAKES		
	BEECHES	8
	CINNABAR	14
	PARSLEY	7
	SPARROWS	7
	WALNUTS	7
		43
MOUNTAIN		
	BANANAS	7
	BISCUIT	14
	BRONZE	9
		30
RIVERS		
	HEADLANDS	7
	LIMES	10
	REDWINGS	12
	RIVERS	12
		41
SEA		
	CLIFFS	14
	ISLANDS	11
	LIMPETS	12
	OYSTERS	7
	PAWPAWS	10
	SEA URCHINS	14
	STARFISH	7
	ULTRAMARINE	9
		84

1 02/02/99

Chapter 4, Section 1, Exercise 5

NATURETRAIL HOLIDAYS									
ANALYSIS OF INCOME									
							BOOKINGS		
PRICE CODE DETAILS								BOOKED(A)	BOOKED(B)
PRICE CODE		A	B	C	D	E			
COST PER WEEK(£)		150.00	200.00	225.00	255.00	300.00	COUNTRY		
							FOREST		
FIXED CHARGE(£)		50.00					LAKES		
							MOUNTAIN		
							RIVERS		
							SEA		
PROPERTY DETAILS									
LOCATION AND PROPERTY CODE	BOOKED(A)	BOOKED(B)	PRICE CODE	TOTAL WEEKS BOOKED	INCOME	TOTAL WEEKS NOT BOOKED			
COUNTRY									
C181	12	12	B						
C34	14	12	B						
C66	14	9	B						
C670	11	14	B						
C777	9	12	B						
C91	14	12	D						
C997	14	14	C						
FOREST									
F129	7	13	A						
F642	7	14	C						
F919	7	12	B						
LAKES									
L654	12	10	C						
L67	7	14	C						
L801	14	14	A						
L802	8	14	B						
L816	7	13	A						
L817	11	11	A						
L855	11	6	B						
L919	7	14	D						
MOUNTAIN									
M30	7	13	A						
M341	7	13	B						
M443	9	11	E						
M45	9	6	A						
M51	14	9	E						
M666	9	11	B						
M88	9	12	E						
M89	11	9	B						
M975	14	14	A						
RIVERS									
R103	14	14	E						
R134	12	14	B						
R21	14	12	C						
R54	12	14	B						
R691	7	12	B						
SEA									
S126	11	12	E						
S16	7	14	C						
S222	14	12	D						
S51	14	14	E						
S555	10	14	C						
S589	14	10	E						
S715	12	12	D						
S89	13	14	D						
				TOTAL(£)					
PROPERTIES PER LOCATION									
LOCATION	NO OF PROPERTIES								
COUNTRY									
FOREST									
LAKES									
MOUNTAIN									
RIVERS									
SEA									

Chapter 4, Section 2, Exercise 11

NATURETRAIL HOLIDAYS									
ANALYSIS OF INCOME									
							BOOKINGS		
		PRICE CODE DETAILS						BOOKED(A)	BOOKED(B)
PRICE CODE		A	B	C	D	E			
COST PER WEEK(£)		150.00	200.00	225.00	255.00	300.00	COUNTRY	88	85
							FOREST	21	39
FIXED CHARGE(£)		50.00					LAKES	77	96
							MOUNTAIN	89	98
							RIVERS	59	66
							SEA	95	102
			PROPERTY DETAILS						
LOCATION AND PROPERTY CODE	BOOKED(A)	BOOKED(B)	PRICE CODE	TOTAL WEEKS BOOKED	INCOME	TOTAL WEEKS NOT BOOKED	LOW(A)		
COUNTRY									
C181	12	12	B	24	4850.00	4	NO		
C34	14	12	B	26	5250.00	2	NO		
C66	14	9	B	23	4650.00	5	NO		
C670	11	14	B	25	5050.00	3	YES		
C777	9	12	B	21	4250.00	7	YES		
C91	14	12	D	26	6680.00	2	NO		
C997	14	14	C	28	6350.00	0	NO		
FOREST									
F129	7	13	A	20	3050.00	8	YES		
F642	7	14	C	21	4775.00	7	YES		
F919	7	12	B	19	3850.00	9	YES		
LAKES									
L654	12	10	C	22	5000.00	6	NO		
L67	7	14	C	21	4775.00	7	YES		
L801	14	14	A	28	4250.00	0	NO		
L802	8	14	B	22	4450.00	6	YES		
L816	7	13	A	20	3050.00	8	YES		
L817	11	11	A	22	3350.00	6	NO		
L855	11	6	B	17	3450.00	11	NO		
L919	7	14	D	21	5405.00	7	YES		
MOUNTAIN									
M30	7	13	A	20	3050.00	8	YES		
M341	7	13	B	20	4050.00	8	YES		
M443	9	11	E	20	6050.00	8	YES		
M45	9	6	A	15	2300.00	13	NO		
M51	14	9	E	23	6950.00	5	NO		
M666	9	11	B	20	4050.00	8	YES		
M88	9	12	E	21	6350.00	7	YES		
M89	11	9	B	20	4050.00	8	NO		
M975	14	14	A	28	4250.00	0	NO		
RIVERS									
R103	14	14	E	28	8450.00	0	NO		
R134	12	14	B	26	5250.00	2	YES		
R21	14	12	C	26	5900.00	2	NO		
R54	12	14	B	26	5250.00	2	YES		
R691	7	12	B	19	3850.00	9	YES		
SEA									
S126	11	12	E	23	6950.00	5	YES		
S16	7	14	C	21	4775.00	7	YES		
S222	14	12	D	26	6680.00	2	NO		
S51	14	14	E	28	8450.00	0	NO		
S555	10	14	C	24	5450.00	4	YES		
S589	14	10	E	24	7250.00	4	NO		
S715	12	12	D	24	6170.00	4	NO		
S89	13	14	D	27	6935.00	1	YES		
				TOTAL(£)	£204,945.00				
PROPERTIES PER LOCATION									
LOCATION	**NO OF PROPERTIES**								
COUNTRY									
FOREST									
LAKES									
MOUNTAIN									
RIVERS									
SEA									

Chapter 4, Section 2, Exercise 12

NATURETRA									
ANALYSIS O									
							BOOKINGS		
				PRICE CODE DETAILS				BOOKED(A)	BOOKED(B)
PRICE CODE		A	B	C	D	E			
COST PER WEEK		150	200	225	255	300	COUNTRY	=SUM(B18:B24)	=SUM(C18:C24)
							FOREST	=SUM(B26:B28)	=SUM(C26:C28)
FIXED CHARGE(£)		50					LAKES	=SUM(B30:B37)	=SUM(C30:C37)
							MOUNTAIN	=SUM(B39:B47)	=SUM(C39:C47)
							RIVERS	=SUM(B49:B53)	=SUM(C49:C53)
							SEA	=SUM(B55:B62)	=SUM(C55:C62)
				PROPERTY DETAILS					
LOCATION AND PROPERTY CODE	BOOKED(A)	BOOKEI	PRICE	TOTAL WEEKS BOOKED	INCOME	TOTAL WEEKS NOT BOOKED	LOW(A)		
COUNTRY									
C181	12	12	B	=SUM(B18:C18)	=E18*LOOKUP(D18,CODE)+$C$10	=28-E18	=IF(B18<C18,"YES","NO")		
C34	14	12	B	=SUM(B19:C19)	=E19*LOOKUP(D19,CODE)+$C$10	=28-E19	=IF(B19<C19,"YES","NO")		
C66	14	9	B	=SUM(B20:C20)	=E20*LOOKUP(D20,CODE)+$C$10	=28-E20	=IF(B20<C20,"YES","NO")		
C670	11	14	B	=SUM(B21:C21)	=E21*LOOKUP(D21,CODE)+$C$10	=28-E21	=IF(B21<C21,"YES","NO")		
C777	9	12	B	=SUM(B22:C22)	=E22*LOOKUP(D22,CODE)+$C$10	=28-E22	=IF(B22<C22,"YES","NO")		
C91	14	12	D	=SUM(B23:C23)	=E23*LOOKUP(D23,CODE)+$C$10	=28-E23	=IF(B23<C23,"YES","NO")		
C997	14	14	C	=SUM(B24:C24)	=E24*LOOKUP(D24,CODE)+$C$10	=28-E24	=IF(B24<C24,"YES","NO")		
FOREST									
F129	7	13	A	=SUM(B26:C26)	=E26*LOOKUP(D26,CODE)+$C$10	=28-E26	=IF(B26<C26,"YES","NO")		
F642	7	14	C	=SUM(B27:C27)	=E27*LOOKUP(D27,CODE)+$C$10	=28-E27	=IF(B27<C27,"YES","NO")		
F919	7	12	B	=SUM(B28:C28)	=E28*LOOKUP(D28,CODE)+$C$10	=28-E28	=IF(B28<C28,"YES","NO")		
LAKES									
L654	12	10	C	=SUM(B30:C30)	=E30*LOOKUP(D30,CODE)+$C$10	=28-E30	=IF(B30<C30,"YES","NO")		
L67	7	14	C	=SUM(B31:C31)	=E31*LOOKUP(D31,CODE)+$C$10	=28-E31	=IF(B31<C30,"YES","NO")		
L801	14	14	A	=SUM(B32:C32)	=E32*LOOKUP(D32,CODE)+$C$10	=28-E32	=IF(B32<C32,"YES","NO")		
L802	8	14	B	=SUM(B33:C33)	=E33*LOOKUP(D33,CODE)+$C$10	=28-E33	=IF(B33<C33,"YES","NO")		
L816	7	13	A	=SUM(B34:C34)	=E34*LOOKUP(D34,CODE)+$C$10	=28-E34	=IF(B34<C34,"YES","NO")		
L817	11	11	A	=SUM(B35:C35)	=E35*LOOKUP(D35,CODE)+$C$10	=28-E35	=IF(B35<C35,"YES","NO")		
L855	11	6	B	=SUM(B36:C36)	=E36*LOOKUP(D36,CODE)+$C$10	=28-E36	=IF(B36<C36,"YES","NO")		
L919	7	14	D	=SUM(B37:C37)	=E37*LOOKUP(D37,CODE)+$C$10	=28-E37	=IF(B37<C37,"YES","NO")		
MOUNTAIN									
M30	7	13	A	=SUM(B39:C39)	=E39*LOOKUP(D39,CODE)+$C$10	=28-E39	=IF(B39<C39,"YES","NO")		
M341	7	13	B	=SUM(B40:C40)	=E40*LOOKUP(D40,CODE)+$C$10	=28-E40	=IF(B40<C40,"YES","NO")		
M443	9	11	E	=SUM(B41:C41)	=E41*LOOKUP(D41,CODE)+$C$10	=28-E41	=IF(B41<C41,"YES","NO")		
M45	9	6	A	=SUM(B42:C42)	=E42*LOOKUP(D42,CODE)+$C$10	=28-E42	=IF(B42<C42,"YES","NO")		
M51	14	9	E	=SUM(B43:C43)	=E43*LOOKUP(D43,CODE)+$C$10	=28-E43	=IF(B43<C43,"YES","NO")		
M666	9	11	B	=SUM(B44:C44)	=E44*LOOKUP(D44,CODE)+$C$10	=28-E44	=IF(B44<C44,"YES","NO")		
M88	9	12	E	=SUM(B45:C45)	=E45*LOOKUP(D45,CODE)+$C$10	=28-E45	=IF(B45<C45,"YES","NO")		
M89	11	9	B	=SUM(B46:C46)	=E46*LOOKUP(D46,CODE)+$C$10	=28-E46	=IF(B46<C46,"YES","NO")		
M975	14	14	A	=SUM(B47:C47)	=E47*LOOKUP(D47,CODE)+$C$10	=28-E47	=IF(B47<C47,"YES","NO")		
RIVERS									
R103	14	14	E	=SUM(B49:C49)	=E49*LOOKUP(D49,CODE)+$C$10	=28-E49	=IF(B49<C49,"YES","NO")		
R134	12	14	B	=SUM(B50:C50)	=E50*LOOKUP(D50,CODE)+$C$10	=28-E50	=IF(B50<C50,"YES","NO")		
R21	14	12	C	=SUM(B51:C51)	=E51*LOOKUP(D51,CODE)+$C$10	=28-E51	=IF(B51<C51,"YES","NO")		
R54	12	14	B	=SUM(B52:C52)	=E52*LOOKUP(D52,CODE)+$C$10	=28-E52	=IF(B52<C52,"YES","NO")		
R691	7	12	B	=SUM(B53:C53)	=E53*LOOKUP(D53,CODE)+$C$10	=28-E53	=IF(B53<C53,"YES","NO")		
SEA									
S126	11	12	E	=SUM(B55:C55)	=E55*LOOKUP(D55,CODE)+$C$10	=28-E55	=IF(B55<C55,"YES","NO")		
S16	7	14	C	=SUM(B56:C56)	=E56*LOOKUP(D56,CODE)+$C$10	=28-E56	=IF(B56<C56,"YES","NO")		
S222	14	12	D	=SUM(B57:C57)	=E57*LOOKUP(D57,CODE)+$C$10	=28-E57	=IF(B57<C57,"YES","NO")		
S51	14	14	E	=SUM(B58:C58)	=E58*LOOKUP(D58,CODE)+$C$10	=28-E58	=IF(B58<C58,"YES","NO")		
S555	10	14	C	=SUM(B59:C59)	=E59*LOOKUP(D59,CODE)+$C$10	=28-E59	=IF(B59<C59,"YES","NO")		
S589	14	10	E	=SUM(B60:C60)	=E60*LOOKUP(D60,CODE)+$C$10	=28-E60	=IF(B60<C60,"YES","NO")		
S715	12	12	D	=SUM(B61:C61)	=E61*LOOKUP(D61,CODE)+$C$10	=28-E61	=IF(B61<C61,"YES","NO")		
S89	13	14	D	=SUM(B62:C62)	=E62*LOOKUP(D62,CODE)+$C$10	=28-E52	=IF(B62<C62,"YES","NO")		
				TOTAL(£)	=SUM(F18:F62)				
PROPERTIES PER									
LOCATION	NO OF PROPERTIES								
COUNTRY	=COUNT(B18:B24)								
FOREST	=COUNT(B26:B28)								
LAKES	=COUNT(B30:B37)								
MOUNTAIN	=COUNT(B39:B47)								
RIVERS	=COUNT(B49:B53)								
SEA	=COUNT(B55:B62)								
AVERAGE	=AVERAGE(B66:B71)								

Chapter 4, Section 3, Exercise 2

PROPERTY DETAILS				
LOCATION AND PROPERTY CODE	TOTAL WEEKS BOOKED	INCOME	TOTAL WEEKS NOT BOOKED	LOW(A)
COUNTRY				
C181	24	4850.00	4	NO
C34	26	5250.00	2	NO
C66	23	4650.00	5	NO
C670	25	5050.00	3	YES
C777	21	4250.00	7	YES
C91	26	6680.00	2	NO
C997	28	6350.00	0	NO
FOREST				
F129	20	3050.00	8	YES
F642	21	4775.00	7	YES
F919	19	3850.00	9	YES
LAKES				
L654	22	5000.00	6	NO
L67	21	4775.00	7	YES
L801	28	4250.00	0	NO
L802	22	4450.00	6	YES
L816	20	3050.00	8	YES
L817	22	3350.00	6	NO
L855	17	3450.00	11	NO
L919	21	5405.00	7	YES
MOUNTAIN				
M30	20	3050.00	8	YES
M341	20	4050.00	8	YES
M443	20	6050.00	8	YES
M45	15	2300.00	13	NO
M51	23	6950.00	5	NO
M666	20	4050.00	8	YES
M88	21	6350.00	7	YES
M89	20	4050.00	8	NO
M975	28	4250.00	0	NO
RIVERS				
R103	28	8450.00	0	NO
R134	26	5250.00	2	YES
R21	26	5900.00	2	NO
R54	26	5250.00	2	YES
R691	19	3850.00	9	YES
SEA				
S126	23	6950.00	5	YES
S16	21	4775.00	7	YES
S222	26	6680.00	2	NO
S51	28	8450.00	0	NO
S555	24	5450.00	4	YES
S589	24	7250.00	4	NO
S715	24	6170.00	4	NO
S89	27	6935.00	1	YES
	TOTAL(£)	£204,945.00		

Chapter 4, Section 3, Exercise 3

PROPERTY DETAILS				
LOCATION AND PROPERTY CODE	**TOTAL WEEKS BOOKED**	**INCOME**	**TOTAL WEEKS NOT BOOKED**	**LOW(A)**
COUNTRY				
C181	=SUM(B18:C18)	=E18*LOOKUP(D18,CODE)+$C$10	=28-E18	=IF(B18<C18,"YES","NO")
C34	=SUM(B19:C19)	=E19*LOOKUP(D19,CODE)+$C$10	=28-E19	=IF(B19<C19,"YES","NO")
C66	=SUM(B20:C20)	=E20*LOOKUP(D20,CODE)+$C$10	=28-E20	=IF(B20<C20,"YES","NO")
C670	=SUM(B21:C21)	=E21*LOOKUP(D21,CODE)+$C$10	=28-E21	=IF(B21<C21,"YES","NO")
C777	=SUM(B22:C22)	=E22*LOOKUP(D22,CODE)+$C$10	=28-E22	=IF(B22<C22,"YES","NO")
C91	=SUM(B23:C23)	=E23*LOOKUP(D23,CODE)+$C$10	=28-E23	=IF(B23<C23,"YES","NO")
C997	=SUM(B24:C24)	=E24*LOOKUP(D24,CODE)+$C$10	=28-E24	=IF(B24<C24,"YES","NO")
FOREST				
F129	=SUM(B26:C26)	=E26*LOOKUP(D26,CODE)+$C$10	=28-E26	=IF(B26<C26,"YES","NO")
F642	=SUM(B27:C27)	=E27*LOOKUP(D27,CODE)+$C$10	=28-E27	=IF(B27<C27,"YES","NO")
F919	=SUM(B28:C28)	=E28*LOOKUP(D28,CODE)+$C$10	=28-E28	=IF(B28<C28,"YES","NO")
LAKES				
L654	=SUM(B30:C30)	=E30*LOOKUP(D30,CODE)+$C$10	=28-E30	=IF(B30<C30,"YES","NO")
L67	=SUM(B31:C31)	=E31*LOOKUP(D31,CODE)+$C$10	=28-E31	=IF(B31<C31,"YES","NO")
L801	=SUM(B32:C32)	=E32*LOOKUP(D32,CODE)+$C$10	=28-E32	=IF(B32<C32,"YES","NO")
L802	=SUM(B33:C33)	=E33*LOOKUP(D33,CODE)+$C$10	=28-E33	=IF(B33<C33,"YES","NO")
L816	=SUM(B34:C34)	=E34*LOOKUP(D34,CODE)+$C$10	=28-E34	=IF(B34<C34,"YES","NO")
L817	=SUM(B35:C35)	=E35*LOOKUP(D35,CODE)+$C$10	=28-E35	=IF(B35<C35,"YES","NO")
L855	=SUM(B36:C36)	=E36*LOOKUP(D36,CODE)+$C$10	=28-E36	=IF(B36<C36,"YES","NO")
L919	=SUM(B37:C37)	=E37*LOOKUP(D37,CODE)+$C$10	=28-E37	=IF(B37<C37,"YES","NO")
MOUNTAIN				
M30	=SUM(B39:C39)	=E39*LOOKUP(D39,CODE)+$C$10	=28-E39	=IF(B39<C39,"YES","NO")
M341	=SUM(B40:C40)	=E40*LOOKUP(D40,CODE)+$C$10	=28-E40	=IF(B40<C40,"YES","NO")
M443	=SUM(B41:C41)	=E41*LOOKUP(D41,CODE)+$C$10	=28-E41	=IF(B41<C41,"YES","NO")
M45	=SUM(B42:C42)	=E42*LOOKUP(D42,CODE)+$C$10	=28-E42	=IF(B42<C42,"YES","NO")
M51	=SUM(B43:C43)	=E43*LOOKUP(D43,CODE)+$C$10	=28-E43	=IF(B43<C43,"YES","NO")
M666	=SUM(B44:C44)	=E44*LOOKUP(D44,CODE)+$C$10	=28-E44	=IF(B44<C44,"YES","NO")
M88	=SUM(B45:C45)	=E45*LOOKUP(D45,CODE)+$C$10	=28-E45	=IF(B45<C45,"YES","NO")
M975	=SUM(B46:C46)	=E46*LOOKUP(D46,CODE)+$C$10	=28-E46	=IF(B46<C46,"YES","NO")
RIVERS	=SUM(B47:C47)	=E47*LOOKUP(D46,CODE)+$C$10	=28-E47	=IF(B47<C47,"YES","NO")
R103				
R134	=SUM(B49:C49)	=E49*LOOKUP(D49,CODE)+$C$10	=28-E49	=IF(B49<C49,"YES","NO")
R21	=SUM(B50:C50)	=E50*LOOKUP(D50,CODE)+$C$10	=28-E50	=IF(B50<C50,"YES","NO")
R54	=SUM(B51:C51)	=E51*LOOKUP(D51,CODE)+$C$10	=28-E51	=IF(B51<C51,"YES","NO")
R691	=SUM(B52:C52)	=E52*LOOKUP(D52,CODE)+$C$10	=28-E52	=IF(B52<C52,"YES","NO")
SEA	=SUM(B53:C53)	=E53*LOOKUP(D53,CODE)+$C$10	=28-E53	=IF(B53<C53,"YES","NO")
S126				
S16	=SUM(B55:C55)	=E55*LOOKUP(D55,CODE)+$C$10	=28-E55	=IF(B55<C55,"YES","NO")
S222	=SUM(B56:C56)	=E56*LOOKUP(D56,CODE)+$C$10	=28-E56	=IF(B56<C56,"YES","NO")
S51	=SUM(B57:C57)	=E57*LOOKUP(D57,CODE)+$C$10	=28-E57	=IF(B57<C57,"YES","NO")
S555	=SUM(B58:C58)	=E58*LOOKUP(D58,CODE)+$C$10	=28-E58	=IF(B58<C58,"YES","NO")
S589	=SUM(B59:C59)	=E59*LOOKUP(D59,CODE)+$C$10	=28-E59	=IF(B59<C59,"YES","NO")
S715	=SUM(B60:C60)	=E60*LOOKUP(D60,CODE)+$C$10	=28-E60	=IF(B60<C60,"YES","NO")
S89	=SUM(B61:C61)	=E61*LOOKUP(D61,CODE)+$C$10	=28-E61	=IF(B61<C61,"YES","NO")
	=SUM(B62:C62)	=E62*LOOKUP(D62,CODE)+$C$10	=28-E62	=IF(B62<C62,"YES","NO")
	TOTAL(£)	=SUM(F18:F62)		

Chapter 4, Section 3, Exercise 5

LOCATION	NO OF PROPERTIES
COUNTRY	7
FOREST	3
LAKES	8
MOUNTAIN	9
RIVERS	5
SEA	8
AVERAGE	7

Chapter 4, Section 3

LOCATION AND PROPERTY CODE	PRICE CODE
COUNTRY	
C670	B
C777	B
FOREST	
F129	A
F642	C
F919	B
LAKES	
L67	C
L802	B
L816	A
L919	D
MOUNTAIN	
M30	A
M341	B
M443	E
M666	B
M88	E
RIVERS	
R134	B
R54	B
R691	B
SEA	
S126	E
S16	C
S555	C
S89	D

Chapter 4, Section 3, Exercise 7

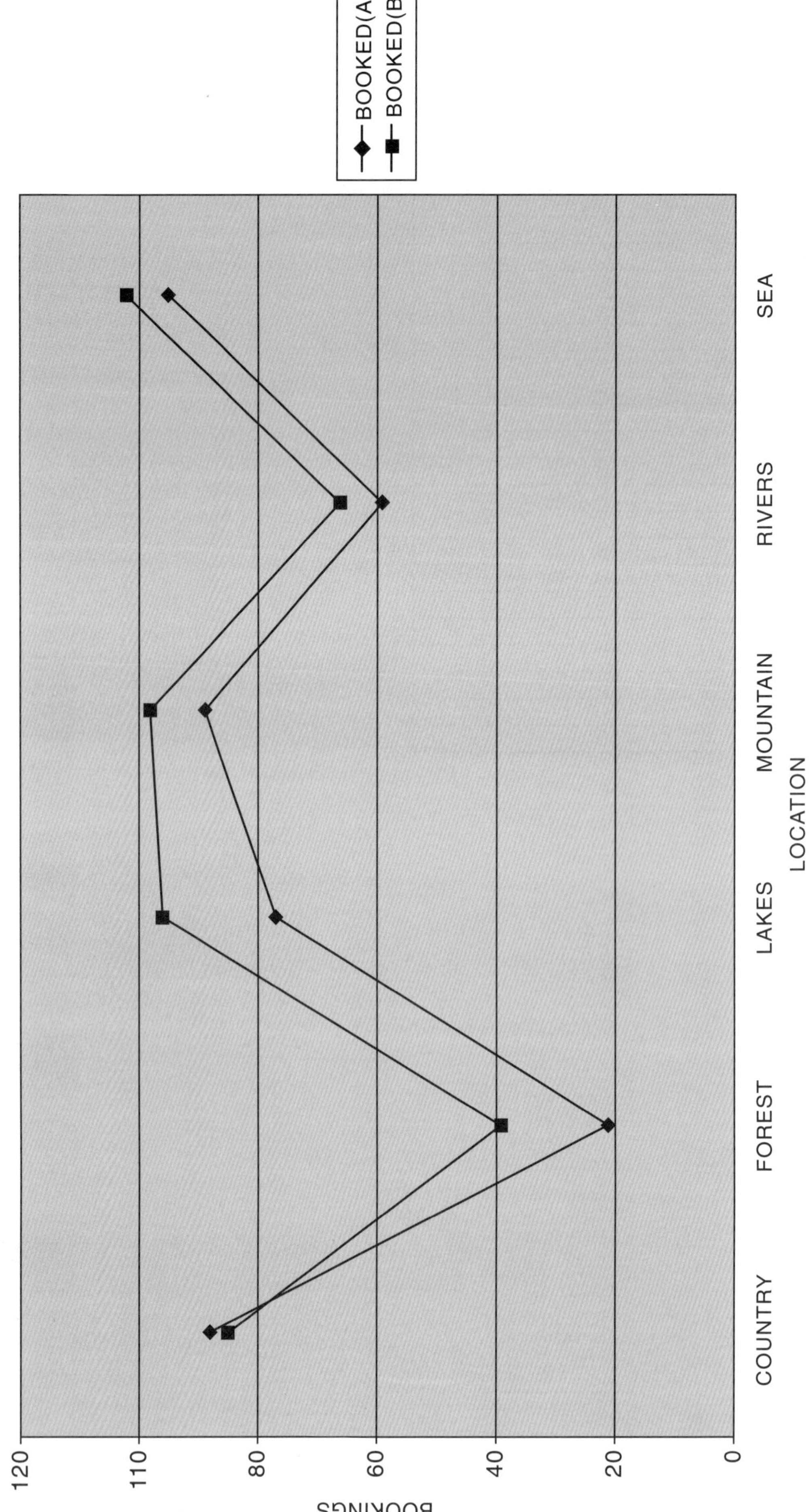

Chapter 4, Section 3, Exercise 8

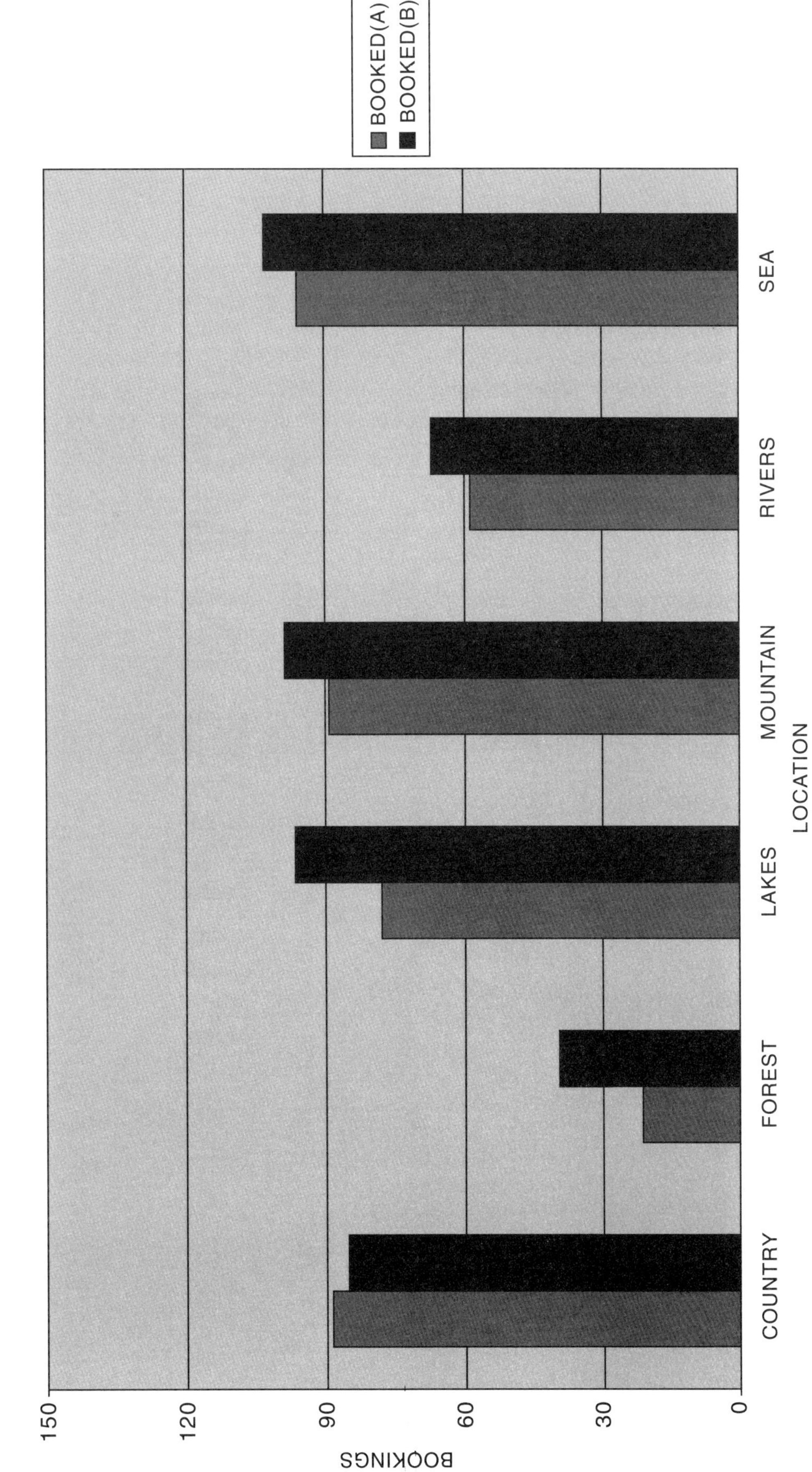

Chapter 5, Section 2, Exercise 9/P5

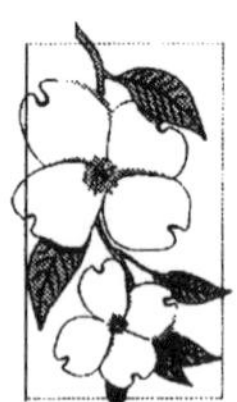

WANT TO UNWIND?

PUT US IN MIND!

Naturetrail Holidays Angela Bessant 9 November 1998

Chapter 5, Section 2, Exercise 9/P1

NATURETRAIL HOLIDAYS

TOTAL RELAXATION

Tel: 01234 29786

Open 7 to 7

Naturetrail Holidays Angela Bessant 9 November 1998

Chapter 5, Section 2, Exercise 9/P2

DELIGHTFUL LOCATIONS

Our holiday homes are situated in some of the most beautiful settings, for example:

- Mountains
- Lakes
- Sea

Naturetrail Holidays　　Angela Bessant　　9 November 1998

Chapter 5, Section 2, Exercise 9/P3

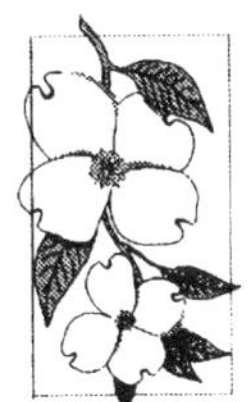

BOOKINGS

Why not take a holiday early in the year when there is usually more choice:

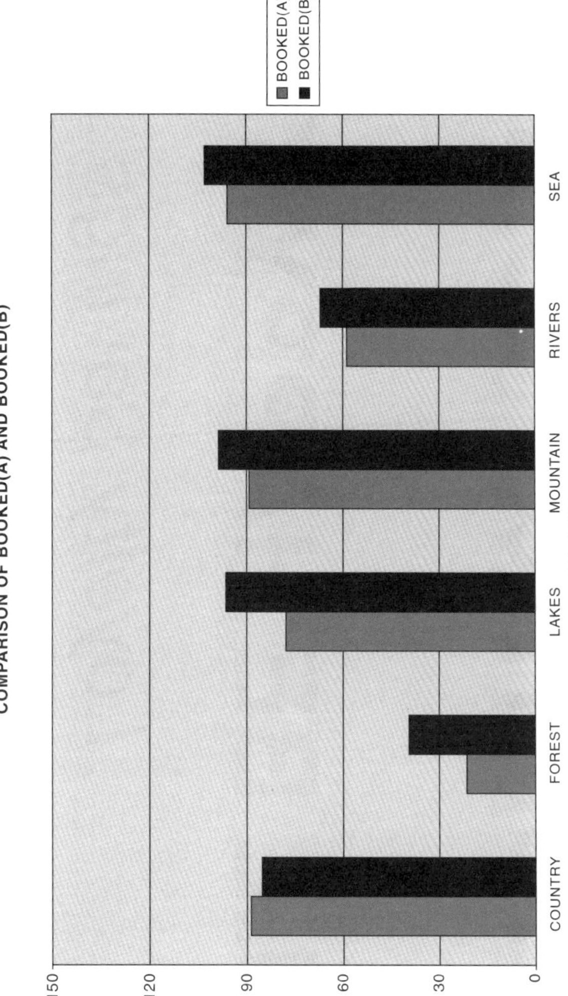

Naturetrail Holidays

Angela Bessant

9 November 1998

Chapter 5, Section 2, Exercise 9/P4

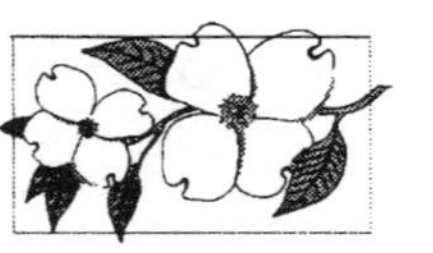

CONTACT US NOW!

WE'LL BE HAPPY TO HELP

Loyalty Savings

We will be continuing our loyalty scheme for the foreseeable future and there is also the chance that you may win one of ten super cash prizes.

Naturetrail Holidays | Angela Bessant | 9 November 1998

Chapter 5, Section 2, Exercise 9

NATURETRAIL HOLIDAYS

TOTAL RELAXATION

Tel: 01234 29786

Open 7 to 7

Naturetrail Holidays   Angela Bessant   9 November 1998

DELIGHTFUL LOCATIONS

Our holiday homes are situated in some of the most beautiful settings, for example:

- Mountains
- Lakes
- Sea

Naturetrail Holidays   Angela Bessant   9 November 1998

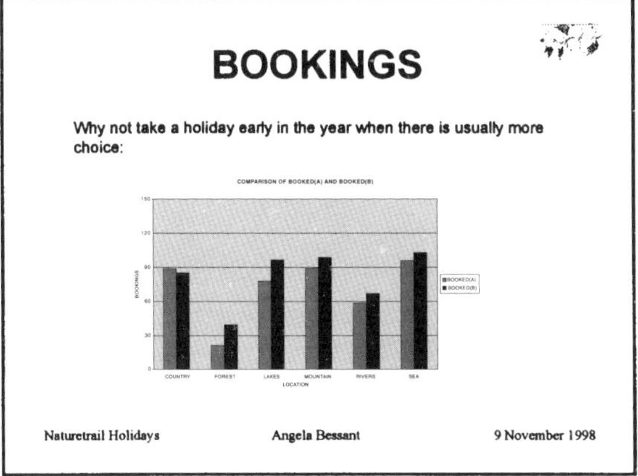

CONTACT US NOW!

WE'LL BE HAPPY TO HELP

Loyalty Savings

We will be continuing our loyalty scheme for the foreseeable future and there is also the chance that you may win one of ten super cash prizes.

Naturetrail Holidays   Angela Bessant   9 November 1998

WANT TO UNWIND?

PUT US IN MIND!

Naturetrail Holidays   Angela Bessant   9 November 1998

Chapter 6, Final Publication

19/01/99

Angela Bessant

Chapter 6, Final Publication ctd

NATURETRAIL HOLIDAYS

If you are looking for a peaceful and relaxing holiday then look no further than Naturetrail Holidays. From small beginnings five years ago when the company had only one location we are now able to offer a choice of six completely different locations. Whatever your idea of the perfect place for a holiday we have the answer.

LOCATIONS

We have holiday cottages in the beautiful unspoilt countryside of the Cotswolds. Here you are able to ramble along the picturesque footpaths and visit the charming villages and small towns that are dotted around this area. Our forest properties are situated in North Wales, close to Betws-y-Coed. There are endless outdoor activities in this area ranging from walking, canoeing or climbing. In Cumbria you will find our lakes cottages - if you like sailing and fishing then this is the place for you. Again in North Wales, situated in the heart of Snowdonia, you will find our mountain complex. There are even trained mountaineers on hand to give you coaching in all aspects of climbing. So don't worry if you're a novice, there are activities ranging from those for beginners right through to the more experienced climber. Cornwall is the setting for our seaside properties. These are located between Boscastle and Newquay. The scenery in this area is second to none. There are wild coastal footpaths, fishing villages and sandy beaches. You will be spoilt for choice for your daily excursions! For those of you who enjoy the tranquillity of a riverside setting, you will find this at our site in Devon. Our properties are situated only 100 metres from the river Dart. Of course also in this area, in addition to riverside activities, there are beautiful moorland walks.

THE CHOICE IS YOURS. We believe that you cannot fail to appreciate the natural beauty that abounds in all of these locations.

PROPERTIES AVAILABLE

Our properties vary in size and we have properties to suit most needs. You can choose from one to four bedrooms, with the maximum occupancy being eight people (there is the possibility that some of our properties can accommodate babies (cots and high chairs can be provided at no extra cost). Please ask the agent when booking.

PRICES

Prices vary depending on the size of the property. This year we have introduced a new system and now if you book for more than

continued

one week, any subsequent weeks are charged at a reduced rate.

The table below shows the prices relating to the different codes:

CODE	COST	EXTRA WEEK
A	£150	£135
B	£200	£185
C	£225	£210
D	£255	£240
E	£300	£285

Why not reserve a property for our early booking period? The properties shown below are on special discount prices (deduct a further 10% from the price shown in the brochure) for this year only:

LOW BOOKINGS PERIOD A

PROPERTY NAME	ASPENS
BOOKED (A)	7
PROPERTY NAME	HEADLANDS
BOOKED (A)	7
PROPERTY NAME	PEANUTS
BOOKED (A)	7
PROPERTY NAME	PUFFINS
BOOKED (A)	5

You can arrive on Friday or Saturday depending on which property you have chosen and at any time before 7 pm. Please let us know if you will be arriving later than this. Staggering arrivals in this way makes it easier to ensure that we have more staff available to give you a warm welcome. You may prefer to travel on a Friday, especially in summer when the roads are usually less congested. Whilst on the subject of transport, you will notice that most of our properties have parking adjacent to them. Where this is not the case your vehicle may be left in the parking areas which are never more than 50 metres away. For unloading purposes, parking outside the property is perfectly acceptable but please remember to move your vehicle as soon as you can since it will cause an obstruction.

Your property will have been fully cleaned and inspected before your arrival which can be anytime after 12 noon. All bed linen is provided but you will need to bring your own towels. All properties are self-catering but to help you settle in, we do provide a small grocery basket containing essentials, such as bread and milk. Should you find that things are not to your liking, please contact us straight away. WE PRIDE OURSELVES ON GIVING YOU THE BEST SERVICE AT ALL TIMES.

LOYALTY SAVINGS

Naturetrail Holidays are pleased to announce an important bonus for customers who have taken holidays with us in the past. We are now able to give substantial discounts on your holiday booking this year. If you book your holiday before the end of January you will be entitled to a 20% discount on the standard cost of your chosen property (subject to its availability). If you book before the end of March you will be entitled to a 10% discount on the standard cost.

We feel that this is a very generous offer and hope that you will be able to make your bookings early to benefit from the maximum savings.

Each 'loyalty' customer will be entered into our prize draw. We will be offering cash prizes ranging from £50 to £500 to those lucky ones picked out at random. If you are eligible for this discount please have your

continued

previous booking reference to hand when you call. If you no longer have your booking reference, don't worry we will be able to look up your details on our database.

HOW TO BOOK

Our properties can be booked from our Head Office by telephoning 01234 29786. We are open from 7 am to 7 pm every day except Sunday. Our regional offices can also help you with any queries that you may have. They are each allocated several properties that are their major concern. Choosing the right accommodation to suit your needs can be difficult and we want to help you make an informed choice. You can rely on our staff giving informative and friendly advice. Our computerised booking system gives instant availability of our properties so that we can suggest an alternative should your first choice be taken. Shown below are the properties dealt with by our Bristol office:

LOCATION	NO OF PROPERTIES
COUNTRY	7
FOREST	3
LAKES	8
MOUNTAIN	9
RIVERS	5
SEA	8
AVERAGE	7

As you can see each regional office deals with properties from all of the locations. Our staff training ensures that all staff have visited the six locations and are aware of the differences between them.

When booking please ensure that you have the following details to hand:

- Reference of Property
- Price Code
- Date Required
- Number in Party
- Vehicle Registration Number
- Credit Card Number
- Former Booking Ref (if applicable)

Here at Naturetrail Holidays we pride ourselves in providing an excellent booking service and we hope that you feel that this level of excellence carries through to all of our operations. We know how important it is that everything runs smoothly so that you are able to relax and enjoy yourselves.

So what are you waiting for? Have another look through our brochure and imagine the fun that you'll have with Naturetrail Holidays.

DON'T DELAY - BOOK TODAY.

We will be continuing our loyalty scheme for the foreseeable future and there is also the chance that you may win one of ten super cash prizes.

Full PRACTICE ASSIGNMENT – section B

Query1 04/02/99

PROPERTY NAME	CODE	LOCATION	OCCUPANTS	BEDROOMS	PETS	TV	BOOKED(A)	BOOKED(B)	PRICE CODE	CHANGE DAY	DATE BOOKED	AGENT
ASPENS	M341	MOUNTAIN	2	1	☐	☐	7	13	B	FRI	24-Sep-99	JANE
HEADLANDS	S122	SEA	4	2	☑	☐	7	10	B	SAT	18-Sep-99	PAUL
PEANUTS	F919	FOREST	4	2	☐	☐	7	12	B	SAT	18-Sep-99	PAUL
PUFFINS	S855	SEA	4	1	☐	☐	5	14	B	SAT	25-Sep-99	MIKE

Page 1

Full Practice Assignment – section B

BOOKINGS PERIOD A

PROPERTY NAME PUFFINS

BOOKED (A) 5

PROPERTY NAME PEANUTS

BOOKED (A) 7

PROPERTY NAME HEADLANDS

BOOKED (A) 7

PROPERTY NAME ASPENS

BOOKED (A) 7

Full Practice Assignment – section B

PROPERTY NAME	LOCATION	BOOKED(A)	PRICE CODE
MARBLE	FOREST	11	C
MISTY	SEA	12	D
MOLLUSCS	SEA	13	D
MUSSELS	SEA	10	C
SEASHORE	SEA	12	E
SHELLFISH	SEA	11	C
SHINGLE	SEA	11	C
SHRIMPS	SEA	7	C
STARFISH	SEA	7	C
SURF	SEA	11	C

Full Practice Assignment – section B

BOOKINGS PER LOCATION

LOCATION	PROPERTY NAME	BOOKED (A)
FOREST		
	MARBLE	11
		11
SEA		
	SURF	11
	STARFISH	7
	SHRIMPS	7
	SHINGLE	11
	SHELLFISH	11
	SEASHORE	12
	MUSSELS	10
	MOLLUSCS	13
	MISTY	12
		94

1 04/02/99

Full Practice Assignment – section C

NATURETRAIL HOLIDAYS

ANALYSIS OF INCOME

PRICE CODE DETAILS

PRICE CODE	A	B	C	D	E
COST PER WEEK(£)	150.00	200.00	225.00	255.00	300.00
FIXED CHARGE(£)	50.00				

BOOKINGS

	BOOKED(A)	BOOKED(B)
COUNTRY	88	85
FOREST	21	39
LAKES	77	96
MOUNTAIN	89	98
RIVERS	62	66
SEA	102	112

PROPERTY DETAILS

LOCATION AND PROPERTY CODE	BOOKED(A)	BOOKED(B)	PRICE CODE	TOTAL WEEKS BOOKED	INCOME	TOTAL WEEKS NOT BOOKED	
COUNTRY							
C181	12	12	B	24	4850.00	4	NO
C34	14	12	B	26	5250.00	2	NO
C66	14	9	B	23	4650.00	5	NO
C670	11	14	B	25	5050.00	3	YES
C777	9	12	B	21	4250.00	7	YES
C91	14	12	D	26	6680.00	2	NO
C997	14	14	C	28	6350.00	0	NO
FOREST							
F129	7	13	A	20	3050.00	8	YES
F642	7	14	C	21	4775.00	7	YES
F919	7	12	B	19	3850.00	9	YES
LAKES							
L654	12	10	C	22	5000.00	6	NO
L67	7	14	C	21	4775.00	7	YES
L801	14	14	A	28	4250.00	0	NO
L802	8	14	B	22	4450.00	6	YES
L816	7	13	A	20	3050.00	8	YES
L817	11	11	A	22	3350.00	6	NO
L855	11	6	B	17	3450.00	11	NO
L919	7	14	D	21	5405.00	7	YES
MOUNTAIN							
M30	7	13	A	20	3050.00	8	YES
M341	7	13	B	20	4050.00	8	YES
M443	9	11	E	20	6050.00	8	YES
M45	9	6	A	15	2300.00	13	NO
M51	14	9	E	23	6950.00	5	NO
M666	9	11	B	20	4050.00	8	YES
M88	9	12	E	21	6350.00	7	YES
M89	11	9	B	20	4050.00	8	NO
M975	14	14	A	28	4250.00	0	NO
RIVERS							
R103	14	14	E	28	8450.00	0	NO
R134	12	14	B	26	5250.00	2	YES
R21	14	12	C	26	5900.00	2	NO
R401	10	12	A	22	3350.00	6	YES
R54	12	14	B	26	5250.00	2	YES
SEA							
S122	7	12	B	17	3450.00	11	YES
S126	11	12	E	23	6950.00	5	YES
S16	7	14	C	21	4775.00	7	YES
S222	14	12	D	26	6680.00	2	NO
S51	14	14	E	28	8450.00	0	NO
S555	10	14	C	24	5450.00	4	YES
S589	14	10	E	24	7250.00	4	NO
S715	12	12	D	24	6170.00	4	NO
S89	13	14	D	27	6935.00	1	YES
				TOTAL(£)	£207,895.00		

PROPERTIES PER LOCATION

LOCATION	NO OF PROPERTIES
COUNTRY	7
FOREST	3
LAKES	8
MOUNTAIN	9
RIVERS	5
SEA	9

Full Practice Assignment – section C

NATURETRAIL HOLIDAYS									
ANALYSIS OF INCOME									
							BOOKINGS		
				PRICE CODE DETAILS					
PRICE CODE		A	B	C	D	E		BOOKED(A)	BOOKED(B)
COST PER WEEK(£)		150	200	225	255	300	COUNTRY	=SUM(B18:B24)	=SUM(C18:C24)
FIXED CHARGE(£)		50					FOREST	=SUM(B26:B28)	=SUM(C26:C28)
							LAKES	=SUM(B30:B37)	=SUM(C30:C37)
							MOUNTAIN	=SUM(B39:B47)	=SUM(C39:C47)
							RIVERS	=SUM(B49:B53)	=SUM(C49:C53)
							SEA	=SUM(B55:B63)	=SUM(C55:C63)
				PROPERTY DETAILS					
LOCATION AND PROPERTY CODE	BOOKED(A)	BOOKED(B)	PRICE CODE	TOTAL WEEKS BOOKED	INCOME	TOTAL WEEKS NOT BOOKED	LOW(A)		
COUNTRY									
C181	12	12	B	=SUM(B18:C18)	=E18*LOOKUP(D18,CODE)+$C$10	=28-E18	=IF(B18<C18,"YES","NO")		
C34	14	12	B	=SUM(B19:C19)	=E19*LOOKUP(D19,CODE)+$C$10	=28-E19	=IF(B19<C19,"YES","NO")		
C66	14	9	B	=SUM(B20:C20)	=E20*LOOKUP(D20,CODE)+$C$10	=28-E20	=IF(B20<C20,"YES","NO")		
C670	11	14	B	=SUM(B21:C21)	=E21*LOOKUP(D21,CODE)+$C$10	=28-E21	=IF(B21<C21,"YES","NO")		
C777	9	12	B	=SUM(B22:C22)	=E22*LOOKUP(D22,CODE)+$C$10	=28-E22	=IF(B22<C22,"YES","NO")		
C91	14	12	D	=SUM(B23:C23)	=E23*LOOKUP(D23,CODE)+$C$10	=28-E23	=IF(B23<C23,"YES","NO")		
C997	14	14	C	=SUM(B24:C24)	=E24*LOOKUP(D24,CODE)+$C$10	=28-E24	=IF(B24<C24,"YES","NO")		
FOREST									
F129	7	13	A	=SUM(B26:C26)	=E26*LOOKUP(D26,CODE)+$C$10	=28-E26	=IF(B26<C26,"YES","NO")		
F642	7	14	C	=SUM(B27:C27)	=E27*LOOKUP(D27,CODE)+$C$10	=28-E27	=IF(B27<C27,"YES","NO")		
F919	7	12	B	=SUM(B28:C28)	=E28*LOOKUP(D28,CODE)+$C$10	=28-E28	=IF(B28<C28,"YES","NO")		
LAKES									
L654	12	10	C	=SUM(B30:C30)	=E30*LOOKUP(D30,CODE)+$C$10	=28-E30	=IF(B30<C30,"YES","NO")		
L67	7	14	C	=SUM(B31:C31)	=E31*LOOKUP(D31,CODE)+$C$10	=28-E31	=IF(B31<C31,"YES","NO")		
L801	14	14	A	=SUM(B32:C32)	=E32*LOOKUP(D32,CODE)+$C$10	=28-E32	=IF(B32<C32,"YES","NO")		
L802	8	14	B	=SUM(B33:C33)	=E33*LOOKUP(D33,CODE)+$C$10	=28-E33	=IF(B33<C33,"YES","NO")		
L816	7	13	A	=SUM(B34:C34)	=E34*LOOKUP(D34,CODE)+$C$10	=28-E34	=IF(B34<C34,"YES","NO")		
L817	11	11	A	=SUM(B35:C35)	=E35*LOOKUP(D35,CODE)+$C$10	=28-E35	=IF(B35<C35,"YES","NO")		
L855	11	6	B	=SUM(B36:C36)	=E36*LOOKUP(D36,CODE)+$C$10	=28-E36	=IF(B36<C36,"YES","NO")		
L919	7	14	D	=SUM(B37:C37)	=E37*LOOKUP(D37,CODE)+$C$10	=28-E37	=IF(B37<C37,"YES","NO")		
MOUNTAIN									
M30	7	13	A	=SUM(B39:C39)	=E39*LOOKUP(D39,CODE)+$C$10	=28-E39	=IF(B39<C39,"YES","NO")		
M341	7	13	B	=SUM(B40:C40)	=E40*LOOKUP(D40,CODE)+$C$10	=28-E40	=IF(B40<C40,"YES","NO")		
M443	9	11	E	=SUM(B41:C41)	=E41*LOOKUP(D41,CODE)+$C$10	=28-E41	=IF(B41<C41,"YES","NO")		
M45	9	6	A	=SUM(B42:C42)	=E42*LOOKUP(D42,CODE)+$C$10	=28-E42	=IF(B42<C42,"YES","NO")		
M51	14	9	E	=SUM(B43:C43)	=E43*LOOKUP(D43,CODE)+$C$10	=28-E43	=IF(B43<C43,"YES","NO")		
M666	9	11	B	=SUM(B44:C44)	=E44*LOOKUP(D44,CODE)+$C$10	=28-E44	=IF(B44<C44,"YES","NO")		
M88	9	12	E	=SUM(B45:C45)	=E45*LOOKUP(D45,CODE)+$C$10	=28-E45	=IF(B45<C45,"YES","NO")		
M89	11	9	B	=SUM(B46:C46)	=E46*LOOKUP(D46,CODE)+$C$10	=28-E46	=IF(B46<C46,"YES","NO")		
M975	14	14	A	=SUM(B47:C47)	=E47*LOOKUP(D47,CODE)+$C$10	=28-E47	=IF(B47<C47,"YES","NO")		
RIVERS									
R103	14	14	E	=SUM(B49:C49)	=E49*LOOKUP(D48,CODE)+$C$10	=28-E49	=IF(B49<C49,"YES","NO")		
R134	12	14	B	=SUM(B50:C50)	=E50*LOOKUP(D50,CODE)+$C$10	=28-E50	=IF(B50<C50,"YES","NO")		
R21	14	12	C	=SUM(B51:C51)	=E51*LOOKUP(D51,CODE)+$C$10	=28-E51	=IF(B51<C51,"YES","NO")		
R401	10	12	A	=SUM(B52:C52)	=E52*LOOKUP(D52,CODE)+$C$10	=28-E52	=IF(B52<C52,"YES","NO")		
R54	12	14	B	=SUM(B53:C53)	=E53*LOOKUP(D53,CODE)+$C$10	=28-E53	=IF(B53<C53,"YES","NO")		
SEA									
S122	7	10	B	=SUM(B55:C55)	=E55*LOOKUP(D55,CODE)+$C$10	=28-E55	=IF(B55<C55,"YES","NO")		
S126	11	12	E	=SUM(B56:C56)	=E56*LOOKUP(D56,CODE)+$C$10	=28-E56	=IF(B56<C56,"YES","NO")		
S16	7	14	C	=SUM(B57:C57)	=E57*LOOKUP(D57,CODE)+$C$10	=28-E57	=IF(B57<C57,"YES","NO")		
S222	14	12	D	=SUM(B58:C58)	=E58*LOOKUP(D58,CODE)+$C$10	=28-E58	=IF(B58<C58,"YES","NO")		
S51	14	14	E	=SUM(B59:C59)	=E59*LOOKUP(D59,CODE)+$C$10	=28-E59	=IF(B59<C59,"YES","NO")		
S555	10	14	C	=SUM(B60:C60)	=E60*LOOKUP(D60,CODE)+$C$10	=28-E60	=IF(B60<C60,"YES","NO")		
S589	14	10	E	=SUM(B61:C61)	=E61*LOOKUP(D61,CODE)+$C$10	=28-E61	=IF(B61<C61,"YES","NO")		
S715	12	12	D	=SUM(B62:C62)	=E62*LOOKUP(D62,CODE)+$C$10	=28-E62	=IF(B62<C62,"YES","NO")		
S89	13	14	D	=SUM(B63:C63)	=E63*LOOKUP(D63,CODE)+$C$10	=28-E63	=IF(B63<C63,"YES","NO")		
				TOTAL(£)	=SUM(F18:F63)				
PROPERTIES PER LOCATION									
LOCATION	NO OF PROPERTIES								
COUNTRY	=COUNT(B18:B24)								
FOREST	=COUNT(B26:B28)								
LAKES	=COUNT(B30:B37)								
MOUNTAIN	=COUNT(B39:B47)								
RIVERS	=COUNT(B49:B53)								
SEA	=COUNT(B55:B63)								

Full Practice Assignment – section C

PROPERTY DETAILS				
LOCATION AND PROPERTY CODE	TOTAL WEEKS BOOKED	INCOME	TOTAL WEEKS NOT BOOKED	LOW(A)
COUNTRY				
C181	24	4850.00	4	NO
C34	26	5250.00	2	NO
C66	23	4650.00	5	NO
C670	25	5050.00	3	YES
C777	21	4250.00	7	YES
C91	26	6680.00	2	NO
C997	28	6350.00	0	NO
FOREST				
F129	20	3050.00	8	YES
F642	21	4775.00	7	YES
F919	19	3850.00	9	YES
LAKES				
L654	22	5000.00	6	NO
L67	21	4775.00	7	YES
L801	28	4250.00	0	NO
L802	22	4450.00	6	YES
L816	20	3050.00	8	YES
L817	22	3350.00	6	NO
L855	17	3450.00	11	NO
L919	21	5405.00	7	YES
MOUNTAIN				
M30	20	3050.00	8	YES
M341	20	4050.00	8	YES
M443	20	6050.00	8	YES
M45	15	2300.00	13	NO
M51	23	6950.00	5	NO
M666	20	4050.00	8	YES
M88	21	6350.00	7	YES
M89	20	4050.00	8	NO
M975	28	4250.00	0	NO
RIVERS				
R103	28	8450.00	0	NO
R134	26	5250.00	2	YES
R21	26	5900.00	2	NO
R401	22	3350.00	6	YES
R54	26	5250.00	2	YES
SEA				
S122	17	3450.00	11	YES
S126	23	6950.00	5	YES
S16	21	4775.00	7	YES
S222	26	6680.00	2	NO
S51	28	8450.00	0	NO
S555	24	5450.00	4	YES
S589	24	7250.00	4	NO
S715	24	6170.00	4	NO
S89	27	6935.00	1	YES
	TOTAL(£)	£ 207,895.00		

Full Practice Assignment – section C

LOCATION	NO OF PROPERTIES
COUNTRY	7
FOREST	3
LAKES	8
MOUNTAIN	9
RIVERS	5
SEA	9

1 04/02/99

Full Practice Assignment – section C

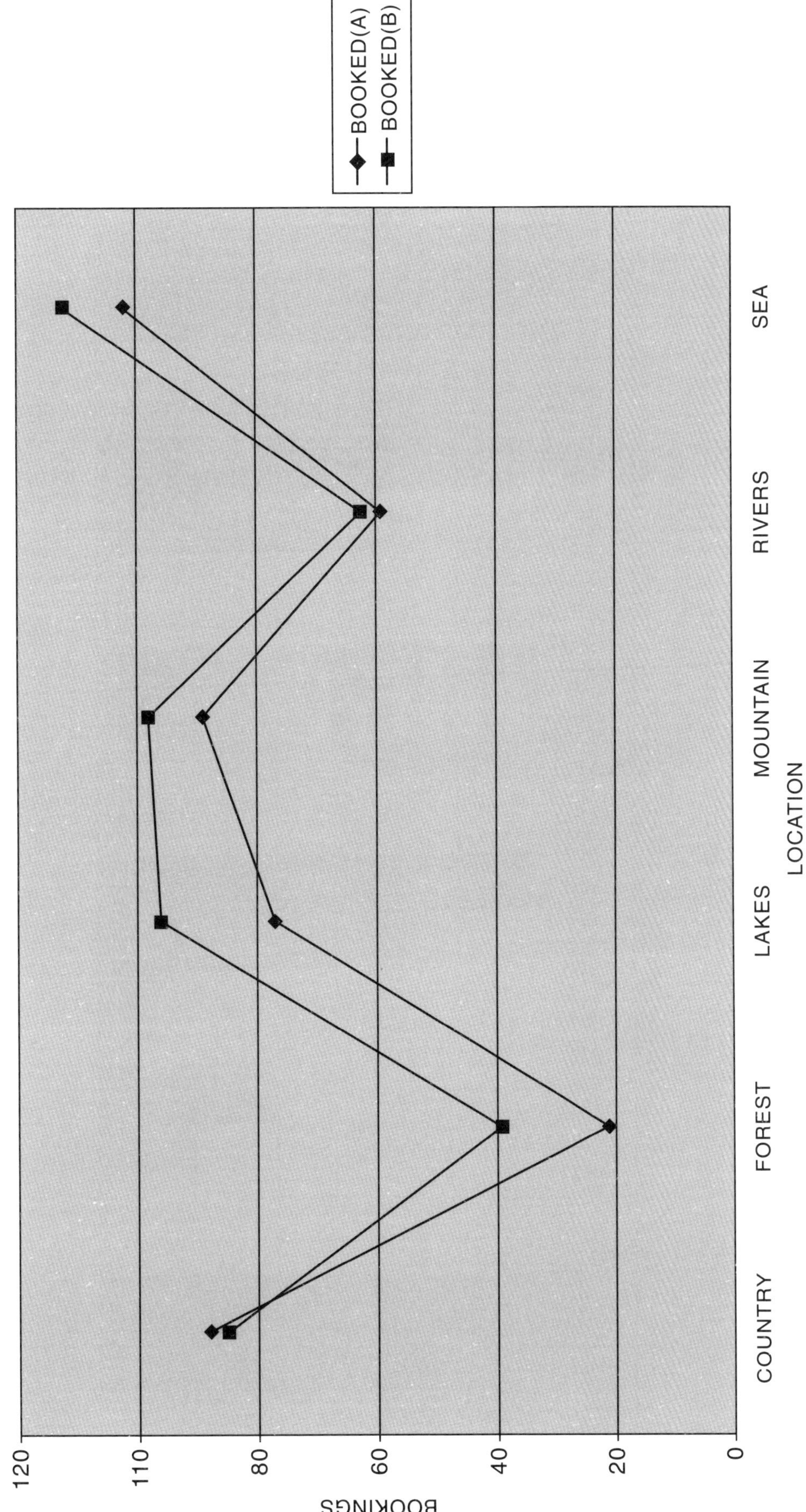

Full Practice Assignment – section C

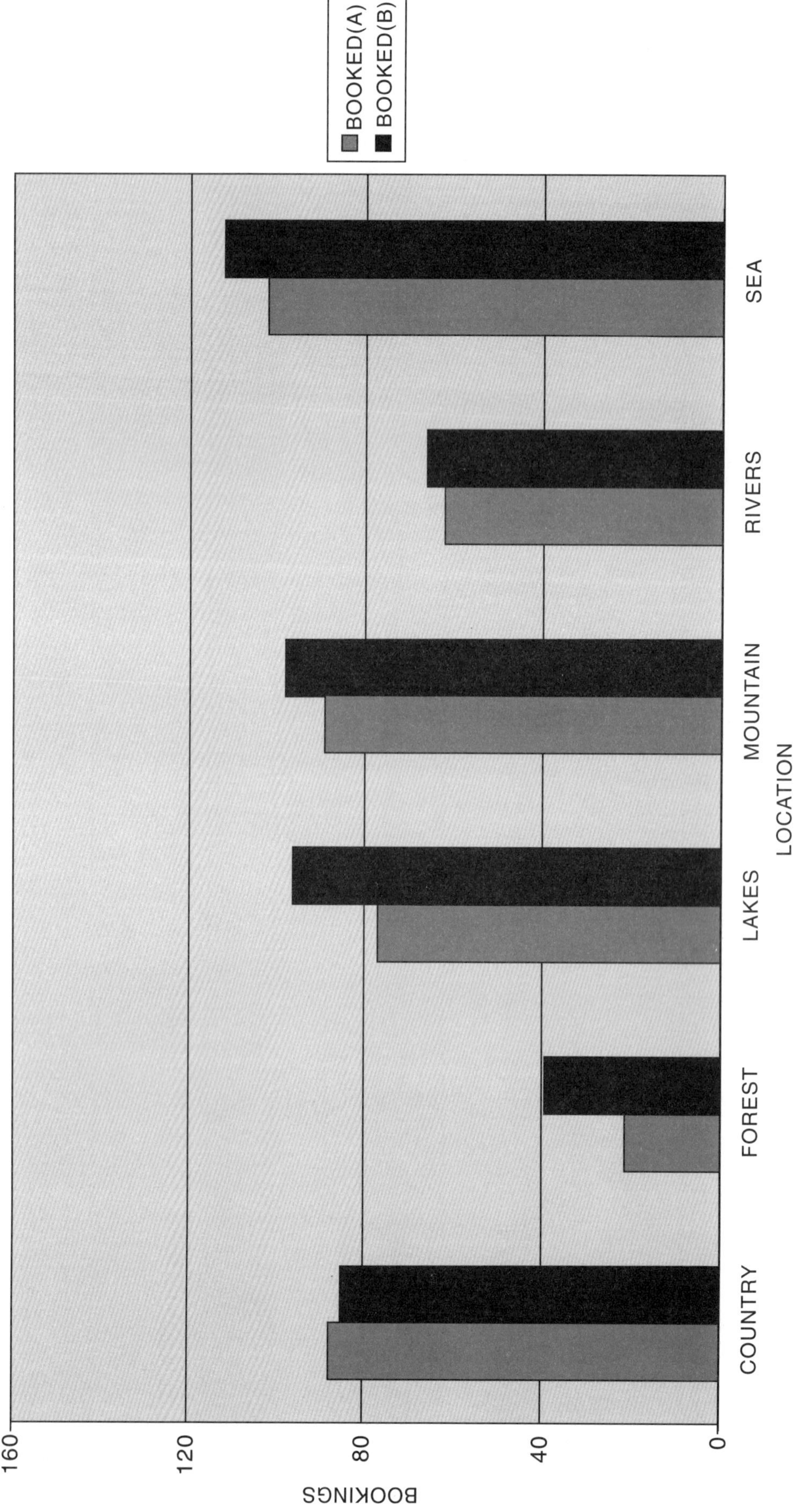

Full Practice Assignment – section C

LOCATION AND PROPERTY CODE	PRICE CODE
COUNTRY	
C670	B
C777	B
FOREST	
F129	A
F642	C
F919	B
LAKES	
L67	C
L802	B
L816	A
L919	D
MOUNTAIN	
M30	A
M341	B
M443	E
M666	B
M88	E
RIVERS	
R134	B
R401	A
R54	B
SEA	
S122	B
S126	E
S16	C
S555	C
S89	D

Full Practice Assignment – section D

Naturetrail Holidays

NATURETRAIL HOLIDAYS

TOTAL RELAXATION

The date

The Designer

Full Practice Assignment – section D

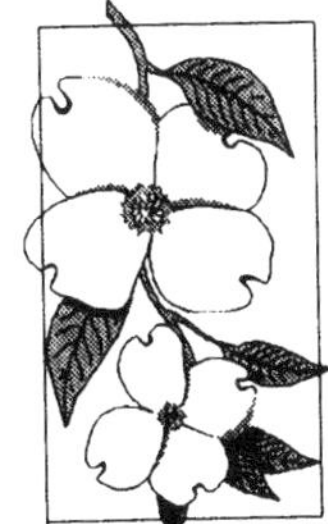

Naturetrail Holidays

A PERFECT HOLIDAY

PHONE NOW

Tel: 01234 29786

Open 7 am to 7 pm

The date

The Designer

Full Practice Assignment – section D

Naturetrail Holidays

BEAUTIFUL LOCATIONS

Our holiday homes are situated in some of the most delightful settings, for example:

- *Rivers*
- *Lakes*
- *Sea*
- *Mountains*

The date

The Designer

Full Practice Assignment – section D

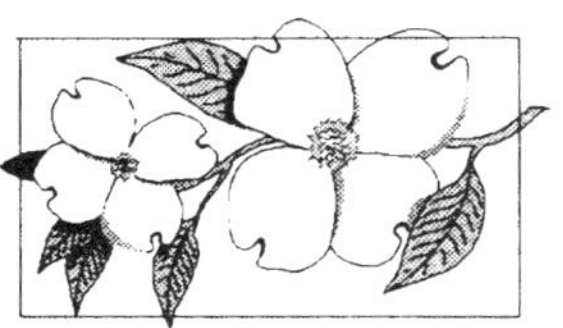

Naturetrail Holidays

RESERVATIONS

Why not take a holiday in the spring when there is usually more choice:

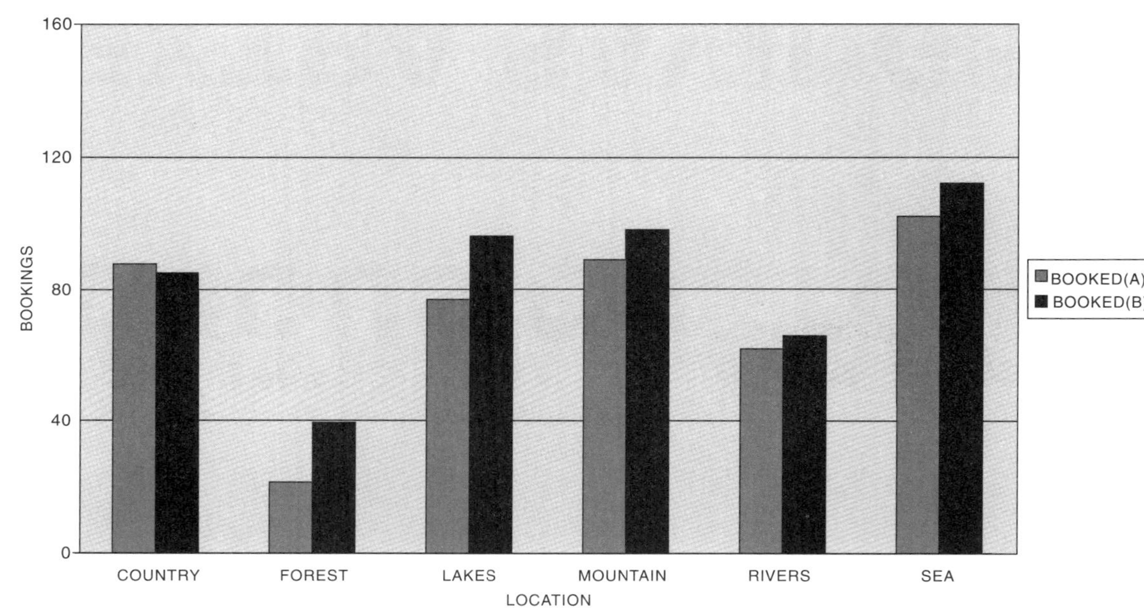

The date

The Designer

Full Practice Assignment – section D

Naturetrail Holidays

PREVIOUS CUSTOMER?

EXTRA SAVINGS!

***Contact** us now!*

We will be continuing our loyalty scheme for the forseeable future and there is also the chance that you may win one of ten super cash prizes.

Full Practice Assignment – section D

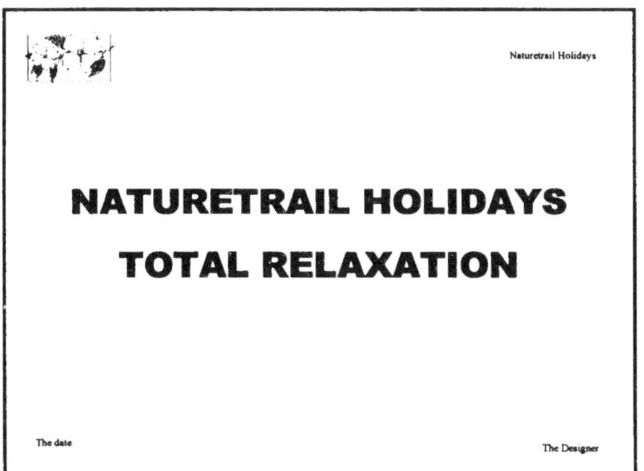

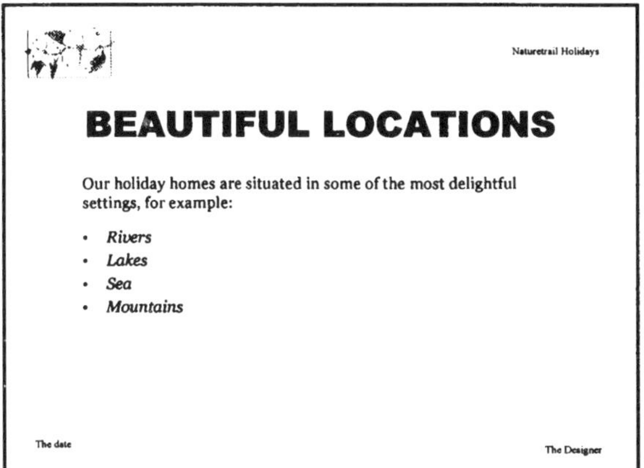

Naturetrail Holidays
BEAUTIFUL LOCATIONS
Our holiday homes are situated in some of the most delightful settings, for example:
• Rivers
• Lakes
• Sea
• Mountains
The date
The Designer

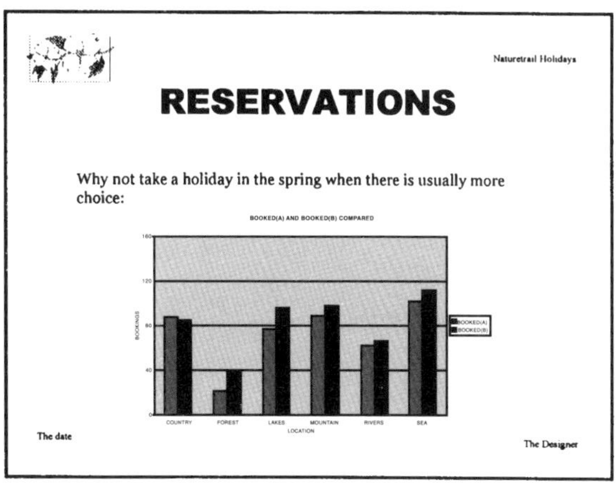

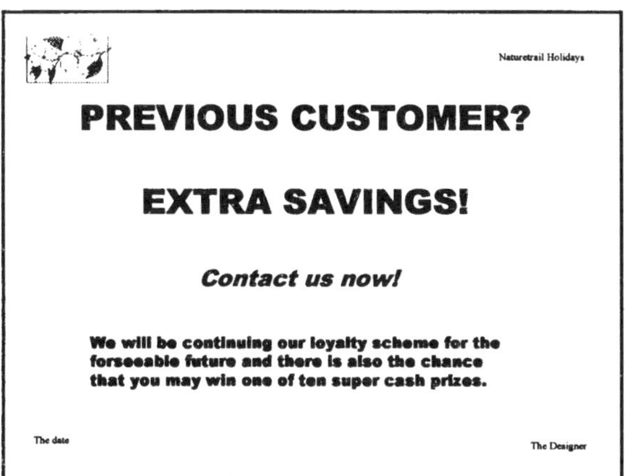

Full Practice Assignment – section D

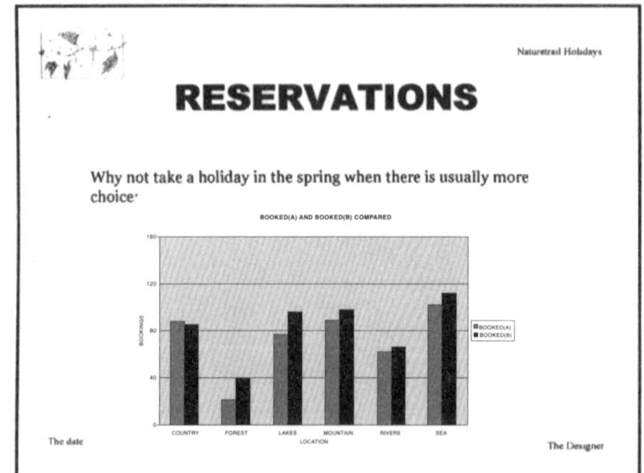

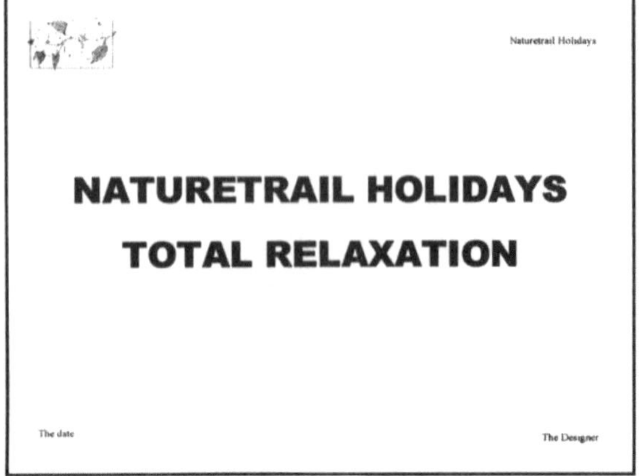

Full Practice Assignment – section F

The Designer

The Date

Full Practice Assignment – section F

2

NATURETRAIL NEWS

If you are looking for a peaceful and relaxing holiday then look no further than Naturetrail Holidays. From small beginnings five years ago when the company had only one location we are now able to offer a choice of six completely different locations. Whatever your idea of the perfect place for a holiday we have the answer.

LOCATIONS

We have holiday cottages in the beautiful unspoilt countryside of the Cotswolds. Here you are able to ramble along the picturesque footpaths and visit the charming villages and small towns that are dotted around this area. Our forest properties are situated in North Wales, close to Betws-y-Coed. There are endless outdoor activities in this area ranging from walking, canoeing or climbing. In Cumbria you will find our lakes cottages - if you like sailing and fishing then this is the place for you. Again in North Wales, situated in the heart of Snowdonia, you will find our mountain complex. There are even trained mountaineers on hand to give you coaching in all aspects of climbing. So don't worry if you're a novice, there are activities ranging from those for beginners right through to the more experienced climber. Cornwall is the setting for our seaside properties. These are located between Boscastle and Newquay. The scenery in this area is second to none. There are wild coastal footpaths, fishing villages and sandy beaches. You will be spoilt for choice for your daily excursions! For those of you who enjoy the tranquillity of a riverside setting you will find this at our site in Devon. Our properties are situated only 100 metres from the river Dart. Of course also in this area, in addition to riverside activities, there are beautiful moorland walks. THE CHOICE IS YOURS. We believe that you cannot fail to appreciate the natural beauty that abounds in all of these locations.

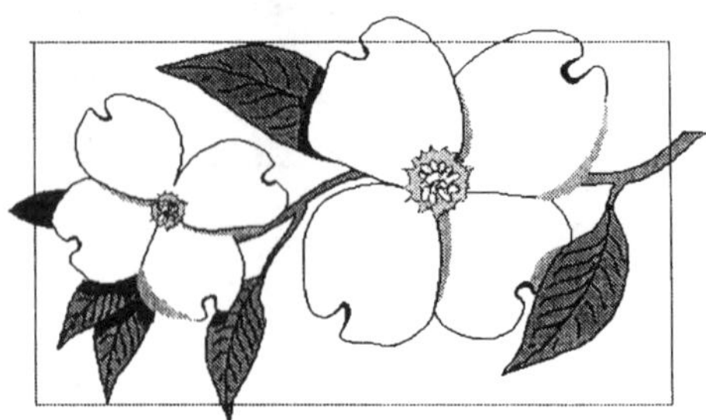

PROPERTIES AVAILABLE

Our properties vary in size and we have properties to suit most needs. You can choose from one to four bedrooms, with the maximum occupancy being eight people (there is the possibility that some of our properties can accommodate babies (cots and high chairs can be provided at no extra cost). Please ask the agent when booking.

PRICES

Prices vary depending on the size of the property. This year we have introduced a new system and now if you book for more than one week, any subsequent weeks are charged at a reduced rate.

The table below shows the prices relating to the different codes:

CODE	COST	EXTRA WEEK
A	£150	£135
B	£200	£185
C	£225	£210
D	£255	£240
E	£300	£285

The Designer

The Date

Full Practice Assignment – section F (contd.)

Why not reserve a property for our early booking period? The properties shown below are on special discount prices (deduct a further 10% from the price shown in the brochure) for this year only:

BOOKINGS PERIOD A

PROPERTY NAME	PUFFINS
BOOKED (A)	5
PROPERTY NAME	PEANUTS
BOOKED (A)	7
PROPERTY NAME	HEADLANDS
BOOKED (A)	7
PROPERTY NAME	ASPENS
BOOKED (A)	7

You can arrive on Friday or Saturday depending on which property you have chosen and at any time before 7 pm. Please let us know if you will be arriving later than this. Staggering arrivals in this way makes it easier to ensure that we have more staff available to give you a warm welcome. You may prefer to travel on a Friday, especially in summer when the roads are usually less congested. Whilst on the subject of transport, you will notice that most of our properties have parking adjacent to them. Where this is not the case your vehicle may be left in the parking areas which are never more than 50 metres away. For unloading purposes, parking outside the property is perfectly acceptable but please remember to move your vehicle as soon as you can since it will cause an obstruction.

Your property will have been fully cleaned and inspected before your arrival which can be anytime after 12 noon. All bed linen is provided but you will need to bring your own towels. All properties are self-catering but to help you settle in, we do provide a small grocery basket containing essentials, such as bread and milk. Should you find that things are not to your liking, please contact us straight away. WE PRIDE OURSELVES ON GIVING YOU THE BEST SERVICE AT ALL TIMES.

LOYALTY SAVINGS

Naturetrail Holidays are pleased to announce an important bonus for customers who have taken holidays with us in the past. We are now able to give substantial discounts on your holiday booking this year.

If you book your holiday before the end of January you will be entitled to a 20% discount on the standard cost of your chosen property (subject to its availability). If you book before the end of March you will be entitled to a 10% discount on the standard cost.

We feel that this is a very generous offer and hope that you will be able to make your bookings early to benefit from the maximum savings.

Each 'loyalty' customer will be entered into our prize draw. We will be offering cash prizes ranging from £50 to £500 to those lucky ones picked out at random. If you are eligible for this discount, please have your previous booking reference to hand when you call. If you no longer have your booking reference, don't worry we will be able to look up your details on our database.

HOW TO BOOK

Our properties can be booked from our Head Office by telephoning 01234 29786. We are open from 7 am to 7 pm every day except Sunday. Our regional offices can also help you with any queries that you may have. They are each allocated several properties that are their major concern. Choosing the right accommodation to suit your needs can be difficult and we want to help you make an informed choice. You can rely on our staff giving informative

Full Practice Assignment – section F (contd.)

and friendly advice. Our computerised booking system gives instant availability of our properties so that we can suggest an alternative should your first choice be taken. Shown below are the properties dealt with by our Bristol office:

LOCATION	NO OF PROPERTIES
COUNTRY	7
FOREST	3
LAKES	8
MOUNTAIN	9
RIVERS	5
SEA	9

As you can see each regional office deals with properties from all of the locations. Our staff training ensures that all staff have visited the six locations and are aware of the differences between them.

When booking please ensure that you have the following details to hand:

- Reference of Property
- Price Code
- Date Required
- Number in Party
- Vehicle Registration Number
- Credit Card Number
- Former Booking Ref (if applicable)

Here at Naturetrail Holidays we pride ourselves in providing an excellent booking service and we hope that you feel that this level of excellence carries through to all of our operations. We know how important it is that everything runs smoothly so that you are able to relax and enjoy yourselves.

So what are you waiting for? Have another look through our brochure and imagine the fun that you'll have with Naturetrail Holidays.

DON'T DELAY - BOOK TODAY.

Appendix

Changing defaults in Word

Office Assistant

To hide the Office Assistant:

1 Right-click on the Office Assistant, click on: **Options** and set them to your preferences. Click on: **OK** (Figure A.1).

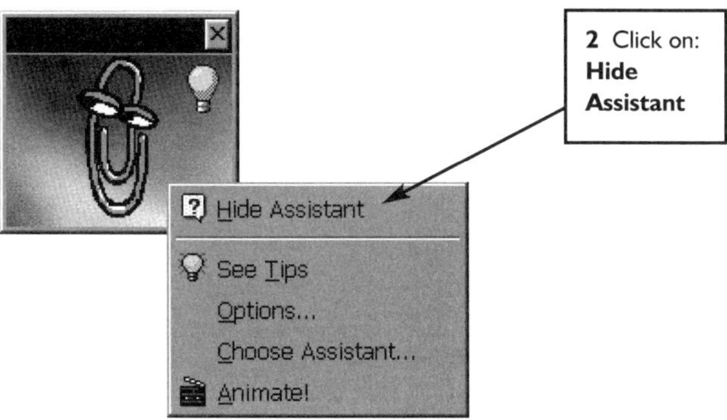

Figure A.1 Hiding the Office Assistant

To turn the Office Assistant on:

1 Click on: the **Office Assistant** toolbar button.
2 Click on: **Options** and set preferences.
3 Click on: **OK**.

Checking spelling and grammar

There are many options available. Throughout the book, I have chosen to check spelling (not spelling and grammar). I have also chosen not to check on an ongoing basis but after I have keyed in the entire document.

The above settings work well with the students I work with. Should you wish to choose other options: from the **Tools** menu, select: **Options**, and then click on: the **Spelling and Grammar** tab. Select your preferences and click on: **OK**.

Changing the unit of measure

To change the unit of measure from inches to centimetres or vice versa:

1 From the **Tools** menu, select: **Options**, and then select the **General** tab.
2 In the **Measurement** units box, click on: the **down arrow** and then the option you want.
3 Click on: **OK**.

Different types of view in Word

Normal View – this is the default. It allows for quick and easy text editing.

Page Layout view – this view allows you to see how objects will be positioned on the printed page. It shows margins, headers and footers, and graphics. This is essential for the integrated assignments for IBT III.

File maintenance within programs

In addition to using Explorer, you can carry out file maintenance within programs as follows.

When opening or saving a file, you are able to gain access to your files within the window (figure A.2). This is common to all programs. This window was opened in Word and displays only Word documents (by default). If you want to see other documents, click on: the **down arrow** next to **Files of type** and make your selection.

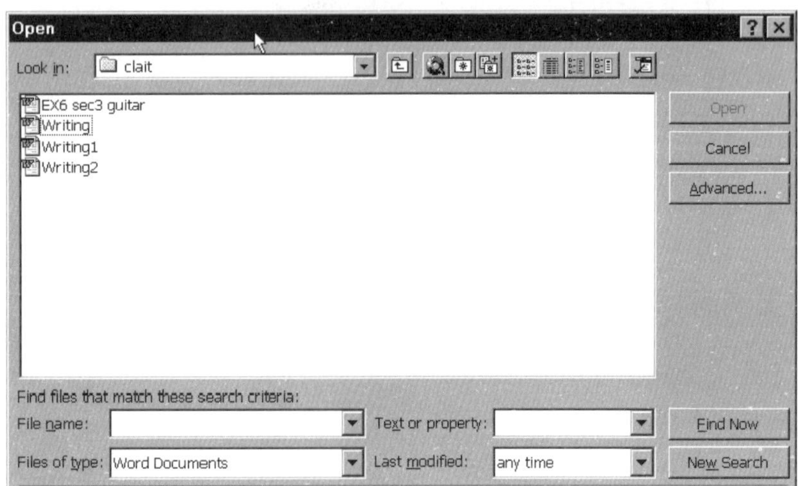

Figure A.2 Open window

The main shortcut buttons that will be useful for IBT III are shown in Figure A.3. Using these will enable you to find out all the details of your files.

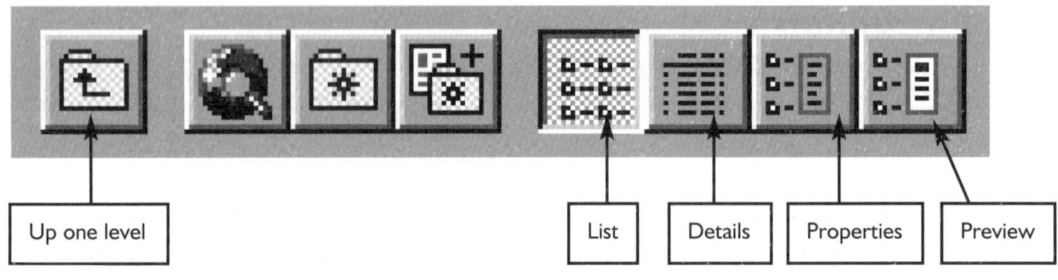

Figure A.3 Shortcut buttons

Right-clicking on a file/folder will bring up the pop-up menu (Figure A.4). This allows you to carry out any of the tasks on the menu.

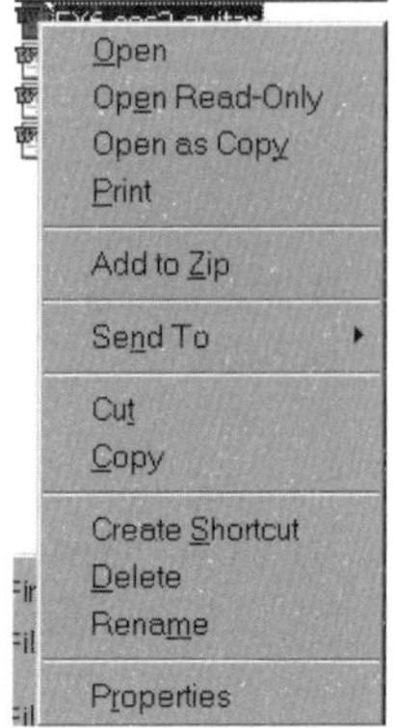

Figure A.4 File/folder pop-up menu

Adding headers and footers in Excel

1 From the **View** menu, select: **Header and Footer...**
2 The Page Setup dialogue box appears. Click on: the **Header/Footer** tab so that it is displayed as below.
3 Click on: **Custom header...** or **Custom Footer...** .
4 The Header dialogue box appears (Figure A.5). Click in the section where you want your name to appear and key in your name. Click in the section where you want the date to appear and key in the date (or click the date button if you are certain that your computer's date is set correctly – the actual date will not be displayed here but you can practise and see what appears on your Print Preview). Click on: **OK**.

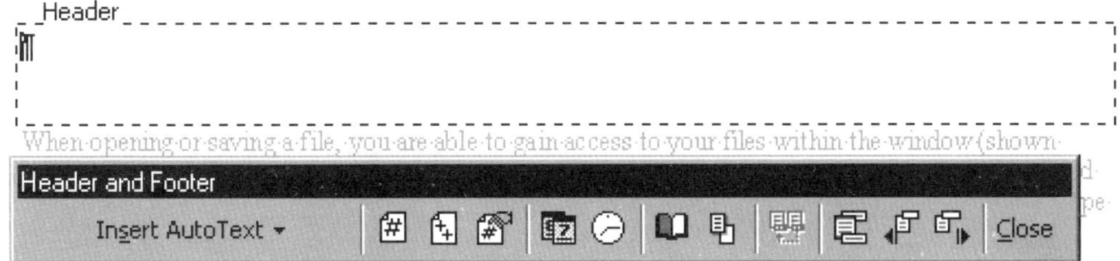

Figure A.5 Header dialogue box

A guide to document layout

When you have edited text, or moved text within an exercise, remember adjustment of line spacing is often necessary. When proofreading pay particular attention to line spacing between paragraphs.

When inserting a sentence within a paragraph, make sure the spacing after any punctuation marks remains consistent. Make the necessary adjustments if required.

Use the spellchecker but do realise its limitations.

Line spacing between paragraphs: Press **Enter** twice to leave one clear line space between paragraphs.

Underlining/underscoring: Underlining should not extend beyond the word. For example:

word is correct   word is incorrect

Punctuation

Be consistent with your spacing after punctuation marks. Use the table below as a guide:

Punctuation	*Mark*	*Number of spaces before/after*
Comma	,	No space before – one space after
Semi-colon	;	No space before – one space after
Colon	:	No space before – two spaces after
Full stop	.	No space before – two spaces after
Exclamation mark	!	No space before – two spaces after
Question mark	?	No space before – two spaces after

Hyphen: No space is left before or after a hyphen, eg dry-clean.

Dash: One space precedes and follows a dash. Never place a dash at the left-hand margin when it is in the middle of a word or a sentence – always place it at the end of the previous line.

Brackets: No spaces are left between brackets and the words enclosed within them – eg (solely for the purposes of assignments).

Keyboard shortcuts that work (nearly) everywhere

Keyboard	**Menu**
F1	Help
F7	Tools, Spelling and Grammar
Ctrl + N	File, New
Ctrl + O	File, Open
Ctrl + S	File, Save
F12	File, Save As
Ctrl + W	File, Close
Ctrl + P	File, Print
Alt + F4	File, Exit
Ctrl + X	Edit, Cut
Ctrl + C	Edit, Copy
Ctrl + V	Edit, Paste
Ctrl + Z	Edit, Undo
Ctrl + A	Edit, Select All
Ctrl + R	Edit, Replace
Esc	Cancels items

Dont't forget! Right-clicking on objects displays pop-up menus in Office 97.

Integrated Business Technology Stage III: File Store Record Sheet

Candidate name ______________ *Name of directory created for IBT III project* [ ]

Section	Step no.	Subdirectory	Filename or reference	Query/report name	Tick here*
Prepare source data					
Set up and produce presentation					
Set up and produce publication					

*Tick the boxes if the files saved are to be used later in the assignment.

Time Log Sheet

Section reference	Time started	Time finished	Date	Total time elapsed	Tutor's signature

Candidates should record the section of the assignment worked on and the time they started and finished. On completion of the assignments section a running total should be kept to ensure the total time taken does *not exceed ten hours.*

HILDON
ESTABLISHED
1989

2006 Awards For Excellence

The winners of the Condé Nast Johansens 2006 Awards for Excellence

The Condé Nast Johansens 2006 Awards for Excellence were presented at the Awards Luncheon held at Jumeirah Carlton Tower, London, on November 14th, 2005. Awards were received by properties from all over the world that represented the finest standards and best value for money in luxury independent travel. An important source of information for these awards was the feedback provided by guests who completed Condé Nast Johansens Guest Survey Reports. Guest Survey Reports can be found on page 382.

Most Excellent Value for Money

Renvyle House Hotel

– Connemara, Galway, p270

"Sitting between mountains and sea on the rugged romantic coast of Connemara; this hotel is a delight. "

Most Excellent Spa

Park Hotel Kenmare & Sámas

– Kenmare, Kerry, p271

"The Sámas experience is magical… your senses are indulged and the body finds a new level of relaxation."

Most Excellent City Hotel

The Cranley

– South Kensington, London, p162

"A wonderful example of a quintessential London town house hotel. Beautiful traditional style with exceptional personal service and possibly the best four-poster beds in London."

Most Excellent London Hotel

Jumeirah Carlton Tower

– Knightsbridge, London, p155

"Simply one of the best hotel experiences in London – service and comfort are paramount."

2006 Awards For Excellence

The winners of the Condé Nast Johansens 2006 Awards for Excellence

Details of all other award winners featured within Condé Nast Johansens 2007 Guides to Country Houses - Great Britain & Ireland; Hotels & Spas - Europe & The Mediterranean; Hotels & Resorts - The Americas, Atlantic, Caribbean & Pacific can be found on-line at www.johansens.com

Most Excellent Country Hotel

Mount Somerset Country House Hotel

- Taunton, Somerset, p186

"A magnificent Regency country hotel overlooking the Somerset countryside, offering superb service and total relaxation."

Condé Nast Johansens Reader Award

Northcote Manor Country House Hotel

- Burrington, Devon, p78

"A wonderful country escape set high above the Taw River Valley. Highly praised by readers for the warm and attentive staff as well the outstanding food."

Champagne Taittinger Wine List of the Year Award Overall Winner

The Cottage in the Wood

- Malvern Wells, Worcestershire, p235

"An outstanding winner with a comprehensive wine list packed full of interesting flavours and vintages. The user-friendly presentation with its informative descriptions enhances guests' experience."

Knight Frank Award for Outstanding Excellence & Innovation

Mr Mark Breen

- The Royal Park Hotel, London, p157

"Mark has impacted the hotel industry with his drive and innovation in the creation of luxury town house hotels through the restoration and refurbishment of period listed buildings."

The Perfect Combination...

Condé Nast Johansens Guides

As well as this Guide, Condé Nast Johansens also publish the following titles:

Recommended Country Houses, Small Hotels, Inns & Restaurants Great Britain & Ireland

Small and often intimate properties that include old coaching inn's, hunting lodges and manors. The emphasis is on personal service and high levels of comfort.

Recommended Hotels & Spas Europe & The Mediterranean

A wonderful choice of properties including châteaux, resorts, charming countryside hotels and stylish city hotels.

Recommended Hotels, Inns, Resorts & Spas The Americas, Atlantic, Caribbean & Pacific

A diverse collection of properties across the region including exotic ocean-front resorts, historic plantation houses and traditional inns.

To purchase Guides please complete the Order Form on page 381, call FREEPHONE 0800 269 397 or visit our Bookshop at www.johansens.com

Condé Nast Johansens Gift Vouchers

Condé Nast Johansens Gift Vouchers make a unique and much valued present for birthdays, weddings, anniversaries, special occasions and as a corporate incentive.

Vouchers are available in denominations of £100, £50, €140, €70, $150, $75 and may be used as payment or part payment for your stay or a meal at any Condé Nast Johansens 2007 recommended property.

To order Gift Vouchers call +44 (0)207 152 3558 or purchase direct at www.johansens.com

England

Recommendations in England appear on pages 14-256

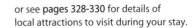

Images from www.britainonview.com

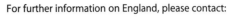

For further information on England, please contact:

Cumbria Tourist Board
Ashleigh, Holly Road, Windermere, Cumbria LA23 2AQ
Tel: +44 (0)15394 44444
Web: www.golakes.co.uk

East of England Tourist Board
Toppesfield Hall , Hadleigh, Suffolk IP7 5DN
Tel: +44 (0)1473 822922
Web: www.visiteastofengland.com

Heart of England Tourism
Larkhill Road, Worcester, Worcestershire WR5 2EZ
Tel: +44 (0)1905 761100
Web: www.visitheartofengland.com

Visit London
6th Floor, 2 More London Riverside, London SE1 2RR
Tel: 0870 156 6366
Web: www.visitlondon.com

One North East Tourism Team
Stelle House, Gold Crest Way, Newburn Riverside,
Newcastle-Upon-Tyne, N15 8NY
Tel: +44 (0)191 375 3000
Web: www.visitnorthumbria.com

North West Tourist Board
Swan House, Swan Meadow Road, Wigan, Lancashire WN3 5BB
Tel: +44 (0)1942 821 222
Web: www.visitnorthwest.com

Tourism South East
40 Chamberlayne Road, Eastleigh, Hampshire, SO50 5JH
Tel: +44 (0)23 8062 5400
Web: www.visistsoutheastengland.com

South West Tourism
Woodwater Park, Exeter, Devon EX2 5WT
Tel: +44 (0)1392 360 050
Web: www.visitsouthwest.co.uk

Yorkshire Tourist Board
312 Tadcaster Road, York, Yorkshire YO24 1GS
Tel: +44 (0)1904 707961
Web: www.ytb.org.uk
Yorkshire and North & North East Lincolnshire.

English Heritage
Customer Services Department , PO Box 569, Swindon SN2 2YP
Tel: +44 (0) 870 333 1181
Web: www.english-heritage.org.uk

Historic Houses Association
2 Chester Street, London SW1X 7BB
Tel: +44 (0)20 7259 5688
Web: www.hha.org.uk

The National Trust
Heelis, Kemble Drive, Swindon, SN2 2NA
Tel: 0870 242 6620
Web: www.nationaltrust.org.uk

or see **pages 328-330** for details of
local attractions to visit during your stay.

The Bath Priory Hotel and Restaurant

WESTON ROAD, BATH, SOMERSET BA1 2XT

Standing in 4 acres of gardens, The Bath Priory Hotel is close to some of England's most famous and finest architecture. Within walking distance of Bath city centre, this Georgian, mellow stone building dates from 1835, when it formed part of a row of fashionable residences on the west side of the city. Visitors will sense the luxury as they enter the hotel; antique furniture, many superb oil paintings and objets d'art add interest to the 2 spacious reception rooms and the elegant drawing room. Well-defined colour schemes lend an uplifting brightness throughout, particularly in the tastefully appointed bedrooms. Enjoy Michelin-Star modern European cuisine in the charming restaurant, under the direction of restaurant manager Vito Scaduto M.C.A, served in 3 interconnecting dining rooms which overlook the gardens. An especially good selection of wines can be recommended to accompany meals. Private functions can be accommodated both in the terrace, pavilion and the orangery. The Roman Baths, Theatre Royal, Museum of Costume and a host of bijou shops offer plenty for visitors to see. The Garden Spa consists of a fitness suite, swimming pool, sauna, steam room and health and beauty suite. The Bath Priory Hotel has a total non-smoking policy.

Our inspector loved: *The attention to detail and the luxurious feel throughout.*

Directions: 1 mile west of the centre of Bath. Please contact the hotel for precise directions.

Web: www.johansens.com/bathpriory
E-mail: mail@thebathpriory.co.uk
Tel: 0870 381 8345
International: +44 (0)1225 331922
Fax: 01225 448276

Price Guide: (incl. full English breakfast) double/twin from £245

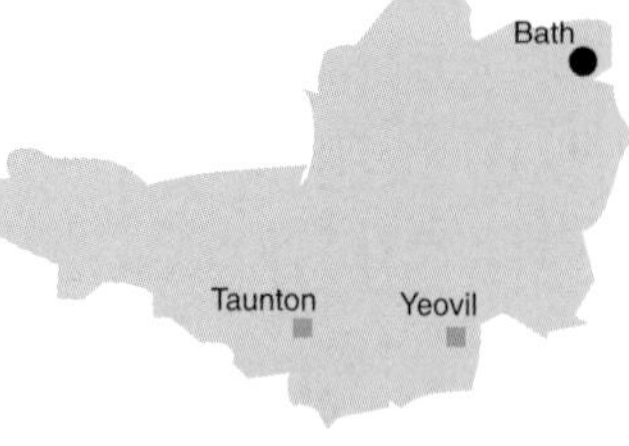

The Bath Spa Hotel

SYDNEY ROAD, BATH, SOMERSET BA2 6JF

Nestling in 7 acres of mature grounds dotted with ancient cedars, formal gardens, ponds and fountains, The Bath Spa Hotel's elegant Georgian façade can only hint at the warmth, style, comfort and attentive personal service. It is a handsome building in a handsome setting with antique furniture, richly coloured carpeting and well defined colour schemes lending an uplifting brightness throughout. The bedrooms are elegantly decorated; the bathrooms are luxuriously appointed in mahogany and marble. The Bath Spa Hotel offers all amenities that guests would expect of a 5-star hotel, for example WiFi, whilst retaining the character of a homely country house. Chef Andrew Hamer's imaginative, contemporary style is the primary inspiration for the award-winning cuisine served in the 2 restaurants. For relaxation there is a fully equipped health and leisure spa which includes an indoor swimming pool, gymnasium, sauna, Jacuzzi, 3 treatment rooms, hair salon and croquet lawn. Apart from the delights of Bath, there is motor racing at Castle Combe and hot air ballooning nearby.

Our inspector loved: *The fabulous new spa.*

Directions: Exit M4 jct 18 onto A46, follow signs to Bath for 8 miles until major roundabout. Turn right onto A4 follow city centre signs for a mile, at first major set of traffic lights turn left towards A36. Over Cleveland Bridge, past Fire Station, turn right at the traffic lights after the pedestrian crossing then next left after Holburne Museum into Sydney Place. The Hotel is 200 yards up the hill on the right.

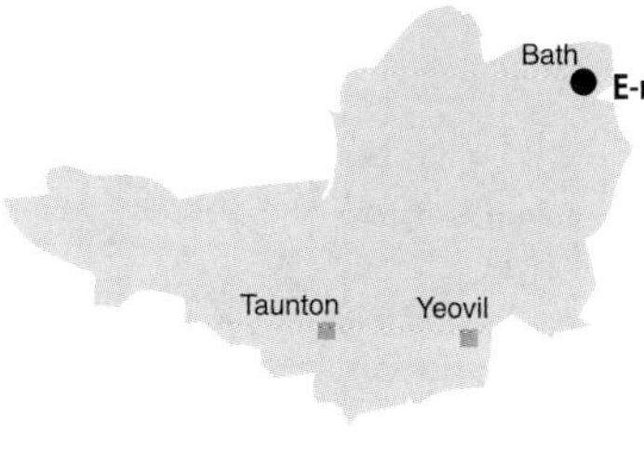

Bath
Taunton
Yeovil

Web: www.johansens.com/bathspa
E-mail: sales.bathspa@macdonald-hotels.co.uk
Tel: 0870 381 8346
International: +44 (0)1225 444424
Fax: 01225 444006

Price Guide:
double/twin £280–£350
4-poster £400–£470

128 130 SPA

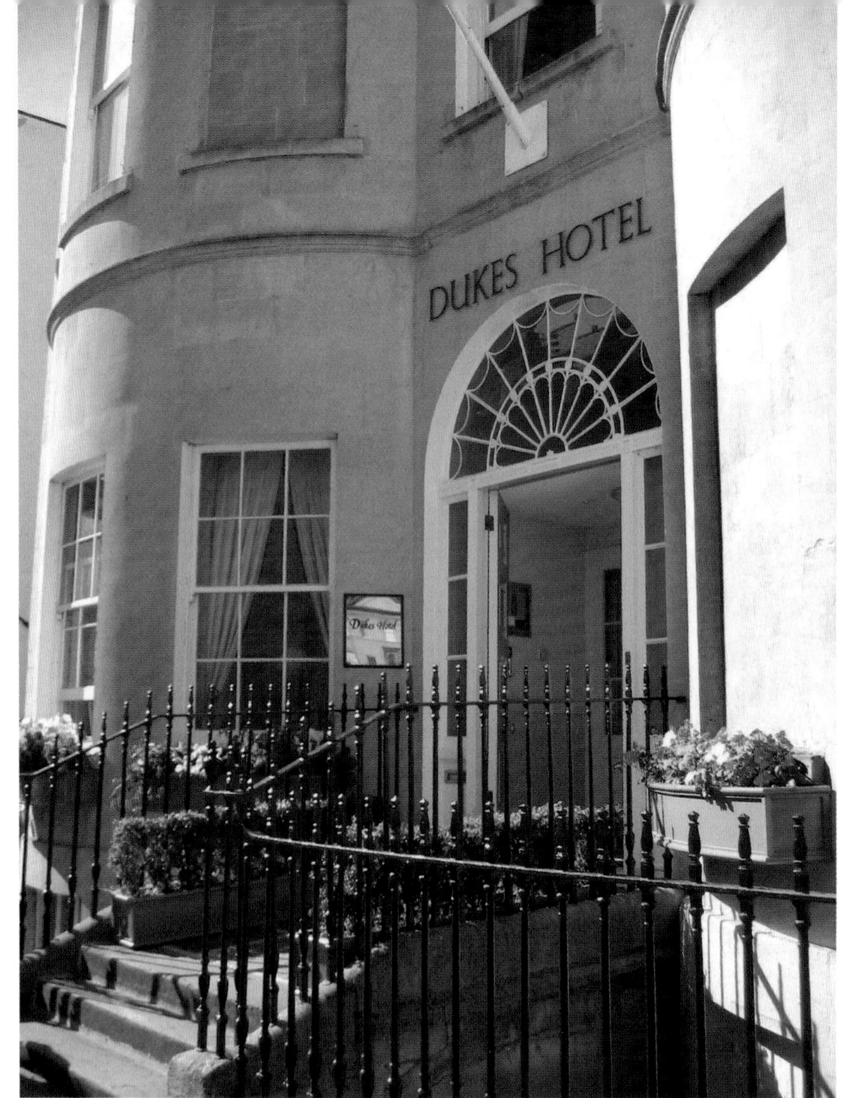

Dukes Hotel

GREAT PULTENEY STREET, BATH, SOMERSET BA2 4DN

Directions: Exit the M4, junction 18 and follow signs for Bath. Turn left at the traffic lights towards Warminster then right at the next traffic lights into Sydney Place. Great Pulteney Street is on the right after approx 150 yards.

Web: www.johansens.com/dukesbath
E-mail: info@dukesbath.co.uk
Tel: 0870 381 8357
International: +44 (0)1225 787960
Fax: 01225 787961

Price Guide:
single £100
double/twin £135–£155
suite £195–£215

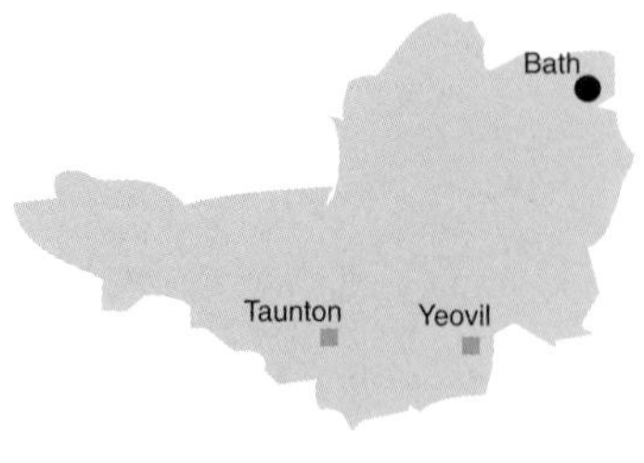

Upon entering the elegant entrance topped with half-moon shaped decorative glass ornamentation edged by slim, black, wrought-iron railings, guests are immediately introduced to the charm, character, style and understated luxury of this Grade I listed town house hotel. Situated in one of the finest and most majestic boulevards in Europe, in the heart of the best preserved Georgian city in Britain, Dukes Hotel is a former Palladian mansion, built from Bath stone and now transformed to its original splendour. The front guest rooms overlook façades inspired by Palladio and rear rooms have views of rolling hills. Each en-suite bedroom and suite is the essence of quality; most have original features such as intricate plasterwork and large sash windows. Fine furniture and fabrics abound throughout. The newly introduced and refurbished Cavendish Restaurant is a light, airy and relaxing venue in which to enjoy superb cuisine prepared by talented chef Richard Allen. The very best of organic and free-range British ingredients, including Cornish lamb, Angus beef and seafood delivered daily from Devon, are on the menu. There are 2 further, smaller dining rooms, complemented by a secluded, walled patio garden, which provides an enviable setting for summer al fresco dining.

Our inspector loved: *The newly decorated Somerset suite right at the top of the house.*

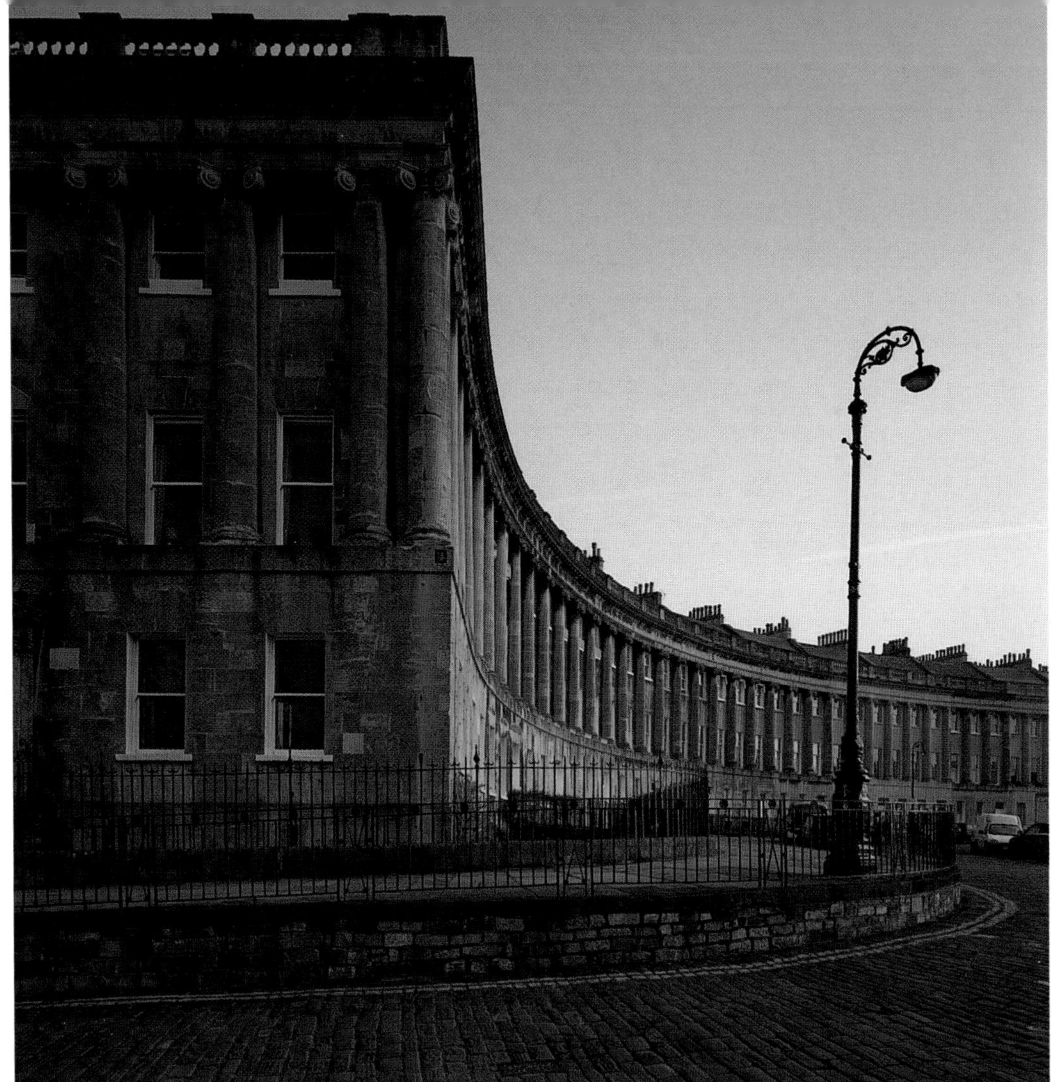

THE ROYAL CRESCENT & BATH HOUSE SPA

16 ROYAL CRESCENT, BATH, SOMERSET BA1 2LS

The Royal Crescent Hotel is a Grade I listed building of the greatest historical and architectural importance and occupies the central 2 houses of one of Europe's finest masterpieces. The Royal Crescent is a sweep of 30 houses with identical façades stretching in a 500ft curve. Built by 1775, the hotel was completely refurbished in 1998 and the work undertaken has restored many of the classical Georgian features with all the additional modern comforts. Each of the 45 bedrooms is equipped with air conditioning, the Cliveden bed, video/compact disc player and personal facsimile machine. Pimpernel's restaurant offers a relaxed and informal dining atmosphere, presenting a contemporary menu. Comprehensively equipped, the secure private boardroom provides self-contained business meeting facilities. Exclusive use of the hotel can be arranged for a special occasion or corporate event. Magnificent views of Bath and the surrounding countryside may be enjoyed from the hotel's vintage river launch or by hot air balloon upon arrangement. The Bath House is a unique spa, in which to enjoy both complementary therapies and holistic massage. Adjacent to this tranquil setting is the gym with cardio-vascular and resistance equipment.

Directions: Detailed directions are available from the hotel on booking.

Web: www.johansens.com/royalcrescent
E-mail: info@royalcrescent.co.uk
Tel: 0870 381 8874
International: +44 (0)1225 823333
Fax: 01225 339401

Bath
Taunton
Yeovil

Price Guide:
(including continental breakfast)
double/twin from £290
suite from £530

Our inspector loved: *The wonderfully relaxing Bath House spa.*

HOMEWOOD PARK

HINTON CHARTERHOUSE, BATH, SOMERSET BA2 7TB

Standing amid 10 acres of beautiful grounds and woodland on the edge of the Limpley Stoke Valley, a designated area of outstanding natural beauty is Homewood Park, one of Britain's finest privately-owned smaller country house hotels. This lovely 19th-century building has an elegant interior, adorned with beautiful fabrics, antiques, oriental rugs and original oil paintings. Lavishly furnished bedrooms offer the best in comfort, style and privacy. Each of them has a charm and character of its own and most have good views over the Victorian garden. The outstanding cuisine has won the hotel an excellent reputation and the à la carte menu uses, wherever possible, produce from local suppliers. A range of carefully selected wines, stored in the hotel's original medieval cellars, lies patiently waiting to augment lunch and dinner. Before or after a meal guests can enjoy a drink in the comfortable bar or drawing rooms, both of which have a log fire during the cooler months. The hotel is well placed for guests to enjoy the varied attractions of the wonderful city of Bath with its unique hot springs, Roman remains, superb Georgian architecture and American Museum. Further afield but within reach are Stonehenge and Cheddar caves.

Our inspector loved: *The lovely traditional country house feel throughout.*

Directions: On the A36, 6 miles from Bath towards Warminster.

Web: www.johansens.com/homewoodpark
E-mail: info@homewoodpark.co.uk
Tel: 0870 381 8605
International: +44 (0)1225 723731
Fax: 01225 723820

Price Guide:
single from £140
double/twin from £180
suites from £300

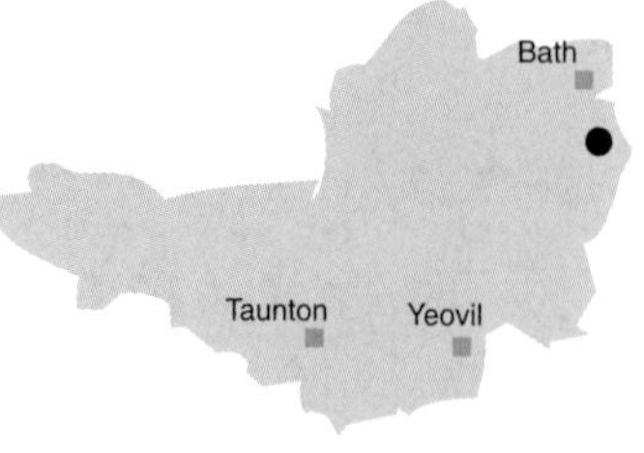

Hunstrete House

HUNSTRETE, NR BATH, SOMERSET BS39 4NS

In a classical English landscape on the edge of the Mendip Hills stands Hunstrete House. This unique hotel, surrounded by lovely gardens, is largely 18th century, although the history of the estate goes back to 963AD. Each of the bedrooms is individually decorated and furnished to a high standard, combining the benefits of a hotel room with the atmosphere of a charming private country house. Many offer uninterrupted views over undulating fields and woodlands. The reception areas exhibit warmth and elegance and are liberally furnished with beautiful antiques. Log fires burn in the hall, library and drawing room through the winter and on cooler summer evenings. The Terrace dining room looks out on to an Italianate, flower-filled courtyard. A highly skilled head chef offers light, elegant dishes using produce from the extensive garden, including organic meat and vegetables. The menu changes regularly and the hotel has an excellent reputation for the quality and interest of its wine list. In a sheltered corner of the walled garden there is a heated swimming pool for guests to enjoy. For the energetic, the all-weather tennis court provides another diversion. The hotel is also available for exclusive use wedding and corporate events with a marquee to seat up to 120 people.

Our inspector loved: *The beautiful setting with deer so close in the surrounding fields and woodland.*

Directions: From Bath take the A4 towards Bristol and then the A368 to Wells.

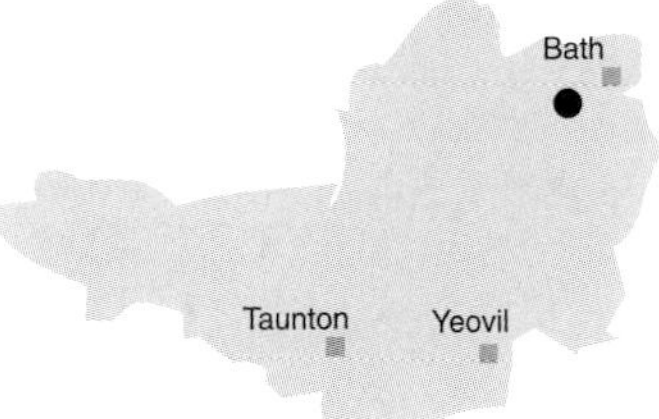

Web: www.johansens.com/hunstretehouse
E-mail: reception@hunstretehouse.co.uk
Tel: 0870 381 8630
International: +44 (0)1761 490490
Fax: 01761 490732

Price Guide:
single from £135
double/twin from £170
suite from £265

The Park

WICK, NEAR BATH BS30 5RN

Nestling in 240 acres of historic natural parkland, The Park is conveniently located between Bristol and the magnificent city of Bath, just 4 miles away. Within the hotel's grounds are 2 championship golf courses filled with mature trees, lakes and modern specification greens. Completely refurbished in 2005, the bedrooms in the picturesque courtyard have been decorated to a very high standard and offer the best in comfort and style; some have four-poster beds. The Park's restaurant, Oakwood, has an open-plan kitchen under the instruction of Chef Mark Treasure, and was originally an old stone Masonic temple. The menu specializes in simple treatment of roasted meats and fish cooked in a wood burning oven. The Park has 8 conference and syndicate rooms that can accommodate up to 200 delegates, and the attractive Park Room, with views over the golf course, can seat up to 130 for a private banquet or wedding reception. This is an ideal location for golf enthusiasts, weekend breaks and corporate stays.

Our inspector loved: *The fabulous newly decorated bedrooms and manor house.*

Directions: From the M4 take junction 18, then the A46 and A420. The entrance to The Park is just off the A420.

Web: www.johansens.com/thepark
E-mail: info@tpresort.com
Tel: 0870 381 8394
International: +44 (0)117 937 2251
Fax: 0117 937 4288

Price Guide:
single from £135
double/twin from £185
luxury from £280

Moore Place Hotel

The Square, Aspley Guise, Milton Keynes, Bedfordshire MK17 8DW

Built in 1786, Moore Place Hotel is a delightful country house hotel set in the centre of the peaceful village of Aspley Guise, and only 1.5 miles from the M1. Sympathetically extended to create extra accommodation, the new wing frames the attractive patio courtyard, rock garden, lily pool and waterfall. In May 2003, an additional 10 guest rooms were opened in the converted, listed cottage; each maintaining a very special character of its own. All 62 bedrooms are well-appointed and offer little extras such as trouser press, hairdryer, welcome drinks and large towelling bathrobes to make each visit special, for both business and leisure travellers alike. The attractive Victorian-style conservatory houses the highly acclaimed Greenhouse Restaurant, which is open to residents as well as non-residents, and serves cuisine rated amongst the best in the area. The menu is traditional English with European influences and is enhanced by a selection of fine wines; private dinners, conferences and special celebrations can be accommodated in 4 private function rooms. Moore Place Hotel is ideally situated for exploring the surrounding countryside and places of interest such as Bletchley Park, Waddesdon Manor, Woburn Abbey and Whipsnade Zoo to name but a few.

Our inspector loved: *The spacious and attractive rooms available in the cottage.*

Directions: Only a 2-minute drive from the M1/junction 13.

Web: www.johansens.com/mooreplace
E-mail: manager@mooreplace.com
Tel: 0870 381 8745
International: +44 (0)1908 282000
Fax: 01908 281888

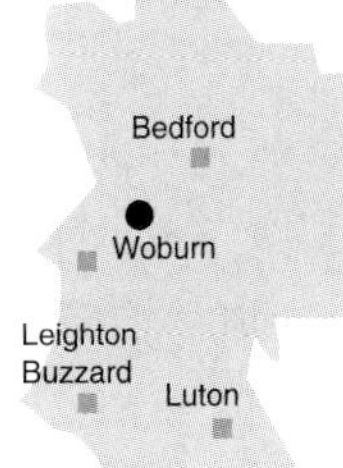

Price Guide:
single £58–£114
double/twin £79–£145
suite £150–£211

The Bear Hotel

41 CHARNHAM STREET, HUNGERFORD, BERKSHIRE RG17 0EL

Directions: Exit the M4 at junction 14 and take the A388 south. After approximately 2½ miles turn right onto the A4 to Hungerford. The Bear Hotel is on the left after the mini-roundabout.

Web: www.johansens.com/bearhotelhungerford
E-mail: info@thebearhotelhungerford.co.uk
Tel: 0870 381 8430
International: +44 (0)1488 682512
Fax: 01488 684357

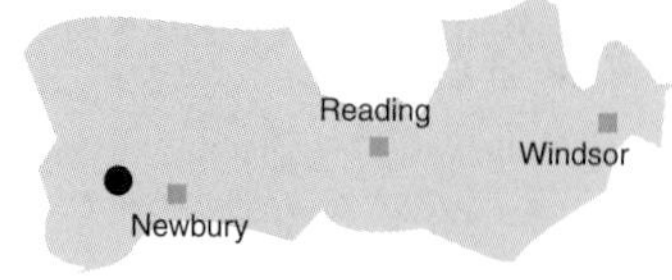

Price Guide: (room only)
standard from £110
double £125-£145
superior/de luxe suite £185

Few hotels can rival the history and charm of this attractive 13th-century inn situated in the ancient market town of Hungerford, a short walk from the picturesque Kennet and Avon Canal. It is one of the oldest in England and once owned by King Henry VIII who gave it to his wives Anne of Cleves in 1540 and Katherine Parr a year later. It was visited by Queen Elizabeth I, William Prince of Orange (the future King William III) and was the Civil War headquarters of Charles I prior to the nearby Battle of Newbury in 1644. Throughout the years The Bear Hotel has seen many changes but always retained its traditional ambience. Today, it is a welcoming, stylish weekend or longer stay venue and as suitable for leisure as for corporate entertaining. The Howat Family owners have invested in an extensive restoration programme since taking over in March 2005, in order to create a contemporary establishment whilst preserving its original features. Bedrooms in the main building as well as around a waterside courtyard have every comfort; many have custom designed furniture and high-tech facilities including flat-screen LCD televisions, broadband and WiFi whilst others are more traditional. The comfortable bar is ideal for lunch or informal suppers and the more stylish restaurant is presided over by award-winning chef, Phil Wild.

Our inspector loved: *The fabulous transformation of this hotel without detriment to its historical roots.*

Fredrick's – Hotel Restaurant Spa

SHOPPENHANGERS ROAD, MAIDENHEAD, BERKSHIRE SL6 2PZ

'Putting people first' is the guiding philosophy behind this sumptuously equipped deluxe hotel. Guests can expect to receive uncompromising service from this second generation family-run establishment. Extensive landscaped gardens furnished with an array of contemporary artwork overlook the fairways and greens of Maidenhead Golf Club. The spectacular addition of Fredrick's exclusive Spa offers the ultimate in relaxation and is the first in the UK equipped with its own private flotation suite. Guests can indulge in restorative treatments such as Rasul or LaStone therapies. In the hotel, minute attention to detail is evident in the luxurious bedrooms, all immaculate with gleaming, marble bathrooms, whilst some of the suites have their own patio or balcony. A quiet drink can be enjoyed in the light airy wintergarden lounge, and in warmer weather on the patio, before entering the 3 AA Rosette air-conditioned restaurant. Gourmet cuisine, which has received recognition from leading guides for many years, is served in elegant surroundings enhanced by a collection of fine art and sculpture. As well as being suitable for relaxation, leisurely spa breaks, romantic stays and fine dining, Fredrick's is perfectly located for conferences and corporate hospitality. Fredrick's is easily accessible from London, Heathrow and the West Country and near to Windsor, Henley, and Ascot .

Directions: Leave the M4 at junction 8/9, take the A404(M) and leave at the first exit 9A signed Cox Green/White Waltham. Turn left into Shoppenhangers Road towards Maidenhead. The entrance to Fredrick's is on the right.

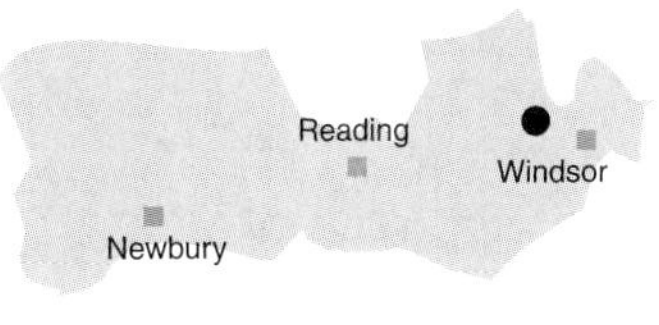

Web: www.johansens.com/fredricks
E-mail: reservations@fredricks-hotel.co.uk
Tel: 0870 381 8531
International: +44 (0)1628 581000
Fax: 01628 771054

Reading
Windsor
Newbury

Price Guide:
single from £215
double/twin from £295
suite from £450

Our inspector loved: *The warm, wonderful welcome and fantastic spa.*

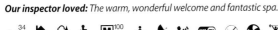

CLIVEDEN

TAPLOW, BERKSHIRE SL6 0JF

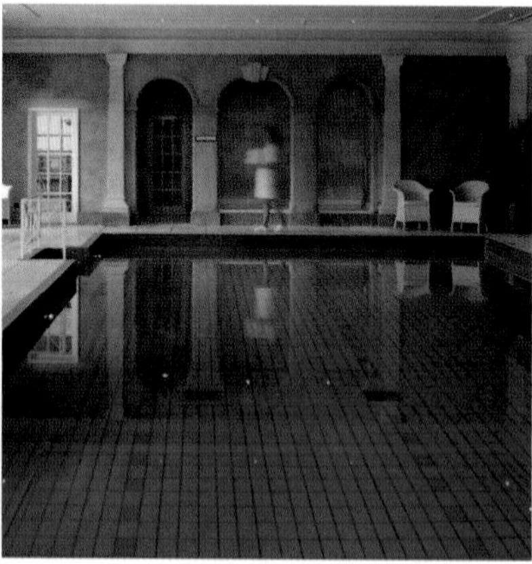

Cliveden is Britain's only 5 Red AA Star hotel that is also a stately home. Set in 376 acres of gardens and parkland on an elevated position overlooking the Thames, Cliveden has been home to a Prince of Wales, 3 dukes, an earl and the Astor family, and has been at the centre of Britain's social and political life for over 300 years. Exquisitely furnished in an English country house style, original works of art and antiques abound, and the French Dining Room is one of the most stunning examples of an 18th-century Rococo interior in this country. Guests seeking privacy may stay in Spring Cottage on the edge of the River Thames, where unrivalled peace is guaranteed. Sample fine dining in the award-winning restaurants, either Michelin-starred Waldo's or The Terrace, which overlooks the Parterre. Enjoy being pampered with treatments in the Pavilion Spa, roam the estate or partake in a river cruise on one of the hotel's vintage launches. Leisure activities include indoor and outdoor swimming, tennis, squash, a gymnasium, golf, horse riding and shooting. 2 well-equipped private boardrooms provide self-contained business meeting facilities. Luxury transfers via helicopter, a Rolls Royce Phantom or Bentley can be arranged. Cliveden is part of the von Essen hotel collection.

Directions: From the M4, jct 7 take the A4 towards Maidenhead. After a few miles, turn right into Berry Hill and follow the road for ¾ mile. Cliveden's drive is on the left-hand side via a grand entrance. Follow the "House Guests"signs.

Web: www.johansens.com/cliveden
E-mail: Reservations@clivedenhouse.co.uk
Tel: 0870 381 8432
International: +44 (0)1628 668561
Fax: 01628 661837

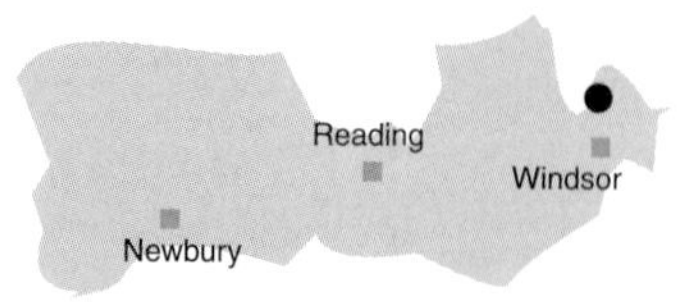

Price Guide: (excluding VAT)
double/twin from £295
suites from £480

Our inspector loved: *The approach...The location...The style.*

DONNINGTON VALLEY HOTEL & GOLF CLUB

OLD OXFORD ROAD, DONNINGTON, NEWBURY, BERKSHIRE RG14 3AG

Donnington Valley Hotel and Spa - "The New Destination!" With 111 beautifully designed bedrooms and suites, an 18-hole golf course and a luxury Health Club and Spa, the hotel is perfectly located in the heart of the Berkshire countryside, yet only minutes from the M4. With its open log fire and stunning grounds and water features, Donnington Valley Hotel is the ideal place to entertain colleagues or friends and enjoy the relaxed ambience. Dine in the award-winning WinePress Restaurant, which offers excellent British cuisine in a welcoming and informal environment. There is also the wooden beamed bar and lounge area, in which guests are offered a more casual dining experience. The brand new Health Club and Spa includes an 18-metre swimming pool, a spa bath, sauna, steam room, aromatherapy room, feature showers, a state-of-the-art gymnasium and seven elegantly designed treatment suites. Special corporate golf days can be arranged and joint spa or golf breaks are also available.

Our inspector loved: *The new additions to this welcoming, superbly run hotel.*

Directions: Leave the M4 at junction 13, go south towards Newbury on the A34 then follow signs for Donnington Castle. The hotel is on the right before reaching the castle.

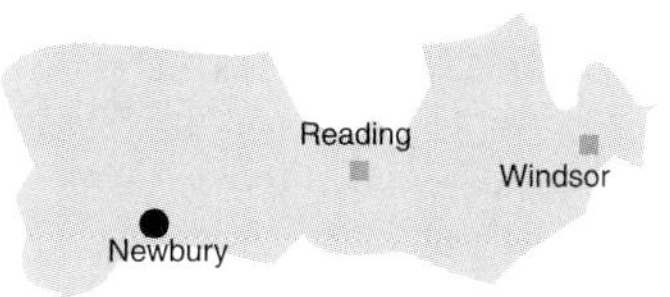

Web: www.johansens.com/donningtonvalley
E-mail: general@donningtonvalley.co.uk
Tel: 0870 381 8484
International: +44 (0)1635 551199
Fax: 01635 551123

Price Guide:
single from £175
double/twin £215
suite from £255

THE VINEYARD AT STOCKCROSS

NEWBURY, BERKSHIRE RG20 8JU

The Vineyard at Stockcross, Sir Peter Michael's "restaurant-with-suites" is a European showcase for the finest Californian wines including those from the Peter Michael Winery. The Head Sommelier, has selected the best from the most highly-prized, family-owned Californian wineries, creating one of the widest, most innovative, international wine lists. Awarded 5 Red Stars and 4 Rosettes by the AA, the modern British cuisine matches the calibre of the wines. John Campbell, Executive Chef, combines a unique blend of flavours and textures to ensure that every dish is an unforgettable multi-sensory feast. This superb food is complemented by a wine list of over 2000 wines, 600 of which are Californian. A stimulating collection of paintings and sculpture includes the keynote piece,"Fire and Water" by William Pye FRBS and "Deconstructing the Grape", a sculpture commissioned for The Vineyard Spa. A vine-inspired steel balustrade elegantly dominates the restaurant and the luxurious interior is complemented by subtle attention to detail throughout with stunning china and glass designs. The 49 well-appointed bedrooms include 31 suites offering stylish comfort with distinctive character. The Vineyard Spa features an indoor pool, spa bath, sauna, steam room, gym and treatment rooms offering a range of ESPA and Choco, Vino and Truffle Therapy treatments.

Our inspector loved: *The attention to detail and sophisticated excellence.*

Directions: From M4, exit Jct13, A34 towards Newbury, then Hungerford exit. 1st roundabout Hungerford exit, 2nd roundabout Stockcross exit. Hotel on right.

Web: www.johansens.com/vineyardstockcross
E-mail: general@the-vineyard.co.uk
Tel: 0870 381 8965
International: +44 (0)1635 528770
Fax: 01635 528398

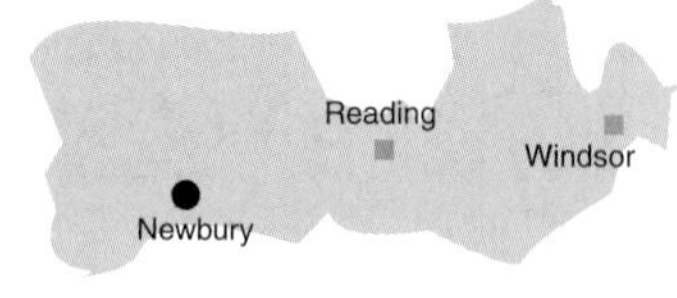

Price Guide: (excluding VAT)
single/double/twin £175–£275
suite £350–£530

The Crab at Chieveley

WANTAGE ROAD, NEWBURY, BERKSHIRE RG20 8UE

Now in its third successful year, The Crab at Chieveley, restaurant and hotel, has deservedly gained a fine reputation. Its owners David and Jackie Barnard are passionate about food and take a genuine delight in providing award-winning cuisine in their fantastic and interesting restaurant – The Crab has been awarded the AA Best Seafood Restaurant Award as well as a Remy. Anyone visiting the The Crab will instantly understand why. Great care is taken in sourcing the freshest fish from Brixham, Newlyn and Looe as well as scallops from the Isle of Skye and home-grown vegetables. Each of the 15 amazing bedrooms is carefully designed and named after the most famous hotels of the world. Choose from the Gleneagles or Cipriani or stay in the Oriental-styled Raffles or tropical Sandy Lane. All the ground floor rooms have a private garden and hot tub. A further 7 bedrooms are to be added in phases with completion due in spring 2007. The Crab is ideal for corporate stays with a difference, weekend breaks, weddings, special events and meetings in the pretty marquee and coach house. The nearby countryside is perfect for walking and visiting Newbury and its racecourse. London Bath and Bristol are within easy reach.

Our inspector loved: *The amazing rooms, energy of the owners and super location.*

Directions: Leave the M4 at junction 13 (taking care not to join the A34 north) and follow signs to Chieveley. Turn left onto Graces Lane and after 1/3 mile turn left into School Road. Turn right at the top of the hill then right onto the B4494. The Crab is on the right after 1/2 mile.

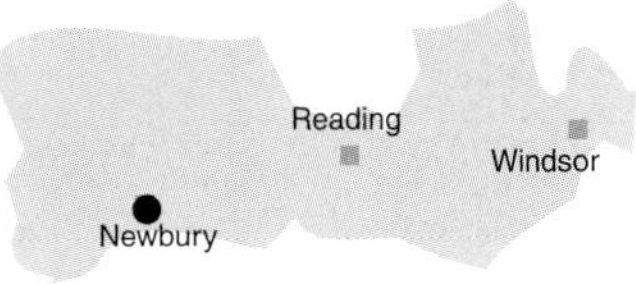

Web: www.johansens.com/crabatchieveley
E-mail: info@crabatchieveley.com
Tel: 0870 381 8318
International: +44 (0)1635 247550
Fax: 01635 247440

Price Guide:
single from £110
double from £150

The Regency Park Hotel

BOWLING GREEN ROAD, THATCHAM, BERKSHIRE RG18 3RP

Directions: Between Newbury and Reading. Leave M4 at Jct12 or 13; the hotel is signposted on A4, on the western outskirts of Thatcham.

Web: www.johansens.com/regencypark
E-mail: info@regencyparkhotel.co.uk
Tel: 0870 381 8852
International: +44 (0)1635 871555
Fax: 01635 871571

Price Guide:
single £95–£229
double/twin £110–£229
suite £233–£385

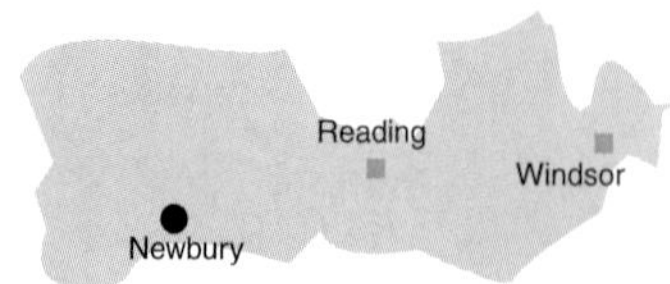

Ideally situated for access to both London and the South West, the Regency Park is a modern and contemporary hotel that takes great pride in providing not only the most sophisticated facilities but combining them with the most attentive service and care. The style is fresh and crisp with an understated elegance throughout, from the airy and spacious bedrooms to the array of meeting venues housed in the Business Centre. "Escape" is the hotels' leisure complex, and true to its name it really is a place where state-of-the-art technology and luxury meet to form an inviting and special feature. The 17m swimming pool and the large health and beauty salon create an instantly relaxing atmosphere where fully qualified staff offer holistic health and beauty treatments. The AA Rosette Watermark Restaurant has a contemporary elegance and attractive views over the waterfall gardens, reflected in its excellent menu of modern flavours and fusions. There is even a children's menu to ensure all guests are catered for. The Parkland Suite is a beautiful setting for any occasion, and with its own entrance and facilities for up to 200 guests it is the ideal place for wedding receptions and parties, as well as conferences and launches. Weekend leisure and spa breaks available.

Our inspector loved: *The consistency of excellence throughout this well run hotel.*

THE FRENCH HORN

SONNING-ON-THAMES, BERKSHIRE RG4 6TN

For over 150 years The French Horn, nestling beside the Thames near the historic village of Sonning with its pretty riverside walks,has provided a charming riverside retreat. Today, although busier on this stretch of the river, it continues that fine tradition of comfortable accommodation and outstanding cuisine in a beautiful setting. It is as ideal for a midweek or weekend break as it is for an executive meeting or private dinner. The bedrooms and suites are traditional and homely and many have river views. The old panelled bar provides an intimate scene for pre-dinner drinks and the Condé Nast Johansens award winning restaurant with its' speciality of locally reared duck, spit roasted here over an open fire. By day the restaurant is a lovely setting for lunch, while by night diners can enjoy the floodlit view of the graceful weeping willows which fringe the river. Dinner is served by candlelight and the cuisine is a mixture of French and English cooking using the freshest ingredients, complemented by The French Horn's fine and extensive wine list. Places of interest in the area include Henley, Windsor Stratfield Saye, and Mapledurham. There are numerous golf courses, equestrian centres and fishing. Shooting can be arranged at Bisley, there are leisure facilities at the local nearby spa as well as The Mill Theatre at Sonning to enjoy.

Our inspector loved: *This lovely traditional hotel with its exceptional restaurant and attentive staff.*

Directions: Leave the M4 at J8/9. Follow A404/M then at Thickets Roundabout turn left on A4 towards Reading for 8 miles. Turn right for Sonning. Cross Thames on B478. Hotel is on right.

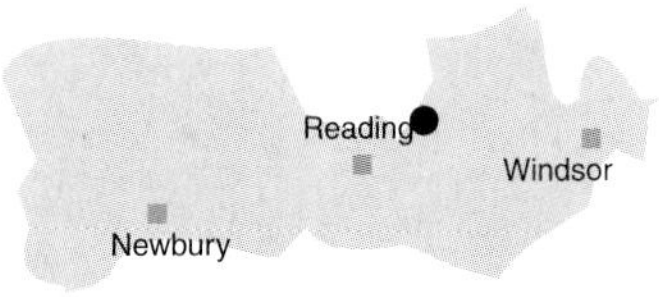

Reading
Windsor
Newbury

Web: www.johansens.com/frenchhorn
E-mail: info@thefrenchhorn.co.uk
Tel: 0870 381 8532
International: +44 (0)1189 692204
Fax: 01189 442210

Price Guide:
single £125–£170
double/twin £160–£215

The Great House

THAMES STREET, SONNING-ON-THAMES, NEAR READING, BERKSHIRE RG4 6UT

Directions: From the M4 exit either at junction 8, 9 or 10 and take the A4. Sonning is situated 2 minutes from the A4 on the B478. The hotel is on the right just before the bridge.

Web: www.johansens.com/greathouse
E-mail: greathouse@btconnect.com
Tel: 0870 381 8374
International: +44 (0)118 9692277
Fax: 0118 9441296

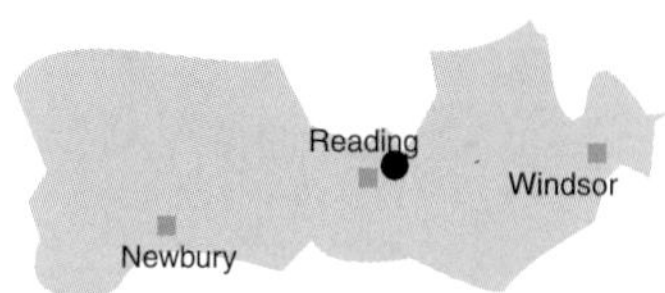

Price Guide:
single £59.50–£149
double £119–£209
suite £129–£229

The enchanting village of Sonning lies on a beautiful stretch of the river, with the Thames path heading towards Oxford and London Bridge in either direction. One of the oldest villages in England it is steeped in history and is surprisingly accessible from London, Heathrow, Reading and the West Country. History enthusiasts will love its proximity to Windsor and bustling Henley, and the hotel itself has an interesting story of its own. Bedrooms are located either in the original White Hart Hotel, 16th century Palace Yard & Hideaway Buildings, 17th century Coach House, 19th century Manor House or the brand new Clocktower Building. Each is individually designed and reflective of its period. One room has a four-poster bed, some are large enough to accommodate families and have river views. The Regatta Bar and Restaurant has a more contemporary feel and serves dishes influenced by the Mediterranean and Pacific Rim; al fresco dining is available in the summer. The Ferrymans Bar has an ambience of a traditional inn with warm fires in winter. There are moorings for up to 4 boats and boat owners are most welcome. The house has a "something for everyone" attitude and is popular for weddings, parties, functions and corporate meetings alike.

Our inspector loved: *The variety of rooms, pretty gardens and riverside location.*

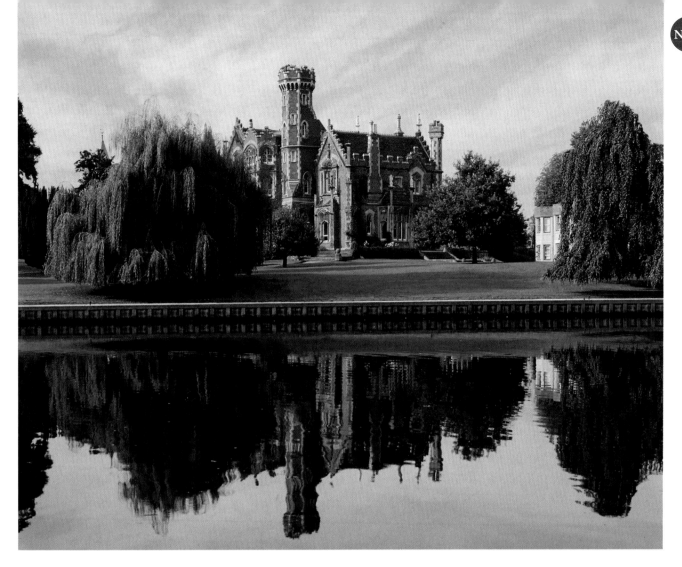

Oakley Court Hotel

WINDSOR ROAD, WATER OAKLEY, WINDSOR, BERKSHIRE SL4 5UR

Few would imagine that this impressive, stately gothic mansion set amidst 35 acres of beautiful grounds could be in such close proximity to central London. Within easy reach of the M25, M4 and M3 Oakley Court is the ideal escape from the city - be it for single days away or longer relaxing breaks. The house was built in classic Victorian gothic style, and its impressive architecture and sweeping lawns reaching down to the Thames have always proved popular: it has been used as the setting for the eccentric St Trinians, and has featured in the Hammer House of Horror films and a production of Dracula. The house was converted into a hotel in 1981 and today remains the epitome of English country-house elegance and style. The 118 impressive bedrooms range from the handsomely furnished Mansion Bedrooms with their imposing four-poster beds, to the River Suites, which overlook the Thames. There is a choice of fine wines and dining in the elegant Oakleaf Restaurant, and its accompanying bar is a welcoming, intimate haven with warm log fires. The sitting room and conservatory are available for private hire, to make Oakley Court a stunning destination for a wedding or summer party. Windsor Castle and Eton College are just a few minutes' drive away, and the delightful riverside towns of Marlow, Bray, Cookham and Henley-on-Thames all within easy reach.

Directions: Oakley Court is situated between Windsor and Maidenhead. Junction 6 or Junction 8/9 of the M4.

Web: www.johansens.com/oakleycourt
E-mail: reservations@oakleycourt.com
Tel: 0870 381 8322
International: +44 (0)1753 609988
Fax: 01628 637011

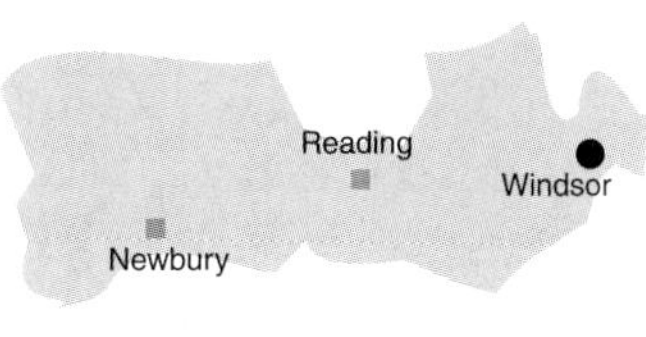

Price Guide:
single from £124
double from £134
suite from £224

Our inspector loved: *The setting, glorious gardens and interesting interior.*

New Hall

WALMLEY ROAD, ROYAL SUTTON COLDFIELD, WEST MIDLANDS B76 1QX

With a history of royal intrigue, forbidden passions and unrequited love spanning 900 years, this is the oldest inhabited moated manor house in England. In the evening flickering candles in the mullioned windows and shimmering reflection of the house in the surrounding moat add to the enchantming and magical ambience. The exceptionally friendly staff offer a warm welcome and set the convivial tone. English aristocratic tradition meets modern living and the attention to detail makes each guest feel special, relaxed and at home. Each of the "special occasion" suites, superior double and single rooms has been tastefully furnished. The Princess Elizabeth Suite, room for Queen Elizabeth I shortly before she was coronated in 1559, features a four-poster bed, separate sitting room and original fireplace, and the open-plan Krug Room, with sumptuous marble bathroom, was designed specifically for Luciano Pavarotti when he stayed here. The Bridge Restaurant and more informal Terrace Room serve delicious menus created from first-class, local produce alongside an extensive, worldwide wine list. The nostalgic cocktail bar features record players and guests can choose from the extensive collection of vinyl or even bring their favourite LP! New Hall Spa offers a wide range of relaxing and restorative therapies. The hotel has a 9 hole par 3 golf course and Belfry's Brabizon Golf course is nearby.

Our inspector loved: *The laid-back ambience, and friendly, attentive staff.*

Directions: From exit 9 of the M42, follow the A4097 (ignoring signs to the A38 Sutton Coldfield). At the B4148 turn right at the traffic lights. New Hall is 1 mile on the left.

Web: www.johansens.com/newhall
E-mail: info@newhalluk.com
Tel: 0870 381 8756
International: +44 (0)121 378 2442
Fax: 0121 378 4637

Price Guide:
single from £120
double/twin from £135
suite from £205

Hartwell House Hotel, Restaurant & Spa

OXFORD ROAD, NEAR AYLESBURY, BUCKINGHAMSHIRE HP17 8NR

Standing in 90 acres of gardens and parkland landscaped by a contemporary of Capability Brown, Hartwell House has both Jacobean and Georgian facades. This beautiful country house is a Grade 1 listed building, and was the residence in exile of King Louis XVIII of France from 1809 to 1814. The large ground floor reception rooms, with oak panelling and decorated ceilings, have antique furniture and fine paintings that evoke the elegance of the 18th century. There are 46 individually designed bedrooms and suites, 30 of which are non smoking in the main house and 16 in the Hartwell Court, the restored 18th century stables. The dining room at Hartwell is the setting for excellent food awarded 3 AA Rosettes and there are also 2 private dining rooms. The Old Rectory, Hartwell with its 2 acres of gardens, tennis court and swimming pool, provides superb accommodation and offers great comfort and privacy. The elegant Hartwell Spa adjacent to the hotel includes an indoor heated pool, whirlpool spa bath, steam room, saunas, gymnasium and 4 beauty salons. Situated in the Vale of Aylesbury, the hotel is only 45 minutes from London Heathrow, one hour from London and 20 miles from Oxford. Blenheim Palace, Waddesdon Manor and Woburn Abbey are just some of the nearby attractions. Dogs are permitted only in Hartwell Court bedrooms. Owned and restored by Historic House Hotels Limited

Directions: Off the A418 between Oxford and Aylesbury. 2 miles from Aylesbury, 20 minutes from M40, Junction 7

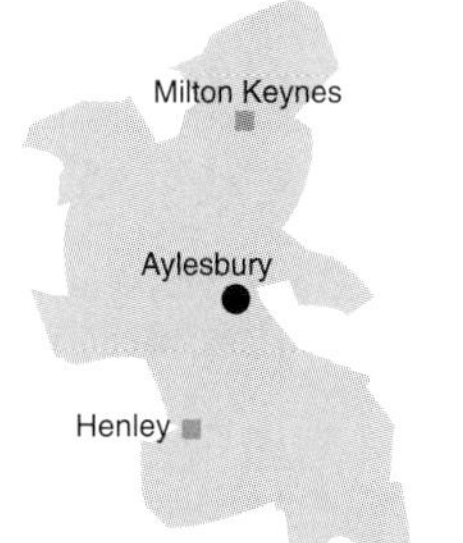

Web: www.johansens.com/hartwellhouse
E-mail: info@hartwell-house.com
Tel: 0870 381 8585
International: +44 (0)1296 747444
Fax: 01296 747450

Price Guide: (inc continental breakfast)
single from £155
double/twin from £280
suites from £380

Our inspector loved: *The sweeping drive and old fashioned grandeur.*

DANESFIELD HOUSE HOTEL AND SPA

HENLEY ROAD, MARLOW-ON-THAMES, BUCKINGHAMSHIRE SL7 2EY

Danesfield House Hotel and Spa is set within 65 acres of gardens and parkland overlooking the River Thames, and boasts panoramic views across the Chiltern Hills. It is the third house since 1664 to occupy this lovely setting and was designed and built in sumptuous style at the end of the 19th century. The house has been fully refurbished and combines Victorian splendour with contemporary touches. The luxury bedrooms are all beautifully and richly decorated and furnished to include many facilities. Guests may relax in the magnificent Grand Hall, with its galleried library, in the sun-lit atrium or comfortable bar before taking dinner in one of the 2 restaurants. The Oak Room and Orangery Brasserie feature the delicious cuisine of Michelin-starred chef Aiden Byrne. Leisure facilities include the award-winning spa with 20m pool, sauna, steam room, gymnasium and superb treatment rooms. Windsor Castle, Marlow, Henley and London are nearby, and the main motorway networks and Heathrow Airport are easily accessible. The hotel has 10 private banqueting and conference rooms.

***Our inspector loved:** This gloriously grand yet comfortable and welcoming hotel with its' friendly staff.*

Directions: Danesfield is situated between Henley-on-Thames and Marlow and is easily accessed by the M4 junction 8/9 and the M40 junction 4.

Web: www.johansens.com/danesfieldhouse
E-mail: sales@danesfieldhouse.co.uk
Tel: 0870 381 8474
International: +44 (0)1628 891010
Fax: 01628 890408

Price Guide:
single £215
double/twin £260
suites £300

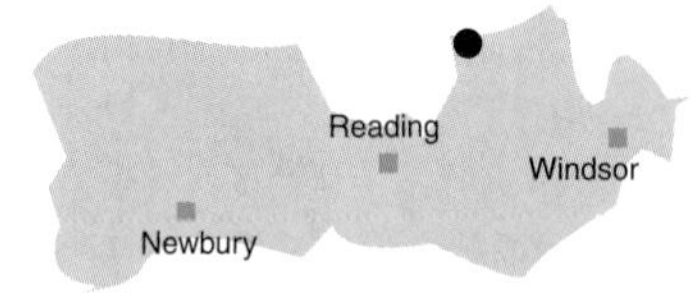

Stoke Park Club

PARK ROAD, STOKE POGES, BUCKINGHAMSHIRE SL2 4PG

Amidst 350 acres of sweeping parkland and gardens, Stoke Park Club is the epitome of elegance and style. For more than 900 years the estate has been at the heart of English heritage, playing host to lords, noblemen, kings and queens. History has left an indelible mark of prestige on the hotel and today it effortlessly combines peerless service with luxury. The magnificence of the Palladian mansion is echoed by the stunningly decorated interior where intricate attention to detail has been paid to the décor with antiques, exquisite fabrics and original paintings and prints ensuring that each room is a masterpiece of indulgence. All 21 individually furnished bedrooms and suites are complemented by marble en-suite bathrooms and some open onto terraces with views over the lakes and gardens. The Park Restaurant, and 8 beautiful function rooms, perfect for entertaining, also continue the theme of tasteful elegance. Since 1908 the hotel has been home to one of the finest 27-hole championship parkland golf courses in the world, Stoke Poges, and an all indulging spa, health and racquet pavilion re-affirms the hotel's position as one of the country's leading sporting venues. Luxury facilities include 11 beauty treatment rooms, indoor swimming pool, state-of-the-art gymnasium and studio and 13 tennis courts. Stoke Park is as ideal for midweek leisure breaks as for corporate events and partner programmes.

Our inspector loved: *The excellent facilities of this gracious country hotel.*

Directions: From the M4 take junction 6 or from the M40 take junction 2 then the A344. At the double roundabout at Farnham Royal take the B416. The entrance is just over 1 mile on the right.

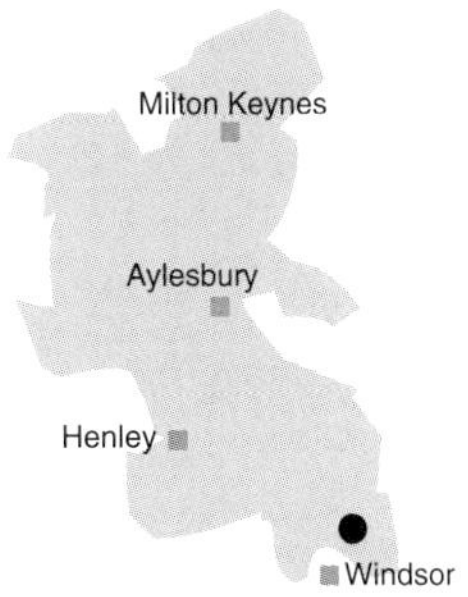

Milton Keynes
Aylesbury
Henley
Windsor

Web: www.johansens.com/stokepark
E-mail: info@stokeparkclub.com
Tel: 0870 381 8915
International: +44 (0)1753 717171
Fax: 01753 717181

Price Guide:
single £285
suite from £595

HOTEL FELIX

WHITEHOUSE LANE, HUNTINGDON ROAD, CAMBRIDGE CB3 0LX

Hotel Felix combines Victorian and modern architecture and sits in landscaped gardens offering peaceful surroundings, yet is within minutes' reach of Cambridge with its famous contrast of high-tech science parks and beautiful medieval university buildings. The furniture in the hotel's public areas is bespoke and the décor is softly neutral with splashes of colour and carefully selected sculptures and artwork. All of the 52 en-suite bedrooms comprise king-sized beds. Rooms have elegant proportions and are light and airy with high ceilings and views over the gardens. A restaurant and adjacent Café Bar act as a focal point and guests experience modern cuisine with a strong European influence or continental coffees and pastries, fine teas, wine and champagne by the glass. Hotel Felix specialises in private corporate and celebration dining and its 4 meeting rooms with natural daylight and both ISDN and WiFi connections will accommodate 34 boardroom and 60 theatre style. Other activities to be enjoyed in Cambridge are visits to Kings College, the Botanical Gardens, Fitzwilliam Museum and punting on the River Cam. Nearby places of interest include Ely, Bury St Edmunds and the races at Newmarket.

Our inspector loved: *The changing collection of original artworks.*

Directions: 1 mile north of Cambridge city centre.

Web: www.johansens.com/felix
E-mail: help@hotelfelix.co.uk
Tel: 0870 381 9056
International: +44 (0)1223 277977
Fax: 01223 277973

Price Guide:
single £136–£186
double/twin £168–£275

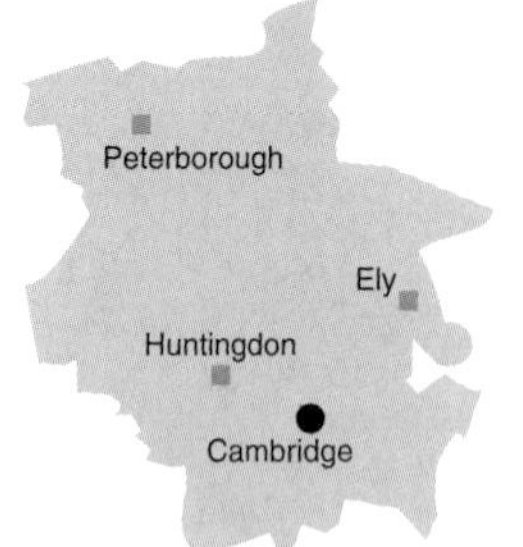

THE ALDERLEY EDGE HOTEL

MACCLESFIELD ROAD, ALDERLEY EDGE, CHESHIRE SK9 7BJ

Built as a family home in 1850 this imposing sandstone building has been skilfully converted into one of Cheshire's finest country house hotels. Privately owned, the award-winning Alderley Edge offers a peaceful and charming ambience in luxuriously comfortable surroundings. Modern facilities excellently combine with those of the past without the house losing any of its appeal of the more graceful and languid era of the mid-19th century. The beautifully appointed guest rooms include opulent Presidential and Bridal Suites, and most have scenic views over the Cheshire Plain or flower-filled garden, a popular venue with summer visitors where cool afternoon drinks or pre-dinner apéritifs are enjoyed. Panoramic views are also a feature of the Alderley Restaurant, which is situated in the elegant conservatory. The kitchen produces the highest standards of cooking using the freshest local seasonal produce. Pot roasted wild halibut, celery & apple mash, muscat & caraway emulsion and a selection of unusual and delicious breads baked each morning. Menus are complemented by a superb wine list that offers over 500 wines and 100 champagnes. Private dining is available, together with wedding, party, reception and meeting accommodation. Nearby are the famous Edge walks, Tatton and Lyme Parks, Quarry Bank Mill and Dunham Massey. Manchester is within easy reach.

Our inspector loved: *The dining experience in the Alderley Restaurant.*

 52   90      

Directions: M6 to M56 Stockport then exit jct 6. Take A538 to Wilmslow and follow signs to Alderley Edge. Turn left onto Macclesfield Rd. The hotel is 200 yards on the right. From M6, jct 18 follow signs to Holmes Chapel and Alderley Edge.

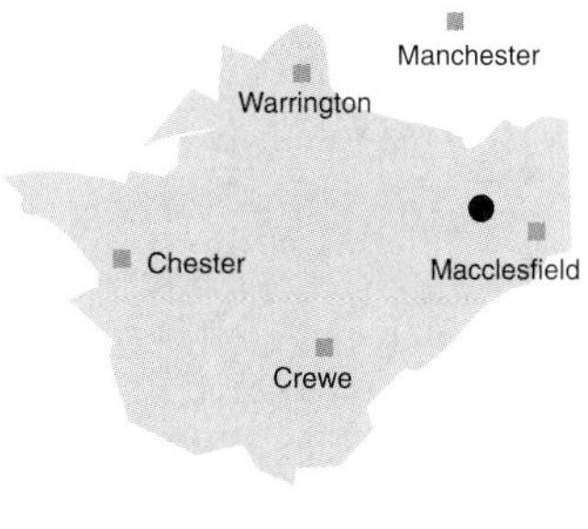

Manchester
Warrington
Chester
Macclesfield
Crewe

Web: www.johansens.com/alderleyedge
E-mail: sales@alderleyedgehotel.com
Tel: 0870 381 8307
International: +44 (0)1625 583033
Fax: 01625 586343

Price Guide:
single £65–£180
double £99–£260
suite from £250

THE CHESTER GROSVENOR AND SPA

EASTGATE, CHESTER, CHESHIRE CH1 1LT

Directions: In the centre of Chester on Eastgate. 24-hour NCP car parking available – follow signs to Grosvenor Shopping Centre Car Park

Web: www.johansens.com/chestergrosvenor
E-mail: hotel@chestergrosvenor.com
Tel: 0870 381 9264
International: +44 (0)1244 324024
Fax: 01244 313246

Price Guide:
double/twin from £195
suite from £395

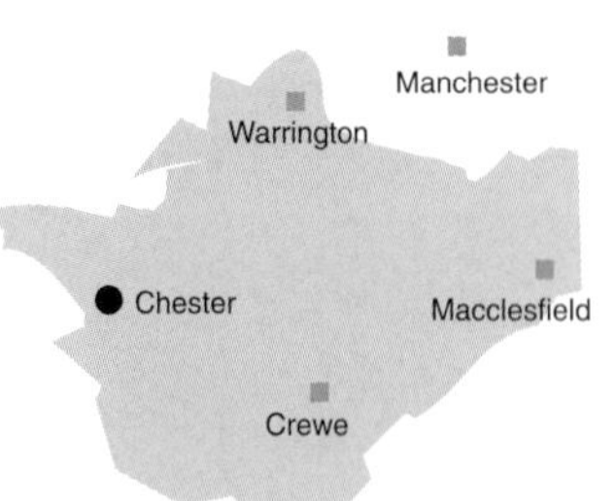

Located in the centre of Chester, this Grade II listed building has a black and white half timbered façade that belies the modern elegance of the interior. Awarded 5 Red Stars from the AA and 5 Stars from the RAC, this highly acclaimed hotel is just a short walk from the medieval galleried streets known as the "Rows", Roman Walls, Chester Cathedral and one of the oldest race courses in England. Each of the air-conditioned 80 guest bedrooms and suites is individually decorated and features a queen or king-size bed. Morning coffee, lunch and afternoon tea are all served in the relaxing and comfortable Library. The Arkle restaurant offers contemporary dining in an atmosphere of supreme elegance and features French cuisine with a modern twist and has one of the most extensive wine cellars in England. The less formal, Parisian-style La Brasserie provides an alternative dining option. The Grosvenor Spa offers both Western and Eastern treatments and comprises 5 treatment rooms. Facilities include: thermal suite, salt grotto, crystal steam room, ice fountain and herb sauna. For the more athletic, there is a fitness centre adjacent to the spa. Conference facilities for up to 250 delegates can be accommodated. Non-smoking policy throughout the hotel.

***Our inspector loved:** The attentive service at this grand hotel in the centre of Chester.*

Green Bough Hotel

60 HOOLE ROAD, CHESTER, CHESHIRE CH2 3NL

Proprietors Janice and Philip Martin have worked ceaselessly to create this friendly, relaxing haven, which is now Chester's premier small luxury hotel. The 15 sumptuous bedrooms and suites have been completely refurbished using Italian wall coverings and fabrics in keeping with the Roman theme which is evident throughout the hotel. Original oil paintings depicting scenes from a bygone era in Pompeii add to the exclusive ambience. Bedrooms feature original antique cast-iron beds and some have four-posters, plasma televisions, CD, DVD players and Jacuzzi baths. There are 7 deluxe bedrooms and 1 master suite in the Lodge. This totally non-smoking hotel enjoys an outstanding reputation reflected in the prestigious awards it has accumulated: England Awards for Excellence 2006 Hotel of the Year Gold Winner, Regional Small Hotel of the Year 2005, RAC Gold Ribbon. The Olive Tree restaurant offers a fine dining experience bringing together an eclectic mix of aromas and flavours to produce imaginative and innovative dishes for the daily changing table d'hôte menu, which is complemented by wines from the extensive cellar. The hotel is located within walking distance of the ancient and historic city of Chester and centrally placed for easy access to Snowdonia, Cumbria, Manchester and Liverpool. There is ample off-road free parking.

Our inspector loved: *The Roman theme prevalent throughout the hotel.*

Directions: Leave M53 at Jct12. Take A56 into Chester for 1 mile. The Green Bough Hotel is on the right.

Web: www.johansens.com/greenbough
E-mail: luxury@greenbough.co.uk
Tel: 0870 381 8571
International: +44 (0)1244 326241
Fax: 01244 326265

Price Guide:
single from £105
double/twin from £150
suites from £250

   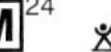  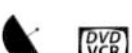   

Nunsmere Hall

TARPORLEY ROAD, OAKMERE, NORTHWICH, CHESHIRE CW8 2ES

Directions: Leave M6 at junction 19, take A556 to Chester (approximately 12 miles). Turn left onto A49. Hotel is 1 mile on left.

Web: www.johansens.com/nunsmerehall
E-mail: reservations@nunsmere.co.uk
Tel: 0870 381 8772
International: +44 (0)1606 889100
Fax: 01606 889055

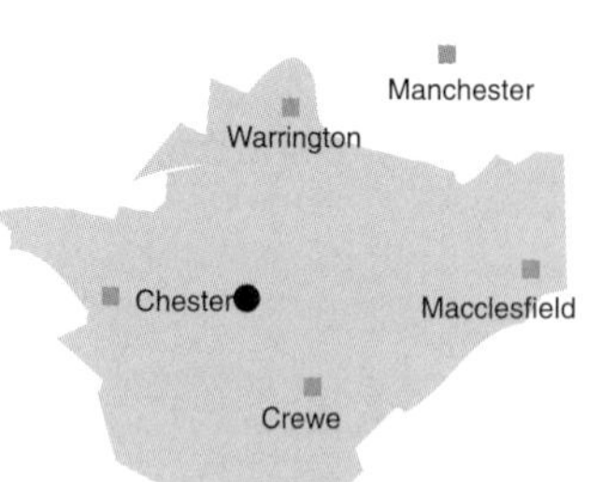

Price Guide:
single £145–£170
double/twin £200–£237
junior suites £260–£360

Set in peaceful Cheshire countryside and surrounded on three sides by a lake, Nunsmere Hall epitomises the elegant country manor where superior standards of hospitality still exist. Wood panelling, antique furniture, exclusive fabrics, Chinese lamps and magnificent chandeliers evoke an air of luxury. The 29 bedrooms and 7 junior suites, most with spectacular views of the lake and gardens, are beautifully appointed with king-size beds, comfortable breakfast seating and marbled bathrooms containing soft bathrobes and toiletries. The Brocklebank, Delamere and Oakmere business suites are air-conditioned, soundproofed and offer excellent facilities for boardroom meetings, private dining and seminars. The restaurant has a reputation for fine food and uses only fresh seasonal produce. Twice County Restaurant of the Year in the Good Food Guide. A snooker room is available and there are several championship golf courses nearby. Oulton Park racing circuit and the Cheshire Polo Club are next door. Golf pitch and putt is available in the grounds. Archery and air rifle shooting by arrangement. Although secluded, Nunsmere is convenient for major towns and routes. AA 3 Red Star and 2 Rosettes.

Our inspector loved: *This elegant country house surrounded by its own lake.*

ROWTON HALL HOTEL, HEALTH CLUB & SPA

WHITCHURCH ROAD, ROWTON, CHESTER, CHESHIRE CH3 6AD

Set in over 8 acres of award-winning gardens, Rowton Hall is located at the end of a leafy lane, only a mile from Chester. Built as a private residence in 1779, it retains many of its original features, including extensive oak panelling, a self-supporting hand-carved staircase, an original Inglenook fireplace and an elegant Robert Adam fireplace. Each luxury bedroom is individually and tastefully decorated with attention to detail, and is equipped with every modern amenity, including private bathroom, satellite television, broadband and voice mail, personal safe, luxury bathrobes, trouser press and hostess tray. Dining in the oak-panelled Langdale Restaurant is a delight; every dish is carefully created using the finest ingredients from local markets and the Hall's gardens to produce exquisite cuisine. Guests can enjoy the new Health Club with swimming pool and spa, relax in the Jacuzzi, sauna and steam room. For the more energetic, a workout in the well-equipped gymnasium and dance studio is available and 2 floodlit all-weather tennis courts are within the grounds. Four main conference and banqueting suites make the Hall an ideal venue for meetings, weddings, private dining or conferences and corporate events for up to 150 guests. Marquee events can be arranged in the gardens. Special offers available.

Directions: From the centre of Chester, take A41 towards Whitchurch. After 3 miles, turn right to Rowton village. The hotel is in the centre of the village.

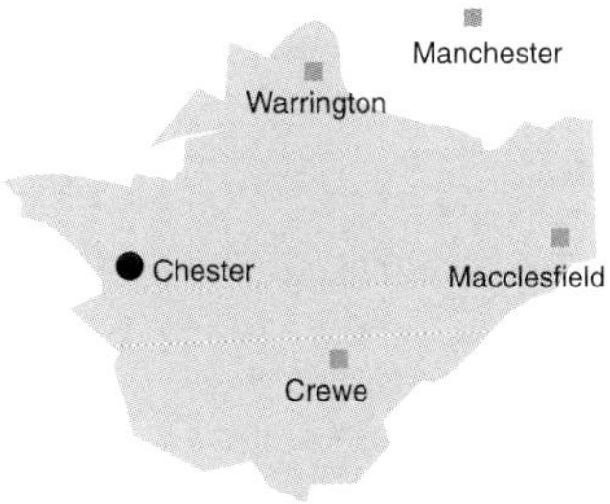

Manchester
Warrington
Chester
Macclesfield
Crewe

Web: www.johansens.com/rowtonhall
E-mail: rowtonhall@rowtonhall.co.uk
Tel: 0870 381 8871
International: +44 (0)1244 335262
Fax: 01244 335464

Price Guide:
single £145
double/twin £145–£205
suites £345–£500

Our inspector loved: *The health club, gym and spa.*

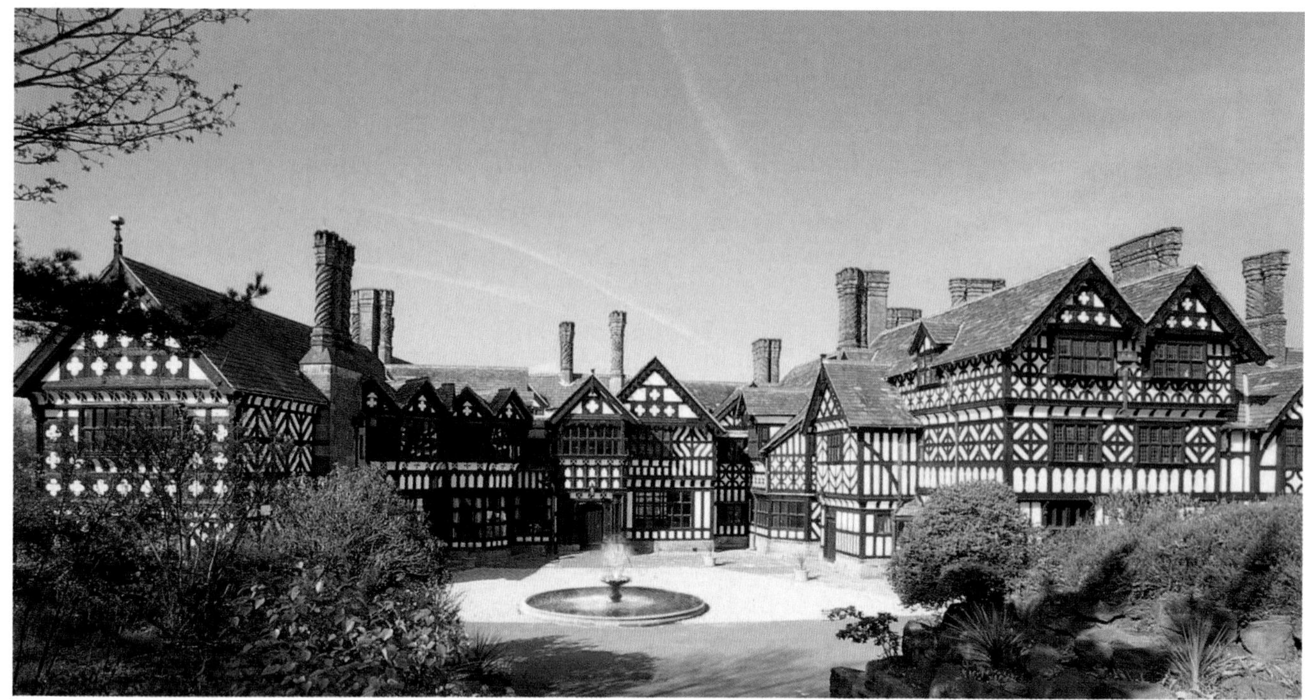

Hillbark Hotel

ROYDEN PARK, FRANKBY, WIRRAL CH48 1NP

Directions: Take M53, jct 3 for A552. Bear right on A551 towards Upton. After the hospital turn left onto Arrowe Brook Road then left onto Arrowe Brook Lane. Straight on at roundabout for ½ mile and Hillbark is on the left.

Web: www.johansens.com/hillbark
E-mail: enquiries@hillbarkhotel.co.uk
Tel: 0870 381 9128
International: +44 (0)151 625 2400
Fax: 0151 625 4040

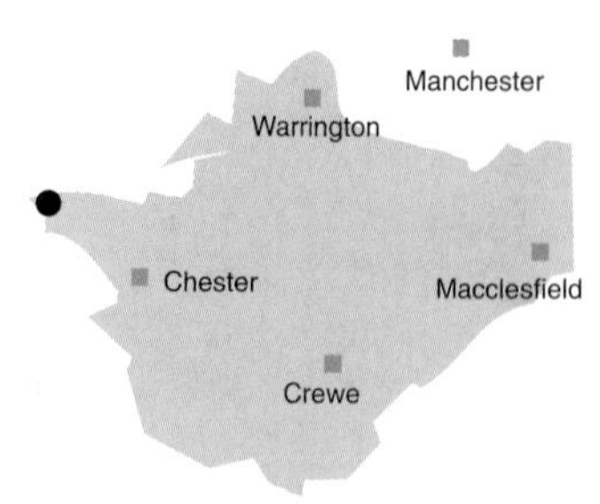

Price Guide:
single from £175
double/twin £175–£250
suite £250–£500

In the heart of the beautiful Wirral Peninsula, just 15 minutes yet seemingly a million miles away from vibrant Liverpool and historic Chester, this Grade II listed hotel provides the finest luxury coupled with discreet yet friendly service. Set in 250 acres of beautiful parkland overlooking the scenic Dee Estuary across to the hills of North Wales, Hillbark's character appearance hides a fascinating history. The house was originally built in 1891 in Birkenhead for the soap manufacturer Robert William Hudson, a founder of Lever Fabergé. It was sold in 1921 to Cunard shipping magnate Sir Ernest Royden, and was then moved in 1928 to its present site, brick by brick, finally being completed in 1931.The house contains many interesting features: the Great Hall has a 1527 Jacobean fireplace from Sir Walter Raleigh's house in Ireland; a set of William Morris stained-glass windows and a pair of 13th-century church screen doors; the library was originally in a stately home in Gloucestershire; and the Yellow Room restaurant contains a 1795 Robert Adam fire surround. Delicious, imaginative haute cuisine is served in the opulent Yellow Room restaurant and stylish Hillbark Grill, with a 300-bin cellar. Suites and bedrooms are individually designed and lavishly furnished. Leisure activities include world-class golf and windsurfing. Rolls-Royce and Bentley cars are available to collect guests from airports and rail stations.

Our inspector loved: *The peace and quiet in this Elizabethan-style house.*

Mere Court Hotel

WARRINGTON ROAD, MERE, KNUTSFORD, CHESHIRE WA16 0RW

This attractive Edwardian house stands in 7 acres of mature gardens and parkland in one of the loveliest parts of Cheshire. Maintained as a family home since being built in 1903, Mere Court has been skilfully restored into a fine country house hotel offering visitors a peaceful ambience in luxury surroundings. Comforts and conveniences of the present mix excellently with the ambience and many original features of the past. The bedrooms have views over the grounds or ornamental lake. All are individually designed and a number of them have a Jacuzzi spa bath and mini bar. Facilities include safes, personalised voice mail telephones and modem points. Heavy ceiling beams, polished oak panelling and restful waterside views are features of the elegant Aboreum Restaurant, which serves the best of traditional English and Mediterranean cuisines. Lighter meals can be enjoyed in the Lounge Bar. The original coach house has been converted into a designated conference centre with state-of-the-art conference suites and syndicate rooms accommodating up to 120 delegates. The addition of the lakeside Conservatory gives the hotel added space for weddings and functions accommodating up to 180 guests. Warrington, Chester, Manchester Airport and many National Trust properties are within easy reach.

Our inspector loved: *The oak-panelled restaurant overlooking the ornamental lake.*

Directions: From M6, exit at junction 19. Take A556 towards Manchester. After 1 mile turn left at traffic lights onto A50 towards Warrington. Mere Court is on the right.

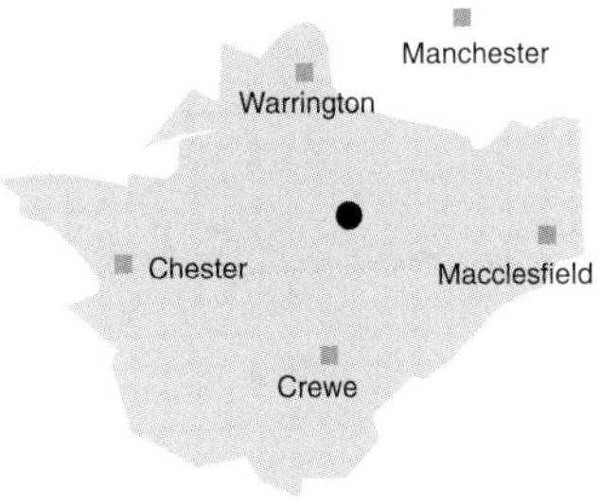

Manchester
Warrington
Chester
Macclesfield
Crewe

Web: www.johansens.com/merecourt
E-mail: sales@merecourt.co.uk
Tel: 0870 381 8727
International: +44 (0)1565 831000
Fax: 01565 831001

Price Guide:
single £130–£152
double/twin £154–£220

The Nare Hotel

CARNE BEACH, VERYAN-IN-ROSELAND, TRURO, CORNWALL TR2 5PF

Peace, tranquillity and stunning sea views make The Nare a real find. Superbly positioned, the hotel overlooks the fine sandy beach of Gerrans Bay, facing south and sheltered by The Nare and St Mawes headlands. In recent years extensive refurbishments have ensured comfort and elegance without detracting from the country house charm of this friendly family-run hotel. All bedrooms are close to the sea, many with patios and balconies taking advantage of the spectacular outlook. In the main dining room guests can enjoy the sea views from 3 sides of the room where local seafood, such as lobster and delicious homemade puddings, are served with Cornish cream, complemented by an interesting range of wines. The Quarterdeck Restaurant is open all day serving morning coffee, light luncheons, cream teas and offers relaxed dining in the evening. The Nare remains the highest rated AA 4 star hotel in the south west with 2 Rosettes for its food. Surrounded by subtropical gardens and National Trust land the hotel's seclusion is ideal for exploring the coastline and villages of the glorious Roseland Peninsula. It is also central for many of Cornwall's beautiful houses and gardens including the famous Heligan. Guests arriving by train or air are met, without charge, by prior arrangement, at Truro Station or Newquay Airport. The hotel is open throughout the year, including Christmas and New Year.

Our inspector loved: *The location, year round facilities and fine dining.*

Directions: Follow the road to St Mawes. 2 miles after Tregony Bridge turn left for Veryan. The hotel is 1 mile beyond Veryan.

Web: www.johansens.com/nare
E-mail: office@narehotel.co.uk
Tel: 0870 381 8755
International: +44 (0)1872 501111
Fax: 01872 501856

Price Guide:
single £95-£195
double/twin £180-£390
suite £330-£554

St Michael's Hotel & Spa

Gyllyngvase Beach, Falmouth, Cornwall TR11 4NB

Set in 4 acres of tranquil, subtropical gardens, with stunning views of the beautiful Cornish coastline, St Michael's Hotel & Spa is a place that guests return to time and time again. The property has undergone an extensive £2.5 million refurbishment programme that has resulted in a state-of-the-art health club and spa, award-winning restaurant and modernized bedrooms, bars and conference suites. The Flying Fish Restaurant focuses on fresh fish and seafood with a menu that regularly changes to utilise the best seasonal Cornish produce. The restaurant overlooks the sea and gardens, with an outside sun terrace for al fresco dining. Set within the gardens, the newly created St Michael's Spa provides an impressive range of health, beauty and relaxation treatments. Guests can also enjoy the sauna, Jacuzzi and steam room, take a dip in the large heated indoor swimming pool, work out in the large fitness suite or relax on the timber sundeck overlooking the sea. The exotic grounds form the perfect backdrop for a magical wedding, and the hotel offers a variety of rooms to suit large conferences or small meetings. Visitors will find plenty to do in the surrounding area with a sandy blue flag beach directly opposite the hotel, the National Maritime Museum a short walk away, and the Eden Project within an hour's drive.

Directions: Take A.39 to Falmouth then follow the signs for "Beaches and Hotels" Turn right at roundabout into Penance Road. At the end turn right into Spernen Wynn Road, then left into Stracey Road after 400 metres. Hotel is on the right.

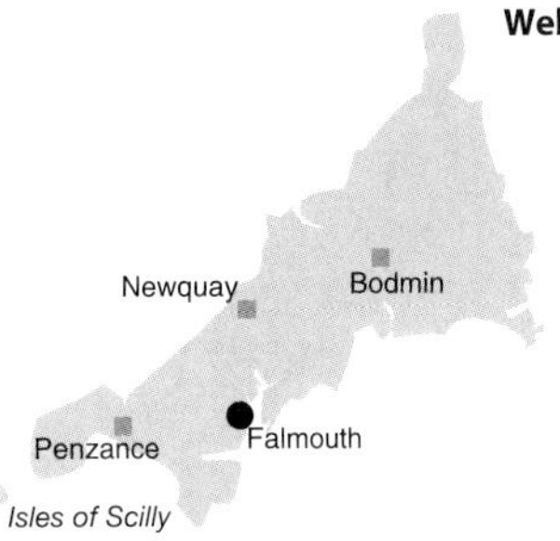

Newquay
Bodmin
Penzance
Falmouth
Isles of Scilly

Web: www.johansens.com/stmichaelsfalmouth
E-mail: info@stmichaelshotel.co.uk
Tel: 0870 381 8399
International: +44 (0)1326 312707
Fax: 01326 211772

Price Guide:
single £45–£120
double/twin £90–£190
suite £150–£230

Our inspector loved: *All the facilities offered.*

BUDOCK VEAN - THE HOTEL ON THE RIVER

NEAR HELFORD PASSAGE, MAWNAN SMITH, FALMOUTH, CORNWALL TR11 5LG

This family-run, 4-star Cornwall Tourist Board Hotel of the Year 2002, 2003 and 2004, is nestled in 65 acres of award-winning gardens and parkland with a private foreshore on the tranquil Helford River. Set in a designated area of breathtaking natural beauty, the hotel is a destination in itself with outstanding leisure facilities and space to relax and be pampered. The AA Rosette restaurant offers excellent cuisine using the finest local produce to create exciting and imaginative 5-course dinners, with fresh seafood being a speciality. On site are a golf course, large indoor swimming pool, tennis courts, a billiard room, boating, fishing, and the Natural Health Spa. Awarded the South West Tourism Large Hotel of the Year 2003. The local ferry will take guests from the hotel's jetty to waterside pubs, to Frenchman's Creek or to hire a boat. The hotel also takes out guests on its own 32-foot "Sunseeker". A myriad of magnificent country and coastal walks from the wild grandeur of Kynance and the Lizard to the peace and tranquillity of the Helford itself, as well as several of the Great Gardens of Cornwall, are in the close vicinity.

Our inspector loved: *The location, the peace, the tranquillity and the new addition of a hot tub overlooking the grounds – a must do experience.*

Directions: From the A39, Truro to Falmouth road, follow the brown tourist signs for Trebah Garden. Budock Vean appears ½ mile after passing Trebah on the left-hand side.

Web: www.johansens.com/budockvean
E-mail: relax@budockvean.co.uk
Tel: 0870 381 8392
International: reservations+44 (0)1326 252100
Fax: 01326 250892

Price Guide: (including dinner)
single £72–£119
double/twin £144–£238
suites £142–£308

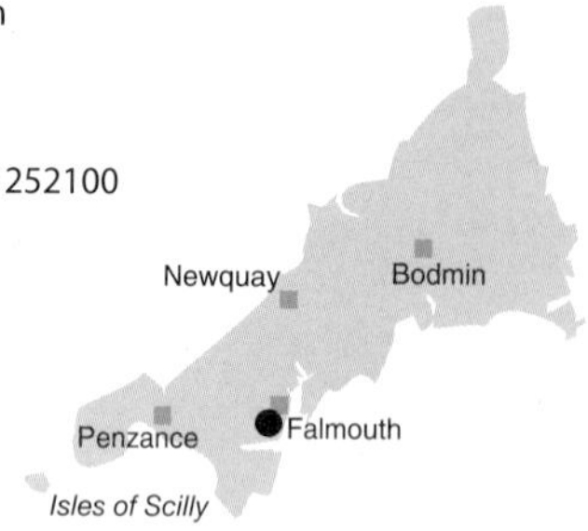

Newquay
Bodmin
Penzance
Falmouth
Isles of Scilly

Meudon Hotel

MAWNAN SMITH, NEAR FALMOUTH, CORNWALL TR11 5HT

Set against a delightfully romantic backdrop of densely wooded countryside between the Fal and Helford Rivers, Meudon Hotel is a unique, family-run, superior retreat with sub-tropical gardens leading to its own private sea beach. The French name originates from a nearby farmhouse built by Napoleonic prisoners of war and called after their eponymous home village in the environs of Paris. 9 acres of sub-tropical gardens are coaxed into early bloom by the Gulf Stream and mild Cornish climate; Meudon is safely surrounded by 200 acres of beautiful National Trust land and the sea. All bedrooms are in a modern wing, have en-suite bathrooms and each enjoys spectacular garden views. Many a guest is enticed by the cuisine to return: the fresh seafood, caught by local fishermen, and the kitchen's commitment to using local Cornish ingredients creates superb dishes alongside wines from a judiciously compiled list. Rich in natural beauty with a myriad of watersports and country pursuits to indulge in, you can play golf free at nearby Falmouth Golf Club and 5 others in Cornwall, sail aboard the hotel's skipperd 34-foot yacht or just laze on the beach.

Our inspector loved: *The newly presented en-suite bedrooms, and magnificent gardens.*

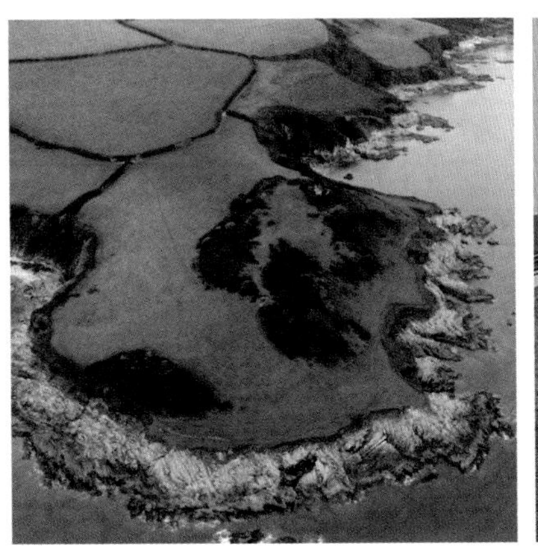

Directions: From Truro A39 towards Falmouth at Hillhead roundabout take 2nd exit. The hotel is 4 miles on the left.

Newquay
Bodmin
Penzance
Falmouth
Isles of Scilly

Web: www.johansens.com/meudon
E-mail: wecare@meudon.co.uk
Tel: 0870 381 8730
International: +44 (0)1326 250541
Fax: 01326 250543

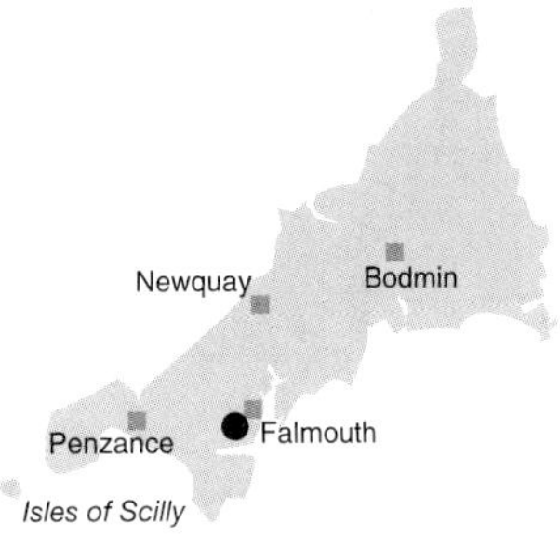

Price Guide: (including dinner)
single £120
double/twin £240
suite £330

Fowey Hall Hotel & Restaurant

HANSON DRIVE, FOWEY, CORNWALL PL23 1ET

Directions: On reaching Fowey, go straight over 3 mini roundabouts and follow the road all the way eventually taking a sharp right bend, take the next left turn and Fowey Hall drive is on the right.

Web: www.johansens.com/foweyhall
E-mail: info@foweyhallhotel.co.uk
Tel: 0870 381 8529
International: +44 (0)1726 833866
Fax: 01726 834100

Price Guide: (min 2 nights incl dinner)
double/twin £170–£300 per night
suite £210–£500 per night

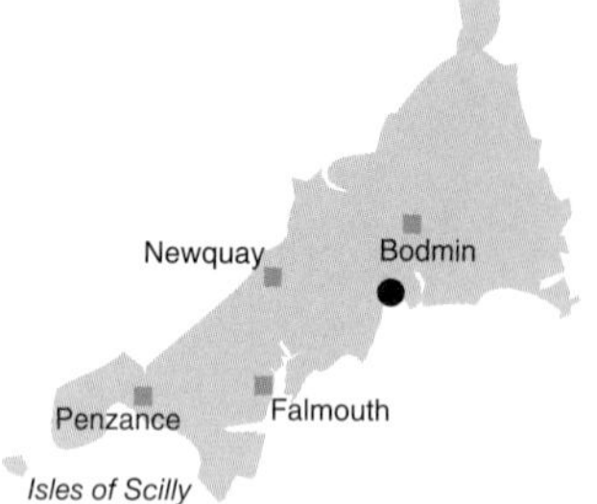

Situated in five acres of beautiful grounds overlooking the Estuary, Fowey Hall Hotel is a magnificent Victorian mansion renowned for its excellent service and comfortable accommodation. The fine panelling and superb plasterwork ceilings add character to the spacious public rooms. Located in either the main house or the Court, the 36 bedrooms include 12, suites and 10 sets of interconnecting rooms. All are well-proportioned with a full range of modern comforts. The panelled dining rooms provide an intimate atmosphere where guests may savour the local delicacies. Using the best of regional produce, the menu comprises tempting seafood and fish specialities. The hotel offers a full complimentary crèche service. Guests may swim in the indoor swimming pool or play croquet in the gardens. Older children have not been forgotten and "The Garage" in the courtyard is well-equipped with table tennis, table football and many other games. Also a cinema room with a 42" plasma screen showing the latest childrens movies. Outdoor pursuits include sea fishing, boat trips and a variety of water sports such as sailing, scuba-diving and windsurfing. Dogs are allowed in the courtyard rooms only. There are several coastal walks for those who wish to explore Cornwall and its beautiful landscape.

Our inspector loved: *The new interconnecting suites.*

Hell Bay

BRYHER, ISLES OF SCILLY, CORNWALL TR23 0PR

Bryher is the smallest community of the Isles of Scilly, 28 miles west of Land's End, and Hell Bay its only hotel. It stands in a spectacular and dramatic setting in extensive lawned grounds on the rugged West Coast overlooking the unbroken Atlantic Ocean. Described as a "spectacularly located getaway-from-it-all destination that is a paradise for adults and children alike" .. and it is. Outdoor heated swimming pool, gym, sauna, spa bath, children's playground, games room and par 3 golf course ensure there is never a dull moment. Daily boat trips are available so that you can discover the islands, the world famous tropical Abbey Garden is on the neighbouring island of Tresco. White sanded beaches abound with an array of water sports available. Dining is an integral part of staying at Hell Bay and the food will not disappoint; as you would expect, seafood is a speciality. Out of season breaks available and open for Christmas and New Year.

***Our inspector loved:** This superb little gem tucked away from the big world offering total peace.*

Directions: The Isles of Scilly are reached by helicopter or boat from Penzance or fixed-wing aircraft from Southampton, Bristol, Exeter, Newquay and Lands End. The hotel can make all necessary travel arrangements and will co-ordinate all transfers to Bryher on arrival.

Web: www.johansens.com/hellbay
E-mail: contactus@hellbay.co.uk
Tel: 0870 381 8591
International: +44 (0)1720 422947
Fax: 01720 423004

Price Guide: (including dinner)
suites £260–£550

TALLAND BAY HOTEL

PORTHALLOW, CORNWALL PL13 2JB

Surrounded by 2 acres of beautiful sub-tropical gardens and with dramatic views over Talland Bay, this lovely old Cornish manor house is a real gem. Each of the 23 bedrooms has its own individual character and is traditionally furnished. Many offer stunning views of the sea and the garden's magnificent Monterey pines. In the bathrooms, fluffy bathrobes and Molton Brown toiletries are just some of the extra touches that are the hotel's hallmark. The award-winning, 3 AA Rosetted restaurant, has gained the accolade Restaurant Newcomer of the Year for Cornwall from the Good Food Guide. The menu is essentially modern British and incorporates high quality, fresh local produce complemented by fine wines specially selected by the owners. The hotel organises a number of exclusive weekends combining gourmet food with superb entertainment – such as an evening of jazz or classical music. Talland Bay is also noted for its splendid Christmas and New Year "house party" breaks. There are fabulous coastal walks all year round while, in summer, putting and croquet can be played on the beautiful lawns and the heated outdoor swimming pool, with its south-facing terrace, is a constant temptation. In the winter, there is a chance to read that favourite book by a roaring log fire.

Our inspector loved: *The location and attention to detail.*

Directions: The hotel is signposted from the A387 Looe–Polperro road.

Web: www.johansens.com/tallandbay
E-mail: info@tallandbayhotel.co.uk
Tel: 0870 381 8937
International: +44 (0)1503 272667
Fax: 01503 272940

Price Guide:
single £75–£105
double/twin £95–£225

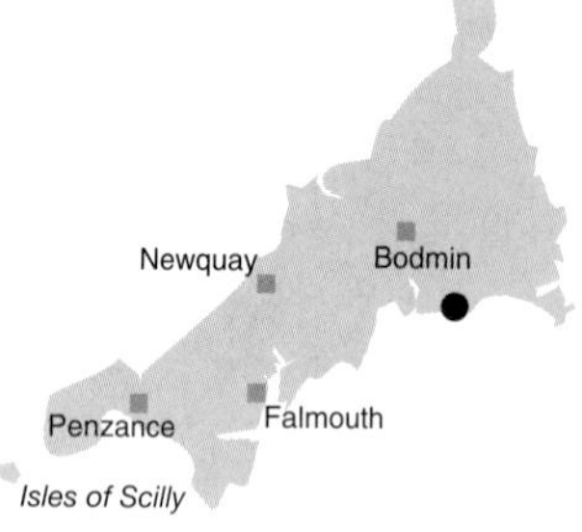

Treglos Hotel

CONSTANTINE BAY, NEAR PADSTOW, CORNWALL PL28 8JH

Built in 1905 as a four-bedroom family home overlooking the sea on the dramatic North Cornwall coast, Treglos was converted into a hotel in 1933 and has been sympathetically expanded and tastefully refurbished by the Barlow family over the past 40 years. Current owners, Jim and Rose, are just as fastidious as their predecessors, ensuring that the highest standards are maintained and that the personal touch is always in evidence. The 4-star AA-rated hotel has 42 delightfully decorated and extremely comfortable rooms and suites with every modern facility. Some have balconies and many offer uninterrupted views over Constantine Bay and Trevose Head. Alternatively, guests have the choice of self-catering facilities in the landscaped gardens consisting of 2 and 4-person apartments and a charming cottage for up to 6. The hotel's two elegant lounges with open fires and a sunny conservatory are perfect for taking tea or relaxing over a drink before or after dining on award-winning cuisine in the restaurant. Leisure facilities include a heated swimming pool and Jacuzzi, snooker room and beauty rooms with a range of treatments. Outdoors there are coastal paths, golden beaches and enchanting little coves. Treglos also has its own holiday golf course, Merlin, which is within a 10-minute drive.

Our inspector loved: *This beautiful coastal country house hotel. Offering total comfort and superb disabled accommodation.*

Directions: From A39 take B3274 or A389 towards Padstow. Then take B3276 towards Newquay. After approximately ¼ mile turn right to Constantine Bay and then right again at Constantine Bay Stores. Treglos is 50 yards on the left.

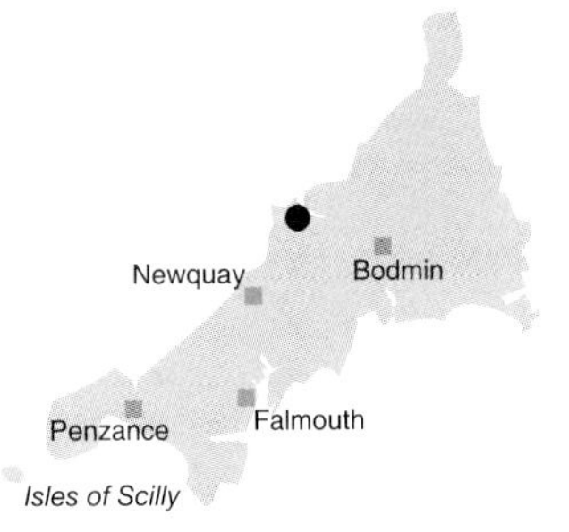

Web: www.johansens.com/treglos
E-mail: stay@tregloshotel.com
Tel: 0870 381 8951
International: +44 (0)1841 520727
Fax: 01841 521163

Price Guide: (including dinner)
single £74–£99.50
double/twin £148–£198
bed and breafast prices on request.

THE ROSEVINE HOTEL

PORTHCURNICK BEACH, PORTSCATHO, ST MAWES, TRURO, CORNWALL TR2 5EW

At the heart of Cornwall's breathtaking Roseland Peninsula, the Rosevine is an elegant and gracious late Georgian hotel that offers visitors complete comfort and peace. The Rosevine stands in its own landscaped grounds overlooking Porthcurnick Beach and town, Portscatho Harbour, a traditional Cornish fishing village. The superbly equipped bedrooms are delightfully designed, with some benefiting from direct access into the gardens and from their own private patio. The award-winning restaurant serves exceptional food, using the freshest seafood and locally grown produce with al fresco dining. After dining, guests can relax in any of the 3 tastefully and comfortably presented lounges, bathe in the spacious indoor heated pool, or read in the hotel's well stocked library. Visitors to the region do not forget the walks to the charming villages dotted along the Roseland Peninsula, and the golden sand of the National Trust maintained beach, which immediately faces the hotel. Children and family holdays are especially catered for. Visitors can sail, canoe or take river trips. The hotel is ideally placed for the Eden Project, Heligan, National Trust gardens and the beautiful Cathedral city of Truro.

Our inspector loved: *The 4 newly refurbished bedrooms, the mouth-watering cuisine and the lovely location.*

Directions: From Exeter take A30 towards Truro. Take the St Mawes turn and the hotel is signed to the left.

Web: www.johansens.com/rosevinehotel
E-mail: info@rosevine.co.uk
Tel: 0870 381 8867
International: +44 (0)1872 580206
Fax: 01872 580230

Price Guide:
single £90–£190
double/twin £175–£250
suite £250–£360

The Lugger Hotel

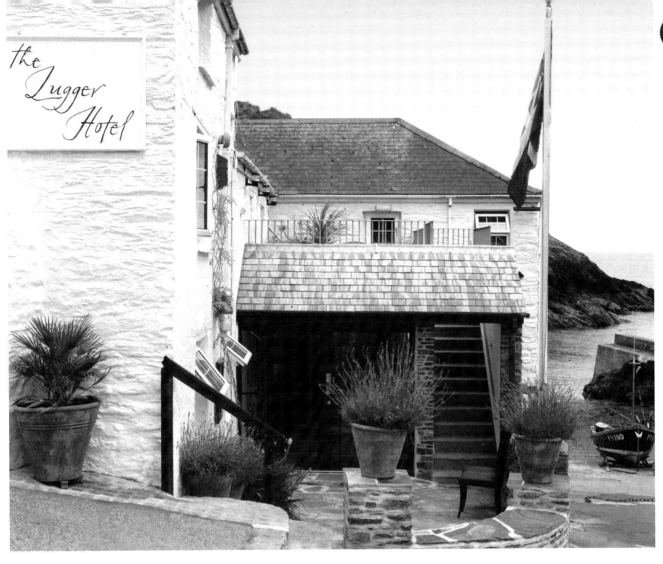

PORTLOE, NEAR TRURO, CORNWALL TR2 5RD

Set on the water's edge and sheltered on 3 sides by green rolling hills tumbling into the sea, this quaint former inn stands in an idyllic setting. Reputedly the haunt of 17th-century smugglers, The Lugger Hotel overlooks a tiny working harbour in the scenic village of Portloe on the unspoilt Roseland Peninsula. It is a conservation area of outstanding beauty and a perfect escape from the stresses of today's hectic world. Seaward views from the hotel are stunning and reaching out from each side are coastal paths leading to secluded coves. Welcoming owners Sheryl and Richard Young have created an atmosphere of total comfort and relaxation whilst retaining its historic ambience. Each bedroom has every amenity, has an en-suite and is tastefully decorated and furnished; some are situated across an attractive courtyard. A great variety of dishes and innovative dinner menus are served in the restaurant overlooking the harbour. Local seafood is a speciality with crab and lobster being particular favourites. The rejuvinating Seboni Spa offers aromatherapy, body wraps, massages, facials and nail treatments and only uses natural products including local herbs, flowers, rocks and the Cornish sea. The sandy stretches of Pendower and Carne, many National Trust properties and gardens such as the Lost Gardens of Heligan and The Eden Project are within easy reach.

Our inspector loved: *This little gem so idyllically tucked away.*

Directions: Turn off the A390 St Austell to Truro onto the B3287 Tregony then take the A3048 signed St Mawes. After 2 miles take the left fork following signs for Portloe.

Newquay
Bodmin
Penzance
Falmouth
Isles of Scilly

Web: www.johansens.com/lugger
E-mail: office@luggerhotel.com
Tel: 0870 381 8708
International: +44 (0)1872 501322
Fax: 01872 501691

Price Guide: (including dinner)
double/twin £220–£420

THE GARRACK HOTEL & RESTAURANT

BURTHALLAN LANE, ST IVES, CORNWALL TR26 3AA

This family-run hotel, secluded and full of character, ideal for a family holiday, is set in 2 acres of gardens with fabulous sea views over Porthmeor Beach, the St Ives Tate Gallery and the old town of St Ives. The bedrooms in the original house are in keeping with the style of the building. The additional rooms are modern in design. All rooms have private bathrooms. Enhanced rooms have either four-poster beds or whirlpool baths. A ground-floor room has been fitted for guests with disabilities. Visitors return year after year to enjoy informal yet professional service, good food and hospitality. The restaurant specialises in seafood especially fresh lobsters. The wine list includes over 70 labels from ten regions. The lounges have books, magazines and board games for all and open fires. The small attractive leisure centre contains a small swimming pool with integral spa, sauna, solarium and fitness area. The hotel has its own car park. Porthmeor Beach, just below the hotel, is renowned for surfing. Riding, golf, bowls, sea-fishing and other activities can be enjoyed locally. St Ives, with its harbour, is famous for artists and for the new St Ives Tate Gallery. Gateway to coastal footpaths. Dogs are welcome by prior arrangement

Our inspector loved: *This family-run relaxed informal hotel overlooking Porthmeor Beach.*

Directions: A30–A3074–B3311–B3306. Go ½ mile, turn left at mini-roundabout, hotel signs are on the left as the road starts down hill.

Web: www.johansens.com/garrack
E-mail: djenquiry@garrack.com
Tel: 0870 381 8536
International: +44 (0)1736 796199
Fax: 01736 798955

Price Guide:
single £70–£90
double/twin £120–£195

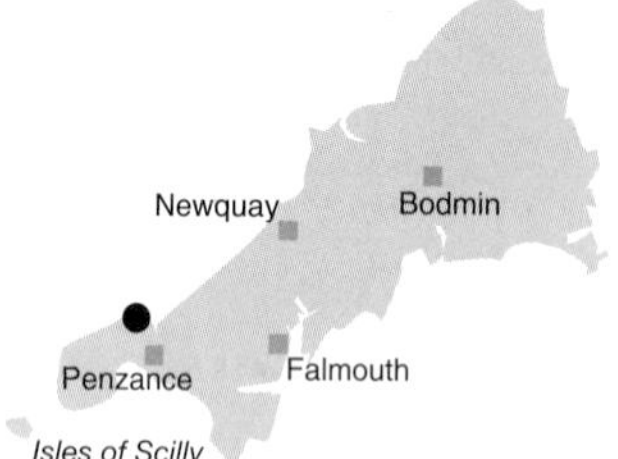

THE WELL HOUSE

ST KEYNE, LISKEARD, CORNWALL PL14 4RN

The West Country is renowned for its welcome and hospitality, and nowhere is this better demonstrated than at The Well House, situated just beyond the River Tamar. The façade of this lovely Victorian country manor, wrapped in rambling wisteria and jasmine trailers, is just one of a continuous series of delights including first-class service, modern luxury and impeccable standards of comfort and cooking. New proprietors Deborah and Richard Farrow continue to pay close attention to the smallest of details, an ethos which has earned the hotel numerous awards including 2 AA Red Stars and the restaurant 3 Rosettes. From the tastefully appointed bedrooms there are rural views and each private bathroom offers luxurious bath linens and toiletries. Continental breakfast can be served in bed or a traditional English breakfast may be taken in the dining room. Menus combine fresh, seasonal produce to create superbly presented dishes such as Cornish crab risotto, oven roasted monkfish and guinea fowl suprême. Tennis and swimming are on-site and the Cornish coastline provides unmatched scenery for walks. The Eden Project and the Lost Gardens of Heligan are a short drive away.

Our inspector loved: *The enthusiasm of the new owners, and wonderful surprises.*

Directions: Leave the A38 at Liskeard and take the A390 to the town centre. Take the B3254 south to St Keyne Well and then follow signs to the hotel.

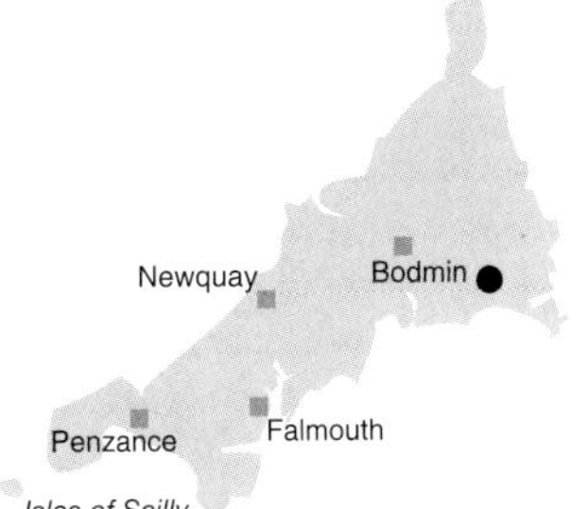

Web: www.johansens.com/wellhouse
E-mail: enquiries@wellhouse.co.uk
Tel: 0870 381 8975
International: +44 (0)1579 342001
Fax: 01579 343891

Price Guide:
single £105–£155
double/twin £145–£205
suite £205–£245

THE IDLE ROCKS HOTEL

HARBOURSIDE, ST MAWES, CORNWALL TR2 5AN

Set on the harbourside of St Mawes, a former fishing village on the tip of Cornwall's Roseland Peninsular, The Idle Rocks Hotel boasts a tranquil location for guests in need of a peaceful environment. From the narrow lanes of fisherman's cottages to the verdant fields leading down to the Cornish beaches, this waterside property enjoys idyllic surrounds. Food is the key criterion and the Water's Edge Restaurant has retained its 2 Rosettes consistently for over 14 years. Every table enjoys picturesque harbour views and serves a menu that is heavily influenced by Cornish sourced produce and seafood specialities. During the day, the best place to be is "On The Rocks" terrace, enjoy morning coffee, light lunches or an afternoon Cornish cream tea. After a sumptuous dinner, the well-appointed bedrooms, most of which offer a sea view, are a pleasure to discover. Housed in either the original building, a restored fisherman's cottage or a Georgian house, the 33 rooms are well-appointed with every modern comfort. Attractions in the nearby area include St Mawes Castle, the Eden Project, Lost Gardens of Heligan, Trelissick and Trebah Gardens. Sea lovers wishing to get closer to nature should take the foot ferry from St Mawes to Falmouth or try a day trip with the local ferry operator.

Our inspector loved: *The location, comfort and food.*

Directions: From St Austell take the A390 signposted Truro then turn left onto the A3287 signposted Tregony. Drive through Tregony then join the A3078 for St Mawes.

Web: www.johansens.com/idlerocks
E-mail: reception@idlerocks.co.uk
Tel: 0870 381 8324
International: +44 (0)1326 270771
Fax: 01326 270062

Price Guide: (including dinner)
single £126–£236
double/twin £168–£318

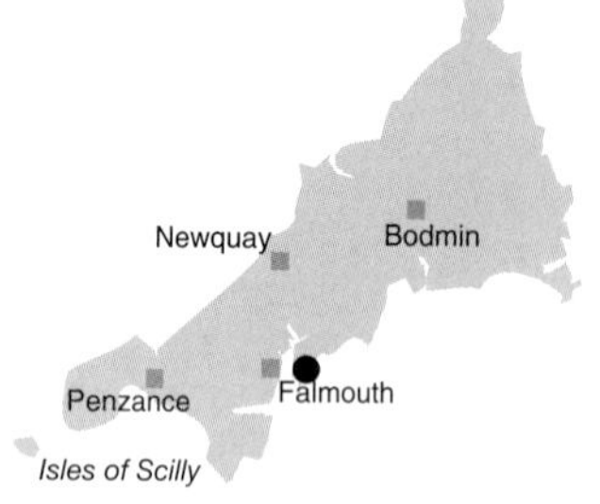

Alverton Manor

TREGOLLS ROAD, TRURO, CORNWALL TR1 1ZQ

Standing in the heart of the cathedral city of Truro and rising majestically over immaculate surrounds, Alverton Manor, awarded 2 AA Rosettes, is the epitome of a mid-19th-century family home. With its handsome sandstone walls, mullioned windows and superb Cornish Delabole slate roof, this elegant and gracious hotel is reminiscent of the splendour of a bygone era and proudly defends its claim to a Grade II* listing. Built for the Tweedy family over 150 years ago, it was acquired by the Bishop of Truro in the 1880s and later occupied by the Sister of the Epiphany before being taken over and restored to its former glory. Owner Michael Sagin and his talented and dedicated staff take pride in not only providing a high standard of service and modern English cuisine but also in enthusiastically maintaining a welcoming and relaxing ambience that attracts guests time and again. A superb entrance hall with a huge, decorative York stone archway leads to rooms that are comfortable in a quiet, elegant way. Lounges are restful, finely furnished, tastefully decorated and warmed by open fires in winter. The dining room is exquisite, and each of the 33 bedrooms has been individually designed to provide a special character, from the intimate to the grand. Golf, sailing and fishing nearby. Special golf and garden breaks available.

Our inspector loved: *The idea of ones own choice of weekend break – you choose and the hotel organises everything.*

Directions: Exit the M5, junction 30 and join the A30 through Devon into Cornwall at Fraddon and join the A39 to Truro.

Web: www.johansens.com/alverton
E-mail: reception@alvertonmanor.co.uk
Tel: 0870 381 9152
International: +44 (0)1872 276633
Fax: 01872 222989

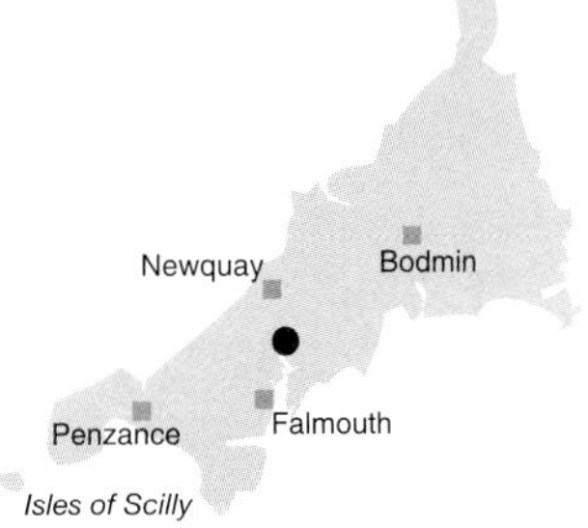

Price Guide:
single £75
double £125-£140
suite £160

Lovelady Shield Country House Hotel

NENTHEAD ROAD, ALSTON, CUMBRIA CA9 3LF

Reached by the A646, one of the worlds 10 best drives and 2½ miles from Alston, England's highest market town, Lovelady Shield, nestles in 3 acres of secluded riverside gardens. Bright log fires in the library and drawing room enhance the hotel's welcoming atmosphere. Owners Peter and Marie Haynes take great care to create a peaceful and tranquil haven where guests can relax and unwind. The 5-course dinners prepared by master chef Barrie Garton, rounded off by homemade puddings and a selection of English farmhouse cheeses, have consistently been awarded AA Rosettes for the past 10 years for food. Many guests first discover Lovelady Shield en route to Scotland. They then return to explore this beautiful and unspoilt part of England and experience the comforts of the hotel. Golf, fishing, shooting, pony-trekking and riding can be arranged locally. The Pennine Way, Hadrian's Wall and the Lake District are within easy reach. Facilities for small conferences and boardroom meetings are available. Open all year, Special Christmas, New Year, and short breaks are offered with special rates for 2 and 3-day stays.

Our inspector loved: *This informal relaxing hotel set in a picturesque valley.*

Directions: The hotel's driveway is by the junction of the B6294 and the A689, 2¼ miles east of Alston.

Web: www.johansens.com/loveladyshield
E-mail: enquiries@lovelady.co.uk
Tel: 0870 381 8705
International: +44 (0)1434 381203
Fax: 01434 381515

Price Guide:
single £75–£125
double/twin £150–£250

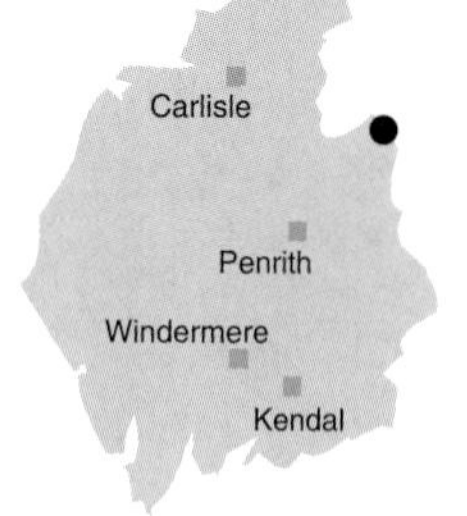

HOLBECK GHYLL COUNTRY HOUSE HOTEL

HOLBECK LANE, WINDERMERE, CUMBRIA LA23 1LU

The saying goes that all the best sites for building a house in England were taken long before the days of the motor car. Holbeck Ghyll has one such prime position. It was built in the early days of the 19th century and is superbly located overlooking Lake Windermere and the Langdale Fells. Today this luxury hotel has an outstanding reputation and is managed personally and expertly by its proprietors, David and Patricia Nicholson. As well as being awarded 4 AA Red Stars they are among an elite who have won an AA Courtesy and Care Award, Country Life Hotel of the Year (2002) and in the 2006 Northern Hospitality Awards were voted Best Hotel. The majority of bedrooms are large and have spectacular and breathtaking lake views. All are refurbished to a very high standard and include decanters of sherry, fresh flowers, fluffy bathrobes and much more. There are 6 rooms in the Lodge and both Madison House and the Miss Potter Suite opened during 2006. The oak-panelled restaurant, awarded a coveted Michelin star and 3 AA Rosettes, is a delightful setting for memorable dining and the meals are classically prepared, with the focus on flavours and presentation, while an extensive wine list reflects quality and variety. The hotel has an all-weather tennis court and a health spa with gym, sauna and treatment facilities.

Our inspector loved: *The delicious dinner in the oak-panelled restaurant with extensive views over Lake Windermere.*

Directions: From Windermere, pass Brockhole Visitors Centre, then after $\frac{1}{2}$ mile turn right into Holbeck Lane. Hotel is $\frac{1}{2}$ mile on left.

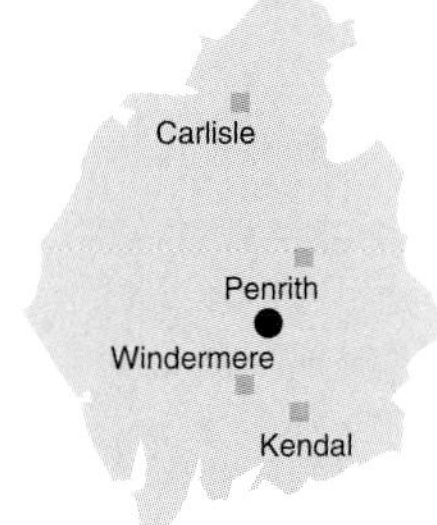

Web: www.johansens.com/holbeckghyll
E-mail: stay@holbeckghyll.com
Tel: 0870 381 8601
International: +44 (0)15394 32375
Fax: 015394 34743

Price Guide: (including 4 course dinner)
single from £135
double/twin £110–£380
suite £240–£470

Rothay Manor

ROTHAY BRIDGE, AMBLESIDE, CUMBRIA LA22 0EH

A short walk from the centre of Ambleside and ¼ mile from Lake Windermere, this Regency country house hotel, set within landscaped gardens, has been personally managed by the Nixon family for 40 years. Renowned for its relaxed, comfortable and friendly atmosphere, each of the 16 bedrooms in the hotel is individually designed, some with balconies overlooking the garden, and there are 3 spacious, private suites, 2 of which are situated within the grounds. Family rooms and suites are also available, and a ground-floor bedroom and one suite designed with particular attention to the comfort of those with disabilities. A varied menu is prepared with flair and imagination using local produce whenever possible, complemented by a personally compiled wine list. Guests are entitled to free use of nearby Low Wood Leisure Club with swimming pool, sauna, steam room, gym, Jacuzzi, squash courts, sunbeds and a health and beauty salon. Local activities such as walking, sightseeing, cycling, sailing, horse riding, golf and fishing (permits available) can be arranged. Alternatively, spend the day cruising on Lake Windermere. Special interest holidays from October-May include: gardening, antiques, walking, bridge, music, painting and Lake District heritage. Small functions and conferences can be catered for and short breaks are available at various times through the year.

Our inspector loved: *Home-made cakes and biscuits at this relaxing oasis.*

Directions: ¼ mile from Ambleside on the A593 to Coniston.
Closed 3rd-27th January.

Web: www.johansens.com/rothaymanor
E-mail: hotel@rothaymanor.co.uk
Tel: 0870 381 8869
International: +44 (0)15394 33605
Fax: 015394 33607

Price Guide:
single £85–£125
double/twin £145–£175
suite £190–£215

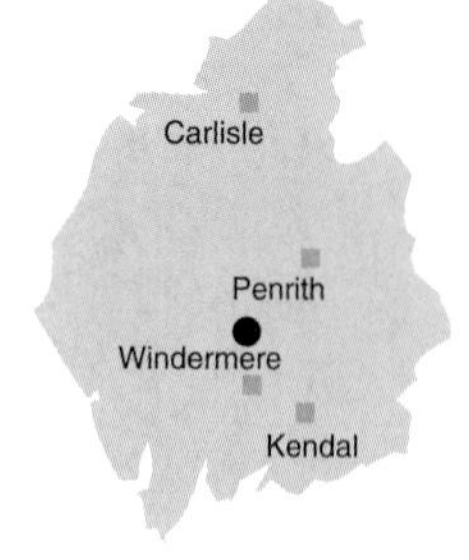

Tufton Arms Hotel

MARKET SQUARE, APPLEBY-IN-WESTMORLAND, CUMBRIA CA16 6XA

This distinguished Victorian coaching inn, owned and run by the Milsom family, has been refurbished to provide a high standard of comfort. The bedrooms evoke the style of the 19th century, when the Tufton Arms became one of the premier hotels in Victorian England. The kitchen is run under the auspices of David Milsom and Lee Braithwaite, who spoil guests for choice with a gourmet dinner menu as well as a grill menu, the restaurant being renowned for its fish dishes. Complementing the cuisine is an extensive wine list. There are conference and meeting rooms including the air-conditioned Hothfield Suite which can accommodate up to 100 people. Appleby, the historic county town of Westmorland, stands in splendid countryside and is ideal for touring the Lakes, Yorkshire Dales and Pennines. It is also a convenient stop-over en route to Scotland. Members of the Milsom family also run The Royal Hotel in Comrie. Superb fishing for wild brown trout on a 24-mile stretch of the main River Eden, salmon fishing can be arranged on the lower reaches of the river. Shooting parties for grouse, duck and pheasant are a speciality. Appleby has an 18-hole moorland golf course.

Our inspector loved: *The "Ian Oats" Scottish sporting paintings for sale in the bar.*

Directions: In centre of Appleby (bypassed by the A66), 38 miles west of Scotch Corner, 13 miles east of Penrith (M6 junction 40), 12 miles from M6 junction 38.

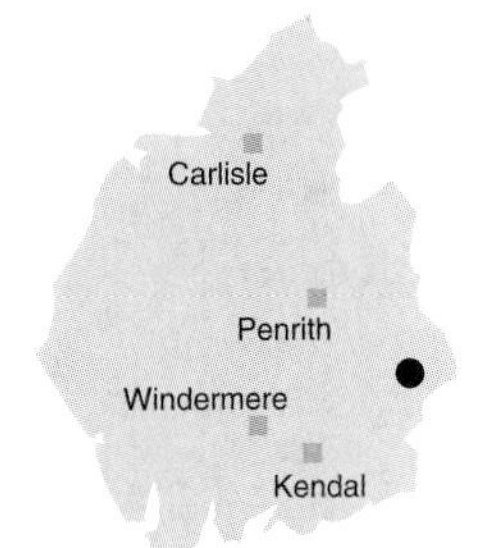

Web: www.johansens.com/tuftonarms
E-mail: info@tuftonarmshotel.co.uk
Tel: 0870 381 8956
International: +44 (0)17683 51593
Fax: 017683 52761

Price Guide:
single £75–£105
double/twin £105–£150
suite £170

FARLAM HALL HOTEL

RELAIS & CHATEAUX

BRAMPTON, CUMBRIA CA8 2NG

Directions: Farlam Hall is 2½ miles east of Brampton on the A689, not in Farlam village.

Web: www.johansens.com/farlamhall
E-mail: farlam@relaischateaux.com
Tel: 0870 381 8581
International: +44 (0)16977 46234
Fax: 016977 46683

Price Guide: (including dinner)
single £150–£175
double/twin £280–£330

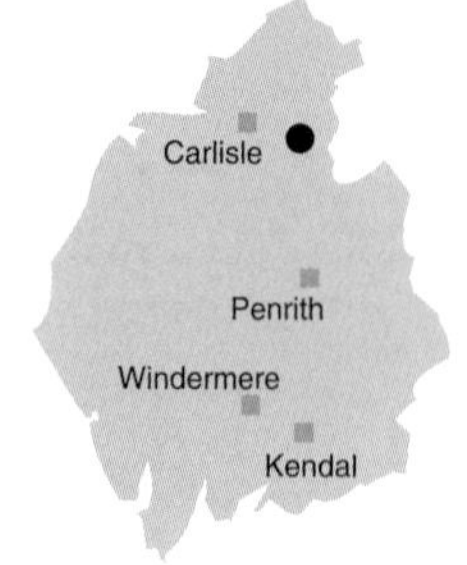

Farlam Hall was opened in 1975 by the Quinion and Stevenson families who over the years have managed to achieve and maintain consistently high standards of food, service and comfort. These standards have been recognised and rewarded by all the major guides and membership of Relais et Châteaux. This old border house, dating in parts from the 17th century, is set in mature gardens, which can be seen from the elegant lounges and dining room, creating a relaxing and pleasing environment. The fine silver and crystal in the dining room complement the quality of the English country house cooking produced by Barry Quinion and his team of chefs. There are 12 individually decorated bedrooms varying in size and shape, some having Jacuzzi baths, one an antique four-poster bed and there are 2 ground floor bedrooms. This area offers many different attractions: miles of unspoilt countryside for walking, 8 golf courses within 30 minutes of the hotel, Hadrian's Wall, Lanercost Priory and Carlisle with its castle, cathedral and museum. The Lake District, Scottish Borders and Yorkshire Dales each make an ideal day's touring. Winter and spring breaks are offered. Closed Christmas.

Our inspector loved: *The Luxurious elegance of this borders hotel.*

Netherwood Hotel

LINDALE ROAD, GRANGE-OVER-SANDS, CUMBRIA LA11 6ET

This dramatic and stately residence was built as a family house in the 19th century, and still retains its family ambience in the careful hands of its long - standing owners, the Fallowfields. Impressive oak panelling is a key feature of the property and provides a marvellous backdrop to the public areas – the lounge, lounge bar and ballroom, where log fires roar in the winter months. All of the bedrooms have en-suite facilities, and many have been furnished to extremely high modern standards; all have picturesque views of the sea, woodland or gardens. The light and airy restaurant is housed in the conservatory area on the first floor of the property, maximising the dramatic views over Morecambe Bay. Here, a daily changing menu of freshly prepared specialities caters for a wide variety of tastes and is complemented by an extensive selection of fine wines. A stunning indoor swimming pool and fitness centre is a delightful haven and a keen favourite with families – the pool even has toys for younger guests - whilst an extensive range of beauty treatments, massage and complementary therapies is available at "Equilibrium", the hotel's health spa. Special breaks available.

Our inspector loved: *The oak panelling in the hall and lounge and the stunning views over Morecambe Bay.*

Directions: Take the M6, exit 36 then the A590 towards Barrow-in-Burness. Then the B5277 into Grange-Over-Sands. The hotel is on the right before the town.

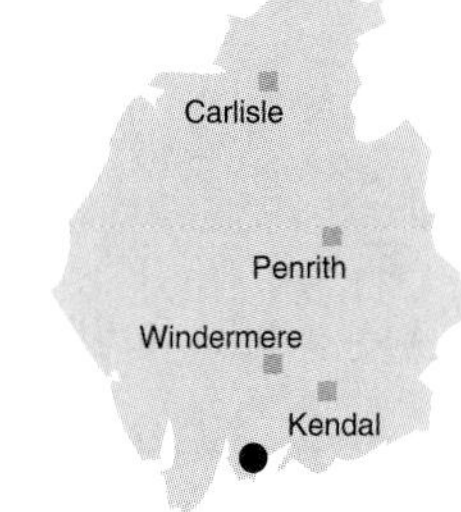

Web: www.johansens.com/netherwood
E-mail: enquiries@netherwood-hotel.co.uk
Tel: 0870 381 8729
International: +44 (0)15395 32552
Fax: 015395 34121

Price Guide:
single £80–£115
double £120-£190

Armathwaite Hall Hotel

BASSENTHWAITE LAKE, KESWICK, CUMBRIA CA12 4RES

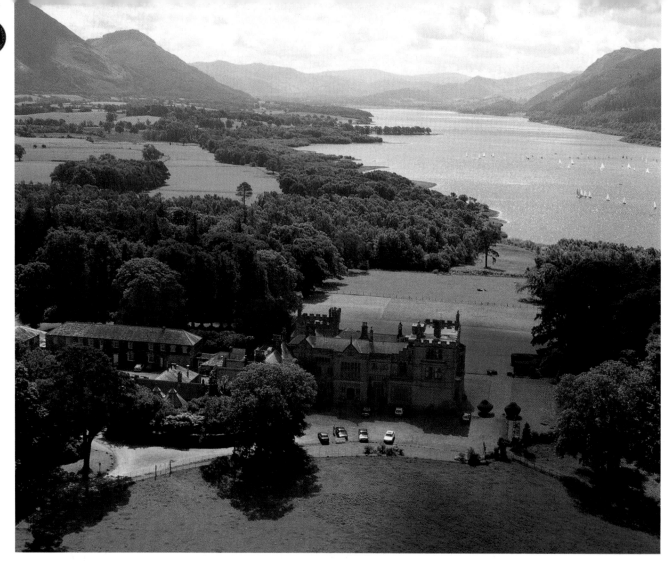

With an awe-inspiring backdrop of Skiddaw Mountain and the surrounding Lakeland fells, on the shores of Bassenthwaite Lake, the romantic Armathwaite Hall is the perfect location for lovers of boating, walking and climbing. Amidst 400 acres of deer park and woodland, this 4-star country house is a tranquil hideaway for those wishing to relax and escape from modern day living, where comfort is intensified by an emphasis on quality and old-fashioned hospitality, as you would expect of a family-owned and run hotel. The timeless elegance of this stately home is complemented by original features such as wood panelling, magnificent stonework, artworks and antiques. Beautiful bedrooms are decorated in a warm, traditional style and guests can arrange to have champagne, chocolates and flowers on their arrival. The Rosette restaurant offers exceptional cuisine created by Master Chef Kevin Dowling, who uses the finest local seasonal produce. In the Spa there is a gym, indoor swimming pool and a holistic Beauty Salon. Clay pigeon shooting, quad bike safaris, falconry, mountain biking, tennis and croquet are all available, with sailing, fishing and golf nearby. Family friendly with a programme of activities for children and the attraction of Trotters World of Animals on the estate, home to many traditional favourites and endangered species.

Our inspector loved: *The spectacular views over Bassenthwaite Lake.*

Directions: Take the M6 to Penrith. At J40 take the A66 to Keswick roundabout then the A591 towards Carlisle. Go 8 miles to Castle Inn junction, turn left and Armanthwaite Hall is 300 yards ahead.

Web: www.johansens.com/armathwaite
E-mail: reservations@armathwaite-hall.com
Tel: 0870 381 8478
International: +44 (0)17687 76551
Fax: 017687 76220

Price Guide:
single £75–£185
double/twin£160–£360

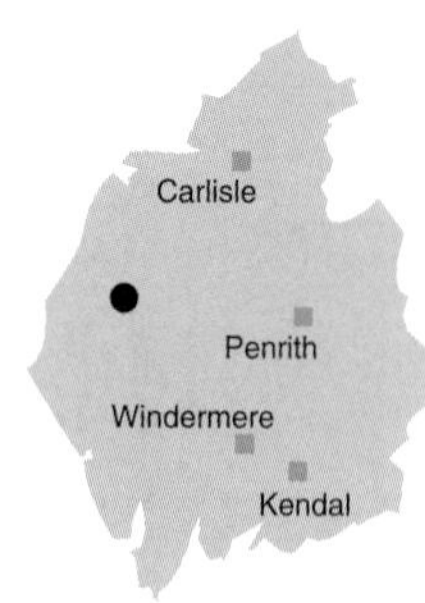

The Lodore Falls Hotel

BORROWDALE, KESWICK, CUMBRIA CA12 5UX

Imagine a place with stunning lake and mountain views – the Lodore Falls Hotel is such a place. Situated in the picturesque Borrowdale Valley with 20 acres of lake frontage and landscaped gardens and with the famous Lodore waterfalls in the grounds, this hotel offers not only a magnificent setting in the heart of the Lake District, but also the very best in hospitality. The 71 en-suite Fell and Lake View Rooms, including family rooms and luxurious suites, some with balconies, have every modern amenity, such as Playstations and Internet access. Light meals and coffee can be enjoyed in the comfortable lounges, whilst the cocktail bar is the ideal venue for a pre-dinner drink. The superb Lake View restaurant serves the best in English and Continental cuisine accompanied by fine wines after a long day exploring the surroundings. Free midweek golf is available at nearby Keswick Golf Club, and the hotel's leisure facilities include an indoor and outdoor swimming pool, sauna, gymnasium, tennis and squash court and beauty salon. In addition to an outdoor children's playground an activity programme is also available for 2 hours daily during school holidays. The hotel's large function suites can accommodate up to 200 guests – ideal for weddings, conferences and meetings.

Our inspector loved: *Having a stroll up to the Lodore Falls before dinner.*

Directions: Take the M6 at junction 40. Take the A66 into Keswick then the B5289 to Borrowdale. After 3 minutes, the hotel is on the left-hand side. The nearest railway station is Penrith.

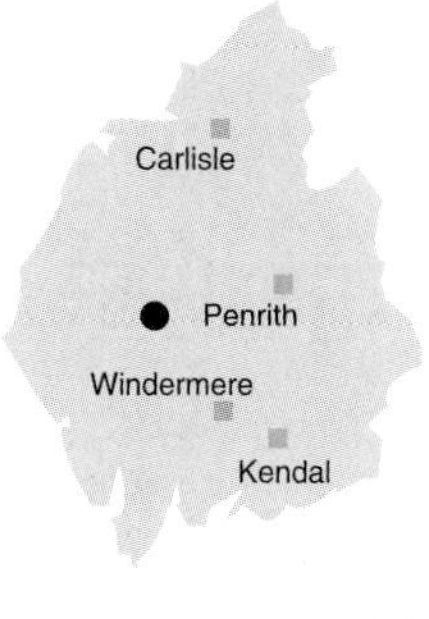

Carlisle
Penrith
Windermere
Kendal

Web: www.johansens.com/lodorefalls
E-mail: lodorefalls@lakedistricthotels.net
Tel: 0870 381 9314
International: +44 (0)17687 77285
Fax: 017687 77343

Price Guide:
single from £72
double from £132
suite from £234

71 200

Sharrow Bay Country House Hotel

HOWTOWN, LAKE ULLSWATER, PENRITH, CUMBRIA CA10 2LZ

Sharrow Bay Country House Hotel is legendary: a founding British member of Relais & Chateaux and reputedly the world's first ever country house hotel, the hotel's reputation as a magical luxury hotel in a breathtakingly beautiful setting has spread worldwide. Nestled in 12 acres of private gardens and woodland on the shore of the stunningly beautiful Lake Ullswater and surrounded by magnificent fells, this is a haven of peace and tranquillity with unrivalled views of the spectacular Ullswater landscape. All the bedrooms are elegantly furnished and guests are guaranteed the utmost comfort. In addition to the main hotel, there are 2 cottages nearby, the Gate House Lodge and Bank House, which offer similarly luxurious accommodation. The view of the lake and fells from the dining room is renowned. The cuisine has won numerous accolades including the highly coveted Michelin Star and is complemented by an award-winning wine list. Dining at Sharrow Bay, be it breakfast, lunch or dinner, or the fabulous afternoon tea, is an experience to be shared and cherished.

Our inspector loved: *The refurbished bedrooms up at Bank House with their stunning views across Lake Ullswater.*

Directions: Take the M6, junction 40, then the A592 to Lake Ullswater, into Pooley Bridge. Take Howtown Road for 2 miles.

Web: www.johansens.com/sharrowbaycountryhouse
E-mail: info@sharrowbay.co.uk
Tel: 0870 381 8891
International: +44 (0)17684 86301/86483
Fax: 017684 86349

Price Guide: (including 6-course dinner and full English breakfast)
single £170–£225
double/twin £350–£440
suites from £460

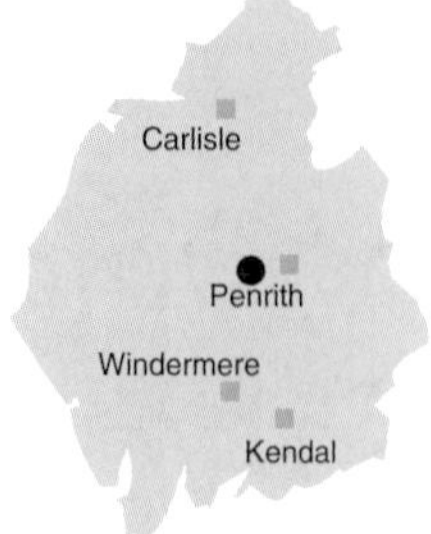

THE INN ON THE LAKE

LAKE ULLSWATER, GLENRIDDING, CUMBRIA CA11 0PE

With its 15 acres of lawns sweeping down to the shore of Lake Ullswater, The Inn on the Lake boasts one of the most spectacular settings in the Lake District. This lovely 19th-century hotel offers a wide range of excellent facilities including sailing from its private jetty, pitch and put and croquet. Guests may relax with a drink in the calm comfort of the lounges downstairs or visit The Rambler's Bar in the grounds for the informal ambience of a Lakeland pub. Superb food is served in the Lake View restaurant. Most of the 46 en-suite bedrooms have stunning views across the Lake or face the dramatic Helvellyn mountain range. The lake-view four-poster rooms are particularly romantic. The hotel can host marriage ceremonies and wedding receptions, and can cater for exclusive private functions as well as conference facilities for up to120 delegates. The list of local activities for children and adults alike is endless: rock climbing, pony trekking, canoeing, windsurfing and fishing. Trips aboard the Ullswater steamers can be organised, and many stunning Lake District walks start from Glenridding.

Our inspector loved: *Strolling across the lawned garden down to Lake Ullswater.*

Directions: Leave the M6 at junction 40, then take the A66 west. At the first roundabout, by Rheged Discovery Centre, head towards Pooley Bridge then follow the shoreline of Lake Ullswater to Glenridding.

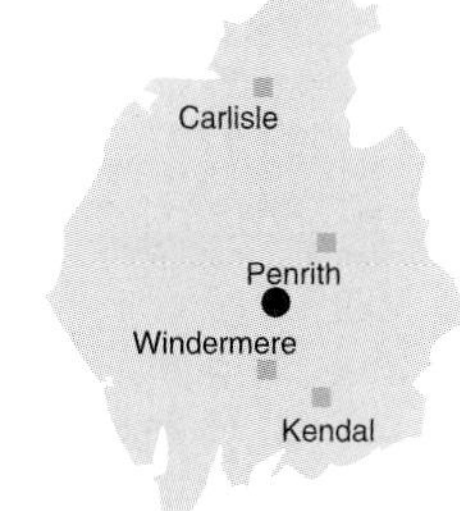

Web: www.johansens.com/innonthelake
E-mail: innonthelake@lakedistricthotels.net
Tel: 0870 381 8640
International: +44 (0)17684 82444
Fax: 017684 82303

Price Guide:
single £75–£130
double £132–£194

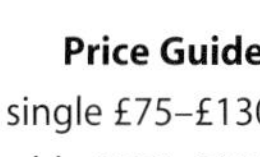

Rampsbeck Country House Hotel

WATERMILLOCK, LAKE ULLSWATER, NR PENRITH, CUMBRIA CA11 0LP

A beautifully situated hotel, Rampsbeck Country House stands in 18 acres of landscaped gardens and meadows leading to the shores of Lake Ullswater. Built in 1714, it first became an hotel in 1947, before the present owners acquired it in 1983. Thomas and Marion Gibb, with the help of Marion's mother, Marguerite MacDowall, completely refurbished Rampsbeck with the aim of maintaining its character and adding only to its comfort. Most of the well-appointed bedrooms have lake and garden views. Three have a private balcony and the suite overlooks the lake. In the elegant drawing room, a log fire burns and French windows lead to the garden. Guests and non-residents are welcome to dine in the intimate candle-lit restaurant. Imaginative menus offer a choice of delicious dishes, carefully prepared by Master Chef Andrew McGeorge and his team. A good bar lunch menu offers light snacks as well as hot food. Guests can stroll through the gardens, play croquet or fish from the lake shore, around which there are designated walks. Lake steamer trips, riding, golf, sailing, wind-surfing and fell-walking are available nearby. Closed January to mid-February. Children and dogs by arrangement only. Special breaks available

Our inspector loved: *The wonderful views of Lake Ullswater and the beautiful landscaped gardens.*

Directions: Leave M6 at junction 40, take A592 to Ullswater. At T-junction at lake turn right; hotel is 1½ miles on left.

Web: www.johansens.com/rampsbeckcountryhouse
E-mail: enquiries@rampsbeck.fsnet.co.uk
Tel: 0870 381 8848
International: +44 (0)17684 86442
Fax: 017684 86688

Price Guide:
single £75–£150
double/twin £120–£260
suite £260

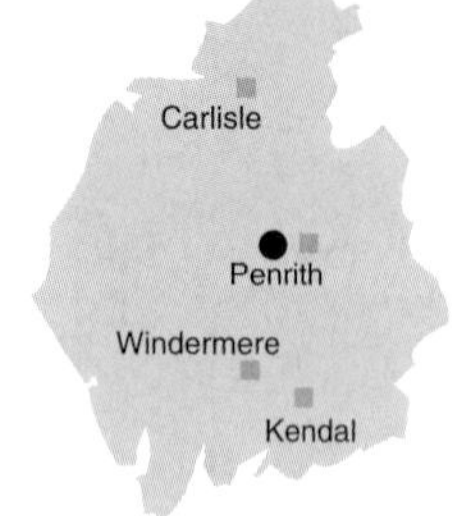

Gilpin Lodge

CROOK ROAD, WINDERMERE, CUMBRIA LA23 3NE

This elegant, luxurious, family-run hotel is set in 20 private acres of woodland, moors and country gardens, 2 miles from Lake Windermere and 12 miles from the M6. The original building, tastefully extended and modernised, dates back to 1901, and the long-standing staff, as much a feature as the Cunliffe Family, ensure a relaxed ambience with friendly, personal care and attention to detail. Fresh flowers, crisp linen, beautiful furniture and log fires in winter are all part of the Gilpin hospitality, and sumptuous bedrooms have en-suite bathrooms with every comfort. Some guest rooms have patio doors, split levels and spa baths while the suites have private gardens and cedarwood hot tubs. The exquisite food has received a Michelin Star, 3 AA Rosettes, 2 Egon Ronay Stars and there are over 300 wines in the recently overhauled wine list. The beautiful gardens are the perfect place in which to savour the beautiful Lakeland scenery. This is Wordsworth and Beatrix Potter country with stately homes, gardens and castles to visit nearby. Guests have free use of a nearby leisure club and Windermere Golf Course is ½ mile away. This is a Relais & Châteaux hotel awarded 4 AA Red Stars, voted in the Top Ten Country Retreats by the AA, an AA Top Ten Small Hotel and is recipient of the English Tourist Council Gold Award. Visit Gilpin Lodge's website for a virtual tour.

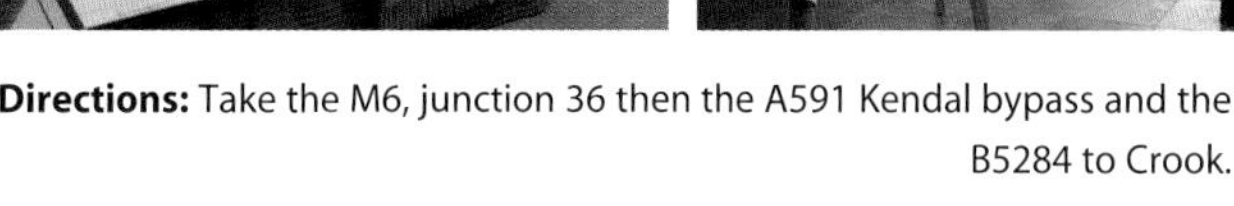

Directions: Take the M6, junction 36 then the A591 Kendal bypass and the B5284 to Crook.

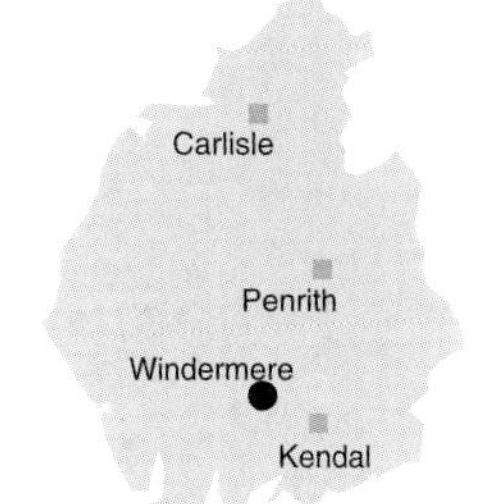

Web: www.johansens.com/gilpinlodge
E-mail: hotel@gilpinlodge.co.uk
Tel: 0870 381 8546
International: +44 (0)15394 88818
Fax: 015394 88058

Price Guide: (including 5-course dinner)
single £175
double/twin £240–£360

Our inspector loved: *The garden suites with private patio and hot tubs.*

LINTHWAITE HOUSE HOTEL

CROOK ROAD, BOWNESS-ON-WINDERMERE, CUMBRIA LA23 3JA

Situated in 14 acres of gardens and woods in the heart of the Lake District, Linthwaite House overlooks Lake Windermere and Belle Isle, with Claife Heights and Coniston Old Man beyond. Here, guests will find themselves amid spectacular scenery, yet only a short drive from the motorway network. The hotel combines stylish originality with the best of traditional English hospitality. Superbly decorated en-suite bedrooms, most of which have lake or garden views. The comfortable lounge is the perfect place to unwind and there is a fire on winter evenings. In the restaurant excellent cuisine features the best of fresh, local produce, accompanied by a fine selection of wines. Within the hotel grounds, there is a 9-hole putting green and a par-3 practice hole. Fly fishermen can fish for brown trout in the hotel tarn. Guests have complimentary use of a private swimming pool and leisure club nearby, while fell walks begin at the hotel's front door. The area around Linthwaite abounds with places of interest: this is Beatrix Potter and Wordsworth country, and there is much to interest the visitor.

Our inspector loved: *Walking through the landscaped gardens up to the tarn with its spectacular views of Lake Windermere.*

Directions: From the M6, junction 36 follow Kendal by-pass for 8 miles. Take the B5284, Crook Road, for 6 miles. 1 mile beyond Windermere Golf Club, Linthwaite House is signposted on the left.

Web: www.johansens.com/linthwaitehouse
E-mail: stay@linthwaite.com
Tel: 0870 381 8694
International: +44 (0)15394 88600
Fax: 015394 88601

Price Guide:
single £120–£150
double/twin £145–£300
suite £280–£320

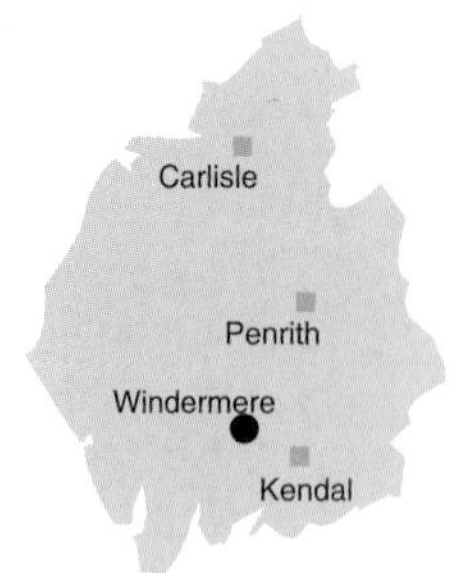

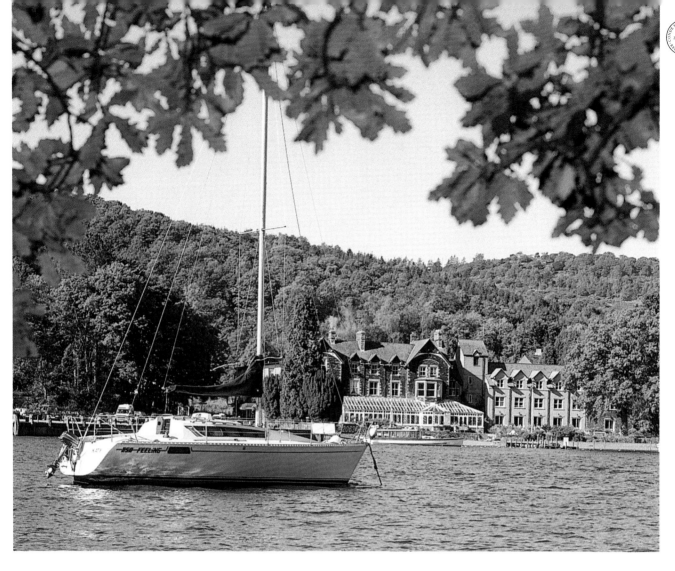

Lakeside Hotel on Lake Windermere

LAKESIDE, NEWBY BRIDGE, CUMBRIA LA12 8AT

Lakeside Hotel offers you a unique location on the water's edge of Lake Windermere. It is a classic, traditional Lakeland hotel offering 4-star facilities and service. All the bedrooms are en suite and enjoy individually designed fabrics and colours, many of the rooms offer breathtaking views of the lake. Guests may dine in either the award-winning Lakeview Restaurant or Ruskin's Brasserie, where extensive menus offer a wide selection of dishes including Cumbrian specialities. The Lakeside Conservatory serves drinks and light meals throughout the day – once there you are sure to fall under the spell of this peaceful location. Berthed next to the hotel there are cruisers which will enable you to explore the lake from the water. To enhance your stay, there is a leisure club including a 17m indoor pool, gymnasium, sauna, steam room and health and beauty suites. The hotel offers a fully equipped conference centre and many syndicate suites allowing plenty of scope and flexibility. Most of all you are assured of a stay in an unrivalled setting of genuine character. The original panelling and beams of the old coaching inn create an excellent ambience, whilst you are certain to enjoy the quality and friendly service. Special breaks available.

Our inspector loved: *Enjoying a delicious afternoon tea in the Lakeside conservatory watching the boats sail by.*

Directions: From the M6, junction 36 join the A590 to Newby Bridge then turn right over bridge towards Hawkshead. The hotel is 1 mile on the right.

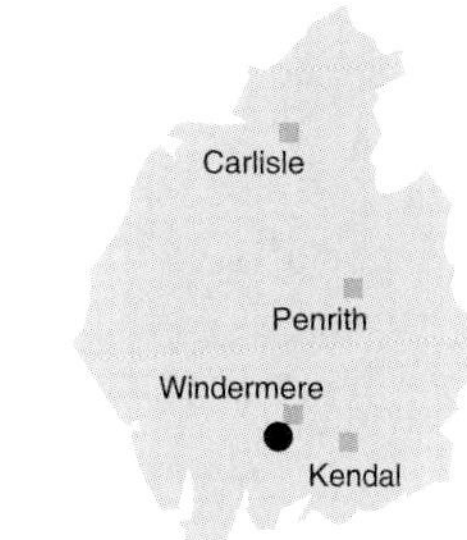

Web: www.johansens.com/lakeside
E-mail: sales@lakesidehotel.co.uk
Tel: 0870 381 8672
International: +44 (0)15395 30001
Fax: 015395 31699

Price Guide:
single from £150
double/twin £185–£295
suite from £325

Callow Hall

MAPPLETON ROAD, ASHBOURNE, DERBYSHIRE DE6 2AA

The Spencer Family welcome guests to this sublime Victorian hall, surrounded by a 44-acre estate overlooking the valleys of Bentley Brook and the Rover Dove. Former proprietors David and Dorothy Spencer have handed the day-to-day running of Callow Hall on to their daughter Emma and son Anthony who invite guests to this retreat with gloriously traditional décor. Fine antiques and fireplaces combine with ornate ceilings to give a sense of grandeur to this country house, while the bedrooms offer comfortable fabrics and striking vistas across the landscape. Gastronomes will be delighted with the fine cuisine served in the formal yet convivial dining room. The Spencers take great pride in home baking, smoking and curing; crafts that have been passed down through the family since 1724. The menu includes local produce such as game and Anthony's passion for wines is evident in the extensive list, which includes over 100 choices. Private parties and banquets can be held in a formal dining room and groups of 20 can meet and eat in a function room, ideal for VIPs. Country pursuits such as trout fishing can be arranged, whilst stately homes including Chatsworth, Hardwick and Kedleston are nearby but the Peak National Park must not be missed.

Our inspector loved: *The fact that Emma and her brother Anthony have taken over seamlessly. It is still very special, unspoilt and very charming.*

Directions: Take the A515 through Ashbourne towards Buxton. At the Bowling Green Inn on the brow of a steep hill, turn left, then take the first right, signposted Mappleton and the hotel is over the bridge on the right.

Web: www.johansens.com/callowhall
E-mail: stay@callowhall.co.uk
Tel: 0870 381 8400
International: +44 (0)1335 300900
Fax: 01335 300512

Price Guide:
single £98–£120
double/twin £145–£195
suite £225

The Izaak Walton Hotel

DOVEDALE, NEAR ASHBOURNE, DERBYSHIRE DE6 2AY

This charming farmhouse dates back to the 17th century, and is idyllically situated with glorious views over the Derbyshire countryside. The River Dove meanders in the valley below and the atmosphere is one of peace and tranquillity. The hotel takes its name from the author of "The Compleat Angler," and great care has been taken to retain the building's character. The bedrooms are individually designed to incorporate interesting period features; the original farmhouse building features oak beams and traditional décor. The AA Rosette-awarded Haddon Restaurant serves a diverse menu of creative interpretations on traditional dishes, which is enhanced by an excellent selection of fine wines from respected worldwide vineyards. The warm and welcoming Dovedale Bar is located in the oldest part of the building and its walls are adorned with interesting fishing memorabilia. Here, guests can enjoy light snacks and informal meals. The hotel has permanent rods on the River Dove and private tuition can be arranged. The Peak District National Park is close by and Chatsworth House, Haddon Hall, Staffordshire Potteries and Alton Towers are within easy access. The hotel welcomes families and is ideal for weddings, family parties, meetings and conferences.

Our inspector loved: *The wonderful views from the restaurant, very theraputic.*

Directions: Dovedale is 2 miles north-west of Ashbourne between the A515 and A52.

Glossop
Sheffield
Chesterfield
Bakewell
Nottingham
Derby

Web: www.johansens.com/izaakwalton
E-mail: reception@izaakwaltonhotel.com
Tel: 0870 381 8642
International: +44 (0)1335 350555
Fax: 01335 350539

Price Guide:
single £110
double/twin £135–£175

HASSOP HALL

HASSOP, NEAR BAKEWELL, DERBYSHIRE DE45 1NS

The recorded history of Hassop Hall reaches back 900 years to the Domesday Book, to a time when the political scene in England was still dominated by the power struggle between the barons and the King, when the only sure access to that power was through possession of land. By 1643, when the Civil War was raging, the Hall was under the ownership of Rowland Eyre, who turned it into a Royalist garrison. It was the scene of several skirmishes before it was recaptured after the Parliamentary victory. Since purchasing Hassop Hall in 1975, Thomas Chapman has determinedly pursued the preservation of its outstanding heritage. Guests can enjoy the beautifully maintained gardens as well as the splendid countryside of the surrounding area. The bedrooms, some of which are particularly spacious, are well furnished and comfortable. A four-poster bedroom is available for romantic occasions. A comprehensive dinner menu offers a wide and varied selection of dishes, with catering for most tastes. As well as the glories of the Peak District, places to visit include Chatsworth House, Haddon Hall and Buxton Opera House. Christmas opening – details on application. Inclusive rates available on request.

Our inspector loved: *So many special points here. For 32 years the Chapmans have delighted and pampered, never faltering on its style.*

Directions: From the M1, exit 29 (Chesterfield), take the A619 to Baslow, then the A623 to Calver. Turn left at the lights to B6001. Hassop Hall is 2 miles on the right.

Web: www.johansens.com/hassophall
E-mail: hassophallhotel@btinternet.com
Tel: 0870 381 8586
International: +44 (0)1629 640488
Fax: 01629 640577

Price Guide: (excluding breakfast)
double/twin £89–£225

EAST LODGE COUNTRY HOUSE HOTEL

ROWSLEY, NR MATLOCK, DERBYSHIRE DE4 2EF

A glorious tree-lined driveway guides visitors to this elegant country house hotel set in the heart of the Peak District National Park. Upon entering the reception hall of this award-winning property, guests are immediately enveloped by a warm, hospitable ambience that prevails throughout the property. The surrounding 10 acres of magnificent grounds create a haven of tranquil privacy making East Lodge an excellent location for weddings and corporate gatherings. David and Joan Hardman, and son Iain, will endeavor to meet any request and ensure that no attention to detail is spared. A no-smoking policy operates throughout the hotel including the en-suite bedrooms, which are thoughtfully designed. Traditional features and contemporary facilities such as Broadband availablity, successfully fuse together, and the luxurious bathrooms boast baths, toiletries and soft, sumptuous towels. In the restaurant, which has been awarded 2 AA Rosettes, Chef Marcus Hall creates interesting and stylish dishes. A romantic garden room and attractive terrace merely add to the rustic charm of this property, easily accessible from Sheffield, Manchester, Nottingham, Derby and London, and is the nearest hotel to the historic Chatsworth House. Fishing on the River Derwent, within the Chatsworth Estate, can be arranged.

Directions: Set back from the A6 in Rowsley village, 3 miles from Bakewell. The hotel entrance is adjacent to the B6012 junction to Sheffield/Chatsworth.

Glossop
Sheffield
Chesterfield
Bakewell
Nottingham
Derby

Web: www.johansens.com/eastlodgecountryhouse
E-mail: info@eastlodge.com
Tel: 0870 381 8496
International: +44 (0)1629 734474
Fax: 01629 733949

Price Guide:
single from £100
double/twin from £150

Our inspector loved: *The tranquil balance of business and leisure.*

THE PEACOCK AT ROWSLEY

ROWSLEY, NEAR MATLOCK, DERBYSHIRE DE4 2EB

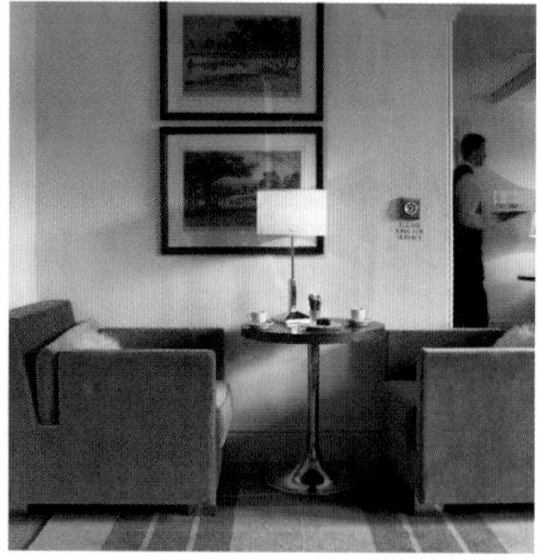

Directions: Take the M1, exit 28 and head for the A6. Rowsley is midway between Matlock and Bakewell. Transfers to and from nearby East Midlands Airport can be organised.

Web: www.johansens.com/peacockrowsley
E-mail: reception@thepeacockatrowsley.com
Tel: 0870 381 8805
International: +44 (0)1629 733518
Fax: 01629 732671

Price Guide:
single from £85
double/twin from £165

Once the Dower House for Haddon Hall, this superb 17th-century country inn has returned to the Haddon Estate after nearly 50 years and remains a renowned historic fishing hostelry with a 3-star AA rating. An exciting refurbishment has been overseen by Lord Edward Manners of Haddon Hall, and today the hotel's eclectic mix of ancient and modern is carried off with great style and charisma. Interiors have been created by the magnificent French designer India Mahdavi, and furnishings are bold featuring contemporary colours and textures. Attractive gardens lead down to the River Derwent and fishermen are spoilt for choice as the River Wye is the only river in the country with wild rainbow trout and brown trout. Catch and drop fishing is observed in all but one area of the River in order to encourage natural breeding; reservations and tuition are arranged at the hotel, where there is a purpose-built drying room. The 2 AA Rosette-awarded restaurant offers fine British cuisine, with a modern influence, and a good selection of bar food is available. Guests have free use of the nearby gym, enjoy beauty treatments by arrangement at Woodlands Fitness Centre, and complimentary golf on the scenic Bakewell golf course can be arranged. Haddon Hall, Chatsworth House, Peak District National Park and Sheffield are all on the doorstep. Children are welcome Mondays to Thursdays.

Our inspector loved: *The harmony of traditional and modern values.*

  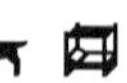     

Riber Hall

MATLOCK, DERBYSHIRE DE4 5JU

There could be few more picturesque settings than this stately Elizabethan manor house standing in its own walled garden in the foothills of the Pennine range. Views over the Peak National Park are outstanding and the atmosphere is one of total tranquillity. Privately owned and managed by the same family for over 35 years the latest round of awards stands testament to their skill and high standards of service. 14 spacious bedrooms are each furnished with period antiques and elegant beds, the majority of which are antique four-poster. Log fires and oak beams of the lounge convey an instant sense of intimacy and timelessness. The restaurant is renowned for its attentive service, game (when in season) and inspired French classical and modern English cuisine. The excellent wine list has also been rated AA Wine Award Finalist in the Top 25 in the UK for 5 consecutive years and was finalist for the Tattinger Condé Nast Johansens wine list award for 2005. This is the perfect setting for both weddings and conferences and there is much to see in the surrounding area for delegates or wedding guests with time to spare. Chatsworth House, Haddon Hall and many world heritage sites are within easy reach. The beautiful Peak District scenery is breathtaking. East Midlands, Sheffield and Birmingham Airports are all nearby.

Our inspector loved: *Sipping coffee in front of the wonderful log fire and absorbing the atmosphere of this wonderful building. Delightful.*

Directions: 20 minutes from junction 28 of the M1, off the A615 at Tansley; 1 mile further to Riber.

Glossop
Sheffield
Chesterfield
Bakewell
Nottingham
Derby

Web: www.johansens.com/riberhall
E-mail: info@riber-hall.co.uk
Tel: 0870 381 8854
International: +44 (0)1629 582795
Fax: 01629 580475

Price Guide:
single £95–£105
double/twin £123–£165

NORTHCOTE MANOR COUNTRY HOUSE HOTEL

BURRINGTON, UMBERLEIGH, DEVON EX37 9LZ

Directions: From Exeter stay on the A377 towards Barnstaple (do not enter Burrington village). The driveway to Northcote Manor is opposite the Portsmouth Arms pub on the A377.

Web: www.johansens.com/northcotemanor
E-mail: rest@northcotemanor.co.uk
Tel: 0870 381 8767
International: +44 (0)1769 560501
Fax: 01769 560770

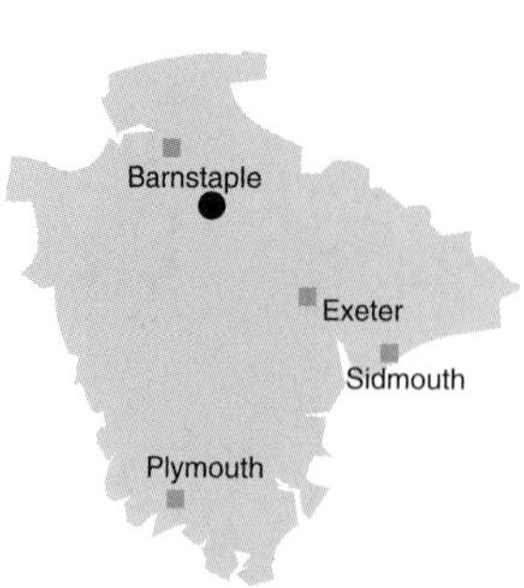

Price Guide:
single from £100
double from £210
suite from £250

This 18th-century manor with grounds high above the Taw River Valley offers an ambience of timeless tranquillity. Situated in 20 acres of peaceful Devonshire countryside, Northcote Manor provides complete relaxation and refreshment. Extensive refurbishment has created 11 luxury bedrooms and suites, resulting in a total redesign of the décor in the spacious sitting rooms, hall and restaurant. One of the south west's leading country houses, the Manor has received a series of accolades: the 2006 Condé Nast Johansens Reader Award, 3 AA Red Stars, Tourist Board Gold Award, 2 AA Rosettes, inclusion on the AA Top 200 Hotels list, the RAC Gold Ribbon Award for the fifth consecutive year and the 2002 Condé Nast Johansens Country Hotel of the Year Award. Exmoor and Dartmoor are within easy reach and guests may visit RHS Rosemoor and the many National Trust properties nearby. A challenging 18-hole golf course is next door whilst outstanding fishing from the Taw River, at the bottom of the drive, can be arranged with the Gillie. The area also hosts some of the best shoots in the country. A tennis court and croquet lawn are on site. Helicopters can land at Eaglescott Airfield, approximately 2 miles away. Special breaks are available.

Our inspector loved: *The conservatory, with oak flooring and slate roof, and beautiful water gardens.*

GIDLEIGH PARK

CHAGFORD, DEVON TQ13 8HH

Gidleigh Park enjoys an outstanding international reputation among connoisseurs for its comfort and gastronomy. It has collected a clutch of top culinary awards including 2 Michelin stars for its imaginative cuisine and the Gidleigh Park wine list is one of the best in Britain. Service throughout the hotel is faultless. The en-suite bedrooms – 2 of them in a converted chapel – are luxuriously furnished with antiques. The public rooms are elegantly appointed and during the cooler months, a fire burns merrily in the lounge's impressive fireplace. Set amid 45 secluded acres in the Teign Valley, Gidleigh Park is 1½ miles from the nearest public road. A croquet lawn, an outdoor tennis court, a bowling lawn and a splendid water garden can be found in the grounds. A 360 yard long, par 52 putting course designed by Peter Alliss was opened in 1995. Guests can swim in the river or explore Dartmoor on foot or in the saddle. There are 14 miles of trout, sea trout and salmon fishing, as well as golf facilities nearby. Gidleigh Park is a Relais & Châteaux member. Totally refurbished for autumn 2006 Gidleigh Park has a total non-smoking policy.

Our inspector loved: *The total peace and tranquillity surrounding this superb hotel.*

Directions: Approach from Chagford: go along Mill Street from Chagford Square. Fork right after 150 yards, cross into Holy Street at factory crossroads and follow lane for 2 miles.

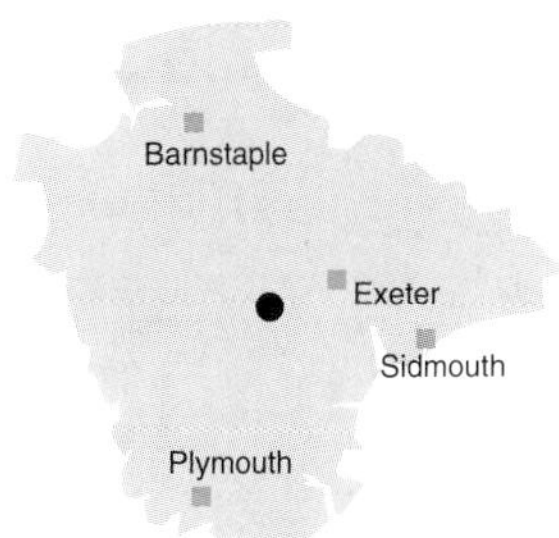

Web: www.johansens.com/gidleighpark
E-mail: gidleighpark@gidleigh.co.uk
Tel: 0870 381 8545
International: +44 (0)1647 432367
Fax: 01647 432574

Price Guide: (including dinner)
single £280–£365
double/twin £440–£1200

Bovey Castle

NORTH BOVEY, DARTMOOR NATIONAL PARK, DEVON TQ13 8RE

Ideally situated within the 368 square miles of Dartmoor National Park and surrounded by moorland, woodlands and rivers, Bovey Castle offers guests the utmost in style, elegance and tranquillity. Built in 1906 for Viscount Hambleden, son of the business baron WH Smith, and transformed into a grand country estate by the 1920s it is now owned by Peter de Savary. Focus on returning this great house to its former glory was then undertaken and remaining true to the standards that the art deco period aspired to has created relaxed luxury and glamour. Sumptuous accommodation in 65 individually designed rooms range from Valley View rooms, with their outlook across Dartmoor, to the triple aspect Chairman's Suites, with views over the gardens, moors and the 1st and 18th holes of the estate's challenging golf course, designed in 1926 to rival Gleneagles and Turnberry. The castle interior is very special with grand oak panelled drawing rooms, ornate broad stairways, a magnificently restored Cathedral Room, with vaulted ceiling, and a superbly crafted Great Hall, which opens onto stone balustraded terraces. The main dining room, where exceptional cuisine is served, is equally impressive in the style of an original art deco Palm Court. Fully equipped spa, indoor swimming pool and many leisure pursuits from riding and shooting to falconry and 25 miles of fishing.

Our inspector loved: *This stunning castle set within breathtaking scenery.*

Directions: Take the M5 and exit at Junction 31 A30 Okehampton, at the first roundabout (Merrymeet) take a left into Whiddon Down left again (A382) signposted Chagford and Moretonhampstead. At the crossroads in Moretonhampstead, turn right towards Postbridge, Bovey Castle is 1.5 miles from Moretonhampstead .

Web: www.johansens.com/boveycastle
E-mail: enquiries@boveycastle.com
Tel: 0870 381 9286
International: +44 (0)1647 445000
Fax: +44 (0)1647 445020

Price Guide:
single from £180
double from £250
suite from £565

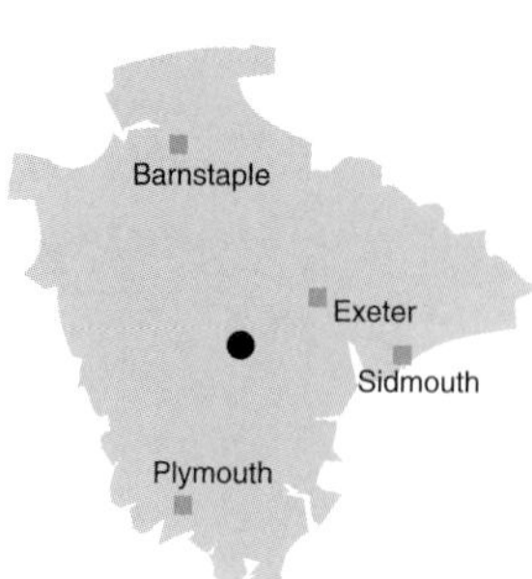

Combe House Hotel & Restaurant

GITTISHAM, HONITON, NEAR EXETER, DEVON EX14 3AD

Awarded Taste of the West - South West Restaurant of the Year 2005, Combe House is a wildly romantic, Grade 1 Elizabethan Manor, hidden in 3,500 acres of private Devon estate, yet close to the World Heritage coastline. Arabian horses and pheasants roam freely beside the mile of winding drive leading from the pretty thatched village of Gittisham. The alluring combination of heritage and a welcoming lived-in feel make this a special place for an indulgent mix of eating, drinking and relaxing in the country. Log fires, treasured antiques and fresh flowers abound and 15 bedrooms and suites, many with breathtaking views, exude style and individuality. In the Restaurant, guests are treated to innovative contemporary cuisine created by 2 Master Chefs of Great Britain, who draw extensively on the West Country's bounteous larder and Combe's own kitchen garden to weave their culinary magic. Add this to interesting wines from the ancient cellars, including a specialist Chablis collection.

Our inspector loved: *The beautifully presented new Linen Suite, quite unique.*

Directions: M5 exit 28 to Honiton and Sidmouth or exit 29 to Honiton. Follow signs to Fenny Bridges and Gittisham (20 mins). A303/A30 exit Honiton, 5 mins.

Web: www.johansens.com/combehousegittisham
E-mail: stay@thishotel.com
Tel: 0870 381 8440
International: +44 (0)1404 540400
Fax: 01404 46004

Price Guide:
single £134
double/twin £164–£178
suite £308–£388

15 M50

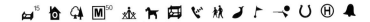

ILSINGTON COUNTRY HOUSE HOTEL

ILSINGTON VILLAGE, NEAR NEWTON ABBOT, DEVON TQ13 9RR

Directions: From the M5 join the A38 at Exeter following Plymouth signs. After approximately 12 miles, exit for Moretonhampstead and Newton Abbot. At the roundabout follow signs for Ilsington.

Web: www.johansens.com/ilsington
E-mail: hotel@ilsington.co.uk
Tel: 0870 381 8635
International: +44 (0)1364 661452
Fax: 01364 661307

Price Guide:
single £92–£98
double/twin £136–£164
suite £166–£174

The Ilsington Country House Hotel stands in 10 acres of beautiful private grounds within the Dartmoor National Park. Run by friendly proprietors, Tim and Maura Hassell, the delightful furnishings and ambience offer a most comfortable environment in which to relax. Stylish bedrooms all boast outstanding views across the rolling pastoral countryside and every comfort and convenience to make guests feel at home. The distinctive candle-lit dining room is perfect for savouring the superb cuisine, awarded 2 AA Rosettes, created by talented chefs from fresh local produce. The library is ideal for an intimate dining party or celebration whilst the conservatory or lounge is the place for morning coffee or a Devon cream tea. There is a fully-equipped, purpose-built gymnasium, heated indoor pool, sauna, steam room and spa. Some of England's most idyllic and unspoilt scenery surrounds Ilsington, with the picturesque villages of Lustleigh and Widecombe-in-the-Moor close by. Guests have easy access to the moors from the hotel. Riding, fishing and many other country pursuits can be arranged. Special breaks are available.

Our inspector loved: *The beautiful new domed ceilinged restaurant with window wall overlooking the moor and views towards the magnificent Hay Tor.*

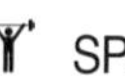

Burgh Island

BIGBURY-ON-SEA, SOUTH DEVON TQ7 4BG

Burgh Island, off the south Devon coast, is a unique and romantic location boasting more proposals of marriage per square inch then any other place in Britain. Linked to the mainland by a tidal beach it has been decorated in genuine art deco design throughout, and is steeped in the style of the 20s and 30s, from the magnificent glass peacock dome of the Palm Court to the cinema room playing black and white classics. Over the years it has welcomed esteemed guests such as Edward VIII and Wallis Simpson, Noel Coward and Agatha Christie. Today, its owners and staff are experts at staging relaxed yet memorable events. Dressing for dinner is expected and when bands are in the house, dancing is encouraged. All of the bedrooms have breathtaking views and beds are fitted with crisp white linen; television is only available in The Library. The restaurant serves modern international dishes, using local suppliers and traditional produce. The nearby 14th-century Pilchards Inn is also available for informal meals. Outdoor pursuits include swimming in the Mermaid natural rock pool, coastal walks, tennis and golf on the Bigbury course.

Our inspector loved: *The breathtaking location and magnificent atmosphere of a bygone era combined with the superb facilities of the 21st century and the flying Devon ensign.*

Directions: From the M5 take the A38 towards Plymouth then exit at Wrangton Cross for the A379 and go through Modbury. Follow signs to Bigbury and Bigbury-on-Sea. At St Anne's Chapel call for further directions.

Web: www.johansens.com/burghisland
E-mail: reception@burghisland.com
Tel: 0870 381 9207
International: +44 (0)1548 810 514
Fax: 01548 810 243

Price Guide: (including dinner)
single £260
double/twin £340
suite £340–£500

LEWTRENCHARD MANOR

LEWDOWN, NEAR OKEHAMPTON, DEVON EX20 4PN

This beautiful Jacobean manor is tucked away within its own estate on rolling Devon hills, and with just 14 exquisite bedrooms is a delightful retreat from city life. Built in 1600 by the Monk family it was later embellished by the Victorian hymn writer Rev Sabine Baring Gould, and today is a stunning example of ornate ceilings, elegant carved oak staircases and leaded light windows. Carefully incorporated family antique pieces and elegant soft furnishings to create a sense of luxury combined with a warmth that is truly welcoming. Each of the bedrooms looks out over the valley, and the oak-panelled dining room with its coffered ceiling provides a stunning backdrop for some excellent cooking and superb wines. The restaurant has won 3 Rosettes for its exquisitely prepared and artistically presented cuisine, which is based on the freshest of local ingredients. The estate offers clay pigeon shooting and rough shooting and fishing, making this an ideal place for weekend parties, as well as an idyllic setting for weddings and functions. Exeter is on the doorstep with its cathedral and sophisticated shops, whilst Devon's numerous tourist attractions are all within easy reach.

Our inspector loved: *The location – the house and beautiful grounds.*

Directions: Take A30 (Okehampton–Bodmin) from Exeter. After 25 miles take the road to Tavistock / Plymouth follow signs to Lewdown from there the Lewtrenchard hotel is signposted .

Web: www.johansens.com/lewtrenchard
E-mail: info@lewtrenchard.co.uk
Tel: 0870 381 9177
International: +44 (0)1566 783222
Fax: 01566 783332

Price Guide:
single £125–£220
double/twin £155–£210
suite £230–£250

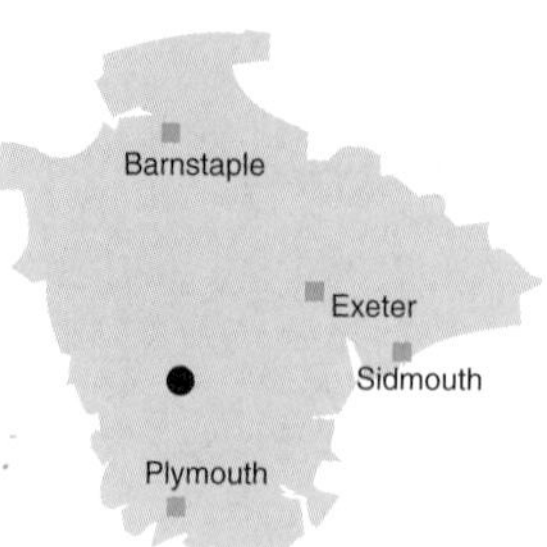

The Arundell Arms

LIFTON, DEVON PL16 0AA

In a lovely valley close to the uplands of Dartmoor, The Arundell Arms is a former coaching inn, which dates back to Saxon times. Its flagstone floors, cosy fires, paintings and antiques combine to create a haven of warmth and comfort in an atmosphere of Old World charm. One of England's best-known sporting hotels for more than half a century, it boasts 20 miles of exclusive salmon and trout fishing on the Tamar, and 5 of its tributaries, and a famous school of fly fishing. Awarded the Good Hotel Guide Sporting Hotel of the Year in 2006. Guests also enjoy a host of other country activities, including hill walking, shooting, riding and golf. The hotel takes great pride in its elegant AA Rosette awarded restaurant, whose gourmet cuisine has gained an international reputation. A splendid base from which to enjoy the wonderful surfing beaches nearby, The Arundell Arms is also well placed for visits to Tintagel and the historic houses and gardens of Devon and Cornwall and the Eden Project. Only 45 minutes from Exeter and Plymouth, it is also ideal for the business executive, reached by major roads from all directions. A spacious conference suite is available.

Our inspector loved: *The warm welcoming ambience throughout.*

Directions: Lifton is approximately ¼ mile off the A30, 2 miles east of Launceston and the Cornish Border.

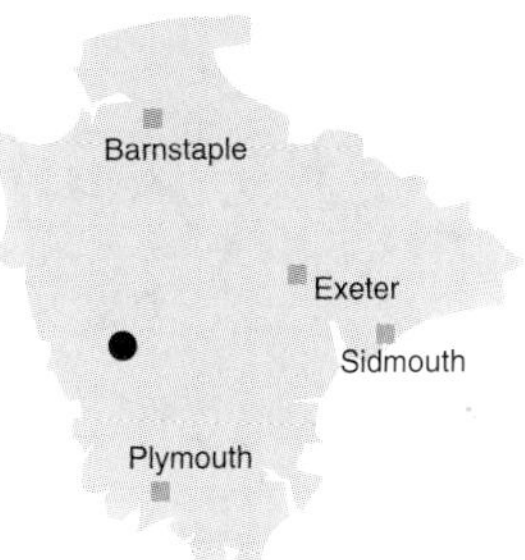

Web: www.johansens.com/arundellarms
E-mail: reservations@arundellarms.com
Tel: 0870 381 8323
International: +44 (0)1566 784666
Fax: 01566 784494

Price Guide:
single from £99
double/twin from £155
superior from £180

SOAR MILL COVE HOTEL

SOAR MILL COVE, SALCOMBE, SOUTH DEVON TQ7 3DS

Owned by the Makepeace family for over 25 years, Soar Mill Cove is situated midway between the historic Port of Dartmouth and The Pilgrim Steps of Plymouth, and is easily accessed by road, rail and regional airlines. Nothing is too much trouble at Soar Mill Cove, where guests are invited to enjoy pampering that only a family-owned hotel can offer. Set within 2,000 acres of National Trust countryside this is arguably the most dramatic seaside setting, with breathtaking views; a hidden gem with a warmth that makes guests return again and again. Idyllically located for peaceful strolls along the golden sand beach, fishing in rock pools and exploring local caves, memories of the beachside holidays Enid Blyton's Famous Five experienced comes to life! Trek the spectacular coastal path or sit back in the passenger seat of the hotel's free tandem whilst sipping from a complimentary flask of hot toddy. Take advantage of the hotel's number of swimming pools and relax with a massage in "The Ocean Spa" before dining on a feast of lobster and crab accompanied by fine wines.

Our inspector loved: *The year on year wonderful new upgrading and as always the breathtaking location.*

Directions: A384 to Totnes, then A381 to Soar Mill Cove.

Web: www.johansens.com/soarmillcove
E-mail: info@soarmillcove.co.uk
Tel: 0870 381 8897
International: +44 (0)1548 561566
Fax: 01548 561223

Price Guide:
single £94–£180
double/twin £180–£240
suite from £216

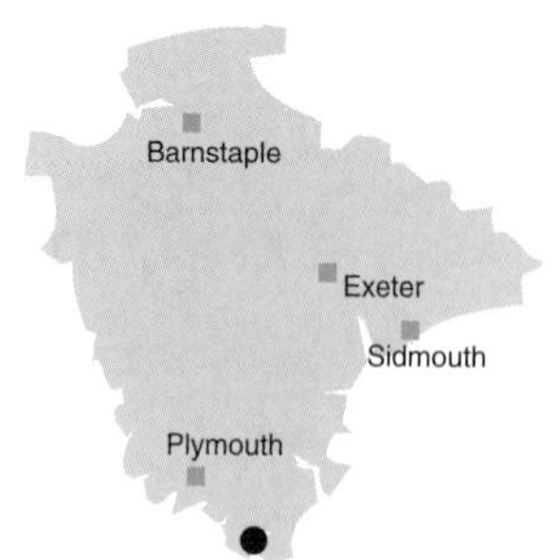

The Tides Reach Hotel

SOUTH SANDS, SALCOMBE, DEVON TQ8 8LJ

This luxuriously appointed hotel is situated in an ideal position for those wishing to enjoy a relaxing or fun-filled break. Facing south in a tree-fringed sandy cove just inside the mouth of the Salcombe Estuary it has an extensive garden on one side, the sea and a safe bathing sandy beach a few steps opposite and, to the rear, a sheltering hill topped by the subtropical gardens of Overbecks. The Tides Reach has been under the supervision of owners, the Edwards family, for more than 39 years and they have built up a reputation for hospitality and courteous service. The atmosphere is warm and friendly, the décor and furnishings tasteful and comfortable. All 35 spacious bedrooms are en-suite, well equipped and decorated with flair and originality. The lawned garden centres around an ornamental lake with waterfall and fountain which is surrounded by landscaped tiers of colourful plants, shrubs and palms. Overlooking it is the restaurant where chef Finn Ibsen's excellent gourmet cuisine has earned AA Rosettes. A superb indoor heated swimming pool is the nucleus of the hotel's leisure complex which includes a sauna, spa bath, gymnasium, squash court, snooker room and hair & beauty salon . The hotel has facilities for windsurfing, sailing and canoeing.

Our inspector loved: *As always the location, warmth of welcome and the refurbished leisure complex.*

Directions: From the M5, exit at junction 30 and join the A38 towards Plymouth. Exit for Totnes and then take the A381.

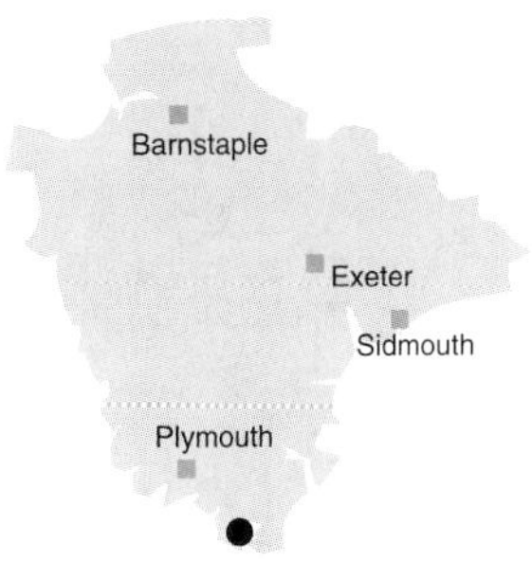

Barnstaple
Exeter
Sidmouth
Plymouth

Web: www.johansens.com/tidesreach
E-mail: enquire@tidesreach.com
Tel: 0870 381 8947
International: +44 (0)1548 843466
Fax: 01548 843954

Price Guide: (including dinner)
single £75–£160
double/twin £140–£330

BUCKLAND-TOUT-SAINTS

GOVETON, KINGSBRIDGE, DEVON TQ7 2DS

Buckland-Tout-Saints is an elegant 300-year-old country house nestled amidst over 4 acres of beautiful landscaped gardens in the heart of idyllic Devon. It is a paradise for nature lovers and a haven for those seeking tranquillity where luxurious accommodation is complemented by excellent service to provide a unique opportunity for guests to relax and enjoy being treated like royalty. 16 individually decorated bedrooms are en suite and have wonderful views over the surrounding countryside. Striking interior design includes sumptuous four-poster beds, stylish and opulent fabrics as well as wonderful attention to detail. Guests are made to feel extremely comfortable: a complimentary daily newspaper is delivered to guests' doors and mineral water, colour television and fluffy bathrobes are supplied. The superb restaurant has won many accolades over the years and offers mouth-watering dishes, both local and exotic, cooked to perfection and accompanied by the finest wines from around the world. There is plenty to do in and around the hotel: read a book or take afternoon tea in front of a roaring wood fire or explore the local area with its historic homes, castles and picturesque villages. The hotel is very close to the sailing and fishing towns of Salcombe, Dartmouth and historic Totnes.

Our inspector loved: *This tucked away gem within The South Hams – beautiful views, wonderful presentation and fine dining.*

Directions: The hotel is signposted from the A381 between Totnes and Kingsbridge.

Web: www.johansens.com/bucklandtoutsaints
E-mail: buckland@tout–saints.co.uk
Tel: 0870 381 8391
International: +44 (0)1548 853055
Fax: 01548 856261

Price Guide:
single from £80
double/twin from £150
suite from £300

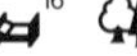       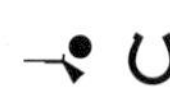  

HOTEL RIVIERA

THE ESPLANADE, SIDMOUTH, DEVON EX10 8AY

A warm welcome awaits guests arriving at this prestigious award-winning hotel. With accolades such as the AA Courtesy and Care Award and the Which? Hotel Guide's Hotel of the Year, it comes as no surprise that Peter Wharton's Hotel Riviera is arguably one of the most comfortable and most hospitable in the region. The exterior, with its fine Regency façade and bow fronted windows complements the elegance of the interior comprising handsome public rooms and beautifully appointed bedrooms, many with sea views. Perfectly located at the centre of Sidmouth's historic Georgian esplanade and awarded 4 stars by both the AA and the RAC, the Riviera is committed to providing the very highest standard of excellence which makes each stay at the property a totally pleasurable experience. Guests may dine in the attractive salon, which affords glorious views across Lyme Bay, and indulge in the superb cuisine, prepared by English and French trained chefs. The exceptional cellar will please the most discerning wine connoisseur. Activities include coastal walks, golf, bowling, croquet, putting, tennis, fishing, sailing, riding and exploring the breathtaking surroundings with its gardens, lush countryside and stunning coastline. Short breaks are available.

Our inspector loved: *The location, overall ambience and first class service.*

Directions: The hotel is situated at the centre of The Esplanade.

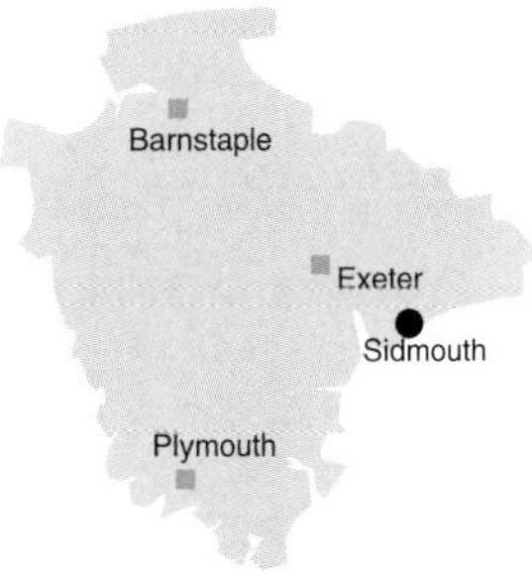

Barnstaple
Exeter
Sidmouth
Plymouth

Web: www.johansens.com/riviera
E-mail: enquiries@hotelriviera.co.uk
Tel: 0870 381 8624
International: +44 (0)1395 515201
Fax: 01395 577775

Price Guide: (including 6 course dinner):
single £104–£156
double/twin £208–£290
suite £314–£334

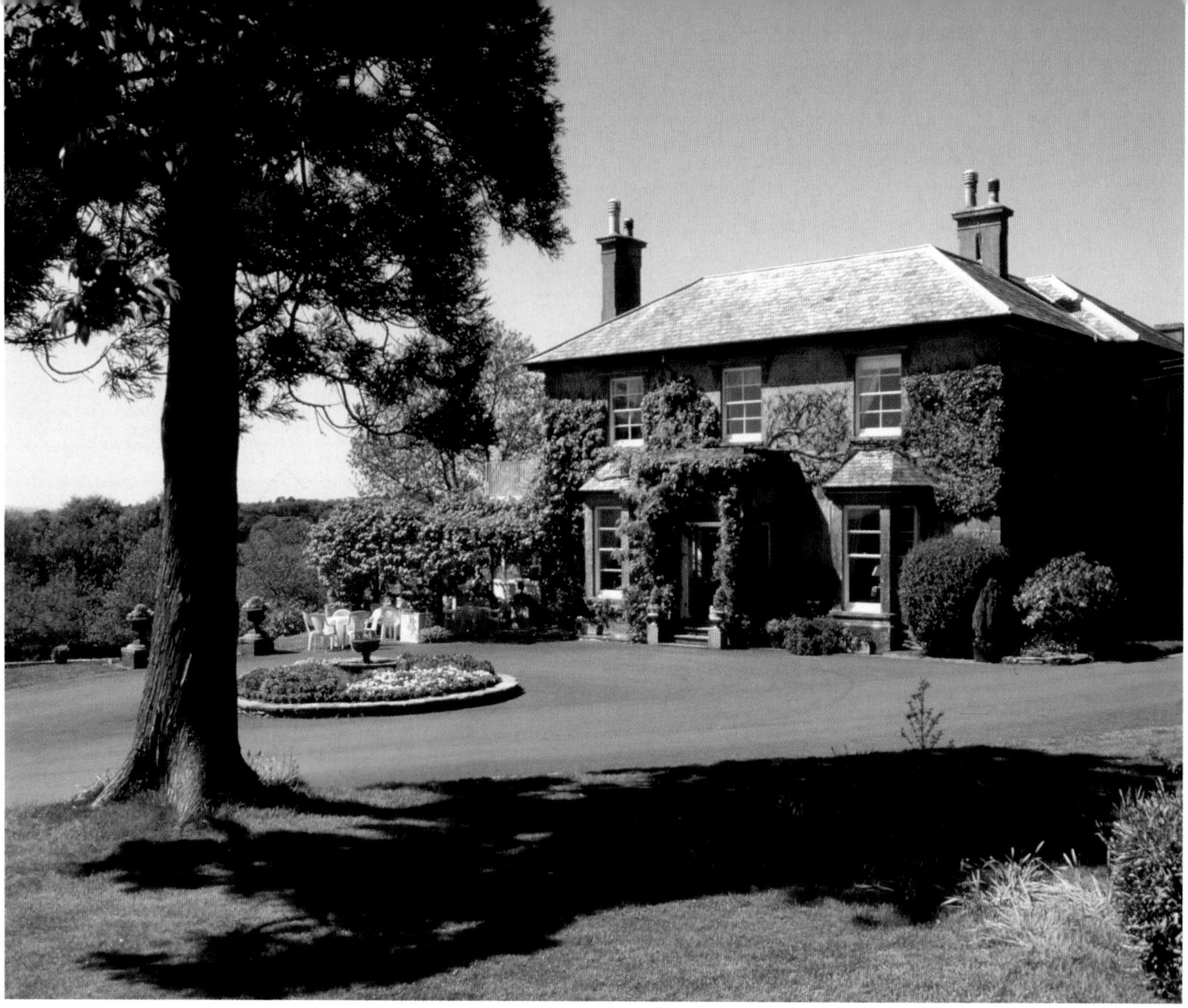

The Horn of Plenty Country House Hotel & Restaurant

GULWORTHY, TAVISTOCK, DEVON PL19 8JD

This enchanting country house hotel is privately owned and run by Paul Roston and Master Chef Peter Gorton, whose warmth and charm extends into the friendly and informal atmosphere created by the young, efficient staff. Set in 5 acres of spectacular gardens and wild orchards, the house oozes character and boasts breathtaking views over the tranquil Tamar Valley. Some of the en-suite bedrooms have balconies, and a host of luxuries includes fluffy towels and robes, handmade chocolates and the scent of fresh flowers, competing with the aroma of woodsmoke from log fires in winter. The heart of The Horn of Plenty is its kitchen and guests are invited to sample a superb selection of food and wine. Fresh produce is sourced locally and menus feature dishes such as steamed John Dory with smoked salmon mousse and tortellini, crisp belly pork with creamed garlic and rosemary polenta, hot ginger sponge pudding with rhubarb compote and a selection of West Country cheeses. The hotel can also accommodate weddings and business events, and cookery courses are available. There are a number of excellent golf courses within easy reach, and other nearby attractions include the Eden Project, Devon and Cornwall coastline and Dartmoor National Park.

Directions: Leave the M5, junction 31 and follow signs for Okehampton then join the A386 for Tavistock. Take the A390 and after 3 miles at Gulworthy Cross pick up the signs for the hotel.

Web: www.johansens.com/hornofplenty
E-mail: enquiries@thehornofplenty.co.uk
Tel: 0870 381 8584
International: +44 (0)1822 832528

Price Guide:
single £130–£220
double/twin £140–£230

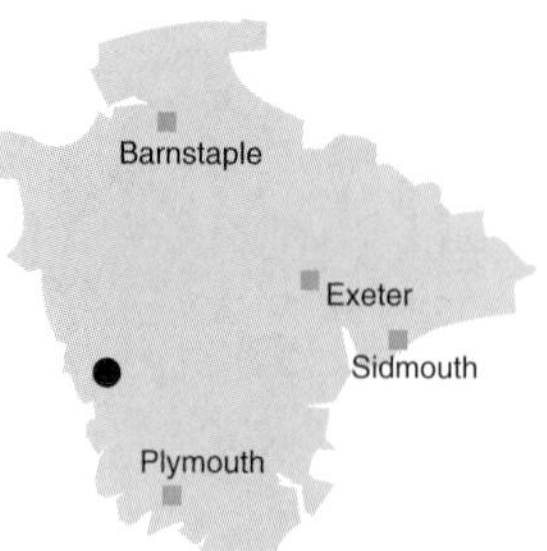

Our inspector loved: *This tucked away retreat offering everything.*

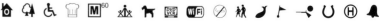

THE PALACE HOTEL

BABBACOMBE ROAD, TORQUAY, DEVON TQ1 3TG

Once the residence of the Bishop of Exeter, the privately owned Palace Hotel is a gracious Victorian building set in 25 acres of beautifully landscaped gardens and woodlands. The comfortable bedrooms are equipped with every modern amenity and there are also elegant, spacious suites available. Most rooms overlook the hotel's magnificent grounds. The main restaurant provides a high standard of traditional English cooking, making full use of fresh, local produce, as well as offering a good variety of international dishes. The cuisine is complemented by a wide selection of popular and fine wines. Light meals are also available from the lounge and during the summer months, a mediterranean-style menu is served on the terrace. A host of sporting facilities has made this hotel famous. These include a short par 3 9-hole championship golf course, indoor and outdoor swimming pools, 2 indoor and 4 outdoor tennis courts, 2 squash courts, saunas, snooker room and a well-equipped fitness suite. Places of interest nearby include Dartmoor, South Hams and Exeter. Paignton Zoo, Bygone's Museum and Kent's Cavern are among the local attractions. Breaks available all year.

***Our inspector loved:** This gracious hotel - beautiful grounds and the fact one can stay on-site and forget the car.*

Directions: From seafront follow signs for Babbacombe. Hotel entrance is on the right.

Barnstaple
Exeter
Sidmouth
Plymouth

Web: www.johansens.com/palacetorquay
E-mail: info@palacetorquay.co.uk
Tel: 0870 381 8798
International: +44 (0)1803 200200
Fax: 01803 299899

Price Guide:
single £69–£84
double/twin £138–£168
executive £236
suite £256–£296

ORESTONE MANOR & THE RESTAURANT AT ORESTONE MANOR

ROCKHOUSE LANE, MAIDENCOMBE, TORQUAY, DEVON TQ1 4SX

Stylishly refurbished as a Colonial manor house, this luxury country house hotel and restaurant is located on the rural fringe of Torquay, with stunning views across the Torbay coastline and Lyme Bay. Built in 1809 this was once the home of painter John Calcott Horsley RA, whose celebrated portrait of his brother-in-law, Isambard Kingdom Brunel, hangs in the National Gallery. He is also renowned for having painted the very first Christmas card. Each guest room has its own décor and character with full amenities and luxury en-suite bathrooms; some have a terrace or balcony. Excellent service and superb food and wine can be enjoyed in the 2 AA Rosette-awarded restaurant. Using only the best seasonal local produce – some from Orestone's gardens – light lunches and afternoon teas are served in the conservatory or on the terrace, whilst a full set lunch and à la carte dinner menu are available in the restaurant. A number of accolades have been forthcoming: listed in the AA's Top 50 with 85% (the highest in the southwest), Michelin star, recipient of a RAC Blue Ribbon, award winner of the English Riviera Hotel of the Year and Les Routiers Southwest Hotel of the Year. Numerous places of interest close by include Dartmoor, Exmoor and National Trust properties and gardens. There is also a wide range of activities and picturesque coastal walks to enjoy.

Our inspector loved: *The location, the fine dining and stylish presentation.*

Directions: About 3 miles north of Torquay on the A379 (Formerly B3199). Take the coast road towards Teignmouth.

Web: www.johansens.com/orestonemanor
E-mail: stay@orestonemanor.com
Tel: 0870 381 8794
International: +44 (0)1803 328098
Fax: 01803 328336

Price Guide:
single £89–£149
double/twin £125–£225

Langdon Court Hotel & Restaurant

DOWN THOMAS, PLYMOUTH, DEVON PL9 0DY

Originally built for Katherine Parr, the sixth wife of Henry VIII, this Grade II listed Tudor manor has even earlier origins, evidence of which can be found in its cellars. Rebuilt in 1648, the house is now surrounded by fields and woodland and has its own Jacobean walled gardens and well-kept lawns. Behind its impressive grey façade lie tiled floors, warmly painted stone walls and classic, uncluttered furnishings. Some of the 12 bedrooms are simply stunning; many have views of the countryside or the gardens. Three function suites: Calmady, Cory and Courtney, are available for wedding receptions, shooting and house parties. An impressive menu is served in the modern brasserie, the bar or on the terrace, specialising in fish and seafood. Throughout the year, the finest produce and organically farmed meats are selected from local suppliers, while the hotel's own kitchen garden provides an assortment of vegetables and herbs, and the cellar holds well-established favourites along with wines from the New World. The hotel has a direct path to the beach at Wembury, access to the coastal paths and is ideally placed for exploring the South Hams countryside, numerous National Trust properties and the Eden project.

Our inspector loved: *The location – a dream to join an inclusive superb house party speciality.*

Directions: From Exeter join the A38 towards Plymouth then take the exit signed Plymouth, Yelverton Plymstock into Brixton. Follow Brixton Tor/Otter Nurseries and carry on the Leyford Lane. Turn left into the hotel's drive.

Web: www.johansens.com/langdon
E-mail: enquiries@langdoncourt.co.uk
Tel: 0870 381 9157
International: +44 (0)1752 862358
Fax: 01752 863428

Price Guide:
single from £85
double from £120

Woolacombe Bay Hotel

SOUTH STREET, WOOLACOMBE, DEVON EX34 7BN

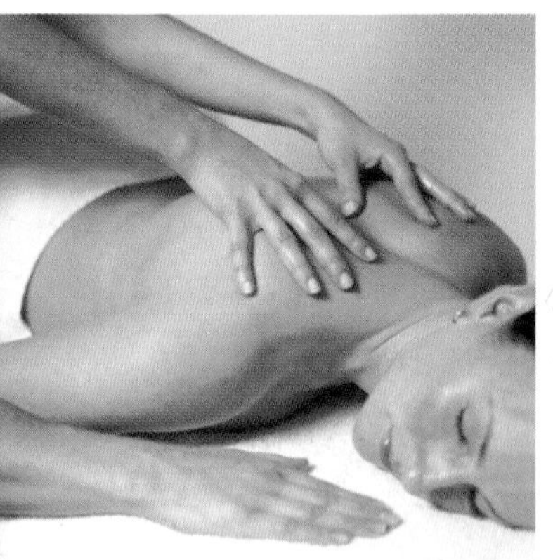

Woolacombe Bay Hotel stands in 6 acres of grounds, leading to 3 miles of golden Blue-flag sand. Built by the Victorians, the hotel has an air of luxury, style and comfort. All rooms are en-suite with satellite TV, baby listening, ironing centre, some with a balcony. Traditional English and French dishes are offered in Doyle's restaurant. Superb in-house recreational amenities include free unlimited use of tennis, squash, indoor and outdoor pools, billiards, bowls, dancing and films, a health suite with steam room, sauna, spa bath with high impulse shower. Power-boating, fishing, shooting and riding can be arranged and preferential rates are offered for golf at nearby golf clubs. The "Hot House" aerobics studio, Haven beauty salon, cardio vascular weights room, solariums, masseurs and beauticians. However, being energetic is not a requirement for enjoying the qualities of Woolacombe Bay. Many of its regulars choose simply to relax in the public rooms and in the grounds, which extend to the rolling surf of the magnificent bay. A drive along the coastal route in either direction will guarantee splendid views. Exmoor's beautiful Doone Valley is an hour away by car. Closed January.

Our inspector loved: *The loction and facilities offered to guests. Superb for families*

Directions: At the centre of the village, off main Barnstaple–Ilfracombe road.

Web: www.johansens.com/woolacombebay
E-mail: woolacombe.bayhotel@btinternet.com
Tel: 0870 381 9007
International: +44 (0)1271 870388
Fax: 01271 870613

Price Guide: (including dinner)
single £92–£152
double/twin £184–£304

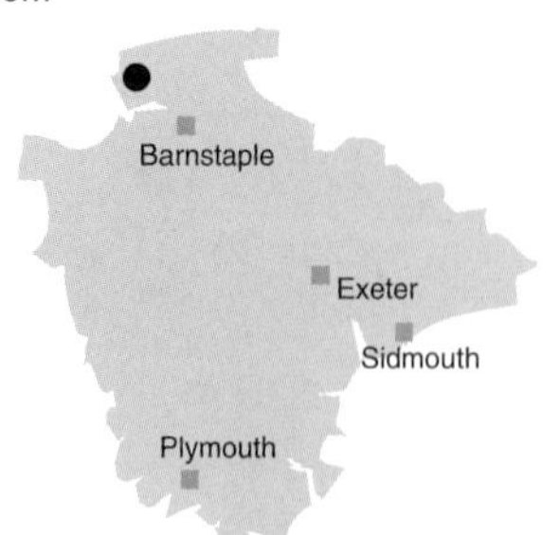

Watersmeet Hotel

MORTEHOE, WOOLACOMBE, DEVON EX34 7EB

In a setting of incomparable beauty the Watersmeet is situated in one of the finest and most dramatic locations in the South West, it commands an elevated position at the waters edge above Combesgate Beach with steps leading directly to the sandy beach. The magnificent views of the rugged coastline to Lundy Island can be enjoyed from the large picture windows in the reception rooms ensuring that guests can admire the ever-changing coastline. Under the ownership of Michael and Amanda James a tasteful refurbishment has transformed the bedrooms, consistent with the high standard of the hotel, to include all accoutrement for luxury living. All boast superb uninterrupted sea views and many have balconies. Award winning imaginative menus combine the use of the finest quality local ingredients with thoughtfully balanced dishes, taken in the pavilion AA Rosette restaurant while admiring the sunsets by candlelight. Lunch and tea may be taken alfresco on the terrace or in the picturesque tea garden. Recreational facilities include heated outdoor and indoor pool with a hot spa and steam room. Scenic coastal walks along National Trust land and Saunton Sands Championship Golf Course are nearby. The excellent reputation of the hotel with the impeccable service, relaxation theme and home from home ambiance continues to attract guests all year round.

Directions: From the M5, junction 27, follow the A361 towards Ilfracombe. Turn left at the roundabout and follow signs to Mortehoe.

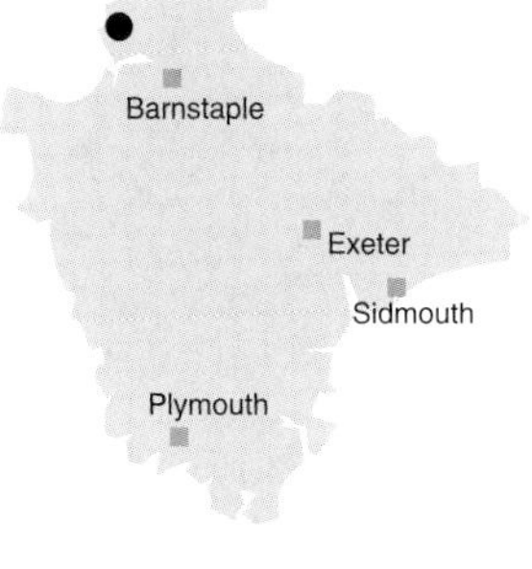

Barnstaple
Exeter
Sidmouth
Plymouth

Web: www.johansens.com/watersmeet
E-mail: info@watersmeethotel.co.uk
Tel: 0870 381 8972
International: +44 (0)1271 870333
Fax: 01271 870890

Price Guide: (including dinner)
single £98–£150
double/twin £140–£285

Our inspector loved: *The breathtaking location and facilities offered.*

Norfolk Royale Hotel

RICHMOND HILL, BOURNEMOUTH, DORSET BH2 6EN

Directions: From the M27, A31 & A338 find the hotel on the right, halfway down Richmond Hill approaching the town centre.

Web: www.johansens.com/norfolkroyale
E-mail: norfolkroyale@englishrosehotels.co.uk
Tel: 0870 381 8765
International: +44 (0)1202 551521
Fax: 01202 299729

Price Guide:
single from £115
double/twin £160–£200
suite from £225

Bournemouth has long been a popular seaside resort and has not lost its unique character. The RAC 4 Star Norfolk Royale Hotel is a fine example of the elegant buildings that grace the town. It is a splendid Edwardian house, once the holiday home of the Duke of Norfolk, after whom it is named. Extensive restoration work throughout the hotel, while enhancing its comfort, has not eliminated the echoes of the past and new arrivals are impressed by the elegant furnishings and courtesy of the staff. The designs of the spacious bedrooms reflect consideration for lady travellers, busy business executives, non-smokers and the disabled. The rich fabrics of the delightful colour schemes contribute to their luxurious ambience. Guests relax in the lounge or attractive club bar, in summer enjoying the gardens or patio – all with waiter service – and delicious breakfasts, lunches and candle-lit dinners are served in the Echoes Restaurant, which has an excellent wine list. The good life includes the pleasures of a pool and spa whilst Bournemouth offers golf courses, tennis, water sports, a casino and theatre. It has a large conference and exhibition centre. Poole Harbour, The New Forest, Thomas Hardy country and long sandy beaches are nearby.

Our inspector loved: *The new function suite and meeting rooms with lots of technology.*

AVONMOUTH HOTEL AND RESTAURANT

95 MUDEFORD, CHRISTCHURCH, DORSET BH23 3NT

Built in the 1830s as a gentleman's residence, this charming, Grade II listed hotel stands in extensive grounds on a quiet area of the waterfront with magnificent views over Mudeford Quay, Hengistbury Head and Christchurch Estuary. Privately owned, it has undergone sympathetic refurbishment, awarded an AA Rosette and offers the highest standards of accommodation, service and cuisine. Each en-suite bedroom is distinctively styled, tastefully furnished and has every home comfort. Guests have a choice of bedrooms in the Georgian main house or in the Orchard Wing, situated in the landscaped garden, which slopes gently down to the harbour edge. Dining in the delightful Quays Restaurant, with its panoramic window views and sunny terrace, is a real pleasure; classic dishes, with a touch of imagination, are prepared by talented executive chef Nigel Popperwell, formerly personal chef to fashion designers Tommy Hilfiger and Valentino and Ainsley Harriott's successor at London's Westbury Hotel. For the more energetic there are sailing and windsurfing in the estuary. Bournemouth and Christchurch's attractions are within easy reach while the lovely walks, rambling trails and villages of the New Forest are just 15 minutes away.

Our inspector loved: *This hotel's dedication to its continuing programme of improvement and refurbishment.*

Directions: From the M25/M3/M27, take the A35 Lyndhurst to Christchurch. At Sainsbury roundabout follow signs to Mudeford. Continue on the main route through the village, past a parade of shops on the right and the hotel is on the left.

Web: www.johansens.com/avonmouth
E-mail: stay@theavonmouth.co.uk
Tel: 0870 381 9333
International: +44 (0)1202 483434
Fax: 01202 479004

Price Guide:
single from £90
double/twin from £120
double/twin with water view from £150

Summer Lodge Country House Hotel, Restaurant & Spa

SUMMER LANE, EVERSHOT, DORSET DT2 0JR

Directions: The turning to Evershot leaves the A37 halfway between Dorchester and Yeovil. Once in the village, turn left into Summer Lane and the hotel entrance is 150 yards on the right.

Web: www.johansens.com/summerlodge
E-mail: summer@relaischateaux.com
Tel: 0870 381 8926
International: +44 (0)20 7589 2412
Fax: 01935 482040

Price Guide:
single from £152.50
double/twin £185–£375
suite/master bedroom £370–£512

Tucked away amidst 4 private, walled acres and the quaint thatched cottages of Wessex, the luxurious Summer Lodge hails back to 1789. Built for the 2nd Earl of Ilchester, Thomas Hardy was commissioned to draw plans for a second floor by the 6th Earl in 1893. Just 2 hours from London by train and 20 minutes from Dorset's Jurassic coast, the impeccably restored 24 gorgeous rooms, suites and cottages - many with fireplaces - combine finest English furnishings and classical art with the latest technology, such as flat-screen televisions and Wi-Fi, and the highest standards of impeccable, friendly service. The award-winning restaurant, under Head Chef Steven Titman and Sommelier of the Year Eric Zweibel, is a delight and the Lodge's own vegetable garden and extensive wine cellar complement the culinary experience. Lighter meals are available in the cosy, well-stocked bar. A sumptuous Dorset cream tea with delights by the 2 pastry chefs is served each afternoon. The spa boasts an indoor heated pool, gymnasium, sauna, beauty salon, whirlpool spa and treatment rooms offering Matis products. Civil weddings, small business meetings and private dining are meticulously catered for. Activities arranged, include golf, shooting, tennis, sailing, fishing, horse riding, racing, scuba diving and visits to various museums and country estates.

Our inspector loved: *The extravagant new garden water features and opulent provision within the house – 63 malts to choose from.*

Stock Hill Country House

STOCK HILL, GILLINGHAM, DORSET SP8 5NR

Set within 11 acres of stunning woodlands and attractive gardens on the borders of Dorset, Somerset and Wiltshire, this remarkable late Victorian mansion is welcoming and elegant, exuding a relaxed charm. Huge oak doors open to reveal a carefully decorated and stunning period interior. Each bedroom mirrors the interesting history and style of the house and offers every comfort expected from a first-class hotel. Guests can snuggle into comfy chairs in the guest lounge where a crackling log fire burns creating a warm homeliness. The refined restaurant is adorned with interesting antiques and curios and has beautiful views over the gardens. Romantic candle-lit tables are perfectly positioned to provide privacy, complemented by attentive and friendly service. The highly-acclaimed food is remarkable and imaginative with a range of European flavours that have earned it many awards. Ingredients are sourced locally and include fresh fish, shellfish and organic vegetables, many harvested from the walled kitchen garden. Sumptuous desserts are a perfect finish to a delectable evening. There are many local attractions of geographical and historical interest nearby: Stourhead Lake and its gardens, the majestic cathedrals of Winchester and Wells, the stunning Dorset coastline, Wookey Caves and the awe-inspiring Stonehenge.

Our inspector loved: *The traditions of service maintained in this most welcoming of hotels.*

Directions: 3 miles south of the A303 on the B3081, just north of Gilingham.

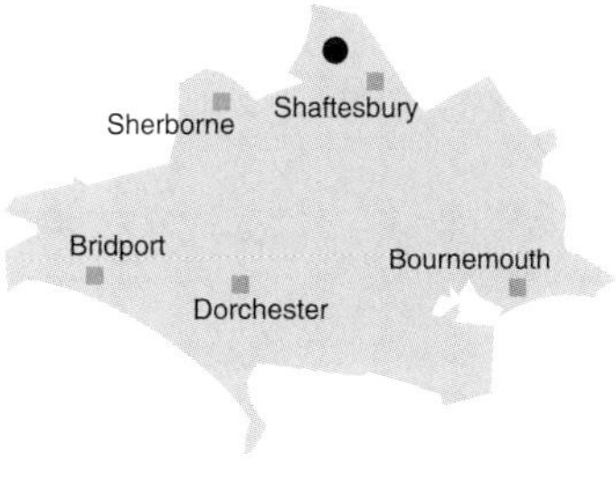

Web: www.johansens.com/stockhillhouse
E-mail: reception@stockhillhouse.co.uk
Tel: 0870 381 8567
International: +44 (0)1747 823626
Fax: 01747 825628

Sherborne
Shaftesbury
Bridport
Bournemouth
Dorchester

Price Guide: (including dinner) double from £270

PLUMBER MANOR

STURMINSTER NEWTON, DORSET DT10 2AF

Directions: Plumber Manor is 2 miles south-west of Sturminster Newton on the Hazelbury Bryan road, off the A357.

Web: www.johansens.com/plumbermanor
E-mail: book@plumbermanor.com
Tel: 0870 381 8829
International: +44 (0)1258 472507
Fax: 01258 473370

Price Guide:
single from £90
double/twin £110–£170

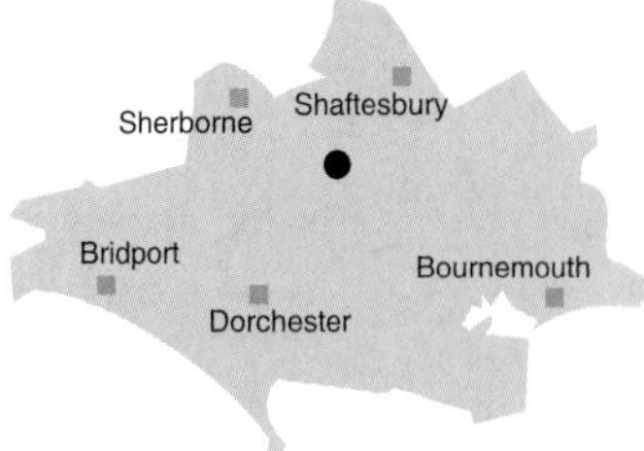

An imposing Jacobean building of local stone, occupying extensive gardens in the heart of Hardy's Dorset, Plumber Manor has been the home of the Prideaux-Brune family since the early 17th century. Leading off a charming gallery, hung with family portraits, are 6 very comfortable bedrooms. The conversion of a natural stone barn lying within the grounds, as well as the courtyard building, has added a further 10 spacious bedrooms, some of which have window seats overlooking the garden and the Develish stream. 3 interconnecting dining rooms comprise the restaurant, where a good choice of imaginative, well-prepared dishes is presented, supported by a wide-ranging wine list. Chef Brian Prideaux-Brune's culinary prowess has been recognised by all the major food guides. Open for dinner every evening and Sunday lunch. The Dorset landscape, with its picture-postcard villages such as Milton Abbas and Cerne Abbas, is close at hand, while Corfe Castle, Lulworth Cove, Kingston Lacy and Poole Harbour are not far away. Riding can be arranged locally; however, if guests wish to bring their own horse to hack or hunt with local packs, the hotel provides free stabling on a do-it-yourself basis. Closed during February.

Our inspector loved: *The quiet and gracious comfort in this exceptional country house.*

THE PRIORY HOTEL

CHURCH GREEN, WAREHAM, DORSET BH20 4ND

Dating from the early 16th century, the one-time Lady St Mary Priory has, for hundreds of years, offered sanctuary to travellers. In Hardy's Dorset, "Far From the Madding Crowd", it placidly stands on the bank of the River Frome in 4½ acres of immaculate gardens. Steeped in history, The Priory has undergone a sympathetic conversion to a hotel, which is charming yet unpretentious. Each bedroom is distinctively styled, with family antiques lending character and many rooms have views of the Purbeck Hills. A 16th-century clay barn has been transformed into the Boathouse, consisting of 4 spacious luxury suites at the river's edge. Tastefully furnished, the drawing room, residents' lounge and intimate bar together create a convivial atmosphere. The Garden Room Restaurant is open for breakfast and lunch (alfresco lunches are served on the terrace in the summertime), while splendid dinners are served in the vaulted stone cellars. There are moorings for guests arriving by boat. Dating back to the 9th century, the market town of Wareham has more than 200 listed buildings. Corfe Castle, Lulworth Cove, Poole and Swanage are all close by with superb walks and beaches.

Our inspector loved: *This truly beautiful building in its delightful riverside garden setting.*

Directions: Wareham is on the A351 to the west of Bournemouth and Poole. The hotel is beside the River Frome at the southern end of the town near the parish church.

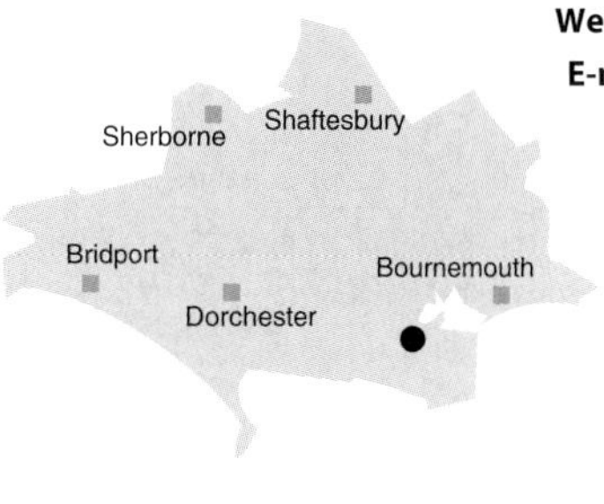

Sherborne
Shaftesbury
Bridport
Bournemouth
Dorchester

Web: www.johansens.com/priorywareham
E-mail: reservations@theprioryhotel.co.uk
Tel: 0870 381 8841
International: +44 (0)1929 551666
Fax: 01929 554519

Price Guide:
single from £168
double/twin £210–£280
suite from £340

Moonfleet Manor

FLEET, WEYMOUTH, DORSET DT3 4ED

Directions: Take the B3157 Weymouth to Bridport Road, then turn off towards the sea at the sign for Fleet.

Web: www.johansens.com/moonfleetmanor
E-mail: info@moonfleetmanorhotel.co.uk
Tel: 0870 381 8744
International: +44 (0)1305 786948
Fax: 01305 774395

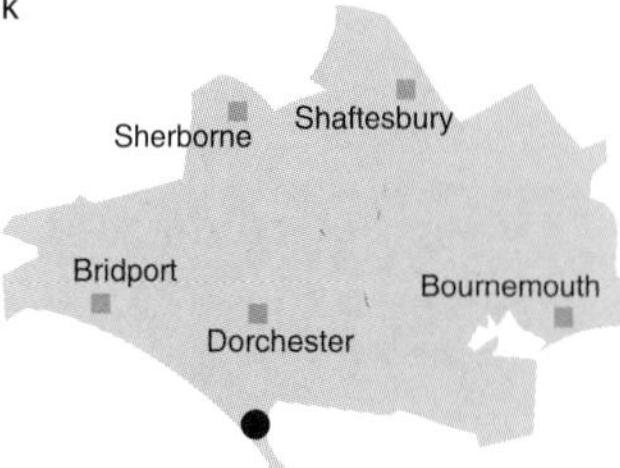

Price Guide:
double/twin £170–£270
suite from £310

Overlooking Chesil Beach, a unique feature of the Dorset coast, Moonfleet Manor is both a luxury hotel and a family resort. The owners have applied the same flair for design evident in their other family friendly properties, Woolley Grange, The Ickworth Hotel and Fowey Hall in Cornwall. The use of a variety of unusual antiques and objects from around the world lends a refreshing and individual style to this comfortable and attractive hotel. Bedrooms are beautifully decorated and furnished and a range of amenities ensures that guests enjoy standards of maximum comfort and convenience. Enthusiastic and attentive staff work hard to ensure that guests feel at home, whatever their age. Moonfleet's dining room, whose décor and style would do credit to a fashionable London restaurant, offers an excellent and varied menu based on fresh local produce but bringing culinary styles from around the world. Facilities at the hotel include an indoor swimming pool with squash and tennis courts for the more energetic. Key places of interest nearby include Abbotsbury, Dorchester, Corfe Castle and Lulworth Cove, whilst in Weymouth itself the Sea Life Park, The Deep Sea Adventure and The Titanic Story are worth a visit.

Our inspector loved: *The real welcome and provision for your children.*

Headlam Hall

HEADLAM, NEAR GAINFORD, DARLINGTON, COUNTY DURHAM DL2 3HA

This magnificent 17th-century Jacobean mansion stands in 4 acres of formal walled gardens. The grand main lawn, ancient beach hedges and flowing waters evoke an air of tranquillity. Located in the picturesque hamlet of Headlam, surrounded by over 200 acres of its own rolling farmland, Headlam Hall offers a special ambience of seclusion and opulence. The traditional bedrooms are all en suite; many are fitted with period furniture. The restaurant serves modern English and Continental cuisine alongside an extensive, well-chosen wine list. Guests may dine in the tasteful surroundings of either the Panelled Room, the Victorian Room, the Patio Room or Conservatory. The main hall features huge stone pillars and a superb original carved oak fireplace, which has dominated the room for over 300 years. The elegant Georgian Drawing Room opens out to a stepped terrace overlooking the main lawn. The hotel also offers extensive conference facilities and a fine ballroom: the Edwardian Suite with its oak floor and glass ceiling, which is able to accommodate up to 150 people. The new Headlam Spa has a swimming pool, outdoor spa pool, sauna, steam room, gym, exercise studio and provides health and beauty treatments and a new Brasserie Bar. There is also a 9-hole golf course, driving range, golf shop, tennis court, croquet lawn, coarse fishing and a snooker room.

Directions: Headlam is 2 miles north of Gainford off A67 Darlington–Barnard Castle road.

Web: www.johansens.com/headlamhall
E-mail: admin@headlamhall.co.uk
Tel: 0870 381 8590
International: +44 (0)1325 730238
Fax: 01325 730790

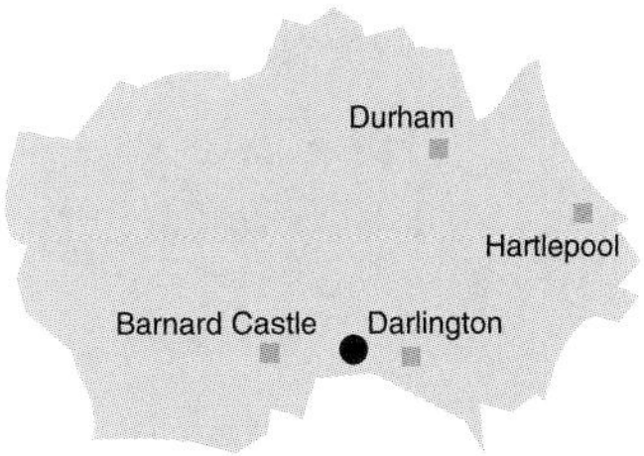

Durham
Hartlepool
Barnard Castle
Darlington

Price Guide:
single £90–£120
double/twin £110–£140
suite from £150

Our inspector loved: *The recent addition of the golf course and spa.*

Five Lakes Hotel, Golf, Country Club & Spa

COLCHESTER ROAD, TOLLESHUNT KNIGHTS, MALDON, ESSEX CM9 8HX

Set in 320 acres, the superb Five Lakes Hotel, Golf, Country Club & Spa successfully combines leisure, health and sports activities with excellent conference and banqueting facilities. Each of the 194 bedrooms are furnished to a high standard offering every comfort and convenience. With two 18-hole golf courses – one of which, the Lakes Course, was designed by Neil Coles MBE – Five Lakes is one of East Anglia's leading golf venues. Guests can take advantage of the indoor and outdoor championship-standard tennis courts; squash and badminton courts; an indoor pool with spa bath, steam room and sauna; gymnasium; jogging trail, snooker and a luxurious Health & Beauty Spa. Two restaurants offer a choice of good food which is complemented by excellent service. Comfortable lounges and 2 bars provide convivial surroundings in which to relax and enjoy a drink. The extensive facilities for conferences, meetings and exhibitions include 18 meeting rooms, a 3,500m^2 exhibition hall holding over 2,000 guests and a dedicated activity field.

Our inspector loved: *The rooms that overlook the natural settings of lakes, flowers and waterfowl.*

Directions: From M25 jct 28 to A12, turn left at the Fox pub at Gt Braxted /Silver End exit or A12 from north, exit at Kelvedon. Follow brown tourist signs to the resort, on the B1026. 32 miles from Stansted Airport.

Web: www.johansens.com/fivelakes
E-mail: enquiries@fivelakes.co.uk
Tel: 0870 381 8524
International: +44 (0)1621 868888
Fax: 01621 869696

Price Guide: (room only)
single £110
double/twin £165
suites £235

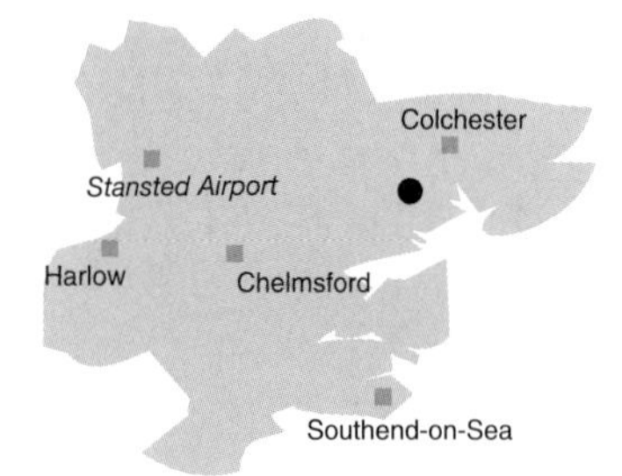

The Swan Hotel At Bibury

BIBURY, GLOUCESTERSHIRE GL7 5NW

The Swan Hotel at Bibury in the South Cotswolds, a 17th-century coaching inn, is a perfect base for both leisurely and active holidays which will appeal especially to motorists, fishermen and walkers. The hotel has its own fishing rights and a moated ornamental garden encircled by its own crystalline stream. Bibury itself is a delightful village, with its honey-coloured stonework, picturesque ponds, the trout-filled River Coln and its utter lack of modern eyesores. When Cotswold Inns and Hotels acquired the Swan they gained a distinctive hotel in the English countryside which acknowledges the needs of the sophisticated modern-day traveller. Oak panelling, plush carpets and sumptuous fabrics create the background for the fine paintings and antiques that grace the interiors. The 18 eccentric bedrooms are superbly appointed with luxury bathrooms and comfortable furnishings. Guests may dine in the Café Swan and the unique Gallery Restaurant. Midweek special rates available.

Our inspector loved: *The newly decorated Gallery restaurant and outside terrace.*

Directions: Bibury is signposted off A40 Oxford–Cheltenham road, on the left hand side. Secure free parking now available next to the hotel.

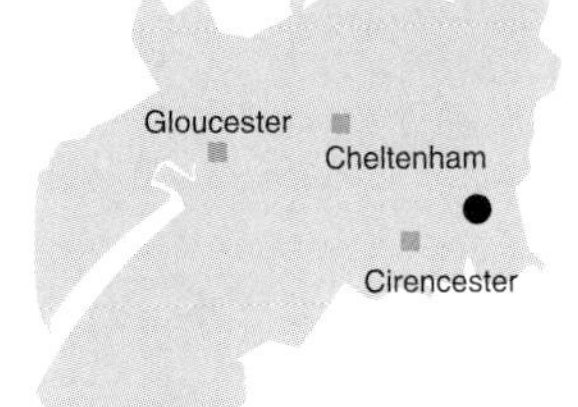

Web: www.johansens.com/swanhotelatbibury
E-mail: info@swanhotel.co.uk
Tel: 0870 381 8931
International: +44 (0)1285 740695
Fax: 01285 740473

Price Guide:
single £99–£155
double/twin £140–£260

The Dial House

THE CHESTNUTS, HIGH STREET, BOURTON-ON-THE-WATER, GLOUCESTERSHIRE GL54 2AN

Built in 1698 from traditional Cotswold stone, The Dial House is the essence of sophisticated English country style offering guests peace and tranquillity, charm, and a spacious, luxurious interior filled with period furnishings such as large inglenook fireplaces, exposed timber beams, monks' chairs, poor boxes, secret cupboards, water wells and stone arches. Surrounded by a secluded lawned garden, highlighted by aromatic flowers and colourful shrub-filled borders and beds, this privately owned, family-run hotel is idyllically situated in a picturesque and unspoiled village where the little River Windrush flows down the main street under "toy town" low bridges beside trees and lawns. Each of the hotel's 13 bedrooms has every detail and accessory to make a guest's stay comfortable and memorable: hand-painted wallpaper, lavish big beds, deep baths, exquisite fabrics, together with television, video, direct dial telephone and state-of-the-art communication links. Mouth-watering cuisine, created from the finest and freshest of local and national produce, is served in intimate dining rooms whose innovative style and high standards have been recognised by 2 AA Rosettes and Which? Hotel of the Year 2005 Most Ravishing Restaurant with Rooms Award. Blenheim Palace, Warwick Castle, the Roman antiquities at Bath and all the delights of Shakespeare country are nearby.

Our inspector loved: *The beautiful newly decorated bar and sitting room.*

Directions: From the A40 take the A429 north towards Stow-on-the-Wold for approximately 3.5 miles.

Web: www.johansens.com/dialhouse
E-mail: info@dialhousehotel.com
Tel: 0870 381 9296
International: +44 (0)1451 822244
Fax: 01451 810126

Price Guide:
single £55–£89
double £120–£160
suite £180

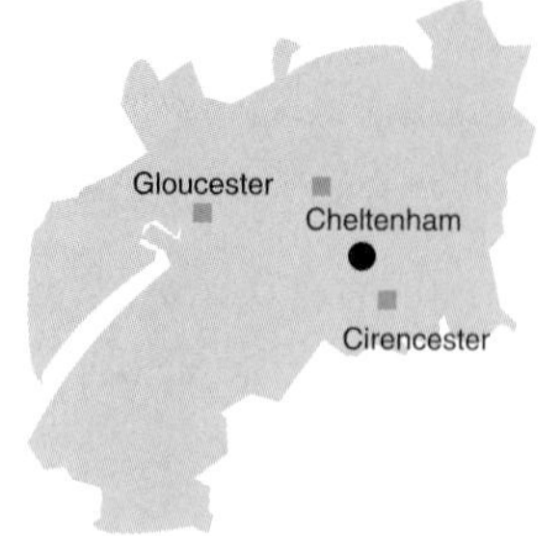

Hotel On The Park

EVESHAM ROAD, CHELTENHAM, GLOUCESTERSHIRE GL52 2AH

Situated in the refined, Regency spa town of Cheltenham, this attractive wisteria-clad town house hotel combines the elegance and attentive, quality service of the past with an impressive 21st-century standard of accommodation and facilities. The imposing white façade, with grand pillared doorway, leads visitors into a charming, luxurious interior, which has a very welcoming, relaxed atmosphere. Bedrooms are traditional with a contemporary twist and delightfully furnished with antiques. The bathrooms are very special and range from an infinity spa bathroom, through to state-of-the-art whirlpool bathrooms and a spa bathroom with aromatherapy/chromatherapy, which either energises or relaxes bathers with aromatics and mood lighting. The infinity bath, with gently cascading water is enhanced by a spectrum cycle of colours that can be controlled according to guests' moods. Parkers the brasserie takes a contemporary approach to food and décor; menus feature imaginative, vibrant cuisine complemented by an unusual and carefully chosen wine list. The public rooms offer comfort and style, and the well-stocked library is popular with those seeking quiet contemplation, a peaceful read or private chat. The town's attractive promenade, exclusive boutiques, theatres and historic attractions are within walking distance, and the Cheltenham National Hunt Racecourse is nearby.

Our inspector loved: *The state-of-the-art bathrooms and lovely bedrooms.*

Directions: The hotel is opposite Pittville Park, a 5-minute walk from the town centre.

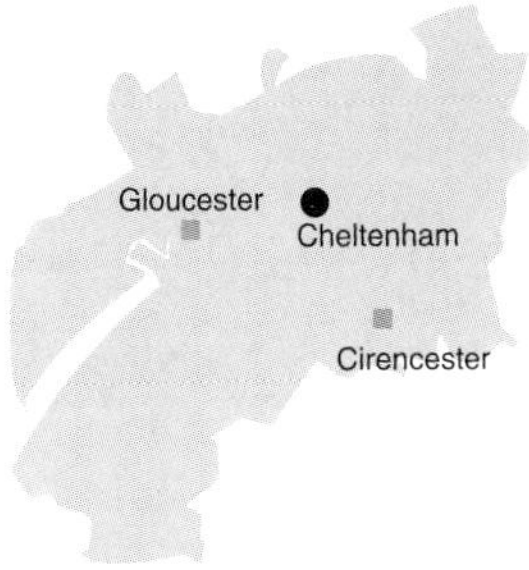

Gloucester
Cheltenham
Cirencester

Web: www.johansens.com/hotelonthepark
E-mail: stay@hotelonthepark.co.uk
Tel: 0870 381 8623
International: +44 (0)1242 518898
Fax: 01242 511526

Price Guide:
single from £106.50
double/twin from £126–£136

The Greenway

SHURDINGTON, CHELTENHAM, GLOUCESTERSHIRE GL51 4UG

Directions: On the outskirts of Cheltenham off the A46 Cheltenham–Stroud road, 2½ miles from the town centre.

Web: www.johansens.com/greenway
E-mail: info@thegreenway.co.uk
Tel: 0870 381 8574
International: +44 (0)1242 862352
Fax: 01242 862780

Price Guide:
single from £99
double/twin £150–£240

Set amidst gentle parkland with the rolling Cotswold hills beyond, The Greenway is an Elizabethan country house with a style that is uniquely its own – very individual and very special. Renowned for the warmth of its welcome, its friendly atmosphere and its immaculate personal service, The Greenway is the ideal place for total relaxation. The public rooms with their antique furniture and fresh flowers are elegant and spacious yet comfortable, with roaring log fires in winter and access to the formal gardens in summer. The 21 bedrooms all have private bathrooms and are individually decorated with co-ordinated colour schemes. Eleven of the rooms are located in the main house with a further ten rooms in the converted Georgian coach house immediately adjacent to the main building. The award-winning conservatory dining room overlooks the sunken garden, providing the perfect backdrop to superb cuisine of international appeal complemented by an outstanding selection of wines. Situated in one of Britain's most charming areas, The Greenway is well placed for visiting the spa town of Cheltenham, the Cotswold villages and Shakespeare country.

Our inspector loved: *The pretty terrace, and the hotel puppy Mr Biggles.*

21 40

Cotswold House Hotel

HIGH STREET, CHIPPING CAMPDEN, GLOUCESTERSHIRE GL55 6AN

Chipping Campden is a nostalgic Cotswold town, unspoilt by the 21st-century, and Cotswold House Hotel is a splendid Regency mansion facing the town square, impressive with colonnades flanking the front door and built in soft local stone. The interior successfully contrasts a witty mix of modern style with the surrounding splendid architecture, including a signature spiral staircase. Original pieces of artwork adorn every room, and modern glass sculptures and award-winning lighting are a feast for the senses. The peaceful bedrooms are individually designed, decorated in warm tones and furnished with contemporary furniture of the utmost quality. Most guest rooms, particularly those in the recently opened Montrose House, include state-of-the-art technology, bathroom TVs, feature lighting, huge baths and luscious toiletries. Cotswold House Hotel is deservedly proud of its kitchen, which has won many accolades. The elegant Juliana's Restaurant serves locally sourced cuisine alongside a cellar book of 150 wines. Informal meals are provided in Hicks' Brasserie. Private functions and conferences for up to 100 can be held in the bespoke Montrose Suite or the intimate Grammar School Suite. Guests can enjoy exploring Chipping Campden's intriguing shops and alleyways. The hotel is a ideal base for Stratford-on-Avon and Oxford, and has parking facilities.

Directions: Chipping Campden is 2 miles north-east of A44, on the B4081.

Web: www.johansens.com/cotswoldhouse
E-mail: reception@cotswoldhouse.com
Tel: 0870 381 8449
International: +44 (0)1386 840330
Fax: 01386 840310

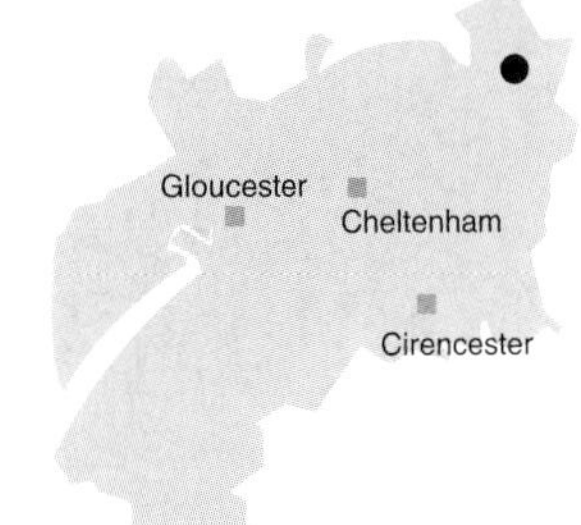

Price Guide:
single from £140
double/twin from £285
cottage room from £395
junior suite from £425
grammar school 2-bed suite from £650

Our inspector loved: *The fabulous lighting and the up to date technology*

The Noel Arms Hotel

HIGH STREET, CHIPPING CAMPDEN, GLOUCESTERSHIRE GL55 6AT

A long tradition of hospitality awaits you at the Noel Arms Hotel. In 1651 the future Charles II rested here after his Scottish army was defeated by Cromwell at the Battle of Worcester, and for centuries the hotel has entertained visitors to the ancient and unspoilt, picturesque Cotswold village of Chipping Campden. Many reminders of the past, fine antique furniture, swords, shields and other mementoes can be found around the hotel. There are 26 en-suite bedrooms in either the main house or in the tastefully constructed new wing, some of which boast luxurious antique four-poster beds and all offering the standards you expect from a country hotel. The restaurant offers an excellent modern British menu including a seasonal selection of fresh local produce, as well as the option of a superb Oriental fusion menu from the hotel's Chinese chef. You may be tempted to choose from the gastropub food available in the conservatory and Dover's Bar, much of which is Cotswold produce. The fine selection of wines from around the world are a delicious accompaniments to any meal. Try some of the traditional cask ales and keg beers. Browse around the delightful array of shops in Chipping Campden or many of the enchanting honey-coloured Cotswold villages, Hidcote Manor Gardens, Cheltenham Spa, Worcester, Oxford and Stratford-upon-Avon which are all close by.

Directions: The Noel Arms is in the centre of Chipping Campden, which is on the B4081, 2 miles east of the A44.

Web: www.johansens.com/noelarms
E-mail: reception@noelarmshotel.com
Tel: 0870 381 8763
International: +44 (0)1386 840317
Fax: 01386 841136

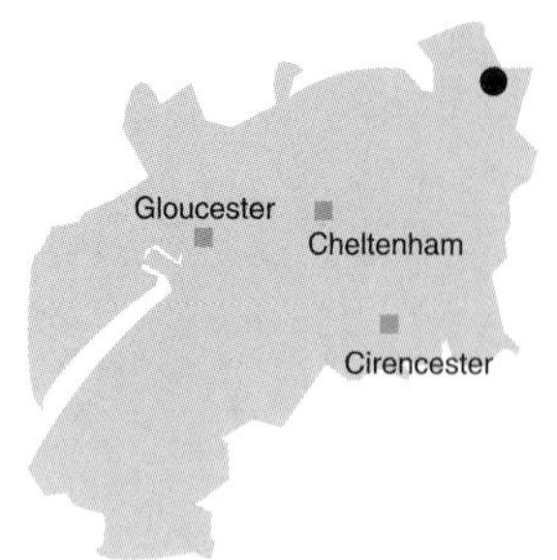

Price Guide:
single £95
double £130–£220

Our inspector loved: *The friendly staff and relaxed atmosphere.*

LOWER SLAUGHTER MANOR

LOWER SLAUGHTER, GLOUCESTERSHIRE GL54 2HP

Queen of the Cotswolds, this magnificently regal manor house is the epitome of luxury and refinement, contemporary design and exemplary service with a uniqueness that positively oozes style. "Designer" rooms, with a chic continental flavour, enhance guests' experience and cleverly complement the history of this exceptional house. The renowned, award-winning cuisine is prepared from the best local produce and offers an outstanding wine list of 800 specially selected wines from the Old and New Worlds. Grade II listed, Lower Slaughter Manor stands in its own private grounds in one of England's prettiest villages. The wonderful grounds comprise a croquet lawn and tennis court, and, within the delightful walled garden, a unique 2-storey dovecote that dates back to the 15th century. An excellent setting for private parties, weddings and civil partnership ceremonies, the Manor is also an inspired venue for business meetings. Visitors may wish to explore the surrounding areas of the Cotswolds, Cheltenham, Stratford, and Warwick and Sudeley Castles.

Our inspector loved: *The wow factor of the Antoinette Room.*

Directions: The Manor is on the right as Lower Slaughter is approached from the A429.

Web: www.johansens.com/lowerslaughtermanor
E-mail: info@lowerslaughter.co.uk
Tel: 0870 381 8706
International: +44 (0)1451 820456
Fax: 01451 822150

Price Guide:
single £175–£375
double/twin £200–£400
suite £350–£400

WASHBOURNE COURT HOTEL

LOWER SLAUGHTER, GLOUCESTERSHIRE GL54 2HS

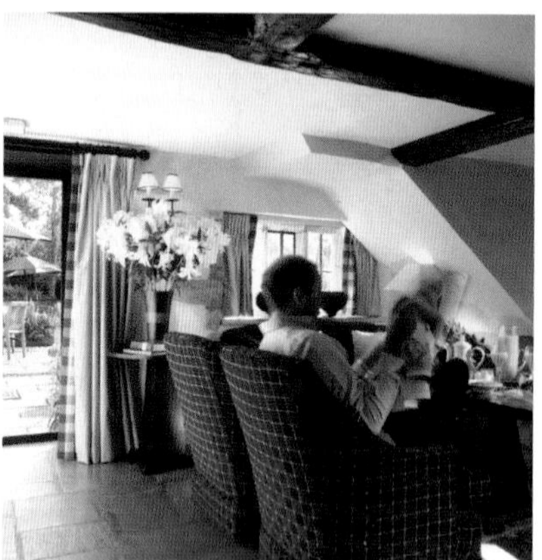

Directions: The hotel is situated ½ a mile from the main A429 Fosseway between Stow-on-the-Wold and Bourton-on-the-Water (signed To the Slaughters).

Web: www.johansens.com/washbournecourt
E-mail: info@washbournecourt.co.uk
Tel: 0870 381 8970
International: +44 (0)1451 822143
Fax: 01451 821045

Price Guide: (including dinner)
single from £115
double/twin from £170

Nestling by the River Eye in the idyllic Cotswolds village of Lower Slaughter, one of the prettiest villages in England, stands Washbourne Court Hotel. This 17th-century hotel is surrounded by 4 acres of private gardens and grounds and effortlessly combines the charm and character of a traditional retreat with contemporary touches and the latest amenities. Beamed ceilings, stone mullioned windows and original open fireplaces delight guests in search of a cosy country bolthole, while the 28 opulent bedrooms include modern fabrics and tasteful colour schemes. Some of the rooms in the main building date back over 400 years and new rooms are located in the Coach House. The cottage suites will please the most discerning traveller. Breakfast, afternoon tea and light meals can be enjoyed on the attractive garden terrace during fine weather. For a more formal experience, the British menu, made from local produce and served in the elegant restaurant or private dining room, must not be missed! The stylish Mayflower meeting room can cater for up to 16 delegates, and the private dining room can accommodate conferences and banquets.

Our inspector loved: *The relaxing atmosphere, and beautiful setting.*

Burleigh Court

BURLEIGH, MINCHINHAMPTON, NEAR STROUD, GLOUCESTERSHIRE GL5 2PF

Built in the 18th century, Burleigh Court Hotel is a former gentleman's manor house nestling on the edge of a steep hillside overlooking the Golden Valley in the heart of the Cotswolds. Comfortable surroundings, quality service, the ambience of a bygone era and a tranquil, relaxed atmosphere are combined with 3½ acres of beautifully tended gardens featuring terraces, ponds, pools, hidden pathways and Cotswold stone walls to create an idyllic setting. All the bedrooms are individually and delightfully furnished, with the highest standard of facilities and stunning scenic views. The coach house bedrooms, located by a Victorian plunge pool, and those within the courtyard gardens provide versatile accommodation for families. The elegant restaurant has a reputation for classical cuisine which utilises only the best local produce, whilst an extensive cellar produces a wine list to satisfy the most demanding palate. For special occasions a private dining room overlooking the rear terrace is available. Burleigh Court is perfectly situated to explore the famous honey-stoned villages of the Cotswolds, the market towns of Minchinhampton, Tetbury, Cirencester, Painswick and Bibury and attractions such as Berkely Castle and Chavenage House.

Our inspector loved: *The well-kept grounds and wonderful views.*

Directions: Leave Stroud on A419 towards Cirencester. After approximately 2½ miles turn right, signposted Burleigh and Minchinhampton. After a further 500 yards turn left and the hotel is signposted.

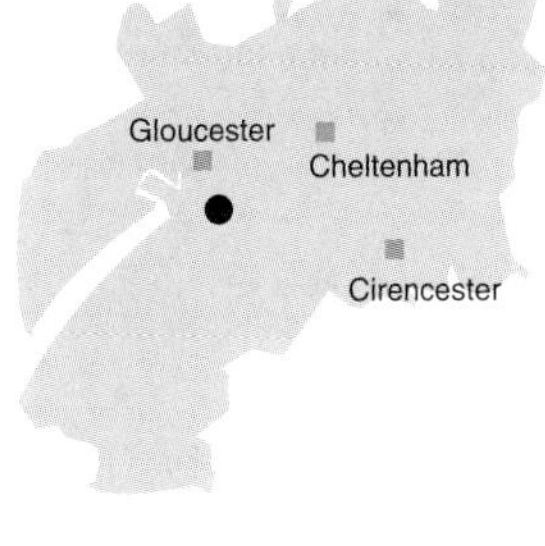

Web: www.johansens.com/burleighgloucestershire
E-mail: info@burleighcourthotel.co.uk
Tel: 0870 381 8664
International: +44 (0)1453 883804
Fax: 01453 886870

Gloucester
Cheltenham
Cirencester

Price Guide:
single £80-£105
double £125-£145
suite £170

THE PAINSWICK HOTEL & OLD RECTORY RESTAURANT

KEMPS LANE, PAINSWICK, GLOUCESTERSHIRE GL6 6YB

Directions: M5 Jct13. Painswick is on A46 between Stroud and Cheltenham, turn into road by the church and continue round the corner, taking the first right. The hotel is at the bottom of the road on the right hand side.

Web: www.johansens.com/painswick
E-mail: reservations@painswickhotel.com
Tel: 0870 381 8797
International: +44 (0)1452 812160
Fax: 01452 814059

Price Guide:
single from £95
double/twin from £145–£220

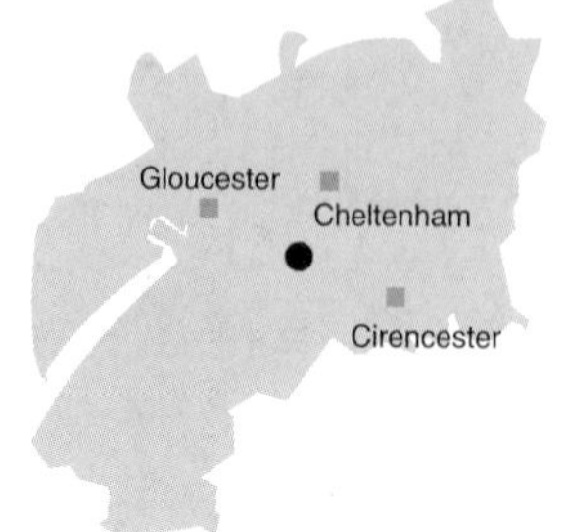

The Painswick Hotel is the perfect location from which to discover the heart of the Cotswolds. A beautiful former rectory built in 1790 in the Palladian style, the hotel is set within the enchanting village of Painswick overlooking stunning countryside. Designed in traditional country house style, emphasis has been placed on providing a relaxing environment with large log fires blazing in winter, and long drinks served on the terrace in summer. There are 19 individually designed bedrooms with rich fabrics and antiques, whilst many have romantic four-poster beds. The bathrooms complement the bedrooms excellently and the sumptuous "his 'n' hers" bathroom should not be missed. Great pride is taken in the dining room where much of the produce is locally sourced and innovative menus are prepared. The fine fare is complemented by a cellar of over 250 wines ranging from French and Italian classics to New World boutiques. The hotel also makes an ideal destination for weddings and private gatherings, but its accessibility to both the M4 and M5 also make it extremely popular for business meetings. London is just 2 hours away and Cardiff and Bristol are within an hour's drive.

Our inspector loved: *The informal, relaxed atmosphere, and the location in a very pretty village.*

Stonehouse Court Hotel

BRISTOL ROAD, STONEHOUSE, GLOUCESTERSHIRE GL10 3RA

Built in 1601, this is an outstanding Grade II listed manor house set in 6 acres of secluded grounds overlooking the Cotswold landscape. An independently owned hotel renowned for providing a personal and professional service, Stonehouse offers the largest conference and meeting venue in the area, catering for up to 150 guests and provides a dedicated team to oversee wedding celebrations. Facilities are available for banquets, product launches, training courses and team-building events as well as intimate civil wedding ceremonies in the picturesque outdoor pagoda and marquees on the lawn. Relaxation and home comforts extend into the individually decorated bedrooms. Some are located in the original Tudor manor house and have fireplaces and mullioned windows with views of the mature gardens. Dinner is served in the lounge or on the terrace, and Henry's restaurant creates a delicious selection of dishes using fine local ingredients. Menus include fillet of line caught sea bass, duet of spring lamb, carrot infused pannacotta and apple and lavender mousse. Easily accessible from the M5, nearby places of interest include Gloucester Cathedral, Westonbirt Arboretum, Slimbridge Wildfowl Trust and the Cheltenham Races. The Stroud Valley offers stunning walks and cycle tracks.

Our inspector loved: *The lovely gardens backing onto the canal with views of the surrounding countryside.*

Directions: Exit the M5 at junction 13 and follow the A419 towards Stroud.

Web: www.johansens.com/stonehousecourt
E-mail: info@stonehousecourt.co.uk
Tel: 0870 381 8631
International: +44 (0)1453 794950
Fax: 0871 871 3241

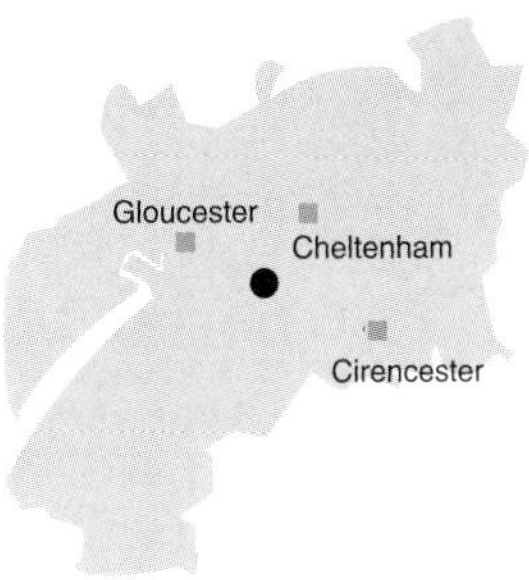

Gloucester
Cheltenham
Cirencester

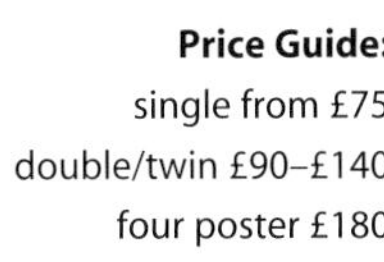

Price Guide:
single from £75
double/twin £90–£140
four poster £180

LORDS OF THE MANOR HOTEL

UPPER SLAUGHTER, NR BOURTON-ON-THE-WATER, GLOUCESTERSHIRE GL54 2JD

Situated in the heart of the Cotswolds, on the outskirts of one of England's most unspoilt and picturesque villages, stands the Lords of the Manor Hotel. Built in the 17th century of honeyed Cotswold stone, the house enjoys splendid views over the surrounding meadows, stream and parkland. For generations the house was the home of the Witts family, who historically had been rectors of the parish. It is from these origins that the hotel derives its distinctive name. Charming, walled gardens provide a secluded retreat at the rear of the house. Each bedroom bears the maiden name of one of the ladies who married into the Witts family; each room is individually and imaginatively decorated with period furniture. The reception rooms are magnificently furnished with fine antiques, paintings, traditional fabrics and masses of fresh flowers. Log fires blaze in cold weather. The heart of this English country house is its dining room, where truly memorable dishes are created from the best local ingredients. Nearby are Blenheim Palace, Warwick Castle, the Roman antiquities at Bath and Shakespeare country.

Our inspector loved: *The feeling of calm and relaxation as soon as you arrive.*

Directions: Upper Slaughter is 2 miles west of the A429 between Stow-on-the-Wold and Bourton-on-the-Water.

Web: www.johansens.com/lordsofthemanor
E-mail: enquiries@lordsofthemanor.com
Tel: 0870 381 8704
International: +44 (0)1451 820243
Fax: 01451 820696

Price Guide:
single from £110
double/twin/suites £170–£320

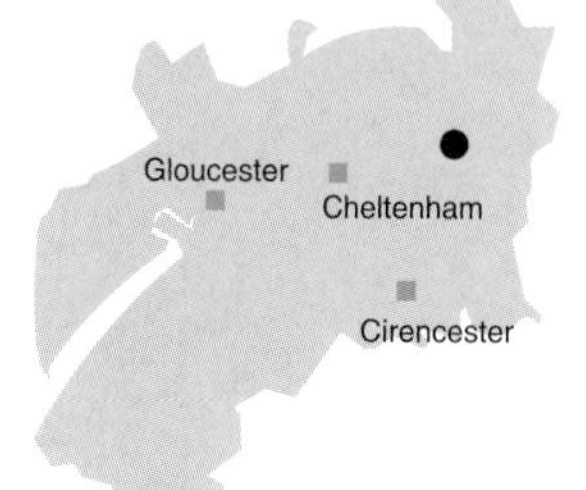

The Grapevine Hotel

SHEEP STREET, STOW-ON-THE-WOLD, GLOUCESTERSHIRE GL54 1AU

Set in the pretty town of Stow-on-the-Wold, regarded by many as the jewel of the Cotswolds, The Grapevine Hotel has an atmosphere which makes visitors feel welcome and at ease. The outstanding personal service provided by a loyal team of staff is perhaps the secret of the hotel's success. The hotel has 22 beautifully furnished bedrooms, including 6 superb garden rooms across the courtyard and offer every facility. Imaginative cuisine is served in the relaxed atmosphere of the Conservatory Restaurant. Awarded 1 AA Rosette for food, the restaurant, like all of the bedrooms, is non-smoking. In addition to fine dining in the Conservatory Restaurant, guests also have the option of eating in the hotel's popular brasserie, La Vigna. La Vigna offers its own extensive menu, with Mediterranean influenced dishes, including pasta, pizzas and tapas, being served alongside more traditional English fare. Al fresco dining is available during the summer months at both restaurants. Whether travelling on business or pleasure, guests will wish to return to The Grapevine time and again. The local landscape offers unlimited scope for exploration to the numerous picturesque villages in the Cotswolds or to the towns of Oxford, Cirencester and Stratford-upon-Avon. Nature enthusiasts will enjoy the beautiful gardens of Hidcote, Kifsgate and Barnsley House nearby. Open over Christmas.

Our inspector loved: *The friendly and welcoming staff.*

Directions: Sheep Street is part of A436 in the centre of Stow-on-the-Wold.

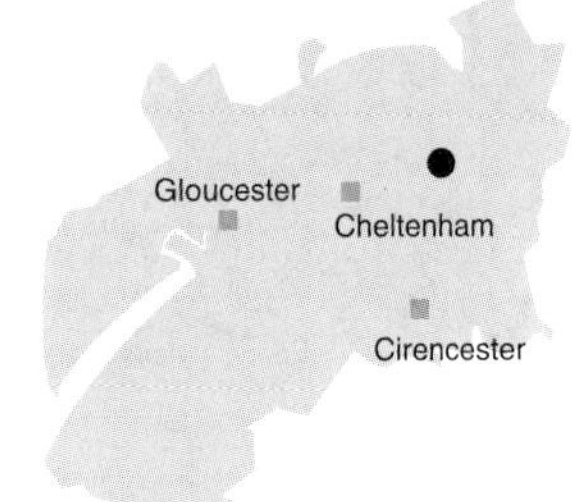

Web: www.johansens.com/grapevine
E-mail: enquiries@vines.co.uk
Tel: 0870 381 8564
International: +44 (0)1451 830344
Fax: 01451 832278

Price Guide:
single from £85
double/twin from £140

Calcot Manor Hotel & Spa

NEAR TETBURY, GLOUCESTERSHIRE GL8 8YJ

Directions: From Tetbury, take the A4135 signposted Dursley; Calcot Manor is on the right after 3½ mile

Web: www.johansens.com/calcotmanor
E-mail: reception@calcotmanor.co.uk
Tel: 0870 381 8398
International: +44 (0)1666 890391
Fax: 01666 890394

Price Guide:
double/twin £185–£225
family room £225
family suite £260

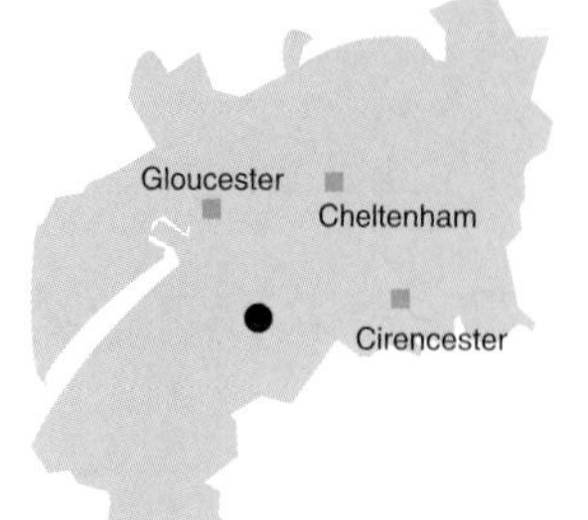

This delightful hotel, built of Cotswold stone, offers tranquillity amidst acres of rolling countryside. In the southern Cotswolds close to the historic town of Tetbury, the building dates back to the 15th century and was a farmhouse until 1983. Its beautiful stone barns and stables include one of the oldest tithe barns in England, built in 1300 by the Cistercian monks from Kingswood Abbey. These buildings form a quadrangle and the stone glistening in the dawn or glowing in the dusk is quite a spectacle. Excellent facilities for families include family suites featuring bunk beds and baby listening devices. The play facility keeps older children entertained with Playstations, X boxes and a small cinema. An Ofsted registered care crèche for younger children is open 7 days a week. Parents can escape to the spa and enjoy the 16m pool, steam room and sauna, gym, outdoor hot tub and beauty treatments. Dinner in the elegant conservatory restaurant is the focus of a memorable stay and the congenial Gumstool Bistro and Bar offers a range of simpler traditional food and local ales. The comprehensive conference facilities include The Barn, a new feature with extra conference rooms including the Thomas Suite with its state-of-the-art digital projection and sound system and a theatre style capacity of 120.

Our inspector loved: *Absolutely ideal for a spa break, a family getaway or a corporate event.*

The Hare and Hounds Hotel

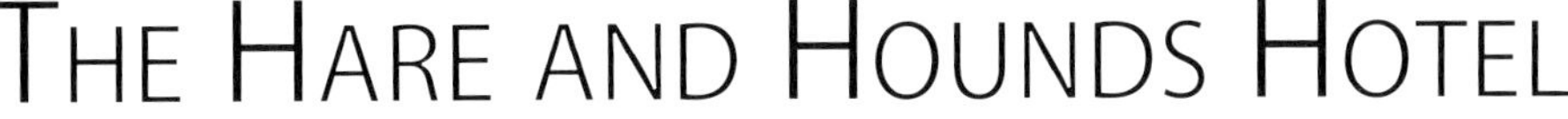

WESTONBIRT, NEAR TETBURY, GLOUCESTERSHIRE GL8 8QL

This charming and extremely welcoming country hotel stands next to the well-known Westonbirt Arboretum, home to approximately 18,000 specimens of trees and 17 miles of meandering paths. The location makes an idyllic setting for quiet getaways; spring and autumn are the most spectacular months for visiting the Arboretum. Historic Bath is only 21 miles away and excellent road and rail links make The Hare and Hounds Hotel accessible from any corner of the UK. The hotel lies in acres of well-tended grounds, and a combination of blazing log fires, polished parquet floors and club-like public rooms lend a particularly convivial atmosphere. There is a choice of elegant, carefully appointed suites, as well as interconnecting, ground floor and large family bedrooms. The delightful Westonbirt Restaurant offers a well-planned menu that will provide something to suit the most varied of palates, and traditional favourites influenced with a Continental flavour. Licensed for civil wedding ceremonies, the Ballroom, adorned with amazing historic tapestries, is a beautiful setting for any reception or dinner dance. There are also a number of well-designed and stylish meeting rooms and suites that cater for up to 200 delegates – most with direct access from both the car park and gardens.

Our inspector loved: *The wonderful location right next to Westonbirt Arboretum and the well tended grounds.*

Directions: 10 miles from the M4, junction 17, Malmesbury, Tetbury and the A433. The hotel is on the right-hand side 2½ miles outside Tetbury.

Web: www.johansens.com/hareandhounds
E-mail: enquiries@hareandhoundshotel.com
Tel: 0870 381 8302
International: +44 (0)1666 880233
Fax: 01666 880241

Price Guide:
single £88–£98
double/twin £123
superior £143
suite £156

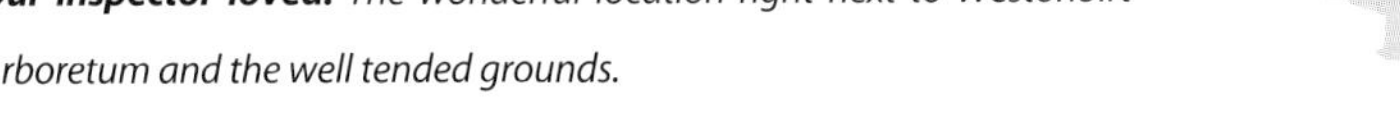

43 200

Corse Lawn House Hotel

CORSE LAWN, NR TEWKESBURY, GLOUCESTERSHIRE GL19 4LZ

Although only 6 miles from the M5 and M50, Corse Lawn is a completely unspoilt, typically English hamlet in a peaceful Gloucestershire backwater. The hotel, an elegant Queen Anne listed building set back from the village green, stands in 12 acres of gardens and grounds and still displays the charm of its historic pedigree. Visitors can be assured of the highest standards of service and cooking: Baba Hine is famous for the dishes she produces. The service here, now in the hands of son Giles, is faultlessly efficient, friendly and personal. As well as the renowned restaurant, there are 3 comfortable drawing rooms, a large lounge bar, a private dining-cum-conference room for up to 45 persons and a similar, smaller room for up to 20. A tennis court, heated indoor swimming pool and croquet lawn adjoin the hotel and most sports and leisure activities can be arranged. Corse Lawn is ideal for exploring the Cotswolds, Malverns and Forest of Dean. Short break rates are always available.

Our inspector loved: *The friendliest of welcomes at this family-run, very pretty traditional country house.*

Directions: Corse Lawn House is situated on the B4211 between the A417 (Gloucester–Ledbury road) and the A438 (Tewkesbury–Ledbury road).

Web: www.johansens.com/corselawn
E-mail: enquiries@corselawn.com
Tel: 0870 381 8448
International: +44 (0)1452 780479/771
Fax: 01452 780840

Price Guide:
single £90
double/twin £140
four-poster £160

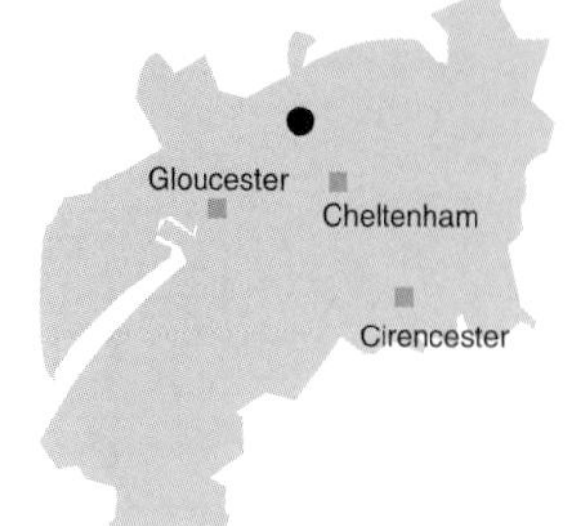

THORNBURY CASTLE

THORNBURY, SOUTH GLOUCESTERSHIRE BS35 1HH

Built in 1511 by Edward Stafford, third Duke of Buckingham, Thornbury Castle was later owned by Henry VIII, who stayed here in 1535 with Anne Boleyn. Today it stands in 15 acres of regal splendour with its vineyard, high walls and the oldest Tudor garden in England. Rich furnishings are displayed against the handsome interior features, including ornate oriel windows, panelled walls and large open fireplaces. The 25 carefully restored bedchambers retain many period details. Thornbury Castle has received many accolades for its luxurious accommodation and excellent cuisine, which includes such delights as Gloucestershire old spot pork, the freshest of south coast fish with local seasonal vegetables, local cheeses and local organic free-range eggs and you will often see the chef picking fresh herbs from the Castle garden. The Castle also provides peaceful and secluded meeting facilities. Thornbury is an ideal base from which to explore Bath, Wales and the Cotswolds. Personally guided tours are available to introduce guests to the little-known as well as the famous places which are unique to the area. In addition, golf may be enjoyed locally and day clay pigeon shooting and archery can be arranged locally.

Our inspector loved: *A unique property with an abundance of historic features and charm.*

Directions: The entrance to the Castle is left of the Parish Church at the lower end of Castle Street which is off Thornbury high street. Look for brown historic signs.

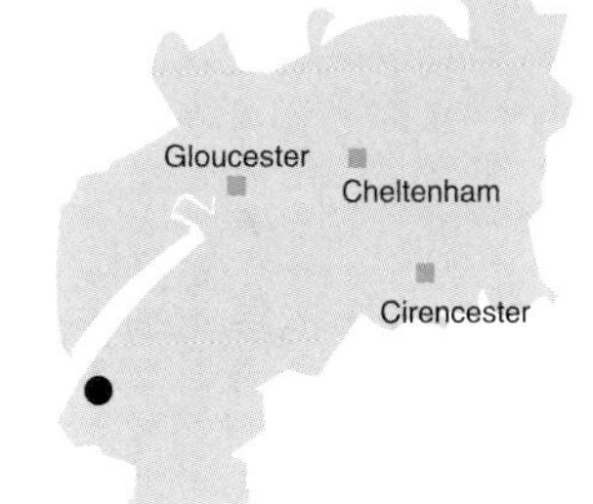

Web: www.johansens.com/thornburycastle
E-mail: info@thornburycastle.co.uk
Tel: 0870 381 8944
International: +44 (0)1454 281182
Fax: 01454 416188

Price Guide:
single from £110
double/twin from £140
suite from £295

ESSEBORNE MANOR

HURSTBOURNE TARRANT, ANDOVER, HAMPSHIRE SP11 0ER

Directions: Midway between Newbury and Andover on the A343, 1½ miles north of Hurstbourne Tarrant.

Web: www.johansens.com/esseborneманor
E-mail: info@essebornemanor.co.uk
Tel: 0870 381 8506
International: +44 (0)1264 736444
Fax: 01264 736725

Price Guide:
single £95–£135
double/twin £120–£180

Esseborne Manor is small and unpretentious, yet stylish. The present house was built at the end of the 19th century and carries the name used to record details of the local village in the Domesday Book. It is set in a pleasing garden amid the rich farmland of the North Wessex Downs in a designated area of outstanding natural beauty. Ian and Lucilla Hamilton, who own the house, have established the restful atmosphere of a private country home where guests can unwind and relax. There are now 20 bedrooms including a luxurious suite with a giant sunken Jacuzzi bath; some of the rooms are reached via a courtyard. There are delightful cottage rooms with their own patio overlooking the garden. The pretty sitting room and cosy library are comfortable areas in which to relax. Head Chef Steve Ratic's fine 2 AA Rosette-awarded cooking is set off to advantage in the new dining room and adjoining bar. There is a spacious meeting and function facility. In the grounds there is a herb garden, an all-weather tennis court, a croquet lawn and plenty of good walking beyond. Nearby Newbury racecourse has a busy programme of steeple-chasing and flat racing. Places to visit include Highclere Castle, Stonehenge, Salisbury, Winchester and Oxford.

Our inspector loved: *The The Hamilton family's commitment to ever improving standards of room provision – every comfort awaits.*

Audleys Wood

ALTON ROAD, BASINGSTOKE, HAMPSHIRE RG25 2JT

This Hampshire retreat, once a Victorian manor house, has been painstakingly converted into an intimate yet chic country hotel. Stained-glass windows are lit by candles, log fires evoke a cosy ambience and the magnificent Stucco ceiling in the Great Hall adds a feeling of grandeur. The 72 bedrooms are the very essence of comfort, with spacious beds draped in soft furnishings and carved wooden cabinets. Special touches include inviting nightcaps on the beside tables and covetable toiletries. Guests can build up an appetite by taking a brisk walk through the surrounding 7 acres of woodland before returning for preprandial drinks, served in the oak-panelled cocktail bar. Appetites can be sated in the recently restyled Gallery Restaurant. The stylish eaterie boasts decorative cast ironwork and an unusual minstrels' gallery. The menu is unashamedly British and draws heavily on the produce of the area while the accompanying wine list offers vintages from across the world. Event planners in search of a country retreat with a twist for corporate events can make use of this property on an exclusive basis. Croquet, horse-riding or exploring the Hampshire countryside and its charming villages are all tempting pastimes.

***Our inspector loved:** The stylish new presentation of the Gallery Restaurant: a fitting setting for delicious food with cheerful staff.*

Directions: The hotel is south of Basingstoke, the M3 and the A339 Alton Road. Leave the M3 at junction 6.

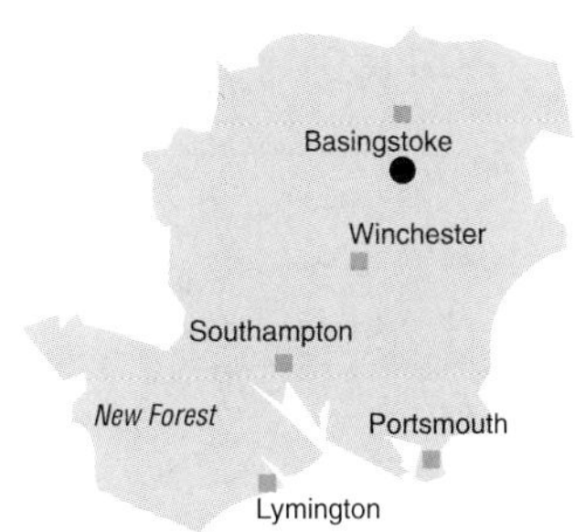

Web: www.johansens.com/audleyswood
E-mail: info@audleyswood.com
Tel: 0870 381 8497
International: +44 (0)1256 817555
Fax: 01256 817500

Price Guide:
double from £129
weekends from £85

Tylney Hall

ROTHERWICK, HOOK, HAMPSHIRE RG27 9AZ

Approaching this hotel in the evening, with its floodlit exterior and forecourt fountain, it is easy to imagine arriving for a party in a private stately home. Grade II listed and set in 66 acres of ornamental gardens and parkland, Tylney Hall typifies the great houses of a bygone era. Apéritifs are taken in the wood-panelled library bar; haute cuisine is served in the glass-domed Oak Room restaurant. The hotel holds RAC and AA food awards and also AA 4 Red Stars and RAC Gold Ribbon. The health and leisure facilities include 2 heated pools and whirlpool, solarium, fitness studio, beauty and hairdressing, sauna, tennis, croquet and snooker, whilst hot-air ballooning, archery, clay pigeon shooting, golf and riding can be arranged. Surrounding the hotel are wooded trails ideal for jogging. Functions for up to 100 people are catered for in the Tylney Suite or Chestnut Suite; more intimate gatherings are available in one of the other 10 private banqueting rooms. Tylney Hall is licensed to hold wedding ceremonies on-site. The cathedral city of Winchester, Wellington Estate, Marwell Zoological Park, Watercress Line and Milestones museum are nearby. Legoland and Windsor Castle are a 40-minute drive away.

Our inspector loved: *The spacious and elegant drawing room, where afternoon tea is a delight.*

Directions: M4/jct 11 towards Hook and Rotherwick, follow signs to the hotel. M3/jct 5, A287 towards Newnham, over the A30 into Old School Road. Left for Newnham then right onto Ridge Lane. Hotel is on the left after 1 mile.

Web: www.johansens.com/tylneyhall
E-mail: reservations@tylneyhall.com
Tel: 0870 381 8958
International: +44 (0)1256 764881
Fax: 01256 768141

Price Guide:
single £140–£430
double/twin £170–£235
suite £270–£460

The Montagu Arms Hotel

BEAULIEU, NEW FOREST, HAMPSHIRE SO42 7ZL

An AA Top 200 Hotel with 3 Red Stars in the heart of the New Forest, yet close to the M27, The Montagu Arms is a delightful hotel that takes great pride in its outstanding service. With 23 beautifully decorated bedrooms and suites, the hotel is a small oasis of luxury, winner of the AA's Courtesy and Care Award England 2003/2004 for its attentive levels of service. Available for exclusive use, the hotel lends itself ideally to both weddings and conferences, able to cater for anything between 10 and 100 people. The Terrace Restaurant overlooks the beautiful and secluded gardens, and head chef Scott Foy is happy to cater for specific occasions and tastes. Under the guidance of Shaun Hill, Director of Cooking, the Oakwood and Paris Rooms provide a more intimate setting for board meetings, family celebrations and private dining. The New Forest is well known for both sailing on the Solent and good riding in the forest; both of these activites are easily arranged by the hotel. The Montagu Arms Hotel has its own fully-crewed luxury 84ft yacht that can accommodate up to 12 guests for a day's sail, possibly reaching Cowes on the Isle of Wight or the famous Needles. The hotel also has strong links with a number of nearby estates where clay pigeon shooting, fishing, and other country pursuits can take place.

Our inspector loved: *The calming ambience of this beautiful conservation village hotel; the perfect base from which to explore the surrounding area.*

Directions: The village of Beaulieu is well signposted and the hotel commands an impressive position at the foot of the main street.

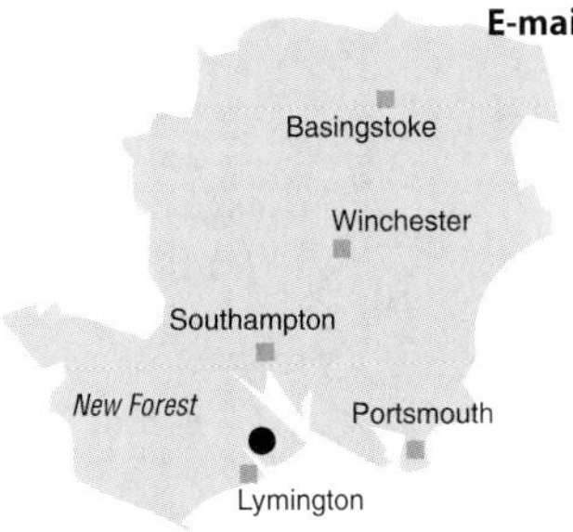

Web: www.johansens.com/montaguarms
E-mail: reservations@montaguarmshotel.co.uk
Tel: 0870 381 8743
International: +44 (0)1590 612324
Fax: 01590 612188

Price Guide: (inclusive terms available)
single from£135
double/twin £185–£273
suites £215–£313

Careys Manor Hotel & Senspa

BROCKENHURST, NEW FOREST, HAMPSHIRE SO42 7RH

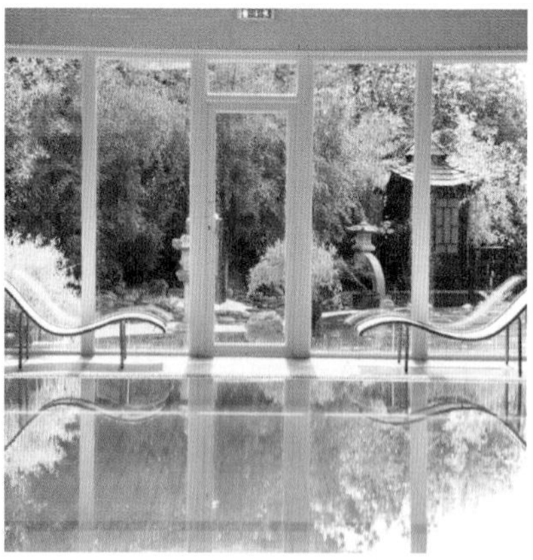

Careys Manor dates from 1888 and is built on the site of a royal hunting lodge used by Charles II. Situated close to the glorious New Forest countryside, the hotel is proud of the personal welcome and care it extends to its visitors. The bedrooms are comfortably appointed and furnished in a range of styles. The old manor house bedrooms are traditional whilst some of the modern Garden wing rooms have balconies and others open directly onto lawns and borders. The hotel offers 3 restaurants: the award-winning two AA Rosette Manor Restaurant, Blaireaus French Bistro and The Zen Garden Thai Restaurant. The superb luxury Thai Spa is set within the grounds and linked to the hotel through charming corridors. A variety of treatments are performed by Eastern and Western therapists and there is a state-of-the-art hydrotherapy pool with several experience rooms and showers, which include amongst others, a mud room, blizzard shower, ice room, tepidarium, laconicum and Vichy shower. Windsurfing, riding and sailing can all be enjoyed locally, whilst Stonehenge, Beaulieu, Broadlands, Salisbury and Winchester are a short distance away. There are comprehensive self-contained conference facilities available.

Our inspector loved: *All the stylish improvements, which rightly gained this hotel its fourth star.*

Directions: From the M27, junction 1, follow the A337 signed to Lymington. Careys Manor is on the left after the 30 mph sign at Brockenhurst.

Web: www.johansens.com/careysmanor
E-mail: stay@careysmanor.com
Tel: 0870 381 8405
International: +44 (0)8707 512305
Fax: 08707 512306

Price Guide:
double/twin £178–£238

LE POUSSIN AT WHITLEY RIDGE

BEAULIEU ROAD, BROCKENHURST, NEW FOREST, HAMPSHIRE SO42 7QL

Set in 25 acres of secluded parkland in the heart of the New Forest, this privately owned Georgian house was once a Royal hunting lodge visited by the Queen Mother. Today it has the ambience of a true country house with the accent on relaxation. The bedrooms are individually decorated, and most have lovely views over open forest. The public rooms are similarly luxurious and elegant and log fires burn on cool evenings. Internationally acclaimed chef patron Alex Aitken, awarded Hampshire Chef of the Year by Hampshire Life Magazine, has re-located his famous Le Poussin restaurant, which holds a Michelin Star and 3 AA Rosettes, in to Whitley Ridge whilst nearby Parkhill undergoes extensive refurbishment and expansion; his innovative, imaginative cuisine is a joy not to be missed. Guests can relax in the grounds or enjoy a game of tennis. Some of the country's best woodland walks are directly accessible from the gardens. Whichever pastime you choose, Whitley Ridge guarantees a restful and enjoyable stay. A number of stately homes, including Broadlands and Wilton House, are within easy reach. Lord Montague's Motor Museum, Buckler's Hard and historic Stonehenge are also within driving distance.

Our inspector loved: *Parquet floors and open fires set the tone – come here for really serious eating.*

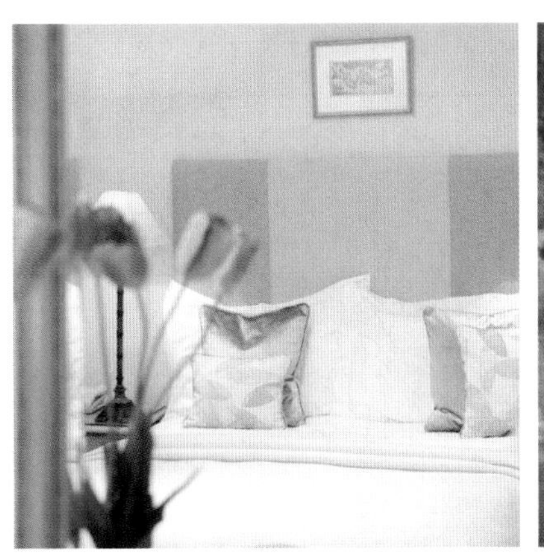

Directions: M27 junction 1. Situated on the B3055, Brockenhurst – Beaulieu

Web: www.johansens.com/poussinwhitleyridge
E-mail: whitley@lepoussin.co.uk
Tel: 0870 381 8994
International: +44 (0)1590 622354
Fax: 01590 622856

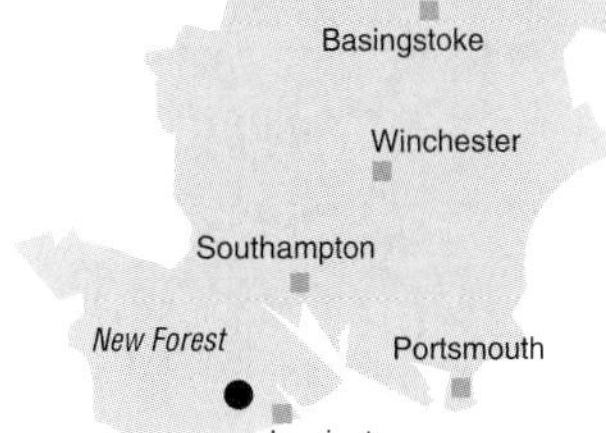

Price Guide:
single from £70
double £110–£220
cottage suite £180–£220

New Park Manor & Bath House Spa

LYNDHURST ROAD, BROCKENHURST, NEW FOREST, HAMPSHIRE SO42 7QH

Directions: New Park Manor is ½ mile off the A337 between Lyndhurst and Brockenhurst, easily reached from the M27, junction 1.

Web: www.johansens.com/newparkmanor
E-mail: info@newparkmanorhotel.co.uk
Tel: 0870 381 8761
International: +44 (0)1590 623467
Fax: 01590 622268

Price Guide:
double/twin £155–£275
four poster £295

Escape from the pressures of a hectic lifestyle in this Grade II listed former Charles II hunting lodge that dates from the 16th century. Within its own clearing, in the heart of the New Forest, New Park is easily accessed from the main Lyndhurst/Lymington road. All bedrooms have views of the surrounding parklands and forest and are individually decorated, in-keeping with the historic nature of the manor. The Forest Rooms are contemporary and have LCD TV screens in the bathrooms! Wandering ponies and wild deer can be seen from the hotel and on the many walks and paths through the forest. The Equestrian Centre, with BHS trained stable crew, heated outdoor pool and gardens, affords the perfect starting point from which to explore the countryside and visit the nearby coast and sailing on the Solent. The new Bath House Spa provides a 16m swimming pool, hydro-pool, rasul, sauna, steam room and sanarium heat room. Guests can also enjoy a wide variety of treatments that are inspired by the rural setting: hay and moss wraps, holistic natural therapies, thermal spa treatments and techno-gym. The Lively Polo Bar serves light meals all day whilst the romantic restaurant has a more extensive menu of traditional British cuisine with a continental twist. The New Forest Room, with its picture windows, makes is a wonderful location for tailor-made parties or functions.

Our inspector loved: *The delightful new spa – very relaxed and stylish.*

      SPA   

Passford House Hotel

MOUNT PLEASANT LANE, LYMINGTON, HAMPSHIRE SO41 8LS

Set in 9 acres of picturesque gardens and rolling parkland, the Passford House Hotel lies midway between the charming New Forest village of Sway and the Georgian splendour of Lymington. Once the home of Lord Arthur Cecil, it is steeped in history and the traditions of leisurely country life. Pleasantly decorated bedrooms include a number of superior rooms, whilst comfort is the keynote in the 4 public lounges. The hotel prides itself on the standard and variety of cuisine served in its delightful restaurant and the extensive menu aims to give pleasure to the most discerning of palates. Meals are complemented by a speciality wine list. The hotel boasts a compact leisure centre, catering for all ages and activities. In addition to 2 heated swimming pools, there is a multi-gym, sauna, pool table, croquet lawn, pétanque and tennis court. Just a short drive away are Beaulieu, the cathedral cities of Winchester and Salisbury and ferry ports to the Isle of Wight and France. The New Forest has numerous golf courses, riding and trekking centres, cycling paths, beautiful walks, and of course sailing on the Solent. Milford-on-Sea, 4 miles away, is the nearest beach.

Our inspector loved: *The relaxed atmosphere with good food and good service.*

Directions: Exit 1/M27, A337 to Brockenhurst. The road runs beneath a railway bridge just before a mini roundabout. Straight over this roundabout, taking the next right immediately before the Tollhouse Pub. Continue along Sway Road for about ¾ mile and bear right into Mount Pleasant Lane.

Basingstoke
Winchester
Southampton
New Forest
Portsmouth
Lymington

Web: www.johansens.com/passfordhouse
E-mail: sales@passfordhousehotel.co.uk
Tel: 0870 381 8804
International: +44 (0)1590 682398
Fax: 01590 683494

Price Guide:
single from £100
double/twin from £180

Chewton Glen

NEW MILTON, NEW FOREST, HAMPSHIRE BH25 6QS

Voted Best Country House Hotel in the World by Gourmet magazine, Chewton Glen is set in 130 acres of gardens, woodland and parkland on the edge of the New Forest, close to the sea. Privately owned Chewton Glen is a haven of tranquillity, luxury and comfort. The wonderful setting of the restaurant, which overlooks the landscaped gardens, adds to the sublime culinary experience created by head chef Luke Matthews, who uses fresh local produce to create surprising and delicious dishes, complemented by an impressive wine list. The 58 sumptuous bedrooms, all individually designed with carefully chosen fabrics, are the ultimate in luxury with fantastic marble bathrooms, cosy bathrobes and views over the surrounding parkland. The stunning Spa opened in spring 2002. In addition to the magnificent 17 metre pool, there are now improved changing rooms with their own steam room and sauna, more treatment rooms, larger gym, hydrotherapy pool and a totally new lounge, buffet and bar with a conservatory and sun terrace. There are indoor and outdoor tennis courts, a 9-hole par 3 golf course and an outdoor swimming pool. Fishing, shooting and riding can be arranged locally.

Our inspector loved: *This fabled icon of unashamed self indulgence.*

Directions: Take A35 from Lyndhurst towards Bournemouth. Turn left at Walkford, then left before roundabout. The hotel is on the right.

Web: www.johansens.com/chewtonglen
E-mail: reservations@chewtonglen.com
Tel: 0870 381 8427
International: +44 (0)1425 275341
US toll free: 1 800 344 5087
Fax: 01425 272310

Price Guide: (room only)
double £205–£460
suites £395–£805

Chilworth Manor

CHILWORTH, SOUTHAMPTON, HAMPSHIRE SO16 7PT

A long, sweeping, tree-lined drive leads visitors to this imposing Edwardian manor house situated in 12 landscaped acres of glorious Hampshire countryside. The mellow, cream coloured stone exterior is highlighted by tall, slim, sparkling wide sash windows and an attractive balustrade. Heavy, dark oak-front doors open into a magnificent galleried hall, which sets the pattern for a rich and gracious interior overhung with a wealth of historical ambience, charm and comfort. There are 26 bedrooms with panoramic estate views in the Manor and 69 in the Garden Wing; all have been refurbished to a high standard, are pleasantly decorated and have every comfort, including 24-hour room service. Dining in the elegant restaurant is a delight, to be sampled leisurely whilst enjoying views over and beyond manicured lawns and colourful flower beds. The hotel's cuisine is innovative and imaginative and complemented by an extensive international wine list. For the energetic there is a jogging route within the grounds and a hard tennis court. Southampton's splendid shopping facilities and nightlife are within easy reach, as is Portsmouth and the cathedral city of Winchester. Extensive purpose-built conference and meeting facilities are available.

Our inspector loved: *The lofty galleried hall with its welcoming open fire.*

Directions: Take the M3 and exit at junction 14. At the roundabout take the third exit towards Romsey (A27). Chilworth Manor is on the left after Clump Inn.

Web: www.johansens.com/chilworth
E-mail: sales@chilworth-manor.co.uk
Tel: 0870 381 9057
International: +44 (0)23 8076 7333
Fax: 023 8076 6392

Price Guide:
single £55-£150
double £110-£165
suite £185-£195

Lainston House Hotel

SPARSHOLT, WINCHESTER, HAMPSHIRE SO21 2LT

Standing majestically in 63 acres of glorious parkland, this exquisite country house hotel provides a perfect retreat for rest and relaxation. Guests are attended to by courteous staff whose service is discreet yet always impeccable. Designed with comfort in mind, each of the elegant bedrooms and suites enjoys a distinctive character and luxurious en-suite facilities. The hotel is able to cater for all manner of special events from small business meetings to large family functions, and exclusive use of the property can be arranged. The principal reception room is the Dawley Barn, which is an attractively converted 17th-century barn, as well as 4 other charming meeting rooms. An unpretentious menu is on offer at The Avenue Restaurant and Al fresco Terrace, where guests dine on succulent, modern English cuisine, in opulent surroundings. For leisure pursuits, patrons have exclusive use of the well-equipped gym and mountain bikes for exploring the local area. Alternatively, laser clay shooting, quad biking or, for those with a head for heights, a flight in a hot-air balloon can be arranged. Lainston House Hotel is easily reached from Waterloo station, Heathrow Airport and central London.

***Our inspector loved:** The warm welcome and magnificent setting of this stunning country house.*

Directions: Lainston House is well signposted off the B3049 Winchester–Stockbridge road, at Sparsholt 2½ miles from Winchester.

Web: www.johansens.com/lainston
E-mail: enquiries@lainstonhouse.com
Tel: 0870 381 8667
International: +44 (0)1962 863588
Fax: 01962 776672

Price Guide:
single from £125
double/twin from £195
suite from £395

CASTLE HOUSE

CASTLE STREET, HEREFORD, HEREFORDSHIRE HR1 2NW

A simply stunning example of Georgian architecture, this elegant hotel lies in the centre of Hereford, 100m from the cathedral, overlooking the old moat. The stately façade is both impressive and immaculate, yet as soon as one steps off the street and into the hotel there is an immediate sense of serene tranquillity undisturbed by the bustling town outside. A grand staircase greets guests in the lobby, which has been attentively decorated in welcoming warm yellows and furnished with traditional pieces of furniture. Each of the bedrooms is individually designed and offers the utmost luxury, and the chic public rooms provide comfort in a stylish environment. La Rive restaurant serves exciting and carefully presented food, with a menu that perfectly balances traditional English ingredients with a European twist such as the fillet of Hereford beef with sweet potato dauphinoise, caramelised shallots and wild mushroom compote. The Left Bank Village is 100 yards from the hotel and is an ideal venue for functions, whilst Castle House itself is the perfect base from which to explore the city, returning to enjoy afternoon tea in the delightful gardens. The staff are welcoming, friendly and thoughtful, ensuring guests' complete relaxation and total enjoyment during their stay.

Our inspector loved: *The luxurious, comfortable bedrooms and excellent food.*

15

Directions: Follow signs for Hereford's City Centre and then City Centre East. From St Owen's Street turn right into St Ethelbert Street and veer right into Castle Street. Hereford Train Station is 1 mile away.

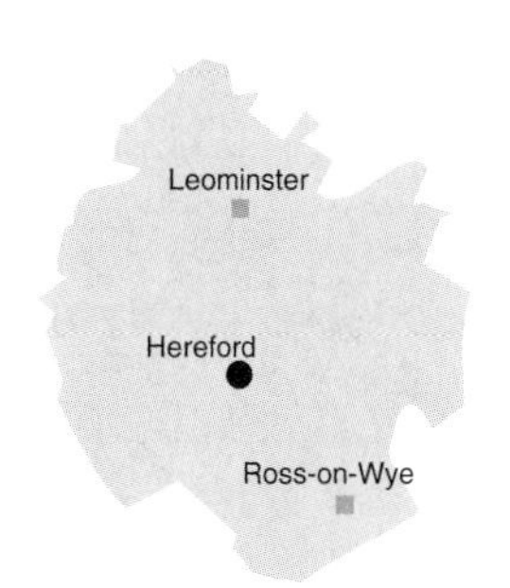

Web: www.johansens.com/castlehse
E-mail: info@castlehse.co.uk
Tel: 0870 381 9206
International: +44 (0)1432 356321
Fax: 01432 365909

Price Guide:
single £120
double £210
suite £221–£258

The Grove Hotel

CHANDLER'S CROSS, HERTFORDSHIRE WD3 4TG

This magnificent 18th-century former home of the Earls of Clarendon stands in 300 acres of Hertfordshire countryside. Painstakingly restored and transformed into an impressive cosmopolitan country estate, just 45 minutes from the centre of London, it has been awarded AA Hotel of the Year 2005, Best UK Spa Retreat 2005, by readers of Condé Nast Traveller, and is host to the World Golf Championships American Express Championships 2006. Providing the best of 21st-century living within peaceful countryside, a personal welcome and sense of sanctuary and refuge is guaranteed. Great attention to detail and quality is balanced with the ethos of pleasure and wellbeing of guests, and the gardens, grounds and woodland walks are superb. The grand interior displays antiques set against modern elegance, fine pictures and quirky touches. Guest rooms and suites are luxuriously appointed: many have balconies or terraces, some have working fireplaces and all boast panoramic garden and parkland views. There are 3 bars, 3 restaurants and a spa with 13 treatment rooms, a saltwater vitality pool, fitness and exercise studios and an 18-hole golf course. The Walled Garden features 2 tennis courts and outdoor pool, croquet lawn and herb garden. Families will benefit from Anouska's Kid's Club, a crèche and day nursery open to children aged 3 months and over.

Directions: From M25 clockwise junction 19, anti-clockwise junction 20.

Web: www.johansens.com/thegrove
E-mail: info@thegrove.co.uk
Tel: 0870 381 8646
International: +44 (0)1923 807807
Fax: +44 (0)1923 221008

Price Guide: (excluding VAT)
double/twin £250–£550
suite £700–£1,000

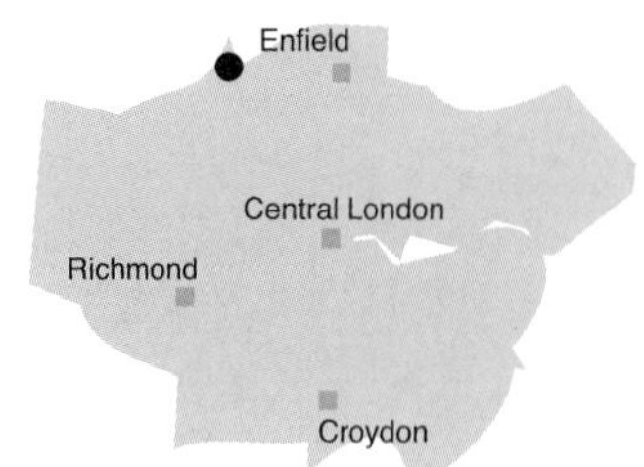

Our inspector loved: *The diverse elements that both surprise and delight.*

West Lodge Park Country House Hotel

Cockfosters Road, Hadley Wood, Barnet, Hertfordshire EN4 0PY

West Lodge Park is a country house hotel which stands in 34 acres of green belt parklands and gardens. These include a lake and an arboretum with hundreds of mature trees. Run by the Beale family for over 60 years, West Lodge Park was originally a gentleman's country seat, rebuilt in 1838 on the site of an earlier keeper's lodge. In the public rooms, antiques, original paintings and period furnishings create a restful atmosphere. All the bright and individually furnished bedrooms, many of which enjoy country views, have a full range of modern amenities. Well presented cuisine is available in the elegant restaurant. Beauty rooms feature Elemis products. Residents enjoy free membership and a free taxi to the nearby leisure centre, which has excellent facilities. Hatfield House and St Albans Abbey are a 15-minute drive away. The hotel is credited with AA 4 stars and 2 Rosettes. Top rating in Hertfordshire, Bedfordshire and North London. Enquire about special offers available.

Our inspector loved: *The stunning arboretum and the diverse programme of special events.*

Directions: The hotel is on the A111, 1 mile north of Cockfosters underground station and 1 mile south of junction 24 on the M25.

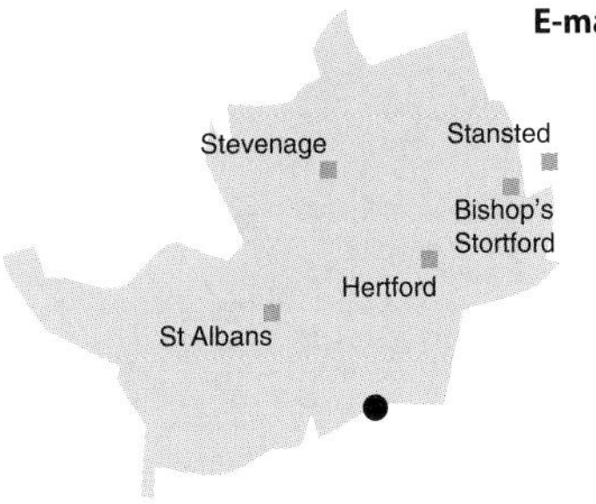

Web: www.johansens.com/westlodgepark
E-mail: westlodgepark@bealeshotels.co.uk
Tel: 0870 381 8978
International: +44 (0)20 8216 3900
Fax: 020 8216 3937

Price Guide:
single £59–£160
double/twin from £115–£180

Down Hall Country House Hotel

HATFIELD HEATH, NEAR BISHOP'S STORTFORD, HERTFORDSHIRE CM22 7AS

Directions: The hotel is 14 miles from the M25, 7 miles from the M11 and Bishop's Stortford Station. Heathrow Airport is 60 miles away; Stansted is 9 miles. There is ample free parking.

Web: www.johansens.com/downhall
E-mail: reservations@downhall.co.uk
Tel: 0870 381 8489
International: +44 (0)1279 731441
Fax: 01279 730416

Price Guide:
single from £60
double/twin from £80
suite from £120

Set in 110 acres of parkland, this Italianate mansion is the perfect choice for those wishing to escape the pressures of everyday life. A peaceful ambience pervades this tastefully restored country house hotel. The well-appointed bedrooms all feature period furnishings; and afford picturesque views across the grounds. Gastronomes will be pleased with the excellent cuisine served in the Grill Room and the new Ibbetsons 2 AA Rosette restaurant. Here, English and French dishes are prepared with only the finest fresh ingredients. The superb on-site sporting facilities include croquet lawn, swimming pool, sauna and whirlpool. Clay pigeon shooting and golf can be arranged nearby. Day excursions include visits to Cambridge, horse racing at Newmarket, Constable Country and the old timbered village of Thaxted. This is an ideal venue for board meetings, conferences, award dinners and corporate hospitality in a secluded environment. The rooms accommodate from 10 delegates boardroom style, up to 180 theatre style and a maximum of 200 for a dinner dance. An executive shuttle is available to and from Stansted Airport subject to availability.

Our inspector loved: *The grandeur of the fresh aromatic flowers and sparkling chandeliers in the lounge.*

St Michael's Manor

ST MICHAEL'S VILLAGE, FISHPOOL STREET, ST ALBANS, HERTFORDSHIRE AL3 4RY

Owned and run by the Newling Ward family for the past 40 years, St Michael's Manor is a rare gem – peaceful, intimate, and set in delightful landscaped grounds. It is also within the historic village of St Michael's and a stone's throw from the magnificent St Albans Abbey. Each of the 30 bedrooms has been individually designed – some have four-poster beds and some are sitting-room suites – and all have an elegance and charm. Many of the bedrooms overlook the award-winning grounds, set in 5 acres, with wide sweeping lawns and a beautiful lake that hosts a variety of wildlife. The Georgian lounge and the award-winning conservatory dining room also overlook the gardens and make a wonderful setting for a tantalising dinner. There is also an excellent variety of vegetarian dishes. Coffee may be served in the Oak Lounge, which dates from 1586, with its fine panelled walls and original Elizabethan ceiling. Hatfield House, the Roman remains of Verulamium and Verulam golf course – the Home of the Ryder Cup – are within easy reach, as is London, which is only 20 minutes away by train. Weekend rates from £60 per person are available.

Our inspector loved: *The new bedrooms - Especially the very surprising bathrooms.*

Directions: Easy access to the M1, junction 6/7, M25, junction 21a - 10 minutes; M4/M40 - 25 minutes; Luton Airport - 20 minutes.

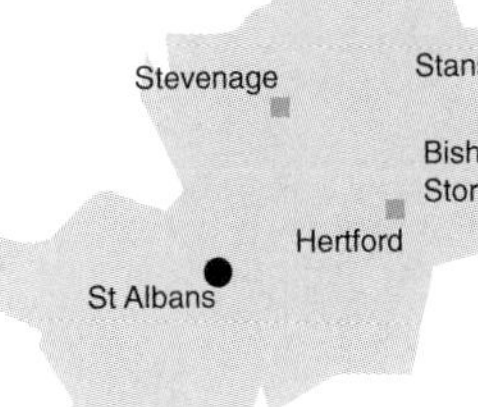

Web: www.johansens.com/stmichaelsmanor
E-mail: reservations@stmichaelsmanor.com
Tel: 0870 381 8906
International: +44 (0)1727 864444
Fax: 01727 848909

Price Guide:
single £145–£230
double/twin £180–£320
suite £250–£310

SOPWELL HOUSE

COTTONMILL LANE, SOPWELL, ST ALBANS, HERTFORDSHIRE AL1 2HQ

Once the country home of Lord Mountbatten's family and surrounded by a peaceful verdant 12-acre estate, Sopwell House is an oasis just minutes from the motorways. The classic reception rooms reflect its illustrious past and the grand panelled ballroom opens out onto the terraces and gardens. The bedrooms, some with four-posters, are spacious and well-equipped. Beautifully designed Mews Suites are ideal for long-stay executives and bridal parties. Superb modern British and International cuisine, complemented by fine wines, are served in the enchanting AA Rosette award-winning Restaurant, whilst the Brasserie offers an informal ambience. The conference and banqueting suites, overlooking the splendid gardens and terrace, are a popular venue for weddings, conferences and special events. The Country Club & Spa, dedicated to health and relaxation, has a full range of fitness facilities and qualified beauty therapists use E'SPA and Clarins.

Our inspector loved: *The extensive facilities and treatments of the spa.*

Directions: Close to M25, M1, M10, A1(M). 15 miles from Luton Airport. 28 miles from Heathrow Airport. From M25 or A414 take A1081 to St Albans. Cross roundabout and turn left after the third set of traffic lights. Hotel is ¼ mile on left.

Web: www.johansens.com/sopwellhouse
E-mail: enquiries@sopwellhouse.co.uk
Tel: 0870 381 8898
International: +44 (0)1727 864477
Fax: 01727 844741

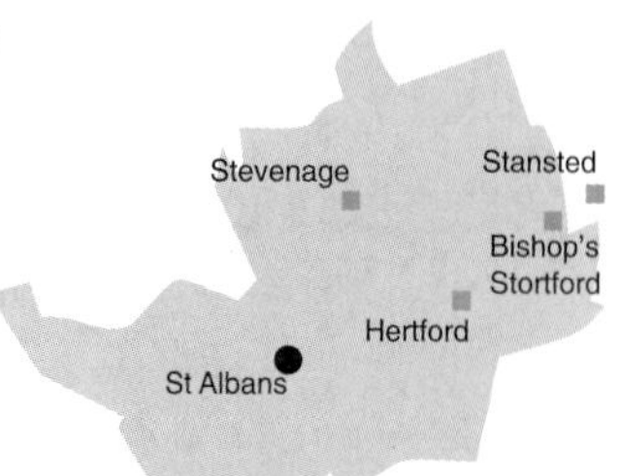

Price Guide: (room only)
single £99–£129
double/twin £169–£185
suites from £205

The Priory Bay Hotel

PRIORY DRIVE, SEAVIEW, ISLE OF WIGHT PO34 5BU

From decades gone by this beautiful site has been built upon by Medieval monks, Tudor farmers and Georgian gentry. Now its medley of buildings has been sympathetically restored and brought to life as a splendid hotel. Situated in a gorgeous open coastal setting to the south of Seaview, the Priory Bay overlooks its own private beach. Everything about it is stylish and elegant, from the impressive arched stone entrance with magnificent carved figures to the delightful, flower-filled gardens with their shady corners and thatched roofed tithe barns. The public rooms are a delight, exquisitely and comfortably furnished, with tall windows framed by rich curtains and liberally filled with vases of flowers. Log fires blaze in open fireplaces during colder months. Each of the 18 comfortable bedrooms is individually decorated and has picturesque views over the gardens. The dining room is establishing a reputation for first-class gastronomy, complemented by a fine wine list. Guests can relax under shady umbrellas in the garden or on the surrounding terraces. For the more energetic guest, there is an outdoor pool and the hotel's adjoining 6-hole golf course. The islands' coastal paths for walking and riding passes the gate, Carisbrooke Castle and Osborne House are nearby.

Our inspector loved: *Friendly hospitality with a smiling and friendly team of staff.*

Directions: Ferry from Portsmouth, Lymington or Southampton to Fishbourne, Yarmouth. Ryde, East or West Cowes. The hotel is on the B3330.

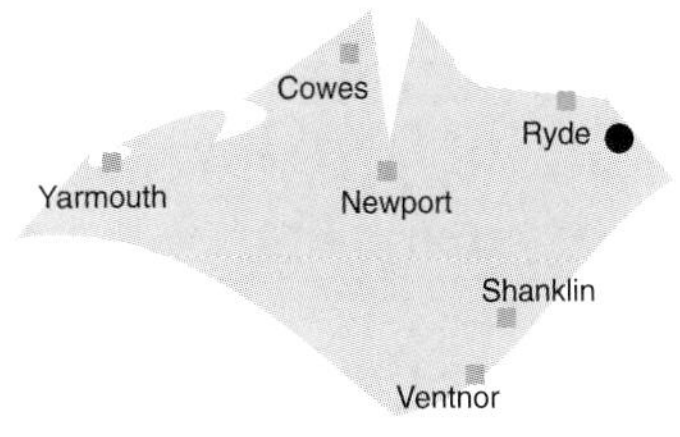

Web: www.johansens.com/priorybayiow
E-mail: enquiries@priorybay.co.uk
Tel: 0870 381 8839
International: +44 (0)1983 613146
Fax: 01983 616539

Price Guide:
single £65–£220
double/twin £110–£260
suite £200–£375

Eastwell Manor

BOUGHTON LEES, NEAR ASHFORD, KENT TN25 4HR

Directions: M20, junction 9. Turn left into Trinity Road over 4 roundabouts turn left onto the A251. The hotel is 1 mile, on the left.

Web: www.johansens.com/eastwellmanor
E-mail: enquiries@eastwellmanor.co.uk
Tel: 0870 381 8498
International: +44 (0)1233 213000
Fax: 01233 635530

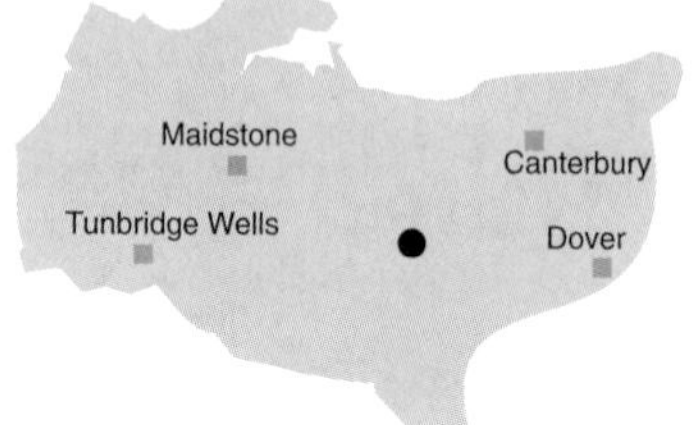

Price Guide:
single From £110
double/twin £140–£295
suites £230–£445

Set in the "Garden of England", Eastwell Manor has a past steeped in history dating back to the 16th century when Richard Plantagenet, son of Richard III, lived on the estate. Surrounded by impressive grounds it encompasses a formal Italian garden, scented rose gardens and attractive lawns and parkland. The magnificent exterior is matched by the splendour of the interior. Exquisite plasterwork and carved oak panelling adorn the public rooms whilst throughout the Manor interesting antique pieces abound. The individually furnished bedrooms and suites, some with fine views across the gardens, feature every possible comfort. There are 19 courtyard apartments giving 39 more bedrooms, all with en-suite facilities. The new health and fitness spa features an indoor and outdoor heated 20m pool, hydrotherapy pool, sauna, steam room, technogym and 15 beauty treatment rooms. Guests can enjoy a choice of dining experiences, fine British cuisine in the Manor Restaurant, and a similar standard of food at the less formal Brasserie. Nearby attractions include the cathedral city of Canterbury, Leeds Castle and several charming market towns. Situated near Ashford Eurostar station, Eastwell is perfect for trips to Paris and Brussels.

Our inspector loved: *The wonderful health spa, its many facilities and unrivalled pampering.*

The Spa

MOUNT EPHRAIM, ROYAL TUNBRIDGE WELLS, KENT TN4 8XJ

The Spa was originally built in 1766 as a country mansion with its own landscaped gardens and 3 beautiful lakes. A hotel for over a century now, it retains standards of service reminiscent of life in Georgian and Regency England. All the bedrooms are individually furnished and many offer spectacular views. Above all else, The Spa prides itself on the excellence of its cuisine. The grand, award-winning Dining Room features the freshest produce from Kentish farms and London markets complemented by a carefully selected wine list. Within the hotel is Spa Health, a magnificent health and leisure centre, which is equipped to the highest standards. Leisure facilities include an indoor heated swimming pool, a fully equipped state-of-the-art resistance gymnasium, cardio-vascular gymnasium, steam room, sauna, beauty and hairdressing salons, floodlit hard tennis court and ½ mile jogging track. The newly established stables include gentle trails and safe paddocks for children to enjoy pony-riding under expert guidance. Special half-board weekend breaks are offered, for a minimum 2-night stay, with rates from £113 per person per night – full details available upon request.

Our inspector loved: *The impressive new generation of refurbished bedrooms.*

Directions: The hotel faces the common on the A264 in Tunbridge Wells.

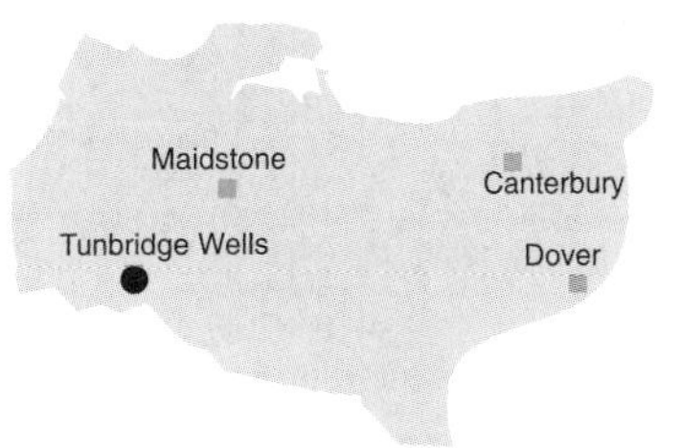

Web: www.johansens.com/spahotel
E-mail: reservations@spahotel.co.uk
Tel: 0870 381 8901
International: +44 (0)1892 520331
Fax: 01892 510575

Price Guide: (room only)
single £103–£113
double/twin £150–£210

Eaves Hall

EAVES HALL LANE, WADDINGTON, CLITHEROE, LANCASHIRE BB7 3JG

Set in the heart of the breathtaking Ribble Valley and within 7 acres of beautiful landscaped gardens, this luxurious, non-smoking, Georgian-style manor house hotel is the ideal getaway for both leisure and business travellers. The original building was constructed in the mid-19th century, and has been altered considerably over the following 50 years to create the grand red brick building of today. The bedrooms and suites are of a high standard; many offer superb views over the gardens. There are also 2 self-catering cottages within the grounds, Peels Cottage and The Lodge, which sleep 4 to 5 people and come with fully-equipped kitchens. A sophisticated, modern à la carte menu based on the finest and freshest ingredients can be enjoyed in the warm and inviting ambience of the restaurant, which is decorated with exquisite artworks and affords splendid views across the picturesque surroundings. Eaves Hall is the ideal location for weddings and small meetings, with a ballroom and a further meeting room accommodating up to 60 people. Guests can enjoy the hotel's first-class bowling green, its pitch 'n' putt and tennis courts, and a snooker room with bar billiards. Set within a 2-hour drive from the Lake District, the hotel is ideally located to explore the numerous attractions of this beautiful corner of the country.

Our inspector loved: *The manicured gardens and grounds of this Georgian Lancashire manor house.*

Directions: M6/junction 31 then A59 towards Clitheroe. At A761 roundabout take Clitheroe bypass, third left for Clitheroe, North and West Bradford and pass through West Bradford. Turn left at T-junction then right into Eaves Hall Lane.

Web: www.johansens.com/eaveshall
E-mail: eaveshall@csma.uk.com
Tel: 0870 381 9198
International: +44 (0)1200 425 271
Fax: 01200 425 131

Price Guide:
single £78–£90
double/twin £120–£140
suite £143–£175

The Gibbon Bridge Hotel

NEAR CHIPPING, FOREST OF BOWLAND, LANCASHIRE PR3 2TQ

This award-winning hotel in the heart of Lancashire in the Forest of Bowland is a welcoming and peaceful retreat. The area, a favourite of the Queen, is now officially recognised as the Centre of the Kingdom! Created in 1982 by resident proprietor Janet Simpson and her late Mother, Margaret, the buildings combine traditional architecture with interesting Gothic masonry. Individually designed and equipped to the highest standard, the 7 bedrooms and 22 suites include four-posters, half-testers, Gothic brass beds and whirlpool baths. The restaurant overlooks the garden and is renowned for traditional and imaginative dishes incorporating home-grown vegetables and herbs. The garden bandstand is perfect for musical repertoires or civil wedding ceremonies. Elegant rooms, lounges and a unique al fresco dining area are available for private dinner parties and wedding receptions. For executive meetings and conference facilities the hotel will offer that "something a bit different". Leisure facilities include a gymnasium, steam room and an all-weather tennis court.

Our inspector loved: *The spectacular landscaped gardens surrounding the bandstand.*

Directions: From the south: M6 Exit 31A, follow signs for Longridge. From the north: M6 Exit 32, follow A6 to Broughton and B5269 to Longridge. At Longridge follow signs for Chipping for approx 3 miles, then follow Gibbon Bridge brown tourism signs.

Web: www.johansens.com/gibbonbridge
E-mail: reception@gibbon-bridge.co.uk
Tel: 0870 381 8544
International: +44 (0)1995 61456
Fax: 01995 61277

Price Guide:
single £80–£120
double/twin £120
suite £150–£250

29 50

Stapleford Park Country House Hotel & Sporting Estate

NR. MELTON MOWBRAY, LEICESTERSHIRE LE14 2EF

A stately home and sporting estate where casual luxury is the byword. This 16th-century house was once coveted by Edward, Prince of Wales, but his mother Queen Victoria forbade him to buy it for fear that his morals would be corrupted by the Leicestershire hunting society! Today, Stapleford Park offers guests and club members a "lifestyle experience" to transcend all others in supreme surroundings with views over 500 acres of parkland. Stapleford Park was voted Top UK Hotel for Leisure Facilities by Condé Nast Traveller, Johansens Most Excellent Business Meeting Venue 2000 and holds innumerable awards for its style and hospitality. Individually designed bedrooms and 2 self-contained cottages have been created by famous names such as Mulberry, Wedgwood, Zoffany and Crabtree & Evelyn. The British with European influences cuisine is carefully prepared to the highest standards and complemented by an adventurous wine list. Sports include fishing, shooting, falconry, riding, tennis and an 18-hole championship golf course designed by Donald Steel. The luxurious Spa with indoor pool, Jacuzzi, sauna and fitness room offers an array of health therapies. 11 elegant function and dining rooms are suited to private dinners, special occasions and corporate hospitality.

Our inspector loved: *The whole Stapleford experience in all its many aspects and don't miss the rare "black" pheasants.*

Directions: By train Kings Cross/Grantham in 1 hour. Take the A1 north to Colsterworth then the B676 via Saxby.

Web: www.johansens.com/staplefordpark
E-mail: reservations@stapleford.co.uk
Tel: 0870 381 8912
International: +44 (0)1572 787 000
Fax: 01572 787 001

Price Guide:
double/twin £250–£465
suites from £575

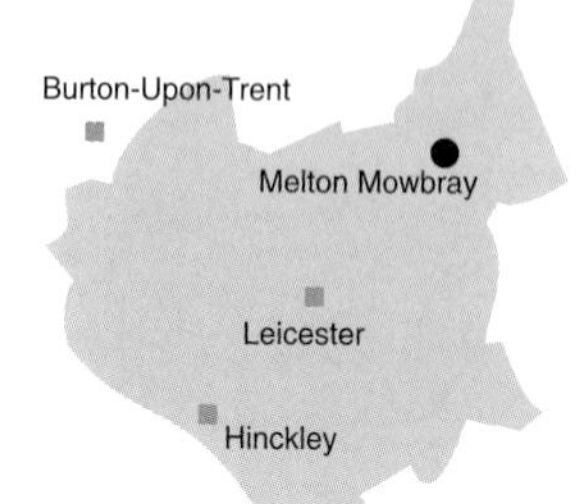

41

41 BUCKINGHAM PALACE ROAD, LONDON SW1W 0PS

This intimate, AA 5 Red Star Hotel is quietly situated, overlooking the Royal Mews and Buckingham Palace Gardens. Adjacent also to St James's Park it is perfectly positioned for access to the City and West End. The hotel reflects a remarkable attention to detail, from its discreet and secluded guest entrance and magnificent architectural features to the beautiful furniture and club-like qualities of its superb day rooms. The 18 de luxe bedrooms and 2 split-level suites are furnished with traditional mahogany and black leather décor. With affordable 5-star service, continental breakfast and a variety of tasty snacks are served in the Executive Lounge. Flooded with natural daylight and comfortable chairs, the Lounge is the perfect place to read, meet or just take a moment to unwind. "41" has the world's most comfortable, handmade English mattresses and pure wool carpets throughout, bathrooms are in marble with bespoke bath and beauty products. Every room features an on-demand entertainment system with movie, music and Internet access with Wi-Fi broadband available. A state-of-the-art boardroom offers ISDN teleconferencing and private dining. 41 offers secretarial support, chauffeur driven cars, butler and chef services. Trafalgar Square, the Houses of Parliament and West End theatres are all nearby.

Our inspector loved: *The Master Suite 4104 with the retractable roof.*

Directions: Victoria Station and Underground links are within minutes' walk; Gatwick Express 30 minutes; Heathrow 40 minutes.

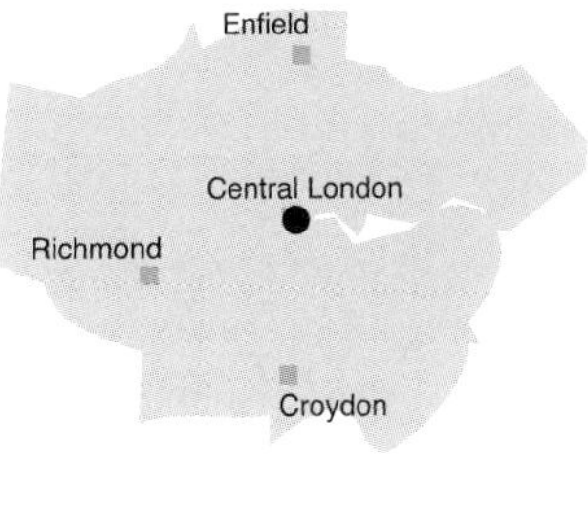

Enfield

Central London

Richmond

Croydon

Web: www.johansens.com/41buckinghampalaceroad
E-mail: book41@rchmail.com
Tel: 0870 381 8300
International: +44 (0)20 7300 0041
Fax: 020 7300 0141

Price Guide:
king bedded from £295
junior suite from £495
master suite from £695

THE MAYFLOWER HOTEL

26-28 TREBOVIR ROAD, LONDON SW5 9NJ

Located in 2 Edwardian town houses, conveniently situated in central London, the interior has been designed in a unique style with a fusion of Eastern influences that create a Colonial atmosphere. Upon entering the relaxing reception area, guests may wish to enjoy the coffee and juice bar and recline in the leather sofas before adjourning to one of the compact guest rooms; ideal accommodation for single travellers and corporate guests, who will benefit from the broadband Internet access. Pale stone, rich, vibrant fabrics with Indian and Oriental antiques abound in the individually styled bedrooms, 4 of which have balconies. Each features high ceilings, wooden flooring, hand-carved wardrobes, bedside tables with ornate beds covered in luxurious Andrew Martin fabrics and digi-boxes. The en-suite bathrooms are stylish and sparkling in slate and chrome with walk-in showers. Complimentary Continental buffet breakfast is served in the basement dining room or on the patio garden. Nearby are the fashionable shopping areas of Knightsbridge and Chelsea and the V&A and The Natural History and Science Museums. The Mayflower Hotel is located close to the famous Earl's Court Exhibition Centre and Earl's Court underground station, which is only a minute's walk away and provides direct access to Heathrow Airport, the City and West End.

Directions: Between Earl's Court Road and Warwick Road. The nearest underground station is Earl's Court.

Web: www.johansens.com/mayflower
E-mail: info@mayflower-group.co.uk
Tel: 0870 381 9195
International: +44 (0)20 7370 0991
Fax: 020 7370 0994

Price Guide:
double £109
family room £130

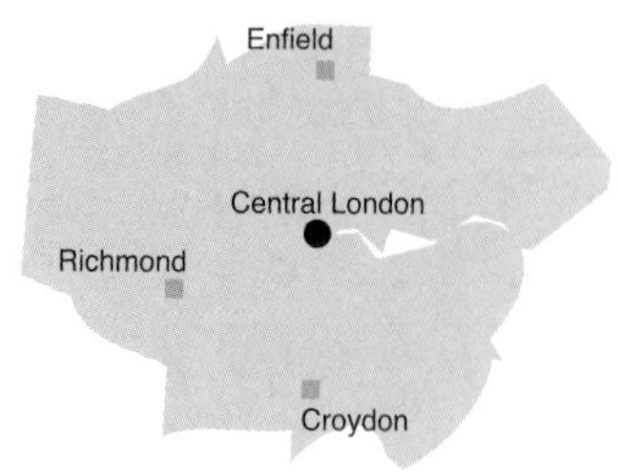

Our inspector loved: *The cool Colonial reception and juice bar.*

Grim's Dyke Hotel

OLD REDDING, HARROW WEALD, MIDDLESEX HA3 6SH

Formerly the country residence of Sir William Gilbert, this award-winning, elegant country retreat is a carefully restored idyll that is well loved for its outstanding musical events. A landmark venue for Gilbert & Sullivan fans, the hotel hosts highly successful opera dinners where all the pieces ever written by the duo are performed throughout the year. Gilbert himself installed several of the building's distinctive features. For those who enjoy the outdoors, there are 120 acres of woodland, sheltered gardens, pathways and waterways surrounding the hotel. The Gilbert Restaurant has a spectacular fireplace that ensures a cosy atmosphere and has 2 Rosettes for its outstanding cuisine. Vegetables are freshly sourced from its own kitchen garden and the honey from its own beehive. Recently refurbished bedrooms in the main house combine the elegance of a bygone age with the convenience of modern facilities; some have four-poster beds to create a romantic ambience and country house style. The rooms in the lodge are of a more contemporary nature and many boast a private patio or balcony overlooking the peaceful gardens. Guests can stroll around the historical town of Pinner, which dates back to the 14th century or take one of the many interesting walks in the local area. Easily accessible by public transport from London.

Our inspector loved: *The magical beauty of the woodland setting.*

Directions: Take the M25, junction 23 then the A1 (London) and A411 (Elstree). Travel over the A41 – A409 (Harrow) and turn right at the second set of traffic lights. The hotel is a 25-minute drive from central London.

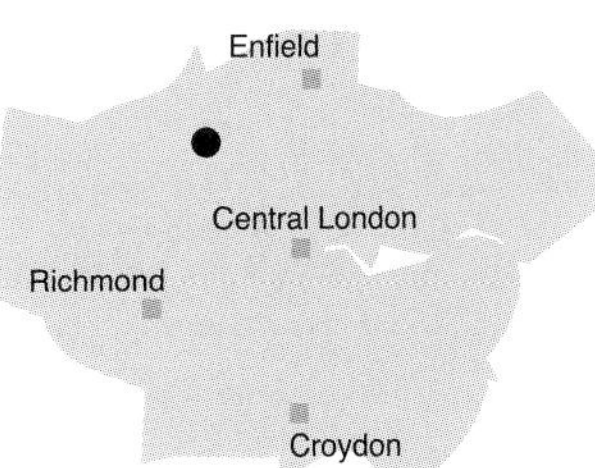

Web: www.johansens.com/grimsdyke
E-mail: reservations@grimsdyke.com
Tel: 0870 381 8486
International: +44 (0)20 8385 3100
Fax: 020 8954 4560

Price Guide:
single from £95
double/twin from £125

HENDON HALL HOTEL

ASHLEY LANE, HENDON, LONDON NW4 1HF

Directions: A 40-minute drive from Heathrow Airport. A 30-minute drive from Luton Airport. The hotel is a 15-minute walk from Hendon Central underground station on the Northern Line.

Web: www.johansens.com/hendonhall
E-mail: info@hendonhall.com
Tel: 0870 381 8518
International: +44 (0)20 8203 3341
Fax: 020 8457 2502

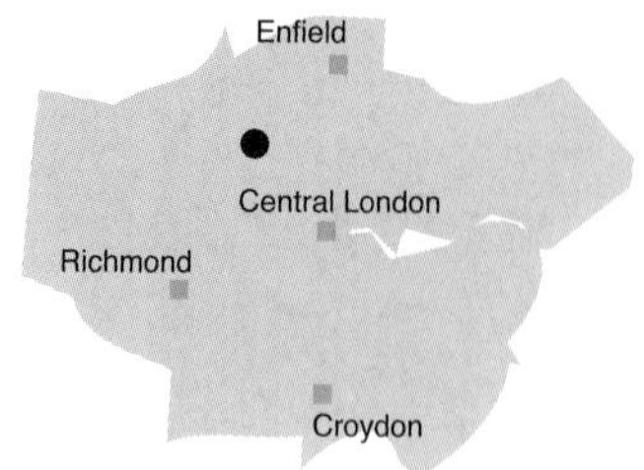

Price Guide:
double £95–£160
deluxe £115–£180
suite £145–£230

This beautiful manor house is steeped in history. Its existence was first recorded in the Domesday Book and has had a succession of historical and literary patrons ever since. It was owned by the actor David Garrick before becoming a girls' school in 1852. The property was first used as a hotel in 1911, and today, is a beautifully restored building in a stunning setting ideal for weddings, conferences and private functions. Carefully incorporating modern luxuries within the traditional framework of the building, there are now 57 bedrooms; each is elegantly designed and fitted with sumptuous soft furnishings. The staff takes great pride in ensuring guests' every comfort and offers the warmest of welcomes. There are 4 conference and function rooms. The Pembroke Suite, named after the 17th-century owners, can accommodate up to 350 guests for a drinks reception, whilst the stunning Johnson and Sheridan rooms are in the original building and can host intimate private dinner dances for 20 or 35 for stand-up receptions. Modern, original English cuisine, created from the best local ingredients and produce, is served in the Fringe Restaurant. There is plenty of free parking available.

Our inspector loved: *The refurbishment of the entire hotel, and the new "Fringe" bistro.*

Kensington House Hotel

15-16 Prince of Wales Terrace, Kensington, London W8 5PQ

This attractive hotel with its architecturally splendid tall, ornate windows and pillared entrance stands grandly on a 19th-century site long associated with style and elegance. Just off Kensington High Street, this charming town house is an ideal base from which to explore London's attractions. Views cover delightful mews houses, leafy streets and out across the City rooftops. The emphasis is on providing informal, professional service in an atmosphere of relaxation and comfort. Each of the 41 intimate bedrooms offers en-suite facilities. Rooms are bright and airy with modern furniture and fittings adding to the fresh, contemporary treatment of a classic design. Home-from-home comforts include crisp linen, duvets and bathrobes. Other features offered: courtesy tray, ceiling fan, voicemail, modem connection and in-room safe. The 2 junior suites can convert into a family room. The stylish Tiger Bar is a popular venue for coffee or cocktails prior to enjoying a delicious dinner, with a menu that draws on a range of influences offering both traditional and modern dishes. The serenity of Kensington Gardens is just a gentle stroll away and some of the capital's most fashionable shops, restaurants and cultural attractions are within walking distance. Weekend rates are available.

Our inspector loved: The great location for shopping and a stroll in the park.

Directions: The nearest underground station is High Street Kensington.

Web: www.johansens.com/kensingtonhouse
E-mail: reservations@kenhouse.com
Tel: 0870 381 8648
International: +44 (0)20 7937 2345
Fax: 020 7368 6700

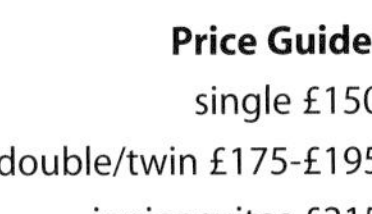

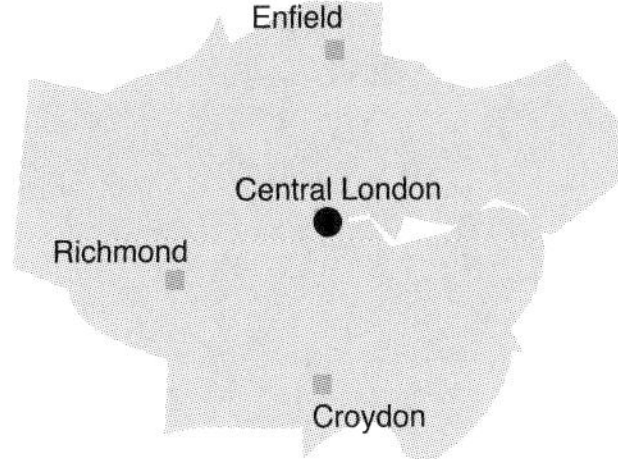

Price Guide:
single £150
double/twin £175-£195
junior suites £215

The Milestone Hotel & Apartments

1 KENSINGTON COURT, LONDON W8 5DL

Directions: Opposite Kensington Palace and adjacent to Hyde Park.

Web: www.johansens.com/milestone
E-mail: bookms@rchmail.com
Tel: 0870 381 8732
International: +44 (0)20 7917 1000
Fax: 020 7917 1010

Price Guide:
double/twin £310–£490
suites £570–£910

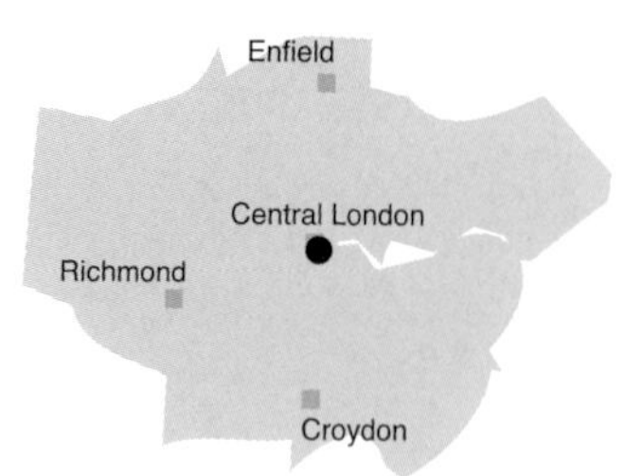

This beautifully appointed Condé Nast Johansens award-winning property is situated directly opposite Kensington Palace with views over Kensington Gardens and Hyde Park. A Victorian showpiece, this unique hotel has been carefully restored to its original splendour whilst incorporating every modern facility. 6 apartments and 57 bedrooms, including 12 suites, are individually designed with antiques, elegant furnishings and some have private balconies. Guests may relax in the comfortable panelled Park Lounge which, in company with all other rooms, provides a 24-hour service. The hotel's restaurant, Cheneston's, the early spelling of Kensington, has an elaborately carved ceiling, original fireplace and ornate windows. The versatile Windsor Suite is perfect for private dining and corporate meetings. The fitness centre offers guests the use of a resistance pool, spa treatment room, sauna, and gymnasium. The traditional bar, Stables, on the ground floor as well as the bright and airy black and white conservatory, are ideal for meeting and entertaining friends. The Milestone is a short walk to the finest shopping areas of Kensington and Knightsbridge which include the antique shops on Church Street and Harrods, and is a brief taxi ride to the West End, the heart of London's Theatreland. The Royal Albert Hall and all the museums in Exhibition Road are also just a stroll away.

Our inspector loved: *The attention to detail in all the stunning rooms.*

Twenty Nevern Square

20 Nevern Square, London SW5 9PD

A unique experience in hospitality awaits guests at this elegant 4-star town house hotel that overlooks a tranquil garden square. Sumptuously restored, the emphasis is on natural materials and beautiful hand-carved beds and furniture. Each of the 20 intimate bedrooms provides white marble, compact en-suite facilities, and is individually designed echoing both Asian and European influences. Guests can choose the delicate silks of the Chinese Room or a touch of opulence in the Rococo Room. The grandeur of the Pasha Suite, complete with four-poster bed and balcony, makes an ideal setting for a special occasion. All rooms have full modern facilities including wide-screen digital TV, CD player, private safe and a separate telephone and Internet/fax connection. Complimentary breakfast is served in the light, bright Conservatory, which opens out to a decked balcony area. Gym facilities are available by arrangement. The location is ideal: close to Earl's Court and Olympia Exhibition Centres and the tube. The Piccadilly Line brings guests arriving at Heathrow in just over 30 minutes. Guests are a mere 10 minutes from London's most fashionable shopping areas, restaurants, theatres and cultural attractions such as the V&A and Science Museums.

Our inspector loved: *The Eastern furniture and colourful fabrics.*

 23   25      

Directions: 2 minutes from Earl's Court station.

Web: www.johansens.com/twentynevernsquare
E-mail: hotel@twentynevernsquare.co.uk
Tel: 0870 381 8957
International: +44 (0)20 7565 9555
Fax: 020 7565 9444

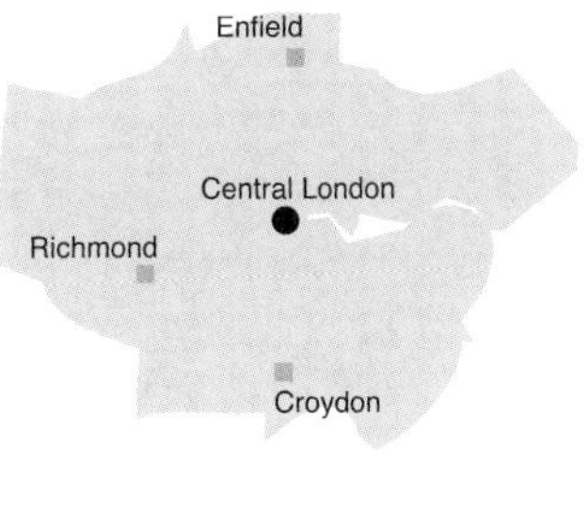

Enfield
Central London
Richmond
Croydon

Price Guide:
double/twin £130–£165
suite £275

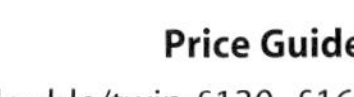

Beaufort House

45 BEAUFORT GARDENS, KNIGHTSBRIDGE, LONDON SW3 1PN

Directions: Beaufort Gardens leads off Brompton Road near Knightsbridge underground station. There is a 24hr car park nearby.

Web: www.johansens.com/beauforthouseapartments
E-mail: info@beauforthouse.co.uk
Tel: 0870 381 8350
International: +44 (0)20 7584 2600
Fax: 020 7584 6532

Price Guide: (excluding VAT)
£225–£695

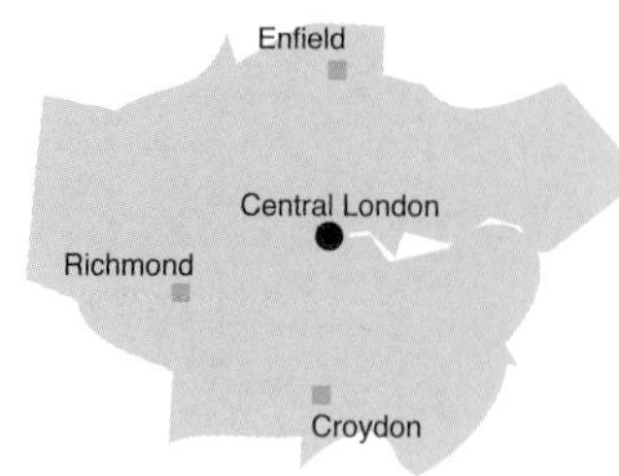

Situated in Beaufort Gardens, a quiet tree-lined Regency cul-de-sac in the heart of Knightsbridge, 250 yards from Harrods, Beaufort House is an exclusive establishment comprising 21 self-contained fully serviced luxury apartments. All the comforts of a first-class hotel are combined with the privacy, discretion and relaxed atmosphere of home. Accommodation ranges in size from an intimate 1- bedroom to a spacious 4-bedroom apartment. Each apartment has been individually and traditionally decorated to the highest standard. All apartments have direct dial telephones with voice mail, personal safes, satellite television, DVD players and high speed broadband access. Some apartments benefit from balconies or patios. The fully equipped kitchens include washer/dryers and many have dishwashers. A daily maid service is included at no additional charge. Full laundry/dry cleaning services are available. A dedicated Guests Services team provides 24 hours coverage and will be happy to organise tours, theatre tickets, restaurant bookings, taxis or chauffeur driven limousines and other services. Complimentary membership at Aquilla's Health Club is offered to all guests during their stay. Awarded 5 stars by the English Tourism Council.

Our inspector loved: *The very English feel to these perfectly located apartments.*

The Capital Hotel & Restaurant

22 Basil Street, Knightsbridge, London SW3 1AT

Voted "Best Hotel for Food" in the UK by Condé Nast Traveller in the 2006 Gold List, Scottish proprietor David Levin created this luxury town house, in its exclusive Knightsbridge address, over 35 years ago. Today it remains the only hotel restaurant to hold 2 coveted Michelin stars. Head Chef Eric Chavot's French-inspired cooking is acclaimed by even the most discriminating of critics and has been described as "faultlessly assured". Menus change frequently with dishes including starters of wild asparagus and poached egg and crab lasagne with langoustine carpaccio, and main courses such as lobster and slow cooked pork belly, pot-roasted pigeon and fillet of sea bass "nicoise". The London Bakery, owned by the Capital Group, supplies all the breads and pastries for the restaurant and afternoon tea served in the Sitting Room. The excellent wine list features wines from the hotel's own vineyard in the Loire Valley in France. The 49 bedrooms are individually decorated with super king-size beds, handmade mattresses, the finest Egyptian cotton sheets, air conditioning and spacious marble bathrooms with power showers. There are 2 suites: the Cadogan and the Eaton, available for private dining. The boutiques of Sloane Street and elegant department stores such as Harrods and Harvey Nichols are all within easy reach.

Our inspector loved: *The Michelin-star restaurant and stunning private dining rooms.*

 49   24     

Directions: A minute's walk from Knightsbridge underground station, on the Piccadilly line.

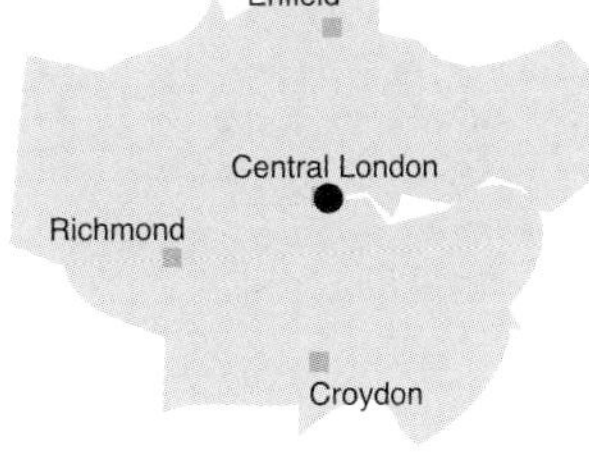

Web: www.johansens.com/capital
E-mail: reservations@capitalhotel.co.uk
Tel: 0870 381 8527
International: +44 (0)20 7589 5171
Fax: 020 7225 0011

Price Guide:
single £175–£210
double/twin £215–£365
suite £390–£850

The Egerton House Hotel

17-19 Egerton Terrace, Knightsbridge, London SW3 2BX

This quiet double fronted Victorian town house hotel in a residential Knightsbridge street has recently been acquired by new owners, and restyled for the 21st century whilst staying true to its original tenets. Each of the 30 air-conditioned rooms and suites is individually designed with an eclectic mix of Italian Rococo and modern contemporary furnishings. As well as en-suite marble bathrooms, exquisite fabrics and original artworks and antiques, some rooms have four-poster beds and most overlook pretty private gardens. High-tech facilities include flat-screen TVs, WiFi and specially programmed Video iPods. 24-hour room service is available and breakfast is served in the dining room on the lower ground floor, which is a stunning space full of glass and light with ivory leather banquette. The reception is truly elegant, graced with stunning paintings by Henri de Toulouse-Lautrec, and the relaxed, cosy drawing room is decorated in soft, muted tones complete with open fire; the addition of a discreet bar lends it a club atmosphere. A selection of drinks, cocktails and light snacks are on offer. The Egerton House Hotel is a leafy 3-minute walk from Harrods and a perfect base for visiting all of central London's attractions.

Our inspector loved: *The superb refurbishment of this classic town house hotel.*

Directions: Located between South Kensington and Knightsbridge underground stations on the Piccadilly Line. 30 minutes from Heathrow.

Web: www.johansens.com/egertonhouse
E-mail: bookeg@rchmail.com
Tel: 0870 381 8559
International: +44 (0)20 7589 2412
Fax: 020 7584 6540

Price Guide:
double £235–£255
suite £295–£395

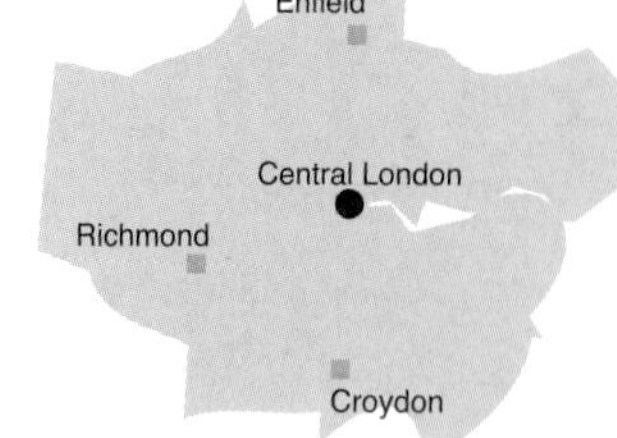

JUMEIRAH CARLTON TOWER

ON CADOGAN PLACE, LONDON SW1X 9PY

In the heart of Knightsbridge, overlooking the private, leafy gardens of Cadogan Place, this 5-star luxury hotel successfully combines ultra modern convenience and facilities with traditional hospitality. The ideal city venue for the leisure and business visitor alike, Harrods and some of the capital's most fashionable shops are within walking distance and the West End and the City can easily be reached by tube or taxi. Beautifully furnished and decorated, an understated elegance pervades the hotel. The stylish and spacious bedrooms, including 58 suites and a Presidential Suite on the 18th floor, are equipped with every amenity and comfort expected from a leading hotel, such as air conditioning, modem access and fax machine. All rooms offer memorable London views. Arguably London's finest, the 184m2 Presidential Suite offers unmatched accommodation and boasts a private sauna, enhanced security and the highest level of personalized service. The hotel is proud of its eclectic mix of restaurants and bars: The Rib Room & Oyster Bar is an acknowledged gourmet delight for those who enjoy the finest steaks or alternatively enjoy the stylish ambience of the exclusive champagne lounge. Other facilities include a range of versatile event rooms and the luxurious rooftop health club and an indoor 20m stainless steel swimming pool.

Our inspector loved: *The Peak Health Club & Spa with some of the best views over London.*

Directions: A 3-minute walk from Knightsbridge tube station (Piccadilly Line). Take Sloane Street/Brompton Road station exit, turn right down Sloane Street then left into Cadogan Place.

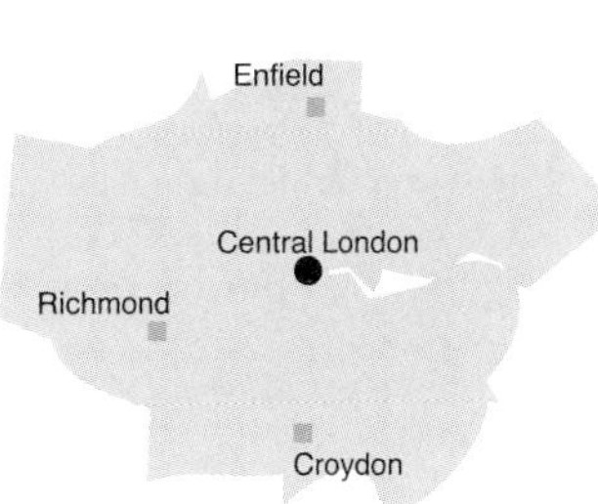

Web: www.johansens.com/carltontower
E-mail: JCTinfo@jumeirah.com
Tel: 0870 381 9326
International: +44 (0)20 7235 1234
Fax: +44 (0)20 7235 9129

Price Guide: (excluding VAT)
double from £375
suite from £525

Jumeirah Lowndes Hotel

21 LOWNDES STREET, KNIGHTSBRIDGE, LONDON SW1X 9ES

Directions: The nearest underground tube stations are Knightsbridge, Hyde Park Corner and Sloane Square.

Web: www.johansens.com/lowndes
E-mail: JLHinfo@jumeirah.com
Tel: 0870 381 9285
International: +44 (0)20 7823 1234
Fax: 020 7235 1154

Price Guide: (room only, excluding VAT)
double from £325
suite from £425

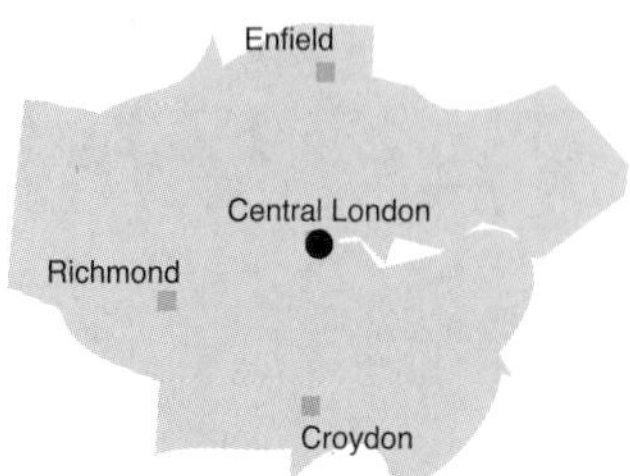

Following an extensive refurbishment, this chic boutique retreat hotel offers guests a luxurious urban sanctuary, ideally situated in London's residential Belgravia, minutes from Hyde Park, Sloane Street and Duke of York Square. One highlight of the renovation is the addition of a new sixth floor comprising 4 one-bedroom suites - 2 of which have balconies - and 5 junior suites. All are themed in blue, silver and grey shades, while the stylish décor of the remaining suites and rooms maximise light and space creating a sense of tranquillity and harmony. In addition, the lobby area has been remodelled to create flowing public areas with an art deco influence, including oak features and limestone flooring in sleek rust tones. The Mimosa Bar & Restaurant serves Mediterranean cuisine with al fresco dining on the terrace overlooking Lowndes Square. An exciting focal point in the heart of the hotel, the bar promises a relaxed yet vibrant atmosphere created by "Lowndes Lounge" grooves. An intimate and flexible event room is available on the ground floor for private dining, cocktail parties and meetings. Throughout the hotel, special touches include luxurious Temple Spa amenities. The central location enables easy access by foot, public transport or taxi to London's major tourist attractions.

Our inspector loved: *The extensive refurbishment.*

The Royal Park

3 WESTBOURNE TERRACE, LANCASTER GATE, HYDE PARK, LONDON W2 3UL

Situated on the doorstep of Hyde Park, this exquisite hotel comprises of 3 Grade II listed Georgian town houses, lovingly restored to their 1840's elegance. There are 48 charming bedrooms, decorated in stunning Regency colours that truly enhance the antique furniture, luxurious linens and handmade beds. Each room boasts a splendid antique writing desk as well as the latest technology including flat-screen television and broadband Internet access. The hotel is adorned with delightful Georgian and Victorian antique pieces, carefully selected by Jonty Hearnden of "The Antiques Roadshow." Upon arrival, guests enter the glorious marble chequered reception with roaring log fire and receive a complimentary glass of sherry or whiskey. Although there is no restaurant, an excellent room service menu is available and breakfast can be served in guests' rooms or in the drawing room. Complimentary traditional English tea is served in the afternoon and a glass of champagne, with canapés, may be enjoyed in the evening. The secluded patio garden at the rear of the hotel is the ideal location to take drinks during the summer months. For small meetings the Green Room can accommodate 10 people. Oxford Street and Notting Hill are both within walking distance.

Our inspector loved: *The pretty light bedrooms and antique furniture.*

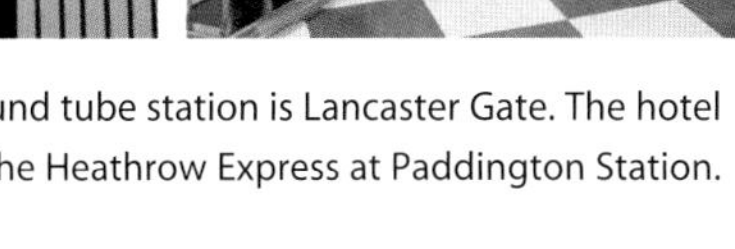

Directions: The nearest underground tube station is Lancaster Gate. The hotel is a 2-minute walk from the Heathrow Express at Paddington Station.

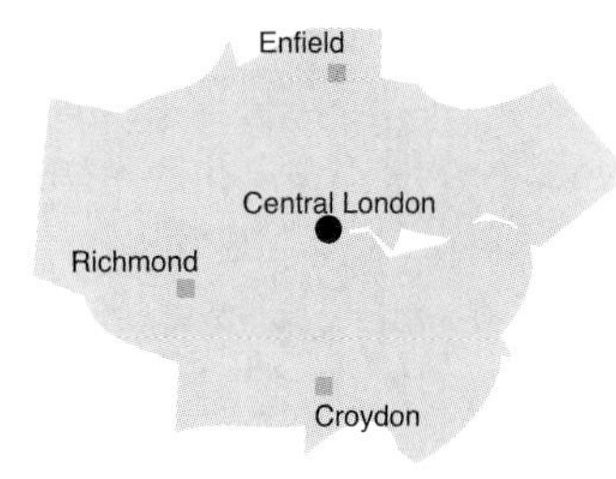

Web: www.johansens.com/royalpark
E-mail: info@theroyalpark.com
Tel: 0870 381 9289
International: +44 (0)20 7479 6600
Fax: 020 7479 6601

Price Guide: (excluding VAT)
double £155–£200
executive £165–£210
four poster £200–£230
suite £215–£305

THE SUMNER

54 UPPER BERKLEY STREET, MARBLE ARCH, LONDON W1H 7QR

This intimate Georgian townhouse reopened in July this year following a total refurbishment to provide guests with opulent accommdation in the heart of the capital. Ideally located for fashionistas wishing to indulge in the delights of Bond Street and South Molton Street and tourists wishing to explore the city on foot, The Sumner is an elegant hotel with every modern comfort and the latest amenities. The 20 bedrooms have been appointed in a contemporary style with minimalist décor including low beds, designer fabrics and chic lighting. All feature air conditioning, flat-screen televisions and free wireless Internet access. The modern breakfast room in the basement serves an extensive buffet before guests embark on their excursions. Upon returning, the cosy sitting room is a favoured place to unwind and in winter, the roaring fireplace provides an added allure. Hyde Park, the Wallace Collection and trendy Soho are all within walking distance of Upper Berkeley Street, while the boutiques of Great Portland Street and Marylebone's bustling restaurant scene can also provide a tempting draw.

Our inspector loved: *The cosy designer siting room.*

Directions: Both Marble Arch tube (Central Line) and Oxford Street are just 2 minutes walk away.

Web: www.johansens.com/thesumner
E-mail: reservations@sumnerhotel.com
Tel: 0870 381 8608
International: +44 (0)20 7723 2244
Fax: 0870 705 8767

Price Guide:
queen from £115
king from £130
de luxe from £145

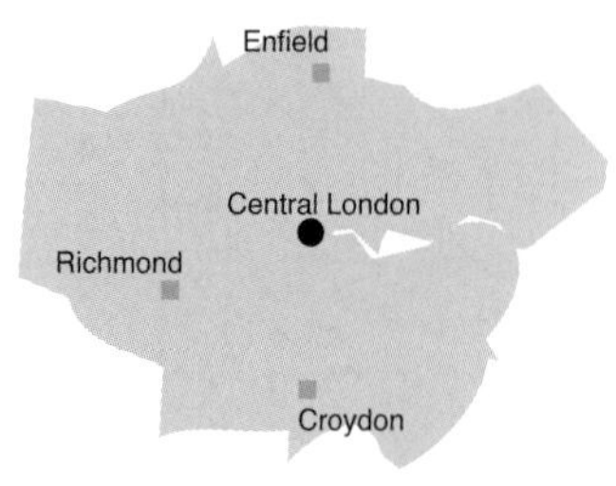

Dorset Square Hotel

39 Dorset Square, Marylebone, London NW1 6QN

One of the first boutique hotels in London, Dorset Square Hotel stands in a prime location for the West End, set in a leafy square that was the original site for Thomas Lord's cricket ground. Today, this Regency town house has been lovingly restored and designed to offer the ultimate in comfort and charm with a chic London edge and customised service. Each of the bedrooms has been perfectly appointed and provides air conditioning, modem ports, flat-screen TVs and extremely well-equipped marble bathrooms. The light and airy Potting Shed Restaurant and Bar exudes character and displays an array of terracotta pots along one wall. The cuisine is a selection of contemporary European/British but for those who prefer to remain in the luxury of their bedrooms, there is also the wonderful "bedroom picnic," a basket laden with cold meats, fresh fruits, cheeses, pastries and chilled champagne. The Thomas Lord meeting room, with large plasma screen, natural daylight and air conditioning, is ideal for intimate meetings, and guests have privileged garden access to the old cricket grounds. The exclusive use of all these facilities for events is available. Live jazz nights are held every Friday, whilst Madame Tussauds, The Planetarium and Regent's Park Zoo are all within a 2-minute walk. Oxford Street, Baker Street and Bond Street are close by, and the City is directly accessible via Baker Street tube station.

Our inspector loved: *This gem of a hotel with its fabulous restaurant.*

Directions: 30 minutes from Heathrow by car and Heathrow Express train via Paddington. 10-15 minutes by taxi from all major train stations

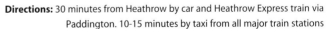

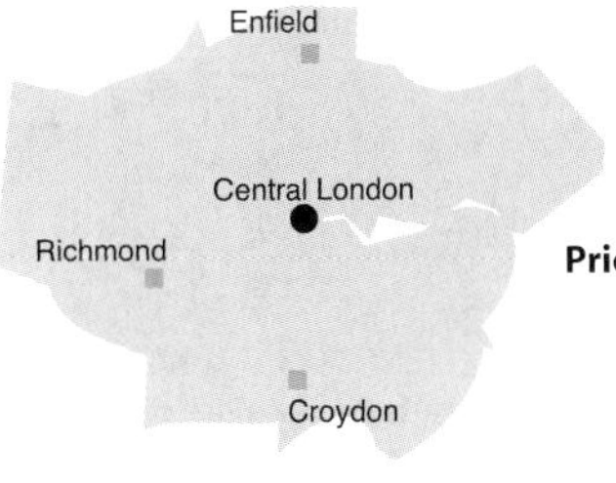

Enfield
Central London
Richmond
Croydon

Web: www.johansens.com/dorsetsquare
E-mail: reservation@dorsetsquare.co.uk
Tel: 0870 381 8488
International: +44 (0)20 7723 7874
Fax: 020 7724 3328

Price Guide: (excluding breakfast and VAT)
single £150
dorset/superior £220
regency/de luxe £260
suite £350

THE MANDEVILLE HOTEL

MANDEVILLE PLACE, LONDON W1U 2BE

Situated in fashionable Marylebone Village, within a few minutes' walk from the shops and art galleries of Oxford Street, Bond Street and Mayfair, as well as the famous auction houses of Sothebys and Christies, this sophisticated hotel exudes style and modern opulence. Highly personalised service and attention to detail ensure that each guest feels at home. The elegant interior design places an emphasis on luxurious comfort and sense of space; magnificent original paintings adorn the walls alongside opulent fabrics and comfortable chairs. All the bedrooms are uniquely decorated with the most up-to-date conveniences and marble bathrooms are equipped with power showers. The penthouse attic suite has its own private terrace, attic bathroom and separate entrance. Red, yellow, green and silver tones enhance the cosy atmosphere of the hotel's stunning saloon, which features an eye-catching silver and glass bar and dark brown suede banquettes. Guests can savour the light bites and mouth-watering finger platters on offer. The superb restaurant has a theatrical theme and bold colour schemes designed by world famous Interior Designer, Stephen Ryan. Delicious modern British cuisine is on the menu accompanied by fine wines. Due to its central location, The Mandeville Hotel is ideal for exploring the many delights of London.

Our inspector loved: *The outrageous bar.*

Directions: The nearest underground station is Bond Street, which is a 5-minute walk away from the hotel.

Web: www.johansens.com/mandeville
E-mail: info@mandeville.co.uk
Tel: 0870 381 8344
International: +44 (0)20 7935 5599
Fax: 020 7935 9588

Price Guide:
single £250
double/twin £275
suite £300

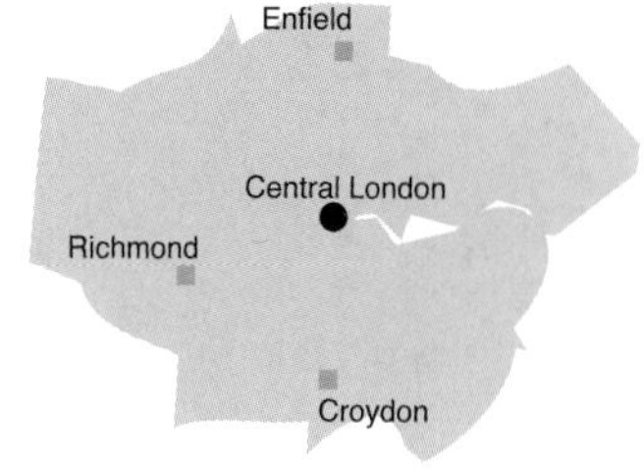

The Richmond Gate Hotel and Restaurant

RICHMOND HILL, RICHMOND-UPON-THAMES, SURREY TW10 6RP

This former Georgian country house stands on the crest of Richmond Hill close to the Royal Park and Richmond Terrace with its commanding views over the River Thames. The 68 stylishly furnished en-suite bedrooms, many with air-conditioning, combine every comfort of the present with the elegance of the past and include several luxury four-poster rooms and suites. Exceptional and imaginative cuisine, complemented by an extensive wine list offering over 60 wines from around the world is served in the sophisticated surroundings of the Gates on the Parks Restaurant. Weddings, business meetings and private dining events can be arranged in a variety of rooms. The beautiful Victorian walled garden provides for summer relaxation. Cedars Health and Leisure Club is accessed through the hotel and includes a 20-metre pool, 6-metre spa, sauna, steam room, aerobics studio, cardiovascular and resistance gymnasia and a health and beauty suite. Richmond is close to London and the West End yet in a country setting. The Borough offers a wealth of visitor attractions, including Hampton Court Palace, Wimbledon, Twickenham Rugby Stadium, Syon House and Park and the Royal Botanic Gardens at Kew.

Our inspector loved: *The decor. It has the welcoming feel of a London club, yet is within a stone's throw of rural Richmond Park.*

Directions: Adjacent to Richmond Park, 7 miles from Heathrow and Central London. Easily reached from the M3, M4 and M25. The nearest underground station is Richmond and there are mainline trains to London Waterloo.

Web: www.johansens.com/richmondgate
E-mail: richmondgate@foliohotels.com
Tel: 0870 381 8855
International: +44 (0)20 8940 0061
Fax: 020 8332 0354

Price Guide:
single £140–£200
double/twin £150–£220
suite from £230

 68  70        SPA

THE CRANLEY

10 BINA GARDENS, SOUTH KENSINGTON, LONDON SW5 0LA

Standing in a quiet, tree-lined street in the heart of Kensington, this charming and sophisticated Victorian town house is an ideal city venue for the leisure and business visitor alike, blending traditional style and service with 21st-century technology. Furnished with beautiful antiques and hand-embroidered linen fabrics, The Cranley has an understated elegance. Striking colour combinations and stone used throughout the bedrooms and reception areas are derived from the original floor in the entrance hall. Recently completely refurbished, The Cranley's bedrooms are now among some of the most comfortable in the Capital. All are delightfully decorated and have king-sized, four-poster or half-tester canopied beds. Each room is light, air-conditioned and has facilities ranging from antique desk, 2 direct dial telephone lines and voicemail to broadband connection. The luxury bathrooms have traditional Victorian-style fittings combined with a lavish use of warm limestone. Guests can enjoy copious continental breakfasts, complimentary English afternoon tea and an evening help-yourself apéritif with canapés. Many of London's attractions are within easy walking distance, including the shops and restaurants of Knightsbridge and the Kings Road.

Our inspector loved: *The beautifully designed rooms and four poster beds.*

Directions: The nearest underground stations are Gloucester Road and South Kensington.

Web: www.johansens.com/cranley
E-mail: info@thecranley.com
Tel: 0870 381 8456
International: +44 (0)20 7373 0123
Fax: 020 7373 9497

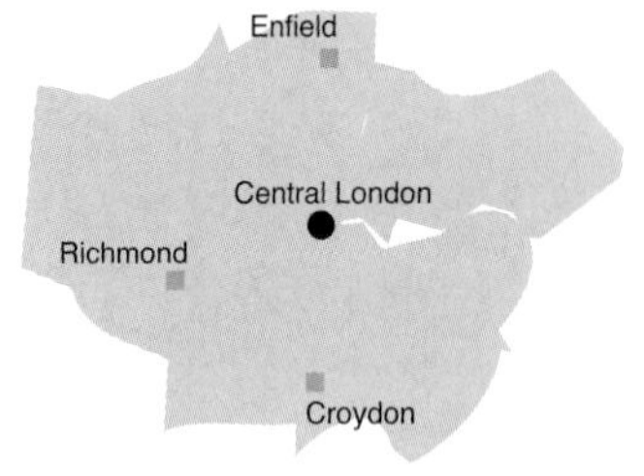

Price Guide: (excluding VAT)
double £155–£200
executive £165–£210
four poster £200–£230
penthouse suite £265–£305

39

Sofitel St James

6 WATERLOO PLACE, LONDON SW1Y 4AN

Located on the corner of Waterloo Place and Pall Mall, this imposing Grade II listed building is the former home of the Cox's and King's bank and has been carefully renovated to create an elegant 5-star hotel. Sofitel acquired the majority of the original artwork from the bank, which is now proudly displayed and balanced out by contemporary design. Bedrooms and suites are sophisticated and equipped with ultra-modern technology, and in the bathrooms black and white marble harmonises with granite tops and chrome fittings. The elegant Rose Lounge is the ideal place for a traditional afternoon tea amidst an eclectic mix of colours and styles, whilst the St James Bar offers the largest selection of Champagnes and cigars in a hotel in London. French flair and refined cuisine are the hallmark of the buzzing Brasserie Roux. Guests can enjoy a pampering session in the hotel's fitness and massage centre complete with treatment rooms and steam room. The hotel's conference and banqueting facilities comprise of 8 rooms including a state-of-the-art boardroom with private dining room as well as a banqueting suite for up to 170 people. Numerous of London's major attractions, Trafalgar Square, Piccadilly Circus and the theatre district are just around the corner.

***Our inspector loved:** The flower decorations in the Lobby, winner of the Villegiature Award 2005 for Best Floral Decoration in Europe - Stunning!*

186

170

 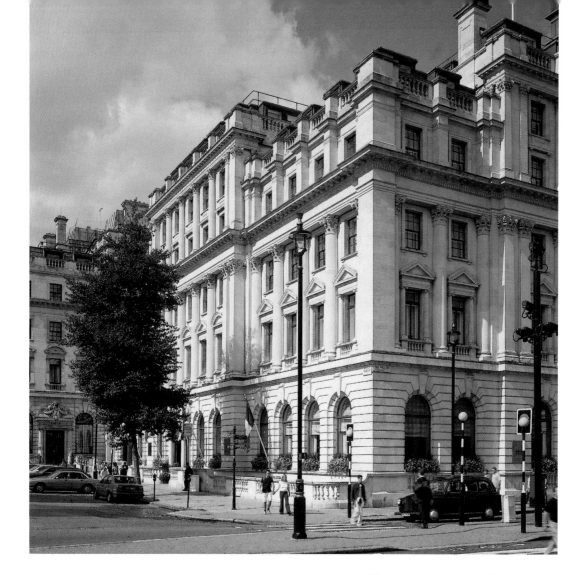

Directions: The nearest underground station is Piccadilly Circus.

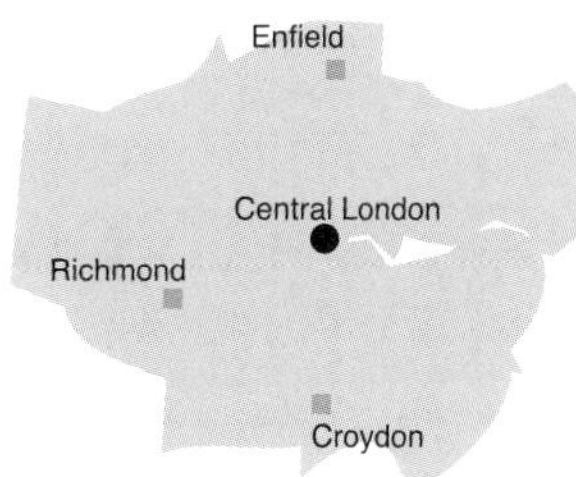

Web: www.johansens.com/stjames
E-mail: H3144@accor.com
Tel: 0870 381 9185
International: +44 (0)20 7747 2200
Fax: +44 (0) 20 7747 2210

Price Guide: (room only, excluding VAT)
single from £305
double from £355
suite £450-£1,200

51 Buckingham Gate

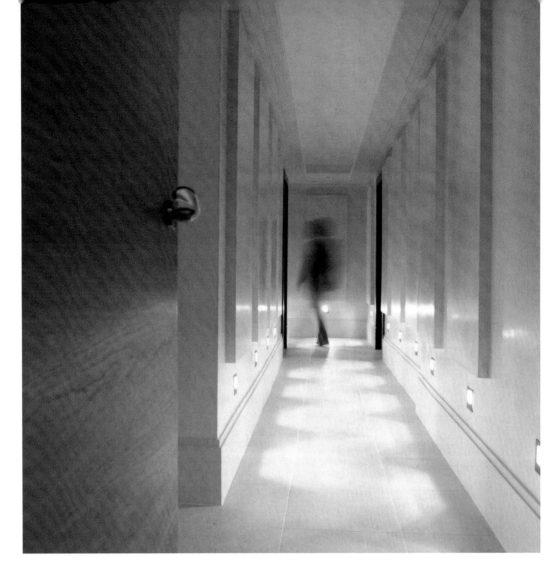

51 BUCKINGHAM GATE, WESTMINSTER, LONDON SW1E 6AF

Close to Buckingham Palace, St James's Park and the Houses of Parliament, 51 Buckingham Gate is contemporary style and luxury on a grand scale. This attractive Victorian town house offers everything the discerning guest could wish for: privacy, relaxation and superb service delivered by multilingual staff which includes a team of Ivor Spencer trained butlers. Guests have a choice of dining options: Quilon, offering southern coastal Indian cuisine, Bank Westminster, Zander Bar and The Library. There are 82 suites and apartments, ranging from junior suites to the 5-bedroom Prime Minister's Suite, which combine contemporary interior design with luxury hotel facilities. De luxe suites offer award-winning bathrooms, whilst designated Ivor Spencer Suites have 16-hour personal butler service, limousine pick-up and an exclusive range of special amenities. Each suite provides sophisticated technology including 2-line speaker telephones, high-speed Internet access, fax/copier/printer, CD and DVD player. Fully-equipped kitchens as well as 24-hour room service are available. A team of talented chefs is also at hand to prepare private dinners. Guests can enjoy the exclusive Spa at Fifty-One which offers Sodashi treatments including a jet lag recovery service and a fully-equipped gymnasium.

Our inspector loved: *The impeccable service and the extremely comfortable beds.*

Directions: The nearest underground stations are St James's Park and Victoria.

Web: www.johansens.com/buckinghamgate
E-mail: info@51-buckinghamgate.co.uk
Tel: 0870 381 8301
International: +44 (0)20 7769 7766
Fax: 020 7828 5909

Price Guide:
suites £405–£975
prime ministers suite p.o.a

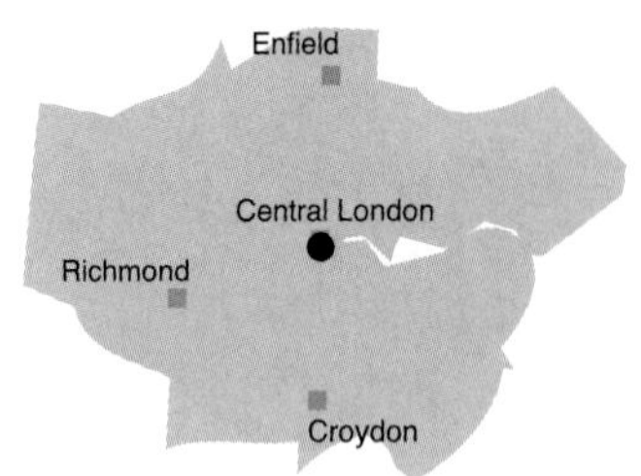

Cannizaro House

WEST SIDE, WIMBLEDON COMMON, LONDON SW19 4UE

Cannizaro House is a captivating Georgian mansion set amidst green sweeping lawns, an ornamental lake and beautiful formal gardens on the edge of Wimbledon Common. Peaceful surroundings create an atmosphere of country living whilst the traditional hospitality of friendly staff make guests feel most welcome. With a long and distinguished history, this elegant hotel has been host to several famous people including King George III, Oscar Wilde, William Pitt and Henry James. Sumptuous interiors are appointed with fine antiques, guilded mirrors and ornate fireplaces, along with a contemporary new light bar. Individually decorated bedrooms are extremely luxurious; some have four-poster beds and views over the grounds and Cannizaro Park. Gentle colour schemes are complemented by opulent fabrics, crisp sheets and rich woodwork. Award-winning modern British and European cuisine is of the finest quality, served in Common restaurant. Afternoon tea may be served on the sunny terrace, and the chic Cannizaro Bar serves cocktails and apéritifs. Several intimate rooms are available for meetings and private dining, including the elegant Queen Elizabeth Room, a popular venue for wedding ceremonies. Ideally located for trips to London city centre and the West End with its many tourist attractions, museums, art galleries and theatres.

Directions: The nearest tube and British Rail station is Wimbledon.

Web: www.johansens.com/cannizarohouse
E-mail: info@cannizarohouse.com
Tel: 0870 381 8402
International: +44 (0)208 879 1464
Fax: 020 8970 2753

Enfield
Central London
Richmond
Croydon

Price Guide:
double/twin from £140
feature room from £170

Our inspector loved: *The recent refurbishment and funky new bar.*

45 120

ETROP GRANGE

THORLEY LANE, MANCHESTER AIRPORT, GREATER MANCHESTER M90 4EG

Hidden away near Manchester Airport lies Etrop Grange, a beautiful country house hotel and restaurant. The original house was built in 1780 and more than 200 years on has been lovingly restored. Today, the hotel enjoys a fine reputation for its accommodation, where the luxury, character and sheer elegance of the Georgian era are evident in every feature. The magnificent award-winning restaurant offers a well balanced mix of traditional and modern English cuisine, complemented by an extensive selection of fine wines. Attention to detail ensures personal and individual service. In addition to the obvious advantage of having an airport within walking distance, the location of Etrop Grange is ideal in many other ways. With a comprehensive motorway network and InterCity stations minutes away, it is accessible from all parts of the UK. Entertainment for visitors ranges from the shopping, sport and excellent nightlife offered by the city of Manchester to golf, riding, clay pigeon shooting, water sports and outdoor pursuits in the immediate countryside. Cheshire also boasts an abundance of stately homes, museums and historical attractions.

Our inspector loved: *The complimentary chauffeur service to Manchester Airport.*

Directions: Leave M56 at junction 5 towards Manchester Airport. Follow signs for Terminal 2. Go up the slip road. At roundabout take first exit, take immediate left and hotel is 400yds on the right.

Web: www.johansens.com/etropgrange
E-mail: etropgrange@corushotels.com
Tel: 0870 381 8507
International: +44 (0)161 499 0500
Fax: 0161 499 0790

Price Guide:
single £89–£179
double/twin £99–£209
suites £136–£240

The Hoste Arms

THE GREEN, BURNHAM MARKET, KING'S LYNN, NORFOLK PE31 8HD

There are few places that feel so utterly comfortable in their surroundings. The Hoste Arms has been skilfully developed by Paul and Jeanne Whittome over several years but it's historic roots dating back to 1720 have never been compromised. Even the rather splendidly named 'Zulu Wing' echoes the comfort, style and attention to detail that its entrepreneurial owners manage so instinctively. A team of 12 bright young chefs create wonderful dishes and menus in a kitchen environment so impressive that it would be the envy of any restaurant in the country. A 300 bin wine list features some of the world's best wines at bargain prices and a new extensive cellar has recently been opened to offer yet another dimension to the experience of this wonderful place. The bedrooms and suites are well appointed and comfortable, featuring Egyptian cotton. Some have air conditioning. The Hoste Arms is well situated to cater for a variety of interests; located in Burnham Market (Chelsea-at-Sea), with its unique line of 40 privately owned shops, there are also several stately homes in the area such as Holkham Hall, Houghton Hall and Sandringham. For nature lovers there are bird sanctuaries, boat trips and miles of unspoilt sandy beaches. Golf enthusiasts have Hunstanton, Brancaster and Cromer.

Our inspector loved: *The exceptional attention to detail in the beautifully furnished bedrooms and the amazingly stylish loos!*

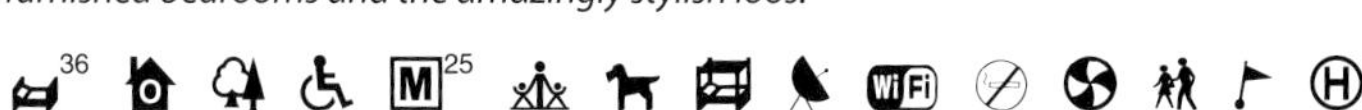

Directions: Burnham Market is 2 miles from A149 on B1155.

King's Lynn
Cromer
Norwich
Great Yarmouth

Web: www.johansens.com/hostearms
E-mail: reception@hostearms.co.uk
Tel: 0870 381 8415
International: +44 (0)1328 738777
Fax: 01328 730103

Price Guide:
single £88–£160
doubles £117–£179
suites £150–£260

Congham Hall

GRIMSTON, KING'S LYNN, NORFOLK PE32 1AH

Dating from the mid-18th century, this stately manor house is set in acres of parkland, orchards and gardens. The conversion from country house to luxury hotel in 1982 was executed with care to enhance the elegance of the classic interiors. The hotel's renowned herb garden grows over 700 varieties of herb, many are used by the chef to create modern English dishes with the accent on fresh local produce and fish from the local Norfolk markets. The hotel's hives even produce the honey for your breakfast table. The beautiful flower displays, homemade pot pourri and roaring log fires blend together to create a welcoming and relaxing atmosphere A programme of events ranging from gardening, antiques and wine masterclasses are now available. Congham Hall is the ideal base from which to tour the spectacular beaches of the north Norfolk coastline, Sandringham, Burnham Market and Holkham Hall.

Our inspector loved: *The wonderful herb garden and personal touches in the rooms (Black Cats – fabrics of course).*

Directions: Go to the A149/A148 interchange northeast of King's Lynn. Follow the A148 towards Sandringham/Fakenham/ Cromer for 100 yards. Turn right to Grimston. The hotel is then 2 miles on the left

Web: www.johansens.com/conghamhall
E-mail: info@conghamhallhotel.co.uk
Tel: 0870 381 8443
International: +44 (0)1485 600250
Fax: 01485 601191

Price Guide:
single from £115
double/twin from £195
suites from £310

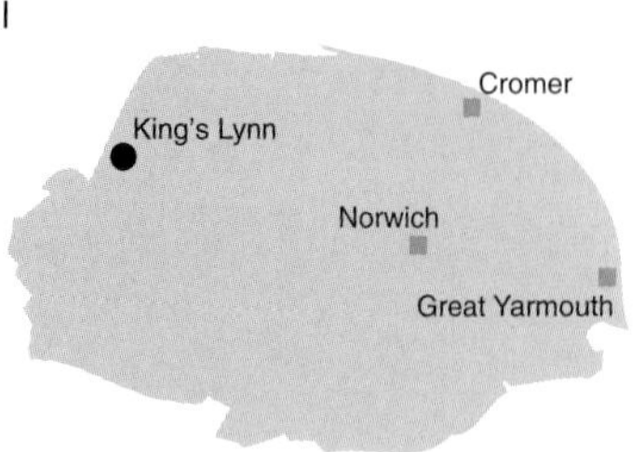

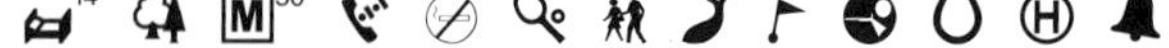

Fawsley Hall

FAWSLEY, NEAR DAVENTRY, NORTHAMPTONSHIRE NN11 3BA

Set in the beautiful Northamptonshire countryside and surrounded by acres of rolling parkland with lakes, landscaped by Capability Brown, Fawsley Hall combines the charm and character of a gracious manor with the facilities and comforts of a modern hotel. The original Tudor manor house opened as a hotel in 1998 but many traces of its illustrious past have been retained, such as the vaulted hall and Queen Elizabeth I chamber. The bedrooms offer a range of Tudor, Georgian, Victorian and "classic modern" styles; many include four-poster beds. The Knightley Restaurant has established a reputation for being the finest in the county and the Old Laundry Bar provides delicious light meals at lunchtime. The spa, in the Georgian cellar, has a beauty salon, fitness studio, steam, sauna and spa bath. There are currently 5 conference and syndicate rooms, which can accommodate up to 80 delegates and the attractive Salvin Suite can seat 140 guests for a banquet. In the spring of 2007 Knightley Court will open adding a further 8 Georgian bedrooms, a cinema, syndicate rooms and a magnificent function room to hold 150 guests for a private dinner, conference or product launch. Sulgrave Manor, ancestral home of George Washington, Althorp, Canons Ashby, Blenheim Palace, Silverstone, Towcester Racecourse, Warwick Castle, Oxford and Stratford-upon-Avon are all nearby.

Directions: Fawsley Hall can be reached by the M40, junction 11 or the M1, junction16. Both are 10 miles from the hotel.

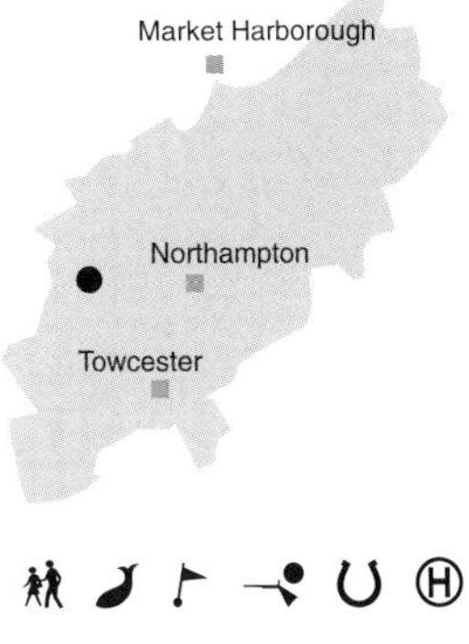

Web: www.johansens.com/fawsleyhall
E-mail: reservations@fawsleyhall.com
Tel: 0870 381 8516
International: +44 (0)1327 892000
Fax: 01327 892001

Market Harborough
Northampton
Towcester

Price Guide:
single from £149
double/twin from £189
suite from £375

Our inspector loved: *The Great Hall with its paintings and fireplace.*

Rushton Hall

RUSHTON, NEAR KETTERING, NORTHAMPTONSHIRE NN14 1RR

Directions: Take the A14 and exit at junction 7. Take the A43 then the A6003 towards Corby Until Rushton. Turn left just after the bridge.

Web: www.johansens.com/rushtonhall
E-mail: enquiries@rushtonhall.com
Tel: 0870 381 8383
International: +44 (0)1536 713001
Fax: 01536 713010

Price Guide:
superior from £140
state room from £180
four poster from £250

This stunning Grade I listed hall was built in the 16th century by Sir Thomas Tresham and a number of well-known aristocratic families have added to the structure over the years. Lying amidst beautifully manicured grounds, and approached by a long sweeping drive through imposing wrought-iron gates, the grand façade is guaranteed to impress arriving guests, and there can be few more spectacular destinations for an event, wedding or a simple weekend getaway. Great care has been taken with the design of the hotel, and the beautiful linen fold panelling and original flooring are complemented by comfortable, stylish furnishings and long, elegant drapes. Many of the bathrooms feature roll-top baths and luxurious fittings. The public rooms are stunning, ranging from the spectacular Great Hall, with vaulted ceiling and beautiful bay window overlooking the grounds, to the more intimate library and delightful drawing room. In all the bedrooms there is a film and music on demand service. Outside, the grounds provide wonderful photographic opportunities; the balcony overlooks the 16th-century courtyard and the magnificent 400-year old stone seat boasts a superb view of the world famous triangular lodge. Within easy access of Market Harborough, Leicester and Northampton, the Hall is ideally located for motorway routes and trains into London

***Our inspector loved:** The magnificence of the tranquil central courtyard.*

        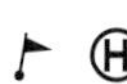 

Whittlebury Hall

WHITTLEBURY, NEAR TOWCESTER, NORTHAMPTONSHIRE NN12 8QH

Whittlebury Hall is a modern building that successfully combines the elegance of classic Georgian architecture with contemporary furnishings and fabrics to create a truly fabulous hotel. The spacious bedrooms are tastefully decorated with modern touches and thoughtful extras; 3 superbly appointed, individually-styled suites have a whirlpool spa bath and shower. Guests may enjoy an apèritif in the aptly named Silverstone Bar where an array of motor racing memorabilia adorns the walls, before sampling the flavours of the informal Italian menu and wine list at Bentleys. Alternatively, the relaxed Astons Restaurant presents meals that blend classic and contemporary cuisine. The 2 AA Rosette-awarded Murrays Restaurant, offers the latest in food trends and fashion. The management training centre comprises 14 suites, 32 syndicate rooms, 6 meeting rooms and a lecture room for up to 450 delegates. Extensive facilities at The Spa and The Leisure Club include a range of heat and ice experiences, a gym, swimming pool and treatment suite where over 60 treatments are available for body, mind and soul. Adjacent to the Hall is the independently owned Whittlebury Park golf course, which offers preferred rates to guests. Motor racing enthusiasts can enjoy racing action at nearby Silverstone. Warwick Castle, Towcester racecourse and Oxford are all easily accessed by car.

Our inspector loved: *The welcoming main lounge complete with open fire.*

Directions: 11 miles from the M1, junction 15A and 17 miles from the M40, junction 10.

Web: www.johansens.com/whittleburyhall
E-mail: sales@whittleburyhall.co.uk
Tel: 0870 381 8995
International: +44 (0)1327 857857
Fax: 01327 857867

Price Guide:
single £130
double/twin £155
suite £280

Marshall Meadows Country House Hotel

BERWICK-UPON-TWEED, NORTHUMBERLAND TD15 1UT

Directions: A1 heading North, take Berwick by-pass and at Meadow House roundabout, head towards Edinburgh. After 300 yards, turn right, indicated by white sign – the hotel is at the end of small side road.

Web: www.johansens.com/marshallmeadows
E-mail: stay@marshallmeadows.co.uk
Tel: 0870 381 8721
International: +44 (0)1289 331133
Fax: 01289 331438

Price Guide:
single £85–£105
double/twin £120–£150
suite £150–£175

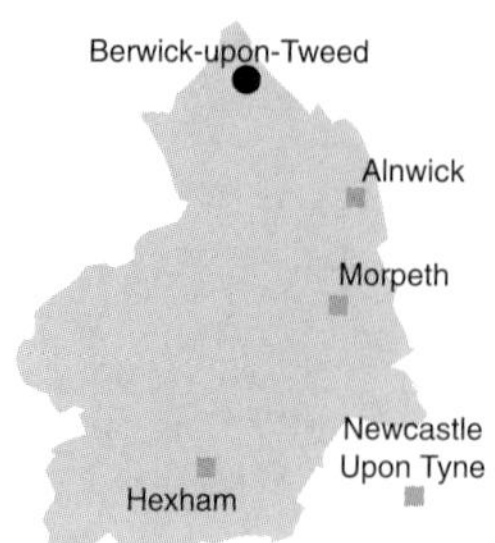

Marshall Meadows can truly boast that it is England's most northerly hotel, just a quarter of a mile from the Scottish border, an ideal base for those exploring the rugged beauty of Northumberland. A magnificent Georgian mansion standing in 15 acres of woodland and formal gardens, Marshall Meadows today is a luxurious retreat, with a country house ambience – welcoming and elegant. It has a burn and small waterfall with attractive woodland walks. This is not a large hotel; there are just 19 bedrooms, each individually designed. Restful harmonious colour schemes, comfortable beds and the tranquillity of its surroundings ensure a good night's sleep! The lounge is delightful, with traditional easy chairs and sofas, overlooking the patio. Ideal for summer afternoon tea. The congenial Duck & Grouse Bar stocks a range of whiskies, beers and fine wines. Marshall Meadows has a galleried restaurant where diners enjoy local game, fresh seafood and good wine. Private dining facilities are also available. Excellent golf, fishing and historic Berwick-on-Tweed are nearby. Short breaks are available throughout the year.

Our inspector loved: *The peaceful country setting in close proximity to the sea and its coastal walks.*

Tillmouth Park

CORNHILL-ON-TWEED, NEAR BERWICK-UPON-TWEED, NORTHUMBERLAND TD12 4UU

This magnificent mansion house, built in 1882 using stones from nearby Twizel Castle, offers the same warm welcome to visitors today as when it was an exclusive private house. Tillmouth Park is situated in 15 acres of mature parkland gardens above the river Till. The generously sized bedrooms are individually designed with period and antique furniture, and are fully appointed with bathrobes, toiletries, hairdryer and trouser press. Most bedrooms offer spectacular views of the surrounding countryside. The wood-panelled, 2 AA Rosette, restaurant serves a fine table d'hôte menu offering contemporary British cuisine, whilst the Bistro is less formal. A well-chosen wine list and a vast selection of malt whiskies complement the cuisine. The elegant, galleried main hall offers country house comfort with open log fires. Tillmouth Park is ideally situated for country pursuits, with fishing on the Tweed and Till and clay shooting available locally. The area also abounds in fine golf courses. Coldstream and Kelso are within easy reach; the Northumbrian coast and Berwick are 15 minutes away, and Flodden Field, Lindisfarne and Holy Island are nearby. There are many stately homes to visit in the area including Floors, Manderston, Paxton and the spectacular Alnwick Garden Project.

Directions: Tillmouth Park is on the A698 Coldstream to Berwick-upon-Tweed road.

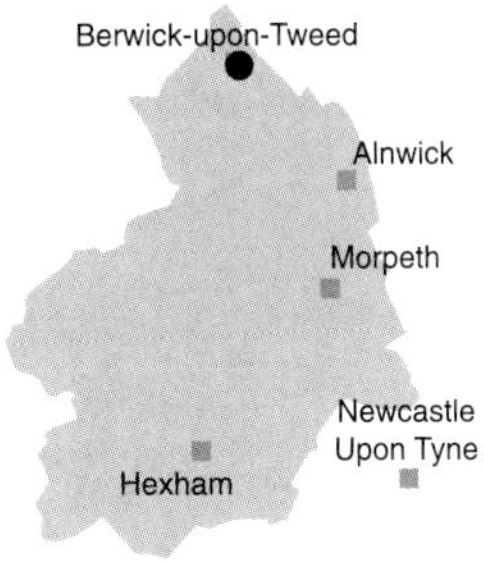

Web: www.johansens.com/tillmouthpark
E-mail: reception@tillmouthpark.f9.co.uk
Tel: 0870 381 8948
International: +44 (0)1890 882255
Fax: 01890 882540

Price Guide:
single £95–£150
twin/double £130–£200

Our inspector loved: *The magnificent galleried main hall.*

Matfen Hall

MATFEN, NEWCASTLE-UPON-TYNE, NORTHUMBERLAND NE20 0RH

Originally built in 1830 by Sir Edward Blackett, Matfen Hall has been carefully restored by Sir Hugh and Lady Blackett. This magnificent family seat lies in the heart of some of Northumberland's most beautiful countryside offering facilities for conferences, weddings, golf, spa and leisure breaks. The Great Hall is awe-inspiring with its stained-glass windows, large pillars and stone floors, whilst each of the bedrooms has an individual character combining modern features with traditional opulence. A huge open fireplace adds charm to the elegantly furnished Drawing Room and the unique Library and Print Room Restaurant serves modern English cuisine, awarded 2 AA Rosettes. The Hall enjoys stunning views of the championship golf course, laid out on a classic parkland landscape with manicured greens and fairways flanked by majestic trees. Rated as one of the finest in the North East it provides a pleasurable test for players of all abilities; there is also a 9-hole, par 3 golf course. The spa offers a wide range of treatments as part of an exclusive association with "comfort zone". Other amenities include a 16m pool, 5 treatment suites featuring a VIP twin treatment room, crystal steam room, salt grotto, herbal sauna, tropical feature shower, ice fountain and gym with the latest techno-gym equipment. Scenic coastal, rural and ancient sites are a drive away and Newcastle is a 20-minute journey.

Directions: From the A1 take the A69 towards Hexham. At Heddon-on-the-Wall take the B6318 towards Chollerford and travel 7 miles, then turn right to Matfen.

Web: www.johansens.com/matfenhall
E-mail: info@matfenhall.com
Tel: 0870 381 8724
International: +44 (0)1661 886500
Fax: 01661 886055

Price Guide: (special breaks available)
single from £105–£190
double from £160–£265

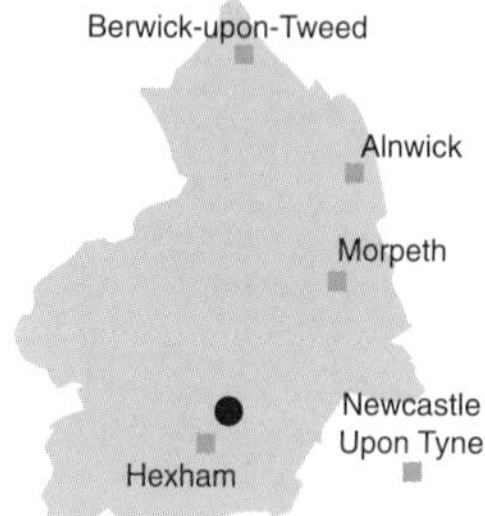

Our inspector loved: *Having a relaxing pamper day in the spa.*

Colwick Hall Hotel

COLWICK PARK, RACECOURSE ROAD, NOTTINGHAM, NOTTINGHAMSHIRE NG2 4BH

There can be few more spectacular settings than this magnificent Palladian-style Georgian country mansion set in acres of parkland overlooking Nottingham Racecourse. Approached via a long sweeping carriage drive, this Grade II listed building has a fascinating history, and it is only in recent years that it has been restored to such elegant splendour. The beautiful grounds have made the hall a prominent destination for functions and summer parties for a number of years; the landscaped lawns and ornamental fountains are unrivalled backdrops for photographs. New in September 2005 were 16 supremely luxurious bedrooms and suites. Each retains the proportions of the original 19th-century building and is consequently extremely spacious with equally generous bathrooms. The original plasterwork and coving has been fully restored and each room features an original cast-iron fireplace and grate, and is furnished with the ultimate elegance and style. The Georgetown Restaurant, with stunning cherub-painted ceiling, is situated in the exquisite front dining room and has a winning formula of delicious award-winning cuisine within an exotic Malaysian inspired setting. The flavours of the Malaysian Malays, Mandarin Chinese and Tamil Indians are all brought together under one roof, and the local house cocktail, the Singapore Sling, is rapidly gaining acclaim.

Directions: Colwick Hall Hotel is situated 2 miles from the city centre. Follow the brown signs for Nottingham Racecourse. Turn into Racecourse Road but continue past the Racecourse entrance and the hotel is 1/4 mile on the right.

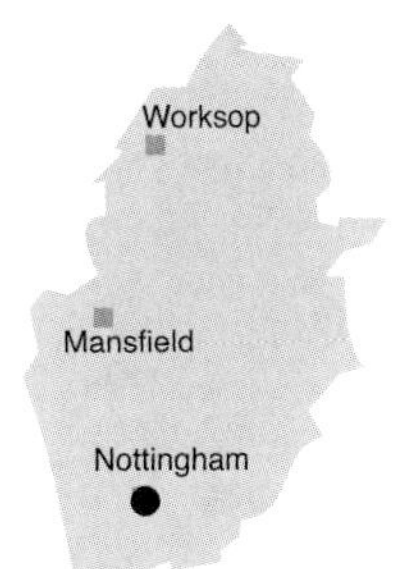

Web: www.johansens.com/colwickhall
E-mail: enquiries@colwickhallhotel.co.uk
Tel: 0870 381 8594
International: +44 (0)115 950 0566
Fax: 0115 924 3797

Price Guide:
single £70–£160
double/twin £80–£180
suite £220–£340

Our inspector loved: *The stunning bedrooms and their vast bathrooms.*

Lace Market Hotel

29-31, HIGH PAVEMENT, THE LACE MARKET, NOTTINGHAM, NOTTINGHAMSHIRE NG1 1HE

Occupying a prime location in Nottingham's city centre, just yards from the most fashionable shops and the National Arena, this privately-owned boutique hotel offers guests outstanding hospitality and service. Lace Market Hotel has a loyal following from the music industry and celebrity A-list, which is not surprising since it boasts luxurious accommodation, stylish rooms for private events, a gastro pub, upmarket brasserie and chic cocktail bar - all under one roof! All 42 bedrooms are individually designed and furnished with unique artwork, and superior rooms and studios have eye catching views from bed and bath alike. The hotel is right next door to the historic church of St Mary the Virgin and is therefore Nottingham's top notch choice for small, understated weddings, civil marriages, civil partnerships and receptions. There is free on-street overnight parking and guests enjoy a generous 30% discount in the adjacent NCP car park. Visitors to Lace Market Hotel will find plenty to do in and around Nottingham and also benefit from complimentary access to nearby Holmes Place Health Club, complete with indoor pool, full gym facilities and fitness classes.

Our inspector loved: *The beautifully appointed bedrooms..*

Directions: Head for the city centre and use Stoney Street NCP car park.

Web: www.johansens.com/lacemarkethotel
E-mail: stay@lacemarkethotel.co.uk
Tel: 0870 381 9325
International: +44 (0)115 852 3232
Fax: 0115 852 3223

Price Guide: (room only)
small single £95
double/twin £119–£139
superior £189
studios £239

Phyllis Court Club

MARLOW ROAD, HENLEY-ON-THAMES, OXFORDSHIRE RG9 2HT

Phyllis Court Club occupies an unrivalled position on the banks of the Thames overlooking the Henley Royal Regatta course. Founded in 1906 by the owner of the house with a group of friends and London businessmen, the house has an intriguing history spanning 6 centuries involving royal patronage. Phyllis Court Club prides itself on retaining the traditions of its illustrious past, whilst guests staying in this fine historic residence today can enjoy a high standard of up-to-date hospitality. Oliver Cromwell slept here and it was also here that William II held his first Royal Court. Years later, when the name Henley became synonymous with rowing, they came as patrons of the Royal Regatta: Prince Albert, King George V and Edward, Prince of Wales. The character of the Court remains unaltered in its hallowed setting, but the comfortable bedrooms, the more formal restaurant, as well as the stunning new Orangery with its contemporary menu and design overlooking the garden and river, are of the latest high quality. Residents become temporary members as the dining areas and bar are open to members only. Ideal for meetings, functions, wedding parties and leisure breaks to include shopping in Henley and glorious riverside walks.

***Our inspector loved:** The bright and airy Orangery, which adds to the splendour of Phyllis Court Club.*

Directions: M40, junction 4 to Marlow or M4, junction 8/9 then follow signposts to Henley-on-Thames. Phyllis Court is on the A4155 between Henley and Marlow.

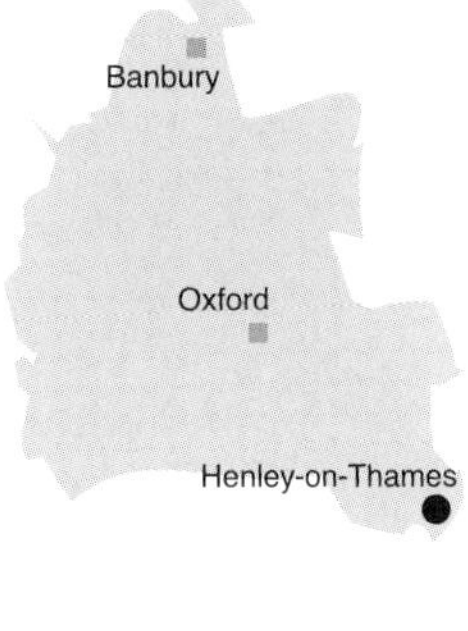

Banbury

Oxford

Henley-on-Thames

Web: www.johansens.com/phylliscourt
E-mail: enquiries@phylliscourt.co.uk
Tel: 0870 381 8822
International: +44 (0)1491 570500
Fax: 01491 570528

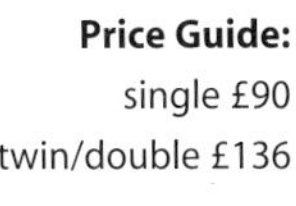

Price Guide:
single £90
twin/double £136

Le Manoir Aux Quat' Saisons

GREAT MILTON, OXFORDSHIRE OX44 7PD

Situated in secluded grounds just 8 miles south of the historic city of Oxford, Le Manoir aux Quat'Saisons is the fulfilment of Chef Patron, Raymond Blanc's vision to create a hotel and restaurant in harmony, where its guests would fine perfection in comfort, cuisine and service. It is regarded as one of the finest hotel and restaurants in Europe and the only country house to have retained 2 Michelin stars for 21 years. This beautiful 15th Century, golden stone, gabled house, set in 7 acres of stunning gardens, with its own organic herb and vegetable gardens has 32 beautifully appointed suites and bedrooms. For everyone with a passion for good food 'The Raymond Blanc Cookery School' provides cookery courses throughout the year. Participation is restricted to 10 guests to ensure the highest level of personal tuition. Participants stay at Le Manoir and their partners are welcome to stay free of charge although their meals and drinks are charged for separately.

Our inspector loved: *The magic of Le Manoir.*

Directions: From London, M40 and turn off at jct 7 (A329 to Wallingford). From the North, leave M40 at jct 8A and follow signs to Wallingford (A329). After 1½ miles, turn right, follow the brown signs for Le Manoir aux Quat' Saisons.

Web: www.johansens.com/lemanoirauxquatsaisons
E-mail: lemanoir@blanc.co.uk
Tel: 0870 381 8682
International: +44 (0)1844 278881
Fax: 01844 278847
USA/Canada Toll free: 1-800-393-5364

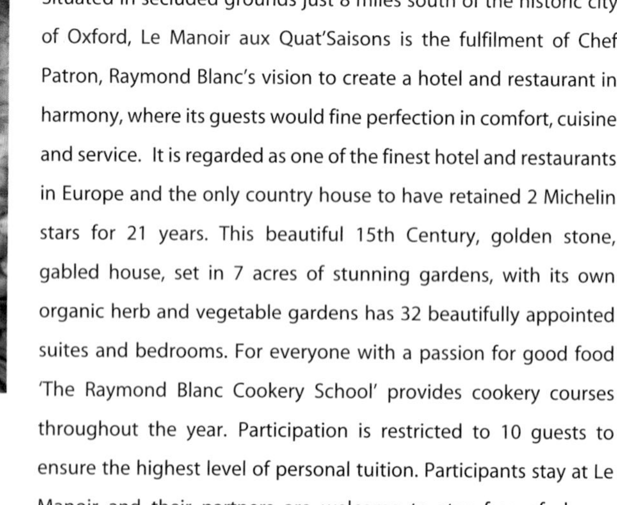

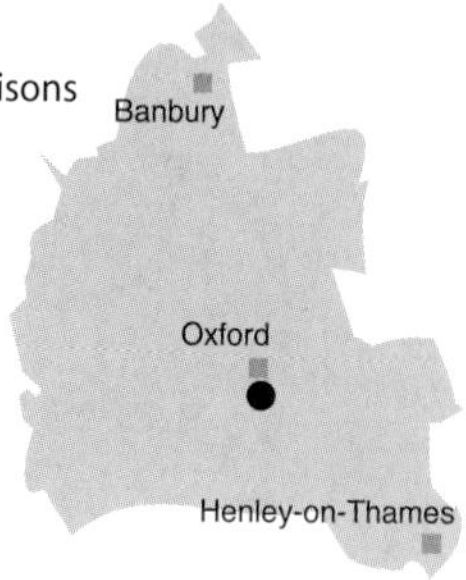

Price Guide:
double/twin £380–£915

Weston Manor

WESTON-ON-THE-GREEN, OXFORDSHIRE OX25 3QL

Imposing wrought-iron gates flanked by sculptured busts surmounting tall grey stone pillars lead into the impressive entrance to this delightful manor house, the showpiece of the lovely village of Weston-on-the Green since the 11th century. The ancestral home of the Earls of Abingdon and Berkshire, and once the property of Henry VIII, today Weston Manor is a popular venue for weddings and corporate occasions. Standing regally in 12 acres of colourful gardens, the manor has been restored to a comfortable country house hotel from which leisure and business visitors can discover the delights of the nearby Cotswold countryside, Oxford, Woodstock, Blenheim Palace and Broughton Castle. Many of the individual bedrooms, including 4 in a cottage and 16 in the coach-house, feature antique furniture; all have garden views and private bathrooms. The restaurant, a magnificent vaulted and oak-panelled Baronial Hall, serves 2 AA Rosette-awarded cuisine; dining in such historic splendour is very much the focus of a memorable stay. The 7 versatile meeting rooms, including the new Osborn suite, have natural daylight and are ideal for exclusive use day and residential conferences and team-building events including laser clay shooting. There is a croquet lawn and secluded, heated outdoor swimming pool.

Our inspector loved: *The combination of historical and contemporary.*

Directions: From the M40, exit at junction 9 onto the A34 towards Oxford. Leave the A34 at the first junction, towards Middleton Stoney. At the mini roundabout turn right onto the B430. The hotel is approx 500m on the left.

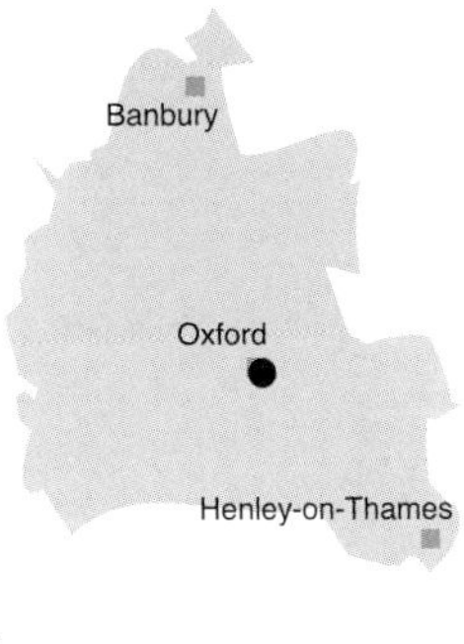

Web: www.johansens.com/westonmanor
E-mail: lesliewood@westonmanor.co.uk
Tel: 0870 381 8981
International: +44 (0)1869 350621
Fax: 01869 350901

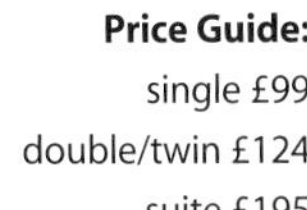

Price Guide:
single £99
double/twin £124
suite £195

The Springs Hotel & Golf Club

NORTH STOKE, WALLINGFORD, OXFORDSHIRE OX10 6BE

Directions: From the M40 take exit 6 onto B4009, through Watlington to Benson; turn left onto A4074 towards Reading. After 2 miles go right onto B4009. The hotel is ½ mile further on the right.

Web: www.johansens.com/springshotel
E-mail: info@thespringshotel.com
Tel: 0870 381 8904
International: +44 (0)1491 836687
Fax: 01491 836877

Price Guide:
single from £95
double/twin from £110
suite from £155

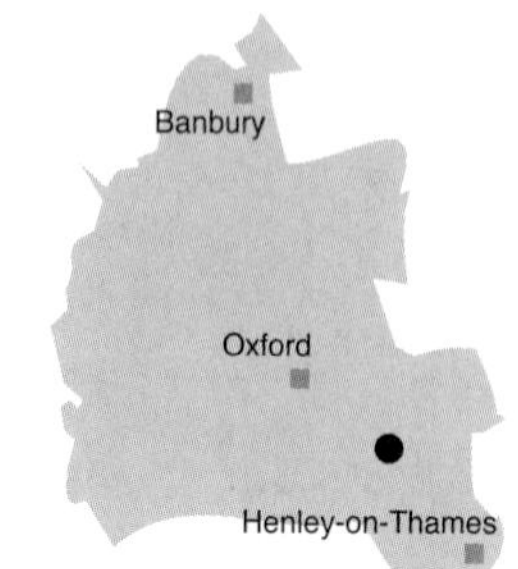

The Springs is a fine old country house which dates from 1874 and is set deep in the heart of the beautiful Thames Valley, yet within easy reach of the motorway networks. One of the first houses in England to be built in the Mock Tudor style, it stands in 6 acres of glorious grounds. The hotel's large south-facing windows overlook a spring-fed lake, from which it takes its name. Many of the comfortable bedrooms and suites offer beautiful views over the lake and lawns, whilst others overlook the quiet woodland that surrounds the hotel. Private balconies provide patios for summer relaxation. The Lakeside restaurant has an intimate atmosphere inspired by its gentle décor and the lovely view of the lake. The award-winning restaurant's menu takes advantage of fresh local produce and a well-stocked cellar of international wines provides the perfect accompaniment to a splendid meal. Leisure facilities include an 18-hole par 72 golf course, clubhouse and putting green, a swimming pool, sauna and touring bicycles. Facilities are as ideal for the corporate guest and teambuilding events as they are for a relaxing break. Oxford, Blenheim Palace and Windsor are nearby and the hotel is conveniently located for racing at Newbury and Ascot as well as the Royal Henley Regatta. Themed weekends are available.

Our inspector loved: *The flexible facilitiies, restaurant views and glorious gardens.*

Hambleton Hall

HAMBLETON, OAKHAM, RUTLAND LE15 8TH

Winner of Johansens Most Excellent Country Hotel Award 1996, Hambleton Hall, originally a Victorian mansion, celebrated its 25th year as a hotel in 2005. Since then its renown has continually grown. It enjoys a spectacular lakeside setting in a charming and unspoilt area of Rutland. The hotel's tasteful interiors have been designed to create elegance and comfort, retaining individuality by avoiding a catalogue approach to furnishing. Delightful displays of flowers, an artful blend of ingredients from local hedgerows and the London flower markets colour the bedrooms. In the Michelin-Starred restaurant, chef Aaron Patterson and his enthusiastic team offer a menu which is strongly seasonal. Grouse, Scottish ceps and chanterelles, partridge and woodcock are all available at just the right time of year, accompanied by the best vegetables, herbs and salads from the Hall's garden. The Croquet Pavilion, a 2-bedroom suite with living room and breakfast room is a luxurious addition to the accommodation options. For the energetic there are lovely walks around the lake and opportunities for tennis and swimming, golf, riding, bicycling, trout fishing, and sailing. Burghley House and Belton are nearby, as are the antique shops of Oakham, Uppingham and Stamford.

Our inspector loved: *The sumptous interior design and colours.*

Directions: In the village of Hambleton, signposted from the A606, 1 mile east of Oakham.

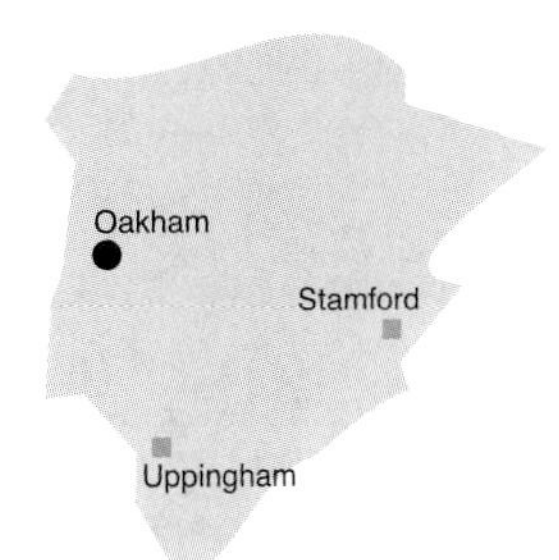

Web: www.johansens.com/hambletonhall
E-mail: hotel@hambletonhall.com
Tel: 0870 381 8582
International: +44 (0)1572 756991
Fax: 01572 724721

Price Guide:
single from £165
double/twin £195–£360
suite £500–£600

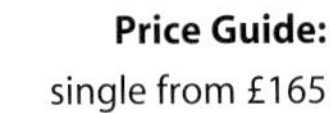

DINHAM HALL

LUDLOW, SHROPSHIRE SY8 1EJ

Built in 1792, Dinham Hall was originally a town residence for a wealthy landowner and today it retains the warmth and calm of a private house. The Georgian building's timeless elegance is enhanced in the public spaces with comfortable sofas, leather armchairs, open fires and fresh flowers. All bedrooms and suites are superbly furnished with views overlooking the gardens or castle and many have a unique history and character including the names of schoolboys inscribed on window ledges from when the building was part of Ludlow College. Chef Dean Banner's food is refreshing and combines local produce and game, when in season, most of which is sourced within a 30-mile radius. Dishes enhance the quality of the finest ingredients, and an excellent lunch menu is on offer, from light snacks and meals to a full menu. The Merchant Suite, with its 14th-century timbers, the Green Room and Orangery are available for private dining. General Manager James Garnett is keen that guests enjoy their visit to the town, described by architectural critics as the most beautiful country town in England. Dinham Hall's location in the heart of Ludlow makes it the ideal base for exploring Shropshire's castles, the Ironbridge Gorge, and the stunning surrounding countryside.

Our inspector loved: *Breakfast: beautifully presented with quality fruit and cereals and the excellent menu. A perfect start to the day.*

Directions: Ludlow is approached via the A49. Dinham Hall is in the centre of town overlooking the castle.

Web: www.johansens.com/dinhamhall
E-mail: info@dinhamhall.co.uk
Tel: 0870 381 8482
International: +44 (0)1584 876464
Fax: 01584 876019

Price Guide:
single from £95
double/twin from £140
suite from £240

Ston Easton Park

STON EASTON, BATH, SOMERSET BA3 4DF

The internationally renowned hotel, Ston Easton Park, is a Grade I Palladian mansion of notable distinction. A showpiece for some exceptional architectural and decorative features of its period, it dates from 1739 and has recently undergone extensive restoration, offering a unique opportunity to enjoy the opulent splendour of the 18th century. A high priority is given to the provision of friendly and unobtrusive service. The hotel has won innumerable awards for its décor, service and food. Jean Monro, an acknowledged expert on 18th-century decoration, supervised the design and furnishing of the interiors, complementing the original features with choice antiques, paintings and objets d'art. Fresh, quality produce, delivered from all parts of Britain, is combined with herbs and vegetables from the Victorian kitchen garden to create English and French dishes. To accompany your meal, a wide selection of rare wines and old vintages is stocked in the house cellars. The grounds, landscaped by Humphry Repton in 1793, consist of romantic gardens and parkland. The 17th-century Gardener's Cottage, close to the main house on the wooded banks of the River Norr, provides private suite accommodation.

Our inspector loved: *The beautiful redecoration to the public rooms and magnificent location.*

Directions: 11 miles south of Bath on the A37 between Bath and Wells.

Web: www.johansens.com/stoneastonpark
E-mail: info@stoneaston.co.uk
Tel: 0870 381 8916
International: +44 (0)1761 241631
Fax: 01761 241377

Price Guide:
single from £145
double/twin £175–£415
four-poster £240–£415

Combe House Hotel

HOLFORD, NEAR BRIDGWATER, SOMERSET TA5 1RZ

Directions: From Bridgwater follow signs for Minehead A39. Holford is 11 miles along the A39. On reaching the village, turn left in front of the Plough Inn and follow the lane to Holford Combe and the hotel.

Web: www.johansens.com/combehouseholford
E-mail: enquiries@combehouse.co.uk
Tel: 0870 381 8621
International: +44 (0)1278 741382

Price Guide:
single £72.50-£95
double £125-£150
suite £140-£165

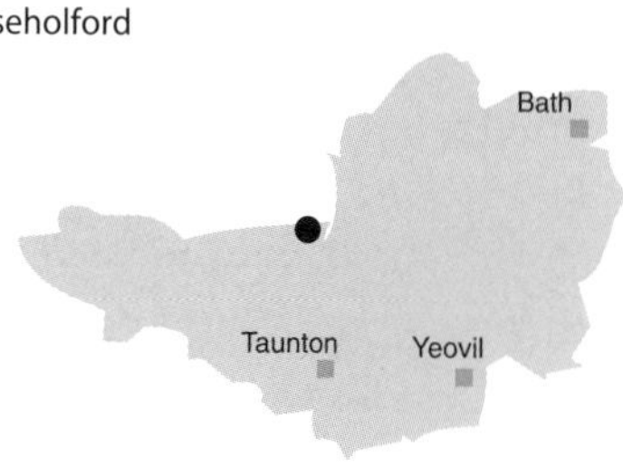

This country house hotel sits within 4 acres of tranquil grounds, which feature a fine variety of shrubs, an ancient yew, a bubbling stream and an organic kitchen garden bursting with vegetables and soft fruit. The surrounding wooded valleys of the Quantock Hills make up the first part of England to be designated an Area of Outstanding Natural Beauty. Many species of wild birds, animals and rare plants can be spotted, and on a summer evening guests can watch scampering rabbits or even catch sight of roe and red deer emerging from the forest to graze. Accommodation ranges from standard to superior rooms with king or super-king-size beds, luxury toiletries, fluffy robes and views over the garden. There is also a four-poster bridal suite. The restaurant has recently been refitted with specially commissioned handmade Cornish oak and walnut furniture, and menus draw on recipes from all over the world combining meat and game from local farms and shoots, fish from Brixham trawlers, shellfish from the Bristol Channel, and of course, Somerset cheeses. The hotel has its own indoor heated pool, sauna, hard tennis court and well-stocked library, alternatively, the Quantocks provide a wonderful variety of walks and the area boasts numerous other attractions.

Our inspector loved: *This little corner of heaven, I did not want to leave!*

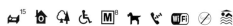

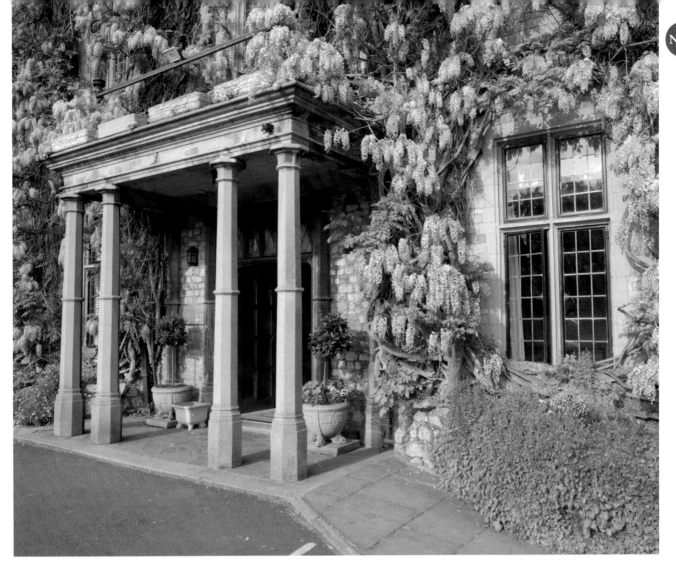

THE CASTLE AT TAUNTON

CASTLE GREEN, TAUNTON, SOMERSET TA1 1NF

Set in the heart of the West Country, The Castle at Taunton has been welcoming travellers to explore the region's plethora of attractions since the 12th century. Run by the Chapman Family for over 50 years, this former Norman fortress serves as a convivial gateway to the land of King Arthur and offers 44 en-suite bedrooms, all of which are individually appointed. Gastronomes will be delighted with the award-winning restaurant whose Head Chef Richard Guest has won a Michelin star, top 25 in the Good Food Guide, 4 RAC Dining Awards and most recently, the accolade of Best Breakfast in England. The ambitious menu includes Brixham crab cakes with marinated cauliflower, red mullet minestrone and a celebration of British beef comprising steamed oxtail pudding, roast fillet of South Devon beef and ox tongue sauce. Conference planners should note that The Castle can cater for meetings up to 100 delegates. Outdoor pursuits abound and fishing, golf, shooting and horse-riding can all be arranged. Exmoor, Glastonbury and Wells are all on The Castle's doorstep while Longleat House and the stunning gardens of Stourhead and Hestercombe are also a pleasure to discover nearby.

Our inspector loved: *The comfort in a fascinating and historical setting.*

Directions: Exit from the M5/junction 25 and follow the brown signs for Castle Hotel within Taunton.

Web: www.johansens.com/castleattaunton
E-mail: reception@the-castle-hotel.com
Tel: 0870 381 8538
International: +44 (0)1823 272671
Fax: 01823 336066

Bath
Taunton
Yeovil

Price Guide:
single from £125
double from £215
suite from £310

Mount Somerset Country House Hotel

HENLADE, TAUNTON, SOMERSET TA3 5NB

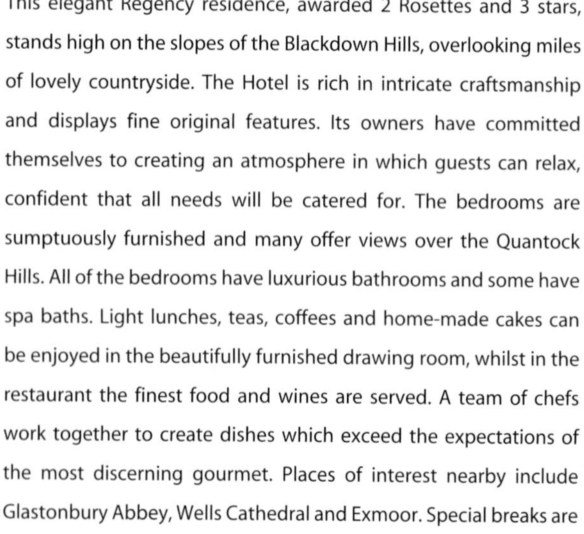

This elegant Regency residence, awarded 2 Rosettes and 3 stars, stands high on the slopes of the Blackdown Hills, overlooking miles of lovely countryside. The Hotel is rich in intricate craftsmanship and displays fine original features. Its owners have committed themselves to creating an atmosphere in which guests can relax, confident that all needs will be catered for. The bedrooms are sumptuously furnished and many offer views over the Quantock Hills. All of the bedrooms have luxurious bathrooms and some have spa baths. Light lunches, teas, coffees and home-made cakes can be enjoyed in the beautifully furnished drawing room, whilst in the restaurant the finest food and wines are served. A team of chefs work together to create dishes which exceed the expectations of the most discerning gourmet. Places of interest nearby include Glastonbury Abbey, Wells Cathedral and Exmoor. Special breaks are available throughout the year.

Our inspector loved: *The delightful newly presented garden room where one can enjoy tempting light lunches.*

Directions: At the M5 exit at junction 25, join the A358 towards Ilminster. Just past Henlade turn right at the sign for Stoke St. Mary. At the T-junction turn left, the Hotel drive is 150 yards on the right.

Web: www.johansens.com/mountsomerset
E-mail: info@mountsomersethotel.co.uk
Tel: 0870 381 8750
International: +44 (0)1823 442500
Fax: 01823 442900

Price Guide:
single from £110–£140
double/twin from £160–£195
suites £190–£225

Bath
Taunton
Yeovil

Bindon Country House Hotel

LANGFORD BUDVILLE, WELLINGTON, SOMERSET TA21 0RU

Occupying a glorious location in 7 acres of tranquil gardens and woodland, this property offers guests a peaceful retreat from a hectic life. Bindon is the quintessential country house hotel with croquet on the lawn, a delightful rose garden and a rediscovered Victorian orangery. Some parts of the building date back to the 17th century, and when current owners Mark and Lynn Jaffa purchased the property in 1996 they undertook a painstaking restoration process to create the wonderful hotel that stands today. The 12 luxurious bedrooms are light, airy and spacious; each has its own character yet enjoys the same sumptuous fabrics, exquisite linens and pampering bathrooms. Acclaimed Head Chef Mike Davies, formerly head chef of a 2 AA Rosette-awarded restaurant and colleague of Head Chef of the Year, Phil Vickery, creates traditional, English dishes with a strong focus on seasonal produce that results in a daily changing table d'hôte menu and seasonally changing à la carte. After a satisfying meal guests may adjourn to the oak-panelled Wellington Bar to enjoy drinks in front of the cosy open fire. Local places of interest include Exmoor, Exeter, Wells, Dartmoor, Bath and Glastonbury with Langford Heath Nature Reserve just a 5-minute walk away. Short breaks from £150, including dinner are available. Exclusive use of the hotel can be arranged on a full, partial or self-catering basis.

***Our inspector loved:** This hidden little gem.*

Directions: 15 minutes from M5, jct 26 drive to Wellington and take B3187 to Langford Budville. Go through the village then right towards Wiveliscombe, right again at the junction and pass Bindon Farm. After 450 yards turn right.

Bath
Taunton
Yeovil

Web: www.johansens.com/bindoncountryhouse
E-mail: stay@bindon.com
Tel: 0870 381 8364
International: +44 (0)1823 400070
Fax: 01823 400071

Price Guide:
single from £95
double/twin £115–£215
suite from £145

Hoar Cross Hall Spa Resort

HOAR CROSS, NR YOXALL, STAFFORDSHIRE DE13 8QS

The only spa resort in a stately home in England. Surrounded by 90 acres of beautiful countryside, lakes and exquisite formal and continental gardens with water features, exotic plants and beautiful flowers, Hoar Cross Hall is a secluded haven and the perfect venue for those who want a peaceful environment in which to be pampered. Oak panelling, tapestries, rich furnishings and paintings adorn the interior. A stunning Jacobean staircase leads to luxurious bedrooms, all with crown tester or four-poster beds and elegant design. Penthouses have private saunas and balconies overlooking the treetops. Breathtaking gilded ceilings and William Morris wallpaper in the original ballroom set the scene for the dining room, where a superb à la carte menu is offered. A tasty breakfast and buffet lunch is served in the Plantation Restaurants overlooking the pools. There are unlimited ways in which visitors can de-stress; yoga, meditation, tai chi, pilates, dance classes and aqua-aerobics are all available and outdoor pursuits include tennis, croquet, archery and a PGA professional golf academy with 9 hole par 3 golf course and driving range. Trained professionals are ready to assist and the spa consists of seawater and hydrotherapy swimming pools, baths, flotation therapy, saunas, a 4000 sq ft gymnasium, steam rooms, water grottos, saunariums, aromatherapy room, aerobics and yoga suites .

Our inspector loved: *The balance of excellent meals and welcoming restaurant combined with serious facilities. Relaxed but so professional.*

Directions: From Lichfield turn off the A51 onto the A515 towards Ashbourne. Go through Yoxall and turn left to Hoar Cross.

Web: www.johansens.com/hoarcrosshall
E-mail: info@hoarcross.co.uk
Tel: 0870 381 8598
International: +44 (0)1283 575671
Fax: 01283 575652

Price Guide: (fully inclusive of spa treatments, breakfast, lunch and dinner)
single £168-£218
double/twin £320-£364
suite £384–£494

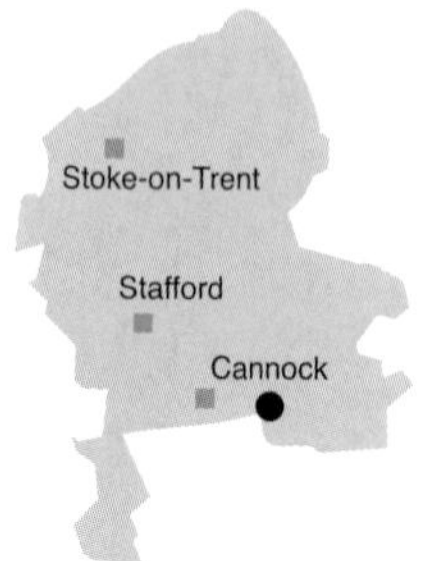

99

160 16

SPA

Brudenell Hotel

THE PARADE, ALDEBURGH, SUFFOLK IP15 5BU

This delightful hotel is the epitome of a charming contemporary seaside hideaway with a light, airy and relaxed ambience. Informal décor and comfortable furnishings complement the occasional piece of driftwood, and welcoming staff attend to your every need. The AA two Rosette awarded restaurant is situated immediately on the seafront and has the feel of an ocean liner. Fresh fish and grills is the speciality. The interior has been cleverly arranged so that the majority of guests can enjoy a stunning panoramic sea view. Decorated in a fresh modern style the spacious bedrooms are well-equipped and many offer either a sea, marsh or river view. Aldeburgh has something for everybody - scenic walks past pastel-coloured houses and fishermen's huts, superb boutique shopping, highly acclaimed restaurants and the annual Aldeburgh Festival. Thorpeness is an unusual and interesting village to explore and also has a splendid golf course. For those interested in history, there are many historic buildings, castles and an abbey in the area. The marshes are a haven for wading birds and birdwatchers or for the more adventurous there is horse riding, archery and rally karting. Access to the hotel is very easy for the less mobile and there is a lift.

Our inspector loved: *Watching the sun glistening on the waves from so many windows.*

Directions: Take the M25, junction 28 onto the A12, then take the A1094 to Aldeburgh. The hotel is on the seafront at the south end of town.

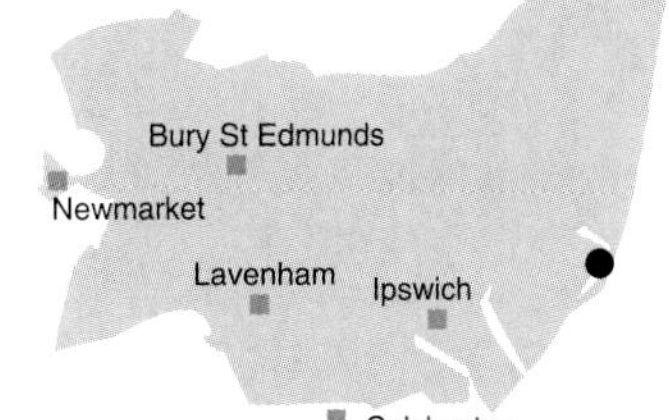

Web: www.johansens.com/brudenell
E-mail: info@brudenellhotel.co.uk
Tel: 0870 381 9182
International: +44 (0)1728 452071
Fax: 01728 454082

Price Guide:
single £68-£105
double £106-£194
deluxe £156–£218

Ravenwood Hall Country Hotel & Restaurant

ROUGHAM, BURY ST EDMUNDS, SUFFOLK IP30 9JA

Nestling within 7 acres of lovely lawns and woodlands deep in the heart of Suffolk lies Ravenwood Hall. Now an excellent country house hotel, this fine Tudor building dates back to 1530 and retains many of its original features. The restaurant, still boasting the carved timbers and huge inglenook from Tudor times, creates a delightfully intimate atmosphere in which to enjoy imaginative cuisine. The menu is a combination of adventurous and classical dishes, featuring some long forgotten English recipes. The Hall's extensive cellars are stocked with some of the finest vintages, along with a selection of rare ports and brandies. A cosy bar offers a less formal setting in which to enjoy some unusual meals. Comfortable bedrooms are furnished with antiques, reflecting the historic tradition of the Hall, although each is equipped with every modern facility. A wide range of leisure facilities is available for guests, including a croquet lawn and heated swimming pool. There are golf courses and woodland walks to enjoy locally; hunting and shooting can be arranged. Places of interest nearby include the famous medieval wool towns of Lavenham and Long Melford; the historic cities of Norwich and Cambridge are within easy reach, as is Newmarket, the home of horse racing.

Our inspector loved: *The huge inglenook fireplaces and the informal reminders of a private country estate.*

Directions: 2 miles east of Bury St Edmunds off the A14 at Rougham, junction 45.

Web: www.johansens.com/ravenwoodhall
E-mail: enquiries@ravenwoodhall.co.uk
Tel: 0870 381 8849
International: +44 (0)1359 270345
Fax: 01359 270788

Price Guide:
single £87.50–£118.50
double/twin £113.50–£170

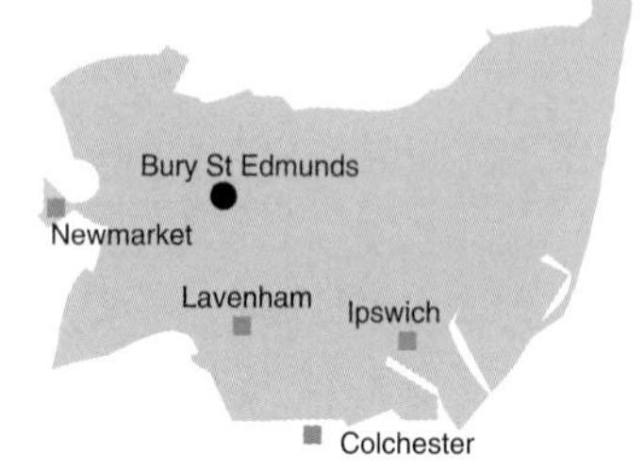

Hintlesham Hall

HINTLESHAM, IPSWICH, SUFFOLK IP8 3NS

The epitome of grandeur, Hintlesham Hall is a house of evolving styles: its splendid Georgian façade belies its 16th-century origins, to which the red-brick Tudor rear of the hall is a testament. The Stuart period also left its mark, in the form of a magnificent carved oak staircase leading to the north wing of the hall. The combination of styles works extremely well, with the lofty proportions of the Georgian reception rooms contrasting with the timbered Tudor rooms. The décor throughout is superb – all rooms are individually appointed in a discriminating fashion. Iced mineral water, toiletries and towelling robes are to be found in each of the comfortable bedrooms. The herb garden supplies many of the flavours for the well-balanced menu which will appeal to the gourmet and the health-conscious alike, complemented by a 300-bin wine list. Bounded by 175 acres of rolling countryside, leisure facilities include an associated 18-hole championship golf course. The Health Club offers a state-of-the-art gymnasium, sauna, steam room, spa bath, tennis and croquet. A full range of E'spa products and services are available in the beauty suite by arrangement. Guests can also explore Suffolk's 16th-century wool merchants' villages, its pretty coast, Constable country and Newmarket

Our inspector loved: *The on going refurbishment programme.*

Directions: Hintlesham Hall is 4 miles west of Ipswich on the A1071 Sudbury road.

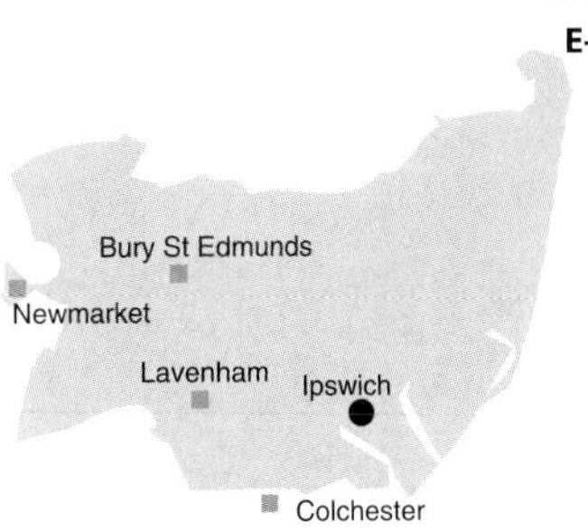

Bury St Edmunds
Newmarket
Lavenham
Ipswich
Colchester

Web: www.johansens.com/hintleshamhall
E-mail: reservations@hintleshamhall.com
Tel: 0870 381 8595
International: +44 (0)1473 652334
Fax: 01473 652463

Price Guide:
single £110–£195
double/twin £140–£280
suite £350–£495

THE SWAN HOTEL

HIGH STREET, LAVENHAM, SUDBURY, SUFFOLK CO10 9QA

Welcoming travellers since 1400 this medieval hotel stands within the heart of the Tudor village of Lavenham. Modern luxury sits comfortably alongside the 15th-century oak beams, panelled walls, flagged floors, log fires and inglenook fires, and the discovery of Medieval wall paintings have influenced the style of the interior, which features mementoes of England's early history hanging on the walls, such as the oldest surviving map of England, circa 1250. Each of the 49 en suite bedrooms has been decorated in calming colour schemes, with natural fabrics evoking the town's wool trade history. Lounge areas invite guests to relax in a soothing atmosphere surrounded by peace and traquillity and the Old Bar, with its brick floor, provides a welcoming retreat. The elegant AA two rosette Gallery Restaurant prides itself on serving imaginative cuisine, created from fresh Suffolk and Norfolk produce accompanied by a comprehensive wine list. During the summer months guests may wish to dine al fresco in the courtyard. 3 large rooms can accommodate executive conferences and are equipped with state-of-the-art facilities and an experienced conference team are on-hand to help. Weddings can also be catered for. The Swan Hotel is a perfect base from which to enjoy an abundance of history, culture and unspoilt countryside.

Our inspector loved: *The newly refurbished dining room.*

Directions: From the A14 at Bury St Edmunds, take the A134 towards Sudbury. Turn onto the A1141 for Lavenham.

Web: www.johansens.com/theswanlavenham
E-mail: info@theswanatlavenham.co.uk
Tel: 0870 381 9280
International: +44 (0)1787 247477
Fax: 01787 248286

Price Guide:
single £52.50–£82.50
double/twin £105–£205
four poster £160–£220
suite £175–£235

The Swan Hotel

MARKET PLACE, SOUTHWOLD, SUFFOLK IP18 6EG

Rebuilt in 1659, following the disastrous fire that destroyed most of the town, The Swan Hotel was remodelled in the 1820s, with further additions made in 1938. The hotel provides every modern amenity and the current extensive refurbishment programme has ensured that a contemporary, stylish sophistication exudes throughout. The refined yet relaxed environment and friendly staff guarantees a most comfortable stay. Many of the bedrooms in the main hotel offer a glimpse of the sea, whilst the stylish garden rooms are clustered around the old bowling green. The elegant Drawing Room is perfect for quiet relaxation; the Reading Room and Southwold Room are also ideal for private functions. The daily menu, created from local produce and organic ingredients, offers dishes ranging from simple, delicious fare through the English classics to the chef's personal specialities as well as a full à la carte menu. An exciting selection of Adnams' wines from all over the world is offered. Southwold is bounded on 3 sides by creeks, marshes and the River Blyth; a paradise for birdwatchers and nature lovers. Little has changed in the town for a century, built around a series of greens there is a fine church, lighthouse and golf course close by. Music lovers flock to nearby Snape Maltings for the Aldeburgh Festival. Dr Hauschka beauty therapy treatments are now available at the hotel.

Our inspector loved: *The refurbished bedrooms especially The Admirals.*

Directions: Southwold is off the A12 Ipswich–Lowestoft Road. The Swan Hotel is in the town centre.

Web: www.johansens.com/swansouthwold
E-mail: swan.hotel@adnams.co.uk
Tel: 0870 381 8929
International: +44 (0)1502 722186
Fax: 01502 724800

Price Guide:
single from £80
double/twin from £140
suite from £200

THE WESTLETON CROWN

THE STREET, WESTLETON, NEAR SOUTHWOLD, SUFFOLK IP17 3AD

With origins that date back to the 12th century, this historic coaching inn provides warm hospitality and a rustic charm that attracts visitors for both business and pleasure. Just a few miles from the Suffolk Heritage Coast, the welcoming ambience is enhanced by the flexible and efficient team that prides itself on making sure each guest is comfortable. Bedrooms are furnished in a fresh country style and have modern en-suite bathrooms; Egyptian cotton bed linen and goose-down duvets are standard luxuries. A variety of guest rooms are available: some are located in the converted stables and cottages, have four-poster beds, luxury doubles or cosy singles. Each room is named after a species of bird, which is depicted in original artwork. Whether a hearty breakfast, lunchtime snack, relaxed or formal meal, the 2 AA Rosette-awarded restaurant serves varied, innovative food created from passion alongside a comprehensive wine list comprising an impressive selection of red, white, rosé, sparkling and dessert wine from all over the world as well as champagne. Dinner may be taken in the parlour, dining room or conservatory. During warmer months, meals may be enjoyed al fresco. A range of local ales is available in the bar. Close to unspoiled heathlands, nature reserves, beaches, wild salt marshes and the quintessential English seaside towns of Aldeburgh and Southwold.

Directions: 2 miles from the A12. Just after the village of Yoxford.

Web: www.johansens.com/westletoncrown
E-mail: info@westletoncrown.co.uk
Tel: 0870 381 8479
International: +44 (0)1728 648777
Fax: 01728 648239

Price Guide:
single from £80
double/twin £95–£160

Our inspector loved: *The welcoming open fires on a chilly day.*

Seckford Hall

WOODBRIDGE, SUFFOLK IP13 6NU

Seckford Hall dates from 1530 and it is said that Elizabeth I once held court here. Furnished as a private house with many fine period pieces, the panelled rooms, beamed ceilings, carved doors and great stone fireplaces are set against the splendour of English oak. Local delicacies such as the house speciality, lobster, feature on the à la carte menu. The original minstrels gallery can be viewed in the banqueting hall, which is now a conference and function suite designed in-keeping with the general style. The Courtyard area was converted from a giant Tudor tithe barn, dairy and coach house; it now incorporates 10 charming cottage-style suites and a leisure complex, which includes a heated swimming pool, exercise machines, spa bath and beauty salon. Alternatively, guests may use the Business Lounge where Internet access and office equipment is available. Set in 34 acres of tranquil parkland with sweeping lawns and a willow-fringed lake, guests may stroll about the grounds or simply relax in the attractive terrace garden. Equipment can be hired for the 18-hole golf course or a gentle walk along the riverside to picturesque Woodbridge, with its tide mill, antique shops and yacht harbours can be enjoyed. Visit the Sutton Hoo burial ship site and museum, Constable country and the Suffolk coast nearby.

Our inspector loved: *Being inspired at the first sight of this beautiful Tudor building with its chimney's and flanking topiary.*

Directions: Remain on the A12 Woodbridge bypass until the blue and white hotel sign.

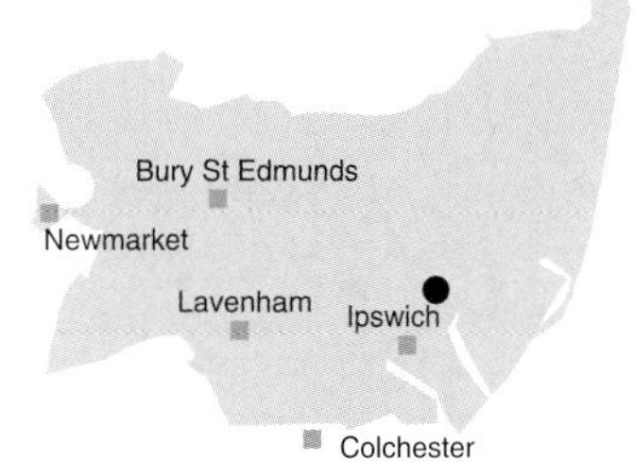

Web: www.johansens.com/seckfordhall
E-mail: reception@seckford.co.uk
Tel: 0870 381 8890
International: +44 (0)1394 385678
Fax: 01394 380610

Price Guide:
single £85–£130
double/twin £135–£210
suite £175–£210

PENNYHILL PARK HOTEL & THE SPA

LONDON ROAD, BAGSHOT, SURREY GU19 5EU

Directions: From the M3 take exit 3 then the A322 towards Bracknell. Turn left onto the A30 signposted to Camberley. 3/4 mile after Bagshot turn right 50 yards past the Texaco garage.

Web: www.johansens.com/pennyhillpark
E-mail: enquiries@pennyhillpark.co.uk
Tel: 0870 381 8815
International: +44 (0)1276 471774
Fax: 01276 473217

Price Guide:
single from £250
double/twin from £250
suite from £320

Set in 125 acres of rolling park yet surprisingly close to London, this is one of Surrey's finest hotels. A long sweeping drive leads to the beautiful ivy-clad mansion which houses the breathtaking spa and Andrew Turner's exciting restaurants. Within easy access of some of the area's historic houses and gardens, there is polo, wine tasting, Wentworth and Twickenham to delight the weekend traveller, and an excellent balance of luxury accommodation and relaxing leisure time. Appointed this year, award-winning Executive Head Chef Andrew Turner has created a real buzz in the kitchen and is poised to place Pennyhill Park Hotel on the culinary map. Quoted as saying, "now is the time to take bold steps and offer a new and astounding dining experience," Andrew and his team now offer a sensational selection of light lunches and leisurely gourmet dinners. The spa will convert the hardened of guests into a spa aficionado. The only destination in the UK to offer a complete thermal sequencing experience, there is a tepidarium, laconium, Turkish hamman, "experience shower," ice cave, plunge pool, herbal saunas and aromatic steam rooms as well as ozone-treated indoor, outdoor and hydrotherapy pools. There are also spacious and beautiful therapy rooms offering a world-class range of natural treatments complemented by the delightful and organic Café Themis.

***Our inspector loved:** The spa, one of the most stylish and luxurious around.*

Great Fosters

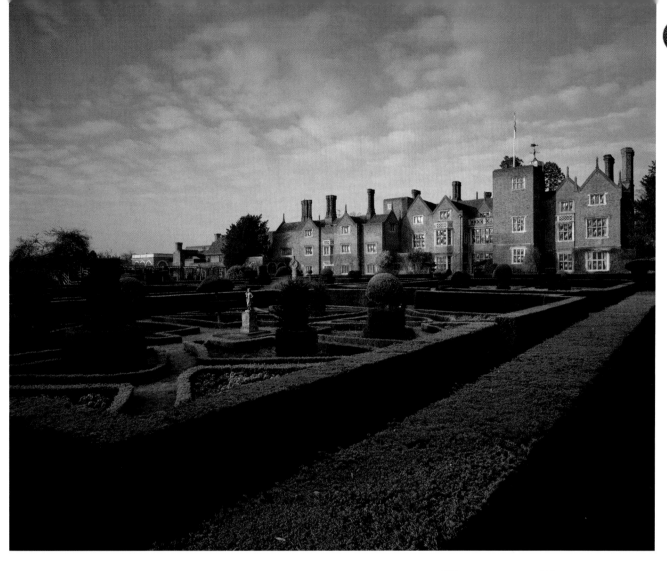

STROUDE ROAD, EGHAM, SURREY TW20 9UR

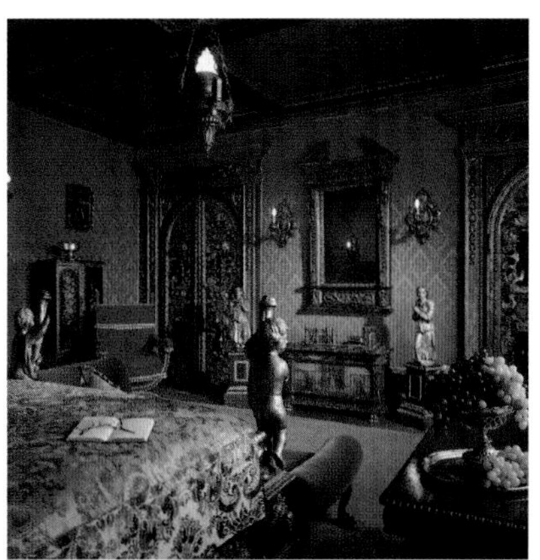

Probably built as a Royal hunting lodge in Windsor Forest, very much a stately home since the 16th century, today Great Fosters is a prestigious hotel within half an hour of both Heathrow Airport and central London. Its past is evident in the mullioned windows, tall chimneys and brick finials, whilst the Saxon moat – crossed by a Japanese bridge – surrounds 3 sides of the formal gardens, complete with topiary, statuary and a charming rose garden. Inside are fine oak beams and panelling, Jacobean chimney pieces, superb tapestries and a rare oakwell staircase leading to the Tower. Some of the guest rooms are particularly magnificent – one Italian styled with gilt furnishings and damask walls, others with moulded ceilings, beautiful antiques and Persian rugs. Guests relax in the bar before enjoying good English and French cooking and carefully selected wines in The Oak Room. Celebrations, meetings and weddings take place in the elegant Orangery and impressive Tithe Barn. Great Fosters is close to polo in Windsor Great Park, racing at Ascot, golf at Wentworth, boating in Henley and pageantry at Windsor Castle, Runnymede and Hampton Court.

Our inspector loved: *The welcoming smell of woodsmoke from the open fires and antique furniture polish on a crips winter's morning was truly magical!*

Directions: M25/J13, head for Egham and watch for brown Historic Buildings signs.

Heathrow
Egham
Kingston upon Thames
Epsom
Guildford
Gatwick

Web: www.johansens.com/greatfosters
E-mail: enquiries@greatfosters.co.uk
Tel: 0870 381 8569
International: +44 (0)1784 433822
Fax: 01784 472455

Price Guide:
single from £120
double/twin from £155
suite from £245

Grayshott Spa

HEADLEY ROAD, GRAYSHOTT, NEAR HINDHEAD, SURREY GU26 6JJ

Directions: Take the M25, junction 10 then the A3 south to Hindhead. Turn right onto the B3002 after the crossroads and traffic lights. 1½ miles after Grayshott village the Spa is on the left.

Web: www.johansens.com/grayshottspa
E-mail: reservations@grayshottspa.com
Tel: 0870 381 8466
International: +44 (0)1428 602020
Fax: 01428 609769

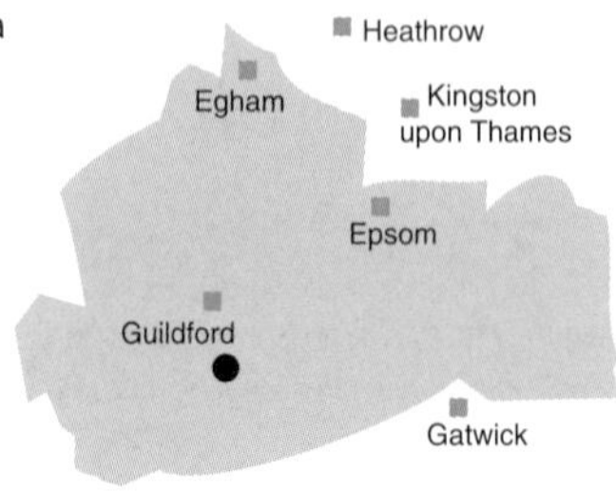

Price Guide: (including meals and use of facilities. minimum 2 night stay)
single from £165
double from £155 per person double occupancy

One hour from London, surrounded by 47 acres of gardens, woodland and lawns alongside 700 acres of National Trust land, stands the majestic Grayshott Spa. A retreat for the stressed, those in need of a health kick or simply those desiring sheer indulgence, Grayshott offers an extensive array of spa packages with friendly, professional staff on-hand to advise personal programmes and exercises to suit the needs of each guest. The spa comprises 36 treatment rooms and boasts a highly acclaimed reputation for its natural therapies. Health consultants, dieticians and a professional fitness team are able to create bespoke sessions and one to one tuition classes in Yoga, Pilates and Tai Chi. Alternatively the golf and tennis academies offer personal training. Before taking dinner in the Dining Room or Conservatory Restaurant, guests may enjoy a drink in Bubbles where a variety of organic wines, champagnes, juices and hot drinks are served. The healthy eating menu at the restaurant upholds the healthy living ethos that is apparent throughout Grayshott Spa. All rooms and new Junior Suites, pictured above, have been tastefully refurbished with style and comfort in mind.

Our inspector loved: *The warm and relaxed atmosphere and the quite splendid facilities available to guests.*

Lythe Hill Hotel & Spa

PETWORTH ROAD, HASLEMERE, SURREY GU27 3BQ

Cradled by the Surrey foothills in a tranquil setting is the enchanting Lythe Hill Hotel & Spa. It is an unusual cluster of ancient buildings – parts of which date from the 14th century. While most of the beautifully appointed accommodation is in the more recently converted part of the hotel, there are 5 charming bedrooms in the Tudor House, including the Henry VIII room with a four-poster bed dated 1614. There are 2 delightful restaurants: the Auberge de France offers classic French cuisine in the oak-panelled room which overlooks the lake and parklands, and the 'Dining Room' has the choice of imaginative English fare. An exceptional wine list offers over 200 wines from more than a dozen countries. The hotel boasts a splendid leisure facility called Amarna (which was voted hotel spa of the year) within the grounds of the hotel. It has a 16 x 8 metre swimming pool, steam room and sauna, gym, hairdressing, treatment rooms and a nail bar. National Trust hillside adjoining the hotel grounds provides interesting walks and views over the surrounding countryside. The area is steeped in history, with the country houses of Petworth, Clandon and Uppark to visit as well as racing at Goodwood and polo at Cowdray Park. Brighton and the south coast are only a short drive away.

Our inspector loved: *The clever use of real English oak in the reception area.*

Directions: Lythe Hill lies about 1½ miles from the centre of Haslemere, east on the B2131.

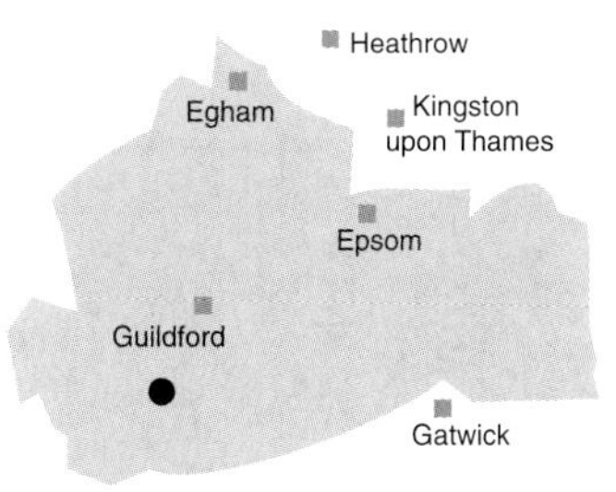

Web: www.johansens.com/lythehill
E-mail: lythe@lythehill.co.uk
Tel: 0870 381 8709
International: +44 (0)1428 651251
Fax: 01428 644131

Price Guide: (room only)
double £160–£295
suite £260–£350

Foxhills

STONEHILL ROAD, OTTERSHAW, SURREY KT16 0EL

Within a staggering 400 acres, one could be excused for imagining themselves deep in the English countryside. At the end of a sweeping rhododendron-clad drive this elegant stone manor house, with 3 golf courses, 11 tennis courts and an array of sporting facilities, offers something for every opportunity. Easily accessible, the manor is minutes from Heathrow and a short train journey from central London. There are 70 bedrooms with a choice of courtyard-style garden rooms and a newly opened wing housing 28 beautifully appointed bedrooms and suites that can be hired exclusively for family parties, weddings or business functions. The meeting rooms have a club-like atmosphere, whilst many other parts of the manor are dedicated family-friendly zones. A stunning spa is due to open at the end of 2007, which will increase the number of swimming pools to 4; the area will be for adults only who will be able to unwind and enjoy being pampered. The new club house overlooks the 18th hole and its outdoor terrace is a popular spot for watching the golfers during a light lunch and drink. In winter months, while away the hours with the live entertainment and savour the informal menu. 2 additional restaurants offer award-winning cuisine. The conservatory-style dining room is perfect for weddings, with its tall, mullioned windows and views.

Our inspector loved: *The new wing: contemporary yet welcoming.*

Directions: From M25 Jct 11, follow signs to Woking. After a dual carriageway, turn left into Guildford Road. 3rd exit at roundabout and immediately right into Foxhills Road. Turn left at the end of the road, Foxhills is on the right.

Web: www.johansens.com/foxhills
E-mail: reservations@foxhills.co.uk
Tel: 0870 381 8530
International: +44 (0)1932 872050
Fax: 01932 874762

Price Guide: (room only)
double/twin from £180
suite from £220

Deans Place Hotel

SEAFORD ROAD, ALFRISTON, EAST SUSSEX BN26 5TW

Deans Place Hotel is situated amongst 4 acres of beautifully landscaped gardens with the rolling South Downs as its backdrop. Upon entering its wrought-iron gates guests will find a world of re-invigorating peace and quiet with experienced and attentive staff on-hand creating an atmosphere of homely sophistication. Comfortable bedrooms have all modern facilities and have views over the meadow and hills beyond; many overlook the heated outdoor pool. Others look out to the garden, croquet lawn and stream. Fine International cuisine, using fresh local produce where possible, is offered by the hotel's excellent chef, whose gourmet artistry provides an unforgettable dining experience within a spacious, light atmosphere. The adjacent Friston Bar is relaxed and comfortable and is an ideal spot for meeting friends over a quiet drink in front of an open log fire. A real treat is the large terrace, where al fresco dining on balmy summer evenings is sublime. There are also outdoor heaters for the cooler spring and autumn nights. Situated on the edge of Alfriston, one of England's prettiest villages, the hotel is easily accessed from the M25, and the bustling seaside towns of Brighton and Eastbourne are nearby. Enjoy the beautiful gardens, a game of croquet or mini putting on the green.

Our inspector loved: *The wonderful downland setting for this delightful traditional country hotel.*

Directions: Just off the A27 through the south side of the village of Alfriston on the left

Web: www.johansens.com/deansplacehotel
E-mail: mail@deansplacehotel.co.uk
Tel: 0870 381 8576
International: +44 (0)1323 870248
Fax: 01323 870918

Price Guide:
single £71–£121
double £88–£197
family £118–£197

The PowderMills

POWDERMILL LANE, BATTLE, EAST SUSSEX TN33 0SP

The PowderMills is an 18th-century listed country house skilfully converted into an elegant hotel. Originally the site of a famous gunpowder works, reputed to make the finest gunpowder in Europe during the Napoleonic wars, the beautiful and tranquil grounds are set amidst 150 acres of parks, lakes and woodlands, and feature a 7-acre specimen fishing lake. Wild geese, swans, ducks, kingfishers and herons abound. Situated close to the historic town of Battle, the hotel adjoins the famous battlefield of 1066, and guests can enjoy a leisurely walk through woodlands and fields to the Abbey. The hotel has been carefully furnished with locally acquired antiques and paintings, and on cooler days log fires burn in the entrance hall and drawing room. There is a range of 40 individually decorated en-suite bedrooms and junior suites in keeping with the style of the house, many with four-poster beds. Fine classical cooking by chef James Penn is served in the 2 AA Rosette-awarded Orangery Restaurant, whilst light meals and snacks are available in the library and conservatory. The location is an ideal base from which to explore the beautiful Sussex and Kent countryside.

Our inspector loved: *The wonderfully relaxed atmosphere and the stunning setting between the lakes.*

Directions: From centre of Battle take the Hastings road south. After ¼ mile turn right into Powdermill Lane. After a sharp bend, the entrance is on the right; cross over the bridge and lakes to reach the hotel.

Web: www.johansens.com/powdermills
E-mail: powdc@aol.com
Tel: 0870 381 8835
International: +44 (0)1424 775511
Fax: 01424 774540

Price Guide:
single from £95
double/twin from £120

Lansdowne Place, Boutique Hotel & Spa

LANSDOWNE PLACE, BRIGHTON, EAST SUSSEX BN3 1HQ

Billing itself as a "touch of a class in Brighton's cosmopolitan hub", Lansdowne Place Hotel certainly lives up to its moniker. Upon entering the spacious lobby of this seafront property, guests can enjoy the stylish blend of contemporary yet classic touches that is omnipresent. The 84 rooms - a testament to the grandeur of Regency Brighton - are appointed with rich fabrics, elegant wallpaper, period lamps and potted orchids; many offer sea views. After a day exploring the charms of England's south coast, guests can relax in the spa and try out the gym, sauna, crystal steam room and relaxation suite before indulging in one of the Espa treatments on offer. These include salt and oil scrubs, aromatherapy facials, Zen spa pedicures and detoxifying algae wraps. Further indulgence comes in the form of the cuisine at the hotel. The Grill features a predominantly French menu made with locally sourced produce and organic and free-range ingredients where possible. An extensive wine list complements the dishes and after the meal, guests can enjoy champagne, cocktails and nightcaps in the attractive lounge bar, either reclining in a Chesterfield or perching on a leopard print bar stool.

Our inspector loved: *The bedrooms: a stylish blend of present day comforts and vibrant colours with excellent bathrooms.*

Directions: Take the M23/A23 into central Brighton and seafront. Turn right (west) at the pier and Landsdowne Place Hotel is on the right immediately after Brunswick Square.

Web: www.johansens.com/lansdowneplace
E-mail: reservations@lansdowneplace.co.uk
Tel: 0870 381 8606
International: +44 (0)1273 736266
Fax: 01273 712304

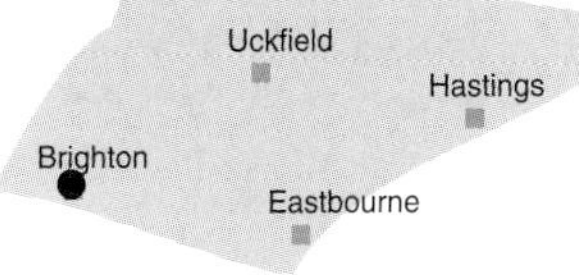

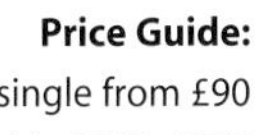

Price Guide:
single from £90
double £140–£350

84 200 SPA

THE GRAND HOTEL

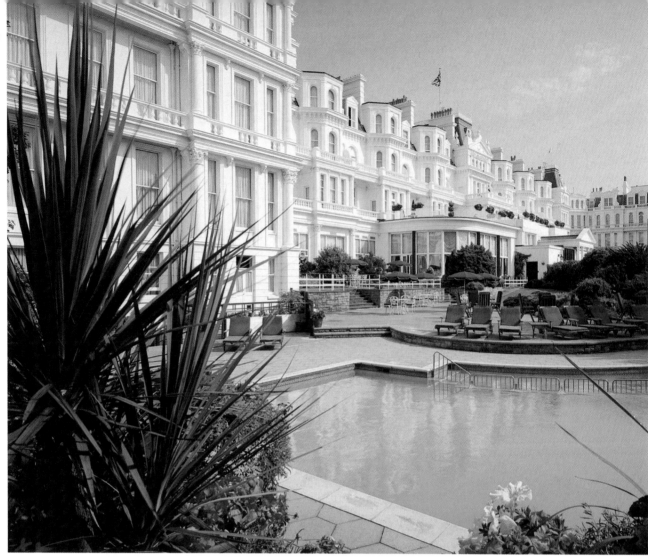

KING EDWARD'S PARADE, EASTBOURNE, EAST SUSSEX BN21 4EQ

Directions: From London take A22 to the south coast and follow signs to Eastbourne, or take the M25 to join the M23 towards Brighton. Take A27 to Lewes then to Eastbourne. The Hotel is at the western end of the seafront.

Web: www.johansens.com/grandeastbourne
E-mail: reservations@grandeastbourne.com
Tel: 0870 381 8560
International: +44 (0)1323 412345
Fax: 01323 412233

Price Guide:
single £140–£430
double/twin £170–£460
suite £300–£460

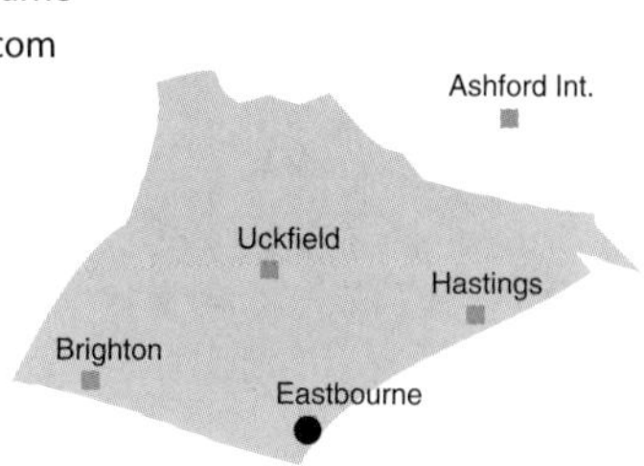

The Grand Hotel is a fine property, steeped in history, which evokes the charm and splendour of the Victorian era. The majestic façade complements the elegant interior whilst the reception rooms are beautifully appointed with rich fabrics and ornaments. Many of the 152 bedrooms are of vast proportions: all being refurbished to include every comfort with attractive bathrooms. The hotel has numerous areas in which to relax and a good choice of restaurants and bars. The Mirabelle in particular achieves exceptional standards of fine dining. The array of new leisure facilities includes both indoor and outdoor pools, gymnasium, sauna, solarium, spa bath, steam room, snooker tables and a hair salon and 8 beauty rooms. Guests may choose to try the nearby racquet and golf clubs. For the meeting organiser, the hotel offers an impressive range of rooms which can cater for a number of business purposes from a board meeting for 12 to a larger conference for up to 300 delegates. Those seeking a peaceful retreat will be pleased with the tranquil atmosphere of Eastbourne. Pastimes include walks along the Downs, sea fishing and trips to the 2 nearby theatres.

Our inspector loved: *This rare truly grand coastal hotel which maintains outstanding levels of service and comfort.*

Ashdown Park Hotel and Country Club

WYCH CROSS, FOREST ROW, EAST SUSSEX RH18 5JR

Ashdown Park is a grand, rambling 19th-century mansion overlooking almost 200 acres of landscaped gardens to the forest beyond. Built in 1867, the hotel is situated within easy reach of Gatwick Airport, London and the South Coast and provides the perfect backdrop for every occasion, from a weekend getaway to a honeymoon or business convention. The hotel is subtly furnished throughout to satisfy the needs of escapees from urban stress. The 106 en-suite bedrooms are beautifully decorated – several with elegant four-poster beds, all with up-to-date amenities. The Anderida restaurant offers a thoughtfully compiled menu and wine list, complemented by discreetly attentive service in soigné surroundings. Guests seeking relaxation can retire to the indoor pool, steam room and sauna, pamper themselves with a massage, before using the solarium, or visiting the beauty salon. Alternatively, guests may prefer to amble through the gardens and nearby woodland paths; the more energetic can indulge in tennis, croquet or use the Fitness Studio and Beauty Therapy. There is also an indoor driving range, a lounge/bar and an 18-hole par 3 golf course with an outdoor driving range.

Our inspector loved: *The impressive and consistent standards maintained by this hotel.*

Directions: East of A22 at Wych Cross traffic lights on road signposted to Hartfield.

Web: www.johansens.com/ashdownpark
E-mail: reservations@ashdownpark.com
Tel: 0870 381 8325
International: +44 (0)1342 824988
Fax: 01342 826206

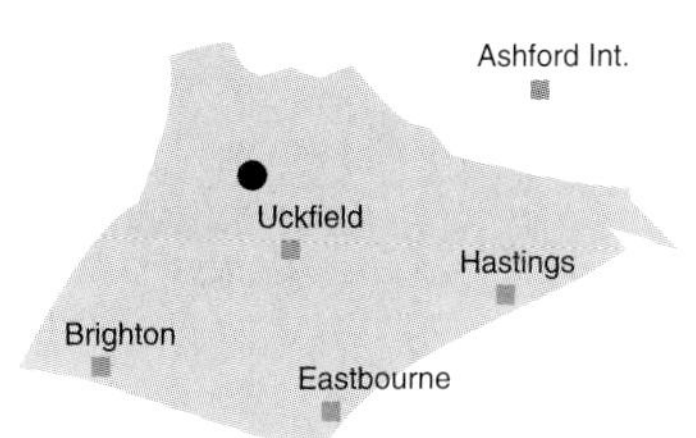

Price Guide:
single £140–£345
double/twin £170–£300
suite £310–£375

Horsted Place Country House Hotel

LITTLE HORSTED, EAST SUSSEX TN22 5TS

Horsted Place enjoys a splendid location amid the peace of the Sussex Downs. This magnificent Victorian Gothic Mansion, which was built in 1851, boasts an interior predominantly styled by the celebrated Victorian architect, Augustus Pugin. In former years the Queen and Prince Philip were frequent visitors. Guests today are invited to enjoy the excellent service offered by a committed staff. The bedrooms provide luxurious décor and every modern comfort. Dining at Horsted is guaranteed to be a memorable experience. Chef Allan Garth offers a daily fixed price menu as well as the seasonal à la carte menu. The Terrace Room is an elegant and airy private function room, licensed for weddings for up to 100 guests. The smaller Morning Room and Library are ideal for boardroom-style meetings and intimate dinner parties, and the self-contained management centre offers privacy and exclusivity for business meetings in a contemporary setting. Places of interest nearby include Royal Tunbridge Wells, Lewes and Glyndebourne. Horsted Place sits at the heart of the West Course of the East Sussex National Golf Club where resident guests enjoy discounted green fees and complimentary use of Horsted Health Club, just a 5 minute drive away. There is an all-weather tennis court and croquet lawn in the hotel grounds

Our inspector loved: *The refurbished dining room offering a menu of delights.*

Directions: The hotel entrance is on the A26 just short of the junction with the A22, 2 miles south of Uckfield and signposted towards Lewes.

Web: www.johansens.com/horstedplace
E-mail: hotel@horstedplace.co.uk
Tel: 0870 381 8609
International: +44 (0)1825 750581
Fax: 01825 750459

Price Guide:
double/twin from £130
suite from £220

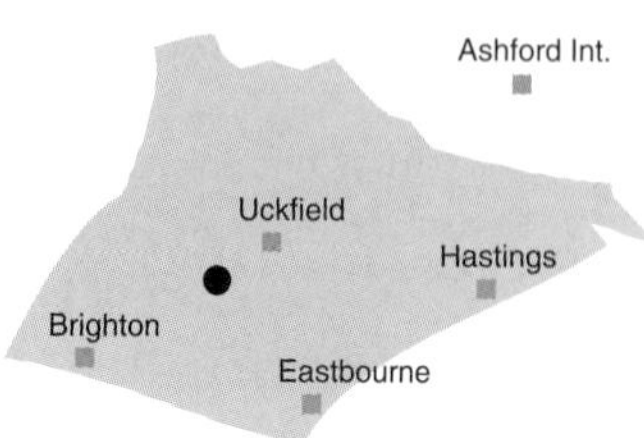

20   80  7      

Newick Park

NEWICK, NEAR LEWES, EAST SUSSEX BN8 4SB

This magnificent Grade II listed Georgian country house, set in over 200 acres of breathtaking parkland and landscaped gardens, overlooks the Longford River and lake and the South Downs. Whilst situated in a convenient location near to the main road and rail routes and only 30 minutes away from Gatwick Airport, Newick Park maintains an atmosphere of complete tranquillity and privacy. The en-suite bedrooms are decorated in a classic style and contain elegant antique furnishings. The exquisite dining room offers a wide choice of culinary delights, carefully devised by the Head Chef, Chris Moore. The convivial bar complements the restaurant with its delicate style and understated elegance. The friendly staff ensure that guests receive a warm welcome and an outstanding level of comfort. The house and grounds are ideal for weddings or conferences and may be hired for exclusive use by larger groups. The Dell gardens, planted primarily in Victorian times, include a rare collection of Royal Ferns. Vibrant and diverse colours saturate the lawns during the changing seasons, courtesy of the various flowers and shrubs encompassing the gardens. The activities on the estate itself include fishing, shooting and tennis, whilst nearby distractions include the East Sussex Golf Club,racing at Goodwood and Glyndebourne Opera House.

Our inspector loved: *All the relaxed comforts offered by this country house.*

Directions: The nearest motorway is the M23, jct 11.

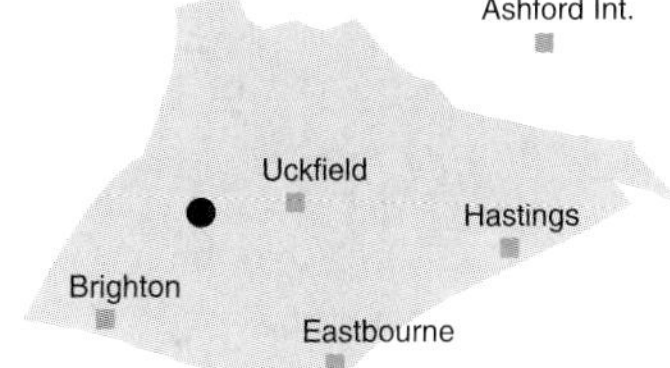

Web: www.johansens.com/newickpark
E-mail: bookings@newickpark.co.uk
Tel: 0870 381 8762
International: +44 (0)1825 723633
Fax: 01825 723969

Price Guide:
single from £125
double/twin from £165

Rye Lodge

HILDER'S CLIFF, RYE, EAST SUSSEX TN31 7LD

Directions: Take the A259 or A268 to Rye. Follow Town Centre signs and go through Landgate Arch (historic stone archway built 1326). The hotel is 100 yards on the right. (The nearest motorway is the M20, junction 10.)

Web: www.johansens.com/ryelodge
E-mail: info@ryelodge.co.uk
Tel: 0870 381 8367
International: +44 (0)1797 223838
Fax: 01797 223585

Price Guide:
single from £85
double £140–£200

Rye Lodge is a traditional hotel in the beautiful town of Rye with stunning views across the Estuary and Romney Marshes. Ideally located close to the High Street, it is surrounded by quaint shops, tea rooms, pubs and restaurants. Almost the entire town has been marked a conservation area of historical interest; its entrance gate was built in 1326. The interior décor of the hotel pays homage to its Edwardian exterior that complements its cosy atmosphere. Several of the spacious deluxe bedrooms benefit from decked roof terraces. Dining in the Terrace Restaurant is a delightful experience: its high ceiling, large windows and elegant Regency-style furniture create a romantic ambience in which to savour delicious dinners by candlelight whilst enjoying the lovely views of the terrace gardens and Estuary. The hotel's Venetian Leisure Centre is a great place to unwind with its sauna and heated indoor swimming pool. Rye is also well known for its hauntings: a ghostly monk is said to parade the hotel's car park and although the owners of 12 years have never seen this cowled spectre, the lands surrounding Rye Lodge were once chapel gardens and monastic cloisters. Bird lovers will relish the coast and marshes nearby.

Our inspector loved: *The presentation of this comfortable hotel; service is the keynote.*

Dale Hill

TICEHURST, NEAR TUNBRIDGE WELLS, EAST SUSSEX TN5 7DQ

Situated in over 350 acres of fine grounds, high on the Kentish Weald, the newly refurbished Dale Hill combines the best in golfing facilities with the style and refinement desired by discerning guests. The décor is enhanced by soft coloured fabrics and carpets, creating a summery impression throughout the year. Golfers have the choice of 2 18-hole courses, a gently undulating 6,093 yards par 70 and a new, challenging championship standard course designed by former US Masters champion Ian Woosnam. Just a 20-minute drive away, under the same ownership as the hotel, is the Nick Faldo designed Chart Hills course hailed as "the best new course in England". Packages allow guests to play both championship courses. Diners enjoy glorious views in a choice of restaurants where traditional award-winning cuisine is complemented by a fine wine list and service. The fully equipped health club features a heated swimming pool and a range of health and fitness facilities. Dale Hill is only a short drive from Tunbridge Wells and its renowned Pantiles shopping walk. Also nearby are medieval Scotney Castle, which dates back to 1380, Sissinghurst, a moated Tudor castle with gardens and Bewl Water, renowned for fly-fishing and water sports.

Our inspector loved: *The attention to every detail – the hotel positively sparkles.*

Directions: From the M25, junction 5, follow the A21 to Flimwell. Then turn right onto the B2087. Dale Hill is on the left.

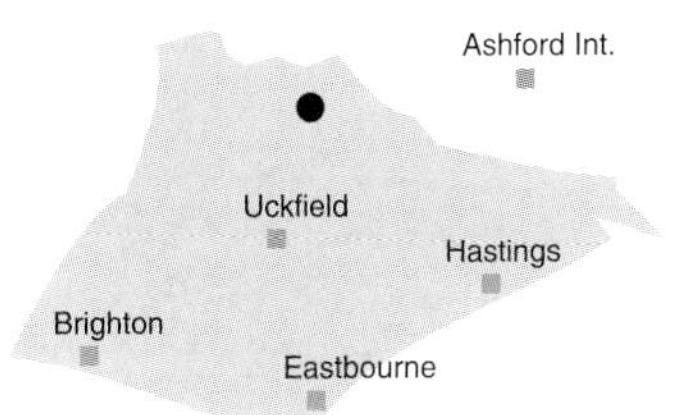

Web: www.johansens.com/dalehill
E-mail: info@dalehill.co.uk
Tel: 0870 381 8471
International: +44 (0)1580 200112
Fax: 01580 201249

Price Guide:
single £110–£130
double/twin £120–£250

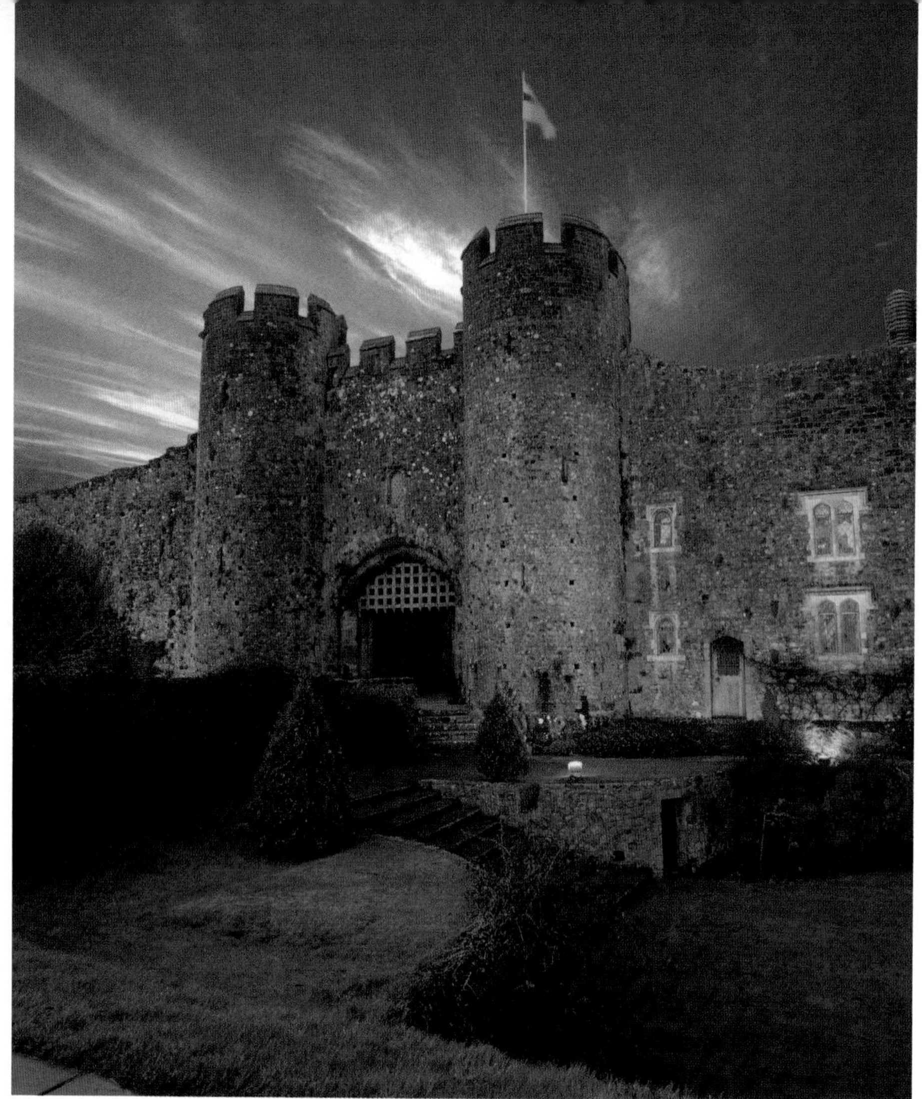

AMBERLEY CASTLE

AMBERLEY, NEAR ARUNDEL, WEST SUSSEX BN18 9LT

Winner of the Condé Nast Johansens Award for Outstanding Excellence and Innovation, Amberley Castle boasts an amazing history spanning over 900 years. Set between the rolling South Downs and the peaceful expanses of the Amberley Wildbrooks, its towering battlements give breathtaking views and massive 14th-century curtain walls and the mighty portcullis bear silent testimony to a fascinating past. Proprietors, Joy and Martin Cummings, have transformed this medieval fortress into a unique country castle hotel. They offer a warm, personal welcome and their hotel provides the ultimate in contemporary luxury, whilst retaining an atmosphere of timelessness. 5 distinctive suites were added recently in the Bishopric by the main gateway. Each room is individually designed and has its own whirlpool bath. The exquisite 12th-century Queen's Room is the perfect setting for the creative cuisine of head chef and his team. Amberley Castle is a natural first choice for romantic or cultural weekends, sporting breaks or confidential executive meetings. Roman ruins, antiques, stately homes, castle gardens, horse-racing and history "everywhere" you look, all within a short distance. It is easily accessible from London and the major air and channel ports.

Our inspector loved: *The battlements, gatehouse, treehouse, moat and peacocks – all combine at this lovely hotel in the countryside.*

Directions: Amberley Castle is on the B2139, off the A29 between Bury and Storrington. Look out for the Union flag, which clearly marks the driveway.

Web: www.johansens.com/amberleycastle
E-mail: info@amberleycastle.co.uk
Tel: 0870 381 8312
International: +44 (0)1798 831992
Fax: 01798 831998

Price Guide: (room only)
double/twin £155–£375
suite £235–£375

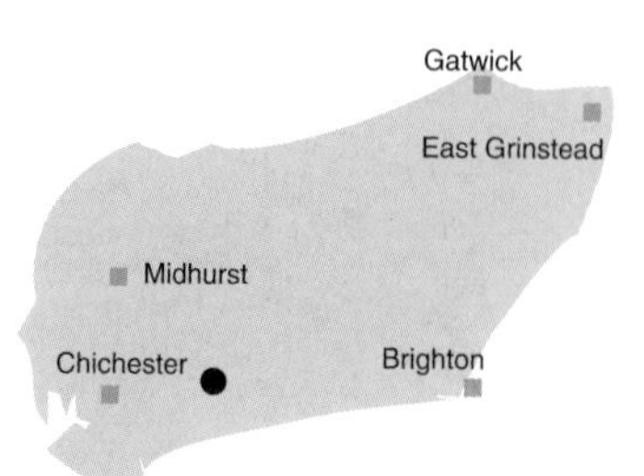

Bailiffscourt Hotel & Health Spa

CLIMPING, WEST SUSSEX BN17 5RW

Bailiffscourt is a perfectly preserved "medieval" house, built in the 1930s using authentic material salvaged from historic old buildings. Gnarled 15th-century beams and gothic mullioned windows combine to recreate a home from the Middle Ages. Set in 30 acres of beautiful pastures and walled gardens, this is a wonderful sanctuary in which to relax or work. Bedrooms are individually decorated and luxuriously furnished, many offer four-poster beds, open log fires and beautiful views over the surrounding countryside. The restaurant serves a varied menu and summer lunches can be taken al fresco in a rose-clad courtyard or in the walled garden; a list of well-priced wines accompanies meals. Private dining rooms are available for weddings, conferences and meetings, and companies can hire the hotel as their "country house" for 2 or 3 days. Bailiffscourt is surrounded by tranquil pastureland and an award-winning health spa featuring an outdoor Californian hot tub, indoor spa pool, sauna, steam room, gym, hammocks and 6 beauty therapy rooms offering 50 Mediterranean treatments. 2 tennis courts and a croquet lawn completes the on-site leisure facilities, whilst a private pathway leads 100yds down to Climping beach, ideal for windsurfing and morning walks. Arundel Castle and Chichester and Goodwood are nearby for classic car driving.

Directions: 3 miles south of Arundel, off the A259.

Gatwick
East Grinstead
Midhurst
Chichester
Brighton

Web: www.johansens.com/bailiffscourt
E-mail: bailiffscourt@hshotels.co.uk
Tel: 0870 381 8333
International: +44 (0)1903 723511
Fax: 01903 723107

Price Guide:
single from £175
double £195–£320
suite £320–£480

Our inspector loved: *This unique hotel and its exquisite new spa.*

MILLSTREAM HOTEL

BOSHAM, NR CHICHESTER, WEST SUSSEX PO18 8HL

A village rich in heritage, Bosham is depicted in the Bayeux Tapestry and King Harold is thought to be buried, alongside King Canute's, daughter in the local Saxon church. Moreover, sailors from the world over navigate their way to Bosham, which is a yachtsman's idyll on the banks of Chichester Harbour. The Millstream, just 300 yards from the harbour, consists of a restored 18th-century malthouse and adjoining cottages linked to The Grange, a small English manor house. Individually furnished bedrooms are complemented by chintz fabrics and pastel décor. The bar, drawing room and the restaurant are all most stylishly refurbished. A stream meanders past the front of the beautiful gardens. Cross the bridge to the 2 delightful new suites in "Waterside" the thatched cottage. Whatever the season, care is taken to ensure that the composition and presentation of the dishes reflect high standards. An appetising luncheon menu is offered and includes local seafood specialities such as: dressed Selsey crab, the Millstream's own home-smoked salmon and grilled fresh fillets of sea bass. During the winter, good-value "Hibernation Breaks" are available.

Our inspector loved: *The unfailing attention to guests needs by General Manager Antony Wallace and his outstanding and long serving team.*

Directions: South of the A259 between Chichester and Havant.

Web: www.johansens.com/millstream
E-mail: info@millstream-hotel.co.uk
Tel: 0870 381 8739
International: +44 (0)1243 573234
Fax: 01243 573459

Price Guide:
single £79–£89
double/twin £138–£158
suite £162–£208

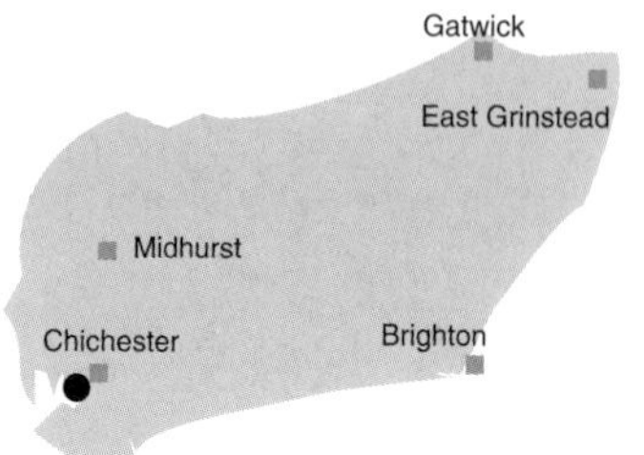

OCKENDEN MANOR

OCKENDEN LANE, CUCKFIELD, WEST SUSSEX RH17 5LD

Set in 9 acres of grounds in the centre of the Tudor village of Cuckfield on the Southern Forest Ridge, this hotel is an ideal base from which to discover Sussex and Kent, the Garden of England. First recorded in 1520, Ockenden Manor has become a hotel of great charm and character. The bedrooms all have their own individual identity: climb your private staircase to Thomas or Elizabeth, look out across the glorious Sussex countryside from Victoria's bay window or choose Charles, with its handsome four-poster bed. The elegant wood-panelled restaurant with its beautiful handpainted ceiling is the perfect setting in which to enjoy the chef's innovative cooking. An outstanding, extensive wine list offers, for example, a splendid choice of first-growth clarets. Spacious and elegantly furnished, the Ockenden Suite welcomes private lunch and dinner parties. A superb conservatory is part of the Ockenden Suite, this opens on to the lawns, where marquees can be set up for summer celebrations. The gardens of Nymans, Wakehurst Place and Leonardslee are nearby, as is the opera at Glyndebourne.

Our inspector loved: *The all-enveloping embrace of this supremely comfortable country house.*

Directions: In the centre of Cuckfield on the A272. Less than 3 miles east of the A23.

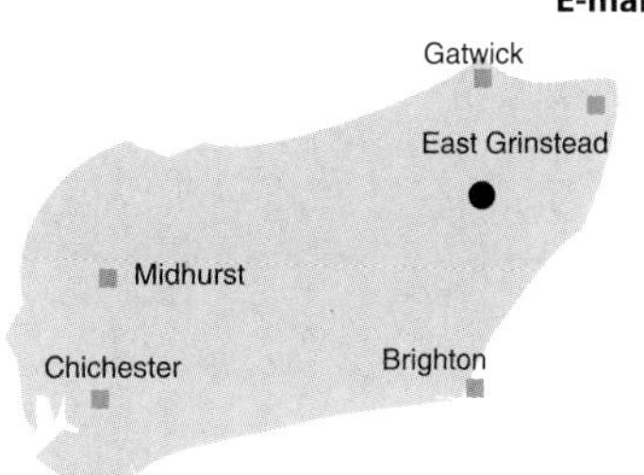

Web: www.johansens.com/ockendenmanor
E-mail: reservations@ockenden-manor.com
Tel: 0870 381 8780
International: +44 (0)1444 416111
Fax: 01444 415549

Price Guide:
single from £105
double/twin from £160
suite from £295

22 50

THE SPREAD EAGLE HOTEL & HEALTH SPA

SOUTH STREET, MIDHURST, WEST SUSSEX GU29 9NH

Dating from 1430, when guests were first welcomed here, The Spread Eagle Hotel is one of England's oldest hotels and is steeped in history; rich in charms, retaining many period features. Those wishing to be pampered will enjoy the superb fitness facilities and excellent standard of service. Located in either the main building or the market house, the 39 en-suite bedrooms, some with four-poster beds, are well-appointed with soft furnishings and fine ornaments. A roaring log fire attracts guests into the historic lounge bar, ideal for relaxing in the afternoons or enjoying an apéritif. Sumptuous modern British cuisine may be savoured in the candle-lit restaurant, complemented by an extensive wine list. Weddings, banquets and meetings are held in the Jacobean Hall and Polo Room. The Aquila Health Spa is an outstanding facility featuring a blue tiled swimming pool as its centrepiece. A Scandinavian sauna, Turkish steam room, hot tub, fitness centre and a range of beauty treatments, aromatherapy and massage are also offered. The stately homes at Petworth, Uppark and Goodwood are all within a short drive, with Chichester Cathedral, the Downland Museum and Fishbourne Roman Palace among the many local attractions. Cowdray Park Polo Club is only 1 mile away.

Our inspector loved: *This magnificent old building where traditional style is the keynote.*

Directions: Midhurst is on the A286 between Chichester and Milford.

Web: www.johansens.com/spreadeaglemidhurst
E-mail: reservations@spreadeagle-midhurst.com.
Tel: 0870 381 8903
International: +44 (0)1730 816911
Fax: 01730 815668

Price Guide:
single £75–£205
double/twin £99–£240

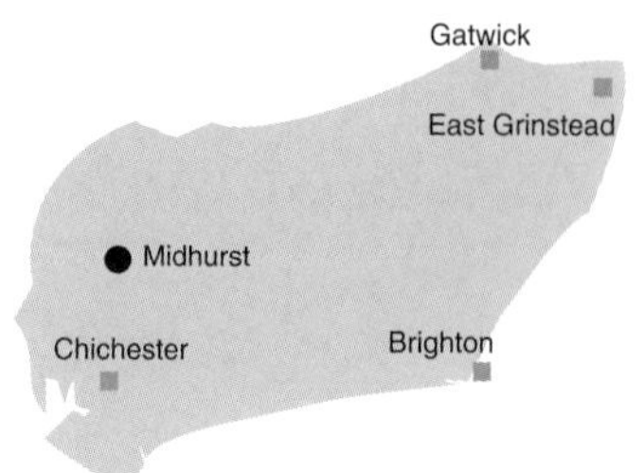

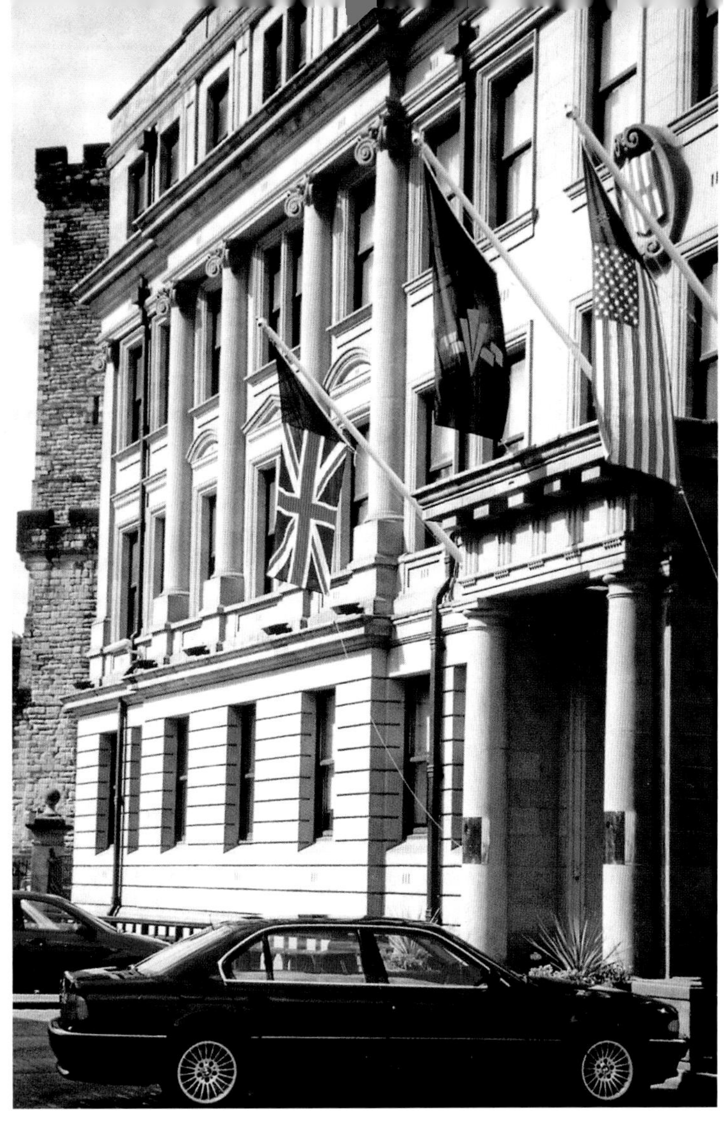

The Vermont Hotel

CASTLE GARTH, NEWCASTLE-UPON-TYNE, TYNE & WEAR NE1 1RQ

The Vermont is Newcastle's only 4-star independent hotel, located next to the Castle, overlooking the Cathedral and the Tyne and Millennium Bridges. This impressive 12 storey, Manhattan-style tower boasts an unrivalled city centre position; a short walk to the main shopping centre, theatres, galleries, universities and main railway station. It has direct access to the Quayside and on site complimentary car parking. The 101 bedrooms and suites are a combination of classical and modern design with 24-hour service expected from a luxury hotel. 7 luxuriously appointed meeting rooms are available for special business occasions and private dining. The Bridge Restaurant is located at the Castle Garth level with spectacular views of the Tyne Bridge, alternatively there is the Redwood Bar, with its fireplace and sofas, open until very late. For those wishing to sample the atmosphere of the famous Quayside, Martha's Bar & Courtyard on the ground floor is the entrance to Newcastle's nightlife. The Vermont is the ideal base from which to explore Newcastle's excellent shops as well as the surrounding areas of Northumberland, Durham and The Borders

Our inspector loved: *Peaceful luxury next to the castle in the centre of Newcastle.*

Directions: Close to the A1(M), and 7 miles from Newcastle International Airport. Contact hotel for detailed directions.

Whitley Bay
Newcastle upon Tyne
Sunderland

Web: www.johansens.com/vermont
E-mail: info@vermont-hotel.co.uk
Tel: 0870 381 8962
International: +44 (0)191 233 1010
Fax: 0191 233 1234

Price Guide:
single/double from £120
suites from £240

101 200

NAILCOTE HALL

NAILCOTE LANE, BERKSWELL, NEAR SOLIHULL, WARWICKSHIRE CV7 7DE

Nailcote Hall is a charming Elizabethan country house hotel set in 15 acres of gardens and surrounded by Warwickshire countryside. Built in 1640, the house was used by Cromwell during the Civil War and was damaged by his troops prior to the assault on Kenilworth Castle. Ideally located in the heart of England, Nailcote Hall is within 15 minutes' drive of the castle towns of Kenilworth and Warwick, Coventry Cathedral, Birmingham International Airport/Station and the NEC. Situated at the centre of the Midlands motorway network, Birmingham city centre, the ICC and Stratford-upon-Avon are less than 30 minutes away. Leisure facilities include indoor swimming pool, gymnasium, solarium and sauna. Outside there are all-weather tennis courts, pétanque, croquet, a challenging 9-hole par-3 golf course and putting green (host to the British Championship Professional Short Course Championship). In the intimate Tudor surroundings of the Oak Room restaurant, chef will delight guests with superb cuisine, whilst the cellar boasts an extensive choice of international wines. En-suite bedrooms offer luxury accommodation and elegant facilities are available for conferences, private dining and corporate hospitality.

Our inspector loved: *This quintessential Elizabethan mansion.*

Directions: Situated 6 miles south of Birmingham International Airport/ NEC on the B4101 Balsall Common–Coventry road.

Web: www.johansens.com/nailcotehall
E-mail: info@nailcotehall.co.uk
Tel: 0870 381 8752
International: +44 (0)2476 466174
Fax: 02476 470720

Price Guide:
single £185
double/twin £200
suite £200–£305

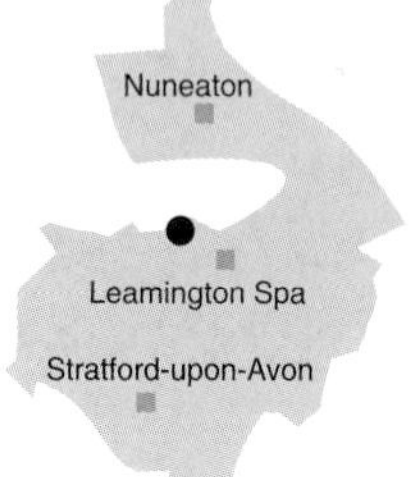

Mallory Court

HARBURY LANE, BISHOPS TACHBROOK, LEAMINGTON SPA, WARWICKSHIRE CV33 9QB

Surrounded by 10 acres of attractive gardens, Mallory Court boasts a truly stunning backdrop across the beautiful Warwickshire countryside and is just a stone's throw away from Stratford-upon-Avon and Warwick Castle. Offering every home comfort, arriving guests are enveloped by the welcoming and tranquil ambience. Guests may begin their evening sipping champagne on the terrace before setting off to visit the Royal Shakespeare Theatre. During the winter season, afternoon tea may be enjoyed in the comfortable lounges beside the burning log fires. The 30 luxurious rooms are enhanced by thoughtful finishing touches and stunning views across the grounds. Modern, English-style dishes are served in the elegant restaurant where chef is happy to create tailor-made menus. Diners may begin with roasted Skye scallops, chicken with Avruga caviar served with marinated cucumber and oyster jus, followed by braised shoulder and roasted fillet of Lighthorne lamb with Provençal vegetables, ending with a hot passion fruit soufflé. September 2005 saw the opening of the more informal, yet excellent brasserie for that lighter menu. This is an ideal venue for weddings and business meetings. Luxury leisure breaks and exclusive use of the hotel are available.

Our inspector loved: *The striking decor and relaxing atmosphere of the brilliant new brasserie.*

Directions: 2 miles south of Leamington Spa on Harbury Lane, just off the B4087 Bishops Tachbrook-Leamington Spa Road. Harbury Lane runs from the B4087 towards Fosse Way. M40, Jct13 from London/Jct14 from Birmingham.

Web: www.johansens.com/mallorycourt
E-mail: reception@mallory.co.uk
Tel: 0870 381 8713
International: +44 (0)1926 330214
Fax: 01926 451714

Price Guide:
double (single occupancy) from £125
double from £135
master rooms from £270

ETTINGTON PARK

ALDERMINSTER, STRATFORD-UPON-AVON, WARWICKSHIRE CV37 8BU

The foundations of Ettington Park date back at least 1000 years. Mentioned in the Domesday Book, Ettington Park rises majestically over 40 acres of Warwickshire parkland, surrounded by terraced gardens and carefully tended lawns, where guests can wander at their leisure to admire the pastoral views. The interiors are beautiful, their striking opulence enhanced by flowers, beautiful antiques and original paintings. Amid these elegant surroundings guests can relax totally, pampered with every luxury. On an appropriately grand scale, the 48 bedrooms and leisure complex, comprising an indoor heated swimming pool,and sauna, make this a perfect choice for the sybarite. The menu reflects the best of English and French cuisine, served with panache in the dining room, with its elegant 18th-century rococo ceiling and 19th-century carved family crests. The bon viveur will relish the fine wine list. Splendid conference facilities are available: the panelled Long Gallery and 12th-century chapel are both unique venues. Clay pigeon shooting, archery and fishing can be arranged on the premises with advanced notice.

Our inspector loved: *Looking back at the stunning neo-gothic building from the River Stour at the edge of the extensive grounds.*

Directions: From M40 junction 15 (Warwick) take A46, A439 signposted Stratford, then left-hand turn onto A3400. Ettington Park is 5 miles south of Stratford-upon-Avon off the A3400.

Web: www.johansens.com/ettingtonpark
E-mail: ettingtonpark@handpicked.co.uk
Tel: 0870 381 8508
International: +44 (0)1789 450123
Fax: 01789 450472

Price Guide:
single from £129
double/twin from £149
suite from £267

The Shakespeare Hotel

CHAPEL STREET, STRATFORD-UPON-AVON, WARWICKSHIRE CV37 6ER

Located in the centre of Stratford-upon-Avon, this hotel is the perfect base for exploring the many quaint houses and villages of the surrounding area, and its black and white gabled Tudor façade is as intriguing as one of the Bard's plays. Inside, the original stone floor of the reception suggests a wealthy style of living that pre-dates the great writer himself. The hotel's ambience is friendly and peaceful and over the years it has become a firm favourite with politicians, diplomats, business people and scholars. There are 74 individually styled en-suite rooms, each named after a character from a Shakespeare play, and those in search of a more luxurious stay can choose from a four-poster bedroom or mini-suite. The 2 AA Rosette David Garrick Restaurant offers fine cuisine in a relaxed setting, while the Quill Bar serves cocktails and a variety of light meals. Afternoon tea can be taken in the lounge, where an open fire blazes in winter. 7 conference suites cater for meetings or banquets of up to 80 people, and the hotel provides a romantic venue for weddings. As well as enjoying Stratford's culture, retail therapy and historical interest, guests are able to use the new Vital Leisure Club at The Alveston Manor.

Our inspector loved: *The oak beams, the flag stone floors and the many open fireplaces.*

Directions: Leave the M40 at Junction 15 Take the A46 and A439 towards Stratford-upon-Avon. It is about 4 miles to Stratford upon Avon and follow the signs for Town Centre.

Nuneaton
Leamington Spa
Stratford-upon-Avon

Web: www.johansens.com/shakespeare
E-mail: sales.shakespeare@macdonald-hotels.co.uk
Tel: 0870 381 8611
International: +44 (0)1789 293636
Fax: 01789 415411

Price Guide:
single £150
double £160
suite £240

Billesley Manor

BILLESLEY, ALCESTER, NR STRATFORD-UPON-AVON, WARWICKSHIRE B49 6NF

This magnificent 4-star 16th-century Manor House is set in 11 acres of its own private parkland and has a unique topiary garden and sun terrace. Centuries of history and tradition with Shakespearian connection welcome guests to this delightful hotel. Billesley Manor has 72 beautiful bedrooms, including four-poster rooms and suites, all of which are en-suite and many with stunning gardens views. Cuisine of the highest standard is served in the Stuart restaurant, awarded 2 AA Rosettes. A selection of rooms for private dining are available for family, friends or business guests. The Cedar Barns offer a new dimension in conference facilities incorporating state-of-the-art equipment in unique and impressive surroundings. A new spa incorporates an impressive indoor heated swimming pool, gym, beauty treatment rooms, sauna, steam room, solarium and healthy eating bistro. Tennis courts, croquet lawn and activity field are also available. The organisation of corporate events such as clay pigeon shooting, archery and quad biking are also on offer. Weekend breaks are available – ideal for visiting the Royal Shakespeare Theatre, Warwick Castle, Ragley Hall and the Cotswolds. Situated in the heart of England, minutes away from Shakespeare's Stratford-upon-Avon and only 23 miles from Birmingham International Airport, the hotel can be easily accessed by air, rail and road.

Directions: Leave M40 at exit 15, follow A46 towards Evesham and Alcester. 4 miles beyond Stratford-upon-Avon turn right to Billesley.

Web: www.johansens.com/billesley
E-mail: bookings@billesleymanor.co.uk
Tel: 0870 381 8363
International: +44 (0)1789 279955
Fax: 01789 764145

Price Guide:
single £125
double/twin from £180
suite £250

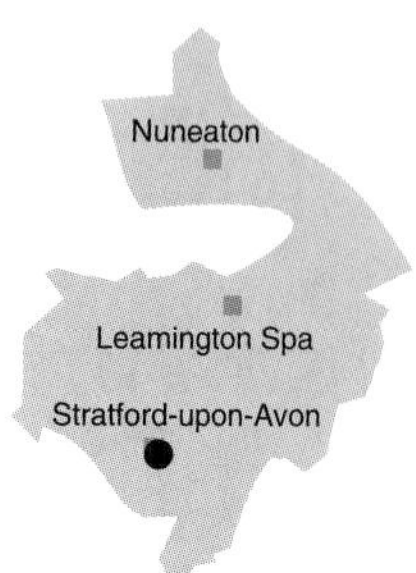

Our inspector loved: *The brilliant bedrooms in the converted tithe barn.*

The Glebe at Barford

CHURCH STREET, BARFORD, WARWICKSHIRE CV35 8BS

"Glebe" means belonging to the Church, which explains why this beautiful Georgian country house is in a unique and quiet position next to the church in Barford, an attractive village in Warwickshire. It is a Grade II listed building, dating back to 1820, with an unusual central atrium and surrounded by gardens. The bedrooms are spacious, comfortable and peaceful. They have all the accessories expected by today's travellers. The restaurant is in an elegant conservatory, green plants adding cool colour. There are excellent table d'hôte and à la carte menus and the wine list has been carefully selected to complement the dishes. The Glebe is an ideal venue for private celebrations and corporate events as it has several well-equipped conference rooms – the Bentley Suite seats 120 people for a banquet and the Directors Suite, with leather armchairs, is ideal for a discreet strategy meeting. Those wishing to be pampered will be pleased with the beauty and sunbed room. Guests appreciate the Glebe Leisure Club with a pool, gymnasium, sauna, steam room and spa facilities. They can play tennis and golf nearby. Ideally situated for Warwick and Stratford races.

Our inspector loved: *The splendid Cedar tree dominating the gravelled forecourt.*

Directions: M40 exit Junction 15 A429 signed Stow. Turning left at mini-roundabout, the hotel is on the right just past the church.

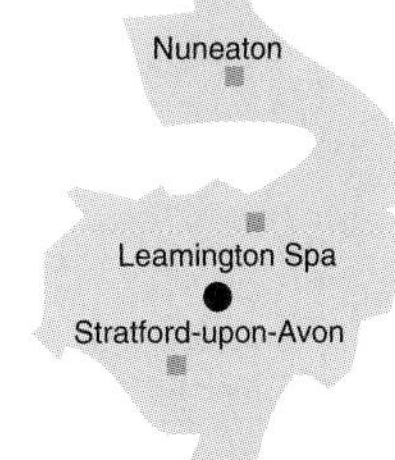

Web: www.johansens.com/glebeatbarford
E-mail: sales@glebehotel.co.uk
Tel: 0870 381 8548
International: +44 (0)1926 624218
Fax: 01926 624625

Price Guide:
single £105
double/twin £125
four poster £135
suite £160

Ardencote Manor Hotel, Country Club & Spa

LYE GREEN ROAD, CLAVERDON, NR WARWICK, WARWICKSHIRE CV35 8LT

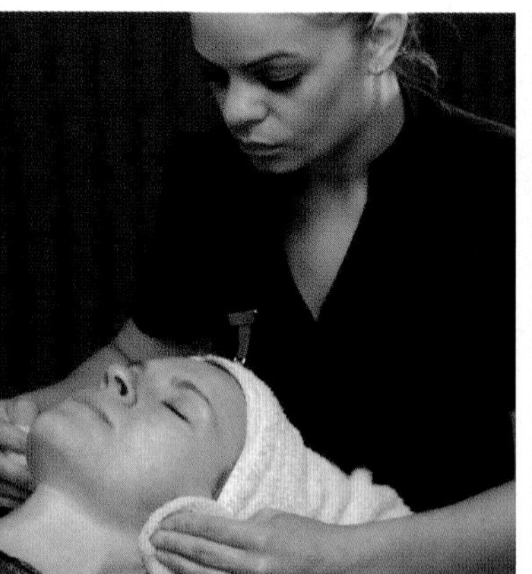

Under private ownership, this former Gentlemen's residence, which was built around 1860, has been sympathetically refurbished and substantially extended to provide a luxury hotel with all modern amenities and comforts, whilst retaining its traditional elegance and appealing intimacy. Set in 42 acres of landscaped grounds in the heart of Shakespeare country, it offers beautifully appointed en-suite accommodation – many rooms have glorious views of the lake and gardens – fine cuisine and extensive sports and leisure facilities, including indoor pool and spa bath, outdoor whirlpool, sauna and steamrooms, squash and tennis courts, fully equipped gymnasia and a 9-hole golf course. The Ardencote Spa is also at the disposal of guests, offering an extensive range of relaxing and holistic treatments. Ardencote Manor's award-winning restaurant, the lakeside Lodge, offers an exciting and innovative menu. Places of interest nearby include the NEC, Warwick Castle (discounted tickets available through hotel), Stratford-upon-Avon and the Cotswolds. Weekend breaks available.

***Our inspector loved:** the many-windowed suites overlooking the lake and golf course.*

Directions: From M40 follow signs to Henley-in-Arden. Lye Green Road is off A4189 Henley-in-Arden/Warwick Road at Claverdon Village Green.

Web: www.johansens.com/ardencote
E-mail: hotel@ardencote.com
Tel: 0870 381 8320
International: +44 (0)1926 843111
Fax: 01926 842646

Price Guide:
single from £105
double from £120
suite £235

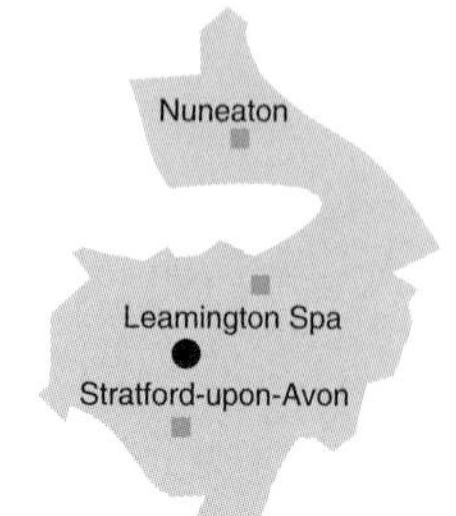

Wroxall Abbey Estate

BIRMINGHAM ROAD, WROXALL, NEAR WARWICK, WARWICKSHIRE CV35 7NB

Nestled in 27 acres of beautifully landscaped gardens within the glorious Warwickshire countryside, Wroxall Abbey Estate is something quite unique. Once the country seat of Sir Christopher Wren, this stunning collection of listed buildings now offers some of the finest hotel and conference facilities. In its entirety, the estate comprises 70 individually designed bedrooms, 15 meeting rooms, public rooms, a bistro, bar, restaurants and marquee. There is somewhere to suit every occasion, be it the elegant mansion, the courtyard building, with landmark clock tower, or the stunning 500m² marquee of flexible entertaining space. The country house-style bedrooms are carefully appointed; each has every modern comfort and amenity. Many have four-poster beds and original marble fireplaces, whilst the bathrooms boast separate walk-in showers and whirlpool baths. There is a first-class range of dining options: the elegant Sonnets restaurant, the informal Bistro, classic Broadwood Bar or the Garden Lounge. Furthermore, the panelled snooker room and bar, as well as the indoor pool complex, have been refurbished to exemplary standards. Sir Christopher Wren's chapel has some breathtaking displays of stained glass windows; there can be few more romantic places to exchange wedding vows.

Our inspector loved: Sir Christopher Wren's "crinkly crankly" walled garden.

Directions: From the M42, exit at junction 5 onto the A4141 to Knowle. Continue towards Warwick for approximately 10 miles and drive through Chadwick End. The entrance to Wroxall Abbey Estate is on the right, 2 miles further on.

Web: www.johansens.com/wroxallcourt
E-mail: info@wroxallestate.com
Tel: 0870 381 9013
International: +44 (0)1926 484470
Fax: 01926 485206

Price Guide:
single £79–£150
double/twin £99–£399

70 300 SPA

LUCKNAM PARK, BATH

COLERNE, CHIPPENHAM, WILTSHIRE SN14 8AZ

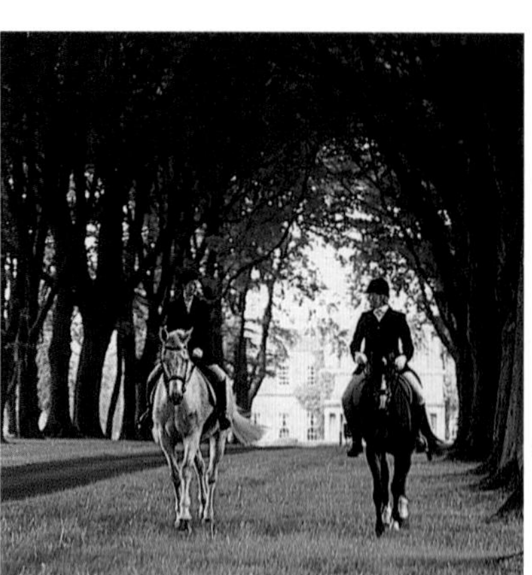

For over 250 years Lucknam Park has been a focus of fine society and aristocratic living, something guests will sense immediately upon their approach along the mile-long avenue lined with beech trees. Built in 1720, this magnificent Palladian mansion is situated just 6 miles from Bath on the southern edge of the Cotswolds. The delicate aura of historical context is reflected in fine art and antiques dating from the late Georgian and early Victorian periods. Award winning food can be savoured in the elegant restaurant, at tables laid with exquisite porcelain, silver and glassware, accompanied with wines from an extensive cellar. Set within the walled gardens of the hotel is the spa, comprising an indoor pool, sauna, steam room, whirlpool spa, gymnasium, beauty salon and snooker room. Numerous activities can be arranged on request, including hot-air ballooning, golf and archery. The Lucknam Park Equestrian Centre, which is situated on the estate, welcomes complete beginners and experienced riders and takes liveries. Bowood House, Corsham Court and Castle Combe are all nearby. Lucknam Park is a member of Relais & Châteaux.

Our inspector loved: *A truly luxurious retreat to get away from it all.*

Directions: 15 minutes from M4, junctions 17 and 18, located between A420 and A4 near the village of Colerne.

Web: www.johansens.com/lucknampark
E-mail: reservations@lucknampark.co.uk
Tel: 0870 381 8707
International: +44 (0)1225 742777
Fax: 01225 743536

Price Guide: (room only)
single/double/twin from £245
suite from £535

Woolley Grange

WOOLLEY GREEN, BRADFORD-ON-AVON, WILTSHIRE BA15 1TX

Woolley Grange is a 17th-century Jacobean stone manor house set in 14 acres of formal gardens and paddocks. Standing on high ground, it affords southerly views of The White Horse at Westbury and beyond. Furnished with flair and an air of eccentricity, a homely atmosphere pervades the hotel alongside pure luxury and well-being. Woolley Grange has gained a reputation for outstanding cuisine; using local farm produce and organically grown fruit and vegetables from the Victorian kitchen gardens, the chef has created a sophisticated style of country house food which aims to revive the focus on flavours. The Orangery provides lighter meals and snacks. Children are particularly welcome and young visitors are not expected to be "seen but not heard." In the Victorian coach house there is a huge games room and a well-equipped nursery with full-time nannies available to look after guests' children 10am–4.45pm every day. A children's lunch and tea are provided daily. Nearby attractions include medieval Bradford-on-Avon, Georgian Bath, Longleat and prehistoric Stonehenge. Riding can be arranged.

Our inspector loved: *The wonderful facilities for children whilst the parents have a relaxing time.*

Directions: From Bath on the A363, fork left onto B3105. From Chippenham take the A4 to Bath, fork left on the B3109 then turn left after the town sign.

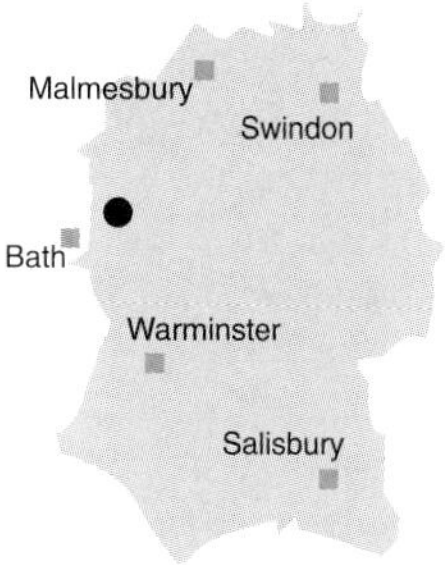

Malmesbury
Swindon
Bath
Warminster
Salisbury

Web: www.johansens.com/woolleygrange
E-mail: info@woolleygrangehotel.co.uk
Tel: 0870 381 8425
International: +44 (0)1225 864705
Fax: 01225 864059

Price Guide:
single £95
double/twin £105–£200
suite from £175–£270

26 35

WHATLEY MANOR

EASTON GREY, MALMESBURY, WILTSHIRE SN16 0RB

Guests staying at this breathtakingly stylish and sophisticated retreat, set amidst 12 acres of superb English gardens, will find a relaxing yet luxurious atmosphere of understated elegance, reminiscent of a friendly, welcoming, private country home. The attention to detail throughout is outstanding. The gardens extend over 26 distinct areas and provide plenty of spaces to escape for relaxation. The 15 bedrooms and 8 suites are individually designed and feature Italian furniture and handmade French wallpaper and are equipped with sound and vision systems. Guests are treated to 2 dining experiences. The intimate dining room offers a truly gastronomic experience, echoing the sumptuous décor of the hotel. While Le Mazot, the informal Swiss interior style brasserie offers a much more relaxed menu and atmosphere. Michelin Starred, Head Chef Martin Burge creates exciting menus using the finest ingredients with a high level of complexity and superb presentation. The award-winning spa, Aquarias, provides a range of luxurious facilities including one of the UK's largest hydrotherapy pools as well as a La Prairie "Art of Beauty" centre. The hotel boasts its own private screening room with seating for up to 40 people. Ideally located for the Georgian city of Bath, Cheltenham and the beautiful Cotswolds, and local attractions such as Westonbirt Arboretum and Beaufort polo club.

Our inspector loved: *The sumptuous luxury throughout – a real treat.*

Directions: The hotel is situated off the B4040, 8 miles from junction 17 of the M4 motorway. 2 hours from London.

Web: www.johansens.com/whatley
E-mail: reservations@whatleymanor.com
Tel: 0870 381 9197
International: +44 (0)1666 822888
Fax: 01666 826120

Price Guide:
single/double/twin from £280
suite from £650

Howard's House

TEFFONT EVIAS, SALISBURY, WILTSHIRE SP3 5RJ

Tucked away in the depths of rural Wiltshire and surrounded by 2 acres of beautiful gardens the fragrance of jasmine exudes through the open windows of the House and the tinkling of the fountain in the lily pond can be gently heard. This charming small country house hotel, run by Noële Thompson, is located in the quintessential English hamlet of Teffon Evias, just 9 miles from Stonehenge. Howard's House is a haven of tranquillity for those seeking to escape the noise and stress of the modern world. The bedrooms are delightfully appointed, with additional touches of fresh fruit, homemade biscuits, plants and up-to-date magazines. The 3 AA Rosette-awarded restaurant is the height of elegance and serves modern British cuisine providing dishes of national acclaim. Cooked with flair and imagination and using home-grown and the best local produce, alfresco dining can be enjoyed during the summer. During winter guests may curl up by the genuine log fire with a good book and a glass of vintage port. Whatever the time of year you are guaranteed the ultimate in country house hospitality. Howard's House is ideally situated for visiting Stonehenge, Old Sarum, Salisbury Cathedral, Wilton House and Stourhead Gardens.

Our inspector loved: *The wonderful smell of fresh flowers as you enter this lovely home from home.*

Directions: From London, turn left off A303. 2 miles after the Wylye intersection follow signs to Teffont and on entering the village join the B3089. Howard's House is signposted.

Web: www.johansens.com/howardshouse
E-mail: enq@howardshousehotel.com
Tel: 0870 381 8627
International: +44 (0)1722 716392
Fax: 01722 716820

Price Guide:
single £105
double/twin £165–£185

THE PEAR TREE AT PURTON

CHURCH END, PURTON, SWINDON, WILTSHIRE SN5 4ED

Dedication to service is the hallmark of this excellent honey-coloured stone hotel nestling in the Vale of the White Horse between the Cotswolds and Marlborough Downs. Owners Francis and Anne Young are justly proud of the many awards for excellence it has received. Surrounded by rolling Wiltshire farmland, The Pear Tree sits majestically in 7½ acres of tranquil grounds on the fringe of the Saxon village of Purton, famed for its unique twin towered Parish Church and the ancient hill fort of Ringsbury Camp. Each of the 17 individually and tastefully decorated bedrooms and suites is named after a character associated with the village, such as Anne Hyde, mother of Queen Mary II and Queen Anne. All are fitted to a high standard and have digital television, hairdryer, trouser press, a safe and a host of other luxuries. The award-winning conservatory restaurant overlooks colourful gardens and is the perfect setting in which to enjoy good English cuisine prepared with style and flair. Cirencester, Bath, Oxford, Avebury, Blenheim Palace, Sudeley Castle and the Cotswolds are all within easy reach.

Our inspector loved: *The beautiful grounds to wander around – and check on the progresss of the newly planted vineyard!.*

Directions: From M4 exit 16 follow signs to Purton and go through the village until reaching a triangle with Spar Grocers opposite. Turn right up the hill and the Pear Tree is on the second left after the Tithe Barn.

Web: www.johansens.com/peartree
E-mail: relax@peartreepurton.co.uk
Tel: 0870 381 8806
International: +44 (0)1793 772100
Fax: 01793 772369

Price Guide:
single £110
double/twin £110–£135
suites £135

BISHOPSTROW HOUSE & SPA

WARMINSTER, WILTSHIRE BA12 9HH

Bishopstrow House is the quintessential Georgian mansion. It combines the intimacy of a grand country hotel retreat with all the benefits of modern facilities and the luxury of the Bishopstrow Spa, which offers a superb range of beauty, fitness and relaxation therapies in addition to Perry Carson's hair styling. A Grade II listed building, Bishopstrow House was built in 1817 and has been sympathetically extended to include indoor and outdoor heated swimming pools, a gymnasium and a sauna. The attention to detail is uppermost in the library, drawing room and conservatory with their beautiful antiques and Victorian oil paintings. The bedrooms are grandly furnished; some have opulent marble bathrooms and whirlpool baths. Skilfully prepared modern British food is served in the Mulberry Restaurant, with lighter meals available in the Mulberry Bar and the conservatory which overlooks 27 acres of gardens. There is fly fishing on the hotel's private stretch of the River Wylye, golf at 5 nearby courses, riding, game and clay pigeon shooting. Longleat House, Wilton House, Stourhead, Stonehenge, Bath, Salisbury and Warminster are within easy reach.

Our inspector loved: *The wonderful mix of facilities for relaxing spa breaks, families or corporate events.*

Directions: Bishopstrow House is south east of Warminster on the B3414 from London via the M3.

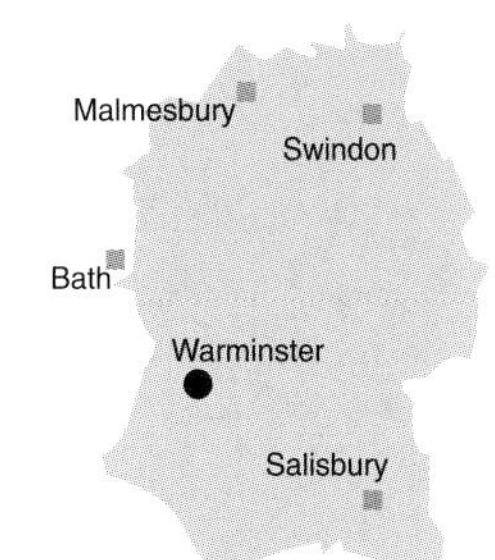

Web: www.johansens.com/bishopstrowhouse
E-mail: info@bishopstrow.co.uk
Tel: 0870 381 8365
International: +44 (0)1985 212312
Fax: 01985 216769

Price Guide:
single £99
double/twin £160–£245
suite from £330

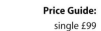

THE ELMS

ABBERLEY, WORCESTERSHIRE WR6 6AT

Built in 1710 by a pupil of Sir Christopher Wren, and converted into a country house hotel in 1946, The Elms has achieved an international reputation for excellence spanning the past half century. Standing impressively between Worcester and Tenbury Wells, this fine Queen Anne mansion is surrounded by beautiful meadows, woodland, hop fields and orchards of cider apples and cherries of the Teme Valley, whose river runs crimson when in flood from bank-side soil tinged with red sandstone. Further to a careful refurbishment in 2005, each of the 16 main house and 5 coach house bedrooms has its own character and provides magnificent views across the landscaped gardens. Guests can enjoy pre-dinner drinks in a comfortable, panelled bar before adjourning to the handsomely furnished restaurant, awarded 2 Rosettes, to be served with sophisticated and imaginative dishes prepeared by Head Chef Daren Bale, complemented by fine wines. The surrounding countryside is ideal for walking, fishing, shooting, golf and horse racing. Within easy reach are the attractions of the market town of Tenbury Wells, Hereford with Mappa Mundi (oldest map in the world), Witley Court, Bewdley and the ancient city of Worcester with its cathedral, county cricket ground and porcelain factory.

Our inspector loved: *This classic Queen Anne building beautifully proportioned inside and out.*

Directions: From the M5, exit at junction 5 (Droitwich) or junction 6 (Worcester) then take the A443 towards Tenbury Wells. The Elms is 2 miles after Great Witley. Do not take Abberley village turning.

Web: www.johansens.com/elmsworcester
E-mail: info@theelmshotel.co.uk
Tel: 0870 381 8304
International: +44 (0)1299 896666
Fax: 01299 896804

Price Guide:
single £70–£145
double/twin £90–£180

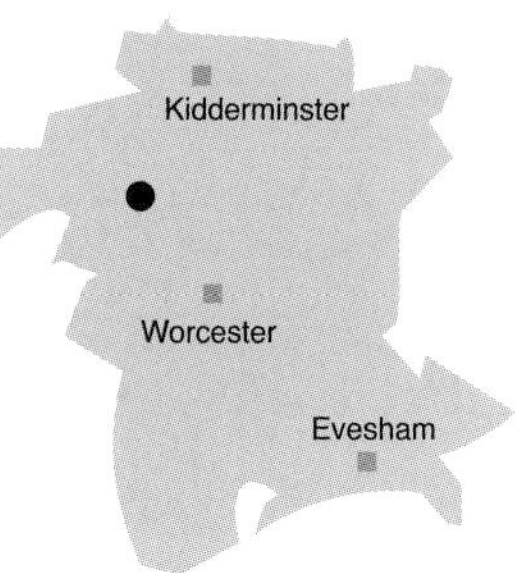

Dormy House

WILLERSEY HILL, BROADWAY, WORCESTERSHIRE WR12 7LF

Dormy House aims to be a home-away-from-home and with its cosy rooms, mouth-watering cuisine, postcard pretty landscape and above all, unstuffy service and ambience, guests will wish this was their own abode. This converted farmhouse dates back to the 17th century and the light stone walls, discreet alcoves and log fires create an inviting atmosphere, which is enhanced by the warm but unobtrusive welcome from the friendly staff. The 45 individually appointed bedrooms are decorated in a quintessential English style and feature rich fabrics, carved headboards and plump scatter cushions. Enjoy the locally-sourced produce served in The Dining Room or al fresco on the new terrace; the gastropub menu in the Barn Owl bar is popular. Activities abound and include relaxing in the sauna and steam room, a round of bar billiards in the games room, swinging a golf club or mallet on the 9-hole putting green or croquet lawn or walking in the circular routes. Cheltenham, Worcester and Stratford-Upon-Avon are nearby, alternatively there is the beautiful Cotswolds countryside on the doorstep. Broadway and Chipping Campden are popular daytrip options.

Our inspector loved: *The luxuriously appointed and spacious bedrooms.*

Directions: The hotel is ½ mile off the A44 between Moreton-in-Marsh and Broadway. Take the turning signposted Saintbury and the hotel is the first building on the left past the picnic area.

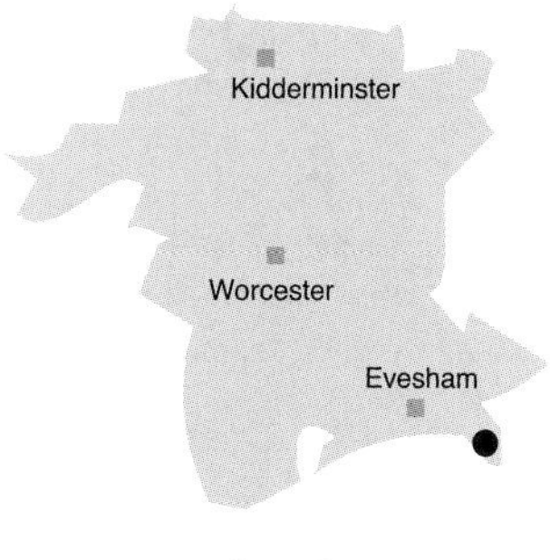

Web: www.johansens.com/dormyhouse
E-mail: reservations@dormyhouse.co.uk
Tel: 0870 381 8487
International: +44 (0)1386 852711
Fax: 01386 858636

Price Guide:
single £120
double/twin £160–£200
suite from £220

BUCKLAND MANOR

RELAIS & CHÂTEAUX

BUCKLAND, NEAR BROADWAY, WORCESTERSHIRE WR12 7LY

The warm glow of Buckland Manor's golden Cotswold stone exterior blends beautifully with the colourful flowers and green shades of the glorious grounds, serving as an appetiser to visitors of the tranquil luxury and history inside those weather-beaten walls. A manor house on the site was first mentioned in the records of Gloucester Abbey in 600AD when the Abbot received it as a gift from Kynred, ruler of Mercia and chief king of the 7 kingdoms of England. Managed by Nigel Power, Buckland retains gracious living and tradition, with the addition of all modern comforts and best service. Guests can relax before log fires in 2 delightfully decorated lounges, one with lovely panelling and a beamed ceiling. The 13 excellently decorated en-suite bedrooms are furnished with luxury fittings and accessories. Some have four-poster beds and fireplaces and all bathrooms use water drawn from the Manor's own spring. Views over the grounds with their small waterfalls, outdoor pool, tennis courts, putting green and croquet lawns are spectacular. The dining room is an oasis of calm, and chef Adrian Jarrad prepares delicious, award-winning cuisine. Broadway Golf Club, Cheltenham race course, Stratford, Stow-on-the-Wold, Warwick and Blenheim are nearby. Buckland Manor is a member of Relais & Châteaux hotels.

Our inspector loved: *The luxurious "Vaulted" room with its double aspect of the glorious grounds.*

Directions: From the M40, exit at junction 8. Take the A40 to Burford, the A424 to Broadway and then the B4632 signposted Winchcombe to Buckland.

Web: www.johansens.com/bucklandmanor
E-mail: info@bucklandmanor.co.uk
Tel: 0870 381 9175
International: +44 (0)1386 852626
Fax: 01386 853557

Price Guide:
single £225-£430
double £235-£440

Brockencote Hall

CHADDESLEY CORBETT, NR KIDDERMINSTER, WORCESTERSHIRE DY10 4PY

The Brockencote estate consists of 70 acres of landscaped grounds surrounding a magnificent hall. There is a gatehouse, half-timbered dovecote, lake, some fine European and North American trees and an elegant conservatory. The estate dates back over three centuries and the style of the building reflects the changes which have taken place in fashion and taste. The hotel has been awarded 3 AA Red Stars, 4 RAC dining awards and is Heart of England Tourist Board Midlands Hotel of the Year silver award 2004. At present, the interior combines classical architectural features with contemporary creature comforts. As in most country houses, each of the bedrooms is different: all have their own character, complemented by tasteful furnishings and décor. The friendly staff provide a splendid service under the supervision of owners Alison and Joseph Petitjean. The Hall specialises in traditional French cuisine with occasional regional and seasonal specialities. Brockencote Hall is an ideal setting for those seeking peace and quiet in an unspoilt corner of the English countryside. Located a few miles south of Birmingham, it is convenient for business people and sightseers alike and makes a fine base for touring historic Worcestershire. Special rates available Sunday to Thursday.

Our inspector loved: *The luxurious light and airy double aspect first floor bedrooms "Teal" and "Kingfisher".*

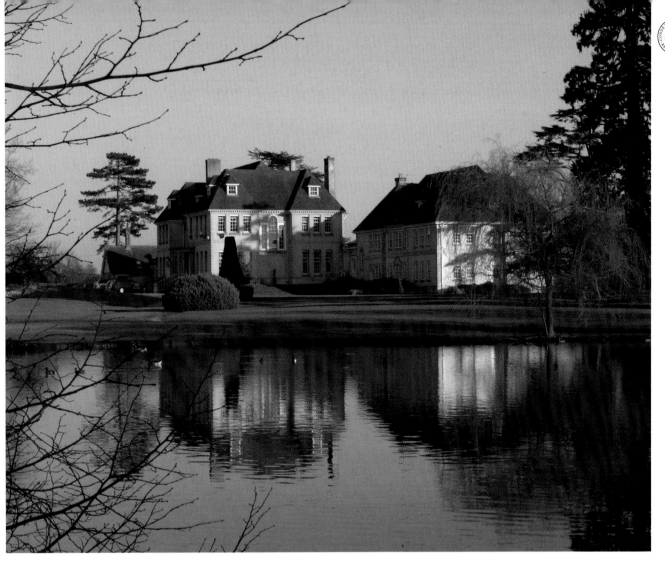

Directions: Exit 4 from M5 or exit 1 from M42 (southbound). Brockencote Hall is set back from A448 at Chaddesley Corbett between Bromsgrove and Kidderminster.

Kidderminster
Worcester
Evesham

Web: www.johansens.com/brockencotehall
E-mail: info@brockencotehall.com
Tel: 0870 381 8382
International: +44 (0)1562 777876
Fax: 01562 777872

Price Guide:
single £93–£140
double/twin £116–£180

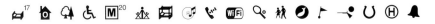

The Evesham Hotel

COOPER'S LANE, OFF WATERSIDE, EVESHAM, WORCESTERSHIRE WR11 1DA

It is the somewhat unconventional atmosphere at the Evesham Hotel that stays in the memory. Originally a Tudor farmhouse, the hotel was extended and converted into a Georgian mansion house in 1809. Unusually, it combines an award-winning welcome for families with the relaxed but efficient style required by business users. For the past 30 years it has been successfully run by the Jenkinson family. Each of the 40 en-suite bedrooms is furnished complete with a teddy bear and a toy duck for the bath. The restaurant offers delicious cuisine from a very imaginative and versatile menu, accompanied by a somewhat unique "Euro-sceptic" wine list (everything but French and German!) offering 100 different grape varieties. The drinks selection is an amazing myriad. The indoor swimming pool has a seaside theme. The peace of the 2½ acre garden belies the hotel's proximity to the town – a 5-minute walk away. In the gardens are six 300-year-old mulberry trees and a magnificent cedar of Lebanon, planted in 1809. The hotel is a good base from which to explore the Cotswolds, Stratford-upon-Avon and the Severn Valley. Closed at Christmas.

Our inspector loved: *So much! The ambience, the themed bedrooms (safari, oriental, horse-racing etc) the "saucy seaside" swimming pool, the unique wine list and range of drinks...*

Directions: Cooper's Lane lies just off Waterside (the River Avon).

Web: www.johansens.com/evesham
E-mail: reception@eveshamhotel.com
Tel: 0870 381 8510
International: +44 (0)1386 765566
Fax: 01386 765443

Price Guide:
single £78–£92
double/twin £128
family suite £173

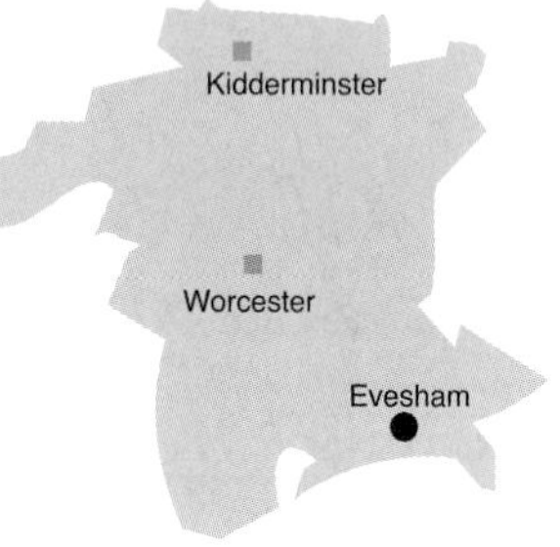

The Cottage in the Wood

HOLYWELL ROAD, MALVERN WELLS, WORCESTERSHIRE WR14 4LG

The Malvern Hills, once the home and inspiration for England's great composer, Sir Edward Elgar, are the setting for The Cottage in the Wood. With its spectacular 30 mile outlook across the Severn Valley, this unique hotel won acclaim from the Daily Mail for having the best view in England. The main house was originally the Dower House to the Blackmore Park estate and accommodation is offered here and in Beech Cottage, an old scrumpy house – and the magnificent new building, "The Pinnacles", named after the hill that rises above, which houses 19 of the traditional-styled bedrooms, many with patios or balconies and giving the best view of all. Owned and run by 2 generations of the Pattin family, the atmosphere is genuinely warm and relaxing. A regularly changing modern English menu is complemented by an almost obsessional wine list of 600 bins. If this causes any over-indulgence, guests can walk to the tops of the Malvern Hills direct from the hotel grounds. Winner of the Condé Nast Johansens/Taittinger wine list award 2006. Good touring base for the Cotswolds, Forest of Dean, black and white villages and many historic houses and castles. Nearby are the Three Counties Showground and the Cathedral cities of Worcester, Gloucester and Hereford.

Directions: 3 miles south of Great Malvern on A449, turn into Holywell Road by post box and hotel sign. Hotel is 250 yards on right.

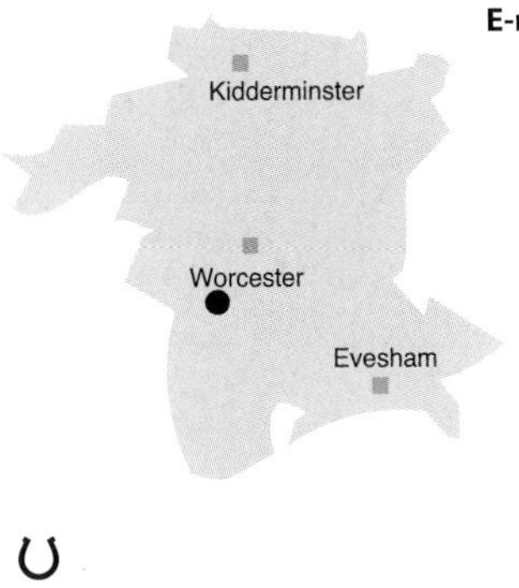

Web: www.johansens.com/cottageinthewood
E-mail: reception@cottageinthewood.co.uk
Tel: 0870 381 8452
International: +44 (0)1684 575859
Fax: 01684 560662

Kidderminster
Worcester
Evesham

Price Guide:
single £79–£115
double/twin £99–£190

Our inspector loved: *The fabulous food and the fantastic view.*

Willerby Manor Hotel

WELL LANE, WILLERBY, HULL, EAST YORKSHIRE HU10 6ER

Directions: Take the M62 towards Hull, which runs into the A63, turn off onto the A164 in the direction of Beverley. Follow the signs to Willerby and then Willerby Manor.

Web: www.johansens.com/willerbymanor
E-mail: willerbymanor@bestwestern.co.uk
Tel: 0870 381 8998
International: +44 (0)1482 652616
Fax: 01482 653901

Price Guide:
single £55–£106
double/twin £85–£135
suite £150–£180

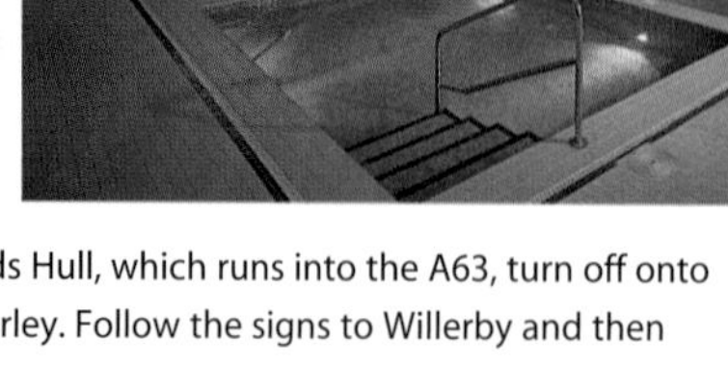

Originally the home of the Edwardian shipping merchant, Sir Henry Salmon, Willerby Manor was bought in the early 1970s by John Townend, a Wine Merchant from Hull. The elegance of the hotel, as it stands today, is testament to the careful work of the Townend family over the years. Furnished in a stylish manner, the public rooms are the essence of comfort. The 50 bedrooms are beautifully decorated with colour co-ordinated fabrics and soft furnishings. Every modern amenity is provided as well as an array of thoughtful extras such as fresh floral arrangements. Restaurant Icon serves modern English food, which is complemented by an extensive well-chosen wine list from the House of Townend. A more informal ambience pervades the Everglades Brasserie where guests may savour bistro-style meals and beverages. Fitness enthusiasts will be delighted with the well-equipped Health Club which includes a 19 metre swimming pool, spacious gymnasium, whirlpool spa bath, an exercise studio with daily classes and a beauty treatment room. The hotel is in a convenient location for those wishing to explore the cities of Hull and York.

Our inspector loved: *Having a relaxing swim in the large pool before dinner.*

The Devonshire Arms Country House Hotel & Spa

BOLTON ABBEY, SKIPTON, NORTH YORKSHIRE BD23 6AJ

The Devonshire reflects its charming setting in the Yorkshire Dales: a welcome escape from a busy and crowded world, peace and quiet, beautiful countryside – the perfect place in which to relax. The hotel is owned by the Duke and Duchess of Devonshire and is set in rolling parkland on their 30,000-acre Bolton Abbey Estate in the Yorkshire Dales National Park. The Dowager Duchess of Devonshire personally supervises the decoration of the interiors which include antiques and paintings from their family home at Chatsworth. Fine dining led by Michelin Star Executive Head Chef Michael Wignall in the elegant Burlington Restaurant is complemented by an outstanding award-winning wine list of over 2,500 fine and rare wines. Alternatively there is the less informal atmosphere of The Devonshire Brasserie and Bar with its lively décor and contemporary art. The Devonshire Health Spa housed in a converted 17th-century barn offers a full range of leisure, health and beauty therapy facilities. There is plenty to do and see on the hotel's doorstep from exploring the ruins of the 12th-century Augustinian Bolton Priory to fly fishing on the river Wharfe. Managing Director, Jeremy Rata, together with General Manager, Eamonn Elliott, lead an enthusiastic team committed to providing a high standard of service and hospitality.

Directions: Off the A59 Skipton–Harrogate road at junction with the B6160

Web: www.johansens.com/devonshirearms
E-mail: reservations@thedevonshirearms.co.uk
Tel: 0870 381 8480
International: +44 (0)1756 718111
Fax: 01756 710564

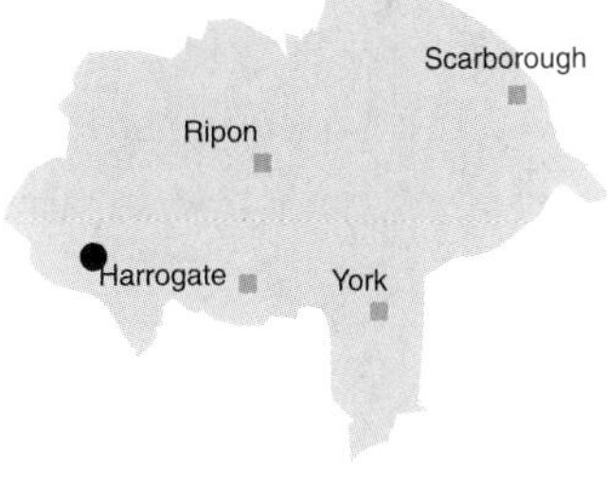

Scarborough
Ripon
Harrogate
York

Price Guide:
single £170–£370
double/twin £215–£370
suite £400

Our inspector loved: *The relaxed, informal and unstuffy ambience.*

         SPA    

GRANTS HOTEL

SWAN ROAD, HARROGATE, NORTH YORKSHIRE HG1 2SS

Towards the end of the last century, Harrogate became fashionable among the gentry, who came to "take the waters" of the famous spa. Today's visitors have one advantage over their Victorian counterparts – they can enjoy the hospitality of Grants Hotel, the creation of Pam and Peter Grant. Their friendly welcome, coupled with high standards of service, ensures a pleasurable stay. All bedrooms are attractively decorated and have en-suite bathrooms. Downstairs, guests can relax in the comfortable lounge or take refreshments out to the terrace gardens. Drinks and light meals are available at all times from Harry Grant's Bar and dinner is served in the French café-style Chimney Pots Bistro, complete with brightly coloured check blinds and cloths and lots of humorous Beryl Cook pictures. Cuisine is basically traditional rustic with a smattering of Oriental influence complemented by the mouth-watering home-made puddings. Located less than 5 minutes' walk from Harrogate's Conference and Exhibition Centre, Grants offers its own luxury meeting and syndicate rooms, the Herriot Suite. The Royal Pump Room Museum and the Royal Baths Assembly Rooms are nearby. Guests have free use of The Academy Health and Leisure Club. Super value breaks available.

Our inspector loved: *The Beryl Cook pictures in the Bistro.*

Directions: Swan Road is in the centre of Harrogate, off the A61 to Ripon.

Web: www.johansens.com/grants
E-mail: enquiries@grantshotel-harrogate.com
Tel: 0870 381 8562
International: +44 (0)1423 560666
Fax: 01423 502550

Price Guide:
single £105–£125
double/twin £110–£160
suites £168

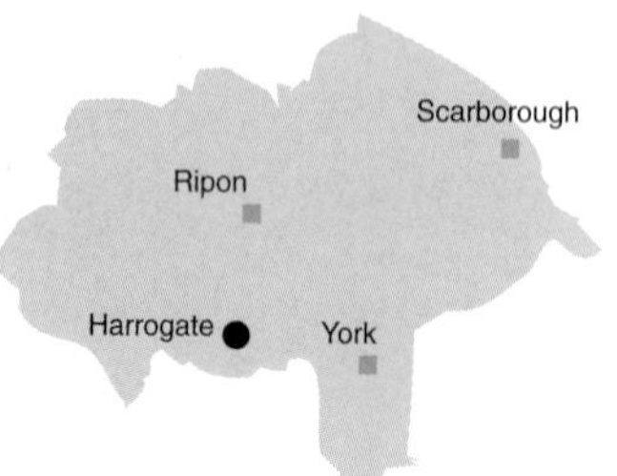

Rudding Park

FOLLIFOOT, HARROGATE, NORTH YORKSHIRE HG3 1JH

Rudding Park's award-winning hotel is just 2 miles from Harrogate town centre. Its setting is superb, surrounded by 230 acres of parkland. The hotel has an elegant façade and entrance, approached by a sweeping driveway. The Regency period house offers fine conference and banqueting rooms, whilst the adjoining hotel has been brilliantly designed and built to harmonise with the original mansion. A warm welcome awaits guests in the pleasant foyer, with its big fireplace and easy chairs. The bedrooms are spacious, with contemporary cherry wood furniture, relaxing colour schemes, many modern accessories and lovely views over the estate. Guests can relax in the Mackaness Drawing Room. The stylish 2 AA Rosette Clocktower Restaurant and Bar are inviting and on sunny days they extend onto the terrace. The food is delicious and the wine list extensive. Leisure facilities are excellent – there is an 18-hole par 72 parkland golf course which has played host to the PGA Mastercard tour series. The golf academy and driving range are ideal for lessons and practice. Hotel guests are welcome to use a local award-winning gym and health club.

Our inspector loved: *The enthusiastic and helpful staff with their attention to detail.*

Directions: Rudding Park is accessible from the A1 north or south, via the A661, just off the A658.

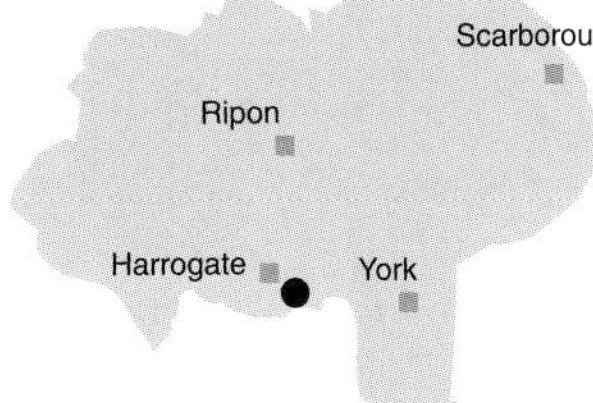

Web: www.johansens.com/ruddingpark
E-mail: sales@ruddingpark.com
Tel: 0870 381 8879
International: +44 (0)1423 871350
Fax: 01423 872286

Price Guide:
single £150–£180
double/twin £170–£200
suite £280–£340

Hob Green Hotel, Restaurant & Gardens

MARKINGTON, HARROGATE, NORTH YORKSHIRE HG3 3PJ

Set in 870 acres of farm and woodland this charming "country house" hotel is only a short drive from the spa town of Harrogate and the ancient city of Ripon. The restaurant has an excellent reputation locally with only the finest fresh local produce being used, much of which is grown in the hotel's own garden. The interesting menus are complemented by an excellent choice of sensibly priced wines. All 12 bedrooms have been individually furnished and tastefully equipped to suit the most discerning guest. The drawing room and hall, warmed by log fires in cool weather, are comfortably furnished with the added attraction of fine antique furniture, porcelain and pictures. Situated in the heart of some of Yorkshire's most dramatic scenery, the hotel offers magnificent views of the valley beyond from all the main rooms. York is only 23 miles away. There is a wealth of cultural and historical interest nearby with Fountains Abbey and Studley Royal water garden and deer park a few minutes' drive. The Yorkshire Riding Centre is in Markington Village. Simply relax in this tranquil place where your every comfort is catered for. Special breaks available.

Our inspector loved: *Strolling around the large lovingly tended Victorian walled herb, vegetable and cutting flower garden.*

Directions: Turn left signposted Markington off the A61 Harrogate to Ripon road, the hotel is 1 mile after the village on the left.

Web: www.johansens.com/hobgreen
E-mail: info@hobgreen.com
Tel: 0870 381 8600
International: +44 (0)1423 770031
Fax: 01423 771589

Price Guide:
single £95–£118
double/twin £110–£155
suite £135–£175

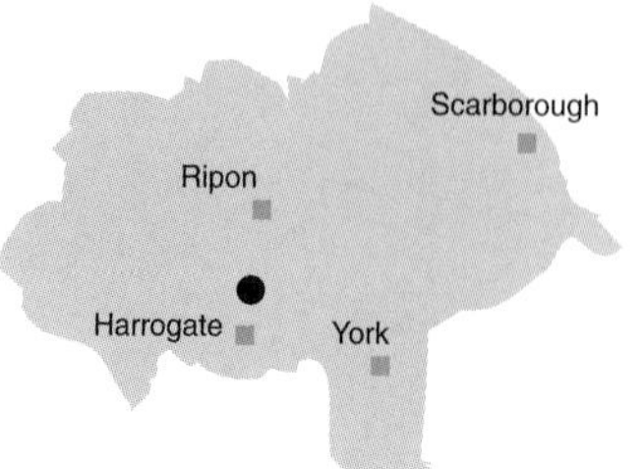

The Boar's Head Hotel

THE RIPLEY CASTLE ESTATE, HARROGATE, NORTH YORKSHIRE HG3 3AY

Imagine relaxing in a luxury hotel at the centre of a historic, private country estate in England's incredibly beautiful North Country. The Ingilby family who have lived in Ripley Castle for 26 generations invite you to enjoy their hospitality at The Boar's Head Hotel. There are 25 luxury bedrooms, individually decorated and furnished, most with king-sized beds. The restaurant's menu is outstanding, presented by a creative and imaginative kitchen brigade and complemented by a wide selection of reasonably priced, good quality wines. There is a welcoming bar serving traditional ales straight from the wood and popular bar meal selections. When staying at The Boar's Head, guests can enjoy complimentary access to the delightful walled gardens and grounds of Ripley Castle, which include the lakes and a deer park. A conference at Ripley is a different experience – using the idyllic meeting facilities available in the Castle, organisers and delegates alike will appreciate the peace and tranquillity of the location, which also offers opportunities for all types of leisure activity in the Deer Park.

Our inspector loved: *The historic Ripley Castle and the pretty village of Ripley.*

Directions: Ripley is very accessible, just 10 minutes from the conference town of Harrogate, 20 minutes from the motorway network and Leeds/Bradford Airport, and 40 minutes from the City of York.

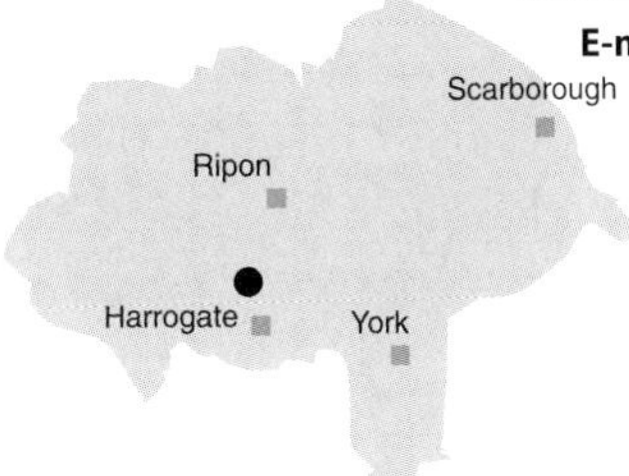

Web: www.johansens.com/boarsheadharrogate
E-mail: reservations@boarsheadripley.co.uk
Tel: 0870 381 8370
International: +44 (0)1423 771888
Fax: 01423 771509

Price Guide:
single £105–£130
double £125–£160

25 150

SIMONSTONE HALL

HAWES, NORTH YORKSHIRE DL8 3LY

Fine cuisine, comfort, peace and tranquillity combine with breathtaking scenery to make any stay at Simonstone Hall totally memorable. This former 18th-century hunting lodge has been lovingly restored and furnished with antiques to create an idyllic retreat for its guests.The hall stands in a beautiful setting with an adjacent 14,000 acres of grouse moors and upland grazing. Many period features have been retained such as the panelled dining room, mahogany staircase with ancestral stained glass windows and a lounge with ornamental fireplace and ceilings. The bedrooms are of the highest standards and offer every comfort including four-poster and sleigh beds. In the restaurant, guests savour the freshest local produce presented with flair and imagination, whilst enjoying stunning views across Upper Wensleydale. An excellent wine list is available to complement any dish. Traditional country cuisine is served in the Game Tavern and The Orangery which provide a particularly warm and informal atmosphere. Simonstone Hall, with its fine views, is the perfect base for enjoying and exploring the hidden Yorkshire Dales. The area abounds with ancient castles, churches and museums. Hardraw Force, England's highest single drop waterfall, which can be heard from the gardens, is only a walk away.

Our inspector loved: *The wonderful setting with stunning views across Upper Wensleydale.*

Directions: Hawes is on A684. Turn north on Buttertubs Pass towards Muker. Simonstone Hall is ½ mile on the left.

Web: www.johansens.com/simonstonehall
E-mail: email@simonstonehall.co.uk
Tel: 0870 381 8895
International: +44 (0)1969 667255
Fax: 01969 667741

Price Guide:
single £55–£100
double/twin £110–£180

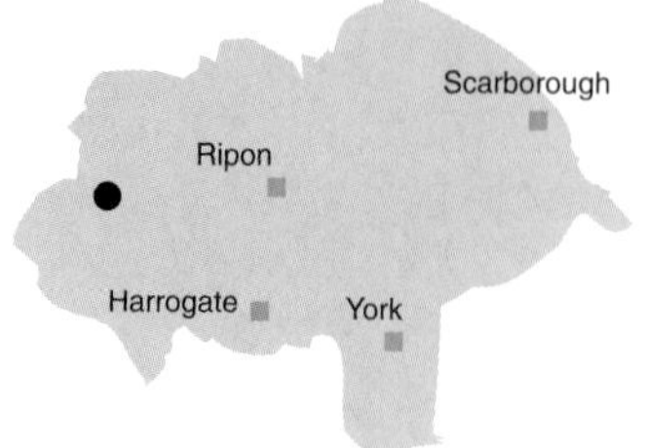

THE FEVERSHAM ARMS HOTEL

HELMSLEY, NORTH YORKSHIRE YO62 5AG

This former coaching inn, standing in the heart of an attractive market town nestling beneath the southern rim of the North Yorkshire Moors National Park, has been carefully redeveloped and furnished by award-winning hotelier Simon Rhatigan, to create a relaxing retreat. The highest standards of hospitality and service are provided in an inviting ambience where elements of the hotel's past and present mingle in complete harmomy. Mousey Thompson furniture and traditional soft leather sofas and armchairs feature comfortably next to contemporary paintings. The 24 en-suite bedrooms, including 12 suites, are individually furnished in a country-chic style. Dining is the heart of the hotel, with the emphasis on game, lamb and the freshest of seafood from nearby Whitby. Guests can enjoy their meals in the lovely conservatory restaurant, in front of open fires in either of the delightfully decorated lounges or, on fine summer days, on the terrace surrounding the open air heated swimming pool. Places of interest nearby include Byland and Rievaulx Abbeys, Helmsley Castle, Castle Howard and Nunnington Hall.

Our inspector loved: *The unique dining experience in the conservatory restaurant, which overlooks the swimming pool.*

Directions: From A1 take A64, then take the York north bypass (A1237) and then B1363. Alternatively, from A1 take A168 signposted Thirsk, then A170.

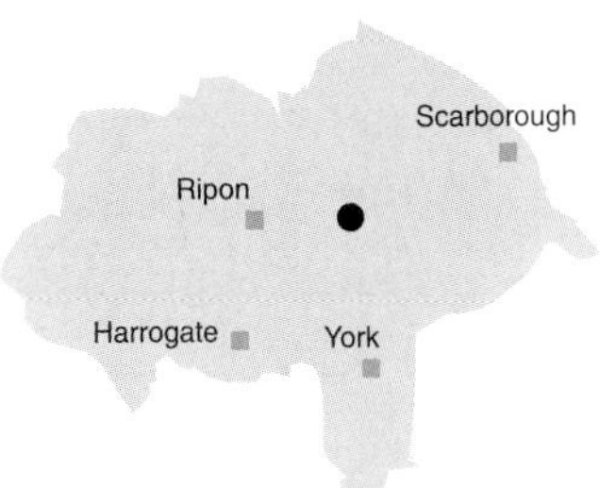

Web: www.johansens.com/fevershamarms
E-mail: info@fevershamarmshotel.com
Tel: 0870 381 9283
International: +44 (0)1439 770766
Fax: 01439 770346

Price Guide:
single £130–£180
double/twin £140–£190
suite £220–£255

THE PHEASANT

HAROME, HELMSLEY, NORTH YORKSHIRE YO62 5JG

Directions: From Helmsley, take the A170 towards Scarborough; after 1/4 mile turn right for Harome. The hotel is near the church in the village.

Web: www.johansens.com/pheasanthelmsley
E-mail: reservations@thepheasanthotel.com
Tel: 0870 381 8821
International: +44 (0)1439 771241
Fax: 01439 771744

Price Guide: (including 5-course dinner)
single £76–£85
double/twin £152–£170

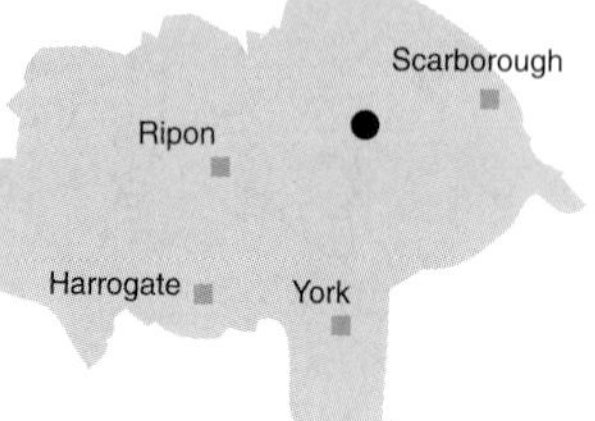

The Pheasant, rich in oak beams and open log fires, offers 2 types of accommodation, some in the hotel and some in a charming, 16th-century thatched cottage. The Binks family, who built the hotel and now own and manage it, have created a friendly atmosphere which is part of the warm Yorkshire welcome that awaits all guests. The bedrooms and suites are brightly decorated in an attractive cottage style, and are all complete with en-suite facilities. Traditional English cooking is the speciality of the restaurant; many of the dishes are prepared using local fresh fruit and vegetables. During summer, guests may relax on the terrace overlooking the pond. An indoor heated swimming pool is an added attraction. Other sporting activities available locally include swimming, riding, golf and fishing. York is a short drive away, as are a host of historic landmarks including Byland and Rievaulx Abbeys and Castle Howard of Brideshead Revisited fame. Also nearby is the magnificent North York Moors National Park. Dogs by arrangement. Closed Christmas, January and February.

Our inspector loved: *The friendly and relaxed ambience in this family-run hotel.*

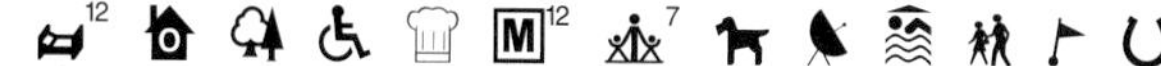

The Crown Spa Hotel

ESPLANADE, SCARBOROUGH, NORTH YORKSHIRE YO11 2AG

The resort's highest rated AA 3-star, The Crown Spa Hotel has long been a bold architectural feature of Scarborough with its commanding position overlooking South Bay beach, the Spa, and the old castle, surrounded by the colourful Esplanade gardens. Since 1845 the hotel has built a solid reputation based on its devotion to quality cuisine and service, with a highly trained and motivated team and a level of comfort that the most discerning traveller expects. Accommodation includes en-suite bedrooms, feature rooms with balconies as well as a luxurious suite with panoramic sea views. Wireless broadband is available throughout, and for business guests a dedicated service is on-hand to ensure events run smoothly. A number of well-equipped conference rooms can cater for exclusive meetings of 5 or 6 people or a full conference for up to 250 delegates. Each restaurant and bar has its own character and style, including the opulent ambience of the "Jewels restaurant" with its international menu served in relaxed, informal surroundings. The hotel's award-winning Crown Spa health club offers fitness, aqua and retreat suites, an indoor pool and hydrotherapy pool together with a sauna, air-conditioned solarium and a well-stocked sports shop. The hotel operates a no-smoking policy throughout except when guests are attending a private event in a function suite.

Our inspector loved: *The lovely views over the South Bay of Scarborough.*

Directions: Take the A64 into Scarborough and at the T -junction outside the Railway Station turn right onto the A165 over the Valley Bridge and follow the signs for South Cliff and on to Belmont Road which leads to the Esplanade.

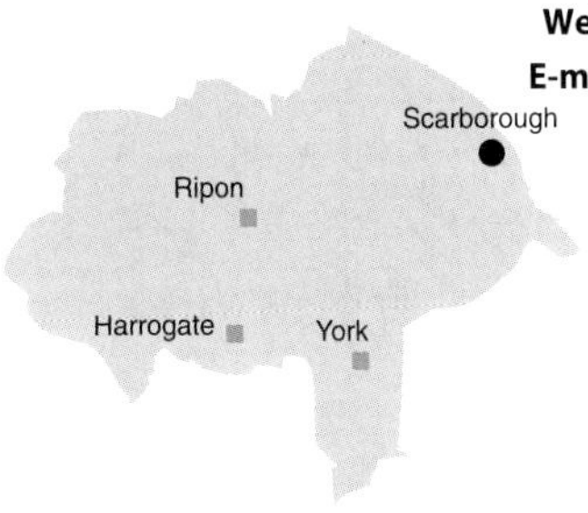

Scarborough
Ripon
Harrogate
York

Web: www.johansens.com/crownspahotel
E-mail: info@crownhotelscarborough.co.uk
Tel: 0870 381 8550
International: +44 (0)1723 357400
Fax: 01723 357404

Price Guide:
single £85
double £130–£190
suite £250

The Royal Hotel

ST NICHOLAS STREET, SCARBOROUGH, NORTH YORKSHIRE YO11 2HE

The AA and RAC 3 Star Royal Hotel has had a long and colourful history since its construction during the peak of Regency elegance in the 1830s, and remains a centrepiece overlooking the South Bay in England's oldest resort town. Many illustrious guests have passed through its doors including Winston Churchill, Charles Laughton and the playwright Alan Ayckbourn, all of whom have suites named after them. Offering a wide range of comfortable contemporary accommodation, en-suite rooms combine the modern and traditional and some have wonderful views over the harbour and the bay. A varied table d'hôte menu, with à la carte options, is served in the grand setting of the Sea View Restaurant, whilst traditional teas and light refreshments are on offer in the extensive lounges and Theatre Bar. A new continental-style café, Café Bliss, means visitors can enjoy a selection of delicacies indoors or al fresco. Once a spa town, Scarborough is close to the North Yorkshire Moors National Park and provides an excellent base for touring the local area, as well as enjoying its own features such as the Victorian Spa Complex.

Our inspector loved: *The original Regency Atrium with its elegant main staircase.*

Directions: From the A1/M1 take A64, continue to the town on Seamer Road. Turn onto Falsgrave towards the town centre. Turn right at the railway station then left at traffic lights and roundabout. The hotel is before the Town Hall.

Web: www.johansens.com/royalscarborough
E-mail: royalhotel@englishrosehotels.co.uk
Tel: 0870 381 9277
International: +44 (0)1723 364333
Fax: 01723 371780

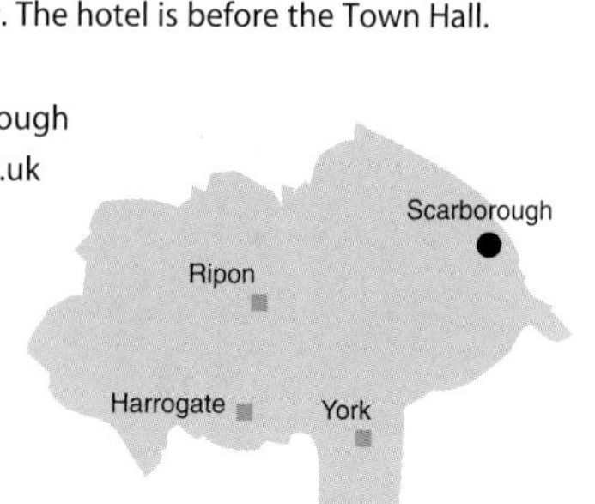

Price Guide:
single from £79
double £140-£199
suite £225-£350

HACKNESS GRANGE

NORTH YORK MOORS NATIONAL PARK, SCARBOROUGH, NORTH YORKSHIRE YO13 0JW

The attractive Georgian Hackness Grange country house lies at the heart of the dramatic North York Moors National Park – miles of glorious countryside with rolling moorland and forests. Set in acres of private grounds, overlooking a tranquil lake, home to many species of wildlife, Hackness Grange is a haven of peace and quiet for guests. The bedrooms are situated in the main house, the courtyard and in the gardens. Whilst the attractive Derwent Restaurant offers a lovely setting for lunch and dinner and you can enjoy creatively prepared cuisine accompanied by wide choice of international wines. For leisure activities, guests can enjoy 9-hole pitch 'n' putt golf, tennis and an indoor heated swimming pool. Hackness Grange is an ideal meeting location for companies wishing to have exclusive use of the hotel for VIP gatherings. It is well positioned for exploring the delights of North Yorkshire; Great Ayton - where Captain Cook first worked as a farm labourer,Goathland with its spectacular waterfalls and Castle Howard the unmistakable setting for "Brideshead Revisited".

Our inspector loved: *The setting and tranquility.*

Directions: Take A64 York road until left turn to Seamer on to B1261, through to East Ayton and Hackness.

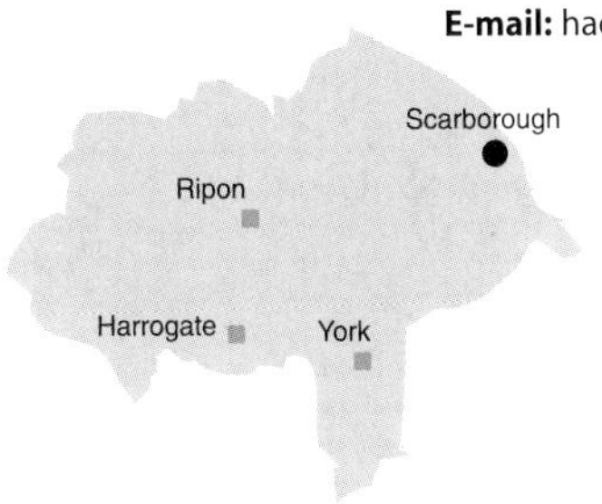

Web: www.johansens.com/hacknessgrange
E-mail: hacknessgrange@englishrosehotels.co.uk
Tel: 0870 381 8578
International: +44 (0)1723 882345
Fax: 01723 882391

Scarborough
Ripon
Harrogate
York

Price Guide:
single from £80
double/twin £135–£180

Wrea Head Country Hotel

SCALBY, NR SCARBOROUGH, NORTH YORKSHIRE YO13 0PB

Directions: Follow the A171 north from Scarborough, past the Scalby Village, until the hotel is signposted. Follow the road past the duck pond and then turn left up the drive.

Web: www.johansens.com/wreaheadcountry
E-mail: wreahead@englishrosehotels.co.uk
Tel: 0870 381 9012
International: +44 (0)1723 378211
Fax: 01723 355936

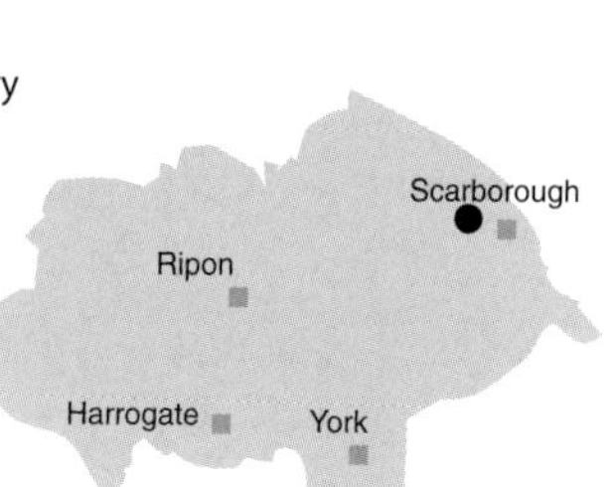

Price Guide:
single from £80
double/twin £140–£180
suite from £200

Wrea Head Country Hotel is an elegant, beautifully refurbished Victorian country house built in 1881 and situated in 14 acres of wooded and landscaped grounds on the edge of the North York Moors National Park, just 3 miles from Scarborough. The house is furnished with antiques and paintings, and the oak-panelled front hall with its inglenook fireplace with blazing log fires in the winter, is very welcoming. All the bedrooms are individually decorated, with most having delightful views of the gardens. The elegant Four Seasons Restaurant is renowned for serving the best traditional English fare using fresh local produce and has a reputation for outstanding cuisine. There are attractive meeting rooms, each with natural daylight, ideal for private board meetings and training courses requiring privacy and seclusion. Scarborough is renowned for its cricket, music and theatre. Wrea Head is a perfect location from which to explore the glorious North Yorkshire coast and country, and special English Rose breaks are offered throughout the year.

Our inspector loved: *The large collection of Pietro Annigoni paintings in the main hall.*

Judges Country House Hotel

KIRKLEVINGTON HALL, KIRKLEVINGTON, YARM, NORTH YORKSHIRE TS15 9LW

Stunningly located within 31 acres of idyllic landscaped gardens and woodlands, this gracious country house hotel is a haven of peace. Its charm and welcoming atmosphere create a sense of intimacy, whilst the warmth of the hotel's luxurious interior design makes it perfect for relaxing and unwinding from the stresses of daily life. Beautiful public rooms are elegantly decorated with opulent fabrics, and guests are surrounded by books, stunning paintings and antiques. The sumptuous bedrooms are extremely comfortable; each includes a foot spa, and a pet goldfish on display. Some guest rooms have Jacuzzi baths and each evening there is a turndown service. Attention to detail and expertly chosen décor enhance the feeling of luxury. A mouth-watering 6-course meal is served in the Conservatory Restaurant, accompanied by the finest of wines. Private dining is available, perfect for parties or the family. The hotel's location makes it ideal for exploring the North East, whilst local attractions include the historic city of Durham, various castles and museums, the races at York and Sedgefield, Croft motor racing circuit and walking in the Cleveland Hills. Various adventure activities can also be organised including horse riding, canoeing, cycling, go karting, off roading and quad biking as well as many others.

Our inspector loved: *The friendly, attentive staff and pet goldfish in every bedroom.*

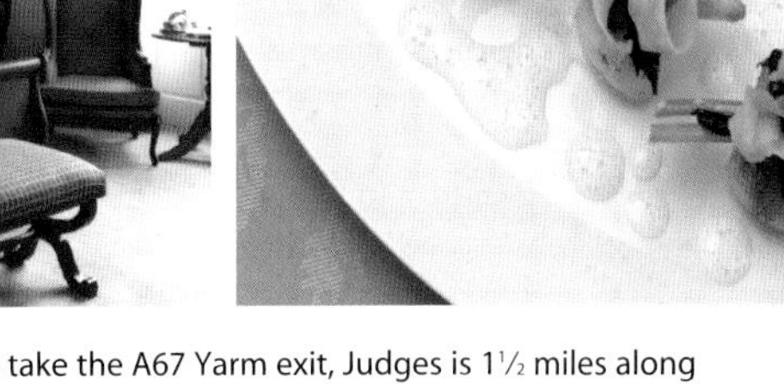

Directions: From the A19 take the A67 Yarm exit, Judges is 1½ miles along the A67 on the left after Kirklevington village.

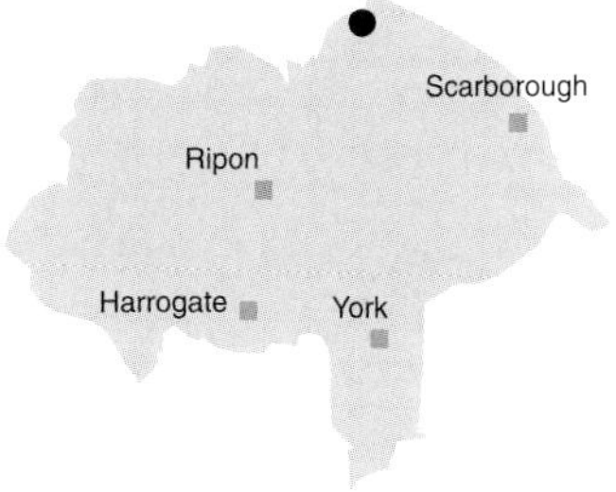

Scarborough
Ripon
Harrogate
York

Web: www.johansens.com/judges
E-mail: enquiries@judgeshotel.co.uk
Tel: 0870 381 9165
International: +44 (0)1642 789000
Fax: 01642 782878

Price Guide:
single £144–£163
double/twin £169–£189

THE GRANGE HOTEL

1 CLIFTON, YORK, NORTH YORKSHIRE YO30 6AA

Set near the ancient city walls, just a short walk from the world-famous Minster, this sophisticated Regency town house has been carefully restored and its spacious rooms richly decorated. Beautiful stone-flagged floors lead to the classically styled reception rooms. The flower-filled Morning Room is welcoming, with its deep sofas and blazing fire in the winter months. Double doors between the panelled library and drawing room can be opened up to create a dignified venue for parties, wedding receptions, meetings or business entertaining. Prints, antiques and English chintz in the bedrooms reflect the proprietor's careful attention to detail. The newly refurbished Ivy Brasserie has an established reputation for first-class gastronomy, incorporating the best in modern British and European cuisine. The Cellar Bar is open for lunch Monday to Saturday and dinner every night until after the theatre closes. For conferences, a computer and fax are available as well as secretarial services. Brimming with history, York's list of attractions includes the National Railway Museum, the Jorvik Viking Centre and the medieval Shambles.

Our inspector loved: *The stunning orchid arrangement in the York stone-paved front hall.*

Directions: The Grange Hotel is on the A19 York–Thirsk road, 400 yards from the city centre.

Web: www.johansens.com/grangeyork
E-mail: info@grangehotel.co.uk
Tel: 0870 381 8561
International: +44 (0)1904 644744
Fax: 01904 612453

Price Guide:
single £115–£180
double/twin £125–£215
suite £260

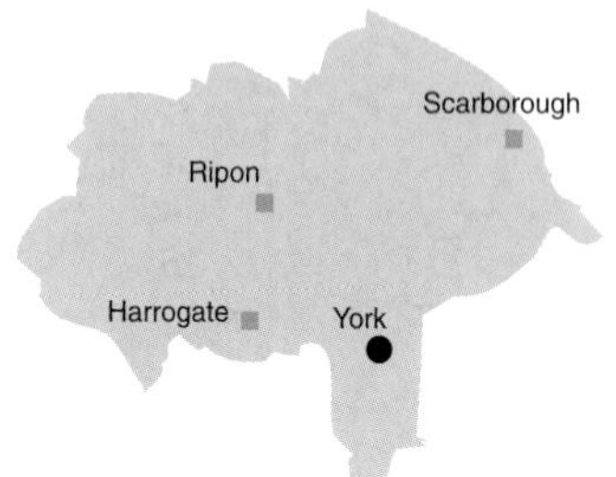

30 M 60

MIDDLETHORPE HALL HOTEL, RESTAURANT & SPA

BISHOPTHORPE ROAD, YORK, NORTH YORKSHIRE YO23 2GB

Middlethorpe Hall is a delightful William III house, built in 1699 for Thomas Barlow, a wealthy merchant and was for a time the home of Lady Mary Wortley Montagu, the 18th-century diarist. The house has been immaculately restored by Historic House Hotels, who have decorated and furnished it in its original style and elegance. There are beautifully designed bedrooms and suites in the main house and the adjacent 18th-century courtyard and a health and fitness spa with pool and treatment rooms. The restaurant, which has been awarded 3 Rosettes from the AA, offers the best in contemporary English cooking. Middlethorpe Hall, which was awarded by the York Tourism Bureau, Hotel of the Year 2005, stands in 26 acres of parkland and overlooks York Racecourse yet is only 1½ miles from the medieval city of York with its fascinating museums, restored streets and world-famous Minster. From Middlethorpe you can visit Yorkshire's famous country houses, like Castle Howard, Beningbrough and Harewood, the ruined Abbeys of Fountains and Rievaulx and explore the magnificent Yorkshire Moors. Helmsley, Whitby and Scarborough are nearby. Special breaks available.

Our inspector loved: *The Spa which is situated in the adjacent cottages and the organic walled garden.*

Directions: Take A64 (T) off A1 (T) near Tadcaster, follow signs to York West, then smaller signs to the Racecourse and Bishopthorpe. Middlethorpe is on the right before the Racecourse.

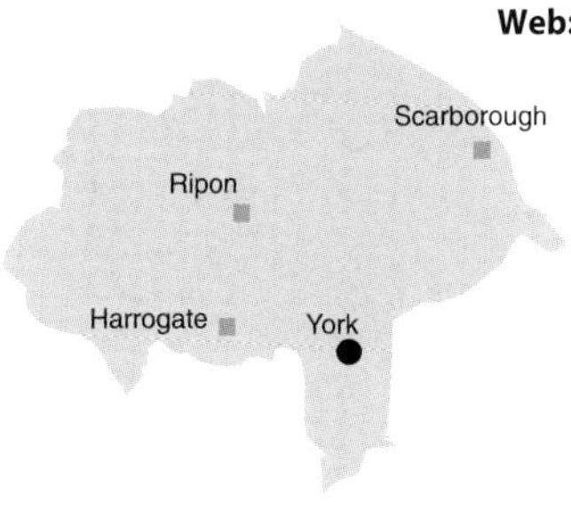

Scarborough
Ripon
Harrogate
York

Web: www.johansens.com/middlethorpehall
E-mail: info@middlethorpe.com
Tel: 0870 381 8731
International: +44 (0)1904 641241
Fax: 01904 620176

Price Guide:
single £115–£160
double/twin £180–£315
suite from £270–£400

THE WORSLEY ARMS HOTEL

HOVINGHAM, NEAR YORK, NORTH YORKSHIRE YO62 4LA

Directions: Hovingham is on the B1257, 8 miles from Malton and Helmsley. 20 minutes north of York.

Web: www.johansens.com/worsleyarms
E-mail: worsleyarms@aol.com
Tel: 0870 381 9011
International: +44 (0)1653 628234
Fax: 01653 628130

Price Guide:
single £85–£105
double/twin £115–£195

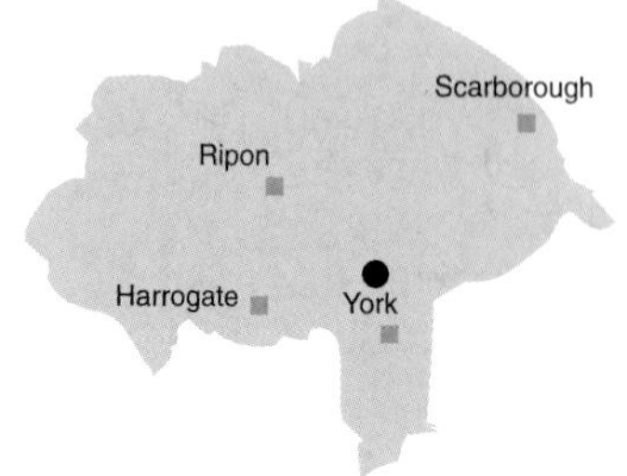

The Worsley Arms is an attractive stone-built Georgian spa hotel in the heart of Hovingham, a pleasant and unspoilt Yorkshire village with a history stretching back to Roman times. The hotel, which overlooks the village green and is set amid delightful gardens, was built in 1841 by the baronet Sir William Worsley and is now owned and personally run by Anthony and Sally Finn. Hovingham Hall, home of the Worsley family and birthplace of the Duchess of Kent, is nearby. Elegant furnishings and open fires create a welcoming atmosphere. The spacious sitting rooms are an ideal place to relax over morning coffee or afternoon tea. The award-winning restaurant offers creatively prepared dishes, including game from the estate, cooked and presented with flair. Guests can visit the wine cellar to browse or choose their wine for dinner. The Cricketers bar provides a more informal setting to enjoy modern cooking at its best. The en-suite bedrooms range in size some with views over the pretty village green. There is plenty to do nearby, including tennis, squash, jogging, golf and scenic walks along nature trails. Guests can explore the beautiful Dales, the North Yorkshire Moors and the spectacular coastline or discover the abbeys, stately homes and castles nearby. Special breaks available.

Our inspector loved: *Walking around the wine cellar choosing the wine for dinner.*

20 M 50 WiFi

Monk Fryston Hall Hotel

MONK FRYSTON, NORTH YORKSHIRE LS25 5DU

A short distance from the A1 and almost equal distance from Leeds and York, this mellow old manor house hotel, built in 1740, is ideal for tourists, business people and those looking for an invitingly secluded spot for a weekend break. The mullioned and transom windows and the family coat of arms above the doorway are reminiscent of Monk Fryston's fascinating past. The bedrooms, ranging from cosy to spacious, have private en-suite bathrooms and are appointed to a high standard. A generous menu offers a wide choice of traditional English dishes with something to suit all tastes. From the Hall, the terrace leads down to an ornamental Italian garden which overlooks a lake and is a delight to see at any time of year. Wedding receptions are held in the oak-panelled Haddon Room with its splendid Inglenook fireplace. The Rutland Room provides a convenient venue for meetings and private parties. York is 17 miles, Leeds 13 miles and Harrogate 18 miles away.

Our inspector loved: *The oak-panelled front hall and bar with open fires in the winter.*

Directions: The Hall is 3 miles off the A1, on the A63 towards Selby in the centre of Monk Fryston.

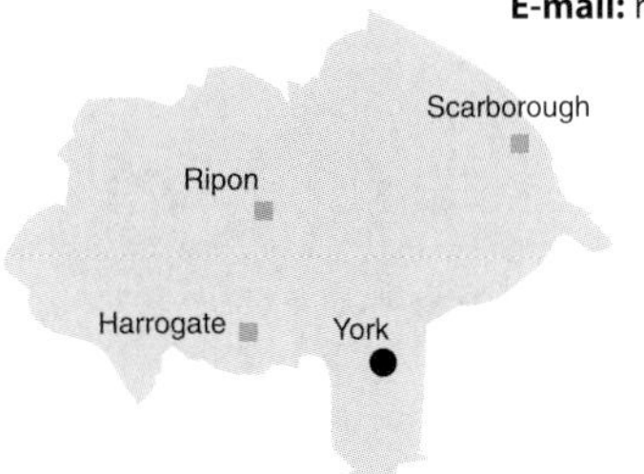

Web: www.johansens.com/monkfrystonhall
E-mail: reception@monkfrystonhallhotel.co.uk
Tel: 0870 381 8741
International: +44 (0)1977 682369
Fax: 01977 683544

Price Guide:
single £95–£165
double/twin £120–£180

Whitley Hall Hotel

ELLIOTT LANE, GRENOSIDE, SHEFFIELD, SOUTH YORKSHIRE S35 8NR

Directions: Leave M1 at junction 35, following signs for Chapeltown (A629), go down hill and turn left into Nether Lane. Go right at traffic lights, then left opposite Arundel pub, then immediately right into Whitley Lane. At fork turn right into Elliott Lane; hotel is on left.

Web: www.johansens.com/whitleyhall
E-mail: reservations@whitleyhall.com
Tel: 0870 381 8993
International: +44 (0)114 245 4444
Fax: 0114 245 5414

Price Guide:
single £70–£110
double/twin £92–£135

Whitley Hall Hotel is a 16th-century ivy clad manor house set in a secluded, wooded valley. Only a short distance from the city of Sheffield, and a 10-minute drive from the M1, Whitley Hall Hotel provides extreme comfort throughout. The sweeping split staircase leads to recently refurbished en-suite bedrooms, individually designed to a very high standard. The restaurant offers an extensive menu of exquisitely cooked food using fresh local produce, offering a table d'hôte and à la carte menus both at lunchtime and in the evening. With its open fires and oak panelling the bar and lounge offer a tranquil relaxing atmosphere to enjoy a glass of wine or other extensive range of beverages. Or step outside and stroll around the 20 acres of land in which Whitley Hall Estate lies, with its ornamental lakes, rolling lawns and mature woodland. Whitley Hall Hotel has its own civil licence and is the perfect setting for weddings and other special occasions large or small conference facilities are also available. Close to the Peak District National Park, Whitley Hall Hotel is an ideal centre from which to explore this fascinating area. Chatsworth House, Hardwick Hall, Bolsover Castle and Haddon Hall are all within easy reach. Special rates are available.

Our inspector loved: *The peacocks fanning their tails in the garden.*

Holdsworth House Hotel & Restaurant

HOLDSWORTH, HALIFAX, WEST YORKSHIRE HX2 9TG

Holdsworth House is a beautiful grade II Jacobean manor house, 3 miles north of Halifax in the heart of Yorkshire's West Riding. Built in 1633, it was acquired by the Pearson family over 40 years ago. With care, skill and professionalism they have created a hotel and restaurant of considerable repute. The interior, with its polished oak panelling and open fireplaces, has been carefully preserved and embellished with fine antiques and paintings. The comfortable lounge opens onto a pretty courtyard and overlooks the parterre and gazebo. The restaurant, with its 2 AA Rosettes, comprises 3 beautifully furnished rooms, ideal for private dinner parties. Exciting modern English and continental cuisine is meticulously prepared and presented using local produce, complemented by a thoughtfully compiled wine list. Each cosy bedroom has its own style, from the split-level suites to the interconnecting rooms for families. This is the perfect base from which to explore the Pennines, the Yorkshire Dales and Haworth, home of the Brontë family. Weekend breaks available.

Our inspector loved: *The cosy, oak-panelled, award-winning restaurant.*

Directions: From M1 Jct42 take M62 west to Jct26. Follow A58 to Halifax (ignore signs to town centre). At Burdock Way roundabout take A629 to Keighley; after 1½ miles go right into Shay Lane; hotel is a mile on right.

Web: www.johansens.com/holdsworthhouse
E-mail: info@holdsworthhouse.co.uk
Tel: 0870 381 8603
International: +44 (0)1422 240024
Fax: 01422 245174

Price Guide:
single £97.50–£155
double/twin £120 –£190
suite £155–£190

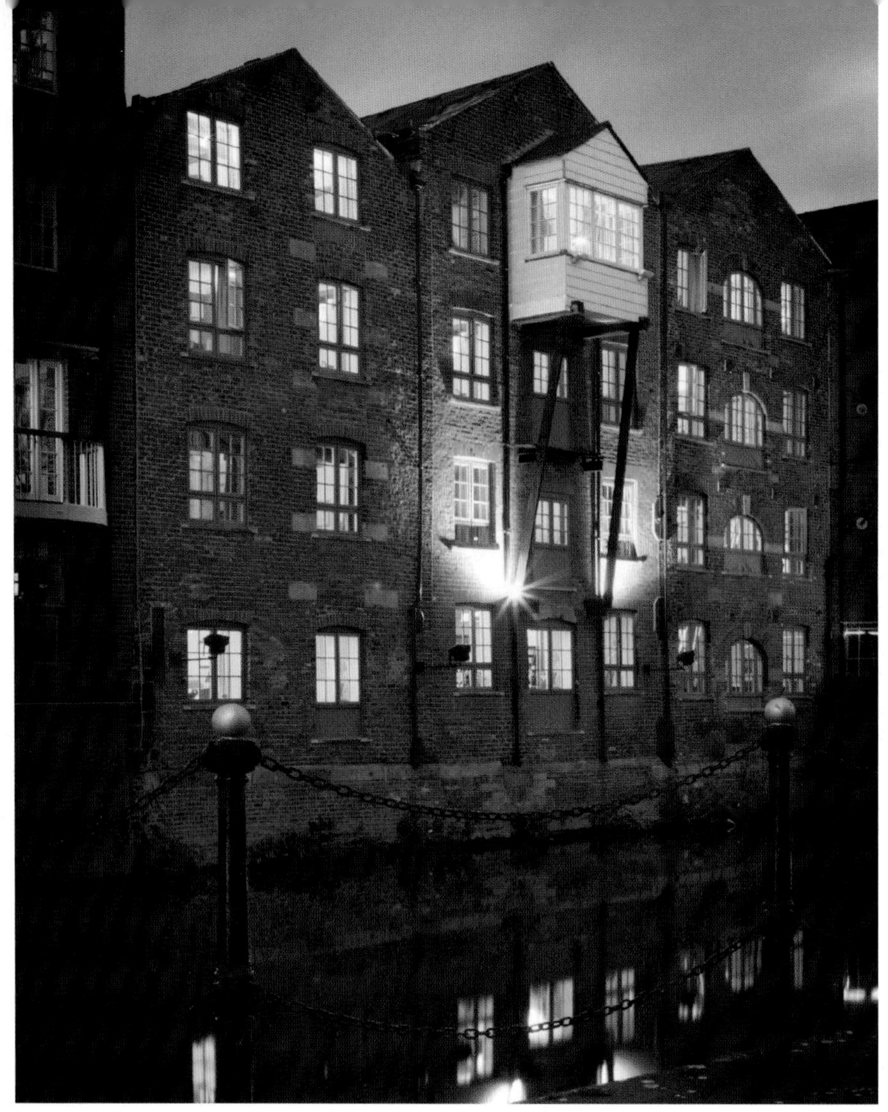

42 The Calls

42 THE CALLS, LEEDS, WEST YORKSHIRE LS2 7EW

Directions: M621, jct 3. Follow City Centre and West Yorkshire Playhouse signs then turn left after Tetley's Brewery then left again onto the City Centre Loop, following City signs. Take jct 15 and The Calls is immediately ahead.

Web: www.johansens.com/42thecalls
E-mail: hotel@42thecalls.co.uk
Tel: 0870 381 8737
International: +44 (0)113 244 0099
Fax: 0113 234 4100

Price Guide:
single £124–£194
double/twin £148–£255
suite from £220

42 the Calls is a remarkable, award-winning hotel situated in the heart of Leeds, alongside the river. Originally a corn mill, this unique hotel takes advantage of many of the original features of the mill, incorporating impressive beams, girders and old machinery into the décor. Each of the 41 bedrooms is imaginatively decorated in an individual style using beautiful fabrics and expert interior design to create a wonderful sense of harmony. Handmade beds and armchairs, a plethora of eastern rugs and extremely lavish bathrooms enhance the feeling of comfort and luxury including interactive plasma television screens. There is an excellent choice of restaurants in the vicinity, including the stylish Brasserie 44, located next door. The hotel does offer round the clock room service or guests may dine in some of of the city's restaurants and simply sign their lunch or dinner to their hotel bill. Shops, offices, galleries and theatres are all within a few minutes' walk from the hotel.

Our inspector loved: *The innovative design of the hotel and the privacy hatches for room service.*

41 M 75

Channel Islands

Recommendations in the Channel Islands appear on pages 258-260

For further information on the Channel Islands, please contact:

Visit Guernsey
PO Box 23, St Peter Port, Guernsey GY1 3AN
Tel: +44 (0)1481 723552
Internet: www.visitguernsey.com

Jersey Tourism
Liberation Square, St Helier, Jersey JE1 1BB
Tel: +44 (0)1534 500777
Internet: www.jersey.com

Sark Tourism
The Visitors Centre, The Avenue, Sark, GY9 0SA
Tel: +44 (0)1481 832345
Internet: www.sark.info

Herm Tourist Office
The White House Hotel, Herm Island via Guernsey GY1 3HR
Tel: +44 (0)1481 722377
Internet: www.herm-island.com

or see **pages 328-330** for details of
local attractions to visit during your stay.

Images from www.britainonview.com

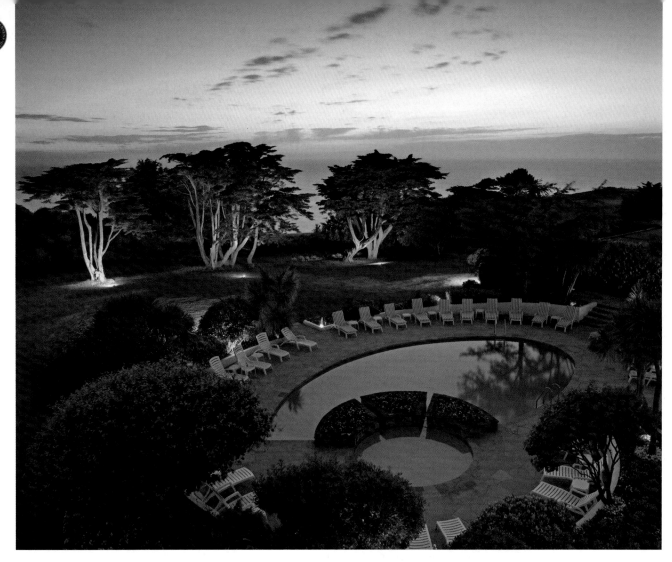

The Atlantic Hotel and Ocean Restaurant

LE MONT DE LA PULENTE, ST BRELADE, JERSEY, CHANNEL ISLANDS JE3 8HE

This is a stunning luxury hotel that offers elegance, grace, comfort, exquisite cuisine and impeccable service. It is excellent in every way, from majestic interior pillars and magnificent wood panelling to sumptuous furnishings, warm décor and perfect location. The Atlantic stands regally in 3 acres of private grounds alongside La Moye Golf Course overlooking the 5-mile sweep of St Ouen's Bay. A multi-million pound refurbishment of the hotel including the enlargement of bedrooms and remodelling of the building's exterior to give a marine flavour, has resulted in even more venue quality and the hotel's elevation to 5-Sun status by Jersey Tourism. No expense has been spared in refurbishing the bedrooms, suites and garden studios. Tastefully decorated, they offer occupants the highest standard of facilities and comfort together with splendid views of the sea or the golf course. Most prestigious and stylish is the spacious Atlantic Suite with its own entrance hall, living room, guest cloakroom and service pantry in addition to the en suite master bedroom. The delightful, award-winning restaurant overlooks the open-air swimming pool and sun terrace. Excellent and imaginative menus showcase the Modern British cuisine with the emphasis on seafood and fresh local produce.

Our inspector loved: *The sumptuous new look throughout with French oak floors and new furnishings.*

Directions: From the airport turn right at the roundabout towards St Brelade (B36). At the traffic lights turn right towards St Ouen's Bay (A13) then right into La Rue de la Sergente (B35). Look out for the hotel sign on your right.

Web: www.johansens.com/atlantic
E-mail: info@theatlantichotel.com
Tel: 0870 381 8330
International: +44 (0)1534 744101
Fax: 01534 744102

Price Guide:
single £145–£185
double/twin £190–£310
suite £350–£550

THE CLUB HOTEL AND SPA

GREEN STREET, ST HELIER, JERSEY, CHANNEL ISLANDS JE2 4UH

The island of St Helier is a breathtaking retreat, dominated by long sandy beaches and intimate bays, and the young Club Hotel and Spa embraces its relationship with these beautiful surroundings. Designed with a contemporary elegance and sense of understated luxury, the serene and tranquil ambience is reflected by the gentle tidal coastline. There are 38 guest rooms and 8 suites; each is furnished to an exceptionally high standard and equipped with the very latest LCD TVs and CD players, whilst the bathrooms have granite surfaces with power showers and sumptuous bathrobes. The Bohemia Restaurant is rapidly gaining an excellent reputation, and has recently been awarded a Michelin Star and 4 AA Rosettes. Fronted by a chic and popular bar, there is a sophisticated atmosphere that complements the fine dining and impeccable, unobtrusive service. The exclusive Club Spa offers an exceptional variety of treatments that are marine-based and harvested in the local gulf of St Malo. Guests are encouraged to savour a slower pace and maximise the benefits of the treatments on offer, as well as enjoying the salt water pool, Rasul Room, salt cabin and herbal steam room. Invigorated and refreshed, guests may wish to explore the island, and abundance of activities such as diving, surfing and sailing. Alternatively, there are numerous beautiful countryside walks.

Our inspector loved: *This superb hotel with its outstanding restaurant.*

 46   30         SPA

Directions: On leaving the airport join the B36 heading for St Helier. At roundabout join the A12 to St Helier then onto A1 for approximately 3½ miles. Continue through the traffic lights towards and into the tunnel. On exiting the tunnel take the second left into Green Street. The hotels is 100 yards on the left.

Web: www.johansens.com/theclubjersey
E-mail: reservations@theclubjersey.com
Tel: 0870 381 8313
International: +44 (0)1534 876500
Fax: 01534 720371

Price Guide:
double/twin from £195
suite from £325

LONGUEVILLE MANOR

ST SAVIOUR, JERSEY, CHANNEL ISLANDS JE2 7WF

Oozing character and charm, this restored 13th-century Norman manor house stands at the foot of a 15-acre wooded valley. The peaceful gardens feature a Victorian greenhouse filled with budding flowers, and vegetable walled gardens. Upon arrival, each room and suite welcomes guests with champagne and homemade shortbread biscuits. Each is individually styled and contains beautiful fabrics, carefully chosen antiques, digital widescreen TVs and DVD/CD players, and are decorated in warm colour schemes. Ground floor bedrooms have private patios that lead out to the gardens and the secluded honeymoon suite contains a four-poster, a dressing room and hand-painted bath for two. Alternatively, there is the private two-bedroomed Cottage, which is located within the grounds and is a self-contained unit with a small kitchen, sitting room and dining room. Boasting many awards for its food and service the Oak Room offers fine dining at its best and an extensive cellar of Old and New wines, which can be chosen with the aid of the Master Sommelier. The Garden Room serves light lunch options and afternoon tea may be enjoyed in the drawing room. The Oak Room is also licensed to hold civil wedding ceremonies and with the beautiful setting of pretty gardens and lake, Longueville Manor is an idyllic wedding location.

Our inspector loved: *The outstanding quality of timeless excellence.*

Directions: On the A3, 1 mile from St Helier.

Web: www.johansens.com/longuevillemanor
E-mail: info@longuevillemanor.com
Tel: 0870 381 8436
International: +44 (0)1534 725501
Fax: 01534 731613

Price Guide:
single from £175
double/twin £230–£480
suite £500–£800

GREGANS CASTLE

BALLYVAUGHAN, CO CLARE, IRELAND

This wonderful, family-run hotel dates back to the 1600s, and today owners Simon and Frederieke Haden welcome guests into its warm, comfortable atmosphere. Careful attention to detail is very much in evidence, from the blazing turf fires to the antique furniture, and the collection of Raymond Piper paintings of local flora. Each of the bedrooms and suites is individually decorated in a relaxing country house style, and public rooms such as the Corkscrew Room and Drawing Room offer conducive areas for enjoying a book, board game or apéritif before dinner. The bay views from the dining room are stunning, and in summer a beautiful light is created by the rays of the setting sun travelling across Galway Bay and striking the limestone mountains. Burren lamb and beef and fresh Atlantic fish appear on the menu daily. Local organic produce is used when available. The Burren is a unique terrain, and provides a home to many rare and rich Alpine and Arctic flowers. Nearby country roads are ideal for cycling and horse riding, whilst beaches and hills are simply waiting to be walked upon. Many golf courses including Lahinch and Doonbeg GC are within easy reach. Only 1 hour from Shannon Airport.

Our inspector loved: *The view over to Ballyvaughan Bay.*

Directions: From Shannon airport take the N18 to Ennis, then N85 to "Fountain Cross" then R476 and R480 to Gregans. From Galway take N18, then N67 to Ballyvaughan. Follow the N67 out of the village and Gregans Castle can be found on the left approx 3 miles away.

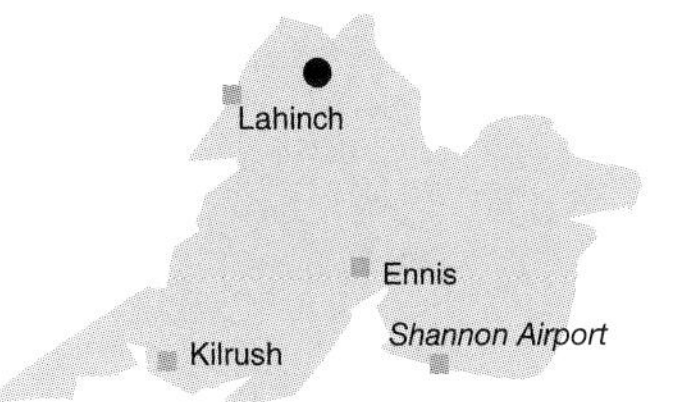

Web: www.johansens.com/gregans
E-mail: stay@gregans.ie
Tel: 00 353 65 7077005
Fax: 00 353 65 7077111

Price Guide: (Euro)
single from €150
double/twin from €190
suite from €295

21 25

LONGUEVILLE HOUSE & PRESIDENTS' RESTAURANT

MALLOW, CO CORK, IRELAND

Directions: Longueville House is 3 miles west of Mallow on the N72 to Killarney. Take the Ballclough junction on the right-hand side and the hotel entrance is 100 yards on the left.

Web: www.johansens.com/longuevillehouse
E-mail: info@longuevillehouse.ie
Tel: 00 353 22 47156
Fax: 00 353 22 47459

Price Guide: (Euro)
single from €110
double/twin from €235

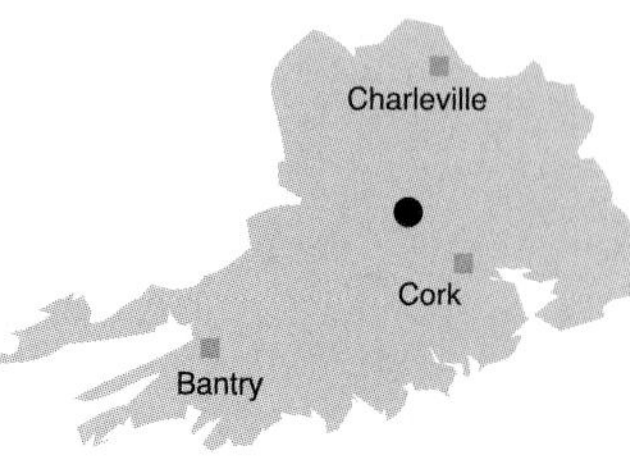

Longueville House is a listed Heritage Georgian manor, built circa1720 and set amidst 500 acres of wooded estate in the heart of Blackwater Valley. Its authentic architectural features and superbly appointed suites and guest rooms offer peaceful sanctuary and a taste of Ireland from the early part of the 18th century. Within the timeless elegance of the Presidents' Restaurant, the finest contemporary French and Irish cuisine is served. The hotel is virtually self-sufficient - a tradition that has remained largely unaltered for almost 300 years - by using fresh produce from the estate's farm, gardens and river, which are expertly prepared and presented under the expert eye of chef and host William O'Callaghan. There is an extensive wine list, with choices from the Old and New Worlds. A "residential" wedding service, in the style of a private house party, can be arranged, including accommodation for guests, a full Irish breakfast and dinner served in the recently restored Victorian conservatory. Consultations and details can be organised by appointment. Personalised corporate events can also be catered for. Amenities on the estate include fly-fishing, winter game and clay pigeon shooting, and Cork Racecourse is just over a kilometre away.

Our inspector loved: *The tranquil atmosphere created by the O'Callaghan family.*

Harvey's Point

LOUGH ESKE, DONEGAL TOWN, CO DONEGAL, IRELAND

Nestling on the edge of Lough Eske against the backdrop of the beautiful Blue Stack Mountains, this is a serene idyll where guests come to unwind and rejuvenate. The architecture blends perfectly with the magnificent surroundings, and opulent accommodation, every modern convenience as well as fresh air and breathtaking scenery are guaranteed. Peaceful, airy bedrooms are elegantly decorated with pure relaxation in mind. There are 4 categories available providing unparalleled luxury: Executive, Deluxe, Premium and Penthouse. An Executive room features a 42-inch plasma screen, separate foyer, lobby and mini-bar, whilst Penthouse Suites each comprise 160m^2 with a living room, lounge, dressing room, bar area, bath jet pool and mini-plasma in the bathroom. Renowned for its superb cuisine, the restaurant is a recipient of the prestigious AA 2 Rosette Award and the RAC Blue Ribbon Award for Excellence. Delicious French dishes are wonderfully imaginative and served with an impressive list of international wines with the finest vintages. The bar is ideal for enjoying a quiet drink whilst the resident pianist enhances the soothing ambience. Donegal is a charming old town with magnificent examples of ancient architecture, stunning gardens, golf courses and arts. Enjoy an energetic hill-walking holiday or merely relax and enjoy the surroundings.

Our inspector loved: *This piece of Switzerland in Ireland.*

Directions: From Donegal Town, take the first left on Killybegs Road at the signpost for Lough Eske and Harvey's Point. Continue for 6km and the hotel is then well signposted at each junction.

Letterkenny

Donegal

Web: www.johansens.com/harveyspoint
E-mail: info@harveyspoint.com
Tel: 00 353 74 972 2208
Fax: 00 353 74 972 2352

Price Guide: (Euro)
single €240
double/twin €290
suite €500

 60      200     

RATHMULLAN HOUSE

RATHMULLAN, LETTERKENNY, CO DONEGAL, IRELAND

Delightfully situated above the shores of peaceful Lough Swilly this attractive former manor is a sanctuary of comfort and relaxation, and an ideal base for exploring the wild and beautiful county of Donegal. Built as a summer house for a Belfast banking family in the 1800s and excellently run as a country hotel by the Wheeler family since 1963, Rathmullan House has all the charm, graciousness and good taste of the 19th-century era. Prize-winning, tree-shaded gardens, leading to a clean sandy beach, provide total serenity and the opportunity to breath fresh Irish air whilst absorbing the dramatic surrounding scenery making this an ideal venue for weddings and small conferences. Inside are 3 elegant sitting-rooms with tall ceilings, marble fireplaces, deep and soft sofas and chairs, fine antiques, oil paintings and overflowing bookcases. The bedrooms vary in décor and facilities, ranging from simple garret rooms for families to luxurious superior rooms with balconies overlooking the garden and Lough Swilly. The dining room, with unusual tented ceiling, is renowned for good food and generous, award-winning breakfasts. Leisure facilities include an indoor heated swimming pool and steam rooms, 2 all-weather tennis courts and a croquet lawn. Nearby are 4 challenging golf courses, deep sea and wreck fishing, boat trips, sailing, horse riding, mountain climbing and miles of beaches to stroll along.

Our inspector loved: *The warmth of welcome at this family run hotel.*

Directions: From Dublin take the N2 and A5. From Belfast take the A6. Drive to Letterkenny and take the road to Ramelton. At the bridge in Ramelton turn right towards Rathmullan. Go through the village and head north. The entrance to the hotel is just beyond the chapel on the right hand side.

Web: www.johansens.com/rathmullanhouse
E-mail: info@rathmullanhouse.com
Tel: 00 353 74 915 8188
Fax: 00 353 74 915 8200

Price Guide: (Euro)
single from €85
double/twin from €170
superior from €210

34 M 80

Merrion Hall Hotel

54-56 Merrion Road, Ballsbridge, Dublin 4

This exclusive Edwardian property is located close to the RDS Convention centre just minutes from downtown Dublin. Merrion Hall shares its neighbourhood with the world's embassies in the fashionable Ballsbridge area of Dublin City. Executive bedrooms, some with four-poster suites, offer air conditioning, whirlpool spas and all the modern comforts expected by the discerning traveller. The hotel's library stocks a fine selection of Irish and international literature, whilst afternoon teas and fine wines are served in the main drawing room. A feature of this Edwardian town house is a very special breakfast, which can be enjoyed in the conservatory, overlooking the terraced garden. There are also numerous restaurants within a short stroll of the hotel, leaving guests utterly spoilt for choice. Near to Lansdowne Road, it is linked to major tourist sites and the business district by the DART electric train. There is a direct luxury coach link to and from Dublin airport. For the corporate guests there is a boardroom, meeting rooms, business facilities and wireless internet access. Residents have complimentary parking on the grounds. The hotel can arrange golfing packages and scenic tours. A member of Ireland's Manor House Hotels

Our inspector loved: *The convenient location of this fine Edwardian house.*

Directions: From the city centre take Merrion Road; the hotel is on the left- hand side overlooking the RDS Convention Centre.

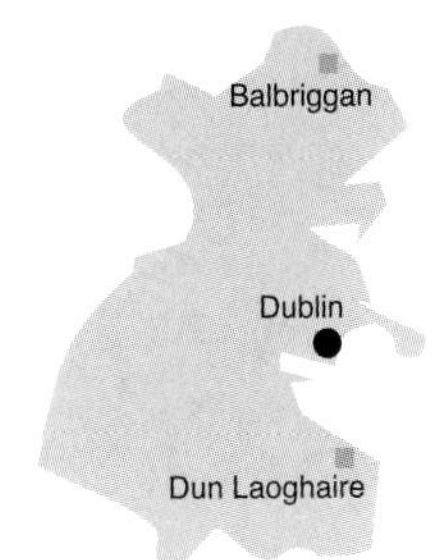

Web: www.johansens.com/merrionhall
E-mail: merrionhall@iol.ie
Tel: 00 353 1 668 1426
Fax: 00 353 1 668 4280

Price Guide: (Euro)
single €106–€139
double/twin €139–€189
de luxe €169–€249
garden suites €239–€349

The Schoolhouse Hotel

2-8 NORTHUMBERLAND ROAD, BALLSBRIDGE, DUBLIN 4

Ideally located within 10 minutes of Dublin city centre, The Schoolhouse Hotel is a refreshing venue that offers something just that little bit more memorable. Closed as a school in 1969, and opened in 1998 following a radical transformation into a modern and stylish hotel, recently refurbished great care has been taken to redesign the property to offer contemporary, luxury 21st-century accommodation with the character of an old schoolhouse in a relaxed, cheerful atmosphere. The Schoolhouse Bar is a lively and popular place for evening drinks, with the sounds of conviviality echoing into its lofty ceilings. Some of the former classrooms now house the Schoolhouse Restaurant, which is rapidly gaining a strong reputation within the city centre. It is the perfect setting for both intimate meals and more formal entertaining. Business meetings take on a new twist at The Schoolhouse: delegates may take inspiration from the learned walls surrounding them, and the proximity to the city centre provides an ideal location for both private parties and more formal conferences. The fashionable shopping area of Grafton Street is minutes walk away and the famous attractions of Trinity College, Merrion Square and St Stephen's Green are all within a stone's throw away.

Our inspector loved: *The unique atmosphere in this recently refurbished old school.*

Directions: A 10-minute walk from Dublin city centre passing Merrion square.

Web: www.johansens.com/schoolhouse
E-mail: reservations@schoolhousehotel.com
Tel: 00 353 1 667 5014
Fax: 00 353 1 667 5015

Price Guide: (Euro)
rooms from €165

Cashel House

CASHEL, CONNEMARA, CO GALWAY, IRELAND

Delightfully situated at the head of Cashel Bay on Ireland's unspoilt west coast, this gleaming white hotel, with the beautiful contrasting backdrop of green-coated Cashel Hill, is a sheltered sanctuary of peace and comfort where guests can relax, unwind and rejuvenate. Built by the owners' great, great grandfather as a family home for Captain Thomas Hazel, an English landowner, it is surrounded by 50 acres of award-winning gardens featuring exotic and exquisite flowering shrubs, secluded woodland walks and clear, tinkling streams. The very welcoming proprietors Dermot and Kay McEvilly, offer luxury, tranquillity and privacy, and nothing is too much trouble. Turf and log fires glow in public areas where the furnishings and décor are the epitome of good taste and comfort. Bedrooms and suites have everything the discerning visitor requires and overlook the hill or garden. In the dining room, Dermot and Kay oversee the preparation and serving of the appetising and imaginative dishes from the constantly changing menu. The emphasis is on local seafood, lamb, beef, game and home-grown vegetables, complemented by a carefully chosen wine list. Visitors may enjoy the hard tennis court, visit the stud farm in the grounds or take a swim in the private beach. Golf, climbing, sea, river and lake fishing can be arranged.

Directions: South off the N59. 1 mile west of Recess.

Web: www.johansens.com/cashelhouse
E-mail: info@cashel-house-hotel.com
Tel: 00 353 95 31001
Fax: 00 353 95 31077

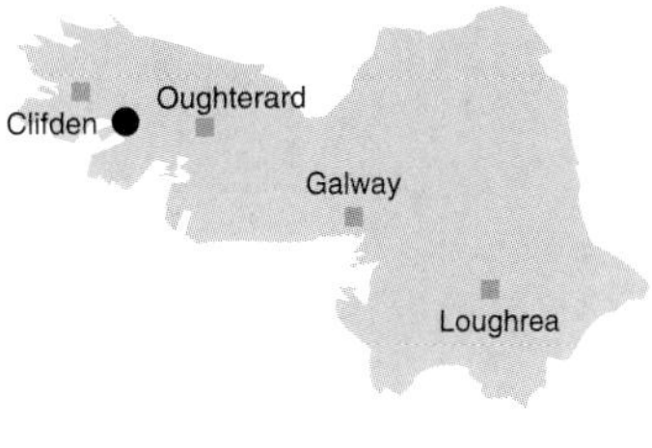

Clifden
Oughterard
Galway
Loughrea

Price Guide: (Euro)
single €85–€125
double/twin €170–€250
suite €230–€310

Our inspector loved: *The beautiful 50-acre garden.*

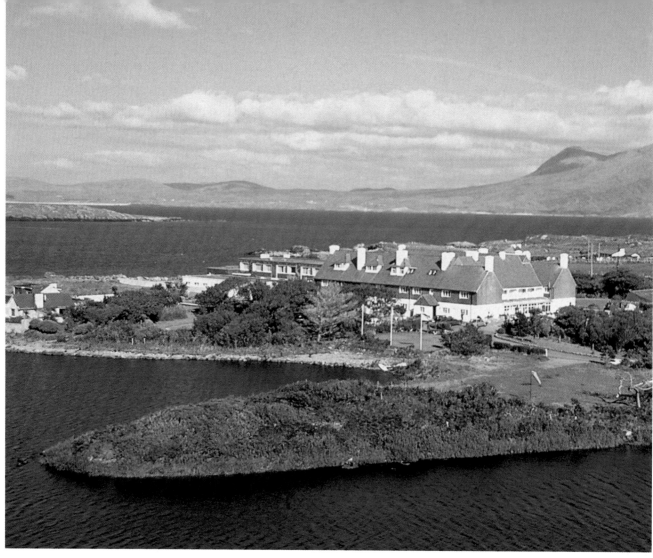

RENVYLE HOUSE HOTEL

CONNEMARA, CO GALWAY, IRELAND

Directions: On the N59 from Galway turn right at Recess, take the Letterfrack turning to Tully Cross and Renvyle is signposted.

Web: www.johansens.com/renvylehouse
E-mail: info@renvyle.com
Tel: 00 353 95 43511
Fax: 00 353 95 43515

Price Guide: (Euro)
single €40
double/twin €80

Renvyle House Hotel has occupied its rugged, romantic position on Ireland's west coast for over 4 centuries. Set between mountains and sea on the unspoilt coast of Connemara, this hardy, beautiful building with its superlative views over the surrounding countryside is just an hour's drive from Galway or Sligo. Originally constructed in 1541, Renvyle has been an established hotel for over 100 years, witnessing in that time a procession of luminaries through its doors – Augustus John, Lady Gregory, Yeats and Churchill, drawn no doubt by an atmosphere as warm and convivial then as it is today. Renvyle now welcomes visitors with turf fires glowing in public areas, wood-beamed interiors and comfortable, relaxed furnishings in the easy rooms. The bedrooms are comfortably appointed and all have been refurbished in the past 4 years. In the dining room, meals from a constantly-changing menu are served with emphasis on local fish and Renvyle lamb. In the grounds activities include tennis, croquet, riding, bowls and golf. Beyond the hotel, there are walks in the heather-clad hills, or swimming and sunbathing on empty beaches.

Our inspector loved: *The relaxed atmosphere at this family friendly hotel.*

Park Hotel Kenmare & Sámas

KENMARE, CO. KERRY, IRELAND

"Mystical," "magical," "wonderful" and "green" are some of the words one would use in relation to describing Ireland. Due to SÁMAS, a Deluxe Destination Spa at the applauded Park Hotel Kenmare, the word "holistic" can be added. Adjoining the hotel and staffed by a professional team, the Spa offers over 60 Holistic treatments combined with heat experiences and relaxation to rejuvenate body, mind and spirit. There are both male and female spas to meet individual, distinctive requirements. Retaining the character and ambience of a past era, the Park Hotel Kenmare combines elegant accommodation and superb amenities with glorious countryside views and is holder of numerous awards, including Egon Ronay and AA 'Hotel of the Year', AA Three Rosettes, RAC Gold Ribbon and Condé Nast Gold List. Bedrooms and suites are furnished in traditional style with fine antiques and objects d'art and have every modern amenity. The elegant dining room, with silver-laden sideboards and views over the terraced gardens, offers acclaimed seasonal à la carte and set dinner menus with a leaning towards local seafood. The hotel has its own 12-seat cinema, tennis and croquet. Adjacent is Kenmare Golf Club's 18-hole parkland course and within easy reach are numerous championship links courses.

Directions: The hotel is in the centre of Kenmare on the N70 or the N71, just 27 miles away from Kerry International Airport.

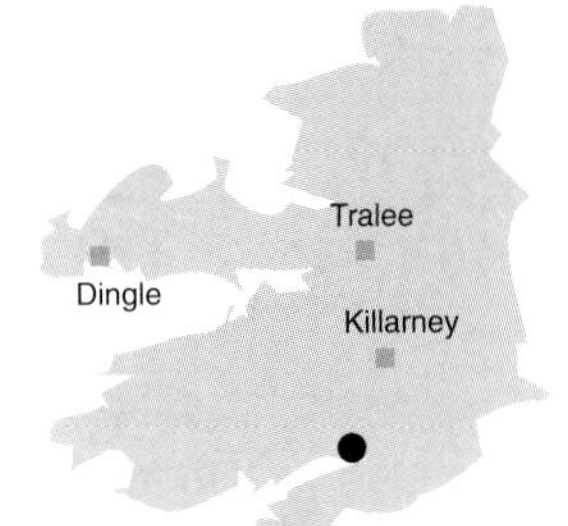

Web: www.johansens.com/parkkenmare
E-mail: info@parkkenmare.com
Tel: 00 353 64 41200
Fax: 00 353 64 41402

Price Guide: (Euro)
double €346–€806

Our inspector loved: *Feeling totally relaxed after a SÀMAS experience.*

SHEEN FALLS LODGE

KENMARE, CO. KERRY, IRELAND

Directions: From Kenmare follow N71 in the direction of Glengarrif and turn left after the Suspension Bridge. Dublin airport is about 5 hours drive away, Shannon airport is 2½ hours travelling time, Cork airport is approx 1¼ hours and Kerry airport is 50 minutes away.

Web: www.johansens.com/sheenfallslodge
E-mail: info@sheenfallslodge.ie
Tel: 00 353 64 41600
Fax: 00 353 64 41386

Price Guide: (Euro)
Deluxe Room €300–€445

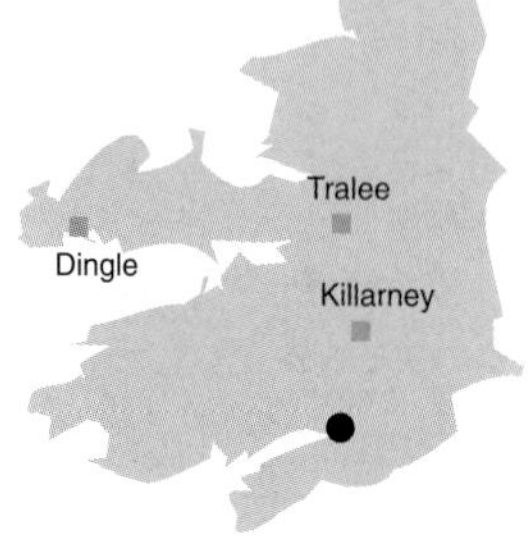

AA Hotel of the Year 2002/2003 and one of Ireland's most romantic, opulent hotels, Sheen Falls Lodge is a haven set within 300 acres of woodlands and crystal, cascading waterfalls. This gracious mansion evokes the atmosphere of a country house, and boasts spacious, luxurious bedrooms with fine linens, restful décor and magnificent views. The differing panoramas of Kenmare Bay and the Sheen waterfalls can be enjoyed from the Sun Lounge, Billiard Room and Library, which holds over 1,200 books. Log fires, sumptuous seating and attentive service complete the essence of utter relaxation. A 5-minute walk along a private avenue, winding down to the water's edge, leads to the Little Hay and Garden thatched cottages. These secluded hideaways are extremely comfortable and offer ultimate privacy. The Green cottage is ideal for families, golfing and corporate visitors; cottage guests may use the hotel's facilities. Enjoy Oscar's bistro, with its Mediterranean influenced menu or the elegant La Cascade, the hotel's signature restaurant, followed by an evening tour of the wine cellar and sample a fine port or whiskey with the sommelier. Activities on the estate include salmon and trout fishing, walking, cycling and hiking. The Health Club, with Jacuzzi and pool, provides a variety of treatments, and there are several excellent golf courses, the Beara Peninsula and the Ring of Kerry nearby.

Our inspector loved: *Sitting on the terrace watching the waterfalls.*

Cahernane House Hotel

MUCKROSS ROAD, KILLARNEY, CO KERRY, IRELAND

A shady tunnel of greenery frames the ¼-mile long drive leading to the welcoming entrance doors at this historic house, a place of peace and tranquillity where time moves at a calming, slow pace. A delightful, family-run hotel, Cahernane is the former home of the Earls of Pembroke and dates back to the 17th century. Standing in gorgeous parklands on the edge of Killarney's National Park, this is a designated area of outstanding beauty with an untamed landscape of lakes, mountains, woodland walks and gardens where giant rhododendrons and tropical plants grow in abundance. The Browne family pride themselves on their hospitality and attentive service that ensures guests enjoy the hotel's charm and grace. Each of the individually designed bedrooms and suites is elegantly furnished, tastefully decorated and has a lovely bathroom; some boast a Jacuzzi. Recipient of 2 AA Rosettes, 3 RAC Ribbons and the RAC White Ribbon, Herbert Room restaurant offers à la carte and table d'hôte menus prepared by chef Pat Karney, whilst less formal dining is enjoyed in the Cellar Bar. The Wine Cellar forms the backdrop to the Cellar Bar and stocks a comprehensive selection. A new spa and conference facility, as well as additional luxury suites, are due to open in 2006. Challenging golf courses, a variety of outdoor pursuits and national treasures such as Muckross House and Ross Castle are within easy reach.

Directions: 1 mile from the town centre on the Muckross Road.

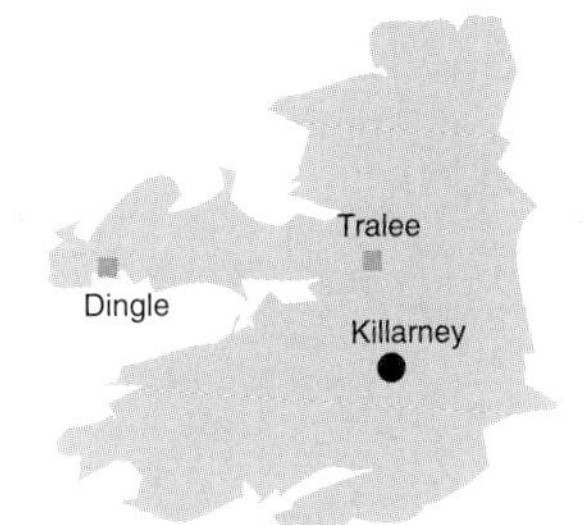

Web: www.johansens.com/cahernane
E-mail: info@cahernane.com
Tel: 00 353 64 31895
Fax: 00 353 64 34340

Price Guide: (Euro)
single €130
double €210
suite €340

Our inspector loved: *The homely feel and attention to residents' comfort.*

Parknasilla Hotel

GREAT SOUTHERN HOTEL, PARKNASILLA, CO. KERRY, IRELAND

County Kerry has an equitable climate from the warm Gulf Stream. Parknasilla is a splendid Victorian mansion surrounded by extensive parkland and subtropical gardens leading down to the seashore. New arrivals appreciate the graceful reception rooms which, like the luxurious bedrooms, look out on the mountains, across the verdant countryside or down to Kenmare Bay. Wonderful damask and chintz harmonize with the period furniture and thoughtful 'extras' have been provided. The bathrooms are lavishly appointed. George Bernard Shaw's many visits are reflected in the names of the inviting Doolittle Bar and the elegant Pygmalion Restaurant. The sophisticated menus always include fish fresh from the sea and the international wine list will please the most discerning guests. Corporate activities and private celebrations are hosted in the traditional Shaw Library or handsome Derryquin Suite. Leisure facilities abound: a private 12-hole golf course with challenging championship courses close by, horse riding, water sports, sailing, clay pigeon shooting and archery. Parknasilla has 7 recommended walks through the estate and its own boat for cruises round the coast. Indoors there is a superb pool, sauna, steam room, Jacuzzi, hot tub, hydrotherapy seaweed baths, aromatherapy and massage

Our inspector loved: *The sensitive modernisation of this Victorian favourite.*

Directions: The hotel is south west of Killarney off N70.

Web: www.johansens.com/parknasilla
E-mail: res@parknasilla-gsh.com
Tel: 00 353 1 2144800
Fax: 00 353 64 45323
UK Freephone: 0800 7316107

Price Guide: (Euro) (room only)
single/double/twin €150–€250
suite €500

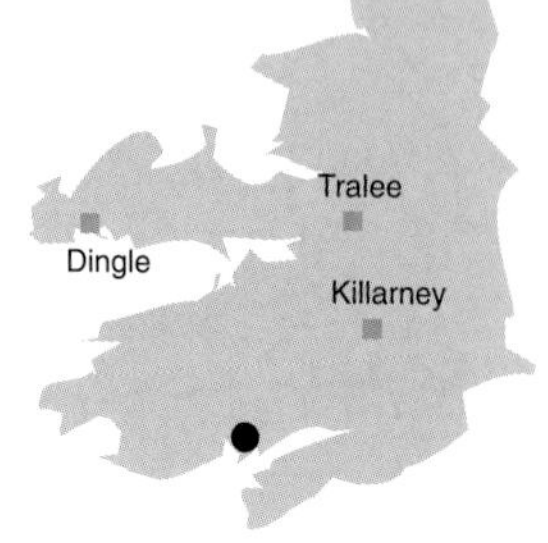

BALLYGARRY HOUSE

KILLARNEY ROAD, TRALEE, CO KERRY, IRELAND

The warmest of welcomes awaits guests at this charming hotel where the ambience is utterly peaceful, comforting and restful. This gracious country retreat, full of character, elegance and style, nestles in 6 acres of lawned gardens edged with colourful flower beds and sprinkled with mature trees at the foot of the majestic Kerry Mountains. Ballygarry House is a family-run property and owner Padraig McGillicudy does everything to help make visitors feel at home. The interior is decorated with rich warm colours, fine antiques, attractive pictures and floral displays, which extend to the glass-fronted entrance. Individually designed en-suite rooms reflect the refinement of the house combined with modern amenities and high-tech services. They are spacious, beautifully appointed and fluffy white bathrobes, luxury toiletries and antique furnishings help create an atmosphere of unhurried tranquillity. Excellent dining can be enjoyed in the sophisticated Brooks restaurant where crisp white linen, attentive service and garden views enhance the gastronomic experience. Lunch is also served in the Leebrook Lounge with al fresco menus offered in the Courtyard during warmer months. The latest addition to the hotel is Nádúr spa, which boasts a hot tub, thermal suite and a range of treatments including traditional Irish seaweed soaks to rejuvenating mud wraps.

Directions: 2 miles from the Tralee town centre on the Killarney Road.

Web: www.johansens.com/ballygarryhouse
E-mail: info@ballygarryhouse.com
Tel: 00 353 66 7123322
Fax: 00 353 66 7127630

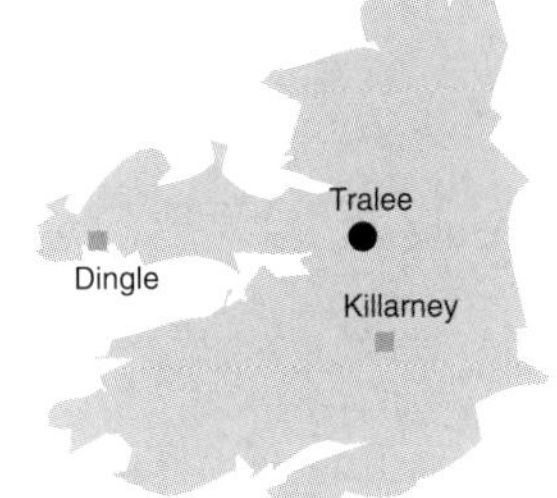

Price Guide: (Euro)
single €100–€130
double/twin €150–€210
suite €190–€350

Our inspector loved: *The individually designed spacious bedrooms.*

KILLASHEE HOUSE HOTEL & VILLA SPA

KILLASHEE, NAAS, CO KILDARE, IRELAND

Directions: 40 minutes from Dublin on the N7/M7 to Naas, then 1 mile along R448 Kilcullen Road.

Web: www.johansens.com/killashee
E-mail: reservations@killasheehouse.com
Tel: 00 353 45 879277
Fax: 00 353 45 879266

Price Guide: (Euro) (per person sharing)
single from €120
double/twin from €90
classic from €110
suites €107.50–€247.50

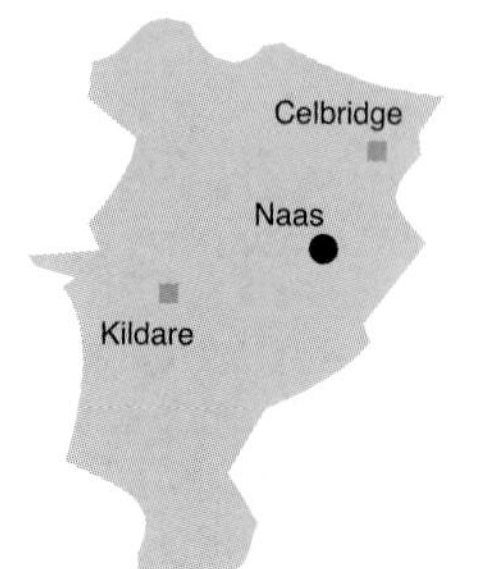

A tall, slim bell tower with steeple peak and an elaborate grey stone Jacobean-style façade, are eye-catching impressions as this prestigious hotel is approached along an elegant curved driveway. Once through the imposing arched entrance door a world of opulence, comfort and tranquillity awaits. Killashee House Hotel & Villa Spa was originally a hunting lodge built in the 1860s for an influential family named Moore, whose coat of arms is visible on the walls. It is a glorious, gracious retreat surrounded by 80 acres of gardens and parkland located 40 minutes from Dublin. Many of the individually designed bedrooms and suites have four-poster beds and stunning views over the gardens and, weather permitting, the Wicklow Mountains. Bedrooms are full of character that reflects the elegance and refinement of the Victorian period, combined with modern amenities and high-tech services expected by today's guest. Traditional Irish and Mediterranean cuisine can be enjoyed in the award-winning Turner's restaurant. For those wishing to work up an appetite or to relax prior to dining, the Country Club and Villa Spa with 25m pool and 18 luxurious treatment rooms offer the ultimate in fitness and pampering, including Elemis and Thalgo treatments. Curragh, Punchestown and Naas racecourses, and several championship golf courses are within easy reach.

Our inspector loved: *The large and luxurious new rooms.*

Mount Juliet Conrad

THOMASTOWN, CO KILKENNY, IRELAND

Mount Juliet Conrad is an architectural gem, a magnificent 18th-century Georgian mansion standing proudly on the banks of the River Nore in the heart of a lush 1,500-acre estate. The entrance doorway leads into an impressive hall featuring elaborate stucco work with bas-reliefs on walls and ceilings. A feeling of opulence pervades all reception rooms, the bars recall a glorious equestrian past whilst the homeliness of the library and drawing rooms provide comfortable venues for relaxation. Afternoon tea or a pre-dinner glass of champagne can be enjoyed in the elegant Majors Room. Jewel in the crown, however, is the exquisite Lady Helen Dining Room, famed for its original stucco plasterwork, pastoral views and superb cuisine. The 32 en-suite guest rooms are individually designed and are full of the character and charm that reflects the quiet good taste and refinement of the Georgian period. Centre of activity for guests is Hunters Yard, which is situated on the edge of a championship golf course, host to the American Express World Golf Championships in 2002 and 2004. The Hunters Yard is the epicentre of the estate's sporting and leisure life and offers stylish dining in Kendals Restaurant and 16 "Club" style rooms which offer direct access to the hotels sybaritic spa. For guests who require a greater degree of space and privacy, there are 10 lodges located beside the magnificent Rose Gardens.

Directions: 16 miles from Kilkenny on the N9 via N10.

Web: www.johansens.com/mountjuliet
E-mail: info@mountjuliet.ie
Tel: 00 353 56 777 3000
Fax: 00 353 56 777 3019

Price Guide: (Euro)
single from €150
double/twin from €230
suite €450

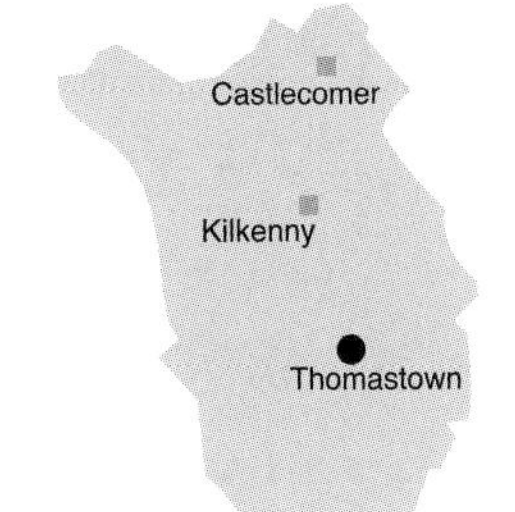

Our inspector loved: *The outstanding golf corse and sporting facilities.*

ASHFORD CASTLE

CONG, CO MAYO

Named the second best hotel in Ireland by Travel and Leisure magazine at the January 2006 World's Best Awards, the 13th-century Ashford Castle stands on the northern shores of Lough Corrib amidst acres of beautiful garden and forests. The former country estate of Lord Ardilaun and the Guinness family, it became a luxury hotel in 1939. There is a variety of restaurants: the award-winning George "V" dining room offering modern and traditional menus, and the gourmet restaurant, the Connaught Room, whose menu features the very best Irish produce in the most romantic and elegant room in the castle. Open Thursday to Sunday inclusive during the high season. The Drawing Room serves lunch, afternoon tea and more casual evening dining. A short stroll across the River Cong and guests arrive at the informal Cullen's at the Cottage, which serves a bistro-style menu where diners can choose a lobster from the tank or a light salad. Open daily from 11am to 9.30pm. Nightly entertainment is provided in the Dungeon Bar. Ashford Castle offers a range of activities including falconry, fishing on Lough Corrib at this Orvis endorsed property, clay pigeon shooting, tennis, an exclusive 9-hole golf course, health centre and treatment rooms. Boat trips can be arranged to the island on Lough Corrib.

Our inspector loved: *The stunning views across Lough Corrib.*

Directions: 30 minutes from Galway on the shore of Lough Corrib, on the left upon entering the village of Cong.

Web: www.johansens.com/ashfordcastle
E-mail: ashford@ashford.ie
Tel: 00 353 94 95 46003
Fax: 00 353 94 95 46260

Price Guide: (Euro)
single/twin/double €232–€680
stateroom/suite €617–€1130

Knockranny House Hotel & Spa

KNOCKRANNY, WESTPORT, CO MAYO, IRELAND

Approached through secluded grounds and mature gardens this impressive Victorian-style hotel and spa immediately evokes images of bygone times as it rises into view against a backdrop of Croagh Patrick Mountain, which towers over the heritage town of Westport and Clew Bay. The opulent charm of a past era coupled with a high standard of facilities has earned Knockranny a reputation as one of Ireland's finest hotels since opening in 1997. Each bedroom is elegantly furnished, warmly decorated, has every home comfort and exudes an ambience of relaxation. De luxe rooms have king-size beds and spa baths and executive suites offer four posters and lounge areas. The new guest rooms are extremely spacious and feature king-size double beds, 32" LCD TVs, Bose surround-sound systems, free broadband Internet access, oversized bathrooms and spa bath as standard. Most of the Grand De luxe rooms overlook the new courtyard whilst the Master Suites have panoramic views over Croagh Patrick, Clew Bay and Westport. Antique furniture and plush seating feature in the drawing room and foyer while the conservatory and library look out to the magnificent scenery. The restaurant is renowned for its quality, contemporary Irish cuisine and fish dishes. A vitality pool with marble columns is at the heart of Spa Salveo, which boasts a serail mud chamber and 12 treatment rooms.

Our inspector loved: *Feeling totally relaxed after a hammam massage.*

Directions: Turn left off the N60 before entering Westport town. Guests staying 2 nights or more will receive a complimentary bottle of house wine and chocolates.

Ballina
Knock Airport
Westport
Ballyhaunis
Galway

Web: www.johansens.com/knockranny
E-mail: info@khh.ie
Tel: 00 353 98 28600
Fax: 00 353 98 28611

Price Guide: (Euro)
single from €120
double/twin from €190
suite from €250

          SPA  

Nuremore Hotel and Country Club

CARRICKMACROSS, CO MONAGHAN, IRELAND

Nestling on the outskirts of Carrickmacross, Nuremore Hotel and Country Club is set in 200 acres of rolling countryside with beautifully landscaped gardens. Its wide range of facilities include a swimming pool, treatment rooms and a health club featuring a gymnasium, spa bath, sauna and steam room. The hotel's renowned 18-hole championship golf course makes superb use of the surrounding lakes and landscape and has been described as one of the most picturesque parkland courses in the country. Resident professional, Maurice Cassidy, is on hand to offer advice and tuition. All 72 bedrooms and suites are beautifully appointed to ensure a generous feeling of personal space, and guests can sample the classic European cuisine, with Irish and French influences, prepared by award-winning Chef Raymond McArdle, "Georgina Campbell's Ireland" Chef of the Year 2005. The restaurant has won Bushmill Guide's Best Ulster Restaurant 2005/06, been awarded 3 AA Rosettes in 2006, listed in Food & Wine magazine and also features in the Bridgestone Guide to Ireland's best 100 restaurants. Ideal for weddings and important meetings, the impressive conference centre constantly evolves to ensure it remains at the cutting edge for business events. Conference and syndicate rooms boast natural lighting, audio-visual equipment, air conditioning, WiFi and fax lines .

Our inspector loved: *The extensive sporting and health facilities.*

Directions: The hotel is ideally located on the main N2 between Dublin and Monaghan. Just a 45-minute drive from Dublin Airport and a 75-minute drive from Belfast.

Web: www.johansens.com/nuremore
E-mail: nuremore@eircom.net
Tel: 00 353 42 9661438
Fax: 00 353 42 9661853

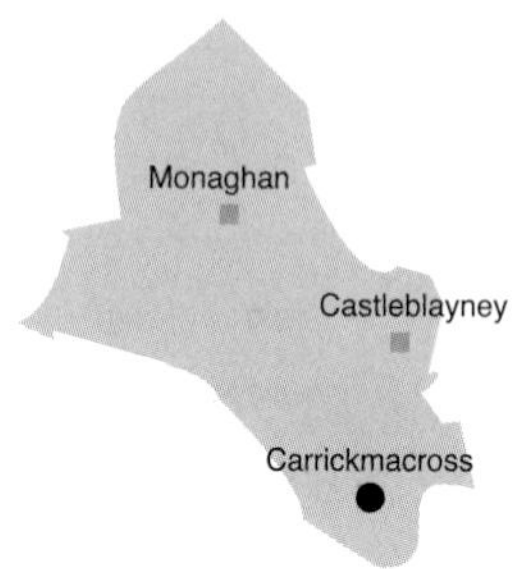

Price Guide: (Euro)
single €150–€200
double/twin €220–€280
suite from €250–€300

MARLFIELD HOUSE

GOREY, CO WEXFORD, IRELAND

Staying at the Condé Nast Johansens award-winning Marlfield House is a memorable experience. Set in 34 acres of woodland and gardens, this former residence of the Earl of Courtown preserves Regency lifestyle in all its graciousness. Built in 1820, and situated 55 miles south of Dublin, it is recognised as one of the finest country houses in Ireland and is supervised by its welcoming hosts and proprietors, Raymond and Mary Bowe and their daughters Margaret and Laura. The State Rooms have been built in a very grand style and have period fireplaces where open fires burn in cooler weather. All of the furniture is antique and the roomy beds are draped with sumptuous fabrics. The bathrooms feature highly polished marble and some have large freestanding bathtubs. There is an imposing entrance hall, luxurious drawing room and an impressive curved Richard Turner conservatory. The kitchen's gastronomic delights have received numerous awards. Located 2 miles from fine beaches and within easy reach of many golf courses including Courtown, Seafield, Woodenbridge, Druids Glen, The European Club and Coolattin, the house is central to many touring high points: Glendalough, Waterford Crystal and Powerscourt Gardens and the medieval city of Kilkenny.

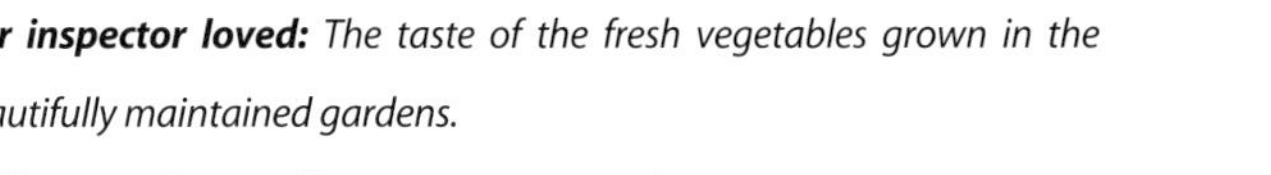

Our inspector loved: *The taste of the fresh vegetables grown in the beautifully maintained gardens.*

Directions: On the Gorey–Courtown road, just over a mile east of Gorey.

Gorey
Enniscorthy
New Ross
Wexford

Web: www.johansens.com/marlfieldhouse
E-mail: info@marlfieldhouse.ie
Tel: 00 353 53 94 21124
Fax: 00 353 53 94 21572

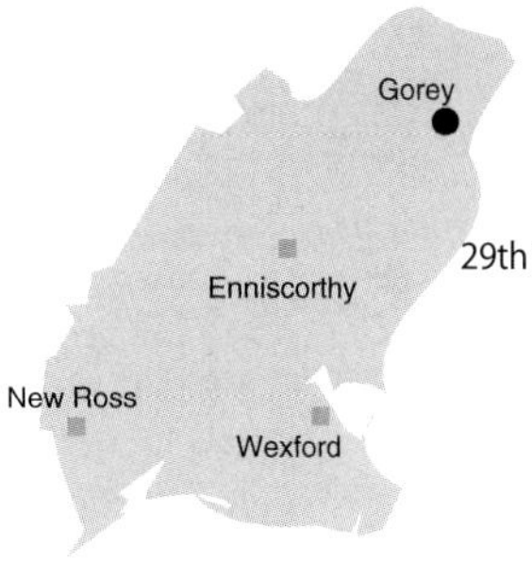

Price Guide: (Euro, closed mid-December - 29th December and 2nd January - end of January)
single from €130
double/twin from €235
state rooms from €405

Scotland

Recommendations in Scotland appear on pages 283-305

For further information on Scotland, please contact:

Visit Scotland
Ocean Point 1, 94 Ocean Drive, Edinburgh, EH6 6JH
Tel: +44 (0)131 332 2433
Internet: www.visitscotland.com

or see **pages 328-330** for details of local attractions to visit during your stay.

Images from www.britainonview.com

Darroch Learg

BRAEMAR ROAD, BALLATER, ABERDEENSHIRE AB35 5UX

4 acres of leafy grounds surround Darroch Learg, situated on the side of the rocky hill which dominates Ballater. The hotel, which was built in 1888 as a fashionable country residence, offers panoramic views over the golf course, River Dee and Balmoral Estate to the fine peaks of the Grampian Mountains. All bedrooms are individually furnished and decorated, providing modern amenities. The reception rooms at Darroch Learg are similarly elegant and welcoming having also been recently refurbished. Log fires create a particularly cosy atmosphere on chilly nights. The food is excellent having been awarded 3 AA Rosettes and the chef was awarded Hotel Chef of the Year in 2005. The wine list is also superb; being a former winner of the AA Wine List of the Year for Scotland and nominated 13th best wine list in the UK by The Top 100 UK Restaurant Wine Lists guide. The views are stunning with a wonderful outlook south over the hills of Glen Muick. The wealth of outdoor activities include walking, riding, mountain-biking, fishing, gliding and skiing as well as exclusive tours around local castles and gardens. There is also the opportunity to have a private luxury safari around nearby Balmoral Castle, the Highland residence of the British sovereign

Our inspector loved: *The personal attention of the charming owners and staff, wonderful understated food, wine and décor.*

Directions: At the western edge of Ballater on the A93.

Web: www.johansens.com/darrochlearg
E-mail: info@darrochlearg.co.uk
Tel: 0870 381 8477
International: +44 (0)13397 55443
Fax: 013397 55252

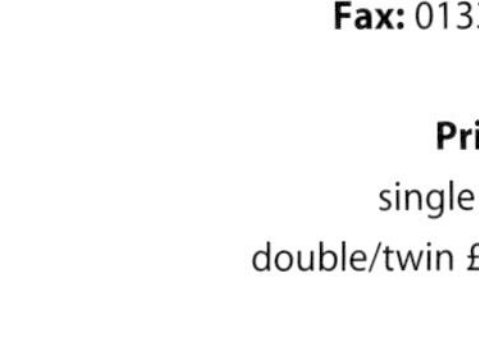

Price Guide:
single £90–£120
double/twin £140–£200

Loch Melfort Hotel & Restaurant

ARDUAINE, BY OBAN, ARGYLL PA34 4XG

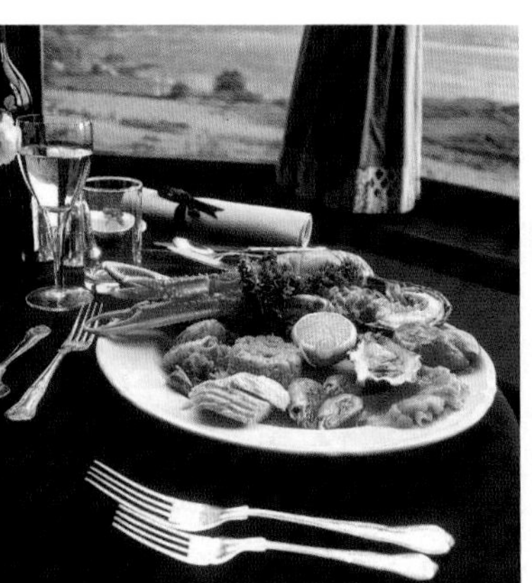

Directions: From Oban take the A816 south for 19 miles. From Loch Lomond area follow A82 then A83, finally A816 north to Arduaine.

Web: www.johansens.com/lochmelfort
E-mail: reception@lochmelfort.co.uk
Tel: 0870 381 8699
International: +44 (0)1852 200233
Fax: 01852 200214

Price Guide: (including dinner)
double/twin £118-£178
superior £138–£218

Spectacularly located on the west coast of Scotland, the Loch Melfort Hotel is a quiet hideaway on Asknish Bay, with the awe-inspiring backdrop of woodlands and the magnificent mountains of Argyll. Friendly staff attend to every need and there is a warm, welcoming atmosphere. Spacious bedrooms are lavishly appointed with bold bright fabrics, comfortable furnishings and have large patio windows overlooking the islands of Jura, Shuna and Scarba. The award-winning restaurant, which has breathtaking views stretching as far as the eye can see, is perfect for a romantic meal. Guests may feast on the sumptuous fresh local fish, shellfish and meat complemented by an extensive selection of fine wines. There is also a mouth-watering array of home-made desserts, delicious ice creams and Scottish cheeses. Skerry Bistro serves informal meals, lunches, suppers and afternoon teas. Outdoor activities include fishing, sailing, riding, windsurfing, walking and mountain biking. Visitors can explore the nearby islands and local places of interest include Mull, Kilchoan Castle, Castle Stalker and the stunning Dunstaffnage Castle (home of Clan Campbell). The Arduaine Gardens, situated adjacent to the hotel, are extremely beautiful and home to a diversity of plants and trees from all over the world. The Marine Sanctuary and Kilmartin Glen are well worth a visit.

***Our inspector loved:** The super views and great food.*

ARDANAISEIG

KILCHRENAN BY TAYNUILT, ARGYLL PA35 1HE

This romantic small luxury hotel, built in 1834, stands alone in a setting of almost surreal natural beauty at the foot of Ben Cruachan. Directly overlooking Loch Awe and surrounded by wild wooded gardens, Ardanaiseig is evocative of the romance and history of the Highlands. Skilful restoration has ensured that this lovely old mansion has changed little since it was built. The elegant drawing room has log fires, bowls of fresh flowers, superb antiques, handsome paintings and marvellous views of the islands in the Loch and of faraway mountains. The traditional library, sharing this outlook, is ideal for postprandial digestifs. The charming bedrooms are peaceful, appropriate to the era of the house, yet equipped thoughtfully with all comforts. True Scottish hospitality is the philosophy of the Ardanaiseig Restaurant, renowned for its inspired use of fresh produce from the Western Highlands. Chef, Gary Goldie won a gold award in the "hotelreviewscotland" 2005 awards. The wine list is magnificent. Artistic guests enjoy the famous 100-acre Ardanaiseig gardens and nature reserve, filled with exotic shrubs and trees brought back from the Himalayas over the years. Brilliant rhododendrons and azaleas add a riot of colour. The estate also offers fishing, boating, tennis and croquet (snooker in the evenings) and exhilarating hill or lochside walks.

Directions: Reaching Taynuilt on the A85, take the B845 to Kilchrenan. Turn left at Kilchronan Inn and continue to the end of the road

Web: www.johansens.com/ardanaiseig
E-mail: ardanaiseig@clara.net
Tel: 0870 381 8319
International: +44 (0)1866 833333
Fax: 01866 833222

Price Guide:
single £80–£125
double/twin £108–£276

Our inspector loved: *The feeling of complete escape and excellent food.*

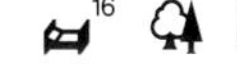        

KIRROUGHTREE HOUSE

NEWTON STEWART, WIGTOWNSHIRE DG8 6AN

Directions: From the A75 Dumfries to Stranraer road. 1 mile east of Newton Stewart turn on to the A712 towards New Galloway. The hotel entrance is 250 metres on the left.

Web: www.johansens.com/kirroughtreehouse
E-mail: info@kirroughtreehouse.co.uk
Tel: 0870 381 8659
International: +44 (0)1671 402141
Fax: 01671 402425

Price Guide:
single £90–£115
double/twin £160–£200
suite £210

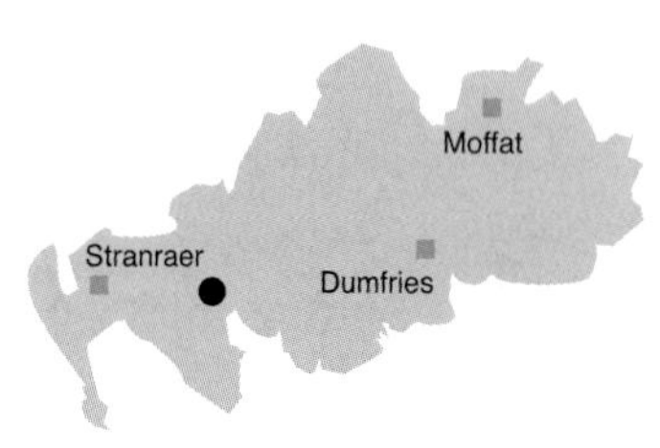

A previous winner of the Johansens Most Excellent Service Award and the Good Hotel Guide's Scottish Hotel of the Year, Kirroughtree House is situated in the foothills of the Cairnsmore of Fleet, on the edge of Galloway Forest Park. Standing in 8 acres of landscaped gardens, guests can relax and linger over the spectacular views. Built by the Heron family in 1719, the oak-panelled lounge, with open fireplace, reflects the style of that period. From the lounge rises the original staircase, where Robert Burns often recited his poems. Each bedroom is well furnished; guests may choose to spend the night in one of the hotel's spacious de luxe bedrooms with spectacular views over the surrounding countryside. Many guests are attracted by Kirroughtree's culinary reputation, awarded 2 AA rosettes – only the finest produce is used to create meals of originality and finesse. An ideal venue for small meetings, family parties and weddings; exclusive use of the hotel can be arranged. Pitch and putt and croquet can be enjoyed in the grounds and the hotel's position makes it an ideal base for great walking expeditions. Residents can play golf on the many local courses and also have use of the exclusive 18-hole course at Cally Palace. Trout and salmon fishing, shooting and deer stalking during the season can all be organised. Short breaks available.

Our inspector loved: *The classic elegance and exceptional service.*

Channings

12-16 SOUTH LEARMONTH GARDENS, EDINBURGH EH4 1EZ

Channings is located on a quiet cobbled street only 10 minutes' walk from the centre of Edinburgh, with easy access to the shops on Princes Street and the timeless grandeur of Edinburgh Castle. The hotel, formerly 5 Edwardian town houses, retains its original features, which have been restored with flair and consideration, and the atmosphere is like that of an exclusive country club. With an ambience of country-style tranquillity, guests can relax in one of the fully refurbished lounges with coffee or afternoon tea served by the friendliest of staff. For those who like to browse, the hotel has an interesting collection of antique prints, furniture, objets d'art, periodicals and books. The atmosphere is perfect for discreet company meetings, small conferences and private or corporate events, which may be held. These may take place in the oak-panelled Library or Kingsleigh. The restaurant offers a varied eating experience. Hubert Lamort Head Chef, has developed an impressive repertoire of Mediterranean inspired dishes. His sound product knowledge results in a colourful menu combining traditional ingredients with simplistic, modern twists.

Our inspector loved: *The location; in the heart of Edinburgh yet overlooking green grass and with the friendliest of staff.*

Directions: Go north-west from Queensferry Street, over Dean Bridge on to Queensferry Road. Take the 3rd turning on the right down South Learmonth Avenue, then turn right at the end into South Learmonth Gardens.

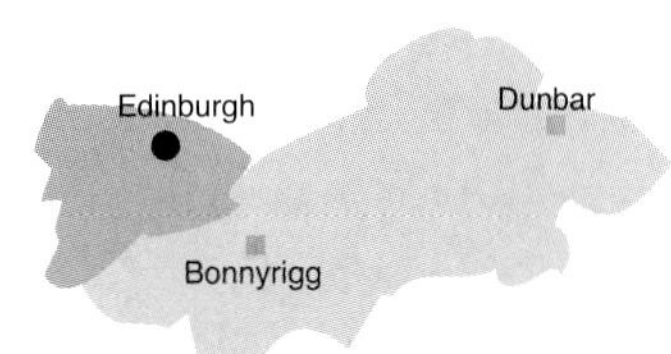

Web: www.johansens.com/channings
E-mail: reserve@channings.co.uk
Tel: 0870 381 8413
International: +44 (0)131 274 7401
Fax: 0131 274 7405

Price Guide:
single £101–£160
double/twin £131–£230
four poster/suite £187–£275

Le Monde Hotel

16 GEORGE STREET, EDINBURGH EH2 2PF

Le Monde Hotel, winner of the Scottish Hotel Design Award 2006, is inspired by some of the most celebrated cities on the planet. With 18 individual suites guests can go globe-trotting from Paris to Tokyo, and even to the depths of Atlantis. From the cutting-edge minimalism of the New York loft apartment to the rich colours and textures of the Marrakech boudoir, each suite features plasma TVs, Egyptian cotton sheets, wireless Internet, huge bathrooms and mini-bars loaded with luxury chocolates and champagne. Elsewhere, Milan, the chic café bar, opens straight onto George Street and combines the style and class of Italy's fashion capital with Edinburgh's Georgian splendour. It provides a glorious setting for breakfast, coffee, lunch and snacks. Vienna, with its grand island bar and cosy seating areas is an ideal meeting place. The unique upstairs Paris bar serves the finest cocktails and delicious food. Club Tokyo, the hotel's sleek, intimate neon flecked nightclub is open until 3am. As Edinburgh's first boutique hotel, bar, brasserie and nightclub, Le Monde Hotel is an excellent addition to Scotland's capital city. Its commitment to high quality standards makes it an ideal location for meetings, parties and corporate events.

Our inspector loved: *The personal, memorable service, and the Valrhona chocolate bonbons!*

Directions: Located on the south side of George Street, between Hanover Street and St Andrews Square.

E-mail: frontoffice@lemondehotel.co.uk
Tel: 0870 381 8610
International: +44 (0)131 270 3900
Fax: 0131 270 3901

Price Guide:
club class experience £195
world class experience £245
different class experience £295

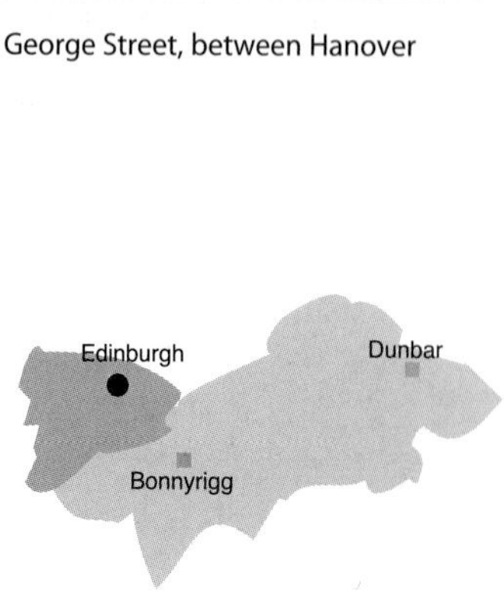

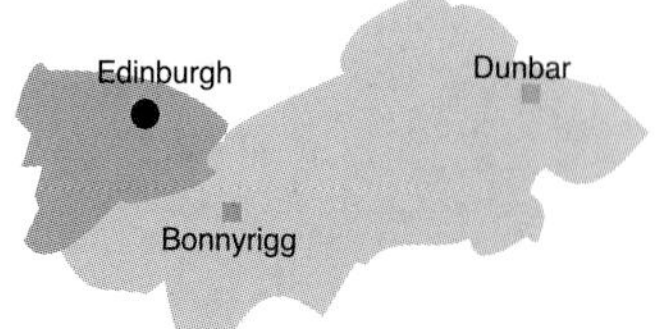

Mar Hall Hotel & Spa

MAR HALL DRIVE, EARL OF MAR ESTATE, BISHOPTON, NEAR GLASGOW PA7 5NW

The solid, impressive and historic Mar Hall Hotel & Spa is a fine example of Gothic architecture. Dominating a superb country estate, the hotel is just a 20-minute drive from Glasgow city centre. From its stone-framed windows guests can marvel and enjoy lush surroundings, which have attracted such figures from the past including Mary Queen of Scots and Robert the Bruce. Built in 1828, the present mansion house was constructed 100 years after the famous Earl of Mar's death and following a restoration it is now one of Scotland's premier five-star hotels. Enveloped by the scenic landscape and clean, crisp air, it is a haven of comfort and impeccable service. 53 lavishly designed bedrooms and suites are decorated in colour schemes of calming blues, rich burgundies and dramatic blacks. And beds, some of which are four-posters, are extremely comfortable with rich, fine fabrics. Elegant public rooms are enhanced by window views of the formal gardens towards the Kilpatrick Hills. Shades of gold and cream set the tone for the relaxing ambience, and excellent cuisine is provided by award-winning Chef Jim Kerr in the Cristal Gourmet Restaurant. Lighter meals can be enjoyed in the Grand Hall and the Café area at the well-equipped spa.

Our inspector loved: *The huge, sumptuous rooms in a supremely tranquil setting only minutes from the city centre.*

Directions: Take the M8 westbound to Erskine Bridge exit and follow signs for Erskine/Bishopton. The driveway is on the right.

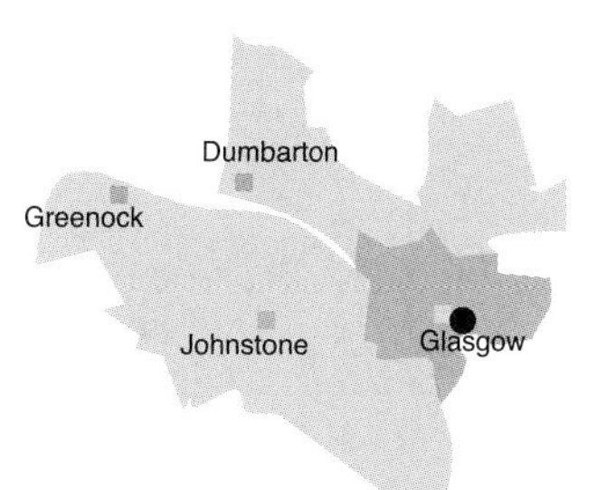

Web: www.johansens.com/marhall
E-mail: sales@marhall.com
Tel: 0870 381 8612
International: +44 (0)141 812 9999
Fax: 0141 812 9997

Price Guide:
single from £135
double/twin £170–£250
suite £250–£495

53 120 SPA

One Devonshire Gardens

1 DEVONSHIRE GARDENS, GLASGOW G12 0UX

Only 10 minutes from the city centre, One Devonshire Gardens is set in the heart of Glasgow's fashionable West End with its tree-lined terraces and Victorian mansions. Quite simply for those who expect and appreciate the finest of standards, this multi-award-winning hotel is situated in a series of converted period townhouses offering luxurious accommodation and exquisite cuisine. It's all about individuality, and all 35 bedrooms have their own distinctive identity, imaginative and unusual use of classic and contemporary furnishings. Public areas reflect the grandeur of a bygone era with antiques and original Scottish artwork throughout, and guests are entrusted to old-fashioned values of genuine personal service in relaxing comfort and style. The terraced garden is perfect for afternoon teas on a sunny day or pre-dinner drinks on a balmy evening. The hotel has a residents only gym, and a personal trainer can be arranged. Guests can also enjoy a range of in-room spa treatments or personalised yoga instruction in the comfort of their own room by prior arrangement. Within walking distance are the lively cafes, bars and boutique shops of the west end, as well as local attractions Kelvingrove Art Gallery, The Hunterian Museum, and Glasgow's landmark Kibble Palace. The hotel's 2 AA Rosette, No5 Restaurant, offers fine dining in intimate and relaxed surroundings.

Our inspector loved: *The incredible effort made to add those little touches that make this hotel the very best there is.*

Directions: From the M8 take junction 17 and follow signs for the A82 Dumbarton/Kelvinside (Great Western Road).

Web: www.johansens.com/onedevonshire
E-mail: reservations@onedevonshiregardens.com
Tel: 0870 381 9146
International: +44 (0)141 3392001
Fax: 0141 3371663

Dumbarton
Greenock
Johnstone
Glasgow

Price Guide: (Continental breakfast £12, full Scottish breakfast £17)
double £135-£295
town house suite from £365
mews suite £925

Royal Marine Hotel

GOLF ROAD, BRORA, SUTHERLAND KW9 6QS

Overlooking the mouth of River Brora, Royal Marine Hotel, designed by Sir Robert Lorimer in 1913, has undergone great restoration to its original antique furniture, woodwork and panelling. Passing under the wooden arches of the entrance hall and ascending the grand staircase, guests step back in time to refined living of a bygone era. All 22 en-suite bedrooms offer modern comfort whilst retaining the ambience of early 20th-century elegance, and the new luxury additions of 24, two bedroomed apartments with magnificent views over Brora Golf Course and the Dornoch Firth. Scottish cuisine is served in the Sir Robert Lorimer Dining Room where fresh seafood, local salmon, meat and game, are all on the menu, complemented by a varied wine list. Less formal meals are taken in Hunter's Bistro where a fine selection of malt whiskies can be sampled and the Garden Room Café Bar in the Leisure Club also serves lighter snacks all day. The Leisure Club features an indoor swimming pool, gymnasium, sauna, steam room and Jacuzzi. There are several golf courses nearby, including Royal Dornoch and the Brora Championship course is just a 1-minute walk from the hotel. Sea angling, walking and hawking expeditions can all be arranged. The hotel maintains 2 fishing boats on Loch Brora, which are available for hire.

Our inspector loved: *This very traditional hotel with excellent facilities and great golf on the doorstep.*

Directions: A 1-hour drive from Inverness. Travel north on the A9, signposted Wick. In Brora cross the bridge and turn right. The hotel is 100 yards on the left.

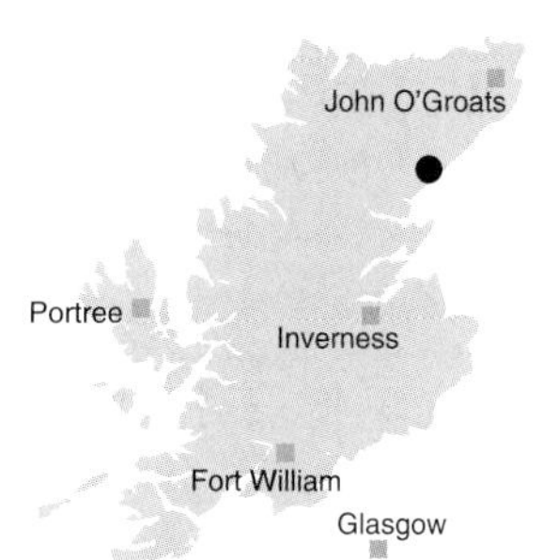

Web: www.johansens.com/royalmarine
E-mail: info@highlandescape.com
Tel: 0870 381 9133
International: +44 (0)1408 621252
Fax: 01408 621181

Price Guide:
single from £79
double £120-£160

INVERLOCHY CASTLE

TORLUNDY, FORT WILLIAM PH33 6SN

Directions: Three miles north-east of Fort William on the A82.

Web: www.johansens.com/inverlochy
E-mail: info@inverlochy.co.uk
Tel: 0870 381 9278
International: +44 (0)1397 702177
Fax: 01397 702953

Price Guide:
single £220-£310
double £300-£410
suite £470-£580

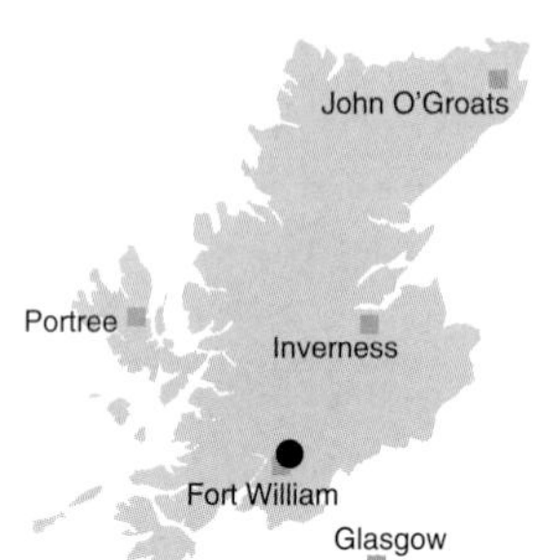

Set amidst gorgeous scenery in the foothills of Ben Nevis, Inverlochy was built in 1863 by the first Lord Abinger, and as a visitor in 1873 Queen Victoria wrote of it, "I never saw a lovelier or more romantic spot." Today, with new manager, Norbert Lieder, the castle is a splendid hotel. A massive reception room has Venetian crystal chandeliers, a Michaelangelo-style ceiling and a handsome staircase leading through to 3 elaborately decorated dining rooms and the Drawing Room, which has views over the castle's private loch and recently underwent a designer makeover. Spacious bedrooms, all with individual furnishings, offer every comfort. Michelin-starred chef Matt Gray, continues to create menus featuring modern British cuisine using the finest local ingredients including local game, hand picked wild mushrooms and scallops from the Isle of Skye. Various outdoor activities are available to guests, such as golf, clay pigeon shooting, guided walking, fly fishing for brown trout, pony trekking and tennis. Stunning places of landscape and history await exploration nearby: the mountains of Glencoe, the falls at Glen Nevis, the monument at Glenfinnan and many more.

Our inspector loved: *The Victorian splendour combining tasteful, contemporary grandeur, great wines and wonderful food.*

BUNCHREW HOUSE HOTEL

INVERNESS IV3 8TA

This splendid 17th-century Scottish mansion, "Hotel on the Shore", is set amidst 20 acres of landscaped gardens and woodlands on the shores of the Beauly Firth. Guests can enjoy breathtaking views of Ben Wyvis and the Black Isle, while just yards from the house the sea laps at the garden walls. Bunchrew has been carefully restored to preserve its heritage, whilst still giving its guests the highest standards of comfort and convenience. A continual schedule of refurbishment is on-going. The bedrooms are beautifully furnished and decorated to enhance their natural features. The elegant panelled drawing room is the ideal place to relax at any time, and during winter log fires lend it an added appeal which has given the hotel 4-star status. In the candle-lit restaurant the traditional cuisine includes prime Scottish beef, fresh lobster and langoustines, locally caught game and venison and freshly grown vegetables which has been rewarded with 2 AA Rosettes. A carefully chosen wine list complements the menu. Local places of interest include Cawdor Castle, Loch Ness, Castle Urquhart and a number of beautiful glens. For those who enjoy sport there is skiing at nearby Aviemore, sailing, cruising, golf, shooting and fishing.

Our inspector loved: *The cosy charm and splendid shore location.*

Directions: From Inverness follow signs to Beauly, Dingwall on the A862. 1 mile from the outskirts of Inverness the entrance to the hotel is on the right.

Web: www.johansens.com/bunchrewhouse
E-mail: welcome@bunchrew-inverness.co.uk
Tel: 0870 381 8393
International: +44 (0)1463 234917
Fax: 01463 710620

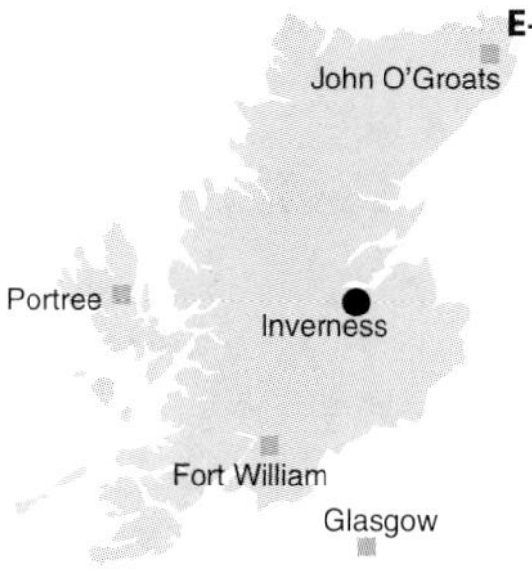

John O'Groats
Portree
Inverness
Fort William
Glasgow

Price Guide:
single £97.50–£137.50
double/twin £145–£240

16 M 80

DRUMOSSIE HOTEL

OLD PERTH ROAD, INVERNESS IV2 5BE

Drumossie Hotel has been totally refurbished in art deco style to create a spacious and unique venue conveniently located minutes from Inverness. It is set within fabulous parklands in a tranquil, natural setting for complete relaxation. The comfortable en-suite bedrooms have been designed in a refined style with luxurious fabrics and warm colour schemes; some rooms feature romantic four-poster beds. Guests will relish the style and splendour of the hotel's excellent restaurant and superior levels of service, where the head chef and his team prepare culinary delights that are sure to please even the most discerning of palates. The extensive wine list features examples from all over the world that are sure to be the perfect accompaniment to every dish. The hotel is able to accommodate up to 450 guests in its magnificent ballroom, with floor to ceiling windows that overlook the gardens. Idyllically located in the heart of the Scottish Highlands, outdoor pursuits abound with hiking, mountain climbing, pony trekking, cycling and off-road driving. There is also cross-country skiing and a dry slope nearby. Water sports include sailing, canoeing, diving and fishing on Loch Ness, famous for its legendary monster. Nearby Cawdor Castle, of Macbeth fame, dates back to the 14th century.

Our inspector loved: *The space away from the bustle of the town.*

Directions: Take the A9 south and after 3½ miles the hotel is signposted.

E-mail: stay@drumossiehotel.co.uk
Tel: 0870 381 8577
International: +44 (0)1463 236451
Fax: 01463 712858

Price Guide:
double/twin £200

NEW

Rocpool Reserve

CULDUTHEL ROAD, INVERNESS, IV2 4AG

Exclusive, modern and elegant, Rocpool Reserve is Inverness's first boutique hotel and restaurant. Located in the centre of the city just a few minutes walk from Inverness castle, guests are made to feel welcome and relaxed in this home-from-home where the contemporary, classic décor provides extreme comfort. With a reoccurring colour scheme of red, black and white, every detail has been considered; even the radiators are designer items. Each guest room is fitted with plasma TVs, DVD players, iPod docking stations and benefits from WiFi. Egyptian linens, king-size beds, and Italian ceramics in the bathrooms, are standard luxury features. Some rooms have a balcony and one room even has a romantic hot tub on the terrace! Cocktail hour in the bar, with its white leather seats and sparkling chandeliers, may tempt guests before taking dinner in the exceptional Reserve Restaurant where indulgently Italian, seasonal menus offer sumptuous dishes that may be enjoyed on the climate controlled balcony, which overlooks the river. Wine from all over the world appears on the extensive list. Inverness boasts fabulous shopping, theatre at Eden Court, numerous pubs and restaurants and golf courses for all levels.

Our inspector loved: *The great modern style. A wonderful statement of a hotel.*

11 14

Directions: From the city centre by the river, take the B861 to Hilton and Culduthel. The hotel is ½ mile on the right

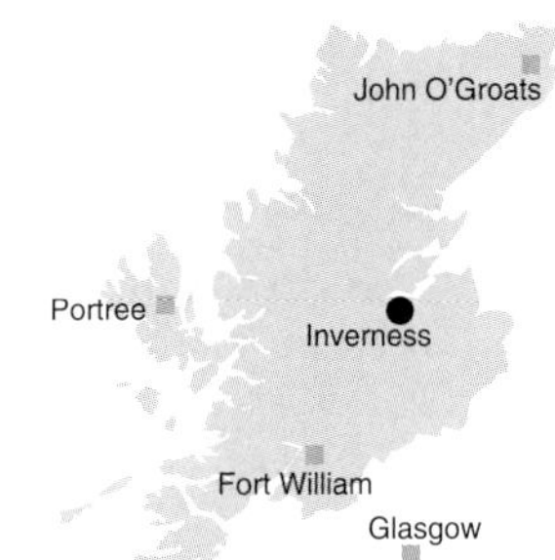

Web: www.johansens.com/rocpool
E-mail: info@rocpool.com
Tel: 0870 381 8434
International: +44 (0)1463 240089
Fax: 01463 248431

Price Guide:
single £95–£230
double £115–£250

Culloden House

CULLODEN, INVERNESS, INVERNESS-SHIRE IV2 7BZ

A majestic circular drive leads to the splendour of this handsome Georgian mansion, battle headquarters of Bonnie Prince Charlie 253 years ago. 3 miles from Inverness, this handsome, totally non-smoking Palladian country house stands in 40 acres of beautiful gardens and peaceful parkland roamed by roe deer. Princes past and present and guests from throughout the world have enjoyed the hotel's ambience and hospitality. Rich furnishings, sparkling chandeliers, impressive Adam fireplaces and ornate plaster reliefs add to the grandness of the luxurious, high-ceilinged rooms. The bedrooms are appointed to the highest standard; many have four-poster beds and Jacuzzis. 4 suites are in the Pavilion Annex, which overlooks a 3-acre walled garden and 2 in the West Pavilion. In the Dining Room guests can savour superb cuisine prepared by Chef Michael Simpson, who trained at Gleneagles Hotel and the Hamburg Conference Centre. There is an outdoor tennis court and indoor sauna and shooting, fishing and pony-trekking can be arranged. Cawdor Castle, the Clava Cairns Bronze Age burial ground and Culloden battlefield are nearby. Awarded AA 4 stars, 2 Rosettes, 4 stars by the Scottish Tourist Board, listed in Condé Nast Traveller's Top 25 UK & Ireland Hotels 2005 and included in the Condé Nast Gold List 2006.

Our inspector loved: *The elegant exterior, and great comfort and service.*

Directions: Leave Inverness on the A96 towards Aberdeen and take the right turn off to Culloden. The hotel is signposted on the left ¾ mile after turning.

Web: www.johansens.com/cullodenhouseinverness
E-mail: info@cullodenhouse.co.uk
Tel: 0870 381 9137
International: +44 (0)1463 790461
Fax: 01463 792181

Price Guide:
single £155–£189
double £210–£260
suite £260–£290

28 60

Cuillin Hills Hotel

PORTREE, ISLE OF SKYE IV51 9QU

Spectacular views of the majestic Cuillin Mountains and Portree Bay on the beautiful Isle of Skye make this hotel the perfect choice for any discerning visitor. Originally built in the 1870s as a hunting lodge, Cuillin Hills Hotel benefits from 15 acres of private mature grounds, which create a secluded setting and tranquil atmosphere. Quality and comfort is a priority, reflected in the beautiful furniture and décor of the lounge, where guests can relax in front of the log fire and sample the extensive choice of malt whiskys. Spacious bedrooms are elegantly furnished and decorated to the highest standard with all modern conveniences. Imaginative and traditional cuisine combine to create award-winning delights, which are served in the stylish restaurant overlooking the bay. Guests may feast on highland game, lobster, scallops and other deliciously fresh local produce as well as tasty homemade desserts. An interesting selection of informal meals are served in the bar. The island's rich history can be discovered through its castles, museums and visitor centres. There is an abundance of beautiful unspoilt coastal paths and woodland walks nearby. The town of Portree is a mere 10 minutes' walk away.

Our inspector loved: *The panoramic position of this well-kept, friendly hotel.*

Directions: Skye can be reached by bridge from Kyle of Localsh or by ferry from Mallaig or Glenelg. From Portree take the A855 to Staffin. After ½ mile take the road to Budhmor.

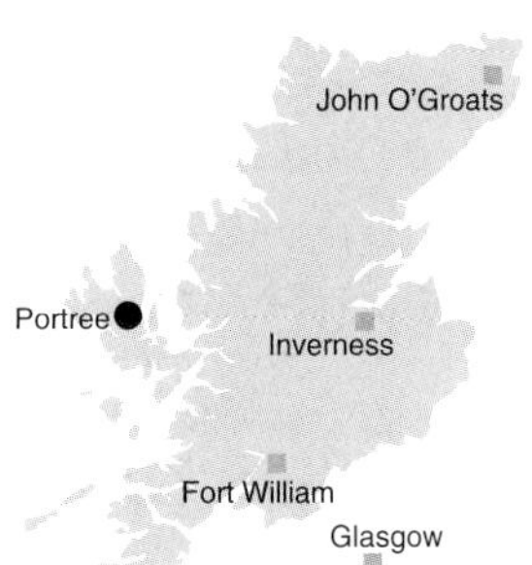

Web: www.johansens.com/cuillinhills
E-mail: info@cuillinhills-hotel-skye.co.uk
Tel: 0870 381 8467
International: +44 (0)1478 612003
Fax: 01478 613092

Price Guide:
single £60–£80
double/twin £120–£230

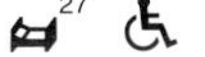 27   140     

LOCH TORRIDON COUNTRY HOUSE HOTEL

TORRIDON, BY ACHNASHEEN, WESTER-ROSS IV22 2EY

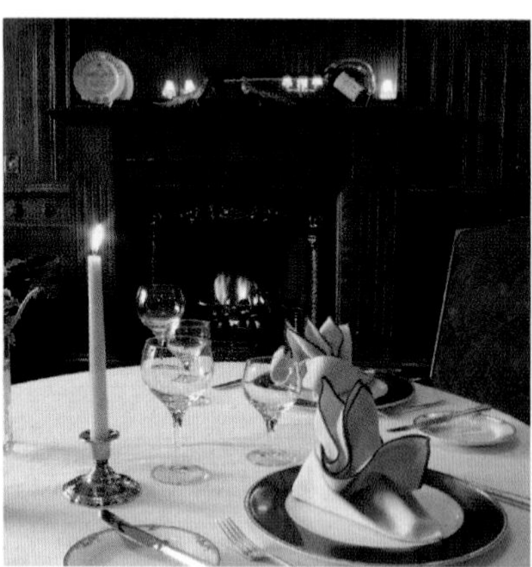

Directions: The hotel is 10 miles from Kinlochewe on the A896. Do not turn off to Torridon village.

Web: www.johansens.com/lochtorridon
E-mail: enquiries@lochtorridonhotel.com
Tel: 0870 381 9136
International: +44 (0)1445 791242
Fax: 01445 712253

Price Guide: (including dinner)
single £115–£160
double/twin £175–£360
master suite £310–£440

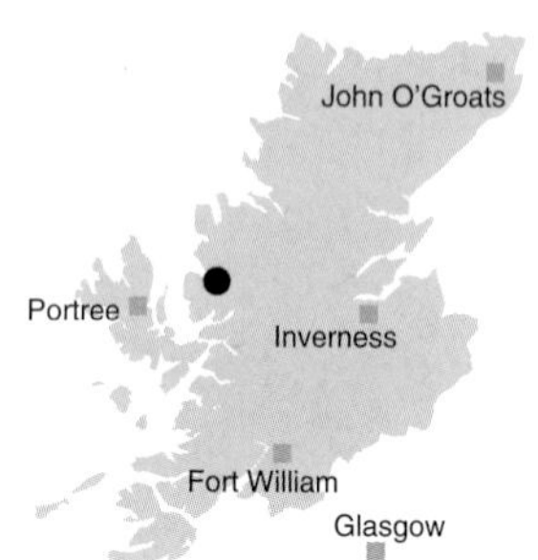

Loch Torridon is gloriously situated at the foot of wooded mountains on the shores of the loch from which it derives its name. Built as a shooting lodge for the first Earl of Lovelace in 1887, in a 58-acre estate containing formal gardens, mature trees and resident Highland cattle. Today, Daniel and Rohaise Rose-Bristow welcome guests into their home offering the best in Highland hospitality. Awarded AA 3 Red Stars, the hotel has 19 bedrooms which are luxuriously decorated. The Victorian kitchen garden provides chef, Kevin Broome, with fresh herbs, salad and a variety of fruits and vegetables. Dinner is served from 7pm - 9pm where a fine dining table d'hôte menu is offered. Guests may begin with white bean and barley slice, wrapped in home cured wild sea salmon with garden beetroot and Marjoram fondue followed by roast fillet and braised aromatic belly free-range Highland pork, chickpea and olive casserole, shallot mash, jus of pork. Providing a seasonal alternative, dinner is also served in the more informal, sister property, Ben Damph Inn with rooms where alternative accommodation is available. Outdoor pursuits include: Guided low and high level walks, kayaking, abseiling, climbing, archery, clay shooting, mountain biking, fishing and opportunities to see otters, seals, deer, eagles and other bird life.

Our inspector loved: *The superb position of this very comfortable country house.*

Dalhousie Castle and Spa

NR EDINBURGH, BONNYRIGG EH19 3JB

For over 700 years Dalhousie Castle has nestled in beautiful parkland, providing warm Scottish hospitality. There are fascinating reminders of a rich and turbulent history, such as the 2 AA Rosette Vaulted Dungeon Restaurant; a delightful setting in which to enjoy classical French and traditional Scottish "Castle Cuisine". 15 of the 29 Castle bedrooms are historically themed and include the James VI, Mary Queen of Scots, Robert the Bruce and William Wallace. The "de Ramseia" suite houses the 500-year-old "Well". There are also 7 en-suite bedrooms in the 100-year-old Lodge. Five carefully renovated function rooms provide a unique setting for conferences for up to 120 delegates, banquets and weddings for up to 100 guests. Extensive parking and a helipad are on site. Dalhousie Castle is only 7 miles from Edinburgh city centre and just 14 miles from the International Airport. The Castle has a Scottish Tourist Board 4 Star classification. The Aqueous Spa includes a hydro pool, Laconium, Ottoman and treatment rooms. The Orangery Restaurant, overlooking the South Esk River, offers contemporary Scottish/European dining. Activities including Dalhousie Castle Falconry with its own mews where guests can enjoy a private display and learn to fly Eagles, Owls, Hawks and Falcons. Clay pigeon shooting can be arranged given prior notice as well as golf at nearby courses.

Our inspector loved: *If you shun modern, soulless accommodation in favour of a bit of up-market sophistication this is the place for you.*

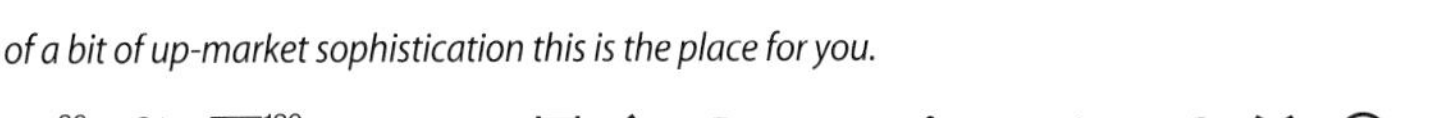

Directions: From Edinburgh on city by pass take the city by pass south to the A7, through Newtongrange. Turn right at the junction onto B704, hotel is ¾ mile and well signposted.

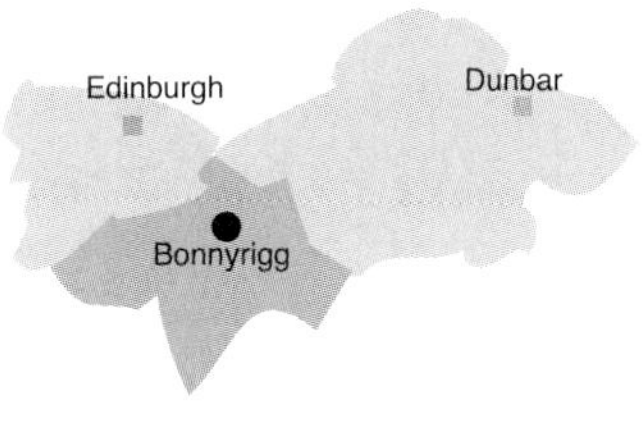

Web: www.johansens.com/dalhousiecastle
E-mail: info@dalhousiecastle.co.uk
Tel: 0870 381 8472
International: +44 (0)1875 820153
Fax: 01875 821936

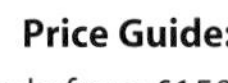

Price Guide:
single from £150
double from £195

THE ROYAL HOTEL

MELVILLE SQUARE, COMRIE, PERTHSHIRE PH6 2DN

Directions: Located in the centre of the village, on the A85.

Web: www.johansens.com/royalcomrie
E-mail: reception@royalhotel.co.uk
Tel: 0870 381 8875
International: +44 (0)1764 679200
Fax: 01764 679219

Price Guide:
single £80–£120
double £130–£170

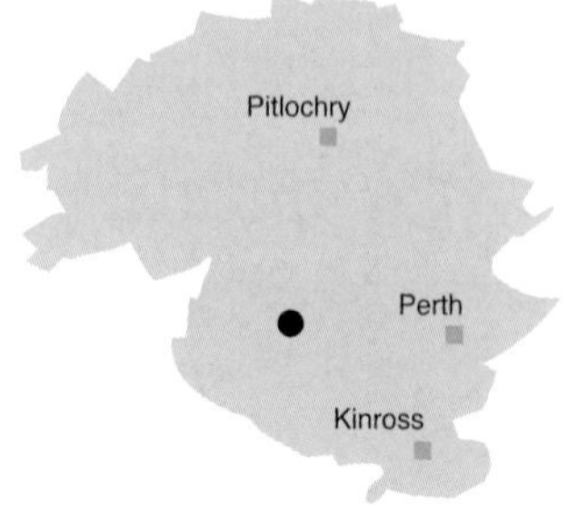

Set in an area of outstanding natural beauty, this former inn was once frequented by personalities such as Rob Roy McGregor and Queen Victoria, whose stay bestowed the name of The Royal Hotel on Comrie's major inn. Its homely yet luxurious and elegant atmosphere is enhanced by open log fires, period furnishings and genuine Highland hospitality provided by the cheerful staff and the Milsom family, who also own the Tufton Arms Hotel, Appleby. The 11 bedrooms have been individually designed and show exceptional attention to detail. Alternatively, guests may rent the apartment within the grounds, which accommodates up to 6 people. An ideal place to unwind, the comfortable Lounge Bar is popular for pre-dinner drinks, which include a choice of over 130 whiskies. Scottish cuisine and fine wines are enjoyed in the conservatory-style Brasserie or the more intimate Royal Restaurant, where chef David Milsom and his team, awarded an AA Rosette, create delicious dishes based on fresh local produce. Located amidst superb walking country, guests may take gentle walks in the nearby Glens and across the hills and moorlands. The hotel has its own stretch of the river Earn for fishing, and fowl or clay pigeon shooting can be arranged. Comrie is surrounded by excellent golf courses from scenic Highland layouts to idyllic parkland settings, such as the famous Gleneagles.

Our inspector loved: *This modern inn "par excellence".*

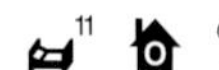      

Kinnaird

KINNAIRD ESTATE, BY DUNKELD, PERTHSHIRE PH8 0LB

With a panoramic vista across the Tay Valley, Kinnaird is surrounded by a beautiful 9,000-acre estate, ideally situated for those seeking a relaxing break or enthusiasts of outdoor pursuits. Built in 1770 this Edwardian mansion boasts 8 individually decorated bedrooms with exquisite fabrics, deep cushioned sofas, gas log fires and opulent bathrooms. In the courtyard are 2 cottages furbished to the same high standard and 4 more cottages located in secluded spots boasting panoramic views. Throughout the house, rare pieces of antique furniture, china and fine paintings abound. The panelled Cedar room is the essence of comfort and enjoys a large open fire where guests enjoy pre-dinner drinks or unwind next door at the full-size billiard table. The newly refurbished restaurant, The Ashtree, with its hand-painted Italian frescoes and ornate fireplace, serves modern classical cuisine created by award-winning chef Trevor Brooks. The well stocked wine cellar maintains an extensive range of wine, liqueurs and malt whiskies. The tranquil beauty room, the Retreat, offers many beauty and holistic treatments including reflexology, aromatherapy and manicures. Other activities include walking, salmon and brown trout fishing, bird-watching, pheasant and partridge shooting, deer stalking and croquet. This historic house holds a civil licence; the gardens are perfect for picturesque photographs.

Our inspector loved: *The spacious rooms, elegance, and amazing food.*

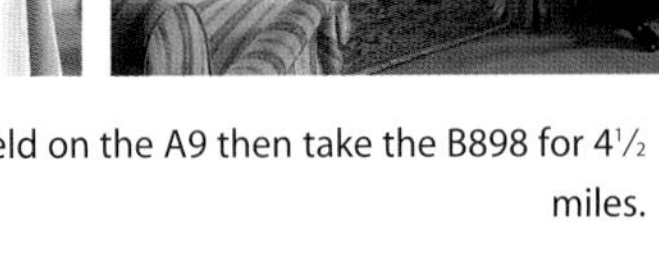

Directions: 2 miles north of Dunkeld on the A9 then take the B898 for 4½ miles.

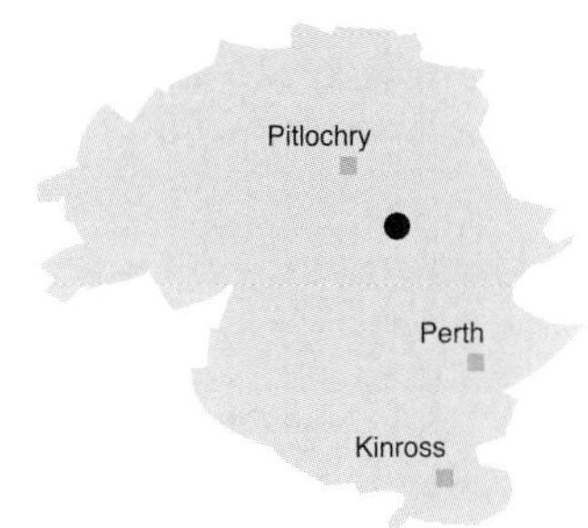

Web: www.johansens.com/kinnaird
E-mail: enquiry@kinnairdestate.com
Tel: 0870 381 9124
International: +44 (0)1796 482440
Fax: 01796 482289

Price Guide: (including dinner)
double/twin £295–£475
winter rates £325 or £275 for
2 or more nights

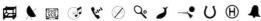

Cromlix House

KINBUCK, BY DUNBLANE, NR STIRLING FK15 9JT

Set in a 2,000-acre estate in the heart of Perthshire, just off the A9, the STB 5 Star Cromlix House is a rare and relaxing retreat. Built as a family home in 1874, much of the house remains unchanged including many fine antiques acquired over the generations. The owners are proud of their tradition of country house hospitality. The individually designed bedrooms and spacious suites have been redecorated with period fabrics to enhance the character and fine furniture whilst retaining the essential feeling of a much loved home. Unpretentious, restful and most welcoming, the large public rooms have open fires. In the restaurant, the finest local produce is used. Cromlix is an ideal venue for small exclusive conferences and business meetings. The private Chapel is a unique feature and perfect for weddings. Cromlix House was one of the AA top 10 hotels in Scotland 2003. Sporting and leisure facilities available nearby include trout and salmon fishing and game shooting in season. There are several challenging golf courses within easy reach including Rosemount, Carnoustie and St. Andrews. The location is ideal for touring the Southern Highlands, with Edinburgh and Glasgow less than an hour away.

Our inspector loved: *The peaceful atmosphere where it's easy to believe you are in your own luxury house.*

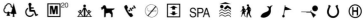

Directions: Cromlix House lies 4 miles north of Dunblane in the village of Kinbuck on the B8033 and 4 miles south of Braco.

Web: www.johansens.com/cromlixhouse
E-mail: reservations@cromlixhouse.com
Tel: 0870 381 8460
International: +44 (0)1786 822125
Fax: 01786 825450

Price Guide:
single £165–£210
double/twin £240–£280
suite £320–£390

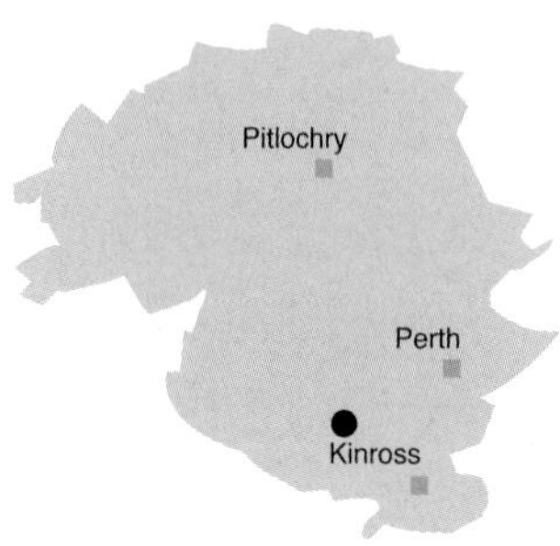

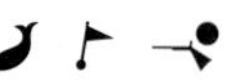

Ballathie House Hotel

KINCLAVEN, STANLEY, PERTHSHIRE PH1 4QN

Set in an estate overlooking the River Tay near Perth, Ballathie House Hotel offers Scottish hospitality in a house of character and distinction. Dating from 1850, this mansion has a French baronial façade and handsome interiors. Overlooking lawns which slope down to the riverside, the drawing room is an ideal place to relax with coffee and the papers or to enjoy a malt whisky after dinner. The premier bedrooms are large and elegant, whilst the standard rooms are designed in a cosy, cottage style. On the ground floor there are several bedrooms suitable for guests with disabilities. Local ingredients such as Tay salmon, Scottish beef, seafood and piquant soft fruits are used to create menus catering for all tastes. The hotel has 2 Rosettes for fine Scottish cuisine. Activities available on the estate include salmon fishing, river walks, croquet and putting. The Riverside Rooms are ideal for both house guests or sportsmen. The area has many good golf courses. Perth, Blairgowrie and Edinburgh are within an hour's drive. STB 4 star and AA 3 Red Stars (Top 200). Dogs are permitted in certain rooms only. 2 day breaks from £99, including breakfast and dinner.

Our inspector loved: *The classical elegance and comfort.*

Directions: From the A93 at Beech Hedges, follow the signs for Kinclaven and Ballathie or take the A9 and turn right 2 miles north of Perth,at the sign for Stanley. The hotel is well signposted from this point and lies 10 miles north of Perth.

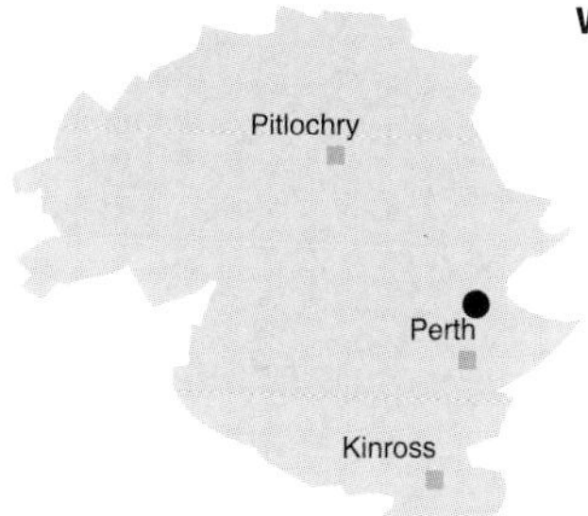

Web: www.johansens.com/ballathiehouse
E-mail: email@ballathiehousehotel.com
Tel: 0870 381 8337
International: +44 (0)1250 883268
Fax: 01250 883396

Price Guide:
single £86–£98
double/twin £172–£196
suite £240–£270

CRINGLETIE HOUSE

EDINBURGH ROAD, PEEBLES EH45 8PL

A distinguished baronial mansion set within 28 acres, Cringletie House is the epitome of style and fine country living. Elegant turrets combine with the traditional red Borders' sandstone to capture the quiet dignity of a bygone era. All of the beautifully appointed bedrooms have been individually decorated and boast breathtaking views over the surrounding Peebleshire countryside. The splendid panelled dining room has an impressive carved oak and marble fireplace, many original artworks and an eye catching hand painted ceiling depicting a heavenly classical scene. Highly acclaimed cuisine is created with flair and imagination with menus designed around the fruits and vegetables available in Scotland's only 17th-century walled kitchen garden. Specialities include deliciously prepared fresh game and fish. Guests can play outdoor chess or boule in the woodland garden, attempt the 9-hole putting green, play lawn croquet or simply stroll around the manicured lawns and lush woodlands surrounding the hotel. Fishing is available on the River Tweed and for golf lovers there is an excellent golf course in Peebles. Other activities such as archery, shooting, quad biking and hot air ballooning can be arranged. Cringletie is a good base from which to explore the rich historical and cultural heritage of the Borders and is only 30 minutes from Edinburgh.

Directions: Take the A703 from Edinburgh towards Peebles. The hotel is on the right approximately 2 miles south of Eddleston village

Web: www.johansens.com/cringletiehouse
E-mail: enquiries@cringletie.com
Tel: 0870 381 9279
International: +44 (0)1721 725750
Fax: 01721 725751

Price Guide:
single £135–£155
double/twin £190–£300

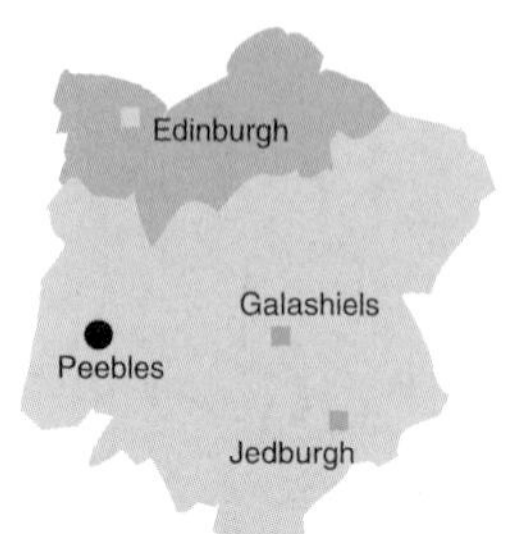

Our inspector loved: *The attention to detail shown by the new owners.*

GLENAPP CASTLE

BALLANTRAE, SCOTLAND KA26 0NZ

Glenapp is an experience rather than "just another hotel". As you turn through the castle gates, Glenapp stands proudly in front of you; imposing, exciting and inviting. The owners, Fay and Graham Cowan, offer a truly Scottish welcome to their glorious Ayrshire home. They bought Glenapp in a state of neglect and spent six years refurbishing it to combine the requirements of the discerning guest with the classic style of the house. No expense has been spared, from the stone fireplaces carved with the family crest to the Castle's own monogrammed china. Head Chef Matt Weedon will prepare exciting, innovative 6-course gourmet dinners using local produce, and fruit, vegetables and herbs straight from the garden. The castle retains many original features as well as personally selected oil paintings and antique furnishings throughout bedrooms, lounges and oak panelled hallways. The 17 en-suite bedrooms are spacious, individually decorated, and furnished to the highest standards, all offering either views of the garden or coastline. The 30-acre gardens contain many rare trees and shrubs and an impressive Victorian glasshouse and walled garden. Tennis and croquet are available in the grounds. Guests may play golf on the local courses including championship courses, and shoot or fish on local estates.

Our inspector loved: *Everything about it - now in its 7th year yet it gets better and better.*

Directions: Glenapp Castle is approximately 15 miles north of Stranraer or 35 miles south of Ayr on A77.

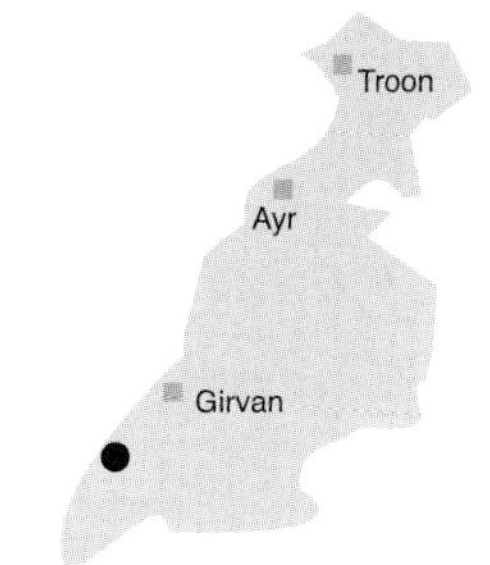

Web: www.johansens.com/glenappcastle
E-mail: enquiries@glenappcastle.com
Tel: 0870 381 8551
International: +44 (0)1465 831212
Fax: 01465 831000

Price Guide: (including dinner)
luxury double/twin from £375
suite from £445
master room from £525

17 20

Wales

Recommendations in Wales appear on pages 307-321

For further information on Wales, please contact:

Wales Tourist Board
Brunel House, 2 Fitzalan Road, Cardiff CF24 0UY
Tel: +44 (0)29 2049 9909
Web: www.visitwales.com

North Wales Tourism
77 Conway Road, Colwyn Bay, Conway LL29 7LN
Tel: +44 (0)1492 531731
Web: www.nwt.co.uk

Mid Wales Tourism
The Station, Machynlleth, Powys SY20 8TG
Tel: (Freephone) 0800 273747
Web: www.visitmidwales.co.uk

South West Wales Tourism Partnership
The Coach House, Aberglasney, Carmarthenshire SA32 8QH
Tel: +44 (0)1558 669091
Web: www.swwtp.co.uk

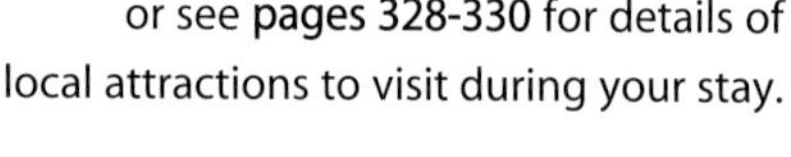

or see **pages 328-330** for details of local attractions to visit during your stay.

Images from www.britainonview.com

Miskin Manor Country House Hotel

MISKIN, NR CARDIFF CF72 8ND

Although its history dates back to the 11th century, Miskin Manor first became a hotel only in 1986, following extensive restoration and refurbishment. Only 10 minutes' drive from central Cardiff and Cardiff Bay and set amid 22 acres of undisturbed parkland, criss-crossed with streams, peace and seclusion are guaranteed. The uncommonly spacious reception rooms have fine fireplaces, panelled walls and elaborate plasterwork ceilings, all enhanced by rich drapery and comfortable furniture. All of the bedrooms have en suite bathrooms and full facilities. In the 1920s, one of the de luxe suites was occupied by the Prince of Wales (later King Edward VIII). First-class Welsh cuisine is served in the restaurant, awarded an AA Rosette and complemented by a comprehensive wine list. Just a short walk away from the hotel, within the grounds, the popular Health Club boasts a glass-backed squash court, badminton and extensive gymnasium, while more gentle pursuits are provided by the solarium, sauna and steam room as well as refreshment facilities. Celebrations, conferences and functions can be catered for, with professional and quality services assured.

Our inspector loved: *The inspector loved the ambience of this friendly hotel, rich with character from the superb restorations of their 11th century origins.*

Directions: From junction 34 of the M4, towards Llantrisant. Drive is ¼ a mile north of the M4.

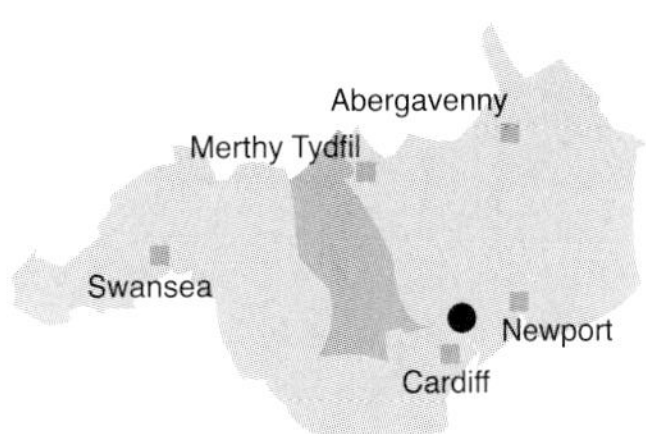

Web: www.johansens.com/miskinmanor
E-mail: info@miskin-manor.co.uk
Tel: 0870 381 8740
International: +44 (0)1443 224204
Fax: 01443 237606

Price Guide:
single from £105
double/twin from £130
four poster from £160
suite from £240

FALCONDALE MANSION HOTEL

LAMPETER, CEREDIGION SA48 7RX

Only 10 miles from Cardigan coast and the beautiful fishing village of Aberaeron, Falcondale, the recent winner of a number of accolades in the hotel trade, is rapidly gaining an excellent reputation and putting this charming area of Wales firmly on the map. One hour from Swansea Airport, and on the outskirts of Lampeter, it is ideally located to enjoy the many coastal walks and unspoilt beaches that lie in the region as well as a number of National Trust properties and the fishing port of Aberaeron. Lampeter is a charming university town: St David's College is the third oldest university and has many interesting small shops. There is a reliable bus service to and from Lampeter, and good road links to Cardiff Airport. The hotel is an elegant Italianate mansion set in14 acres of secluded countryside with a wonderful mix of ornamental woods and sweeping elegant lawns. Available for exclusive use and tailor-made private and corporate events, there are 20 guest rooms, and recent refurbishment has ensured that they are stylishly decorated with accompanying luxurious bathrooms. With a Welsh head chef supported by an English, French and South African team, the cuisine is imaginative yet traditionally Welsh with an international flavour using locally sourced produce; the vegetarian options are excellent. Both fine dining and more informal eating in the Brasserie can be enjoyed.

Our inspector loved: *Its two dining options and interesting menus.*

Directions: Exit the M4 and take the A485 towards Carmarthen. Turn left at the T-junction to Lampeter and drive through the town towards Cardigan. Turn right just before the Murco petrol garage into the South Drive.

Web: www.johansens.com/falcondale
E-mail: info@falcondalehotel.com
Tel: 0870 381 9235
International: +44 (0)1570 422910
Fax: 01570 423559

Price Guide:
single from £95
double/twin from £130

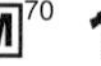

Bodysgallen Hall & Spa

LLANDUDNO, NORTH WALES LL30 1RS

Nestling in 200 acres of parkland to the south of Llandudno and west of Pydew Mountain, Grade I listed Bodysgallen Hall & Spa exudes a mixture of history, great comfort and sophistication. With spectacular views of Snowdonia and Conwy Castle it provides all that is best in country house hospitality. Bodysgallen has grown and developed from a 13th-century fortified tower into one of the grandest family houses in Wales and is now a superb, charismatic hotel. Large, beautiful gardens include a 17th-century parterre of box hedges filled with scented herbs, a rockery with cascade, a superbly restored formal walled rose garden and several follies. Within these beautiful grounds is a cluster of 16 self-contained cottages. The 18 comfortable bedrooms inside the house, including the brand new Principle Suites, are individually and stylishly furnished and are non-smoking. Most of the rooms have selected Sky TV channels and some have air conditioning. The antique furnished entrance hall and first-floor drawing rooms, with large fireplaces and splendid oak panelling, are particularly appealing, as are the 2 dining rooms where 3 AA Rosette award-winning Head Chef John Williams serves imaginative cuisine. A short walk through the garden takes guests to the health and fitness spa with indoor swimming pool - children under 8 are not permitted in the pool outside specific swimming times.

Our inspector loved: *This enchanting oasis with its wealth of history.*

Directions: On the A470, 1 mile from the intersection with the A55. Llandudno is a mile further on the A470.

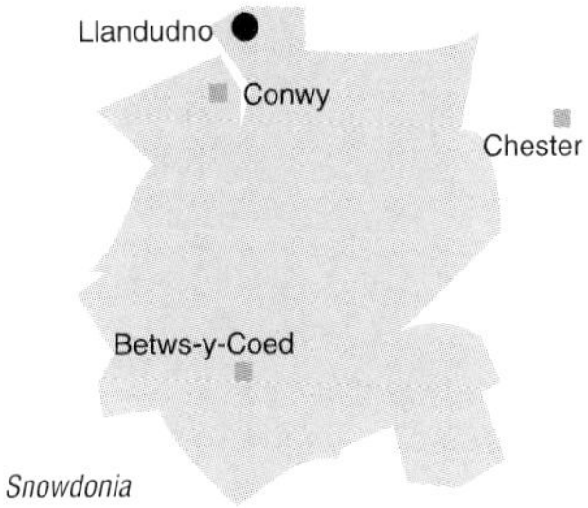

Llandudno
Conwy
Chester
Betws-y-Coed
Snowdonia

Web: www.johansens.com/bodysgallenhall
E-mail: info@bodysgallen.com
Tel: 0870 381 8372
International: +44 (0)1492 584466
Fax: 01492 582519

Price Guide:
single from £125
double/twin from £175
suite from £195

St Tudno Hotel & Restaurant

NORTH PROMENADE, LLANDUDNO, NORTH WALES LL30 2LP

Without doubt one of the most delightful small hotels to be found on the coast of Britain, St Tudno Hotel & Restaurant, a former winner of the Johansens Hotel of the Year Award for Excellence, offers a very special experience. The hotel has been elegantly and lovingly furnished with meticulous attention to detail, and provides a particularly warm welcome generated by the Bland family over the past 35 years. Each beautifully co-ordinated bedroom has been individually designed with many thoughtful extras; half are equipped with spa baths. The bar lounge and sitting room, which overlook the sea, have an air of Victorian charm, and the Rosette award-winning, air-conditioned Terrace Restaurant is regarded as one of Wales' leading restaurants. This AA Red Star Hotel has won a host of other prestigious awards: Best Seaside Resort Hotel in Great Britain (Good Hotel guide); Welsh Hotel of the Year; Runner up for Johansens Tattinger Wine List Award 2004; the AA's Wine Award for Wales 2004 and even an accolade for having the Best Hotel Loos in Britain! St Tudno is ideally situated for visits to Snowdonia, Conwy and Caernarfon Castles, and glorious winter walks on the Great Orme, Bodnant Gardens and Anglesey. Llandudno's excellent theatre is only a short walk away. Golf, riding, dry-slope skiing and tobogganing can all be enjoyed locally, and the hotel has a heated indoor pool.

Our inspector loved: *The pool, such a pleasure within this special place.*

Directions: The hotel is located on the promenade opposite the pier entrance and gardens. Car parking and garages are available for up to 12 cars.

Web: www.johansens.com/sttudno
E-mail: sttudnohotel@btinternet.com
Tel: 0870 381 8907
International: +44 (0)1492 874411
Fax: 01492 860407

Price Guide:
single from £75
double/twin £94–£220
suite from £250

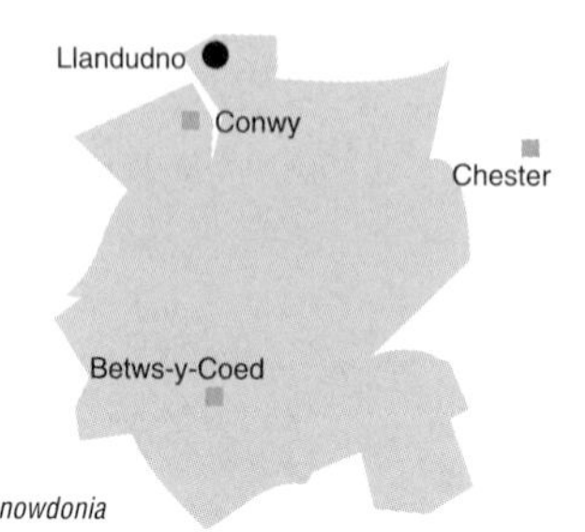

Wild Pheasant Hotel

BERWYN ROAD, LLANGOLLEN, DENBIGHSHIRE LL20 8AD

Some of the most spectacular scenery in Wales lies along the tranquil Vale of Llangollen, threaded by the River Dee. The stunning Horseshoe Pass meaders between the mountains of Llantysilio and Eglwyseg, and these, with the heights of Berwyn and Castell Dinas Branis, provide an impressive backdrop to the town. The Wild Pheasant is a short walk from the centre of this town, famous for the scene of the International Musical Eisteddfod, which is held every July and attracts 120,000 visitors. Dating back to the 19th century, this highly acclaimed hotel has been sympathetically updated, renovated and extended to provide a luxury retreat with all modern amenities and an eclectic blend of contemporary and traditional design. Guest rooms retain country house charm and the atmosphere of a bygone era whilst offering every home comfort; most have spectacular views. En-suite bedrooms, in the original part of the hotel, combine tradition, style and comfort; 2 have four-poster beds. Space and good taste are the hallmarks of the 15 luxury rooms in the wing extension; 1 of the 3 suites has a hot tub on its balcony. Excellent dining options include a Rosette-awarded restaurant and the more informal Bistro Bar. Fully-equipped spa and comprehensive conference facilities are available. The Daily Post Small Business Award Winner 2005.

Our inspector loved: *The excellent range of bedrooms from traditional simplicity to opulent modernity. True value for money.*

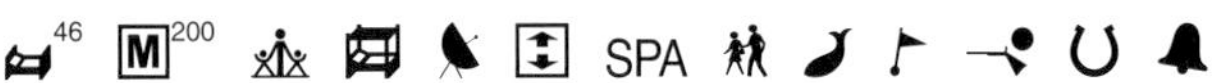

Directions: From the north take the M6 then the M56 to Chester. Follow the A483 past Wrexham and take the A5 to Langollen. From the south take the M6 then the M54 past Shrewsbury onto the A5 to Langollen.

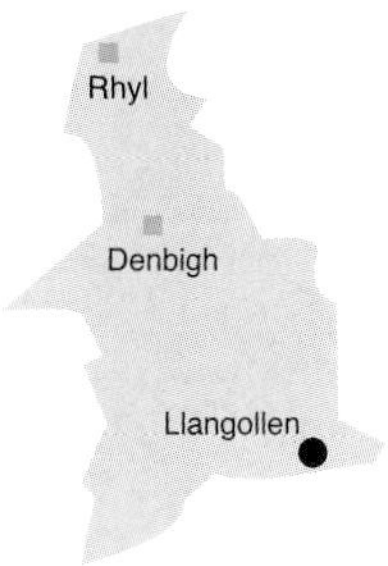

Web: www.johansens.com/wildpheasant
E-mail: wild.pheasant@talk21.com
Tel: 0870 381 8633
International: +44 (0)1978 860629
Fax: 01978 861837

Price Guide:
single £42–£84
double/twin £84–£168
suite £208–£248

PALÉ HALL

PALÉ ESTATE, LLANDDERFEL, BALA, GWYNEDD LL23 7PS

Directions: Situated off the B4401 Corwen to Bala Road, Palé Hall is 4 miles from Llandrillo.

Web: www.johansens.com/palehall
E-mail: enquiries@palehall.co.uk
Tel: 0870 381 8799
International: +44 (0)1678 530285
Fax: 01678 530220

Price Guide:
single £85–£140
double/twin £115–£200

Set in acres of peaceful, tranquil woodland on the edge of Snowdonia National Park, Palé Hall is a magnificent building, beautifully preserved, and provides the opportunity to sample a true country house lifestyle. Shooting parties are a regular occurrence on the surrounding estates, whilst fishing on the Dee is available on-site. A venture with Land Rover Experience also enables guests to experience off-road driving in their preferred choice of 4-wheel drive, whilst the less adventurous can walk for miles on the beautiful Palé Estate. The staff at Palé Hall carefully maintains the beautiful period interior of the building including the galleried staircase and painted ceilings, which have survived largely due to the house's unusual electricity system. Supplied by a turbine powered by water, Palé's 18 electric fires were left burning during 22 years of unoccupancy! Queen Victoria and Winston Churchill have stayed at the Hall. The 17 individually designed suites with luxurious bathrooms, one of which features a steam shower, have breathtaking views of the surrounding scenery. The 2 AA Rosette-awarded restaurant serves seasonal table d'hôte menus complemented by a fine wine selection. The hotel can be hired for exclusive use, and with the wonderful setting, this is an ideal venue for small conferences, product launches and weddings. Smoking is prohibited throughout.

Our inspector loved: *The bathrooms, and tasteful traditional decor.*

Penmaenuchaf Hall

PENMAENPOOL, DOLGELLAU, GWYNEDD LL40 1YB

Climbing the long tree-lined driveway guests arrive at Penmaenuchaf Hall to behold its idyllic setting. With stunning panoramic views across the spectacular Mawddach Estuary and wooded mountain slopes in the distance, this handsome Victorian mansion is an exceptional retreat. Set within the Snowdonia National Park, the 21-acre grounds encompass lawns, a formal sunken rose garden, a water garden and woodland. The beautiful interiors feature oak and mahogany panelling, stained-glass windows, log fires in winter, polished Welsh slate floors and freshly cut flowers. There are 12 non-smoking luxurious bedrooms, some with four-poster and half-tester beds; all have interesting views. A newly created bedroom boasts a balcony that takes full advantage of the magnificent scenery. In the restaurant guests can choose from an imaginative menu prepared with the best seasonal produce complemented by an extensive list of wines. An elegant panelled dining room can be used for private dinners or meetings. Penmaenuchaf Hall is perfect for a totally relaxed holiday: for recreation, guests can fish for trout and salmon along 10 miles of the Mawddach River, try mountain biking or take part in a range of watersports, enjoy scenic walks, visit sandy beaches and historic castles and take trips on narrow-gauge railways.

Our inspector loved: *The fact that every year the hotel continually evolves whilst retaining the pleasure it gives to all that pass through its door.*

Directions: The hotel is off the A493 Dolgellau–Tywyn road, about 2 miles from Dolgellau.

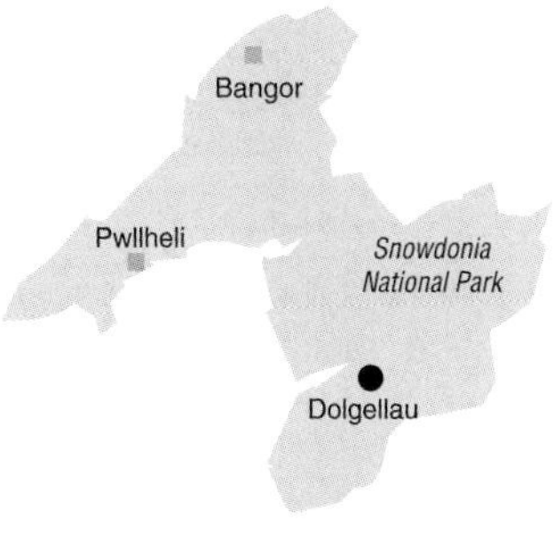

Bangor
Pwllheli
Snowdonia National Park
Dolgellau

Web: www.johansens.com/penmaenuchafhall
E-mail: relax@penhall.co.uk
Tel: 0870 381 8813
International: +44 (0)1341 422129
Fax: 01341 422787

Price Guide:
single £75–£135
double/twin £130–£200
special offers with early bookings available

LLANSANTFFRAED COURT HOTEL

LLANVIHANGEL GOBION, ABERGAVENNY, MONMOUTHSHIRE NP7 9BA

Llansantffraed Court, the Les Routiers Hotel of the Year for Wales and the Marches 2005-2006, is a perfect retreat from the fast pace of modern life. This elegant Georgian-style country house hotel, part of which dates back to the 14th century, is set in spacious grounds on the edge of the Brecon Beacons and the Wye Valley. Guests are provided with the highest level of personal, yet unobtrusive service. Most of the tastefully decorated and luxuriously furnished bedrooms offer views over the gardens and ornamental trout lake. One guest room has a four-poster bed, whilst others feature oak beams and dormer windows. An excellent reputation is enjoyed by the 2 AA Rosette restaurant; the menus reflect the changing seasons and the availability of fresh local produce. The exquisite cuisine is complemented by fine wines. Afternoon tea can be taken in the lounge where guests enjoy a blazing log fire during the cooler months and savour the views of the South Wales countryside. A range of excellent facilities is available for functions, celebrations and meetings. Llansantffraed Court is an ideal base for exploring the diverse history and beauty of the area and there are plenty of opportunities to take advantage of energetic or relaxing pursuits including golf, trekking, walking and salmon and trout fishing. The new Clay Pigeon Shooting School offers international standard tuition for beginners.

Our inspector loved: *The surrounding rolling parkland.*

Directions: From M4 J24 (Via A449) off B4598 (formerly A40 old road) Leave A40 D/C at Abergavenny or Raglan. Follow signs to Clytha and the hotel is approx 4½ miles away.

Web: www.johansens.com/llansantffraedcourt
E-mail: reception@llch.co.uk
Tel: 0870 381 8697
International: +44 (0)1873 840678
Fax: 01873 840674

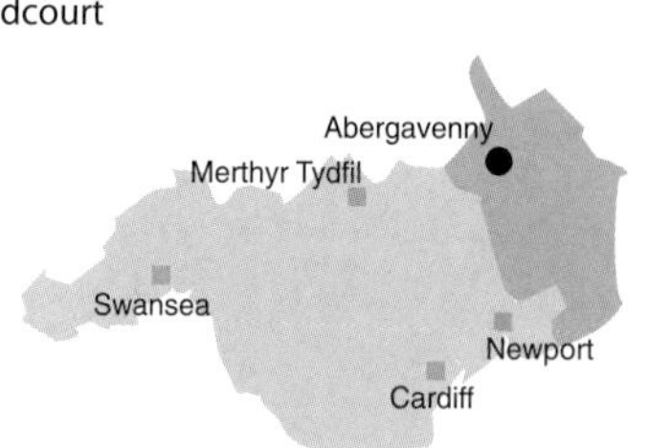

Price Guide:
single £86–£97
double/twin £115–£175
suites £175

Allt-Yr-Ynys Hotel

WALTERSTONE, NEAR ABERGAVENNY, HR2 0DU

Nestling in the foothills of the Black Mountains, on the fringes of the Brecon Beacons National park, Allt-yr-Ynys is an impressive Grade II 16th-century manor house hotel. The Manor was the home of the Cecil family whose ancestry dates back to Rhodri Mawr, King of Wales in the 8th century. A more recent Cecil was Lord Burleigh, Chief Minister to Queen Elizabeth I, portrayed by Sir Richard Attenborough in the recent film, "Elizabeth". Features of this interesting past still remain and include moulded ceilings, oak panelling and beams and a 16th-century four-poster bed in the Jacobean suite. However, whilst the charm and the character of the period remains, the house has been sympathetically adapted to provide all the comforts expected of a modern hotel. The former outbuildings have been transformed into spacious and well-appointed guest bedrooms. Fine dining is offered in the award-winning restaurant and the conference/function suite accommodates up to 200 guests. Facilities include a heated pool, Jacuzzi, clay pigeon shooting range and private river fishing. Pastimes include exploring the scenery, historic properties and plethora of tourist attractions.

***Our inspector loved:** The spacious individually decorated bedrooms, all with glorious secluded views of the countryside.*

Directions: 5 miles north of Abergavenny on A465 Abergavenny/ Hereford trunk road, turn west at Old Pandy Inn in Pandy. After 400 metres turn right down lane at grey/green barn. The hotel is on the right after 400 metres.

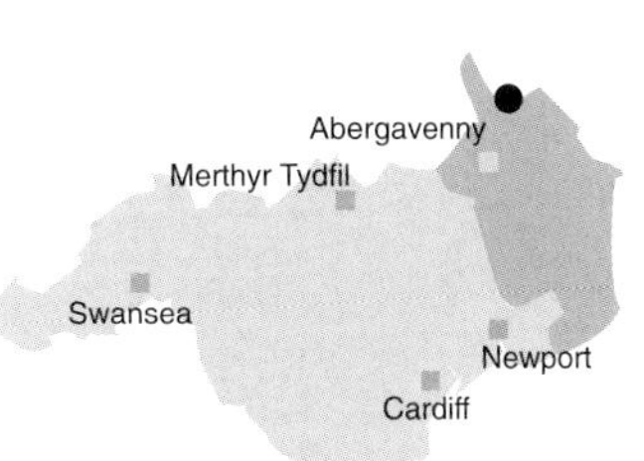

Web: www.johansens.com/alltyrynys
E-mail: reception@allthotel.co.uk
Tel: 0870 381 8309
International: +44 (0)1873 890307
Fax: 01873 890539

Price Guide: (per room)
single £75–£110
double/twin £125–£160
suite from £150

WARPOOL COURT HOTEL

ST DAVID'S, PEMBROKESHIRE SA62 6BN

Originally built as St David's Cathedral Choir School in the 1860s, Warpool Court enjoys spectacular scenery at the heart of the Pembrokeshire National Park, with views over the coast and St Bride's Bay to the islands beyond. First converted to a hotel over 40 years ago, continuous refurbishment has ensured all its up-to-date comforts are fit for the new century. All 25 bedrooms have immaculate en-suite facilities of which 14 enjoy sea views. The 2 AA Rosette restaurant enjoys a splendid reputation. Imaginative menus, including vegetarian, offer a wide selection of modern and traditional dishes. Local produce, including Welsh lamb and beef, is used whenever possible, with crab, lobster, sewin and sea bass caught just off the coast. Salmon and mackerel are smoked on the premises. The hotel gardens are ideal for a peaceful stroll or an after-dinner drink in the summer. There is a covered heated swimming pool (open April to the end of October) and an all-weather tennis court in the grounds. A path from the hotel leads straight on to the Pembrokeshire Coastal Path, with its rich variety of wildlife and spectacular scenery. Boating and water sports are available locally. St David's Peninsula offers a wealth of history and natural beauty and has inspired many famous artists. Closed in January.

Directions: The hotel is signposted from the centre of St David's.

Web: www.johansens.com/warpoolcourt
E-mail: info@warpoolcourthotel.com
Tel: 0870 381 8968
International: +44 (0)1437 720300
Fax: 01437 720676

Price Guide:
single £105–£120
double/twin £170–£250

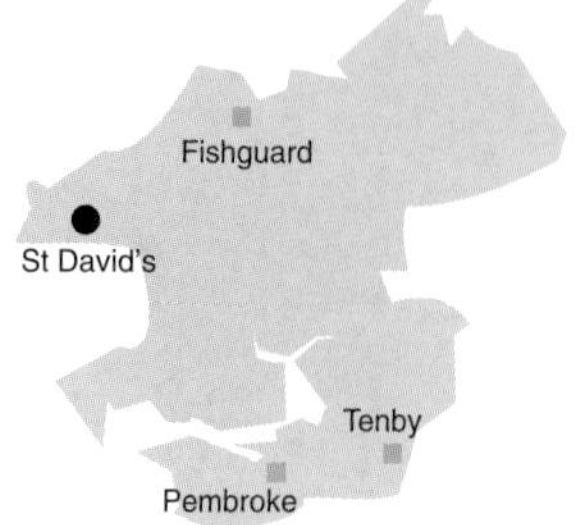

Our inspector loved: *The spectacular views of the coast from the dining room complementing the superb 2 Rosette cuisine.*

Penally Abbey

PENALLY, TENBY, PEMBROKESHIRE SA70 7PY

Built on the site of an ancient abbey, this listed country house stands in 5 acres of garden and woodland on the edge of Pembrokeshire National Park. It is an impressive hotel with wisteria-clad stone walls enhanced by decorative windows through which guests enjoy panoramic views over the gardens to Carmathen Bay and Caldey Island. Penally Abbey comprises 3 limestone buildings, all delightfully furnished to combine the best of the old with the modern. Abbey House, the original house, is reminiscent of a country seat: a superbly proportioned lounge features an Adams fireplace, comfortable leather Chesterfields and family photographs. Enchanting bedrooms are adorned with period pieces, and a sun-catching conservatory leads to the garden terrace. Adjoining is the intimate and quaint Coach House, a converted stable block, with 4 bedrooms decorated in a cottage style; each room has it own entrance. Next door is the newly renovated and uncluttered St Deiniol's Lodge; bedrooms feature urban chic, rich wooden furniture, leather sofas and marble bathrooms. High coved ceilings, large ogee head windows, hand-carved fireplaces and crystal chandeliers heighten the relaxing ambience of the restaurant where fresh seasonal delicacies are enjoyed. Water skiing, surfing and sailing can be arranged nearby.

Our inspector loved: *The romantic location, and outstanding accommodation ranging from classic contemporary to period four posters.*

Directions: Penally Abbey is situated adjacent to the church on Penally village green.

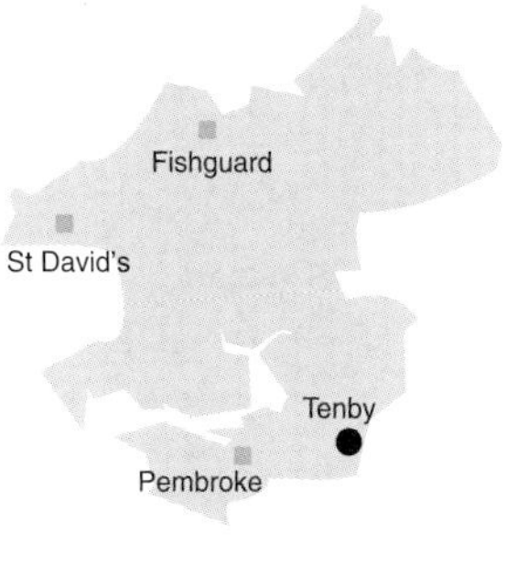

Fishguard
St David's
Tenby
Pembroke

Web: www.johansens.com/penallyabbey
E-mail: penally.abbey@btinternet.com
Tel: 0870 381 8810
International: +44 (0)1834 843033
Fax: 01834 844714

Price Guide:
single £120
double/twin £135–£170
suite £195–£200

Lamphey Court Hotel

LAMPHEY, NR TENBY, PEMBROKESHIRE SA71 5NT

Idyllically located for enjoying spectacular coastal walks and the pretty resorts of Tenby and Saundersfoot, Lamphey Court Hotel is a welcoming country house with excellent facilities. The well-proportioned, richly decorated public rooms are in-keeping with the era when the house was built. The attractive bedrooms offer an extremely high standard of comfort; family suites are located in a former coach house with generously sized rooms and extra space for families. The formal, candlelit Georgian restaurant offers a dinner menu featuring locally caught fish such as Teifi salmon and freshwater Bay lobster. The light and airy Conservatory Restaurant provides a more informal alternative for lunch and lighter meals. Guests may take advantage of the hotel's modern leisure spa, with its large indoor swimming pool overlooking the gardens and floodlit tennis courts, spa pool, saunas and a gymnasium. Skilled therapists provide a range of treatments. The Pembrokeshire National Park offers an unprecedented choice of activities close by including golf, sailing, fishing and cycling. Alternatively, visit the medieval Bishop's Palace located within the hotel grounds.

Our inspector loved: *The extensive leisure centre offering an indoor swimming pool, well equipped gymnasium, hairdresser, sauna and solarium.*

Directions: From M4 to Carmarthen links with M5, M50 and major trunk roads. From Carmarthen follow A40 to St Clears, then follow the A477 towards Pembroke. Turn left at Milton Village for Lamphey and watch for sign at the crossroads

Web: www.johansens.com/courtpembroke
E-mail: info@lampheycourt.co.uk
Tel: 0870 381 8675
International: +44 (0)1646 672273
Fax: 01646 672480

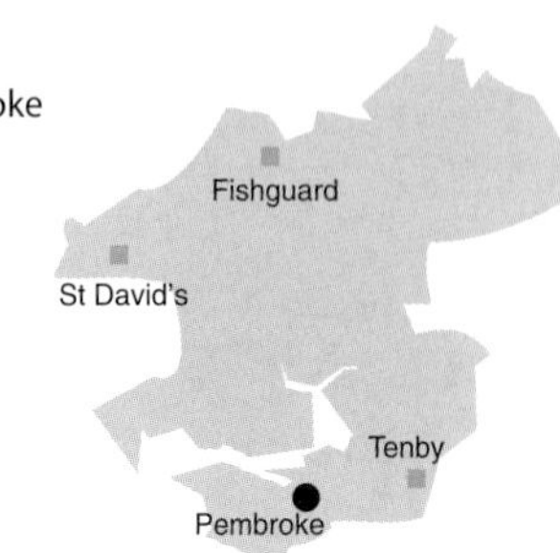

Price Guide:
single £80–£100
double/twin £115–£160

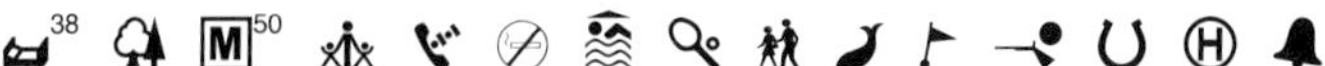

Llangoed Hall

LLYSWEN, BRECON, POWYS LD3 0YP

With a spectacular location by the Brecon Beacons and the Black Mountains and close to the world book centre of Hay-on-Wye, Llangoed Hall has been transformed into a luxurious but welcoming hideaway. Guests in search of a home-away-from-home will be impressed with General Manager Calum Milne's attention to detail and the discreet and professional service from his attentive staff. A timeless and understated elegance pervades the property, which is enhanced by Sir Bernard Ashley's exclusive Elanbach fabrics and the 23 exquisitely refurbished bedrooms that feature cast iron baths, Roberts radios and 17th-century antique mirrors. An eclectic collection of art adorns the interior and is sure to delight true enthusiasts. In the restaurant, head chef Sean Ballington serves local produce including Welsh lamb and salmon whilst the resident wine expert, Regine Ashley, selects accompanying vintages from a distinguished list. Corporate groups in search of a private location can hire Llangoed Hall on an exclusive basis. Outside, the maze has been restored to its former glory and the beautiful gardens complement the breathtaking surrounds. Fishing, rock-climbing and 4x4 driving are some of the many activities that can be enjoyed nearby.

Our inspector loved: *The ongoing evolution of Llangoed Hall. Its charm is to be cherished. A true balance of centries*

Directions: 9 miles west of Hay and 11 miles north of Brecon on the A470. Bristol and Cardiff Airports just under an hour away.

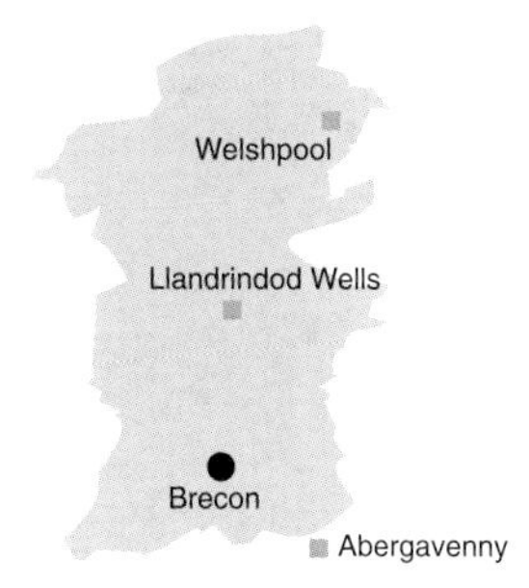

Web: www.johansens.com/llangoedhall
E-mail: enquiries@llangoedhall.com
Tel: 0870 381 8696
International: +44 (0)1874 754525
Fax: 01874 754545

Price Guide:
single from £140
double/twin from £180
suite from £340

LAKE VYRNWY HOTEL

LAKE VYRNWY, MONTGOMERYSHIRE SY10 0LY

Lush forest, wild moorland, rugged mountains and shimmering lake; this stunning country house hotel boasts breathtaking views in all directions. An idyllic haven for country-lovers, Lake Vyrnwy Hotel is set within 24,000 acres of the Vyrnwy Estate, on the hillsides of the Berwyn Mountain Range, easily accessible from the Northwest, Midlands and London. Each of the comfortable guest rooms is individually decorated and some have Jacuzzis, balconies and luxury four-poster beds fitted with sumptuous linen. Guests may dine in the unpretentious atmosphere of the AA Rosette-awarded Tower Restaurant whilst enjoying fine contemporary cuisine. The emphasis is placed on fresh local produce, in fact, the hotel uses organic lamb taken from the surrounding estate along with the hotel's game, shot during the season. With its superb location the hotel offers 9 interesting and diverse leisure activities, making it an ideal location for conferences and corporate team-building exercises. Exhilarating white water rafting, clay shooting, archery and fishing can all be arranged. There is something for everybody and tailor-made packages for any occasion can be organised. The spa is due to open in May/June 2007.

Our inspector loved: *Watching the amazing changes of weather on the lake whilst enjoying a relaxing Welsh breakfast.*

Directions: From Shrewsbury take the A458 to Welshpool then turn right onto the B4393 just after Ford (signposted to Lake Vyrnwy 28 miles).

Web: www.johansens.com/lakevyrnwy
E-mail: res@lakevyrnwy.com
Tel: 0870 381 8671
International: +44 (0)1691 870 692
Fax: 01691 870 259

Price Guide:
single £90–£155
double/twin £120–£190
suite £190–£220

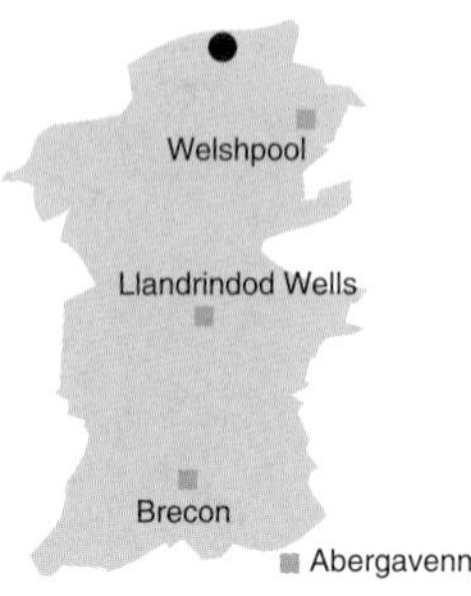

The Lake Country House and Spa

LLANGAMMARCH WELLS, POWYS LD4 4BS

A trout leaping up from a serene lake, carpets of wild flowers bobbing in the breeze and badgers ambling by the woods nearby are all sights to be savoured at this glorious country house, surrounded by 50 acres of unspoilt grounds. This hidden gem in Powys, Mid Wales, is a haven for wildlife enthusiasts with over 100 bird-nesting boxes within the grounds and ample opportunities for salmon and trout fishing and horse-riding. Decadent lounges with fine antiques, sumptuous sofas and rich paintings invite guests to discover this charming property, and the bedrooms are individually appointed with period furnishings, scatter cushions and ornate mirrors. 19 being in the main building and 12 suites in the lodge. Traditional Welsh teas are served in the drawing room by roaring log fires in the winter or beneath the chestnut tree in the summer and Welsh cakes, light chocolate sponges and melting scones with homemade jams and cream are some of the many treats to savour. Fresh produce and herbs from the garden are used in the Condé Nast Johansens award-winning restaurant whilst the superb wine list boasts over 300 choices. In addition to the outdoor pursuits and the historic sights nearby, the spa, gym and swimming pool, is situated by the lake providing an inspired setting for those wishing to unwind.

Our inspector loved: *It and could stay a week, menus so well balanced, totally comfortable. blissfully relaxing.*

Directions: From the A483 follow signs to Llangammarch Wells and then to the hotel.

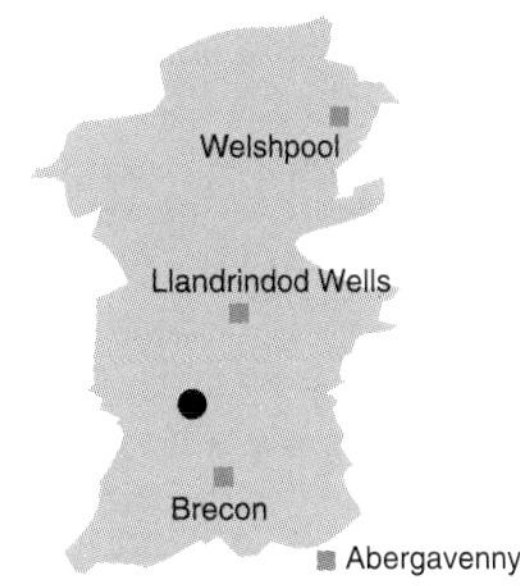

Web: www.johansens.com/lakecountryhouse
E-mail: info@lakecountryhouse.co.uk
Tel: 0870 381 8668
International: +44 (0)1591 620202
Fax: 01591 620457

Price Guide:
single £120
double/twin £160–£200
suite £200–£250

Mini Listings Country Houses

Condé Nast Johansens are delighted to recommend over 200 country houses, small hotels, inns and restaurants across Great Britain & Ireland.

Call 0800 269 397 or see the order forms on page 381 to order Guides.

England

Bath & North East Somerset

The County Hotel - 18/19 Pulteney Road, Bath, Somerset BA2 4EZ. Tel: 0870 381 8455

The Ring O' Roses - Stratton Road, Holcombe, Near Bath BA3 5EB. Tel: 0870 381 9181

Bedfordshire

▼

Cornfields Restaurant & Hotel - Wilden Road, Colmworth, Bedfordshire MK44 2NJ. Tel: 0870 381 8340

Mill House Hotel with Riverside Restaurant - Mill House, Mill Road, Sharnbrook, Bedfordshire MK44 1NP. Tel: 0870 381 9189

Berkshire

Cantley House - Milton Road, Wokingham, Berkshire RG40 5QG. Tel: 0870 381 9233

The Christopher Hotel - High Street, Eton, Windsor, Berkshire SL4 6AN. Tel: 0870 381 8526

The Cottage Inn - Maidens Green, Winkfield, Berkshire SL4 4SW. Tel: 0870 381 9234

The Inn on the Green, Restaurant with Rooms - The Old Cricket Common, Cookham Dean, Berkshire SL6 9NZ. Tel: 0870 381 8639

L'ortolan Restaurant - Church Lane, Shinfield, Reading, Berkshire RG2 9BY. Tel: 0870 381 8349

The Leatherne Bottel Riverside Restaurant - The Bridleway, Goring-on-Thames, Berkshire RG8 0HS. Tel: 0870 381 8685

The Royal Oak Restaurant - Paley Street, Maidenhead, Berkshire SL6 3JN. Tel: 0870 381 8396

Stirrups Country House Hotel - Maidens Green, Windsor, Berkshire RG42 6LD. Tel: 0870 381 9238

Buckinghamshire

Bull & Butcher - Turville, Buckinghamshire RG9 6QU. Tel: 0870 381 8451

The Dinton Hermit - Water Lane, Ford, Aylesbury, Buckinghamshire HP17 8XH. Tel: 0870 381 9295

The Ivy House - London Road, Chalfont-St-Giles, Buckinghamshire HP8 4RS. Tel: 0870 381 9236

Cambridgeshire

The Tickell Arms - 1 North Road, Whittlesford, Cambridgeshire CB2 4NZ. Tel: 0870 381 8634

Cheshire

Broxton Hall - Whitchurch Road, Broxton, Chester, Cheshire CH3 9JS. Tel: 0870 381 8387

Cornwall

Chandlers Waterside Apartment - 30A Passage Street, Fowey, Cornwall PL23 1DE. Tel: 0870 381 9204

Highland Court Lodge - Biscovey Road, Biscovey, Near St Austell, Cornwall PL24 2HW. Tel: 0870 381 9290

The Hundred House Hotel & Fish in the Fountain Restaurant - Ruan Highlanes, Near Truro, Cornwall TR2 5JR. Tel: 0870 381 9205

Lower Barn - Bosue, St Ewe, Cornwall PL26 6ET. Tel: 0870 381 8565

The Old Coastguard Hotel - Mousehole, Penzance, Cornwall TR19 6PR. Tel: 0870 381 8522

Primrose Valley Hotel - Primrose Valley, Porthminster Beach, St Ives, Cornwall TR26 2ED. Tel: 0870 381 9377

Rose-In-Vale Country House Hotel - Mithian, St Agnes, Cornwall TR5 0QD. Tel: 0870 381 8 537

Tredethy House - Helland Bridge, Wadebridge, Cornwall PL30 4QS. Tel: 0870 381 9142

Trehellas House Hotel & Restaurant - Washaway, Bodmin, Cornwall PL30 3AD. Tel: 0870 381 8953

Trelawne Hotel - The Hutches Restaurant - Mawnan Smith, Near Falmouth, Cornwall TR11 5HT. Tel: 0870 381 8954

Trevalsa Court Country House Hotel & Restaurant - School Hill, Mevagissey, St Austell, Cornwall PL26 6TH. Tel: 0870 381 8955

Wisteria Lodge & Apartments - Boscundle, Tregrehan, St Austell, Cornwall PL25 3RJ. Tel: 0870 381 9183

Cumbria

Broadoaks Country House - Bridge Lane, Troutbeck, Windermere, Cumbria LA23 1LA. Tel: 0870 381 8380

Crosby Lodge Country House Hotel - High Crosby, Crosby-on-Eden, Carlisle, Cumbria CA6 4QZ. Tel: 0870 381 8461

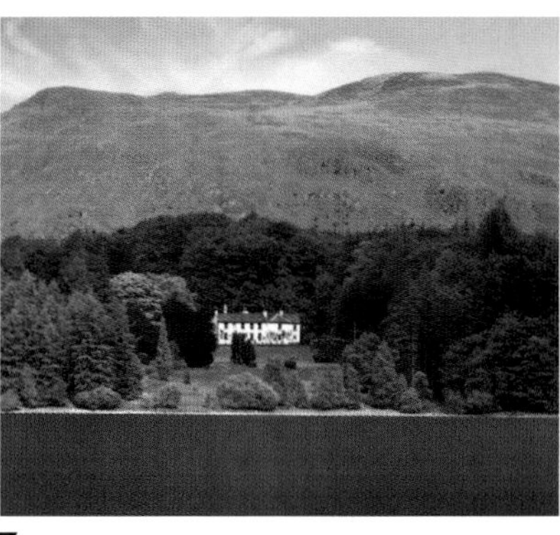

▼

Dale Head Hall Lakeside Hotel - Thirlmere, Keswick, Cumbria CA12 4TN. Tel: 0870 381 8470

Fayrer Garden House Hotel - Lyth Valley Road, Bowness-on-Windermere, Cumbria LA23 3JP. Tel: 0870 381 8517

Hipping Hall - Cowan Bridge, Kirkby Lonsdale, Cumbria LA6 2JJ. Tel: 0870 381 8632

Lake House Hotel - Lake Road, Waterhead Bay, Ambleside, Cimbria LA22 0HD. Tel: 0870 381 8492

The Leathes Head - Borrowdale, Keswick, Cumbria CA12 5UY. Tel: 0870 381 8686

Linthwaite House Hotel - Crook Road, Bowness-on-Windermere, Cumbria LA23 3JA. Tel: 0870 381 8694

Nent Hall Country House Hotel - Alston, Cumbria CA9 3LQ. Tel: 0870 381 9210

The Pheasant - Bassenthwaite Lake, Nr Cockermouth, Cumbria CA13 9YE. Tel: 0870 381 9227

The Queen's Head Hotel - Main Street, Hawkshead, Cumbria LA22 0NS. Tel: 0870 381 8844

Temple Sowerby House Hotel and Restaurant - Temple Sowerby, Penrith, Cumbria CA10 1RZ. Tel: 0870 381 8942

Underwood - The Hill, Millom, Cumbria LA18 5EZ. Tel: 0870 381 8959

West Vale Country House & Restaurant - Far Sawrey, hawkshead, Ambleside, Cumbria LA22 0LQ. Tel: 0870 381 9378

The Wheatsheaf @ Brigsteer - Brigsteer, Kendal, Cumbria LA8 8AN. Tel: 0870 381 8495

Derbyshire

The Chequers Inn - Froggatt Edge, Hope Valley, Derbyshire S32 3ZJ. Tel: 0870 381 8422

Dannah Farm Country House - Bowman's Lane, Shottle, Nr Belper, Derbyshire DE56 2DR. Tel: 0870 381 8476

Mini Listings Country Houses

Condé Nast Johansens are delighted to recommend over 200 country houses, small hotels, inns and restaurants across Great Britain & Ireland. Call 0800 269 397 or see the order forms on page 381 to order Guides.

The Plough Inn - Leadmill Bridge, Hathersage, Derbyshire S30 1BA. Tel: 0870 381 8827

The Wind in the Willows - Derbyshire Level, Glossop, Derbyshire SK13 7PT. Tel: 0870 381 9001

Devon

▼

Combe House Hotel & Restaurant - Gittisham, Honiton, Near Exeter, Devon EX14 3AD. Tel: 0870 381 8440

Heddon's Gate Hotel - Martinhoe, Parracombe, Barnstaple, Devon EX31 4PZ. Tel: 0870 381 8549

Hewitt's - Villa Spaldi - North Walk, Lynton, Devon EX35 6HJ. Tel: 0870 381 8593

Home Farm Hotel - Wilmington, Nr Honiton, Devon EX14 9JR. Tel: 0870 381 8604

Ilsington Country House Hotel - Ilsington Village, Near Newton Abbot, Devon TQ13 9RR. Tel: 0870 381 8635

Kingston House - Staverton, Near Totnes, Devon TQ9 6AR. Tel: 0870 381 8655

Lydford House - Lydford, Near Okehampton, Devon EX20 4AU. Tel: 0870 381 8525

Mill End - Dartmoor National Park, Chagford, Devon TQ13 8JN. Tel: 0870 381 8734

The New Inn - Coleford, Near Crediton, Devon EX17 5BZ. Tel: 0870 381 8757

Yeoldon House Hotel - Durrant Lane, Northam, Nr Bideford EX39 2RL. Tel: 0870 381 9019

Dorset

The Bridge House Hotel - Prout Bridge, Beaminster, Dorset DT8 3AY. Tel: 0870 381 8379

The Grange at Oborne - Oborne, Nr Sherborne, Dorset DT9 4LA. Tel: 0870 381 9240

La Fleur de Lys - Bleke Street, Shaftesbury, Dorset SP7 8AW. Tel: 0870 381 8454

Yalbury Cottage Hotel - Lower Bockhampton, Dorchester, Dorset DT2 8PZ. Tel: 0870 381 9015

Essex

The Crown House - Great Chesterford, Saffron Walden, Essex CB10 1NY. Tel: 0870 381 8465

The Pump House Apartment - 132 Church Street, Great Burstead, Essex CM11 2TR. Tel: 0870 381 8842

Gloucestershire

Bibury Court - Bibury Court, Bibury, Gloucestershire GL7 5NT. Tel: 0870 381 8360

Charlton Kings Hotel - Charlton Kings, Cheltenham, Gloucestershire GL52 6UU. Tel: 0870 381 8416

Lower Brook House - Blockley, Nr Moreton-in-Marsh, Gloucestershire GL56 9DS. Tel: 0870 381 9297

Lypiatt House - Lypiatt Road, Cheltenham, Gloucestershire GL50 2QW. Tel: 0870 381 8622

The Malt House - Broad Campden, Gloucestershire GL55 6UU. Tel: 0870 381 8714

Three Choirs Vineyards Estate - Newent, Gloucestershire GL18 1LS. Tel: 0870 381 8946

The Wild Duck Inn - Drakes Island, Ewen, Cirencester, Gloucestershire GL7 6BY. Tel: 0870 381 8997

Hampshire

Langrish House - Langrish, Near Petersfield, Hampshire GU32 1RN. Tel: 0870 381 8679

The Mill At Gordleton - Silver Street, Hordle, Nr Lymington, New Forest, Hampshire SO41 6DJ. Tel: 0870 381 8558

The Nurse's Cottage - Station Road, Sway, Lymington, New Forest, Hampshire SO41 6BA. Tel: 0870 381 8774

Herefordshire

Aylestone Court - Aylestone Hill, Hereford, Herefordshire HR1 1HS. Tel: 0870 381 8641

Ford Abbey - Pudleston, Nr Leominster, Herefordshire HR6 0RZ. Tel: 0870 381 9144

Glewstone Court - Near Ross-on-Wye, Herefordshire HR9 6AW. Tel: 0870 381 8556

Moccas Court - Moccas, Herefordshire HR2 9LH. Tel: 0870 381 8406

Seven Ledbury - 11 The Hormend, Ledbury, Herefordshire HR8 1BN. Tel: 0870 381 8653

The Swan at Hay - Church Street, Hay-on-Wye, Herefordshire HR3 5DQ. Tel: 0870 381 8628

The Verzon - Hereford Road, Trumpet, Nr Ledbury, Herefordshire HR8 2PZ. Tel: 0870 381 9348

Wilton Court Hotel - Wilton, Ross-on-Wye, Herefordshire HR9 6AQ. Tel: 0870 381 9000

Hertfordshire

Redcoats Farmhouse Hotel and Restaurant - Redcoats Green, Near Hitchin, Hertfordshire SG4 7JR. Tel: 0870 381 8851

The White House and Lion & Lamb Bar & Restaurant - Smiths Green, Dunmow Road, Takeley, Bishop's Stortford, Hertfordshire CM22 6NR. Tel: 0870 381 9334

Isle of Wight

The Hambrough - Hambrough Road, Ventnor, Isle of Wight PO38 1SQ. Tel: 0870 381 8658

Koala Cottage - Church Hollow, Godshill, Isle of Wight PO38 3DR. Tel: 0870 381 8503

Rylstone Manor - Rylstone Gardens, Shanklin, Isle of Wight PO37 6RG. Tel: 0870 381 8882

Winterbourne Country House - Bonchurch Village Road, Bonchurch, Isle of Wight PO38 1RQ. Tel: 0870 381 8504

Kent

Little Silver Country Hotel - Ashford Road, St Michaels, Tenterden, Kent TN30 6SP. Tel: 0870 381 8424

▼

Romney Bay House Hotel - Coast Road, Littlestone, New Romney, Kent TN28 8QY. Tel: 0870 381 8863

Wallett's Court Hotel & Spa - West Cliffe, St Margaret's-at-Cliffe, Dover, Kent CT15 6EW. Tel: 0870 381 8966

Lancashire

Ferrari's Restaurant & Hotel - Thornley, Longridge, Preston, Lancashire PR3 2TB. Tel: 0870 381 8459

The Inn at Whitewell - Forest Of Bowland, Clitheroe, Lancashire BB7 3AT. Tel: 0870 381 8638

Springfield House Hotel - Wheel lane, Pilling, Near Preston PR3 6HL. Tel: 0870 381 9213

Mini Listings Country Houses

Condé Nast Johansens are delighted to recommend over 200 country houses, small hotels, inns and restaurants across Great Britain & Ireland.
Call 0800 269 397 or see the order forms on page 381 to order Guides.

Tree Tops Country House Restaurant & Hotel - Southport Old Road, Formby, Nr Southport, Merseyside L37 0AB. Tel: 0870 381 8950

Leicestershire

Horse & Trumpet - Old Green, Medbourne, Near Market Harborough, Leicestershire LE16 8DX. Tel: 0870 381 9340

Sysonby Knoll Hotel - Asfordby Road, Melton Mowbray, Leicestershire LE13 0HP. Tel: 0870 381 9352

Lincolnshire

▼

Bailhouse Hotel - 34 Bailgate, Lincoln, Lincolnshire LN1 3AP. Tel: 0870 381 9212

The Crown Hotel - All Saints Place, Stamford, Lincolnshire PE9 2AG. Tel: 0870 381 8464

The Dower House Hotel - Manor Estate, Woodhall Spa, Lincolnshire LN10 6PY. Tel: 0870 381 9214

Washingborough Hall - Church Hill, Washingborough, Lincoln LN4 1BE. Tel: 0870 381 8971

Norfolk

Beechwood Hotel - Cromer Road, North Walsham, Norfolk NR28 0HD. Tel: 0870 381 8353

Broom Hall Country Hotel - Richmond Road, Saham Toney, Thetford, Norfolk IP25 7EX. Tel: 0870 381 8384

Brovey Lair - Carbrooke Road, Ovington, Thetford, Norfolk IP25 6SD. Tel: 0870 381 8385

Elderton Lodge Hotel & Langtry Restaurant - Gunton Park, Thorpe Market, Near North Walsham, Norfolk NR11 8TZ. Tel: 0870 381 8502

The Gin Trap Inn - 6 High Street, Ringstead, Hunstanton, Norfolk PE36 5JU. Tel: 0870 381 9376

The Great Escape Holiday Company - The Granary, Docking, Kings Lynn, Norfolk PE31 8LY. Tel: 0870 381 8568

Idyllic Cottages At Vere Lodge - South Raynham, Fakenham, Norfolk NR21 7HE. Tel: 0870 381 8961

The Kings Head Hotel - Great Bircham, King's Lynn, Norfolk PE31 6RJ. Tel: 0870 381 9203

The Neptune Inn & Restaurant - 85 Old Hunstanton Road, Old Hunstanton, Norfolk PE36 6HZ. Tel: 0870 381 9374

The Old Rectory - 103 Yarmouth Road, Norwich, Norfolk NR7 0HF. Tel: 0870 381 8784

The Stower Grange - School Road, Drayton, Norwich, Norfolk NR8 6EF. Tel: 0870 381 8921

Northamptonshire

The Falcon Hotel - Castle Ashby, Northamptonshire NN7 1LF. Tel: 0870 381 8512

The New French Partridge - Horton, Near Northampton, Northamptonshire NN7 2AP. Tel: 0870 381 9201

The Windmill at Badby - Main Street, Badby, Daventry, Northamptonshire NN11 3AN. Tel: 0870 381 9002

Northumberland

Waren House Hotel - Waren Mill, Bamburgh, Northumberland NE70 7EE. Tel: 0870 381 8967

Nottinghamshire

Cockliffe Country House Hotel - Burnt Stump Country Park, Burnt Stump Hill, Nottinghamshire NG5 8PQ. Tel: 0870 381 8435

Langar Hall - Langar, Nottinghamshire NG13 9HG. Tel: 0870 381 8676

Restaurant Sat Bains with Rooms - Lenton Lane, Trentside, Nottingham, Nottinghamshire NG7 2SA. Tel: 0870 381 8351

Oxfordshire

Burford Lodge Hotel & Restaurant - Oxford Road, Burford, Oxfordshire OX18 4PH. Tel: 0870 381 8473

The Dashwood Hotel & Restaurant - South Green, Heyford Road, Kirtlington, Oxfordshire OX5 3HJ. Tel: 0870 381 8378

Duke Of Marlborough Country Inn - Woodleys, Woodstock, Oxford OX20 1HT. Tel: 0870 381 9219

Fallowfields - Kingston Bagpuize With Southmoor, Oxfordshire OX13 5BH. Tel: 0870 381 8513

The Feathers - Market Street, Woodstock, Oxfordshire OX20 1SX. Tel: 0870 381 8519

The Jersey Arms - Middleton Stoney, Bicester, Oxfordshire OX25 4AD. Tel: 0870 381 8644

The Kings Head Inn & Restaurant - The Green, Bledington, Nr Kingham, Oxfordshire OX7 6XQ. Tel: 0870 381 8654

The Lamb Inn - Sheep Street, Burford, Oxfordshire OX18 4LR. Tel: 0870 381 8674

The Plough Hotel, Game & Seafood Restaurant - Bourton Road, Clanfield, Oxfordshire OX18 2RB. Tel: 0870 381 8826

The Spread Eagle Hotel - Cornmarket, Thame, Oxfordshire OX9 2BW. Tel: 0870 381 8902

Rutland

▼

Barnsdale Lodge - The Avenue, Rutland Water, Near Oakham, Rutland LE15 8AH. Tel: 0870 381 8342

The Lake Isle Restaurant & Townhouse Hotel - 16 High Street East, Uppingham, Rutland LE15 9PZ. Tel: 0870 381 8670

Shropshire

Pen-Y-Dyffryn Country Hotel - Rhydycroesau, Near Oswestry, Shropshire SY10 7JD. Tel: 0870 381 8809

Soulton Hall - Near Wem, Shropshire SY4 5RS. Tel: 0870 381 8899

Somerset

Ashwick Country House Hotel - Dulverton, Somerset TA22 9QD. Tel: 0870 381 8327

Bellplot House Hotel & Thomas's Restaurant - High Street, Chard, Somerset TA20 1QB. Tel: 0870 381 8339

Beryl - Wells, Somerset BA5 3JP. Tel: 0870 381 8358

Compton House - Townsend, Axbridge, Somerset BS26 2AJ. Tel: 0870 381 8441

Farthings Hotel & Restaurant - Hatch Beauchamp, Near Taunton, Somerset TA3 6SG. Tel: 0870 381 8515

Glencot House - Glencot Lane, Wookey Hole, Near Wells, Somerset BA5 1BH. Tel: 0870 381 8552

Karslake Country House & Restaurant - Halse Lane, Winsford, Exmoor National Park, Somerset TA24 7JE. Tel: 0870 381 9134

Three Acres Country House - Three Acres, Brushford, Dulverton, Somerset TA22 9AR. Tel: 0870 381 9229

Mini Listings Country Houses

Condé Nast Johansens are delighted to recommend over 200 country houses, small hotels, inns and restaurants across Great Britain & Ireland. Call 0800 269 397 or see the order forms on page 381 to order Guides.

Suffolk

▼

Clarice House - Horringer Court, Horringer Road, Bury St Edmunds Suffolk IP29 5PH. Tel: 0870 381 8431

The Ickworth Hotel and Apartments - Horringer, Bury St Edmunds, Suffolk IP29 5QE. Tel:

Surrey

Chase Lodge - 10 Park Road, Hampton Wick, Kingston-upon-Thames, Surrey KT1 4AS. Tel: 0870 381 8419

Great Tangley Manor - Wonersh Common, Wonersh, Near Guildford, Surrey GU5 0PT. Tel: 0870 381 8677

East Sussex

The Hope Anchor Hotel - Watchbell Street, Rye, East Sussex TN31 7HA. Tel: 0870 381 8607

West Sussex

Crouchers Country Hotel & Restaurant - Birdham Road, Apuldram, Near Chichester, West Sussex PO20 7EH. Tel: 0870 381 8462

The Mill House Hotel - Mill Lane, Ashington, West Sussex RH20 3BX. Tel: 0870 381 8735

Warwickshire

Nuthurst Grange - Hockley Heath, Warwickshire B94 5NL. Tel: 0870 381 8776

Wiltshire

Beechfield House - Beanacre, Wiltshire SN12 7PU. Tel: 0870 381 8643

The George Inn - Longbridge Deverill, Warminster, Wiltshire BA12 7DG. Tel: 0870 381 8542

The Lamb at Hindon - High Street, Hindon, Wiltshire SP3 6DP. Tel: 0870 381 9208

The Old Manor Hotel - Trowle, Near Bradford-on-Avon, Wiltshire BA14 9BL. Tel: 0870 381 8782

Stanton Manor Hotel & Gallery Restaurant - Stanton Saint Quintin, Near Chippenham, Wiltshire SN14 6DQ. Tel: 0870 381 8910

Widbrook Grange - Widbrook, Bradford-on-Avon, Near Bath, Wiltshire BA15 1UH. Tel: 0870 381 8996

Worcestershire

The Broadway Hotel - The Green, Broadway, Worcestershire WR12 7AA. Tel: 0870 381 8381

Colwall Park - Colwall, Near Malvern, Worcestershire WR13 6QG. Tel: 0870 381 8437

The Old Rectory - Ipsley Lane, Ipsley, Near Redditch, Worcestershire B98 0AP. Tel: 0870 381 9169

The Peacock Inn - Worcester Road, Boraston, Tenbury Wells, Worcestershire WR15 8LL. Tel: 0870 381 8514

The White Lion Hotel - High Street, Upton-upon-Severn, Near Malvern, Worcestershire WR8 0HJ. Tel: 0870 381 8989

North Yorkshire

The Austwick Traddock - Austwick, Via Lancaster, North Yorkshire LA2 8BY. Tel: 0870 381 8331

The Devonshire Fell - Burnsall, Skipton, North Yorkshire BD23 6BT. Tel: 0870 381 8554

Dunsley Hall - Dunsley, Whitby, North Yorkshire YO21 3TL. Tel: 0870 381 8494

Hob Green Hotel, Restaurant & Gardens - Markington, Harrogate, North Yorkshire HG3 3PJ. Tel: 0870 381 8600

The Red Lion - By The Bridge At Burnsall, Near Skipton, North Yorkshire BD23 6BU. Tel: 0870 381 8850

Stow House Hotel - Aysgarth, Leyburn, North Yorkshire DL8 3SR. Tel: 0870 381 8920

The Wensleydale Heifer - West Witton, Wensleydale, North Yorkshire DL8 4LS. Tel: 0870 381 8625

West Yorkshire

Hey Green Country House Hotel - Waters Road, Marsden, West Yorkshire HD7 6NG. Tel: 0870 381 8652

Channel Islands

Guernsey

▼

La Sablonnerie - Little Sark, Sark, Channel Islands GY9 0SD. Tel: 0870 381 8666

The White House - Herm Island, Guernsey, Channel Islands GY1 3HR. Tel: 0870 381 8988

Ireland

Galway

St Clerans Manor House - Craughwell, Co Galway, Ireland. Tel: 00 353 91 846555

Kerry

Brook Lane Hotel - Kenmare, Co Kerry, Ireland. Tel: 00 353 64 42077

Sligo

Coopershill House - Riverstown, Co Sligo, Ireland. Tel: 00 353 71 9165108

MINI LISTINGS COUNTRY HOUSES

Condé Nast Johansens are delighted to recommend over 200 country houses, small hotels, inns and restaurants across Great Britain & Ireland.

Call 0800 269 397 or see the order forms on page 381 to order Guides.

Scotland

Angus

Castleton House Hotel - Glamis, By Forfar, Angus DD8 1SJ. Tel: 0870 381 8411

Argyll & bute

Highland Cottage - Breadalbane Street, Tobermory, Isle of Mull PA75 6PD. Tel: 0870 381 9184

Dumfries & Galloway

Balcary Bay Hotel - Auchencairn, Nr Castle Douglas, Dumfries & Galloway DG7 1QZ. Tel: 0870 381 8334

Fife

The Peat Inn - Peat Inn, by Cupar, Fife KY15 5LH. Tel: 0870 381 8673

Highland

The Bridge Hotel - Dunrobin Street, Helmsdale, Sutherland KW8 6JA. Tel: 0870 381 8645

Corriegour Lodge Hotel - Loch Lochy, By Spean Bridge, Inverness-shire PH34 4EA. Tel: 0870 381 8447

Dunain Park Hotel - Inverness, IV3 8JN. Tel: 0870 381 8433

▼

Forss House Hotel - Forss, Near Thurso, Caithness KW14 7XY. Tel: 0870 381 8321

Greshornish House Hotel - Edinbane, by Portree, Isle of Skye IV51 9PN. Tel: 0870 381 8656

Hotel Eilean Iarmain - Sleat, Isle of Skye IV43 8QR. Tel: 0870 381 8619

Ruddyglow Park - Loch Assynt, By Lairg, Sutherland IV27 4HB. Tel: 0870 381 8457

The Steadings at The Grouse & Trout - Flichity, Farr, South Loch Ness, Inverness IV2 6XD. Tel: 0870 381 9138

Toravaig House Hotel - Knock Bay, Sleat, Isle of Skye IV44 8RE. Tel: 0870 381 9344

Moray

Knockomie Hotel - Grantown Road, Forres, Morayshire IV36 2SG. Tel: 0870 381 8663

Perth & Kinross

Cairn Lodge Hotel - Orchil Road, Auchterarder, Perthshire PH3 1LX. Tel: 0870 381 9284

The Four Seasons Hotel - Lochside, St Fillans, Perthshire PH6 2NF. Tel: 0870 381 8528

Scottish Borders

Castle Venlaw - Edinburgh Road, Peebles EH45 8QG. Tel: 0870 381 8410

South Ayrshire

Culzean Castle - The Eisenhower Apartment - Maybole, Ayrshire KA19 8LE. Tel: 0870 381 8469

Western Isles

Amhuinnsuidhe Castle - Amhuinnsuidhe Castle Estate, Isle of Harris HS3 3AS. Tel: 0870 381 8408

Wales

Cardiff

The Inn at the Elm Tree - St Brides, Wentlooge, Nr Newport NP10 8SQ. Tel: 0870 381 8637

Carmarthenshire

Ty Mawr Country Hotel - Brechfa, Carmarthenshire SA32 7RA. Tel: 0870 381 9318

Ceredigion

Conrah Country House Hotel - Rhydgaled, Chancery, Aberystwyth, Ceredigion SY23 4DF. Tel: 0870 381 8444

Conwy

Sychnant Pass House - Sychnant Pass Road, Conwy LL32 8BJ. Tel: 0870 381 8936

Tan-Y-Foel Country House - Capel Garmon, Nr Betws-y-Coed, Conwy LL26 0RE. Tel: 0870 381 8938

Glamorgan

Egerton Grey - Porthkerry, Nr Cardiff, Vale Of Glamorgan CF62 3BZ. Tel: 0870 381 8501

Gwynedd

Bae Abermaw - Panorama Hill, Barmouth, Gwynedd LL42 1DQ. Tel: 0870 381 8332

Hotel Maes-Y-Neuadd - Talsarnau, Near Harlech, Gwynedd LL47 6YA. Tel: 0870 381 9332

Plas Dolmelynllyn - Ganllwyd, Dolgellau, Gwynedd LL40 2HP. Tel: 0870 381 8825

Porth Tocyn Country House Hotel - Abersoch, Pwllheli, Gwynedd LL53 7BU. Tel: 0870 381 8832

Monmouthshire

The Bell At Skenfrith - Skenfrith, Monmouthshire NP7 8UH. Tel: 0870 381 8354

The Crown At Whitebrook - Whitebrook, Monmouthshire NP25 4TX. Tel: 0870 381 8563

Pembrokeshire

Wolfscastle Country Hotel & Restaurant - Wolf's Castle, Haverfordwest, Pembrokeshire SA62 5LZ. Tel: 0870 381 9162

Powys

Glangrwyney Court - Glangrwyney, Nr Crickhowell, Powys NP8 1ES. Tel: 0870 381 8547

Historic Houses, Castles & Gardens

Incorporating Museums & Galleries

We are pleased to feature over 140 places to visit during your stay at a Condé Nast Johansens recommended hotel.

England

Bedfordshire

▼

Woburn Abbey - Woburn, Bedfordshire MK17 9WA. Tel: 01525 290333

Berkshire

Mapledurham House - The Estate Office, Mapledurham, Reading, Berkshire RG4 7TR. Tel: 01189 723350

Buckinghamshire

Doddershall Park - Quainton, Aylesbury, Buckinghamshire HP22 4DF. Tel: 01296 655238

Nether Winchendon Mill - Nr Aylesbury, Buckinghamshire HP18 0DY. Tel: 01844 290199

Stowe Landscape Gardens - Stowe, Buckingham, Buckinghamshire MK18 5EH. Tel: 01280 822850

Waddesdon Manor - Waddesdon, Nr Aylesbury, Buckinghamshire HP18 0JH. Tel: 01296 653226

Cambridgeshire

The Manor - Hemingford Grey, Huntingdon, Cambridgeshire PE28 9BN. Tel: 01480 463134

Oliver Cromwell's House - 29 St Mary's Street, Ely, Cambridgeshire CB7 4HF. Tel: 01353 662062

Cheshire

Arley Hall & Gardens - Arley, Northwich, Cheshire CW9 6NA. Tel: 01565 777353

Dorfold Hall - Nantwich, Cheshire CW5 8LD. Tel: 01270 625245

Rode Hall and Gardens - Rode Hall, Scholar Green, Cheshire ST7 3QP. Tel: 01270 873237

Co Durham

The Bowes Museum - Barnard Castle, Co Durham DL12 8NP. Tel: 01833 690606

Raby Castle - Staindrop, Darlington, Co Durham DL2 3AH. Tel: 01833 660202

Cumbria

Isel Hall - Cockermouth, Cumbria CA13 0QG.

Muncaster Castle , Gardens & Owl Centre- Ravenglass, Cumbria CA18 1RQ. Tel: 01229 717614

Derbyshire

Haddon Hall - Bakewell, Derbyshire DE45 1LA. Tel: 01629 812855

Melbourne Hall & Gardens - Melbourne, Derbyshire DE73 8EN. Tel: 01332 862502

Renishaw Hall Gardens - Renishaw, Nr Sheffield, Derbyshire S21 3WB. Tel: 01246 432310

Devon

Bowringsleigh - Kingbridge, Devon TQ7 3LL. Tel: 01548 852014

Downes Estate at Crediton - Devon EX17 3PL. Tel: 01392 439046

Dorset

Moignes Court - Moreton Road, Owermoigne, Dorchester, Dorset DT2 8HY. Tel: 01305 853 300

Essex

The Gardens of Easton Lodge - Warwick House, Easton Lodge, Gt Dumnow, Essex CM6 2BB. Tel: 01371 876979

Ingatestone Hall - Hall Lane, Ingatestone, Essex CM4 9NR. Tel: 01277 353010

Gloucestershire

Cheltenham Art Gallery & Museum - Clarence Street, Cheltenham, Gloucestershire GL50 3JT. Tel: 01242 237431

Hardwicke Court - Nr Gloucester, Gloucestershire GL2 4RS. Tel: 01452 720212

Mill Dene Garden - Blockley, Moreton-in-Marsh, Gloucestershire GL56 9HU. Tel: 01386 700 457

Sezincote - Nr Moreton-in-Marsh, Gloucestershire GL56 9AW. Tel: 01386 700444

Hampshire

Beaulieu - John Montagu Building, Beaulieu, Hampshire SO42 7ZN. Tel: 01590 612345

Beaulieu Vineyard and Estate - Beaulieu Estate, John Montagu Building, Beaulieu, Hampshire SO42 7ZN. Tel: 01590 612345

Gilbert White's House and The Oates Museum - Selborne, Nr Alton, Hampshire GU34 3JH. Tel: 01420 511275

Greywell Hill House - Greywell, Hook, Hampshire RG29 1DG. Tel: 01256 703565

Pylewell House - South Baddesley, Lymington, Hampshire SO41 5SJ. Tel: 01725 513004

Herefordshire

Kentchurch Court - Kentchurch, Nr Pontrilas, Hereford, Herefordshire HR2 0DB. Tel: 01981 240228

Hertfordshire

Ashridge - Ringshall, Berkhamsted, Hertfordshire HP4 1NS. Tel: 01442 841027

Hatfield House, Park & Gardens - Hatfield, Hertfordshire AL9 5NQ. Tel: 01707 287010

Isle of Wight

Deacons Nursery - Moor View, Godshill, Isle of Wight PO38 3HW. Tel: 01983 840750

Kent

Belmont House and Gardens - Belmont Park, Throwley, Nr Faversham, Kent ME13 0HH. Tel: 01795 890202

Cobham Hall - Cobham, Kent DA12 3BL. Tel: 01474 823371

Groombridge Place Gardens - Groombridge, Tunbridge Wells, Kent TN3 9QG. Tel: 01892 861444

Hever Castle & Gardens - Hever, Nr Edenbridge, Kent TN8 7NG. Tel: 01732 865224

Knole - Sevenoaks, Kent TN15 0RP. Tel: 01732 462100

Marle Place Gardens and Gallery - Marle Place Road, Brenchley, Nr Tonbridge, Kent TN12 7HS. Tel: 01892 722304

Mount Ephraim Gardens - Hernhill, Nr Faversham, Kent ME13 9TX. Tel: 01227 751496

The New College of Cobham - Cobhambury Road, Cobham, Nr Gravesend, Kent DA12 3BG. Tel: 01474 814280

Penshurst Place & Gardens - Penshurst, Nr Tonbridge, Kent TN11 8DG. Tel: 01892 870307

Lancashire

Stonyhurst College - Stonyhurst, Clitheroe, Lancashire BB7 9PZ. Tel: 01254 827084/826345

Townhead House - Slaidburn, Via CLitheroe, Lancashire BBY 3AG. Tel: 01772 421566

London

Dulwich Picture Gallery - Gallery Road, London SE21 7AD. Tel: 020 8299 8711

Handel House Museum - 25 Brook Street, London W1K 4HB. Tel: 020 7495 1685

Pitzhanger Manor House and Gallery - Walpole Park, Mattock Lane, Ealing, London W5 5EQ. Tel: 020 8567 1227

Sir John Soane's Museum - 13 Lincoln's Inn Fields, London WC2A 3BP. Tel: 020 7405 2107

Merseyside

Knowsley Hall - Knowsley Park, Prescot, Merseyside L32 4AG. Tel: 0151 489 4827

Middlesex

Syon House - Syon Park, London Road, Brentford, Middlesex TW8 8JF. Tel: 020 8560 0882

Norfolk

Fairhaven Woodland and Water Garden - School Road, South Walsham, Norwich, Norfolk NR13 6EA. Tel: 01603 270449

Walsingham Abbey Grounds - , Walsingham, Norfolk NR22 6BP. Tel: 01328 820259

Northamptonshire

Cottesbrooke Hall and Gardens - Cottesbrooke, Northampton, Northamptonshire NN6 8PF. Tel: 01604 505808

Haddonstone Show Garden - The Forge House, Church Lane, East Haddon, Northamptonshire NN6 8DB. Tel: 01604 770711

Northumberland

Chillingham Castle - Nr Wooler, Northumberland NE66 5NJ. Tel: 01668 215359

Chipchase Castle - Chipchase, Wark on Tyne, Hexham, Northumberland NE48 3NT. Tel: 01434 230203

Seaton Delaval Hall - Seaton Sluice, Whitley Bay, Northumberland NE26 4QR. Tel: 0191 237 1493 / 0786

Nottinghamshire

Newstead Abbey - Ravenshead, Nottinghamshire NG15 8NA. Tel: 01623 455 900

Oxfordshire

Blenheim Palace - Woodstock, Oxfordshire OX20 1PX. Tel: 08700 602080

Kingston Bagpuize House - Kingston Bagpuize, Abingdon, Oxfordshire OX13 5AX. Tel: 01865 820259

Sulgrave Manor - Manor Road, Sulgrave, Banbury, Oxfordshire OX17 2SD. Tel: 01295 760205

Wallingford Castle Gardens - Castle Street, Wallingford, Oxfordshire OX10 0AL. Tel: 01491 835373

Shropshire

Shipton Hall - Shipton, Much Wenlock, Shropshire TF13 6JZ. Tel: 01746 785225

Weston Park - Weston-under-Lizard, Nr Shifnal, Shropshire TF11 8LE. Tel: 01952 852100

Somerset

The American Museum in Britain - Claverton Manor, Bath, Somerset BA2 7BD. Tel: 01225 460503

Cothay Manor & Gardens - Greenham, Wellington, Somerset TA21 0JR. Tel: 01823 672283

Great House Farm - Wells Road, Theale, Wedmore, Somerset BS28 4SJ. Tel: 01934 713133

Number 1 Royal Crescent - 1 Royal Crescent, Bath, Somerset BA1 2LR. Tel: 01225 428126

Staffordshire

The Ancient High House - Greengate Street, Stafford, Staffordshire ST16 2JA. Tel: 01785 619131

Izaak Walton's Cottage - Shallowford, nr. Stafford, Staffordshire ST15 0PA. Tel: 01785 760 278

Stafford Castle - Newport Road, Stafford, Staffordshire ST16 1DJ. Tel: 01785 257 698

Whitmore Hall - Whitmore, Newcastle-under-Lyme, Staffordshire ST5 5HW. Tel: 01782 680478

Suffolk

Kentwell Hall - Long Melford, Sudbury, Suffolk CO10 9BA. Tel: 01787 310207

Newbourne Hall - Newbourne, Nr. Woodbridge, Suffolk IP12 4NP. Tel: 01473 736277

Otley Hall - Hall Lane, Otley, Suffolk IP6 9PA. Tel: 01473 890264

Surrey

Claremont House - Claremont Drive, Esher, Surrey KT10 9LY. Tel: 01372 473623

Guildford House Gallery - 155, High Street, Guildford, Surrey GU1 3AJ. Tel: 01483 444740

Loseley Park - Guildford, Surrey GU3 1HS. Tel: 01483 304440

Painshill Park - Portsmouth Road, Cobham, Surrey KT11 1JE. Tel: 01932 868113

East Sussex

Bentley Wildfowl & Motor Museum - Halland, Nr Lewes, Sussex BN8 5AF. Tel: 01825 840573

Charleston - Firle, Lewes, East Sussex BN8 6LL. Tel: 01323 811626

Firle Place - Firle, Nr Lewes, East Sussex BN8 6LP. Tel: 01273 858307

Garden and Grounds of Herstmonceux Castle - Herstmonceux Castle, Hailsham, East Sussex BN27 1RN. Tel: 01323 833816

Merriments Gardens - Hurst Green, East Sussex TN19 7RA. Tel: 01580 860666

Preston Manor - Preston Drove, Brighton, East Sussex BN1 6SD. Tel: 01273 292770

Royal Pavilion - Brighton, East Sussex BN1 1EE. Tel: 01273 290900

West Sussex

Denmans Garden - Clock House, Denmans Lane, Fontwell, West Sussex BN18 0SU. Tel: 01243 542808

Goodwood House - Goodwood, Chichester, West Sussex PO18 0PX. Tel: 01243 755000

High Beeches Gardens - High Beeches, Handcross, West Sussex RH17 6HQ. Tel: 01444 400589

Leonardslee - Lakes & Gardens - Lower Beeding, Horsham, West Sussex RH13 6PP. Tel: 01403 891212

Uppark - South Harting, Petersfield, West Sussex GU31 5QR. Tel: 01730 825415

West Dean Gardens - West Dean , Chichester, West Sussex PO18 0QZ. Tel: 01243 818210

Worthing Museum & Art Gallery - Chapel Road, Worthing, West Sussex BN11 1HP. Tel: 01903 239999

Warwickshire

Arbury Hall - Nuneaton, Warwickshire CV10 7PT. Tel: 024 7638 2804

The Shakespeare Houses - The Shakespeare Birthplace Trust, The Shakespeare Centre, Henley Street, Stratford-upon-Avon, Warwickshire CV37 6QW. Tel: 01789 201845

West Midlands

Barber Institute of Fine Arts - The University of Birmingham, Edgbaston, Birmingham, West Midlands B15 2TS. Tel: 0121 414 7333

The Birmingham Botanical Gardens and Glasshouses - Westbourne Road, Edgbaston, Birmingham, West Midlands B15 3TR. Tel: 0121 454 1860

Wiltshire

▼ **Salisbury Cathedral** - Visitor Services, 33 The Close, Salisbury, Wiltshire SP1 2EJ. Tel: 01722 555120

Worcestershire

Harvington Hall - Harvington, Kidderminister, Worcestershire DY10 4LR. Tel: 01562 777846

Little Malvern Court - Nr Malvern, Worcestershire WR14 4JN. Tel: 01684 892988

Spetchley Park Gardens - Spetchley, Worcester, Worcestershire WR5 1RS. Tel: 01453 810303

East Riding of Yorkshire

Burton Agnes Hall & Gardens - Burton Agnes, Driffield, East Yorkshire YO25 4NB. Tel: 01262 490324

Historic Houses, Castles & Gardens

Incorporating Museums & Galleries

www.historichouses.co.uk

Historic Houses Castles & Gardens incorporating Museums&Galleries

North Yorkshire

Duncombe Park - Helmsley, York, North Yorkshire YO62 5EB. Tel: 01439 770213

The Forbidden Corner - Tupgill Park Estate, Coverham, Nr Middleham, North Yorkshire DL8 4TJ. Tel: 01969 640638

Fountains Abbey & Studley Royal - Ripon, North Yorkshire HG4 3DY. Tel: 01765 608888

Norton Conyers - Wath, Nr Ripon, North Yorkshire HG4 5EQ. Tel: 01765 640333

Ripley Castle - Ripley Castle Estate, Harrogate, North Yorkshire HG3 3AY. Tel: 01423 770152

Skipton Castle - Skipton, North Yorkshire BD23 1AW. Tel: 01756 792442

West Yorkshire

Bramham Park - Bramham, Wetherby, West Yorkshire LS23 6ND. Tel: 01937 846000

Harewood House - Harewood, Leeds, West Yorkshire LS17 9LG. Tel: 0113 218 1010

Ledston Hall - Hall Lane, Ledstone, Castleford, West Yorkshire WF10 2BB. Tel: 01423 523 423

Northern Ireland

Co Down

Seaforde Gardens - Seaforde, Downpatrick, Co Down BT30 8PG. Tel: 028 4481 1225

Ireland

Co Cork

Bantry House & Gardens - Bantry, Co Cork. Tel: 00 353 2 750 047

Co Dublin

Ardgillan Castle - Balbriggan, Co Dublin. Tel: 00 353 1 849 2212

Co Kildare

The Irish National Stud, Garden & House Museum - Tully, Kildare Town, Co Kildare. Tel: 00 353 45 521617

Co Offaly

Birr Castle Demesne & Ireland's Historic Science Centre - Birr, Co Offaly. Tel: 00 353 57 91 20336

Co Waterford

Lismore Castle Gardens - Lismore, Co Waterford. Tel: 00 353 58 54424

Co Wexford

Kilmokea Country Manor & Gardens - Great Island, Campile, Co Wexford. Tel: 00 353 51 388109

Co Wicklow

Mount Usher Gardens - Ashford, Co Wicklow. Tel: +353 404 40205

Scotland

Argyll

Inveraray Castle - Inveraray, Argyll PA32 8XE. Tel: 01499 302203

Ayrshire

Kelburn Castle and Country Centre - South Offices, Kelburn, Fairlie, Ayrshire KA29 0BE. Tel: 01475 568685

Dumfries

Drumlanrig Castle, Gardens and Country Park - Thornhill, Dumfries DG3 4AQ. Tel: 01848 330248

Orkney Islands

Balfour Castle - Shapinsay, Orkney Islands KW17 2DY. Tel: 01856 711282

Peebles

Traquair House - Innerleithen, Peebles EH44 6PW. Tel: 01896 830323

Perthshire

Scone Palace - Perth, Perthshire PH2 6BD. Tel: 01738 552300

Scottish Borders

Bowhill House & Country Park - Bowhill, Selkirk, Scottish Borders TD7 5ET. Tel: 01750 22204

Manderston - Duns, Berwickshire, Scottish Borders TD11 3PP. Tel: 01361 882636

Strathclyde

Mount Stuart - Isle of Bute, Strathclyde PA20 9LR. Tel: 01700 503877

West Lothian

Hopetoun House - South Queensferry, Nr Edinburgh West Lothian EH30 9SL. Tel: 0131 331 2451

Newliston - Kirkliston, West Lothian EH29 9EB. Tel: 0131 333 3231

Wigtownshire

Ardwell Estate Gardens - Ardwell House, Stranraer DG9 9LY. Tel: 01776 860227

Wales

Conway

Bodnant Garden - Tal-y-Cafn, Nr Colwyn Bay, Conway LL28 5RE. Tel: 01492 650460

Dyfed

Pembroke Castle - Pembroke, Dyfed SA71 4LA. Tel: 01646 681510

Flintshire

Golden Grove - Llanasa, Nr. Holywell, Flintshire CH8 9NA. Tel: 01745 854452

Gwynedd

Plas Brondanw Gardens - Menna Angharad, Plas Brondanw, Llanfrothen, Gwynedd LL48 6SW. Tel: 01766 770484

Monmouthshire

Usk Castle - Castle House, Monmouth Road, Usk, Monmouthshire NP15 1SD. Tel: 01291 672563

Pembrokeshire

St Davids Cathedral - The Close, St. David's, Pembrokeshire SA62 6RH. Tel: 01437 720199

France

Château de Chenonceau - Chenonceaux, 37150. Tel: 00 33 2 47 23 90 07

Château de Thoiry - Thoiry, Yvelines 78770 . Tel: 00 33 1 34 87 53 65

Mini Listings Europe

Condé Nast Johansens are delighted to recommend over 430 properties across Europe and The Mediterranean.
Call 0800 269 397 or see the order forms on page 381 to order guides.

Austria

KÄRNTEN (VELDEN)
Seeschlössl Velden, Klagenfurter Strasse 34, 9220 Velden, Austria. Tel: +43 4274 2824

Belgium

ANTWERP
Firean Hotel, Karel Oomsstraat 6, 2018 Antwerp, Belgium. Tel: +32 3 237 02 60

AS
Hostellerie Mardaga, 121 Stationsstraat, 3665 As, Belgium. Tel: +32 89 65 62 65

BRUGES
Hotel Die Swaene, 1 Steenhouwersdijk (Groene Rei), 8000 Bruges, Belgium. Tel: +32 50 34 27 98

KNOKKE~HEIST
Romantik Hotel Manoir du Dragon, Albertlaan 73, 8300 Knokke~Heist, Belgium. Tel: +32 50 63 05 80

KORTRIJK
Grand Hotel Damier, Grote Markt 41, 8500 Kortrijk, Belgium. Tel: +32 56 22 15 47

TURNHOUT
Hostellerie Ter Driezen, 18 Herentalsstraat, 2300 Turnhout, Belgium. Tel: +32 14 41 87 57

Croatia

DUBROVNIK
Grand Villa Argentina, Frana Supila 14, 20000 Dubrovnik, Croatia. Tel: +385 20 44 0555

TROGIR
Villa Lavandula, Put Salduna 3, 21220 Trogir, Croatia. Tel: +385 21 798 330

Czech Republic

PRAGUE
Alchymist Grand Hotel and Spa, Trziste 19, Malá Strana, 11800 Prague, Czech Republic. Tel: +420 257 286 011/016

PRAGUE
Aria Hotel Prague, Trziste 9, 118 00 Prague 1, Czech Republic. Tel: +420 225 334 111

PRAGUE
Art Hotel Prague, Nad Královskou Oborou 53, 170 00 Prague 7, Czech Republic. Tel: +420 233 101 331

PRAGUE
Bellagio Hotel Prague, U Milosrdnych 2, 110 00 Prague 1, Czech Republic. Tel: +420 221 778 999

PRAGUE
Golden Well Hotel, U Zlaté studne 166/4, 118 00 Prague 1, Czech Republic. Tel: +420 257 011 213

PRAGUE
Hotel Hoffmeister & Lily Wellness and Spa, Pod Bruskou 7, Malá Strana, 11800 Prague 1, Czech Republic. Tel: +420 251 017 111

PRAGUE
Nosticova Residence, Nosticova 1, Malá Strana, 11800 Prague, Czech Republic. Tel: +420 257 312 513/516

PRAGUE
Romantik Hotel U Raka, Cerninská 10/93, 11800 Prague 1, Czech Republic. Tel: +420 2205 111 00

Estonia

PÄRNU
Ammende Villa , Mere Pst 7, 80010 Pärnu, Estonia. Tel: +372 44 73 888

France

ALSACE~LORRAINE (COLMAR)
Hôtel Les Têtes, 19 Rue des Têtes, BP 69, 68000 Colmar, France. Tel: +33 3 89 24 43 43

ALSACE~LORRAINE (COLMAR)
Romantik Hotel le Maréchal, 4 Place Six Montagnes Noires, Petite Venise, 68000 Colmar, France. Tel: +33 3 89 41 60 32

ALSACE~LORRAINE (CONDÉ NORTHEN)
Domaine de la Grange de Condé, 41 rue des Deux Nied, 57220 Condé Northen, France. Tel: +33 3 87 79 30 50

ALSACE~LORRAINE (GÉRARDMER - VOSGES)
Hostellerie les Bas Rupts Le Chalet Fleuri, 181 Route de la Bresse, 88400 Gérardmer, Vosges, France. Tel: +33 3 29 63 09 25

ALSACE~LORRAINE (GUEBWILLER)
Hostellerie St Barnabé, 68530 Murbach - Buhl, Guebwiller, France. Tel: +33 3 89 62 14 14

ALSACE~LORRAINE (JUNGHOLTZ)
Romantik Hotel les Violettes, Thierenbach, BP 69, 68500 Jungholtz, France. Tel: +33 3 89 76 91 19

ALSACE~LORRAINE (LA WANTZENAU)
Romantik Hotel Relais de la Poste, 21 rue du Général~de~Gaulle, 67610 La Wantzenau, France. Tel: +33 3 88 59 24 80

ALSACE~LORRAINE (OBERNAI)
Hotel à la Cour d'Alsace, 3 Rue de Gail, 67210 Obernai, France. Tel: +33 3 88 95 07 00

ALSACE~LORRAINE (ROUFFACH)
Château d'Isenbourg, 68250 Rouffach, France. Tel: +33 3 89 78 58 50

ALSACE~LORRAINE (STRASBOURG - OSTWALD)
Château de L'Ile, 4 Quai Heydt, 67540 Strasbourg - Ostwald, France. Tel: +33 3 88 66 85 00

ALSACE~LORRAINE (STRASBOURG)
Romantik Hotel Beaucour-Baumann, 5 Rue des Bouchers, 67000 Strasbourg, France. Tel: +33 3 88 76 72 00

ALSACE~LORRAINE (THIONVILLE)
Romantik Hotel L'Horizon, 50 Route du Crève~Cœur, 57100 Thionville, France. Tel: +33 3 82 88 53 65

BRITTANY (BILLIERS)
Domaine de Rochevilaine, Pointe de Pen Lan, BP 69, 56190 Billiers, France. Tel: +33 2 97 41 61 61

BRITTANY (DINARD)
Villa Reine Hortense, 19, rue de la Malouine, 35800 Dinard, France. Tel: +33 2 99 46 54 31

BRITTANY (LA GOUESNIÈRE - SAINT~MALO)
Château de Bonaban, 35350 La Gouesnière, France. Tel: +33 2 99 58 24 50

BRITTANY (MISSILLAC)
Hôtel de La Bretesche, Domaine de la Bretesche, 44780 Missillac, France. Tel: +33 2 51 76 86 96

BRITTANY (MOËLAN~SUR~MER)
Manoir de Kertalg, Route de Riec~Sur~Belon, 29350 Moëlan~sur~Mer, France. Tel: +33 2 98 39 77 77

BRITTANY (NIVILLAC - LA ROCHE~BERNARD)
Domaine de Bodeuc, Route de Saint~Dolay, 56130 Nivillac, La Roche~Bernard, France. Tel: +33 2 99 90 89 63

BRITTANY (PERROS~GUIREC)
Hotel l'Agapa & Spa, 12, Rue des Bons Enfants, 22700 Perros~Guirec, France. Tel: +33 2 96 49 01 10

BRITTANY (SAINT~MALO - PLEVEN)
Manoir du Vaumadeuc, 22130 Pleven, BP 69, France. Tel: +33 2 96 84 46 17

BRITTANY (TREBEURDEN)
Ti al Lannec, 14 Allée de Mezo~Guen, 22560 Trebeurden, France. Tel: +33 2 96 15 01 01

BURGUNDY - FRANCHE~COMTÉ (AVALLON)
Château de Vault de Lugny, 11 Rue du Château, 89200 Vault de Lugny, France. Tel: +33 3 86 34 07 86

BURGUNDY - FRANCHE~COMTÉ (CHOREY~LES~BEAUNE)
Ermitage de Corton, R.N. 74, 21200 Chorey~les~Beaune, France. Tel: +33 3 80 22 05 28

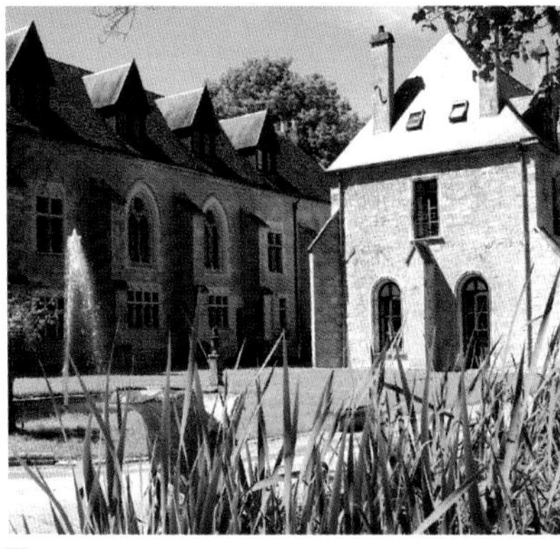

▼

BURGUNDY - FRANCHE~COMTÉ (LA BUSSIÈRE~SUR~OUCHE)
Abbaye de la Bussière, 21360 La Bussière~sur~Ouche, Côte d'Or, France. Tel: +33 3 80 49 02 29

BURGUNDY - FRANCHE~COMTÉ (MONT~SAINT~JEAN)
Château les Roches, Rue de Glanot, 21320 Mont~Saint~Jean, France. Tel: +33 3 80 84 32 71

BURGUNDY - FRANCHE~COMTÉ (POLIGNY)
Hostellerie des Monts de Vaux, Les Monts de Vaux, 39800 Poligny, France. Tel: +33 3 84 37 12 50

BURGUNDY - FRANCHE~COMTÉ (VOUGEOT)
Château de Gilly, Gilly~les~Cîteaux, 21640 Vougeot, France. Tel: +33 3 80 62 89 98

CHAMPAGNE~ARDENNES (DOLANCOURT)
Le Moulin du Landion, 5 rue Saint~Léger, 10200 Dolancourt, France. Tel: + 33 3 25 27 92 17

CHAMPAGNE~ARDENNES (ETOGES~EN~CHAMPAGNE)
Château d'Etoges, 51270 Etoges~en~Champagne, France. Tel: +33 3 26 59 30 08

CHAMPAGNE~ARDENNES (FÈRE~EN~TARDENOIS)
Château de Fère, 02130 Fère~en~Tardenois, France. Tel: +33 3 23 82 21 13

CHAMPAGNE~ARDENNES (SAINTE~PREUVE)
Domaine du Château de Barive, 02350 Sainte~Preuve, France. Tel: +33 3 23 22 15 15

CÔTE D'AZUR (AUPS)
Bastide du Calalou, Village de Moissac-Bellevue, 83630 Aups, France. Tel: +33 4 94 70 17 91

CÔTE D'AZUR (ÈZE VILLAGE)
Château Eza, Rue de la Pise, 06360 Èze Village, France. Tel: +33 4 93 41 12 24

CÔTE D'AZUR (GRASSE)
Bastide Saint~Mathieu, 35 Chemin de Blumenthal, 06130 Saint~Mathieu, Grasse, France. Tel: +33 4 97 01 10 00

CÔTE D'AZUR (LE RAYOL - CANADEL~SUR~MER)
Le Bailli de Suffren, Avenue des Américains, Golfe de Saint~Tropez, 83820 Le Rayol - Canadel~Sur~Mer, France. Tel: +33 4 98 04 47 00

Mini Listings Europe

Condé Nast Johansens are delighted to recommend over 430 properties across Europe and The Mediterranean.
Call 0800 269 397 or see the order forms on page 381 to order guides.

CÔTE D'AZUR (RAMATUELLE)
La Ferme d'Augustin, Plage de Tahiti, 83350 Ramatuelle, Near Saint~Tropez, France. Tel: +33 4 94 55 97 00

CÔTE D'AZUR (SAINT~PAUL~DE~VENCE)
Le Mas d'Artigny, Route de la Colle, 06570 Saint~Paul~de~Vence, France. Tel: +33 4 93 32 84 54

CÔTE D'AZUR (SAINT~RAPHAËL)
La Villa Mauresque, 1792 route de la Corniche, 83700 Saint~Raphaël, France. Tel: +33 494 83 02 42

CÔTE D'AZUR (VENCE)
Hôtel Cantemerle, 258 Chemin Cantemerle, 06140 Vence, France. Tel: +33 4 93 58 08 18

LOIRE VALLEY (AMBOISE)
Château de Pray, Route de Chargé, 37400 Amboise, France. Tel: +33 2 47 57 23 67

LOIRE VALLEY (AMBOISE)
Le Choiseul, 36 Quai Charles Guinot, 37400 Amboise, France. Tel: +33 2 47 30 45 45

LOIRE VALLEY (AMBOISE)
Le Manoir les Minimes, 34 Quai Charles Guinot, 37400 Amboise, France. Tel: +33 2 47 30 40 40

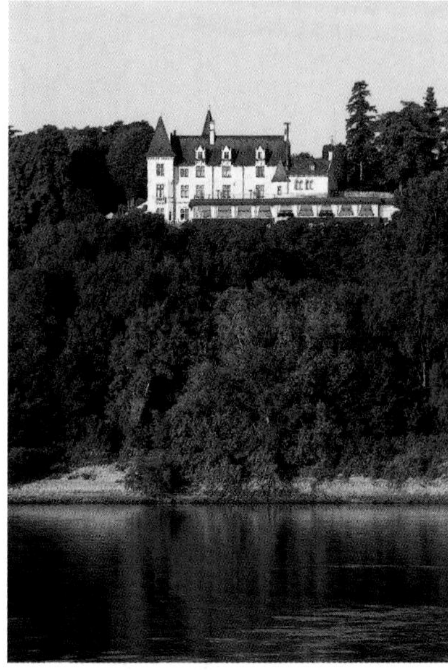

▼

LOIRE VALLEY (CHÊNEHUTTE~LES~TUFFEAUX)
Le Prieuré, 49350 Chênehutte~les~Tuffeaux, France. Tel: +33 2 41 67 90 14

LOIRE VALLEY (LUYNES, NEAR TOURS)
Domaine de Beauvois, Le Pont Clouet, Route de Cléré~les~Pins, 37230 Luynes, France. Tel: +33 2 47 55 50 11

LOIRE VALLEY (MONTBAZON, NEAR TOURS)
Château d'Artigny, 37250 Montbazon, France. Tel: +33 2 47 34 30 30

LOIRE VALLEY (MONTBAZON, NEAR TOURS)
Domaine de la Tortinière, Route de Ballan~Miré, 37250 Montbazon, France. Tel: +33 2 47 34 35 00

LOIRE VALLEY (SAINT~CALAIS)
Château de la Barre, 72120 Conflans sur Anille, France. Tel: +33 2 43 35 00 17

LOIRE VALLEY (SAINTE~MAURE~DE~TOURAINE)
Hostellerie des Hauts de Sainte~Maure, 2-4 avenue du Général~de~Gaulle, 37800 Sainte~Maure~de~Touraine, France. Tel: +33 2 47 65 50 65

MIDI~PYRÉNÉES (CARCASSONNE - MIREPOIX)
Relais Royal, 8 Rue Maréchal Clauzel, 09500 Carcassonne - Mirepoix, France. Tel: +33 5 61 60 19 19

MIDI~PYRÉNÉES (CARCASSONNE~FLOURE)
Château de Floure, 1, Allée Gaston Bonheur, 11800 Floure, France. Tel: +33 4 68 79 11 29

NORMANDY (BAYEUX - PORT~EN~BESSIN)
Château la Chenevière, Escures-Commes, 14520 Port~en~Bessin, France. Tel: +33 2 31 51 25 25

NORMANDY (CAMBREMER)
Château les Bruyères, Route du Cadran, 14340 Cambremer, France. Tel: +33 2 31 32 22 45

NORMANDY (COUTANCES~MONTPINCHON)
Le Castel, 50210 Montpinchon, France. Tel: +33 2 33 17 00 45

NORMANDY (CRICQUEBOEUF)
Manoir de la Poterie, Spa "Les Thermes", Chemin Paul Ruel, 14113 Cricqueboeuf, France. Tel: +33 2 31 88 10 40

NORMANDY (ETRETAT)
Domaine Saint~Clair, Le Donjon, Chemin de Saint~Clair, 76790 Etretat, France. Tel: +33 2 35 27 08 23

NORMANDY (SAINT~CHRISTOPHE~SUR~CONDE)
Château la Thillaye, 27450 Saint~Christophe~Sur~Conde, France. Tel: +33 2 32 56 07 24

NORTH - PICARDY (ALBERT)
Hôtel Royal Picardie, Avenue du Général Leclerc, 80300 Albert, France. Tel: +33 3 22 75 37 00

NORTH - PICARDY (BETHUNE - GOSNAY)
La Chartreuse du Val Saint~Esprit, 62199 Gosnay, France. Tel: +33 3 21 62 80 00

NORTH - PICARDY (CALAIS - RECQUES~SUR~HEM)
Château de Cocove, 62890 Recques~sur~Hem, France. Tel: +33 3 21 82 68 29

NORTH - PICARDY (DOULLENS - REMAISNIL)
Château de Remaisnil, 80600 Remaisnil, France. Tel: +33 3 22 77 07 47

NORTH - PICARDY (LILLE)
Carlton Hotel, Rue de Paris, 59000 Lille, France. Tel: +33 3 20 13 33 13

PARIS (CHAMPS~ELYSÉES)
Hôtel de Sers, 41, Avenue Pierre 1er de Serbie, 75008 Paris, France. Tel: +33 1 53 23 75 75

PARIS (CHAMPS~ELYSÉES)
Hôtel San Régis, 12 Rue Jean Goujon, 75008 Paris, France. Tel: +33 1 44 95 16 16

PARIS (CHAMPS~ELYSÉES)
La Trémoille, 14 Rue de la Trémoille, 75008 Paris, France. Tel: +33 1 56 52 14 00

PARIS (CONCORDE)
Hôtel de Crillon, 10, Place de La Concorde, 75008 Paris, France. Tel: +33 1 44 71 15 00

PARIS (ÉTOILE - PORTE MAILLOT)
Hôtel Duret, 30 rue Duret, 75116 Paris, France. Tel: +33 1 45 00 42 60

PARIS (ÉTOILE - PORTE MAILLOT)
La Villa Maillot, 143 Avenue de Malakoff, 75116 Paris, France. Tel: +33 1 53 64 52 52

PARIS (INVALIDES)
Hôtel le Tourville, 16 Avenue de Tourville, 75007 Paris, France. Tel: +33 1 47 05 62 62

PARIS (JARDIN DU LUXEMBOURG)
Le Relais Médicis, 23 Rue Racine, 75006 Paris, France. Tel: +33 1 43 26 00 60

PARIS (JARDIN DU LUXEMBOURG)
Le Sainte~Beuve, 9 Rue Sainte~Beuve, 75006 Paris, France. Tel: +33 1 45 48 20 07

PARIS (MADELEINE)
Hôtel le Lavoisier, 21 rue Lavoisier, 75008 Paris, France. Tel: +33 1 53 30 06 06

PARIS (MADELEINE)
Hôtel Opéra Richepanse, 14 Rue du Chevalier de Saint~George, 75001 Paris, France. Tel: +33 1 42 60 36 00

PARIS (MARAIS)
Hôtel du Petit Moulin, 29-31 Rue de Poitu, 75003 Paris, France. Tel: +33 1 42 74 10 10

PARIS (SAINT~GERMAIN)
Hôtel Duc de Saint~Simon, 14 rue de Saint~Simon, 75007 Paris, France. Tel: +33 1 44 39 20 20

PARIS (SAINT~GERMAIN)
Hôtel le Saint~Grégoire, 43 Rue de L'Abbé Grégoire, 75006 Paris, France. Tel: +33 1 45 48 23 23

PARIS REGION (AUGERVILLE LA RIVIÈRE)
Château d'Augerville, Place du Château, 45330 Augerville la Riviere, France. Tel: +33 2 38 32 12 07

PARIS REGION (BARBIZON)
Hostellerie du Bas-Breau, 22 Rue Grande, 77630 Barbizon, France. Tel: +33 1 60 66 40 05

PARIS REGION (BERCHERE~SUR~VESGRES)
Château de Berchères, 18 rue de Château, 28260 Berchères~sur~Vesgres, France. Tel: +33 2 37 82 28 22

PARIS REGION (GRESSY~EN~FRANCE - CHANTILLY)
Le Manoir de Gressy, 77410 Gressy~en~France, Chantilly, Near Roissy, Charles de Gaulles Airport, Paris, France. Tel: +33 1 60 26 68 00

PARIS REGION (SAINT~GERMAIN~EN~LAYE)
Cazaudehore la Forestière, 1 Avenue du Président Kennedy, 78100 Saint~Germain~en~Laye, France. Tel: +33 1 30 61 64 64

PARIS REGION (SAINT~SYMPHORIEN~LE~CHÂTEAU)
Château d'Esclimont, 28700 Saint~Symphorien~Le~Château, France. Tel: +33 2 37 31 15 15

POITOU-CHARENTES (CHÂTEAUBERNARD)
Château de L'Yeuse, 65 Rue de Bellevue, Quartier de L'Echassier, 16100 Châteaubernard, France. Tel: +33 5 45 36 82 60

POITOU-CHARENTES (LA ROCHELLE)
Hotel "Résidence de France", 43 Rue Minage, 17000 La Rochelle, France. Tel: +33 5 46 28 06 00

POITOU-CHARENTES (MARTHON)
Château de la Couronne, 16380 Marthon, France. Tel: +33 5 45 62 29 96

POITOU-CHARENTES (MASSIGNAC)
Domaine des Etangs, 16310 Massignac, France. Tel: +33 5 45 61 85 00

POITOU-CHARENTES (SAINT~PREUIL)
Relais de Saint~Preuil, Lieu-dit Chez Riviere, 16130 Saint~Preuil, France. Tel: +33 5 45 80 80 08

PROVENCE (GORDES)
Les Mas des Herbes Blanches, Joucas, 84220 Gordes, France. Tel: +33 4 90 05 79 79

PROVENCE (LE PARADOU - LES BAUX~DE~PROVENCE)
Domaine le Hameau des Baux, Chemin de Bourgeac, 13520 Le Paradou, France. Tel: +33 4 90 54 10 30

PROVENCE (LES BAUX~DE~PROVENCE)
Oustau de Baumanière, 13520 Les Baux~de~Provence, France. Tel: +33 4 90 54 33 07

PROVENCE (PORT CAMARGUE)
Le Spinaker, Pointe de la Presqu'île, Port Camargue, 30240 Le Grau~du~Roi, France. Tel: +33 4 66 53 36 37

PROVENCE (SABRAN - BAGNOLS~SUR~CÈZE)
Château de Montcaud, Combe, Bagnols~sur~Cèze, 30200 Sabran, Near Avignon, France. Tel: +33 4 66 89 60 60

Mini Listings Europe

Condé Nast Johansens are delighted to recommend over 430 properties across Europe and The Mediterranean.
Call 0800 269 397 or see the order forms on page 381 to order guides.

PROVENCE (SAINT~RÉMY~DE~PROVENCE)
Château des Alpilles, Route Départementale 31, Ancienne Route du Grès, 13210 Saint~Rémy~de~Provence, France. Tel: +33 4 90 92 03 33

PROVENCE (SAINT~SATURNIN~LES~APT)
Domaine des Andéols, 84490 Saint~Saturnin~lès~Apt, France. Tel: +33 4 90 75 50 63

RHÔNE~ALPES (CONDRIEU)
Le Beau Rivage, 2 rue du Beau-Rivage, 69420 Condrieu, France. Tel: +33 4 74 56 82 82

RHÔNE~ALPES (DIVONNE~LES~BAINS)
Château de Divonne, 01220 Divonne~les~Bains, France. Tel: +33 4 50 20 00 32

RHÔNE~ALPES (DIVONNE~LES~BAINS)
Domaine de Divonne, Avenue des Thermes, 01220 Divonne~les~Bains, France. Tel: +33 4 50 40 34 34

RHÔNE~ALPES (LES GETS)
Chalet Hôtel La Marmotte, 61 Rue du Chêne, 74260 Les Gets, France. Tel: +33 4 50 75 80 33

RHÔNE~ALPES (MEGÈVE)
Le Fer à Cheval, 36 route du Crêt d'Arbois, 74120 Megève, France. Tel: +33 4 50 21 30 39

RHÔNE~ALPES (SCIEZ~SUR~LÉMAN)
Château de Coudrée, Domaine de Coudrée, Bonnatrait, 74140 Sciez~sur~Léman, France. Tel: +33 4 50 72 62 33

SOUTH WEST (BIARRITZ)
Hôtel du Palais, 1 Avenue de L'Impératrice, 64200 Biarritz, France. Tel: +33 5 59 41 64 00

SOUTH WEST (RIBERAC - DORDOGNE)
Château le Mas de Montet, Petit-Bersac, 24600 Ribérac, Dordogne, France. Tel: +33 5 53 90 08 71

SOUTH WEST (SAINTE~RADEGONDE - SAINT~EMILION)
Château de Sanse, 33350 Sainte~Radegonde, France. Tel: +33 5 57 56 41 10

SOUTH-WEST (SOURZAC-DORDOGNE)
Le Chaufourg~en~Périgord, 24400 Sourzac, Périgord, Dordogne, France. Tel: +33 5 53 81 01 56

WESTERN LOIRE (CHALLAIN~LA~POTHERIE)
Château de Challain, 49440 Challain~la~Potherie, France. Tel: +33 2 41 92 74 26

WESTERN LOIRE (CHAMPIGNÉ - ANGERS)
Château des Briottières, 49330 Champigné, France. Tel: +33 2 41 42 00 02

Great Britain

ENGLAND (BERKSHIRE)
The Crab at Chieveley, Wantage Road, Newbury, Berkshire RG20 8UE, England. Tel: +44 1635 247550

ENGLAND (BERKSHIRE)
The French Horn, Sonning on Thames, Berkshire RG4 6TN, England. Tel: +44 1189 692 204

ENGLAND (CHESHIRE)
Hillbark Hotel, Royden Park, Frankby, Wirral, Cheshire CH48 1NP, England. Tel: +44 151 625 2400

ENGLAND (DEVON)
Soar Mill Cove Hotel, Soar Mill Cove, Salcombe, South Devon TQ7 3DS. Tel: +44 1548 561566

ENGLAND (EAST SUSSEX)
Ashdown Park Hotel, Wych Cross, Forest Row, East Sussex, RH18 5JR, England. Tel: +44 1342 824988

ENGLAND (EAST SUSSEX)
The Grand Hotel, King Edward's Parade, Eastbourne, East Sussex BN21 4EQ, England. Tel: +44 1323 412345

ENGLAND (EAST SUSSEX)
Rye Lodge, Hilder's Cliff, Rye, East Sussex TN31 7LD, England. Tel: +44 1797 223838

ENGLAND (HAMPSHIRE)
Tylney Hall, Rotherwick, Hook, Hampshire RG27 9AZ, England. Tel: +44 1256 764881

ENGLAND (LONDON)
The Cranley, 10 Bina Gardens, South Kensington, London SW5 0LA, England. Tel: +44 20 7373 0123

ENGLAND (LONDON)
Jumeirah Carlton Tower, On Cadogan Place, London SW1X 9PY, England. Tel: +44 20 7235 1234

ENGLAND (LONDON)
Jumeirah Lowndes Hotel, 21 Lowndes Street, Knightsbridge, London SW1X 9ES, England. Tel: +44 20 7823 1234

ENGLAND (LONDON)
The Mayflower Hotel, 26-28 Trebovir Road, London SW5 9NJ, England. Tel: +44 20 7370 0991

ENGLAND (LONDON)
The Royal Park, 3 Westbourne Terrace, Lancaster Gate, Hyde Park, London W2 3UL, England. Tel: +44 20 7479 6600

ENGLAND (LONDON)
Twenty Nevern Square, 20 Nevern Square, London SW5 9PD, England. Tel: +44 20 7565 9555

ENGLAND (OXFORDSHIRE)
Phyllis Court Club, Marlow Road, Henley-on-Thames, Oxfordshire RG9 2HT, England. Tel: +44 1491 570 500

ENGLAND (STAFFORDSHIRE)
Hoar Cross Hall Spa Resort, Hoar Cross, Near Yoxall, Staffordshire DE13 8QS, England. Tel: +44 1283 575671

ENGLAND (WEST SUSSEX)
Amberley Castle, Amberley, Near Arundel, West Sussex BN18 9LT, England. Tel: +44 1798 831 992

Greece

ATHENS
Astir Palace Vouliagmeni, 40 Apollonos Street, 166 71 Vouliagmeni, Athens, Greece. Tel: +30 210 890 2000

ATHENS
Hotel Pentelikon, 66 Diligianni Street, 14562 Athens, Greece. Tel: +30 2 10 62 30 650

CHIOS
Argentikon, Kambos, 82100 Chios, Greece. Tel: +30 227 10 33 111

CORFU
Villa de Loulia, Peroulades, Corfu, Greece. Tel: +30 266 30 95 394

CRETE
Athina Luxury Villas, Ksamoudochori, Platanias, 73014 Chania, Crete, Greece. Tel: +30 28210 20960

CRETE
Elounda Gulf Villas & Suites, Elounda, 72053 Crete, Greece. Tel: +30 28410 90300

CRETE
Elounda Peninsula All Suite Hotel, 72053 Elounda, Crete, Greece. Tel: +30 28410 68012

CRETE
Pleiades Luxurious Villas, Plakes, 72100 Aghios Nikolaos, Crete, Greece. Tel: +30 28410 90450

CRETE
St Nicolas Bay Hotel, PO Box 47, 72100 Aghios Nikolaos, Crete, Greece. Tel: +30 2841 025041

KAVALA
Imaret, 30-32 Poulidou Street, 65110 Kavala, Greece. Tel: +30 2510 620 151-55

LEFKADA
Pavezzo Country Retreat, Katouna, Lefkada, Greece. Tel: +30 26450 71782

MYKONOS
Apanema, Tagoo, Mykonos, Greece. Tel: +30 22890 28590

MYKONOS
Tharroe of Mykonos, Mykonos Town, Angelica, 84600 Mykonos, Greece. Tel: +30 22890 27370

RHODES
Fashion Hotel, Medieval City, 26 Panetiou Avenue, 85100 Rhodes, Greece. Tel: +30 22410 70773/4

RHODES
Melenos Lindos, Lindos, 85107 Rhodes, Greece. Tel: +30 224 40 32 222

SANTORINI
Alexander's Boutique Hotel of Oia, 84702 Oia, Santorini, Greece. Tel: +30 22860 71818

SANTORINI
Canaves Suites & Hotel, Oia, 87402 Santorini, Greece. Tel: +30 22860 71453/71128

▼

SANTORINI
Fanari Villas, Oia, 84702 Santorini, Greece. Tel: +30 22860 71007

SPETSES, NEAR ATHENS
Orloff Resort, Spetses Island, Old Harbour, 18050 Spetses, Greece. Tel: +30 229 807 5444/5

Ireland

DUBLIN
Aberdeen Lodge, 53-55 Park Avenue, Ballsbridge, Dublin 4, Ireland. Tel: +353 1 283 8155

Italy

CAMPANIA (AMALFI COAST & NAPLES)
Furore Inn Resort & Spa, Via Dell'Amore, 84010 Furore, Amalfi Coast, Italy. Tel: +39 089 830 4711

CAMPANIA (RAVELLO)
Hotel Villa Maria, Via S. Chiara 2, 84010 Ravello (SA), Italy. Tel: +39 089 857255

CAMPANIA (SORRENTO)
Grand Hotel Cocumella, Via Cocumella 7, 80065 Sant'Agnello, Sorrento, Italy. Tel: +39 081 878 2933

EMILIA ROMAGNA (PARMA)
Palazzo Dalla Rosa Prati, Strada al Duomo 7, 43100 Parma, Italy. Tel: +39 0521 386 429

Mini Listings Europe

Condé Nast Johansens are delighted to recommend over 430 properties across Europe and The Mediterranean.
Call 0800 269 397 or see the order forms on page 381 to order guides.

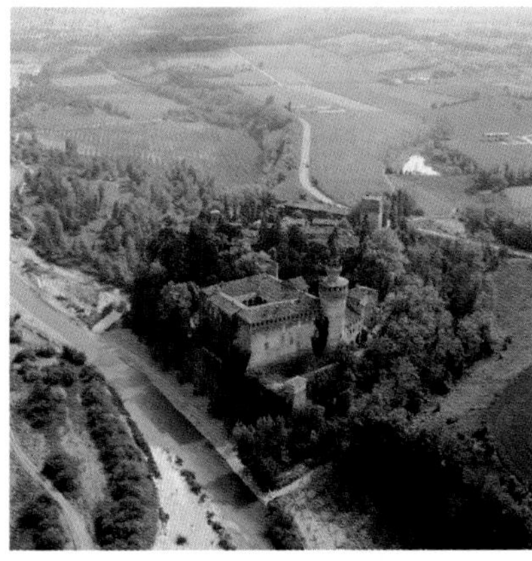

▼

EMILIA ROMAGNA (PIACENZA - BORGO DI RIVALTA)
Torre di San Martino - Historical Residence, Loc. Borgo di Rivalta, 29010 Gazzola, Piacenza, Italy. Tel: +39 0523 972002

EMILIA ROMAGNA (REGGIO EMILIA)
Hotel Posta (Historical Residence), Piazza del Monte, 2, 42100 Reggio Emilia, Italy. Tel: +39 05 22 43 29 44

EMILIA ROMAGNA (RICCIONE - ADRIATIC COAST)
Hotel des Nations, Lungomare Costituzione 2, 47838 Riccione (RN), Italy. Tel: +39 0541 647878

EMILIA ROMAGNA (SAN MARINO REPUBLIC)
Hotel Titano , Contrada del Collegio 31, 47890 San Marino (RSM), San Marino Republic. Tel: +378 99 10 07

LAZIO (CIVITA CASTELLANA)
Relais Falisco, Via Don Minzoni 19, 01033 Civita Castellana (VT), Italy. Tel: +39 0761 54 98

LAZIO (ORTE)
La Locanda della Chiocciola, Loc. Seripola SNC, 01028 Orte, Italy. Tel: +39 0761 402 734

LAZIO (PALO LAZIALE - ROME)
La Posta Vecchia Hotel Spa, Palo Laziale, 00055 Ladispoli, Rome, Italy. Tel: +39 0699 49501

LAZIO (ROME)
Hotel Aventino, Via San Domenico 10, 00153 Rome, Italy. Tel: +39 06 5745 231

LAZIO (ROME)
Hotel dei Borgognoni, Via del Bufalo 126 (Piazza di Spagna), 00187 Rome, Italy. Tel: +39 06 6994 1505

LAZIO (ROME)
Hotel dei Consoli, Via Varrone 2/d, 00193 Roma, Italy. Tel: +39 0668 892 972

LAZIO (ROME)
Hotel Fenix, Viale Gorizia 5/7, 00198 Rome, Italy. Tel: +39 06 8540 741

LAZIO (ROME)
Villa Spalletti Trivelli, via Piacenza 4, 00184 Rome, Italy. Tel: +39 06 48907934

LIGURIA (FINALE LIGURE)
Hotel Punta Est, Via Aurelia 1, 17024 Finale Ligure (SV), Italy. Tel: +39 019 600611

LIGURIA (MONEGLIA)
Abbadia San Giorgio - Historical Residence, Piazzale San Giorgio, 16030 Moneglia (GE), Italy. Tel: +39 0185 491119

LIGURIA (PORTOFINO)
Hotel San Giorgio - Portofino House, Via del Fondaco, 11, 16034 Portofino (Genova), Italy. Tel: +39 0185 26991

LIGURIA (SAN REMO COAST - DIANO MARINA)
Grand Hotel Diana Majestic, Via Oleandri 15, 18013 Diano Marina (IM), Italy. Tel: +39 0183 402 727

LIGURIA (SANTA MARGHERITA - PORTOFINO COAST)
Grand Hotel Miramare, Via Milite Ignoto, 30, 16038 Santa Margherita Ligure - Genova, Liguria, Italy. Tel: +39 0185 287013

LIGURIA (SESTRI LEVANTE)
Hotel Vis à Vis, Via della Chiusa 28, 16039 Sestri Levante (GE), Italy. Tel: +39 0185 42661

LOMBARDY (BELLAGIO - LAKE COMO)
Grand Hotel Villa Serbelloni, Via Roma 1, 22021 Bellagio, Lake Como, Italy. Tel: +39 031 950 216 or +39 031 956 450

LOMBARDY (BORMIO-BAGNI NUOVI - VALTELLINA)
Bagni di Bormio Spa Resort, Località Bagni Nuovi, 23038 Valdidentro (Sondrio), Italy. Tel: +39 0342 901890

LOMBARDY (CANTELLO - VARESE)
Albergo Madonnina, Largo Lanfranco da Ligurno 1, 21050 Cantello - Varese, Italy. Tel: +39 0332 417 731

LOMBARDY (ISEO HILLS - LAKE ISEO)
I Due Roccoli Relais, Via Silvio Bonomelli, Strada per Polaveno, 25049 Iseo (Brescia), Italy. Tel: +39 030 9822 977/8

LOMBARDY (LAKE GARDA - GARDONE RIVIERA)
Grand Hotel Gardone Riviera, Via Zanardelli 84, 25083 Gardone Riviera (BS), Lake Garda, Italy. Tel: +39 0365 20261

LOMBARDY (LAKE GARDA - SALÒ)
Hotel Bellerive, Via Pietro da Salò 11, 25087 Salò (BS), Italy. Tel: +39 0365 520 410

LOMBARDY (LIVIGNO - VALTELLINA)
Hotel Marzia, Via Pedrana 388, 23030 Livigno (SO), Italy. Tel: +39 0342 996 020

LOMBARDY (MILAN - FRANCIACORTA)
L'Albereta Relais & Châteaux, Via Vittorio Emanuele II, no 23, 25030 Erbusco (Bs), Italy. Tel: +39 030 7760 550

LOMBARDY (MILAN - MONZA)
Hotel de la Ville, Viale Regina Margherita 15, 20052 Monza (MI), Italy. Tel: +39 039 3942 1

LOMBARDY (MILAN)
Petit Palais maison de charme, Via Molino delle Armi 1, 20123 Milan, Italy. Tel: +39 02 584 891

MARCHE (CASTEL DI LUCO - ACQUASANTA TERME)
Castel di Luco, Acquasanta Terme, Frazione Castel di Luco, 63041 (AP), Italy. Tel: +39 0736 802319

PIEMONTE (ALAGNA - MONTE ROSA)
Hotel Cristallo, Piazza degli Alberghi, 13021 Alagna (VC), Italy. Tel: +39 0163 922 822/23

PIEMONTE (CLAVIERE)
Hotel Bes, Via Nazionale 18, 10050 Claviere (TO), Italy. Tel: +39 0122 878735

PIEMONTE (GAVI)
Albergo L'Ostelliere, Frazione Monterotondo 56, 15065 Gavi (AL), Piedmont, Italy. Tel: +39 0143 607 801

PIEMONTE (LAKE MAGGIORE - BELGIRATE)
Villa dal Pozzo d'Annone, Strada Statale del Sempione 5, 28832 Belgirate (VB), Lake Maggiore, Italy. Tel: +39 0322 7255

PIEMONTE (LAKE MAGGIORE - CANNOBIO)
Hotel Pironi, Via Marconi 35, 28822 Cannobio, Lake Maggiore (VB), Italy. Tel: +39 0323 70624

PIEMONTE (LAKE MAGGIORE - STRESA)
Hotel Villa Aminta, Via Sempione Nord 123, 28838 Stresa (VB), Italy. Tel: +39 0323 933 818

PIEMONTE (PENANGO - ASTI - MONFERRATO)
Relais Il Borgo, Via Biletta 60, 14030 Penango (AT), Italy. Tel: +39 0141 921272

PUGLIA (MARTINA FRANCA)
Relais Villa San Martino, Via Taranto, Zona G - 59, 74015 Martina Franca (TA), Italy. Tel: +39 080 480 5152

SARDINIA (ALGHERO)
Villa Las Tronas, Lungomare Valencia 1, 07041 Alghero (SS), Italy. Tel: +39 079 981 818

SARDINIA (PORTO CERVO - COSTA SMERALDA)
Grand Hotel in Porto Cervo, Località Cala Granu, 07020 Porto Cervo (SS), Italy. Tel: +39 0789 91533

SARDINIA (SANTA MARGHERITA DI PULA - CAGLIARI)
Villa del Parco and Spa at Forte Village, SS 195, Km 39.600, Santa Margherita di Pula, 09010 Cagliari, Italy. Tel: +39 070 92171

SICILY (AEOLIAN ISLANDS - LIPARI)
Grand Hotel Arciduca, Via G Franza, 98055 Lipari (ME), Isole Eolie, Italy. Tel: +39 090 9812 136

SICILY (AEOLIAN ISLANDS - SALINA)
Hotel Signum, Via Scalo 15, 98050 Salina~Malfa, Italy. Tel: +39 090 9844 222

SICILY (CALATABIANO)
Castello di San Marco, Via San Marco 40, 95011 Calatabiano, Taormina (CT), Italy. Tel: +39 095 641 181

SICILY (MODICA)
Palazzo Failla Hotel, Via Blandini 5, 97010 Modica (RG), Italy. Tel: +39 0932 941 059

SICILY (RAGUSA IBLA)
Locanda Don Serafino, Via XI Febbraio, 15 Ragusa Ibla, Italy. Tel: +39 0932 220 065

SICILY (TAORMINA MARE)
Grand Hotel Atlantis Bay, Via Nazionale 161, Taormina Mare (ME), Italy. Tel: +39 0942 618 011

SICILY (TAORMINA MARE)
Grand Hotel Mazzarò Sea Palace, Via Nazionale 147, 98030 Taormina (ME), Italy. Tel: +39 0942 612 111

SICILY (TAORMINA RIVIERA - MARINA D'AGRO)
Baia Taormina Hotel - Resort & Spa, Statale dello Ionio, Km 39, 98030 Marina d'Agro, Taormina Riviera (ME), Italy. Tel: +39 0942 756 292

TRENTINO - ALTO ADIGE / DOLOMITES (BOLZANO - FIÈ ALLO SCILIAR)
Romantik Hotel Turm, Piazza della Chiesa 9, 39050 Fiè Allo Sciliar (Bz), Italy. Tel: +39 0471 725014

TRENTINO - ALTO ADIGE / DOLOMITES (BOLZANO - NOVA LEVANTE)
Posthotel Cavallino Bianco, Via Carezza 30, 39056 Nova Levante (Bz), Dolomites, Italy. Tel: +39 0471 613113

TRENTINO - ALTO ADIGE / DOLOMITES (COLFOSCO - CORVARA)
Romantik Hotel Art Hotel Cappella, Str. Pecei 17, Alta Badia - Dolomites, 39030 Colfosco - Corvara (BZ), Italy. Tel: +39 0471 836183

TRENTINO - ALTO ADIGE / DOLOMITES (MERANO)
Castel Fragsburg, Via Fragsburg 3, 39012 Merano, Italy. Tel: +39 0473 244071

TRENTINO - ALTO ADIGE - DOLOMITES (VAL BADIA)
Hotel Gardena Grodnerhof, Str. Vidalong 3, 39046 Ortisei, Italy. Tel: +39 0471 796 315

TUSCANY (AMBRA - CHIANTI ARETINO)
Le Case Del Borgo - Tuscan Luxury Living, Loc. Duddova, 52020 Ambra (Arezzo), Italy. Tel: +39 055 991 871

TUSCANY (CASTAGNETO CARDUCCI - MARINA)
Tombolo Talasso Resort, Via del Corallo 3, 57024 Marina di Castagneto Carducci (LI), Italy. Tel: +39 0565 74530

TUSCANY (CORTONA)
Villa Marsili, Viale Cesare Battisti 13, 52044 Cortona (Arezzo), Italy. Tel: +39 0575 605 252

TUSCANY (ELBA ISLAND - PORTOFERRAIO)
Hotel Villa Ottone, Loc. Ottone, 57037 Portoferraio (LI), Isola d'Elba, Italy. Tel: +39 0565 933 042

TUSCANY (FLORENCE - BORGO SAN LORENZO)
Monsignor Della Casa Country Resort, Via di Mucciano 16, 50032 Borgo San Lorenzo, Florence, Italy. Tel: +39 055 840 821

Mini Listings Europe

Condé Nast Johansens are delighted to recommend over 430 properties across Europe and The Mediterranean.
Call 0800 269 397 or see the order forms on page 381 to order guides.

TUSCANY (FLORENCE)
Casa Howard, 18 via della Scala, Piazza Santa Maria Novella, Florence, Italy. Tel: +39 066 992 4555

TUSCANY (FLORENCE)
Hotel Lorenzo Il Magnifico, Via Lorenzo Il Magnifico 25, 50129 Florence, Italy. Tel: +39 055 463 0878

TUSCANY (FLORENCE)
Marignolle Relais & Charme, Via di S Quirichino a Marignolle 16, 50124 Florence, Italy. Tel: +39 055 228 6910

TUSCANY (FLORENCE)
Relais Piazza Signoria, Via Vacchereccia 3, 50122 Florence, Italy. Tel: +39 055 3987239

TUSCANY (FLORENCE)
Relais Santa Croce, Via Ghibellina 15, 50122 Florence, Italy. Tel: +39 055 2342230

TUSCANY (FLORENCE)
Residenza del Moro, Via del Moro 15, 50123 Florence, Italy. Tel: +39 055 290884

TUSCANY (FLORENCE)
Villa Montartino, Via Gherardo Silvani 151, 50125 Florence, Italy. Tel: +39 055 223520

TUSCANY (FORTE DEI MARMI)
Hotel Byron, Viale A Morin 46, 55042 Forte dei Marmi (LU), Italy. Tel: +39 0584 787 052

TUSCANY (LORO CIUFFENNA - AREZZO)
Relais Villa Belpoggio (Historical House), Via Setteponti Ponente 40, 52024 Loro Ciuffenna, Arezzo, Italy. Tel: +39 055 9694411

TUSCANY (LUCCA - PIETRASANTA)
Albergo Pietrasanta - Palazzo Barsanti Bonetti, Via Garibaldi 35, 55045 Pietrasanta (Lucca), Italy. Tel: +39 0584 793 727

TUSCANY (LUCCA - SAN LORENZO A VACCOLI)
Albergo Villa Marta, Via del Ponte Guasperini 873, San Lorenzo a Vaccoli, 55100 Lucca, Italy. Tel: +39 0583 37 01 01

TUSCANY (MONTEBENICHI - CHIANTI AREA)
Country House Casa Cornacchi, Loc. Montebenichi, 52021 Arezzo, Tuscany, Italy. Tel: +39 055 998229

TUSCANY (PISA)
Hotel Relais Dell'Orologio, Via della Faggiola 12/14, 56126 Pisa, Italy. Tel: +39 050 830 361

TUSCANY (POGGI DEL SASSO - MAREMMA)
Castello di Vicarello, Loc. Vicarello, 58044 Poggi del Sasso (GR), Italy. Tel: +39 0564 990 718

TUSCANY (PORTO ERCOLE - ARGENTARIO)
Il Pellicano Hotel & Spa, Loc. Sbarcatello, 58018 Porto Ercole (Gr), Tuscany, Italy. Tel: +39 0564 858111

TUSCANY (ROCCATEDERIGHI - GROSSETO)
Pieve di Caminino (Historical Residence), Via Prov. di Peruzzo, 58028 Roccatederighi - Grosseto, Italy. Tel: +39 0564 569 736/7 or +39 3933 356 605

TUSCANY (SIENA - ASCIANO)
Hotel Borgo CasaBianca, Località Casabianca, 53041 Asciano (SI), Italy. Tel: +39 0577 704 362

TUSCANY (SIENA - LOCALITA BAGNAIA)
Borgo La Bagnaia Resort, Spa and Events Venue, Strada Statale 223 Km 12, 53016 Localita Bagnaia - Siena, Italy. Tel: +39 0577 813000

TUSCANY (SIENA - MONTEPULCIANO)
Relais Dionora, Via Vicinale di Poggiano, 53040 Montepulciano (Siena), Italy. Tel: +39 0578 717 496

TUSCANY (SIENA - MONTEPULCIANO)
Villa di Poggiano, Via di Poggian 7, 53045 Montepulciano (Siena), Tuscany, Italy. Tel: +39 0578 758292

TUSCANY (SIENA - MONTERIGGIONI - STROVE)
Castel Pietraio, Strada di Strove 33, 53035 Monteriggioni, Italy. Tel: +39 0577 300020

TUSCANY (SIENA - PIEVESCOLA)
Relais la Suvera (Dimora Storica), 53030 Pievescola - Siena, Italy. Tel: +39 0577 960 300

TUSCANY (VIAREGGIO)
Hotel Plaza e de Russie, Piazza d'Azeglio 1, 55049 Viareggio (LU), Italy. Tel: +39 0584 44449

UMBRIA (ASSISI - ARMENZANO)
Romantik Hotel le Silve di Armenzano, 06081 Loc. Armenzano, Assisi (PG), Italy. Tel: +39 075 801 9000

UMBRIA (ASSISI - TORDANDREA)
San Crispino Resort & Spa, Loc Tordandrea - Assisi, Tordandrea (PG), Italy. Tel: +39 075 804 3257

UMBRIA (CORTONA - PETRIGNANO)
Relais Alla Corte del Sole, Loc. I Giorgi, 06061 Petrignano del Lago (PG), Italy. Tel: +39 075 9689008

UMBRIA (GUBBIO)
Castello di Petroia, Località Scritto di Gubbio, Petroia, 06020 Gubbio (Pg), Italy. Tel: +39 075 92 02 87

▼

UMBRIA (ORVIETO - ALLERONA)
I Casali di Monticchio, Vocabolo Monticchio 34, 05011 Allerona, Orvieto (TR), Italy. Tel: +39 0763 62 83 65

UMBRIA (PERUGIA - DERUTA)
L'Antico Forziere , Via della Rocca 2, 06051 Casalina Deruta (PG), Italy. Tel: +39 075 972 4314

UMBRIA (PERUGIA - PIEVE SAN QUIRICO)
Le Torri di Bagnara (Medieval Historical Residences), Strada della Bruna 8, 06080 Pieve San Quirico, Perugia, Italy. Tel: +39 075 579 2001 and +39 335 6408 549

UMBRIA (PERUGIA - SAN MARTINO)
Alla Posta dei Donini, Via Deruta 43, 06079 San Martino in Campo (PG), Italy. Tel: +39 075 609 132

UMBRIA (UMBERTIDE - CALZOLARO)
La Preghiera, Via del Refari, 06018 (PG), Calzolaro, Umbertide, Italy. Tel: +39 075 9302428

VALLE D'AOSTA (COURMAYEUR - MONT BLANC)
Mont Blanc Hotel Village, Localita La Croisette 36, 11015 La Salle (AO), Valle d'Aosta, Italy. Tel: +39 0165 864 111

VALLE D'AOSTA (GRESSONEY~LA~TRINITE)
Hotel Jolanda Sport, Loc. Edelboden 31, Gressoney~La~Trinite, 11020 Gressoney La Trinita (Aosta), Italy. Tel: +39 0125 366 140

VENETO (BASSANO DEL GRAPPA)
Hotel Villa Ca' Sette, Via Cunizza da Romano 4, 36061 Bassano del Grappa, Italy. Tel: +39 0424 383 350

VENETO (LAKE GARDA - VERONA - BARDOLINO)
Color Hotel, Via Santa Cristina 5, 37011 Bardolino (VR), Italy. Tel: +39 045 621 0857

VENETO (LAKE GARDA - VERONA - PESCHIERA DEL GARDA)
Ai Capitani Hotel, Via Castelletto 2/4, Peschiera del Garda (VR), Italy. Tel: +39 045 6400782 or 7553071

VENETO (LAKE GARDA - VERONA - SAN VIGILIO)
Locanda San Vigilio, Località San Vigilio, 37016 Garda (VR), Italy. Tel: +39 045 725 66 88

VENETO (LIDO DI JESOLO)
Park Hotel Brasilia, Via Levantina, 30017 Lido di Jesolo, Italy. Tel: +39 0421 380851

VENETO (ROLLE DI CISON DI VALMARINO)
Foresteria Duca di Dolle, Via Piai Orientale 5, 31030 Rolle di Cison di Valmarino (TV), Italy. Tel: +39 0438 975 809

VENETO (TREVISO - ASOLO)
Albergo Al Sole, Via Collegio 33, 31011 Asolo, Treviso, Italy. Tel: +39 0423 951 332

VENETO (VENICE - LIDO)
Albergo Quattro Fontane - Residenza d'Epoca, Via Quattro Fontane 16, 30126 Lido di Venezia, Venice, Italy. Tel: +39 041 526 0227

VENETO (VENICE)
Ca Maria Adele, Dorsoduro 111, 30123 Venice, Italy. Tel: +39 041 52 03 078

VENETO (VENICE)
Hotel Flora, San Marco 2283/A, 30124 Venice, Italy. Tel: +39 041 52 05 844

VENETO (VENICE)
Hotel Giorgione, SS Apostoli 4587, 30131 Venice, Italy. Tel: +39 041 522 5810

VENETO (VENICE)
Hotel Sant' Elena Venezia, Calle Buccari 10, Sant' Elena, 30132 Venice, Italy. Tel: +39 041 27 17 811

VENETO (VENICE)
Londra Palace, Riva degli Schiavoni, 4171, 30122 Venice, Italy. Tel: +39 041 5200533

VENETO (VENICE)
Novecento Boutique Hotel, San Marco 2684, 30124 Venice, Italy. Tel: +39 041 24 13 765

VENETO (VERONA - COSTERMANO)
Locanda San Verolo, Località San Verolo, 37010 Costermano (VR), Italy. Tel: +39 045 720 09 30

VENETO (VERONA - SAN PIETRO IN CARIANO)
Villa Giona, Via Cengia 8, 37029 San Pietro in Cariano (VR), Italy. Tel: +39 045 685 50 11

VENETO (VERONA - VALPOLICELLA)
Relais la Magioca, Via Moron 3, 37024 Negrar - Valpolicella (VR), Italy. Tel: +39 045 600 0167

VENETO (VERONA)
Hotel Gabbia d'Oro (Historical Residence), Corso Porta Borsari 4A, 37121 Verona, Italy. Tel: +39 045 8003060

Latvia

JURMALA
TB Palace Hotel & Spa, Pilsonu Street 8, Jurmala, LV-2015, Latvia. Tel: +371 714 7094

RIGA
Hotel Bergs, Bergs Bazaar, Elizabetes Street 83/85, 1050, Riga, Latvia. Tel: +371 777 09 00

Lithuania

VILNIUS
Grotthuss Hotel, Ligoninės 7, 01134 Vilnius, Lithuania. Tel: +370 5 266 0322

VILNIUS
The Narutis Hotel, 24 Pilies Street, 01123 Vilnius, Lithuania. Tel: +370 5 2122 894

MINI LISTINGS EUROPE

Condé Nast Johansens are delighted to recommend over 430 properties across Europe and The Mediterranean.
Call 0800 269 397 or see the order forms on page 381 to order guides.

Luxembourg

REMICH
Hotel Saint~Nicolas, 31 Esplanade, 5533 Remich, Luxembourg. Tel: +35 226 663

Montenegro

ST. STEFAN
Villa Montenegro, 2 Vukice Mitrovic Str, 86312 St. Stefan, Montenegro. Tel: +381 86 468 802

The Netherlands

AMSTERDAM
Ambassade Hotel, Herengracht 341, 1016 Amsterdam, The Netherlands. Tel: +31 20 5550222

NOORD BRABANT - BREDA
Bliss Hotel, Torenstraat 9, 4811 XV Breda, The Netherlands. Tel: +31 076 533 5980

▼

SANTPOORT - AMSTERDAM
Duin & Kruidberg Country Estate, Duin en Kruidbergerweg 60, 2071 Santpoort, Amsterdam, The Netherlands. Tel: +31 23 512 1800

VREELAND
Hotel Restaurant de Nederlanden, Duinkerken 3, 3633 EM, Vreeland aan de Vecht, The Netherlands. Tel: +31 294 232 326

ZEELAND - VEERE
Auberge de Campveerse Toren, Kaai 2, 4351 AA Veere, The Netherlands. Tel: +31 0118 501 291

Poland

Hotel Copernicus, ul. Kanonicza 16, 31-002 Kraków, Poland. Tel: +48 12 424 34 00/1/2

Portugal

ALENTEJO (BORBA - ESTREMOZ)
Monte da Fornalha, Borba - Estremoz, Portugal. Tel: +351 268 840 314

ALENTEJO (BORBA)
Casa do Terreiro do Poço, Largo dos Combatentes da Grande Guerra 12, 7150-152 Borba, Portugal. Tel: +351 917 256077

ALENTEJO (ÉVORA)
Convento do Espinheiro Heritage Hotel & Spa, Canaviais, 7005-839 Évora, Portugal. Tel: +351 266 788 200

ALENTEJO (MÉRTOLA)
Estalagem São Domingos, Rua Dr Vargas, Mina de São Domingos, 7750-171 Mértola, Portugal. Tel: +351 286 640 000

ALENTEJO (MONTEMOR~O~NOVO)
Monte do Chora Cascas, Apt 296, 7050-013 Montemor~o~Novo, Portugal. Tel: +351 266 899 690

ALENTEJO (REDONDO)
Convento de São Paulo, Aldeia da Serra, 7170-120 Redondo, Portugal. Tel: +351 266 989 160

ALGARVE (ALMANCIL)
Hotel Quinta do Lago, 8135-024 Almancil, Algarve, Portugal. Tel: +351 289 350 350

▼

ALGARVE (GARRÃO)
Quinta Jacintina, Garrão de Cima, 8135-025 Almancil, Portugal. Tel: +351 289 350 090

ALGARVE (LAGOS)
Villa Esmeralda, Porto de Mós, 8600 Lagos, Portugal. Tel: +351 282 760 430

BEIRAS (MARIALVA - MÊDA)
Casas do Côro, Marialvamed Turismo Histórico e Lazer Lda, Largo do Côro, 6430-081 Marialva, Mêda, Portugal Tel: +351 91 755 2020

LISBON & TAGUS VALLEY (CASCAIS)
Albatroz Palace, Luxury Suites, Rua Frederico Arouca 100, 2750-353 Cascais, Lisbon, Portugal. Tel: +351 21 484 73 80

LISBON & TAGUS VALLEY (CASCAIS)
Hotel Cascais Mirage, Av. Marginal, No 8554, 2754-536 Cascais, Portugal. Tel: +351 210 060 600

LISBON & TAGUS VALLEY (CASCAIS)
Senhora da Guia, Estrada do Guincho, 2750-642 Cascais, Portugal. Tel: +351 214 869 239

LISBON & TAGUS VALLEY (LISBON)
As Janelas Verdes, Rua das Janelas Verdes 47, 1200-690 Lisbon, Portugal. Tel: +351 21 39 68 143

LISBON & TAGUS VALLEY (LISBON)
Heritage Av. Liberdade, Avenida da Liberdade 28, 1250-145 Lisbon, Portugal. Tel: +351 213 404 040

LISBON & TAGUS VALLEY (LISBON)
Hotel Britania, Rua Rodrigues Sampaio 17, 1150-278 Lisbon, Portugal. Tel: +351 21 31 55 016

MADEIRA (FUNCHAL)
Quinta da Bela Vista, Caminho do Avista Navios 4, 9000 Funchal, Madeira, Portugal. Tel: +351 291 706 400

MADEIRA (PONTA DO SOL)
Estalagem da Ponta do Sol, Quinta da Rochinha, 9360 Ponta do Sol, Madeira, Portugal. Tel: +351 291 970 200

OPORTO & NORTHERN PORTUGAL (ERVEDOSA DO DOURO)
Quinta de San José, 5130-123 Ervedosa do Douro, Portugal. Tel: +351 254 420000 or +351 917 220450

OPORTO & NORTHERN PORTUGAL (PINHÃO)
Vintage House, Lugar da Ponte, 5085-034 Pinhão, Portugal. Tel: +351 254 730 230

OPORTO & NORTHERN PORTUGAL (VIANA DO CASTELO)
Casa da Torre das Neves, Lugar de Neves, Vila de Punhe 4905-653, Viana do Castelo, Portugal. Tel: +351 266 197 390

OPORTO & NORTHERN PORTUGAL (VIDAGO)
Vidago Palace Hotel & Golf, Parque de Vidago, 5425-307 Vidago, Portugal. Tel: +351 276 990 900

Slovakia

SALGOVCE - PIESTANY
The Château, Salgovce 28, 95606 Slovakia. Tel: +421 385 395 155

Slovenia

BLED
Hotel Golf , Cankarjeva 4, 4260 Bled, Slovenia. Tel: +386 4579 1700

Spain

ANDALUCÍA (ANTEQUERA - LA JOYA)
Hotel La Fuente del Sol, Paraje Rosas Bajas, 29260 La Joya, Antequera, Spain Tel: +34 95 12 39 823

ANDALUCÍA (ARCOS DE LA FRONTERA)
Hacienda el Santiscal, Avda. El Santiscal 129 (Lago de Arcos), 11638 Arcos de La Frontera, Spain. Tel: +34 956 70 83 13

ANDALUCÍA (ARCOS DE LA FRONTERA)
Hotel Cortijo Faín, Carretera de Algar Km 3, 11630 Arcos de la Frontera, Cádiz, Spain. Tel: +34 956 704 131

ANDALUCÍA (BENAHAVÍS - MARBELLA)
Gran Hotel Benahavís, Huerta de Rufino s/n, 29679 Benahavís, Málaga, Spain. Tel: +34 902 504 862

ANDALUCÍA (CORDOBA)
Hospes Palacio del Bailío, Ramirez de las Casas Deza 10-12, 14001 Cordoba, Spain. Tel: +34 957 498 993

ANDALUCÍA (ESTEPONA)
Gran Hotel Elba Estepona & Thalasso Spa, Urb. Arena Beach, Ctra. Estepona-Cádiz 151, 29680 Estepona, Spain. Tel: +34 952 809 200

ANDALUCÍA (GAUCIN)
Hotel Casablanca, Calla Teodoro de Molina, No 12, 29480 Gaucin, Málaga, Spain. Tel: +34 952 151 019

ANDALUCÍA (GRANADA - COSTA TROPICAL)
Casa de los Bates, Carretera Nacional 340 Málaga - Almeria, Km 329, 5 Salobreña - Motril, Provincia de Granada, Spain. Tel: +34 958 349 495

ANDALUCÍA (GRANADA)
Barceló la Bobadilla *** GL,** Finca La Bobadilla, Apto. 144, 18300 Loja, Granada, Spain. Tel: +34 958 32 18 61

ANDALUCÍA (GRANADA)
El Ladrón de Agua, Carrera del Darro 13, 18010 Granada, Spain. Tel: +34 958 21 50 40

ANDALUCÍA (GRANADA)
Hospes Palacio de los Patos, C/ Solarillo de Gracia 1, 18002 Granada, Andalucía, Spain. Tel: +34 958 536 516

ANDALUCÍA (GRANADA)
Hotel Casa Morisca, Cuesta de la Victoria 9, 18010 Granada, Spain. Tel: +34 958 221 100

ANDALUCÍA (GRANADA)
Hotel Palacio de Santa Inés, Cuesta de Santa Inés 9, 18010 Granada, Spain. Tel: +34 958 22 23 62

ANDALUCÍA (GRANADA)
Palacio de los Navas, Calle Navas 1, 18009 Granada, Spain. Tel: +34 958 21 57 60

Mini Listings Europe

Condé Nast Johansens are delighted to recommend over 430 properties across Europe and The Mediterranean.
Call 0800 269 397 or see the order forms on page 381 to order guides.

ANDALUCÍA (GRANADA)
Santa Isabel la Real, Santa Isabel La Real 19, 18010 Granada, Spain. Tel: +34 958 294 658

ANDALUCÍA (JEREZ DE LA FRONTERA)
Casa Viña de Alcantara, Ctra. de Arcos Km 7.8, Jerez (Cádiz), Spain. Tel: +34 956 393 010

ANDALUCÍA (MÁLAGA)
El Molino de Santillán, Ctra. de Macharaviaya, Km 3, 29730 Rincón de la Victoria, Málaga, Spain. Tel: +34 952 40 09 49

ANDALUCÍA (MÁLAGA)
Hotel Molina Lario, Molina Lario 22, 29015 Málaga, Spain. Tel: +34 952 06 002

ANDALUCÍA (MARBELLA)
Gran Hotel Guadalpin Banús, c/ Edgar Neville, s/n 29660 Nueva Andalucía, Marbella, Málaga, Spain. Tel: +34 952 89 94 04 or +34 952 89 97 00

ANDALUCÍA (MARBELLA)
Gran Hotel Guadalpin Marbella, Blvd. Príncipe Alfonso de Hohenlohe, 29600 Marbella, Málaga, Spain Tel: +34 952 89 94 04 or +34 952 89 94 00

ANDALUCÍA (MARBELLA)
Vasari Resort & Spa, Urb. La Alzambra, Edif. Vasari Center, 29660 Marbella, Málaga, Spain. Tel: +34 952 907 806

ANDALUCÍA (MIJAS~COSTA)
Gran Hotel Guadalpin Byblos, Urbanización Mijas Golf, 29650 Mijas, Málaga, Spain. Tel: +34 952 89 94 04 or +34 952 89 94 03

ANDALUCÍA (RONDA)
Hotel Molino del Arco, Partido de los Frontones s/n, 29400 Ronda, Málaga, Spain. Tel: +34 952 114 017

ANDALUCÍA (SEVILLA - CAZALLA DE LA SIERRA)
Palacio de San Benito, c/San Benito S/N, 41370 Cazalla de La Sierra, Sevilla, Spain. Tel: +34 954 88 33 36

ANDALUCÍA (SEVILLA - ÉCIJA)
Hotel Palacio de Los Granados, Emilio Castelar 42, 41400 Écija, Sevilla, Spain. Tel: +34 955 905 344

ANDALUCÍA (SEVILLA - GUILLENA)
Hotel Cortijo Águila Real, Ctra. Guillena-Burguillos Km 4, 41210 Guillena, Sevilla, Spain. Tel: +34 955 78 50 06

ANDALUCÍA (SEVILLA - LAS CABEZAS)
Cortijo Soto Real, Ctra. Las Cabezas - Villamartin Km 13, 41730 Las Cabezas de San Juan, Sevilla, Spain. Tel: +34 955 869 200

ANDALUCÍA (SEVILLA - OSUNA)
Palacio Marqués de la Gomera, C/ San Pedro 20, 41640 Osuna, Sevilla, Spain. Tel: +34 95 4 81 22 23

ANDALUCÍA (SEVILLA - SANLÚCAR LA MAYOR)
Hacienda Benazuza el Bulli Hotel, C/Virgin de las Nieves S/N, 41800 Sanlúcar La Mayor, Seville, Spain. Tel: +34 955 70 33 44

ANDALUCÍA (SEVILLA)
Casa No 7, Calle Virgenes No 7, 41004 Sevilla, Spain. Tel: +34 954 221 581

ANDALUCÍA (SEVILLA)
Hospes las Casas del Rey de Baeza, C/Santiago, Plaza Jesús de la Redención 2, 41003 Sevilla, Spain. Tel: +34 954 561 496

ANDALUCÍA (SOTOGRANDE)
Hotel Almenara, A-7 (National Road), 11310 Sotogrande, Spain. Tel: +34 956 58 20 00 or +34 902 18 18 36

ANDALUCÍA (ÚBEDA)
Palacio de la Rambla, Plaza del Marqués 1, 23400 Úbeda~Jaén, Spain. Tel: +34 953 75 01 96

ARAGÓN (TRAMACASTILLA DE TENA)
Hotel el Privilegio de Tena, Plaza Mayor, 22663 Tramacastilla de Tena, Aragón, Spain. Tel: +34 974 487 206

ARAGÓN (VALDERROBRES)
La Torre del Visco, 44587 Fuentespalda, Teruel, Spain. Tel: +34 978 76 90 15

ASTURIAS (CANGAS DE ONÍS)
Hotel La Cepada, Avenida Contranquil s/n, 33550 Cangas de Onís, Spain. Tel: +34 985 84 94 45

ASTURIAS (VILLAMAYOR)
Palacio de Cutre, La Goleta S/N, Villamayor, 33583 Infiesto, Asturias, Spain. Tel: +34 985 70 80 72

BALEARIC ISLANDS (IBIZA)
Atzaró Agroturismo, Ctra. San Juan, Km 15, 07840 Santa Eulalia, Ibiza, Balearic Islands Tel: +34 971 33 88 38

BALEARIC ISLANDS (IBIZA)
Can Lluc, Crta. Santa Inés, km 2, 07816 San Rafael, Ibiza, Balearic Islands. Tel: +34 971 198 673

BALEARIC ISLANDS (IBIZA)
Cas Gasi, Camino Viejo de Sant Mateu s/n, PO Box 117, 07814 Santa Gertrudis, Ibiza, Balearic Islands. Tel: +34 971 197 700

BALEARIC ISLANDS (MALLORCA)
Blau Porto Petro Beach Resort & Spa, Avenida des Far 12, 07691 Porto Petro (Santanyi), Mallorca, Balearic Islands. Tel: +34 971 648 282

BALEARIC ISLANDS (MALLORCA)
Ca's Xorc, Carretera de Deià, Km 56.1, 07100 Sóller, Mallorca, Balearic Islands. Tel: +34 971 63 82 80

BALEARIC ISLANDS (MALLORCA)
Can Simoneta, Ctra. de Artá a Canyamel km 8, Finca Torre de Canyamel, 07580 Capdepera, Mallorca, Balearic Islands. Tel: +34 971 816 110

BALEARIC ISLANDS (MALLORCA)
Hospes Maricel, Carretera d'Andratx 11, 07181 Cas Català, (Calvià) Mallorca, Balearic Islands. Tel: +34 971 707 744

BALEARIC ISLANDS (MALLORCA)
Hotel Aimia, Santa Maria del Camí, 1 07108 Port de Sóller, Mallorca, Spain. Tel: +34 971 631 200

BALEARIC ISLANDS (MALLORCA)
Hotel Cala Sant Vicenç, c/Maressers 2, Cala Sant Vicenç, 07469 Pollença, Mallorca, Spain. Tel: +34 971 53 02 50

BALEARIC ISLANDS (MALLORCA)
Hotel Dalt Murada, C/ Almudaina 6-A, 07001 Palma de Mallorca, Mallorca, Balearic Islands. Tel: +34 971 425 300

BALEARIC ISLANDS (MALLORCA)
Hotel Migjorn, Poligono 18, Parcela 477, Campos, Mallorca, Spain. Tel: +34 971 650 668

BALEARIC ISLANDS (MALLORCA)
Hotel Tres, C/ Apuntadores 3, 07012 Palma de Mallorca, Balearic Islands, Spain. Tel: +34 971 717 333

BALEARIC ISLANDS (MALLORCA)
La Reserva Rotana, Cami de Sa Vall, Km 3, Apart. Correos 69, 07500 Manacor, Mallorca, Spain. Tel: +34 971 84 56 85

BALEARIC ISLANDS (MALLORCA)
Palacio Ca Sa Galesa, Carrer de Miramar 8, 07001 Palma de Mallorca, Balearic Islands. Tel: +34 971 715 400

BALEARIC ISLANDS (MALLORCA)
Read's Hotel & Spa, Carretera Viejo de Alaro S/n, Santa María 07320, Mallorca, Balearic Islands. Tel: +34 971 14 02 61

BALEARIC ISLANDS (MALLORCA)
Son Brull Hotel & Spa, Ctra. Palma - Pollença, MA 2200 - Km 49.8, 07460 Pollença, Mallorca, Spain. Tel: +34 971 53 53 53

BALEARIC ISLANDS (MALLORCA)
Valldemossa Hotel & Restaurant, Ctra. Vieja de Valldemossa s/n, 07170 Valldemossa, Mallorca, Balearic Islands. Tel: +34 971 61 26 26

CANARY ISLANDS (FUERTEVENTURA)
Hotel Elba Palace Golf, Urb. Fuerteventura Golf Club, Ctra. de Jandia, km11, 35610 Antigua, Fuerteventura, Canary Islands. Tel: +34 928 16 39 22

CANARY ISLANDS (FUERTEVENTURA)
Kempinski Atlantis Bahía Real, Avenida Grandes Playas s/n, 35660 Corralejo, Fuerteventura, Canary Islands. Tel: +34 928 53 64 44

CANARY ISLANDS (GRAN CANARIA)
Gran Hotel Lopesan Costa Meloneras, C/Mar Mediterráneo 1, 35100 Maspalomas, Gran Canaria, Canary Islands. Tel: +34 928 12 81 00

CANARY ISLANDS (GRAN CANARIA)
Gran Hotel Lopesan Villa del Conde, C/Mar Mediterráneo 7, Urbanización Costa Meloneras, 35100 Maspalomas, Gran Canaria, Canary Islands. Tel: +34 928 563 200

CANARY ISLANDS (LANZAROTE)
Caserío de Mozaga, Mozaga 8, 35562 San Bartolomé, Lanzarote, Canary Islands. Tel: +34 928 520 060

CANARY ISLANDS (LANZAROTE)
Princesa Yaiza Suite Hotel Resort, Avenida Papagayo s/n, 35570 Playa Blanca, Yaiza, Lanzarote, Canary Islands. Tel: +34 928 519 222

▼

CANARY ISLANDS (TENERIFE)
Abama, Carretera General TF-47, Km 9, 38687 Guía de Isora, Tenerife, Canary Islands. Tel: +34 922 126 000

CANARY ISLANDS (TENERIFE)
Gran Hotel Bahía del Duque Resort *** G.Lujo,** C/Alcalde Walter Paetzmann, s/n, 38660 Costa Adeje, Tenerife, Canary Islands. Tel: +34 922 74 69 00

CANARY ISLANDS (TENERIFE)
Hotel Jardín Tropical, Calle Gran Bretaña, 38670 Costa Adeje, Tenerife, Canary Islands. Tel: +34 922 74 60 00

CANARY ISLANDS (TENERIFE)
Hotel las Madrigueras, Golf Las Américas, 38660 Playa de Las Américas, Tenerife, Canary Islands. Tel: +34 922 77 78 18

CANARY ISLANDS (TENERIFE)
Jardín de la Paz, Calle de Acentejo 48-52, 38370 La Matanza, Tenerife, Canary Islands. Tel: +34 922 578 818

CASTILLA LA MANCHA (BELVÍS DE LA JARA)
Finca Canturias, Ctra. Alcaudete - Calera, Km 12, 45660 Belvís de la Jara, Toledo, Spain. Tel: +34 925 59 41 08

CASTILLA Y LEÓN (SALAMANCA - TOPAS)
Castillo de Buen Amor, Carretera National 630 Km 317.6, 37799 Topas, Salamanca, Spain. Tel: +34 923 355 002

CASTILLA Y LEÓN (SALAMANCA - VALDERÓN)
Hacienda Zorita, Carretera Salamanca-Ledesma, Km 8.7, 37115 Valderón, Salamanca, Spain. Tel: +34 923 129 400

Mini Listings Europe

Condé Nast Johansens are delighted to recommend over 380 properties across Europe and The Mediterranean.
Call 0800 269 397 or see the order forms on page 425 to order guides.

CASTILLA Y LEÓN (SALAMANCA)
Hotel Rector, c/Rector Esperabé 10-Apartado 399, 37008 Salamanca, Spain. Tel: +34 923 21 84 82

CATALUÑA (ALCANAR)
Tancat de Codorniu, Ctra. N340, Km 1059, 43530 Alcanar, Spain. Tel: +34 977 737 194

CATALUÑA (BARCELONA)
Gallery Hotel, C/ Rosselló 249, 08008 Barcelona, Spain. Tel: +34 934 15 99 11

CATALUÑA (BARCELONA)
Grand Hotel Central, Via Laietana 30, 08003 Barcelona, Spain. Tel: +34 93 295 79 00

CATALUÑA (BARCELONA)
Hotel Casa Fuster, Passeig de Gràcia 132, 08008 Barcelona, Spain. Tel: +34 93 255 30 00

CATALUÑA (BARCELONA)
Hotel Claris, Pau Claris 150, 08009 Barcelona, Spain. Tel: +34 93 487 62 62

CATALUÑA (BARCELONA)
Hotel Cram, C/ Aribau 54, 8011 Barcelona, Spain. Tel: +34 93 216 77 00

CATALUÑA (BARCELONA)
Hotel Duquesa de Cardona, Paseo Colon 12, 08002 Barcelona, Spain. Tel: +34 93 268 90 90

CATALUÑA (BARCELONA)
Hotel Gran Derby, Calle Loreto 28, 08029 Barcelona, Spain. Tel: +34 93 445 2544

CATALUÑA (BARCELONA)
Hotel Granados 83, c/ Enric Granados 83, 08008 Barcelona, Spain. Tel: +34 93 492 96 70

CATALUÑA (BARCELONA)
Hotel Omm, Rosselló 265, 08008 Barcelona, Spain. Tel: +34 93 445 40 00

CATALUÑA (BARCELONA)
Hotel Pulitzer, C/Bergara 8, 08002 Barcelona, Spain. Tel: +34 93 481 67 67

CATALUÑA (BEGUR)
El Convent Begur, c/del Racó 2, sa Riera, 17255 Begur, Spain. Tel: +34 972 62 30 91

CATALUÑA (BOLVIR DE CERDANYA)
Torre del Remei, Camí Reial s/n, 17539 Bolvir de Cerdanya, Gerona, Spain. Tel: +34 972 140 182

CATALUÑA (COSTA BRAVA)
Hotel Rigat, Av. America 1, Playa de Fenals, 17310 Lloret de Mar, Costa Brava, Gerona, Spain. Tel: +34 972 36 52 00

CATALUÑA (COSTA BRAVA)
Hotel Santa Marta, Playa de Santa Cristina, 17310 Lloret de Mar, Spain. Tel: +34 972 364 904

CATALUÑA (LA GARRIGA)
Gran Hotel Balneario Blancafort, Mina 7, 08530 La Garriga (Barcelona), Spain. Tel: +34 93 860 56 00

CATALUÑA (LA SELVA DEL CAMP)
Mas Passamaner, Camí de la Serra 52, 43470 La Selva del Camp (Tarragona), Spain. Tel: +34 977 766 333

CATALUÑA (ROSES)
Romantic Villa - Hotel Vistabella , Cala Canyelles Petites, PO Box 3, 17480 Roses (Gerona), Spain. Tel: +34 972 25 62 00

CATALUÑA (SITGES)
Dolce Sitges Hotel, Av. Cami de Miralpeix 12, Sitges 08870, Spain. Tel: +34 938 109 000

CATALUÑA (SITGES)
San Sebastian Playa Hotel, Calle Port Alegre 53, 08870 Sitges (Barcelona), Spain. Tel: +34 93 894 86 76

EXTREMADURA (BADAJOZ - ZAFRA)
Casa Palacio Conde de la Corte, Plaza Pilar Redondo 2, 06300 Zafra (Badajoz), Spain. Tel: +34 924 563 311

EXTREMADURA (JERTE - CÁCERES)
Tunel del Hada Hotel & Spa, Travesía de la Fuente Nueva 2, 10612 Jerte (Cáceres), Spain. Tel: +34 927 470 000

MADRID (MADRID)
Antiguo Convento, C/ de Las Monjas, s/n Boadilla del Monte, 28660 Madrid, Spain. Tel: +34 91 632 22 20

MADRID (MADRID)
Gran Meliá Fénix, Hermosilla 2, 28001 Madrid, Spain. Tel: +34 91 431 67 00

MADRID (MADRID)
Hotel Orfila, C/Orfila, No 6, 28010 Madrid, Spain. Tel: +34 91 702 77 70

MADRID (MADRID)
Hotel Quinta de los Cedros, C/Allendesalazar 4, 28043 Madrid, Spain. Tel: +34 91 515 2200

MADRID (MADRID)
Hotel Urban, Carrera de San Jerónimo 34, 28014 Madrid, Spain. Tel: +34 91 787 77 70

MADRID (MADRID)
Hotel Villa Real, Plaza de las Cortes 10, 28014 Madrid, Spain. Tel: +34 914 20 37 67

PAIS VASCO (ARMINTZA)
Hotel Arresi, Portugane 7, 48620 Armintza, Spain. Tel: +34 94 68 79 208

VALENCIA (ALICANTE)
Hospes Amérigo, C/ Rafael Altamira 7, 03002 Alicante, Spain. Tel: +34 965 14 65 70

VALENCIA (ALICANTE)
Hotel Sidi San Juan & Spa, Playa de San Juan, 03540 Alicante, Spain. Tel: +34 96 516 13 00

VALENCIA (ALQUERIAS - CASTELLÓN)
Torre la Mina, C/ La Regenta 1, 12539 Alquerias-Castellón, Spain. Tel: +34 964 57 1746/0180

VALENCIA (BENICÀSSIM)
Hotel Termas Marinas el Palasiet, Partida Cantallops s/n, 12560 Benicàssim, Castellón, Costa del Azahar, Spain. Tel: +34 964 300 250

VALENCIA (DÉNIA)
La Posada del Mar, Plaça de les Drassanes, 1-2 03700 Dénia, Spain. Tel: +34 96 643 29 66

VALENCIA (JÁTIVA - XÀTIVA)
Hotel Mont Sant, Subida Al Castillo, s/n Játiva - Xàtiva, 46800 Valencia, Spain. Tel: +34 962 27 50 81

VALENCIA (TÁRBENA)
Casa Lehmi , El Buscarró 1-3, E-03518 Tárbena, Alicante, Spain. Tel: +34 96 588 4018

VALENCIA (VALENCIA)
Hospes Palau de la Mar, Navarro Reverter 14, 46004 Valencia, Spain. Tel: +34 96 316 2884

VALENCIA (VALENCIA)
Hotel Sidi Saler & Spa, Playa el Saler, 46012 Valencia, Spain. Tel: +34 961 61 04 11

VALENCIA (VILAMARXANT)
Mas de Canicattí, Ctra. de Pedralba, Km 2.9, 46191 Vilamarxant, Valencia, Spain. Tel: +34 96 165 05 34

Switzerland

LUGANO
Villa Sassa - Hotel & Spa, Via Tesserete 10, 6900 Lugano, Switzerland. Tel: +41 91 911 41 11

WEGGIS - LAKE LUCERNE
Park Hotel Weggis, Hertensteinstrasse 34, 6353 Weggis, Switzerland. Tel: +41 41 392 05 05

ZÜRICH
Alden Hotel Spügenschloss, Splügenstrasse 2, Genferstrasse, 8002 Zürich, Switzerland. Tel: +41 1 289 99 99

Turkey

ANTALYA
The Marmara Antalya, Eski Lara Yolu No 136, Sirinyali, Antalya, Turkey. Tel: +90 242 249 36 00

BODRUM PENINSULA - MUGLA
Divan Bodrum Palmira, Kelesharim Caddesi 6, Göltürkbükü, Mugla, 48483 Bodrum, Turkey. Tel: +90 252 377 5601

BODRUM
The Marmara Bodrum, Suluhasan Caddesi, Yokusbasi, Mevkii No 18, PO Box 199, 48400 Bodrum, Turkey. Tel: +90 252 313 8130

ÇESME - IZMIR
Degirmen Otel, Degirmen Sok 3, Alaçati, Çesme, Izmir, Turkey. Tel: +90 232 716 6714

GÖREME - CAPPADOCIA
Cappadocia Cave Suites, Gafferli Mahallesi, unlü Sokak, 50180 Göreme - Nevsehir, Turkey. Tel: +90 384 271 2800

▼

ISTANBUL
Ajia Hotel, Ahmet Rasim Pasa Yalisi, Çubuklu Caddesi, No 27, Kanlica, Istanbul, Turkey. Tel: +90 216 413 9300

ISTANBUL
The Marmara Istanbul, Taksim Meydani, Taksim, 34437 Istanbul, Turkey. Tel: +90 212 251 4696

ISTANBUL
The Marmara Pera, Mesrutiyet Caddesi, Tepebasi, 34430 Istanbul, Turkey. Tel: +90 212 251 4646

ISTANBUL
Sumahan On The Water, Kulelí Caddesi No 51, Çengelköy, 34684 Istanbul, Turkey. Tel: +90 216 422 8000

KALEIÇI - ANTALYA
Tuvana Residence, Tuzcular Mahallesi, Karanlik Sokak 7, 07100 Kaleiçi - Antalya, Turkey. Tel: +90 242 247 60 15

KALKAN - ANTALYA
Villa Mahal, PO Box 4 Kalkan, 07960 Antalya, Turkey. Tel: +90 242 844 32 68

KAS - ANTALYA
Villa Hotel Tamara, Çururbag Yarimadasi, Kas, Antalya, Turkey. Tel: +90 242 836 3273

SAPANCA - ADAPAZARI
Richmond Nua Wellness - Spa, Sahilyolu, 54600 Sapanca, Adapazari, Turkey. Tel: +90 264 582 2100

ÜRGÜP - CAPPADOCIA
Sacred House, Karahandere Mahallesi, Barbaros Hayrettin Sokak, No 25, 50400 Ürgüp, Turkey. Tel: +90 384 341 7102

Mini Listings The Americas

Condé Nast Johansens are delighted to recommend 310 properties across The Americas, Atlantic, Caribbean and Pacific.
Call 0800 269 397 or see the order forms on page 381 to order guides.

Recommendations in Canada

CANADA - BRITISH COLUMBIA (SALT SPRING ISLAND)

Hastings House Country Estate
160 Upper Ganges Road, Salt Spring Island, British Columbia V8K 2S2
Tel: +1 250 537 2362
Fax: +1 250 537 5333
Web: www.johansens.com/hastingshouse

CANADA - BRITISH COLUMBIA (TOFINO)

The Wickaninnish Inn
Box 250, Tofino, British Columbia V0R 2Z0
Tel: +1 250 725 3100
Fax: +1 250 725 3110
Web: www.johansens.com/wickaninnish

CANADA - BRITISH COLUMBIA (VANCOUVER)

The Sutton Place Hotel Vancouver
845 Burrard Street, Vancouver, British Columbia V6Z 2K6
Tel: +1 604 682 5511
Fax: +1 604 682 5513
Web: www.johansens.com/suttonplacebc

CANADA - BRITISH COLUMBIA (VANCOUVER)

Wedgewood Hotel & Spa
845 Hornby Street, Vancouver, British Columbia V6Z 1V1
Tel: +1 604 689 7777
Fax: +1 604 608 5348
Web: www.johansens.com/wedgewoodbc

CANADA - BRITISH COLUMBIA (VICTORIA)

Villa Marco Polo Inn
1524 Shasta Place, Victoria, British Columbia V8S 1X9
Tel: +1 250 370 1524
Fax: +1 250 370 1624
Web: www.johansens.com/villamarcopolo

CANADA - NEW BRUNSWICK (ST ANDREWS BY-THE-SEA)

Kingsbrae Arms
219 King Street, St. Andrews By-The-Sea, New Brunswick E5B 1Y1
Tel: +1 506 529 1897
Fax: +1 506 529 1197
Web: www.johansens.com/kingsbraearms

CANADA - ONTARIO (CAMBRIDGE)

Langdon Hall Country House Hotel & Spa
1 Langdon Drive, Cambridge, Ontario N3H 4R8
Tel: +1 519 740 2100
Fax: +1 519 740 8161
Web: www.johansens.com/langdonhall

CANADA - ONTARIO (NIAGARA-ON-THE-LAKE)

Riverbend Inn & Vineyard
16104 Niagara River Parkway, Niagara-on-the-Lake, Ontario L0S 1J0
Tel: +1 905 468 8866
Fax: +1 905 468 8829
Web: www.johansens.com/riverbend

CANADA - ONTARIO (TORONTO)

Windsor Arms
18 St. Thomas Street, Toronto, Ontario M5S 3E7
Tel: +1 416 971 9666
Fax: +1 416 921 9121
Web: www.johansens.com/windsorarms

CANADA - QUÉBEC (QUÉBEC CITY)

Auberge Saint-Antoine
8, Rue Saint-Antoine, Québec City, Québec G1K 4C9
Tel: +1 418 692 2211
Fax: +1 418 692 1177
Web: www.johansens.com/saintantoine

CANADA - QUÉBEC (MONT-TREMBLANT)

Hôtel Quintessence
3004 chemin de la chapelle, Mont-Tremblant, Québec J8E 1E1
Tel: +1 819 425 3400
Fax: +1 819 425 3480
Web: www.johansens.com/quintessence

CANADA - QUÉBEC (LA MALBAIE)

La Pinsonnière
124 Saint-Raphaël, La Malbaie, Québec G5A 1X9
Tel: +1 418 665 4431
Fax: +1 418 665 7156
Web: www.johansens.com/lapinsonniere

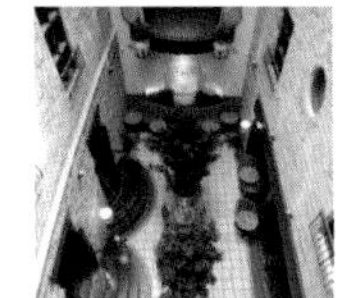

CANADA - QUÉBEC (MONTRÉAL)

Hôtel Nelligan
106 rue Saint-Paul Ouest, Montréal, Québec H2Y 1Z3
Tel: +1 514 788 2040
Fax: +1 514 788 2041
Web: www.johansens.com/nelligan

CANADA - QUÉBEC (MONTRÉAL)

Le Place d'Armes Hôtel & Suites
55 rue Saint-Jacques Ouest, Montréal, Québec H2Y 3X2
Tel: +1 514 842 1887
Fax: +1 514 842 6469
Web: www.johansens.com/hotelplacedarmes

Recommendations in Mexico

MEXICO - BAJA CALIFORNIA NORTE (TECATE)

Rancho La Puerta
Tecate, Baja California Norte
Tel: +52 665 654 9155
Fax: +52 665 654 1108
Web: www.johansens.com/rancholapuerta

MEXICO - BAJA CALIFORNIA SUR (CABO SAN LUCAS)

Esperanza
Km. 7 Carretera Transpeninsular, Punta Ballena, Cabo San Lucas, Baja California Sur 23410
Tel: +52 624 145 6400
Fax: +52 624 145 6499
Web: www.johansens.com/esperanza

MEXICO - BAJA CALIFORNIA SUR (LOS CABOS)

Marquis Los Cabos
Lote 74, Km. 21.5 Carretera Transpeninsular, Fraccionamiento Cabo Real, Los Cabos, Baja California Sur 23400
Tel: +52 624 144 2000
Fax: +52 624 144 2001
Web: www.johansens.com/marquisloscabos

MEXICO - BAJA CALIFORNIA SUR (SAN JOSE DEL CABO)

Casa Natalia
Blvd. Mijares 4, San Jose Del Cabo, Baja California Sur 23400
Tel: +52 624 14671 00
Fax: +52 624 14251 10
Web: www.johansens.com/casanatalia

Mini Listings The Americas

Condé Nast Johansens are delighted to recommend 310 properties across The Americas, Atlantic, Caribbean and Pacific.
Call 0800 269 397 or see the order forms on page 381 to order guides.

MEXICO - BAJA CALIFORNIA SUR (SAN JOSE DEL CABO)

One & Only Palmilla

Km 7.5 Carretera Transpeninsular, San Jose Del Cabo, Baja California Sur 23400
Tel: +52 624 146 7000
Fax: +52 624 146 7001
Web: www.johansens.com/oneandonlypalmilla

MEXICO - COLIMA (COLIMA)

Hacienda de San Antonio

Municipio de Comala, Colima, Colima 28450
Tel: +52 312 314 9554
Fax: +52 312 313 4254
Web: www.johansens.com/sanantonio

MEXICO - DISTRITO FEDERAL (MEXICO CITY)

Casa Vieja

Eugenio Sue 45 (Colonia Polanco), Mexico Distrito Federal 11560
Tel: +52 55 52 82 0067
Fax: +52 55 52 81 3780
Web: www.johansens.com/casavieja

MEXICO - ESTADO DE MEXICO (MALINALCO)

Casa Limon

Rio Lerma 103, Barrio de Santa María, Malinalco, Estado de Mexico 524040
Tel: +52 714 147 0256
Fax: +52 714 147 0619
Web: www.johansens.com/casalimon

MEXICO - GUANAJUATO (GUANAJUATO)

Quinta Las Acacias

Paseo de la Presa 168, Guanajuato, Guanajuato 36000
Tel: +52 473 731 1517
Fax: +52 473 731 1862
Web: www.johansens.com/acacias

MEXICO - GUANAJUATO (SAN MIGUEL DE ALLENDE)

Dos Casas

Calle Quebrada 101, San Miguel de Allende, Guanajuato 37700
Tel: +52 415 154 4073
Fax: +52 415 154 4958
Web: www.johansens.com/doscasas

MEXICO - GUANAJUATO (SAN MIGUEL DE ALLENDE)

La Puertecita Boutique Hotel

Santo Domingo 75 Col. Los Arcos, San Miguel de Allende, Guanajuato 37740
Tel: +52 415 152 5011
Fax: +52 415 152 5505
Web: www.johansens.com/lapuertecita

MEXICO - GUERRERO (ZIHUATANEJO)

Villa del Sol

Playa La Ropa, P.O. Box 84, Zihuatanejo, Guerrero 40880
Tel: +52 755 555 5500
Fax: +52 755 554 2758
Web: www.johansens.com/villadelsol

MEXICO - JALISCO (PUERTA VALLARTA / COSTA ALEGRE)

Las Alamandas Resort

Carretera Barra de Navidad - Puerto Vallarta km 83.5, Col. Quemaro, Jalisco 48850
Tel: +52 322 285 5500
Fax: +52 322 285 5027
Web: www.johansens.com/lasalamandas

MEXICO - JALISCO (PUERTO VALLARTA)

Casa Velas

Pelicanos 311, Fracc. Marina Vallarta, Puerto Vallarta, Jalisco 48354
Tel: +52 322 226 9585
Fax: +52 322 226 6690
Web: www.johansens.com/casavelas

MEXICO - JALISCO (PUERTO VALLARTA)

Hacienda San Angel

Miramar 336, Col. Centro Puerto Vallarta, Jalisco 48300
Tel: +52 322 222 2692
Fax: +52 322 223 1941
Web: www.johansens.com/sanangel

MEXICO - MICHOACÁN (MORELIA)

Hotel Los Juaninos

Morelos Sur 39, Centro, Morelia, Michoacán 58000
Tel: +52 443 312 00 36
Fax: +52 443 312 00 36
Web: www.johansens.com/juaninos

MEXICO - MICHOACÁN (MORELIA)

Hotel Virrey de Mendoza

Av. Madero Pte. 310, Centro Histórico, Morelia, Michoacán 58000
Tel: +52 44 33 12 06 33
Fax: +52 44 33 12 67 19
Web: www.johansens.com/hotelvirrey

MEXICO - MICHOACÁN (MORELIA)

Villa Montaña Hotel & Spa

Patzimba 201, Vista Bella, Morelia, Michoacán 58090
Tel: +52 443 314 02 31
Fax: +52 443 315 14 23
Web: www.johansens.com/montana

MEXICO - NAYARIT (NUEVO VALLARTA)

Grand Velas All Suites & Spa Resort

Av. Cocoteros 98 Sur, Nuevo Vallarta, Nayarit 63735
Tel: +52 322 226 8000
Fax: +52 322 297 2005
Web: www.johansens.com/grandvelas

MEXICO - OAXACA (OAXACA)

Casa Oaxaca

Calle García Vigil 407, Centro, Oaxaca, Oaxaca 68000
Tel: +52 951 514 4173
Fax: +52 951516 4412
Web: www.johansens.com/oaxaca

MEXICO - OAXACA (OAXACA)

Hacienda Los Laureles - Spa

Hidalgo 21, San Felipe del Agua, Oaxaca, Oaxaca 68020
Tel: +52 951 501 5300
Fax: +52 951 501 5301 or +52 951 520 0890
Web: www.johansens.com/laureles

MEXICO - PUEBLA (CHOLULA)

La Quinta Luna

3 sur 702, San Pedro Cholula, Puebla 72760
Tel: +52 222 247 8915
Fax: +52 222 247 8916
Web: www.johansens.com/quintaluna

MEXICO - QUERÉTARO (QUERÉTARO)

La Casa de la Marquesa

Madero 41, Querétaro, Centro Histórico 7600
Tel: +52 442 212 0092
Fax: +52 442 212 0098
Web: www.johansens.com/marquesa

MEXICO - QUINTANA ROO (PLAYA DEL CARMEN)

Royal Hideaway Playacar

Lote Hotelero No. 6, Mza 6 Fracc., Playacar, Playa del Carmen, Quintana Roo 77710
Tel: +52 984 873 4500
Fax: +52 984 873 4507
Web: www.johansens.com/royalhidewaway

Mini Listings The Americas

Condé Nast Johansens are delighted to recommend 310 properties across The Americas, Atlantic, Caribbean and Pacific.
Call 0800 269 397 or see the order forms on page 381 to order guides.

MEXICO - QUINTANA ROO (PUERTO MORELOS)

Ceiba del Mar Spa Resort
Costera Norte Lte. 1, S.M. 10, MZ. 26, Puerto Morelos, Quintana Roo 77580
Tel: +52 998 872 8060
Fax: +52 998 872 8061
Web: www.johansens.com/ceibademar

MEXICO - QUINTANA ROO (TULUM)

Casa Nalum
Sian Ka'an Biosphere Reserve, Quintana Roo
Tel: +52 984 806 4905
Web: www.johansens.com/casanalum

MEXICO - YUCATÁN (MÉRIDA)

Hacienda Xcanatun - Casa de Piedra
Carretera Mérida-Progreso, Km 12, Mérida, Yucatán 97302
Tel: +52 999 941 0273
Fax: +52 999 941 0319
Web: www.johansens.com/xcanatun

Recommendations in U.S.A

U.S.A. - ARIZONA (GREER)

Hidden Meadow Ranch
620 Country Road 1325, Greer, Arizona 85927
Tel: +1 928 333 1000
Fax: +1 928 333 1010
Web: www.johansens.com/hiddenmeadow

U.S.A. - ARIZONA (PARADISE VALLEY / SCOTTSDALE)

The Hermosa Inn
5532 North Palo Cristi Road, Paradise Valley, Arizona 85253
Tel: +1 602 955 8614
Fax: +1 602 955 8299
Web: www.johansens.com/hermosa

U.S.A. - ARIZONA (PARADISE VALLEY / SCOTTSDALE)

Sanctuary on Camelback Mountain
5700 East McDonald Drive, Scottsdale, Arizona 85253
Tel: +1 480 948 2100
Fax: +1 480 483 7314
Web: www.johansens.com/sanctuarycamelback

U.S.A. - ARIZONA (SEDONA)

Amara Creekside Resort
310 North Highway 89A, Sedona, Arizona 86336
Tel: +1 928 282 4828
Fax: +1 928 282 4825
Web: www.johansens.com/amaracreekside

U.S.A. - ARIZONA (SEDONA)

L'Auberge de Sedona
301 L'Auberge Lane, Sedona, Arizona 86336
Tel: +1 928 282 1661
Fax: +1 928 282 2885
Web: www.johansens.com/laubergedesedona

U.S.A. - ARIZONA (SEDONA)

Sedona Rouge Hotel & Spa
2250 West Highway 89A, Sedona, Arizona 86336
Tel: +1 928 203 4111
Fax: +1 928 203 9094
Web: www.johansens.com/sedonarouge

U.S.A. - ARIZONA (TUCSON)

Arizona Inn
2200 East Elm Street, Tucson, Arizona 85719
Tel: +1 520 325 1541
Fax: +1 520 881 5830
Web: www.johansens.com/arizonainn

U.S.A. - ARIZONA (TUCSON)

Tanque Verde Ranch
14301 East Speedway Boulevard, Tucson, Arizona 85748
Tel: +1 520 296 6275
Fax: +1 520 721 9427
Web: www.johansens.com/tanqueverde

U.S.A. - ARIZONA (WICKENBURG)

Rancho de los Caballeros
1551 South Vulture Mine Road, Wickenburg, Arizona 85390
Tel: +1 928 684 5484
Fax: +1 928 684 9565
Web: www.johansens.com/caballeros

U.S.A. - CALIFORNIA (ATASCADERO)

The Carlton Hotel
6005 El Camino Real, Atascadero, California 93422
Tel: +1 805 461 5100
Fax: +1 805 461 5116
Web: www.johansens.com/carltoncalifornia

U.S.A. - CALIFORNIA (BIG SUR)

Post Ranch Inn
Highway 1, P.O. Box 219, Big Sur, California 93920
Tel: +1 831 667 2200
Fax: +1 831 667 2512
Web: www.johansens.com/postranchinn

U.S.A. - CALIFORNIA (BIG SUR)

Ventana Inn and Spa
Highway 1, Big Sur, California 93920
Tel: +1 831 667 2331
Fax: +1 831 667 2419
Web: www.johansens.com/ventana

U.S.A. - CALIFORNIA (CARMEL-BY-THE-SEA)

L'Auberge Carmel
Monte Verde at Seventh, Carmel-by-the-Sea, California 93921
Tel: +1 831 624 8578
Fax: +1 831 626 1018
Web: www.johansens.com/laubergecarmel

U.S.A. - CALIFORNIA (CARMEL-BY-THE-SEA)

Tradewinds Carmel
Mission Street at Third Avenue, Carmel-by-the-Sea, California 93921
Tel: +1 831 624 2776
Fax: +1 831 624 0634
Web: www.johansens.com/tradewinds

U.S.A. - CALIFORNIA (EUREKA)

The Carter House Inns
301 L Street, Eureka, California 95501
Tel: +1 707 444 8062
Fax: +1 707 444 8067
Web: www.johansens.com/carterhouse

U.S.A. - CALIFORNIA (GLEN ELLEN)

The Gaige House
13540 Arnold Drive, Glen Ellen, California 95442
Tel: +1 707 935 0237
Fax: +1 707 935 6411
Web: www.johansens.com/gaige

Mini Listings The Americas

Condé Nast Johansens are delighted to recommend 310 properties across The Americas, Atlantic, Caribbean and Pacific.
Call 0800 269 397 or see the order forms on page 381 to order guides.

U.S.A. - CALIFORNIA (HEALDSBURG)

The Grape Leaf Inn
539 Johnson Street, Healdsburg, California 95448
Tel: +1 707 433 8140
Fax: +1 707 433 3140
Web: www.johansens.com/grapeleaf

U.S.A. - CALIFORNIA (KENWOOD)

The Kenwood Inn and Spa
10400 Sonoma Highway, Kenwood, California 95452
Tel: +1 707 833 1293
Fax: +1 707 833 1247
Web: www.johansens.com/kenwoodinn

U.S.A. - CALIFORNIA (LA JOLLA)

Estancia La Jolla Hotel & Spa
9700 North Torrey Pines Road, La Jolla, California 92037
Tel: +1 858 202 3389
Fax: +1 858 202 3399
Web: www.johansens.com/estancialajolla

U.S.A. - CALIFORNIA (LOS ANGELES)

Hotel Bel-Air
701 Stone Canyon Road, Los Angeles, California 90077
Tel: +1 310 472 1211
Fax: +1 310 909 1611
Web: www.johansens.com/belair

U.S.A. - CALIFORNIA (LOS OLIVOS)

The Fess Parker Wine Country Inn
2860 Grand Avenue, Los Olivos, California 93441
Tel: +1 805 688 7788
Fax: +1 805 688 1942
Web: www.johansens.com/fessparker

U.S.A. - CALIFORNIA (MENDOCINO)

The Stanford Inn By The Sea
Coast Highway One & Comptche-Ukiah Road, Mendocino, California 95460
Tel: +1 707 937 5615
Fax: +1 707 937 0305
Web: www.johansens.com/stanford

U.S.A. - CALIFORNIA (MILL VALLEY)

Mill Valley Inn
165 Throckmorton Avenue, Mill Valley, California 94941
Tel: +1 415 389 6608
Fax: +1 415 389 5051
Web: www.johansens.com/millvalleyinn

U.S.A. - CALIFORNIA (MONTEREY)

Old Monterey Inn
500 Martin Street, Monterey, California 93940
Tel: +1 831 375 8284
Fax: +1 831 375 6730
Web: www.johansens.com/oldmontereyinn

U.S.A. - CALIFORNIA (NAPA VALLEY)

1801 First Inn
1801 First Street, Napa, California 94559
Tel: +1 707 224 3739
Fax: +1 707 224 3932
Web: www.johansens.com/1801inn

U.S.A. - CALIFORNIA (NAPA)

Milliken Creek Inn & Spa
1815 Silverado Trail, Napa, California 94558
Tel: +1 707 255 1197
Fax: +1 707 255 3112
Web: www.johansens.com/milliken

U.S.A. - CALIFORNIA (OAKHURST)

Château du Sureau & Spa
48688 Victoria Lane, Oakhurst, California 93644
Tel: +1 559 683 6860
Fax: +1 559 683 0800
Web: www.johansens.com/chateausureau

U.S.A. - CALIFORNIA (PASO ROBLES)

The Villa Toscana
4230 Buena Vista, Paso Robles, California 93446
Tel: +1 805 238 5600
Fax: +1 805 238 5605
Web: www.johansens.com/villatoscana

U.S.A. - CALIFORNIA (RANCHO SANTA FE)

The Inn at Rancho Santa Fe
5951 Linea del Cielo, Rancho Santa Fe, California 92067
Tel: +1 858 756 1131
Fax: +1 858 759 1604
Web: www.johansens.com/ranchosantafe

U.S.A. - CALIFORNIA (SAN DIEGO)

Tower23 Hotel
723 Felspar, San Diego, California 92109
Tel: +1 858 270 2323
Fax: +1 858 274 2333
Web: www.johansens.com/tower23

U.S.A. - CALIFORNIA (SAN FRANCISCO BAY AREA)

Inn Above Tide
30 El Portal, Sausalito, California 94965
Tel: +1 415 332 9535
Fax: +1 415 332 9535
Web: www.johansens.com/innabovetide

U.S.A. - CALIFORNIA (SAN FRANCISCO)

The Union Street Inn
2229 Union Street, San Francisco, California 94123
Tel: +1 415 346 0424
Fax: +1 415 922 8046
Web: www.johansens.com/unionstreetsf

U.S.A. - CALIFORNIA (SANTA BARBARA)

Harbor View Inn
28 West Cabrillo Boulevard, Santa Barbara, California 93101
Tel: +1 805 963 0780
Fax: +1 805 963 7967
Web: www.johansens.com/harborview

U.S.A. - CALIFORNIA (SANTA YNEZ)

The Santa Ynez Inn
3627 Sagunto Street, Santa Ynez, California 93460-0628
Tel: +1 805 688 5588
Fax: +1 805 686 4294
Web: www.johansens.com/santaynez

U.S.A. - CALIFORNIA (SONOMA)

Ledson Hotel & Harmony Restaurant
480 First Street East, Sonoma, California 95476
Tel: +1 707 996 9779
Fax: +1 707 996 9776
Web: www.johansens.com/ledsonhotel

U.S.A. - CALIFORNIA (ST. HELENA)

Meadowood
900 Meadowood Lane, St. Helena, California 94574
Tel: +1 707 963 3646
Fax: +1 707 963 3532
Web: www.johansens.com/meadowood

MINI LISTINGS THE AMERICAS

Condé Nast Johansens are delighted to recommend 310 properties across The Americas, Atlantic, Caribbean and Pacific.
Call 0800 269 397 or see the order forms on page 381 to order guides.

U.S.A. - COLORADO (BOULDER)

The Bradley Boulder Inn
2040 16th Street, Boulder, Colorado 80302
Tel: +1 303 545 5200
Fax: +1 303 440 6740
Web: www.johansens.com/bradleyboulderinn

U.S.A. - COLORADO (DENVER)

Castle Marne Bed & Breakfast Inn
1572 Race Street, Denver, Colorado 80206
Tel: +1 303 331 0621
Fax: +1 303 331 0623
Web: www.johansens.com/castlemarne

U.S.A. - COLORADO (ESTES PARK)

Taharaa Mountain Lodge
P.O. Box 2586, Estes Park, Colorado 80517
Tel: +1 970 577 0098
Fax: +1 970 577 0819
Web: www.johansens.com/taharaa

U.S.A. - COLORADO (MANITOU SPRINGS)

The Cliff House at Pikes Peak
306 Cañon Avenue, Manitou Springs, Colorado 80829
Tel: +1 719 685 3000
Fax: +1 719 685 3913
Web: www.johansens.com/thecliffhouse

U.S.A. - COLORADO (MONTROSE)

Elk Mountain Resort
97 Elk Walk, Montrose, Colorado 81401
Tel: +1 970 252 4900
Fax: +1 970 252 4913
Web: www.johansens.com/elkmountain

U.S.A. - COLORADO (STEAMBOAT SPRINGS)

Vista Verde Guest Ranch
P.O. Box 770465, Steamboat Springs, Colorado 80477
Tel: +1 970 879 3858
Fax: +1 970 879 6814
Web: www.johansens.com/vistaverderanch

U.S.A. - COLORADO (VAIL)

The Tivoli Lodge at Vail
386 Hanson Ranch Road, Vail, Colorado 81657
Tel: +1 970 476 5615
Fax: +1 970 476 6601
Web: www.johansens.com/tivoli

U.S.A. - COLORADO (VAIL)

Vail Mountain Lodge & Spa
352 East Meadow Drive, Vail, Colorado 81657
Tel: +1 970 476 0700
Fax: +1 970 476 6451
Web: www.johansens.com/vailmountain

U.S.A. - CONNECTICUT (GREENWICH)

Delamar Greenwich Harbor
500 Steamboat Road, Greenwich, Connecticut 06830
Tel: +1 203 661 9800
Fax: +1 203 661 2513
Web: www.johansens.com/delamar

U.S.A. - CONNECTICUT (STONINGTON)

The Inn at Stonington
60 Water Street, Stonington, Connecticut 06378
Tel: +1 860 535 2000
Fax: +1 860 535 8193
Web: www.johansens.com/stonington

U.S.A. - DELAWARE (REHOBOTH BEACH)

The Bellmoor
Six Christian Street, Rehoboth Beach, Delaware 19971
Tel: +1 302 227 5800
Fax: +1 302 227 0323
Web: www.johansens.com/thebellmoor

U.S.A. - DELAWARE (REHOBOTH BEACH)

Boardwalk Plaza Hotel
Olive Avenue & The Boardwalk, Rehoboth Beach, Delaware 19971
Tel: +1 302 227 7169
Fax: +1 302 227 0561
Web: www.johansens.com/boardwalkplaza

U.S.A. - DELAWARE (WILMINGTON)

Inn at Montchanin Village
Route 100 & Kirk Road, Montchanin, Delaware 19710
Tel: +1 302 888 2133
Fax: +1 302 888 0389
Web: www.johansens.com/montchanin

U.S.A. - DISTRICT OF COLUMBIA (WASHINGTON)

The Hay Adams
Sixteenth & H. Streets N.W., Washington D.C. 20006
Tel: +1 202 638 6600
Fax: +1 202 638 2716
Web: www.johansens.com/hayadams

U.S.A. - FLORIDA (COCONUT GROVE)

Grove Isle Hotel & Spa
Four Grove Isle Drive, Coconut Grove, Florida 33133
Tel: +1 305 858 8300
Fax: +1 305 858 5908
Web: www.johansens.com/groveisle

U.S.A. - FLORIDA (DAYTONA BEACH SHORES)

The Shores Resort & Spa
2637 South Atlantic Avenue, Daytona Beach Shores, Florida 32118
Tel: +1 386 767 7350
Fax: +1 386 760 3651
Web: www.johansens.com/shoresresort

U.S.A. - FLORIDA (FISHER ISLAND)

Fisher Island Hotel & Resort
One Fisher Island Drive, Fisher Island, Florida 33109
Tel: +1 305 535 6000
Fax: +1 305 535 6003
Web: www.johansens.com/fisherisland

U.S.A. - FLORIDA (JUPITER)

Jupiter Beach Resort & Spa
5 North A1A, Jupiter, Florida 33477-5190
Tel: +1 561 746 2511
Fax: +1 561 744 1741
Web: www.johansens.com/jupiterbeachresort

U.S.A. - FLORIDA (KEY WEST)

Ocean Key Resort
Zero Duval Street, Key West, Florida 33040
Tel: +1 305 296 7701
Fax: +1 305 292 7685
Web: www.johansens.com/oceankey

U.S.A. - FLORIDA (KEY WEST)

Simonton Court Historic Inn & Cottages
320 Simonton Street, Key West, Florida 33040
Tel: +1 305 294 6386
Fax: +1 305 293 8446
Web: www.johansens.com/simontoncourt

Mini Listings The Americas

Condé Nast Johansens are delighted to recommend 310 properties across The Americas, Atlantic, Caribbean and Pacific.
Call 0800 269 397 or see the order forms on page 381 to order guides.

U.S.A. - FLORIDA (KEY WEST)

Sunset Key Guest Cottages
245 Front Street, Key West, Florida 33040
Tel: +1 305 292 5300
Fax: +1 305 292 5395
Web: www.johansens.com/sunsetkey

U.S.A. - FLORIDA (MARCO ISLAND/NAPLES)

Marco Beach Ocean Resort
480 South Collier Boulevard, Marco Island, Florida 34145
Tel: +1 239 393 1400
Fax: +1 239 393 1401
Web: www.johansens.com/marcobeach

U.S.A. - FLORIDA (MIAMI BEACH)

Hotel Victor
1144 Ocean Drive, Miami Beach, Florida 33139
Tel: +1 305 428 1234
Fax: +1 305 421 6281
Web: www.johansens.com/hotelvictor

U.S.A. - FLORIDA (NAPLES)

LaPlaya Beach & Golf Resort
9891 Gulf Shore Drive, Naples, Florida 34108
Tel: +1 239 597 3123
Fax: +1 239 597 8283
Web: www.johansens.com/laplaya

U.S.A. - FLORIDA (ORLANDO)

Portofino Bay Hotel
5601 Universal Boulevard, Orlando, Florida 32819
Tel: +1 407 503 1000
Fax: +1 407 503 1010
Web: www.johansens.com/portofinobay

U.S.A. - FLORIDA (PONTE VEDRA BEACH)

The Lodge & Club at Ponte Vedra Beach
607 Ponte Vedra Boulevard, Ponte Vedra Beach,Florida 32082
Tel: +1 904 273 9500
Fax: +1 904 273 0210
Web: www.johansens.com/ponteverdrabeach

U.S.A. - FLORIDA (SANTA ROSA BEACH)

WaterColor Inn and Resort
34 Goldenrod Circle, Santa rosa Beach, Florida 32459
Tel: +1 850 534 5000
Fax: +1 850 534 5001
Web: www.johansens.com/watercolor

U.S.A. - FLORIDA (ST. PETE BEACH)

Don CeSar Beach Resort
3400 Gulf Boulevard, St. Pete Beach, Florida 33706
Tel: +1 727 360 1881
Fax: +1 727 367 3609
Web: www.johansens.com/doncesar

U.S.A. - GEORGIA (ADAIRSVILLE)

Barnsley Gardens Resort
597 Barnsley Gardens Road, Adairsville, Georgia 30103
Tel: +1 770 773 7480
Fax: +1 770 877 9155
Web: www.johansens.com/barnsleygardens

U.S.A. - GEORGIA (CUMBERLAND ISLAND)

Greyfield Inn
Cumberland Island, Georgia
Tel: +1 904 261 6408
Fax: +1 904 321 0666
Web: www.johansens.com/greyfieldinn

U.S.A. - GEORGIA (SAVANNAH)

The Ballastone
14 East Oglethorpe Avenue, Savannah, Georgia 31401-3707
Tel: +1 912 236 1484
Fax: +1 912 236 4626
Web: www.johansens.com/ballastone

U.S.A. - GEORGIA (SAVANNAH)

Eliza Thompson House
5 West Jones Street, Savannah, Georgia 31401
Tel: +1 912 236 3620
Fax: +1 912 238 1920
Web: www.johansens.com/elizathompsonhouse

U.S.A. - GEORGIA (SAVANNAH)

The Gastonian
220 East Gaston Street, Savannah, Georgia 31401
Tel: +1 912 232 2869
Fax: +1 912 232 0710
Web: www.johansens.com/gastonian

U.S.A. - HAWAII (BIG ISLAND)

The Palms Cliff House
28-3514 Mamalahoa Highway 19, P.O. Box 189, Honomu, Hawaii 96728-0189
Tel: +1 808 963 6076
Fax: +1 808 963 6316
Web: www.johansens.com/palmscliff

U.S.A. - HAWAII (BIG ISLAND)

Shipman House
131 Ka'iulani Street, Hilo, Hawaii 96720
Tel: +1 808 934 8002
Fax: +1 808 934 8002
Web: www.johansens.com/shipman

U.S.A. - HAWAII (MAUI)

Hotel Hana-Maui and Honua Spa
5031 Hana Highway, Hana, Maui, Hawaii 96713
Tel: +1 808 248 8211
Fax: +1 808 248 7202
Web: www.johansens.com/hanamaui

U.S.A. - IDAHO (KETCHUM)

Knob Hill Inn
960 North Main Street, P.O. Box 800, Ketchum, Idaho 83340
Tel: +1 208 726 8010
Fax: +1 208 726 2712
Web: www.johansens.com/knobhillinn

U.S.A. - KANSAS (LAWRENCE)

The Eldridge Hotel
701 Massachusetts, Lawrence, Kansas 66044
Tel: +1 785 749 5011
Fax: +1 785 749 4512
Web: www.johansens.com/eldridge

U.S.A. - LOUISIANA (NEW ORLEANS)

Hotel Maison de Ville
727 Rue Toulouse, New Orleans, Louisiana 70130
Tel: +1 504 561 5858
Fax: +1 504 528 9939
Web: www.johansens.com/maisondeville

U.S.A. - LOUISIANA (NEW ORLEANS)

The Lafayette Hotel
600 St. Charles Avenue, New Orleans, Louisiana 70130
Tel: +1 504 524 4441
Fax: +1 504 962 5537
Web: www.johansens.com/lafayette

Mini Listings The Americas

Condé Nast Johansens are delighted to recommend 310 properties across The Americas, Atlantic, Caribbean and Pacific.
Call 0800 269 397 or see the order forms on page 381 to order guides.

U.S.A. - LOUISIANA (NEW ORLEANS)

The St. James Hotel
330 Magazine Street, New Orleans, Louisiana 70130
Tel: +1 504 304 4000
Fax: +1 504 304 4444
Web: www.johansens.com/stjamesno

U.S.A. - MAINE (GREENVILLE)

The Lodge At Moosehead Lake
Lily Bay Road, P.O. Box 1167, Greenville, Maine 04441
Tel: +1 207 695 4400
Fax: +1 207 695 2281
Web: www.johansens.com/lodgeatmooseheadlake

U.S.A. - MAINE (KENNEBUNKPORT)

The White Barn Inn
37 Beach Avenue, Kennebunkport, Maine 04043
Tel: +1 207 967 2321
Fax: +1 207 967 1100
Web: www.johansens.com/whitebarninn

U.S.A. - MAINE (PORTLAND)

Portland Harbor Hotel
468 Fore Street, Portland, Maine 04101
Tel: +1 207 775 9090
Fax: +1 207 775 9990
Web: www.johansens.com/portlandharbor

U.S.A. - MARYLAND (EASTON)

Inn at 202 Dover
202 E. Dover Street, Easton, Maryland 21601
Tel: +1 410 819 8007
Fax: +1 410 819 3368
Web: www.johansens.com/innat202dover

U.S.A. - MARYLAND (FROSTBURG)

Savage River Lodge
1600 Mt. Aetna Road, Frostburg, Maryland 21532
Tel: +1 301 689 3200
Fax: +1 301 689 2746
Web: www.johansens.com/savageriver

U.S.A. - MARYLAND (ST. MICHAELS)

Five Gables Inn & Spa
209 North Talbot Street, St. Michaels, Maryland 21663
Tel: +1 410 745 0100
Fax: +1 410 745 2903
Web: www.johansens.com/fivegables

U.S.A. - MASSACHUSETTS (BOSTON)

The Charles Street Inn
94 Charles Street, Boston, Massachusetts 02114
Tel: +1 617 314 8900
Fax: +1 617 371 0009
Web: www.johansens.com/charlesstreetinn

U.S.A. - MASSACHUSETTS (BOSTON)

Clarendon Square Inn
198 West Brookline Street, Boston, Massachusetts 02118
Tel: +1 617 536 2229
Fax: +1 617 536 2993
Web: www.johansens.com/clarendonsquare

U.S.A. - MASSACHUSETTS (BOSTON)

Hotel Commonwealth
500 Commonwealth Avenue, Boston, Massachusetts 02215
Tel: +1 617 933 5000
Fax: +1 617 266 6888
Web: www.johansens.com/commonwealth

U.S.A. - MASSACHUSETTS (BOSTON)

The Lenox
61 Exeter Street at Boylston, Boston, Massachusetts 02116
Tel: +1 617 536 5300
Fax: +1 617 267 1237
Web: www.johansens.com/lenox

U.S.A. - MASSACHUSETTS (BOSTON)

Nine Zero Hotel
90 Tremont Street, Boston, Massachusetts 02108
Tel: +1 617 772 5800
Fax: +1 617 772 5810
Web: www.johansens.com/ninezero

U.S.A. - MASSACHUSETTS (CAMBRIDGE)

Hotel Marlowe
25 Edwin H. Land Boulevard, Cambridge, Massachusetts 02141
Tel: +1 617 868 8000
Fax: +1 617 868 8001
Web: www.johansens.com/marlowe

U.S.A. - MASSACHUSETTS (CAPE COD)

The Crowne Pointe Historic Inn & Spa
82 Bradford Street, Provincetown, Cape Cod, Massachusetts 02657
Tel: +1 508 487 6767
Fax: +1 508 487 5554
Web: www.johansens.com/crownepointe

U.S.A. - MASSACHUSETTS (CAPE COD)

Wequassett Inn Resort and Golf Club
On Pleasant Bay, Chatham, Cape Cod, Massachusetts 02633
Tel: +1 508 432 5400
Fax: +1 508 430 3131
Web: www.johansens.com/wequassett

U.S.A. - MASSACHUSETTS (EDGARTOWN)

The Charlotte Inn
27 South Summer Street, Edgartown, Massachusetts 02539
Tel: +1 508 627 4151
Fax: +1 508 627 4652
Web: www.johansens.com/charlotte

U.S.A. - MASSACHUSETTS (IPSWICH)

The Inn at Castle Hill
280 Argilla Road, Ipswich, Massachusetts 01938
Tel: +1 978 412 2555
Fax: +1 978 412 2556
Web: www.johansens.com/castlehill

U.S.A. - MASSACHUSETTS (LENOX)

Blantyre
16 Blantyre Road, P.O. Box 995, Lenox, Massachusetts 01240
Tel: +1 413 637 3556
Fax: +1 413 637 4282
Web: www.johansens.com/blantyre

U.S.A. - MASSACHUSETTS (LENOX)

Cranwell Resort, Spa & Golf Club
55 Lee Road, Route 20, Lenox, Massachusetts 01240
Tel: +1 413 637 1364
Fax: +1 413 637 4364
Web: www.johansens.com/cranwell

U.S.A. - MASSACHUSETTS (MARTHA'S VINEYARD)

Winnetu Oceanside Resort
31 Dunes Road, Edgartown, Massachusetts 02539
Tel: +1 978 443 1733
Fax: +1 978 443 0479
Web: www.johansens.com/winnetu

Mini Listings The Americas

Condé Nast Johansens are delighted to recommend 310 properties across The Americas, Atlantic, Caribbean and Pacific.
Call 0800 269 397 or see the order forms on page 381 to order guides.

U.S.A. - MISSISSIPPI (JACKSON)

Fairview Inn & Restaurant
734 Fairview Street, Jackson, Mississippi 39202
Tel: +1 601 948 3429
Fax: +1 601 948 1203
Web: www.johansens.com/fairviewinn

U.S.A. - MISSISSIPPI (NATCHEZ)

Monmouth Plantation
36 Melrose Avenue, Natchez, Mississippi 39120
Tel: +1 601 442 5852
Fax: +1 601 446 7762
Web: www.johansens.com/monmouthplantation

U.S.A. - MISSISSIPPI (NESBIT)

Bonne Terre Country Inn
4715 Church Road West, Nesbit, Mississippi 38651
Tel: +1 662 781 5100
Fax: +1 662 781 5466
Web: www.johansens.com/bonneterre

U.S.A. - MISSISSIPPI (VICKSBURG)

Anchuca Historic Mansion & Inn
1010 First East Street, Vicksburg, Mississippi 39183
Tel: +1 601 661 0111
Fax: +1 601 631 0501
Web: www.johansens.com/anchuca

U.S.A. - MISSOURI (BRANSON)

Chateau on the Lake
415 North State Highway 265, Branson, Missouri 65616
Tel: +1 417 334 1161
Fax: +1 417 339 5566
Web: www.johansens.com/chateaulake

U.S.A. - MISSOURI (KANSAS CITY)

The Raphael Hotel
325 Ward Parkway, Kansas City, Missouri 64112
Tel: +1 816 756 3800
Fax: +1 816 802 2131
Web: www.johansens.com/raphael

U.S.A. - MISSOURI (RIDGEDALE)

Big Cedar Lodge
612 Devil's Pool Road, Ridgedale, Missouri 65739
Tel: +1 417 335 2777
Fax: +1 417 335 2340
Web: www.johansens.com/bigcedar

U.S.A. - MONTANA (BIG SKY)

The Big EZ Lodge
7000 Beaver Creek Road, Big Sky, Montana 59716
Tel: +1 406 995 7000
Fax: +1 406 995 7007
Web: www.johansens.com/bigez

U.S.A. - MONTANA (DARBY)

Triple Creek Ranch
5551 West Fork Road, Darby, Montana 59829
Tel: +1 406 821 4600
Fax: +1 406 821 4666
Web: www.johansens.com/triplecreek

U.S.A. - NEW HAMPSHIRE (JACKSON VILLAGE)

The Wentworth
Jackson Village, New Hampshire 03846
Tel: +1 603 383 9700
Fax: +1 603 383 4265
Web: www.johansens.com/wentworth

U.S.A. - NEW HAMPSHIRE (PLAINFIELD)

Home Hill
703 River Road, Plainfield, New Hampshire 03781
Tel: +1 603 675 6165
Fax: +1 603 675 5220
Web: www.johansens.com/homehill

U.S.A. - NEW HAMPSHIRE (WHITEFIELD / WHITE MOUNTAINS)

Mountain View, The Grand Resort & Spa
Mountain View Road, Whitefield, New Hampshire 03598
Tel: +1 603 837 2100
Fax: +1 603 837 8884
Web: www.johansens.com/mountainview

U.S.A. - NEW MEXICO (ESPAÑOLA)

Rancho de San Juan
P.O. Box 4140, Highway 285, Española, New Mexico 87533
Tel: +1 505 753 6818
Fax: +1 505 753 6818
Web: www.johansens.com/ranchosanjuan

U.S.A. - NEW MEXICO (SANTA FE)

Inn and Spa at Loretto
211 Old Santa Fe Trail, Santa Fe, New Mexico 87501
Tel: +1 505 988 5531
Fax: +1 505 984 7968
Web: www.johansens.com/innatloretto

U.S.A. - NEW MEXICO (TAOS)

El Monte Sagrado Living Resort & Spa
317 Kit Carson Road, Taos, New Mexico 87571
Tel: +1 505 758 3502
Fax: +1 505 737 2985
Web: www.johansens.com/elmontesagrado

U.S.A. - NEW YORK (BANGALL)

The Inn at Bullis Hall
P.O. Box 630, Bangall (Stanfordville), New York 12506
Tel: +1 845 868 1665
Fax: +1 845 868 1441
Web: www.johansens.com/bullishall

U.S.A. - NEW YORK (BOLTON LANDING)

The Sagamore
110 Sagamore Road, Bolton Landing, New York 12814
Tel: +1 518 644 9400
Fax: +1 518 644 2851
Web: www.johansens.com/sagamore

U.S.A. - NEW YORK (BUFFALO)

Mansion on Delaware
414 Delaware Avenue, Buffalo, New York 14202
Tel: +1 716 886 3300
Fax: +1 716 883 3923
Web: www.johansens.com/mansionondelaware

U.S.A. - NEW YORK (EAST AURORA)

The Roycroft Inn
40 South Grove Street, East Aurora, New York 14052
Tel: +1 716 652 5552
Fax: +1 716 655 5345
Web: www.johansens.com/roycroftinn

U.S.A. - NEW YORK (LAKE PLACID)

Whiteface Lodge
7 Whiteface Inn Lane, Lake Placid, New York 12946
Tel: +1 518 523 0500
Fax: +1 518 523 0559
Web: www.johansens.com/whiteface

Mini Listings The Americas

Condé Nast Johansens are delighted to recommend 310 properties across The Americas, Atlantic, Caribbean and Pacific.
Call 0800 269 397 or see the order forms on page 381 to order guides.

U.S.A. - NEW YORK (NEW YORK CITY)

Hotel Plaza Athénée

37 East 64th Street, New York, New York 10021
Tel: +1 212 734 9100
Fax: +1 212 772 0958
Web: www.johansens.com/athenee

U.S.A. - NEW YORK (NEW YORK CITY)

The Inn at Irving Place

56 Irving Place, New York, New York 10003
Tel: +1 212 533 4600
Fax: +1 212 533 4611
Web: www.johansens.com/irvingplace

U.S.A. - NEW YORK (TARRYTOWN)

Castle On The Hudson

400 Benedict Avenue, Tarrytown, New York 10591
Tel: +1 914 631 1980
Fax: +1 914 631 4612
Web: www.johansens.com/hudson

U.S.A. - NEW YORK (VERONA)

The Lodge at Turning Stone

5218 Patrick Road, Verona, New York 13478
Tel: +1 315 361 8525
Fax: +1 315 361 8686
Web: www.johansens.com/turningstone

U.S.A. - NEW YORK/LONG ISLAND (EAST HAMPTON)

The Baker House 1650

181 Main Street, East Hampton, New York 11937
Tel: +1 631 324 4081
Fax: +1 631 329 5931
Web: www.johansens.com/bakerhouse

U.S.A. - NEW YORK/LONG ISLAND (EAST HAMPTON)

The Mill House Inn

31 North Main Street, East Hampton, New York 11937
Tel: +1 631 324 9766
Fax: +1 631 324 9793
Web: www.johansens.com/millhouse

U.S.A. - NEW YORK/LONG ISLAND (SOUTHAMPTON)

1708 House

126 Main Street, Southampton, New York 11968
Tel: +1 631 287 1708
Fax: +1 631 287 3593
Web: www.johansens.com/1708house

U.S.A. - NORTH CAROLINA (ASHEVILLE)

Inn on Biltmore Estate

One Antler Hill Road, Asheville, North Carolina 28803
Tel: +1 828 225 1600
Fax: +1 828 225 1629
Web: www.johansens.com/biltmore

U.S.A. - NORTH CAROLINA (BLOWING ROCK)

Gideon Ridge Inn

202 Gideon Ridge Road, Blowing Rock,
North Carolina 28605
Tel: +1 828 295 3644
Fax: +1 828 295 4586
Web: www.johansens.com/gideonridge

U.S.A. - NORTH CAROLINA (CHARLOTTE)

Ballantyne Resort

10000 Ballantyne Commons Parkway, Charlotte,
North Carolina 28277
Tel: +1 704 248 4000
Fax: +1 704 248 4005
Web: www.johansens.com/ballantyneresort

U.S.A. - NORTH CAROLINA (DUCK)

The Sanderling Resort & Spa

1461 Duck Road, Duck, North Carolina 27949
Tel: +1 252 261 4111
Fax: +1 252 261 1638
Web: www.johansens.com/sanderling

U.S.A. - NORTH CAROLINA (HIGHLANDS)

Inn at Half Mile Farm

P.O. Box 2769, 214 Half Mile Drive, Highlands,
North Carolina 28741
Tel: +1 828 526 8170
Fax: +1 828 526 2625
Web: www.johansens.com/halfmilefarm

U.S.A. - NORTH CAROLINA (HIGHLANDS)

Old Edwards Inn and Spa

445 Main Street, Highlands, North Carolina 28741
Tel: +1 828 526 8008
Fax: +1 828 526 8301
Web: www.johansens.com/oldedwards

U.S.A. - NORTH CAROLINA (NEW BERN)

The Aerie Inn

509 Pollock Street, New Bern, North Carolina 28562
Tel: +1 252 636 5553
Fax: +1 252 514 2157
Web: www.johansens.com/aerieinn

U.S.A. - NORTH CAROLINA (PITTSBORO)

The Fearrington House

2000 Fearrington Village Center, Pittsboro,
North Carolina 27312
Tel: +1 919 542 2121
Fax: +1 919 542 4202
Web: www.johansens.com/fearrington

U.S.A. - NORTH CAROLINA (RALEIGH - DURHAM)

The Siena Hotel

1505 E. Franklin Street, Chapel Hill, North Carolina 27514
Tel: +1 919 929 4000
Fax: +1 919 968 8527
Web: www.johansens.com/siena

U.S.A. - NORTH CAROLINA (TRYON)

Pine Crest Inn and Restaurant

85 Pine Crest Lane, Tryon, North Carolina 28782
Tel: +1 828 859 9135
Fax: +1 828 859 9136
Web: www.johansens.com/pinecrestinn

U.S.A. - OHIO (CINCINNATI)

The Cincinnatian Hotel

601 Vine Street, Cincinnati, Ohio 45202-2433
Tel: +1 513 381 3000
Fax: +1 513 651 0256
Web: www.johansens.com/cincinnatian

U.S.A. - OKLAHOMA (OKLAHOMA CITY)

Colcord Hotel

15 North Robinson, Oklahoma City, Oklahoma 73102
Tel: +1 405 601 4300
Fax: +1 405 208 4399
Web: www.johansens.com/colcord

U.S.A. - OKLAHOMA (TULSA)

Hotel Ambassador

1345 South Main Street, Tulsa, Oklahoma 74119
Tel: +1 918 587 8200
Fax: +1 918 587 8208
Web: www.johansens.com/ambassador

Mini Listings The Americas

Condé Nast Johansens are delighted to recommend 310 properties across The Americas, Atlantic, Caribbean and Pacific.
Call 0800 269 397 or see the order forms on page 381 to order guides.

U.S.A. - OREGON (ASHLAND)

The Winchester Inn & Restaurant

35 South Second Street, Ashland, Oregon 97520
Tel: +1 541 488 1113
Fax: +1 541 488 4604
Web: www.johansens.com/winchester

U.S.A. - OREGON (PORTLAND)

The Benson Hotel

309 Southwest Broadway, Portland, Oregon 97205
Tel: +1 503 228 2000
Fax: +1 503 471 3920
Web: www.johansens.com/benson

U.S.A. - OREGON (PORTLAND)

The Heathman Hotel

1001 S.W. Broadway, Portland, Oregon 97205
Tel: +1 503 241 4100
Fax: +1 503 790 7110
Web: www.johansens.com/heathman

U.S.A. - PENNSYLVANIA (BRADFORD)

Glendorn

1000 Glendorn Drive, Bradford, Pennsylvania 16701
Tel: +1 814 362 6511
Fax: +1 814 368 9923
Web: www.johansens.com/glendorn

U.S.A. - PENNSYLVANIA (FARMINGTON)

Nemacolin Woodlands

1001 LaFayette Drive, Farmington, Pennsylvania 15437
Tel: +1 724 329 8555
Fax: +1 724 329 6947
Web: www.johansens.com/nemacolin

U.S.A. - PENNSYLVANIA (HERSHEY)

The Hotel Hershey & Spa

100 Hotel Road, Hershey, Pennsylvania 17033
Tel: +1 717 533 2171
Fax: +1 717 534 3165
Web: www.johansens.com/hershey

U.S.A. - PENNSYLVANIA (LEOLA)

Leola Village Inn & Suites

38 Deborah Drive, Route 23, Leola, Pennsylvania 17540
Tel: +1 717 656 7002
Fax: +1 717 656 7648
Web: www.johansens.com/leolavillage

U.S.A. - PENNSYLVANIA (PHILADELPHIA)

Rittenhouse 1715, A Boutique Hotel

1715 Rittenhouse Square, Philadelphia, Pennsylvania 19103
Tel: +1 215 546 6500
Fax: +1 215 546 8787
Web: www.johansens.com/rittenhouse

U.S.A. - PENNSYLVANIA (POCONOS)

Skytop Lodge

One Skytop, Skytop, Pennsylvania 18357
Tel: +1 570 595 8905
Fax: +1 570 595 7285
Web: www.johansens.com/skytop

U.S.A. - RHODE ISLAND (NEWPORT)

The Chanler at Cliff Walk

117 Memorial Boulevard, Newport, Rhode Island 02840
Tel: +1 401 847 1300
Fax: +1 401 847 3620
Web: www.johansens.com/chanler

U.S.A. - RHODE ISLAND (PROVIDENCE)

Hotel Providence

311 Westminster Street, Providence, Rhode Island 02903
Tel: +1 401 861 8000
Fax: +1 401 861 8002
Web: www.johansens.com/providence

U.S.A. - SOUTH CAROLINA (BLUFFTON)

The Inn at Palmetto Bluff

476 Mount Pelia Road, Bluffton, South Carolina 29910
Tel: +1 843 706 6500
Fax: +1 843 706 6550
Web: www.johansens.com/palmettobluff

U.S.A. - SOUTH CAROLINA (CHARLESTON)

The Boardwalk Inn at Wild Dunes Resort

5757 Palm Boulevard, Isle of Palms, South Carolina 29451
Tel: +1 843 886 6000
Fax: +1 843 886 2916
Web: www.johansens.com/boardwalk

U.S.A. - SOUTH CAROLINA (CHARLESTON)

Charleston Harbor Resort & Marina

20 Patriots Point Road, Charleston, South Carolina 29464
Tel: +1 843 856 0028
Fax: +1 843 856 8333
Web: www.johansens.com/charlestonharbor

U.S.A. - SOUTH CAROLINA (CHARLESTON)

Woodlands Resort & Inn

125 Parsons Road, Summerville, South Carolina 29483
Tel: +1 843 875 2600
Fax: +1 843 875 2603
Web: www.johansens.com/woodlandssc

U.S.A. - SOUTH CAROLINA (KIAWAH ISLAND)

The Sanctuary at Kiawah Island Golf Resort

One Sanctuary Beach Drive, Kiawah Island,
South Carolina 29455
Tel: +1 843 768 6000
Fax: +1 843 768 5150
Web: www.johansens.com/sanctuary

U.S.A. - SOUTH CAROLINA (PAWLEYS ISLAND)

Litchfield Plantation

Kings River Road, Box 290, Pawleys Island,
South Carolina 29585
Tel: +1 843 237 9121
Fax: +1 843 237 1688
Web: www.johansens.com/litchfieldplantation

U.S.A. - SOUTH CAROLINA (TRAVELERS REST)

La Bastide

10 Road Of Vines, Travelers Rest, South Carolina 29210
Tel: +1 864 836 8463
Fax: +1 864 836 4820
Web: www.johansens.com/labastide

U.S.A. - TENNESSEE (WALLAND)

Blackberry Farm

1471 West Millers Cove Road, Walland,
Great Smoky Mountains, Tennessee 37886
Tel: +1 865 380 2260
Fax: +1 865 681 7753
Web: www.johansens.com/blackberryfarm

U.S.A. - TEXAS (AUSTIN)

The Mansion at Judges' Hill

1900 Rio Grande, Austin, Texas 78705
Tel: +1 512 495 1800
Fax: +1 512 691 4461
Web: www.johansens.com/judgeshill

Mini Listings The Americas

Condé Nast Johansens are delighted to recommend 310 properties across The Americas, Atlantic, Caribbean and Pacific.
Call 0800 269 397 or see the order forms on page 381 to order guides.

U.S.A. - TEXAS (GRANBURY)

The Inn on Lake Granbury
205 West Doyle Street, Granbury, Texas 76048
Tel: +1 817 573 0046
Fax: +1 817 573 0047
Web: www.johansens.com/lakegranbury

U.S.A. - TEXAS (SAN ANTONIO)

The Havana Riverwalk Inn
1015 Navarro, San Antonio, Texas 78205
Tel: +1 210 222 2008
Fax: +1 210 222 2717
Web: www.johansens.com/havanariverwalkinn

U.S.A. - TEXAS (WAXAHACHIE)

The Chaska House
716 West Main Street, Waxahachie, Texas 75165
Tel: +1 972 937 3390
Fax: +1 972 937 1780
Web: www.johansens.com/chaskahouse

U.S.A. - UTAH (MOAB)

Sorrel River Ranch Resort & Spa
Highway 128 Mile 17, H.C. 64 BOX 4000, Moab, Utah 84532
Tel: +1 435 259 4642
Fax: +1 435 259 3016
Web: www.johansens.com/sorrelriver

U.S.A. - VERMONT (BARNARD)

Twin Farms
P.O. Box 115, Barnard, Vermont 05031
Tel: +1 802 234 9999
Fax: +1 802 234 9990
Web: www.johansens.com/twinfarms

U.S.A. - VERMONT (KILLINGTON)

Mountain Top Inn & Resort
195 Mountain Top Road, Chittenden, Vermont 05737
Tel: +1 802 483 2311
Fax: +1 802 483 6373
Web: www.johansens.com/mountaintopinn

U.S.A. - VERMONT (WARREN)

The Pitcher Inn
275 Main Street, P.O. Box 347, Warren, Vermont 05674
Tel: +1 802 496 6350
Fax: +1 802 496 6354
Web: www.johansens.com/pitcherinn

U.S.A. - VIRGINIA (ABINGDON)

The Martha Washington Inn
150 West Main Street, Abingdon, Virginia 24210
Tel: +1 276 628 3161
Fax: +1 276 628 8885
Web: www.johansens.com/themartha

U.S.A. - VIRGINIA (CHARLOTTESVILLE)

200 South Street Inn
200 South Street, Charlottesville, Virginia 22901
Tel: +1 434 979 0200
Fax: +1 434 979 4403
Web: www.johansens.com/200southstreetinn

U.S.A. - VIRGINIA (GLOUCESTER)

The Inn at Warner Hall
4750 Warner Hall Road, Gloucester, Virginia 23061
Tel: +1 804 695 9565
Fax: +1 804 695 9566
Web: www.johansens.com/warnerhall

U.S.A. - VIRGINIA (IRVINGTON)

Hope and Glory Inn
65 Tavern Road, Irvington, Virginia 22480
Tel: +1 804 438 6053
Fax: +1 804 438 5362
Web: www.johansens.com/hopeandglory

U.S.A. - VIRGINIA (MIDDLEBURG)

The Goodstone Inn & Estate
36205 Snake Hill Road, Middleburg, Virginia 20117
Tel: +1 540 687 4645
Fax: +1 540 687 6115
Web: www.johansens.com/goodstoneinn

U.S.A. - VIRGINIA (STAUNTON)

Frederick House
28 North New Street, Staunton, Virginia 24401
Tel: + 1 540 885 4220
Fax: +1 540 885 5180
Web: www.johansens.com/frederickhouse

U.S.A. - VIRGINIA (WASHINGTON METROPOLITAN AREA)

Morrison House
116 South Alfred Street, Alexandria, Virginia 22314
Tel: +1 703 838 8000
Fax: +1 703 684 6283
Web: www.johansens.com/morrisonhouse

U.S.A. - WASHINGTON (BELLINGHAM)

The Chrysalis Inn and Spa
804 10th Street, Bellingham, Washington 98225
Tel: +1 360 756 1005
Fax: +1 360 647 0342
Web: www.johansens.com/chrysalis

U.S.A. - WASHINGTON (FRIDAY HARBOR)

Friday Harbor House
130 West Street, Friday Harbor, Washington 98250
Tel: +1 360 378 8455
Fax: +1 360 378 8453
Web: www.johansens.com/fridayharbor

U.S.A. - WASHINGTON (LEAVENWORTH)

Run of the River Inn and Refuge
9308 E. Leavenworth Road, Leavenworth, Washington 98826
Tel: +1 509 548 7171
Fax: 1 509 548 7547
Web: www.johansens.com/runoftheriver

U.S.A. - WASHINGTON (SPOKANE)

The Davenport Hotel and Tower
10 South Post Street, Spokane, Washington 99201
Tel: +1 509 455 8888
Fax: +1 509 624 4455
Web: www.johansens.com/davenport

U.S.A. - WASHINGTON (UNION)

Alderbrook Resort & Spa
10 East Alderbrook Drive, Union, Washington 98592
Tel: +1 360 898 2200
Fax: +1 360 898 4610
Web: www.johansens.com/alderbrook

U.S.A. - WASHINGTON (WOODINVILLE)

The Herbfarm
14590 North East 145th Street, Woodinville, Washington 98072
Tel: +1 425 485 5300
Fax: +1 425 424 2925
Web: www.johansens.com/herbfarm

Mini Listings The Americas

Condé Nast Johansens are delighted to recommend 310 properties across The Americas, Atlantic, Caribbean and Pacific.
Call 0800 269 397 or see the order forms on page 381 to order guides.

U.S.A. - WEST VIRGINIA (WHITE SULPHUR SPRINGS)

The Greenbrier

300 West Main Street, White Sulphur Springs, West Virginia 24986
Tel: +1 304 536 1110
Fax: +1 304 536 7818
Web: www.johansens.com/greenbrier

U.S.A. - WISCONSIN (CHETEK)

Canoe Bay

P.O. Box 28, Chetek, Wisconsin 54728
Tel: +1 715 924 4594
Fax: +1 715 924 2078
Web: www.johansens.com/canoebay

U.S.A. - WISCONSIN (DELAFIELD)

The Delafield Hotel

415 Genesee Street, Delafield, Wisconsin 53018
Tel: +1 262 646 1600
Fax: +1 262 646 1613
Web: www.johansens.com/delafield

U.S.A. - WYOMING (CHEYENNE)

Nagle Warren Mansion

222 East 17Th Street, Cheyenne, Wyoming 82001
Tel: +1 307 637 3333
Fax: +1 307 638 6879
Web: www.johansens.com/naglewarrenmansion

U.S.A. - WYOMING (DUBOIS)

Brooks Lake Lodge

458 Brooks Lake Road, Dubois, Wyoming 82513
Tel: +1 307 455 2121
Fax: +1 307 455 2221
Web: www.johansens.com/brookslake

U.S.A. - WYOMING (GRAND TETON NATIONAL PARK)

Jenny Lake Lodge

Inner Park Loop Road, Grand Teton National Park, Wyoming 83013
Tel: +1 307 543 3300
Fax: +1 307 543 3358
Web: www.johansens.com/jennylake

U.S.A. - WYOMING (TETON VILLAGE)

Teton Mountain Lodge

3385 W. Village Drive, Teton Village, Wyoming 83025
Tel: +1 307 734 7111
Fax: +1 307 734 7999
Web: www.johansens.com/teton

Recommendations in Central America

COSTA RICA - GUANACASTE (ISLITA)

Hotel Punta Islita

Guanacaste
Tel: +506 231 6122
Fax: +506 231 0715
Web: www.johansens.com/hotelpuntaislita

COSTA RICA - GUANACASTE (PLAYA CONCHAL)

Paradisus Playa Conchal

Bahía Brasilito, Playa Conchal, Santa Cruz, Guanacaste
Tel: +506 654 4123
Fax: +506 654 4181
Web: www.johansens.com/paradisusplayaconchal

COSTA RICA - PUNTARENAS (MANUEL ANTONIO)

Gaia Hotel & Reserve

Km 2.7 Carretera Quepos, Manuel Antonio
Tel: +506 777 9797
Fax: +506 777 9126
Web: www.johansens.com/gaiahr

HONDURAS - ATLÁNTIDA (LA CEIBA)

The Lodge at Pico Bonito

A. P. 710, La Ceiba, Atlántida, C. P. 31101
Tel: +504 440 0388
Fax: +504 440 0468
Web: www.johansens.com/picobonito

Recommendations in South America

ARGENTINA - BUENOS AIRES (CIUDAD DE BUENOS AIRES)

1555 Malabia House

Malabia 1555, C1414DME Buenos Aires
Tel: +54 11 4832 3345
Fax: +54 11 4832 3345
Web: www.johansens.com/malabiahouse

ARGENTINA - BUENOS AIRES (CIUDAD DE BUENOS AIRES)

LoiSuites Recoleta Hotel

Vicente López 1955 – C1128ACC, Ciudad de Buenos Aires
Tel: +54 11 5777 8950
Fax: +54 11 5777 8999
Web: www.johansens.com/loisuites

ARGENTINA - PATAGONIA (ISLA VICTORIA)

Hosteria Isla Victoria

Isla Victoria, Parque Nacional Nahuel Huapi, C.C. 26 (R8401AKU)
Tel: +54 43 94 96 05
Fax: +54 11 43 94 95 99
Web: www.johansens.com/islavictoria

ARGENTINA - PATAGONIA (VILLA LA ANGOSTURA)

Correntoso Lake & River Hotel

Av. Siète Lagos 4505, Villa La Angostura, Neuquén
Tel: +54 2944 15 619728
Web: www.johansens.com/correntoso

BRAZIL - ALAGOAS (SÃO MIGUEL DOS MILAGRES)

Pousada do Toque

Rua Felisberto de Ataide, Povoado do Toque, São Miguel dos Milagres, Alagoas
Tel: +55 82 3295 1127
Fax: +55 82 3295 1127
Web: www.johansens.com/pousadadotoque

BRAZIL - BAHIA (ITACARÉ)

Txai Resort

Rod. Ilhéus-Itacaré km 48, Itacaré, Bahia 45530-000
Tel: +55 73 2101 5000
Fax: +55 73 2101 5251
Web: www.johansens.com/txairesort

BRAZIL - BAHIA (PORTO SEGURO FRANCOSO)

Estrela d'Agua

Estrada Arraial d'Ajuda - Trancoso S/No, Trancoso Porto Seguro, Bahia 45818-000
Tel: +55 73 3668 1030
Fax: +55 73 3668 1030
Web: www.johansens.com/estreladagua

Mini Listings South America

Condé Nast Johansens are delighted to recommend 310 properties across The Americas, Atlantic, Caribbean and Pacific.

Call 0800 269 397 or see the order forms on page 381 to order guides.

BRAZIL - BAHIA (PRAIA DO FORTE)

Praia do Forte Eco Resort & Thalasso Spa

Avenida do Farol, Praia do Forte - Mata de São João, Bahia
Tel: +55 71 36 76 40 00
Fax: +55 71 36 76 11 12
Web: www.johansens.com/praiadoforte

BRAZIL - MINAS GERAIS (TIRADENTES)

Pousada dos Inconfidentes

Rua João Rodrigues Sobrinho 91, 36325-000, Tiradentes, Minas Gerais
Tel: +55 32 3355 2135
Fax: +55 32 3355 2135
Web: www.johansens.com/inconfidentes

BRAZIL - MINAS GERAIS (TIRADENTES)

Solar da Ponte

Praça das Mercês S/N, Tiradentes, Minas Gerais 36325-000
Tel: +55 32 33 55 12 55
Fax: +55 32 33 55 12 01
Web: www.johansens.com/solardaponte

BRAZIL - PERNAMBUCO (PORTO DE GALINHAS)

Nannai Beach Resort

Rodovia PE-09, acesso à Muro Alto, Km 3, Ipojuca, Pernambuco 55590-000
Tel: +55 81 3552 0100
Fax: +55 81 3552 1474
Web: www.johansens.com/nannaibeach

BRAZIL - RIO DE JANEIRO (ANGRA DOS REIS)

Sítio do Lobo

Ponta do Lobo, Ilha Grande, Angra dos Reis, Rio de Janeiro
Tel: +55 21 2227 4138
Fax: +55 21 2267 7841
Web: www.johansens.com/sitiodolobo

BRAZIL - RIO DE JANEIRO (ARMAÇÃO DOS BÚZIOS)

Pérola Búzios

Av. José Bento Ribeiro Dantas, 222, Armação dos Búzios, Rio de Janeiro 28950-000
Tel: +55 22 2620 8507
Fax: +55 22 2623 9015
Web: www.johansens.com/perolabuzios

BRAZIL - RIO DE JANEIRO (BÚZIOS)

Casas Brancas Boutique-Hotel & Spa

Alto do Humaitá 10, Armação dos Búzios, Rio de Janeiro 28950-000
Tel: +55 22 2623 1458
Fax: +55 22 2623 2147
Web: www.johansens.com/casasbrancas

BRAZIL - RIO DE JANEIRO (BÚZIOS)

Glenzhaus Lodge

Rua 1 - Quadra F - Lote 27/28, Armação dos Búzios, Rio de Janeiro 28950-000
Tel: +55 22 2623 2823
Fax: +55 22 2623 5293
Web: www.johansens.com/glenzhaus

BRAZIL - RIO DE JANEIRO (ENGENEIRO PAULO DE FRONTIN)

Vivenda Les 4 Saisons

Rua João Cordeiro da Costa E silva, 5, Caixa Postal 127, Engenheiro Paulo de Frontin, Rio de Janeiro 26650-000
Tel: +55 24 2463 2892
Fax: +55 24 2463 1395
Web: www.johansens.com/4saisons

BRAZIL - RIO DE JANEIRO (PETRÓPOLIS)

Parador Santarém Marina

Estrada Correia da Veiga, 96, Petrópolis, Rio de Janeiro 25745-260
Tel: +55 24 2222 9933
Fax: +55 24 2222 9933
Web: www.johansens.com/paradorsantarem

BRAZIL - RIO DE JANEIRO (PETRÓPOLIS)

Solar do Império

Koeler Avenue, 376- Centro, Petrópolis, Rio de Janeiro
Tel: +55 24 2103 3000
Fax: +55 24 2242 0034
Web: www.johansens.com/solardoimperio

BRAZIL - RIO DE JANEIRO (PETRÓPOLIS)

Tankamana EcoResort

Estrada Júlio Cápua, S/N Vale Do Cuiabá, Itaipava - Petrópolis, Rio De Janeiro 25745-050
Tel: +55 24 2222 9181
Fax: +55 24 2222 9181
Web: www.johansens.com/tankamana

BRAZIL - RIO DE JANEIRO (RIO DE JANEIRO)

Hotel Marina All Suites

Av. Delfim Moreira, 696, Praia do Leblon, Rio de Janeiro 22441-000
Tel: +55 21 2172 1001
Fax: +55 21 2172 1110
Web: www.johansens.com/marinaallsuites

BRAZIL - RIO GRANDE DO SUL (SAO FRANCISCO DE PAULA)

Pousada Do Engenho

Rua Odon Cavalcante, 330, São Francisco de Paula 95400-000, Rio Grande do Sul
Tel: +55 54 3244 1270
Fax: +55 54 3244 1270
Web: www.johansens.com/pousadadoengenho

BRAZIL - RIO GRANDE DO SUL (GRAMADO)

Kurotel

Rua Nacões Unidas 533, P.O. Box 65, Gramado, Rio Grande do Sul 95670-000
Tel: +55 54 3295 9393
Fax: +55 54 3286 1203
Web: www.johansens.com/kurotel

BRAZIL - SANTA CATARINA (GOVERNADOR CELSO RAMOS)

Ponta dos Ganchos

Rua Eupídio Alves do Nascimento, 104, Governador Celso Ramos, Santa Catarina 88190-000
Tel: +55 48 3262 5000
Fax: +55 48 3262 5046
Web: www.johansens.com/pontadosganchos

BRAZIL - SÃO PAULO (CAMPOS DO JORDÃO)

Hotel Frontenac

Av. Dr. Paulo Ribas, 295 Capivari, Campos do Jordão 12460-000
Tel: +55 12 3669 1000
Fax: +55 12 3669 1009
Web: www.johansens.com/frontenac

CHILE - ARAUCANIA (PUCON)

Hotel Antumalal

Carretera Pucon-Villarka Highway at Km 2 from Pucon
Tel: +5645 441 011
Fax: +5645 441 013
Web: www.johansens.com/antumalal

CHILE - COLCHAGUA (SAN FERNANDO)

Hacienda Los Lingues

Km 124.5, Ruta 5 Sur + 5km Al Oriente, 6a Region, Colchagua
Tel: +562 431 0510
Fax: +562 431 0501
Web: www.johansens.com/loslingues

CHILE - PATAGONIA (PUERTO GUADAL)

Hacienda Tres Lagos

Carretera Austral Sur Km 274, Localidad Lago Negro, Puerto Guadal
Tel: + 56 2 333 41 22 and + 56 67 411 323
Fax: + 56 2 334 52 94 and + 56 67 411 323
Web: www.johansens.com/treslagos

Mini Listings Atlantic / Caribbean

Condé Nast Johansens are delighted to recommend 310 properties across The Americas, Atlantic, Caribbean and Pacific.
Call 0800 269 397 or see the order forms on page 381 to order guides.

PERU - LIMA PROVINCIAS (YAUYOS)

Refugios Del Peru - Viñak Reichraming
Santiago de Viñak, Yauyos, Lima
Tel: +51 1 421 6952
Fax: +51 1 421 8476
Web: www.johansens.com/refugiosdelperu

Recommendations in the Atlantic

ATLANTIC - BAHAMAS (GRAND BAHAMA ISLAND)

Old Bahama Bay Resort & Yacht Harbour
West End, Grand Bahama Island, Bahamas
Tel: +1 242 350 6500
Fax: +1 242 346 6546
Web: www.johansens.com/oldbahamabay

ATLANTIC - BAHAMAS (HARBOUR ISLAND)

Rock House
Bay & Hill Street, Harbour Island, Bahamas
Tel: +1 242 333 2053
Fax: +1 242 333 3173
Web: www.johansens.com/rockhouse

ATLANTIC - BERMUDA (HAMILTON)

Rosedon Hotel
P.O. Box Hm 290, Hamilton Hmax, Bermuda
Tel: +1 441 295 1640
Fax: +1 441 295 5904
Web: www.johansens.com/rosedonhotel

ATLANTIC - BERMUDA (HAMILTON)

Waterloo House
P.O. Box H.M. 333, Hamilton H.M. B.X., Bermuda
Tel: +1 441 295 4480
Fax: +1 441 295 2585
Web: www.johansens.com/waterloohouse

ATLANTIC - BERMUDA (PAGET)

Horizons and Cottages
33 South Shore Road, Paget, P.G.04, Bermuda
Tel: +1 441 236 0048
Fax: +1 441 236 1981
Web: www.johansens.com/horizonscottages

ATLANTIC - BERMUDA (SOMERSET)

Cambridge Beaches
Kings Point, Somerset, Bermuda
Tel: +1 441 234 0331
Fax: +1 441 234 3352
Web: www.johansens.com/cambridgebeaches

ATLANTIC - BERMUDA (SOUTHAMPTON)

The Reefs
56 South Shore Road, Southampton, Bermuda
Tel: +1 441 238 0222
Fax: +1 441 238 8372
Web: www.johansens.com/thereefs

ATLANTIC - BERMUDA (WARWICK)

Surf Side Beach Club
90 South Shore Road, Warwick, Bermuda
Tel: +1 441 236 7100
Fax: +1 441 236 9765
Web: www.johansens.com/surfside

Recommendations in the Caribbean

CARIBBEAN - ANGUILLA (RENDEZVOUS BAY)

CuisinArt Resort & Spa
P.O. Box 2000, Rendezvous Bay, Anguilla
Tel: +1 264 498 2000
Fax: +1 264 498 2010
Web: www.johansens.com/cuisinartresort

CARIBBEAN - ANTIGUA (ST. JOHN'S)

Blue Waters
P.O. Box 257, St. John's Antigua
Tel: +44 870 360 1245
Fax: +44 870 360 1246
Web: www.johansens.com/bluewaters

CARIBBEAN - ANTIGUA (ST. JOHN'S)

The Inn at English Harbour
English Harbour, Antigua
Tel: +1 268 460 1014
Fax: +1 268 460 1603
Web: www.johansens.com/innatenglishharbour

CARIBBEAN - ANTIGUA (ST. JOHN'S)

Curtain Bluff
P.O. Box 288, St. John's, Antigua
Tel: +1 268 462 8400
Fax: +1 268 462 8409
Web: www.johansens.com/curtainbluff

CARIBBEAN - ANTIGUA (ST. JOHN'S)

Galley Bay
Five Islands, St. John's, Antigua
Tel: +1 954 481 8787
Fax: +1 954 481 1661
Web: www.johansens.com/galleybay

CARIBBEAN - BARBADOS (CHRIST CHURCH)

Little Arches
Enterprise Beach Road, Christ Church, Barbados
Tel: +1 246 420 4689
Fax: +1 246 418 0207
Web: www.johansens.com/littlearches

CARIBBEAN - BARBADOS (ST. JAMES)

Coral Reef Club
St. James, Barbados
Tel: +1 246 422 2372
Fax: +1 246 422 1776
Web: www.johansens.com/coralreefclub

CARIBBEAN - BARBADOS (ST. JAMES)

Lone Star
Mount Standfast, St. James, Barbados
Tel: +1 246 419 0599
Fax: +1 246 419 0597
Web: www.johansens.com/lonestar

CARIBBEAN - BARBADOS (ST. JAMES)

The Sandpiper
Holetown, St. James, Barbados
Tel: +1 246 422 2251
Fax: +1 246 422 0900
Web: www.johansens.com/sandpiper

Mini Listings Caribbean / Pacific

Condé Nast Johansens are delighted to recommend 310 properties across The Americas, Atlantic, Caribbean and Pacific.

Call 0800 269 397 or see the order forms on page 381 to order guides.

CARIBBEAN - BARBADOS (ST. PETER)

Cobblers Cove

Speightstown, St. Peter, Barbados
Tel: +1 246 422 2291
Fax: +1 246 422 1460
Web: www.johansens.com/cobblerscove

CARIBBEAN - BARBADOS (ST. PETER)

Little Good Harbour

Shermans, St. Peter, Barbados
Tel: +1 246 439 3000
Fax: +1 246 439 2020
Web: www.johansens.com/goodharbour

CARIBBEAN - BONAIRE

Harbour Village Beach Club

Kaya Gobernador N. Debrot No. 71, Bonaire, Netherlands Antilles
Tel: +1 305 567 9509
Fax: +1 305 648 0699
Web: www.johansens.com/harbourvillage

CARIBBEAN - BRITISH VIRGIN ISLANDS (VIRGIN GORDA)

Biras Creek Resort

North Sound, Virgin Gorda, British Virgin Islands
Tel: +1 310 440 4225
Fax: +1 310 440 4220
Web: www.johansens.com/birascreek

CARIBBEAN - CURAÇAO (WILLEMSTAD)

Avila Hotel on the beach

Penstraat 130, Willemstad, Curaçao, Netherlands Antilles
Tel: +599 9 461 4377
Fax: +599 9 461 1493
Web: www.johansens.com/avilabeach

CARIBBEAN - DOMINICAN REPUBLIC (PUERTO PLATA)

Casa Colonial Beach & Spa

P.O. Box 22, Puerto Plata, Dominican Republic
Tel: +1 809 320 3232
Fax: +1 809 320 3131
Web: www.johansens.com/casacolonial

CARIBBEAN - GRENADA (ST. GEORGE'S)

Spice Island Beach Resort

Grand Anse Beach, St. George's, Grenada
Tel: +1 473 444 4423/4258
Fax: +1 473 444 4807
Web: www.johansens.com/spiceisland

CARIBBEAN - JAMAICA (MONTEGO BAY)

Half Moon

Montego Bay, Jamaica
Tel: +1 876 953 2211
Fax: +1 876 953 2731
Web: www.johansens.com/halfmoongolf

CARIBBEAN - JAMAICA (MONTEGO BAY)

Round Hill Hotel and Villas

P.O. Box 64, Montego Bay, Jamaica
Tel: +1 876 956 7050
Fax: +1 876 956 7505
Web: www.johansens.com/roundhill

CARIBBEAN - JAMAICA (MONTEGO BAY)

Tryall Club

P.O. Box 1206, Montego Bay, Jamaica
Tel: +1 800 238 5290
Fax: +1 876 956 5673
Web: www.johansens.com/tryallclub

CARIBBEAN - JAMAICA (ORACABESSA)

Goldeneye

Oracabessa, St. Mary, Jamaica
Tel: +1 876 975 3354
Fax: +1 876 975 3620
Web: www.johansens.com/goldeneye

CARIBBEAN - MARTINIQUE (LE FRANÇOIS)

Cap Est Lagoon Resort & Spa

97240 Le François, Martinique
Tel: +596 596 54 80 80
Fax: +596 596 54 96 00
Web: www.johansens.com/capest

CARIBBEAN - NEVIS (CHARLESTOWN)

Montpelier Plantation Inn

Montpelier Estate, Charlestown, Nevis
Tel: +1 869 469 3462
Fax: +1 869 469 2932
Web: www.johansens.com/montpelierplantation

CARIBBEAN - PUERTO RICO (RINCÓN)

Horned Dorset Primavera

Apartado 1132, Rincón, Puerto Rico 00677
Tel: +1 787 823 4030
Fax: +1 787 823 5580
Web: www.johansens.com/horneddorset

CARIBBEAN - SAINT-BARTHÉLEMY (GRAND CUL DE SAC)

Hotel Guanahani & Spa

Grand Cul de Sac, 97133 Saint-Barthélemy
Tel: +590 590 27 66 60
Fax: +590 590 27 70 70
Web: www.johansens.com/guanahani

CARIBBEAN - SAINT-BARTHÉLEMY (GRAND CUL DE SAC)

Le Toiny

Anse de Toiny 97133, Saint-Barthélemy
Tel: +590 590 27 88 88
Fax: +590 590 27 89 30
Web: www.johansens.com/letoiny

CARIBBEAN - SAINT-BARTHÉLEMY (GUSTAVIA)

Carl Gustaf Hotel

Rue des Normands, Gustavia, 97099 Saint-Barthélemy
Tel: +590 590 29 79 00
Fax: +590 590 27 82 37
Web: www.johansens.com/carlgustaf

CARIBBEAN - ST. LUCIA (SOUFRIÈRE)

Ladera

Soufrière, St. Lucia
Tel: +1 758 459 7323
Fax: +1 758 459 5156
Web: www.johansens.com/ladera

CARIBBEAN - ST. LUCIA (SOUFRIÈRE)

Anse Chastanet

Soufrière, St. Lucia
Tel: +1 758 459 7000
Fax: +1 758 459 7700
Web: www.johansens.com/ansechastanet

CARIBBEAN - ST. LUCIA (SOUFRIÈRE)

Jade Mountain at Anse Chastanet

Soufrière, St. Lucia
Tel: +1 758 459 4000
Fax: +1 758 459 4002
Web: www.johansens.com/jademountain

Mini Listings Caribbean / Pacific

Condé Nast Johansens are delighted to recommend 310 properties across The Americas, Atlantic, Caribbean and Pacific.
Call 0800 269 397 or see the order forms on page 381 to order guides.

CARIBBEAN - ST. MARTIN (BAIE LONGUE)

La Samanna
P.O. Box 4077, 97064 St. Martin - CEDEX
Tel: +590 590 87 64 00
Fax: +590 590 87 87 86
Web: www.johansens.com/lasamanna

CARIBBEAN - THE GRENADINES (MUSTIQUE)

Firefly
Mustique Island, St. Vincent & The Grenadines
Tel: +1 784 488 8414
Fax: +1 784 488 8514
Web: www.johansens.com/firefly

CARIBBEAN - THE GRENADINES (PALM ISLAND)

Palm Island
St. Vincent & The Grenadines
Tel: +1 954 481 8787
Fax: +1 954 481 1661
Web: www.johansens.com/palmisland

CARIBBEAN - TURKS & CAICOS (PROVIDENCIALES)

Grace Bay Club
P.O. Box 128, Providenciales, Turks & Caicos Islands
Tel: +1 649 946 5050
Fax: +1 649 946 5758
Web: www.johansens.com/gracebayclub

CARIBBEAN - TURKS & CAICOS (PROVIDENCIALES)

Parrot Cay
P.O. Box 164, Providenciales, Turks & Caicos Islands
Tel: +1 649 946 7788
Fax: +1 649 946 7789
Web: www.johansens.com/parrotcay

CARIBBEAN - TURKS & CAICOS (PROVIDENCIALES)

Point Grace
P.O. Box 700, Providenciales, Turks & Caicos Islands
Tel: +1 649 946 5096
Fax: +1 649 946 5097
Web: www.johansens.com/pointgrace

CARIBBEAN - TURKS & CAICOS (PROVIDENCIALES)

Turks & Caicos Club
P.O. Box 687, West Grace Bay Beach, Providenciales, Turks & Caicos Islands
Tel: +1 649 946 5800
Fax: +1 649 946 5858
Web: www.johansens.com/turksandcaicos

CARIBBEAN - TURKS & CAICOS (PROVIDENCIALES)

The Somerset
Princess Drive, Providenciales, Turks & Caicos Islands
Tel: +1 649 946 5900
Fax: +1 649 946 5944
Web: www.johansens.com/somersetgracebay

Recommendations in the Pacific

PACIFIC - FIJI ISLANDS (LABASA)

Nukubati Island
P.O. Box 1928, Labasa, Fiji Islands
Tel: +61 2 93888 196
Fax: +61 2 93888 204
Web: www.johansens.com/nukubati

PACIFIC - FIJI ISLANDS (LAUTOKA)

Blue Lagoon Cruises
183 Vitogo Parade, Lautoka, Fiji Islands
Tel: +679 6661 622
Fax: +679 6664 098
Web: www.johansens.com/bluelagooncruises

PACIFIC - FIJI ISLANDS (QAMEA ISLAND)

Qamea Resort & Spa
P.A. Matei, Tavenui, Fiji Islands
Tel: +679 888 0220
Fax: +679 888 0092
Web: www.johansens.com/qamea

PACIFIC - FIJI ISLANDS (SAVUSAVU)

Jean-Michel Cousteau Fiji Islands Resort
Lesiaceva Point, SavuSavu, Fiji Islands
Tel: +415 788 5794
Web: www.johansens.com/jean-michelcousteau

PACIFIC - FIJI ISLANDS (SIGATOKA)

Myola Plantation
P.O. Box 638, Sigatoka, Fiji Islands
Tel: +679 652 1084
Fax: +679 652 0899
Web: www.johansens.com/myola

PACIFIC - FIJI ISLANDS (TOBERUA ISLAND)

Toberua Island Resort
P.O. Box 3332, Nausori, Fiji Islands
Tel: +679 347 2777
Fax: +679 347 2888
Web: www.johansens.com/toberuaisland

PACIFIC - FIJI ISLANDS (UGAGA ISLAND)

Royal Davui
P.O. Box 3171, Lami, Fiji Islands
Tel: +679 336 1624
Fax: +679 336 1253
Web: www.johansens.com/royaldavui

PACIFIC - FIJI ISLANDS (YAQETA ISLAND)

Navutu Stars Resort
P.O. Box 1838, Lautoka, Fiji Islands
Tel: +679 664 0553 and +679 664 0554
Fax: +679 666 0807
Web: www.johansens.com/navutustars

PACIFIC - FIJI ISLANDS (YASAWA ISLAND)

Yasawa Island Resort
P.O. Box 10128, Nadi Airport, Nadi, Fiji Islands
Tel: +679 672 2266
Fax: +679 672 4456
Web: www.johansens.com/yasawaisland

Index by Property

▼

▼

▼

Index by Property

INDEX BY LOCATION

London

England

A

B

C

D

Index by Location

INDEX BY LOCATION

Y

Channel Islands

Northern Ireland

Ireland

Scotland

Wales

SPA Dedicated Spa facilities

England

Channel Islands

Ireland

▼

Scotland

Wales

Outdoor pool

England

Channel Islands

Ireland

Hotels with heated indoor swimming pool

England

Index by Activity

▼

Channel Islands

Ireland

Scotland

Wales

Golf course on-site

England

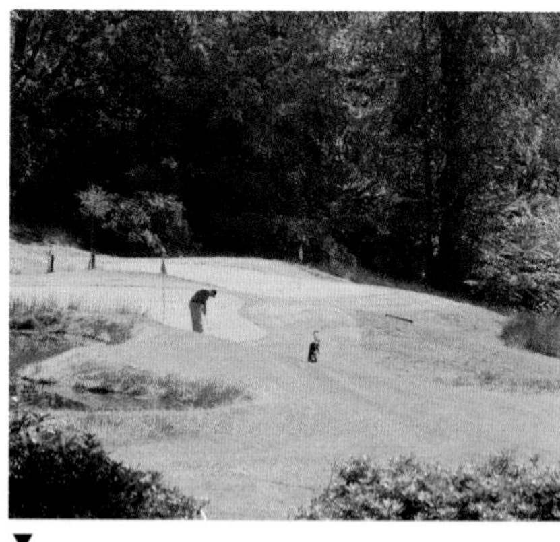

▼

Ireland

Scotland

Wales

Fishing on-site

England

▼

Ireland

Scotland

Wales

Shooting on-site

England

Ireland

Scotland

Wales

M200 Conference facilities for 200 delegates or more

England

▼

Ireland

Scotland

Wales

Index by Consortium

Pride Of Britain members

England

▼

Scotland

Wales

Leading Hotels of the World

England

Ireland

Small Luxury Hotels Of The World members

England

Channel Islands

Ireland

Scotland

▼

Ireland's Blue Book

N Ireland

Ireland

Relais & Châteaux members

England

▼

Channel Islands

Ireland

Scotland

North West England

Hotel location shown in red (hotel) or purple (spa hotel) with page number

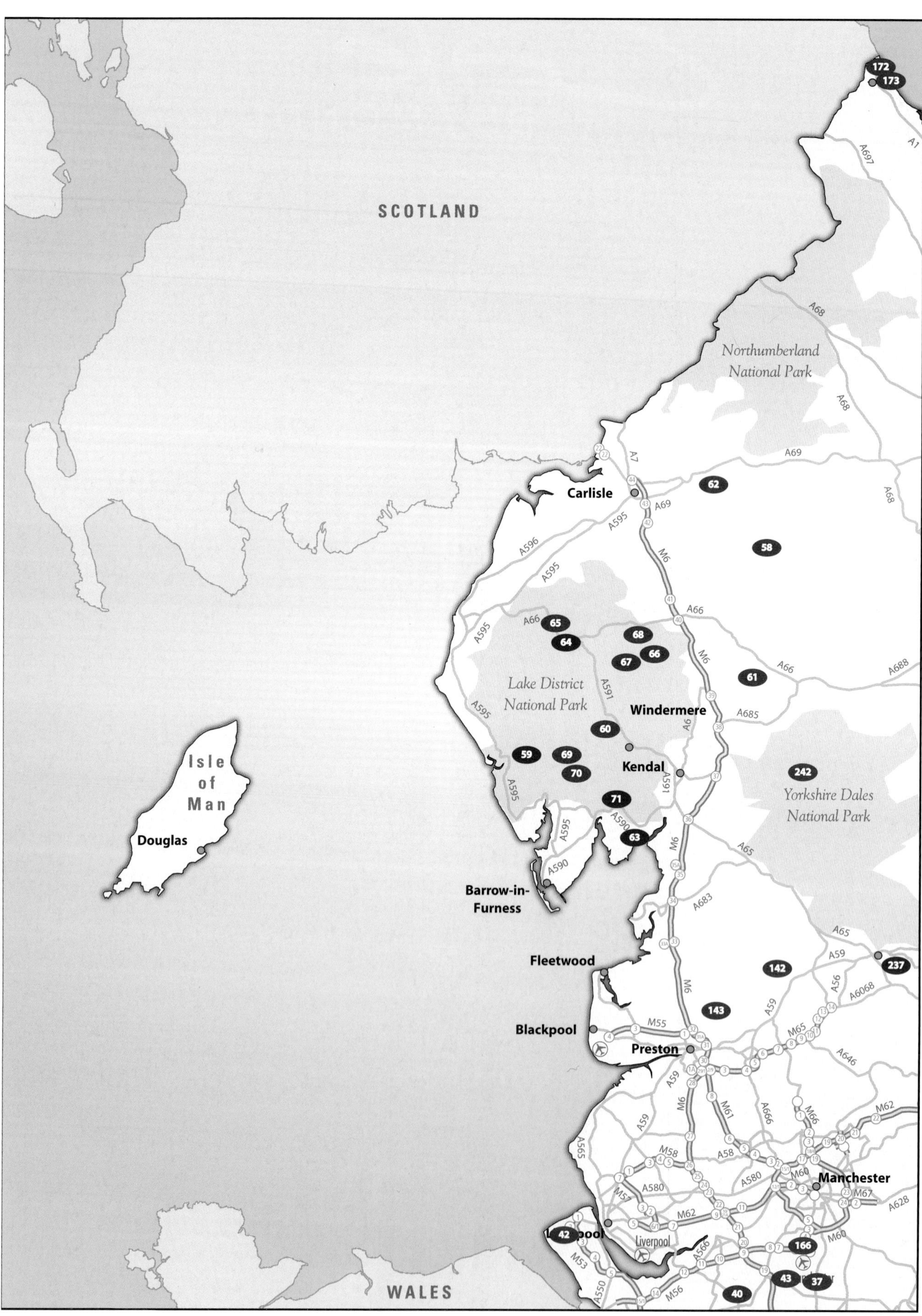

North East England

Hotel location shown in red (hotel) or purple (spa hotel) with page number

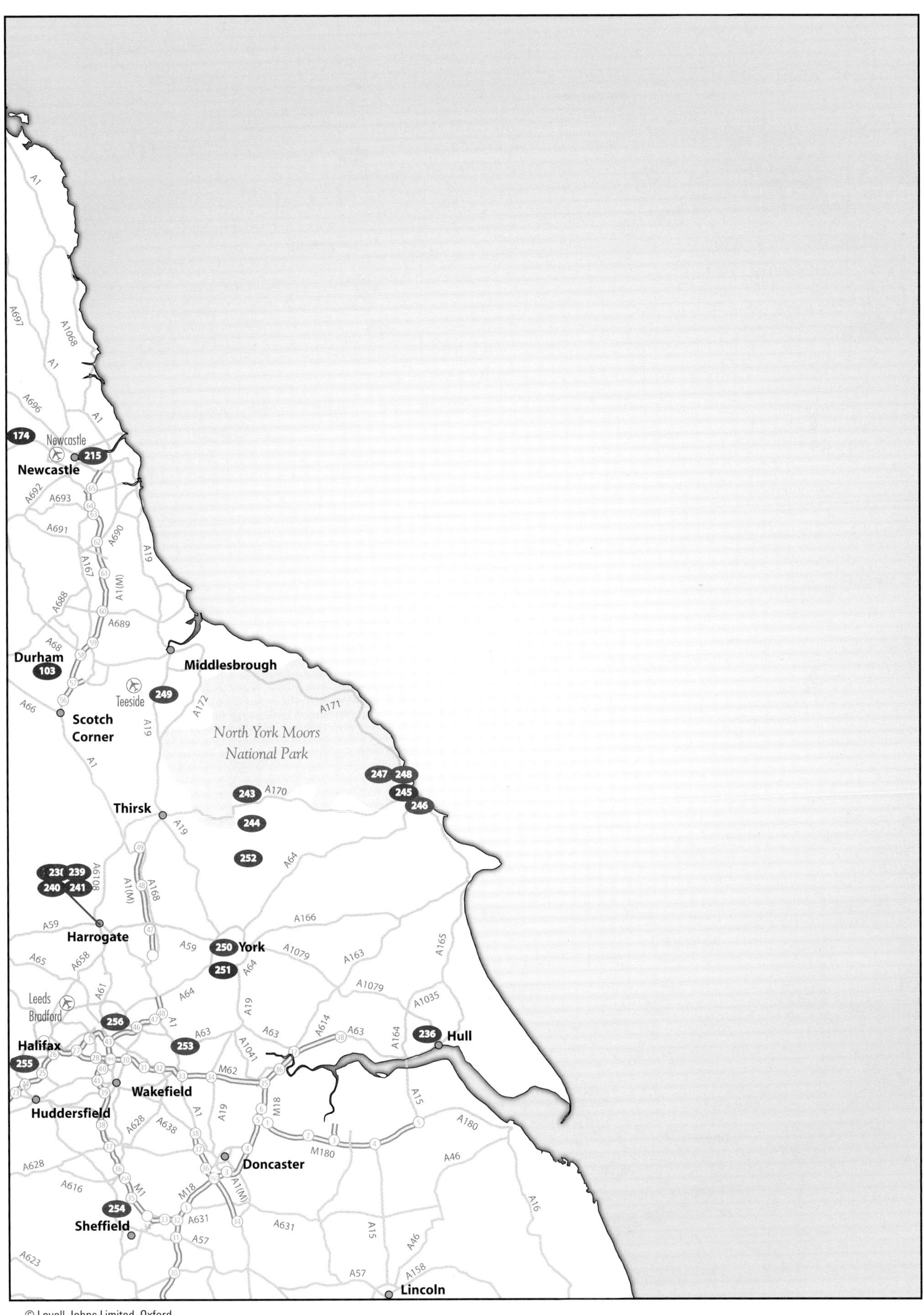

Central England

Hotel location shown in red (hotel) or purple (spa hotel) with page number

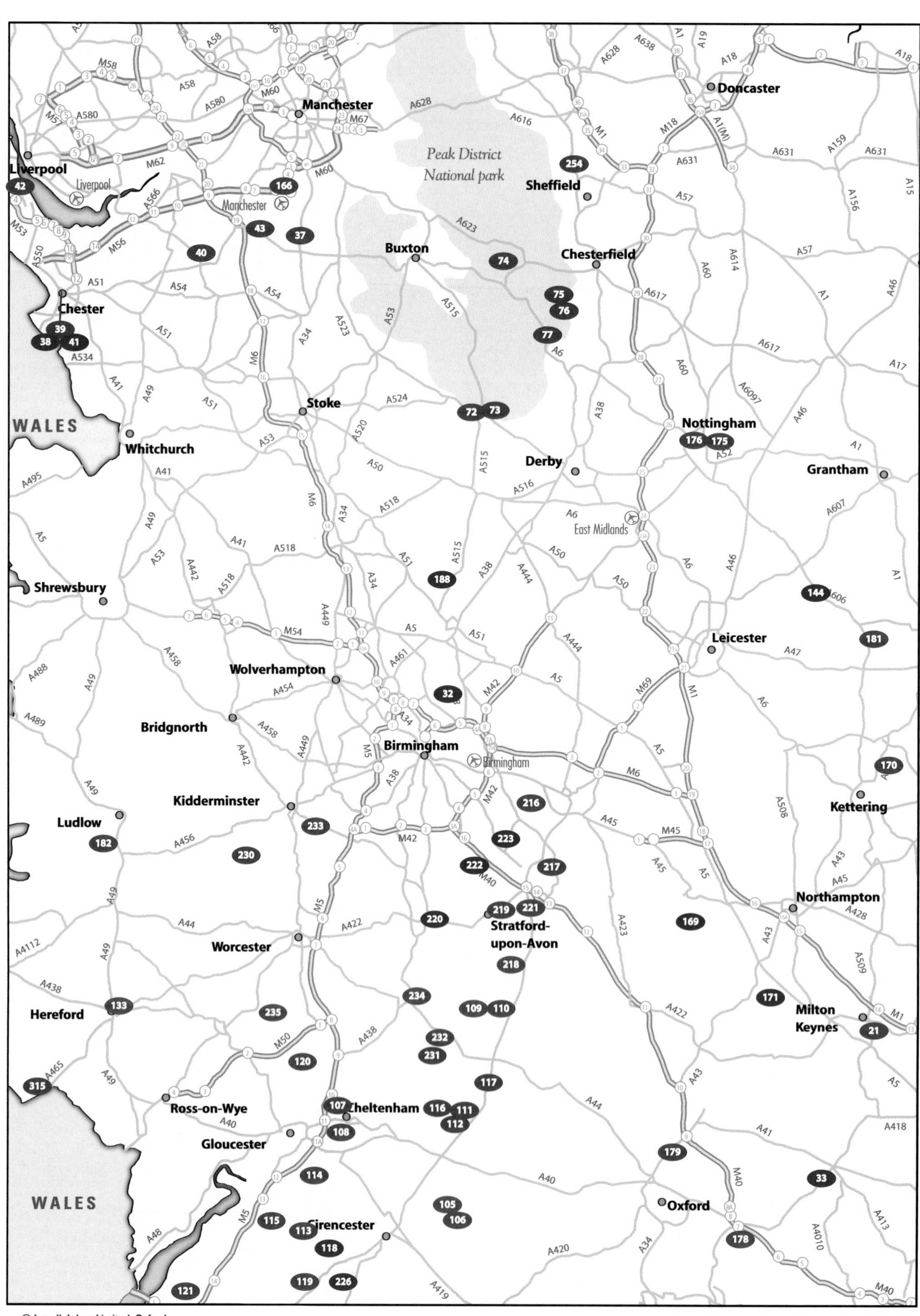

Eastern England

Hotel location shown in red (hotel) or purple (spa hotel) with page number

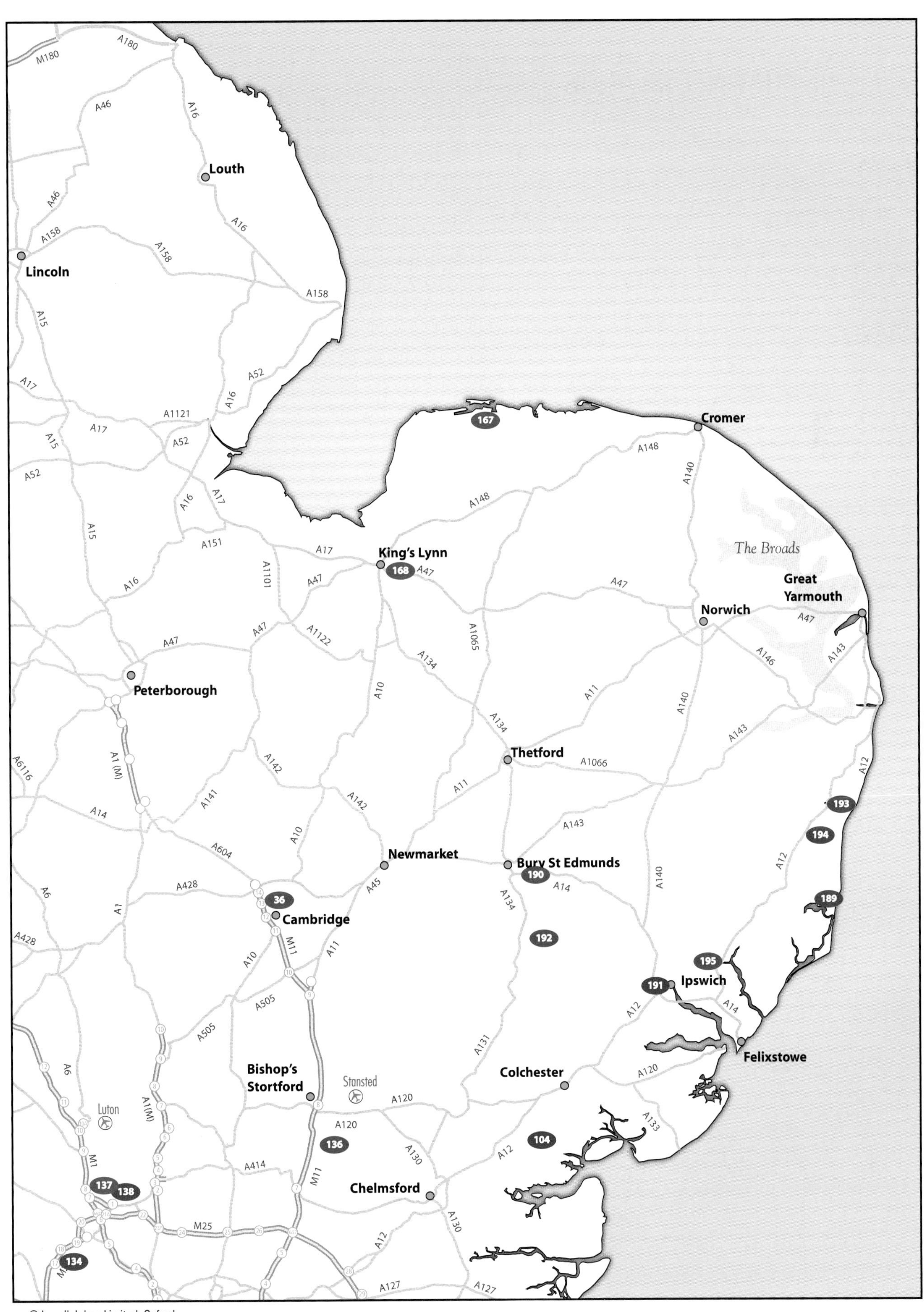

Channel Islands & South West England

Hotel location shown in red (hotel) or purple (spa hotel) with page number

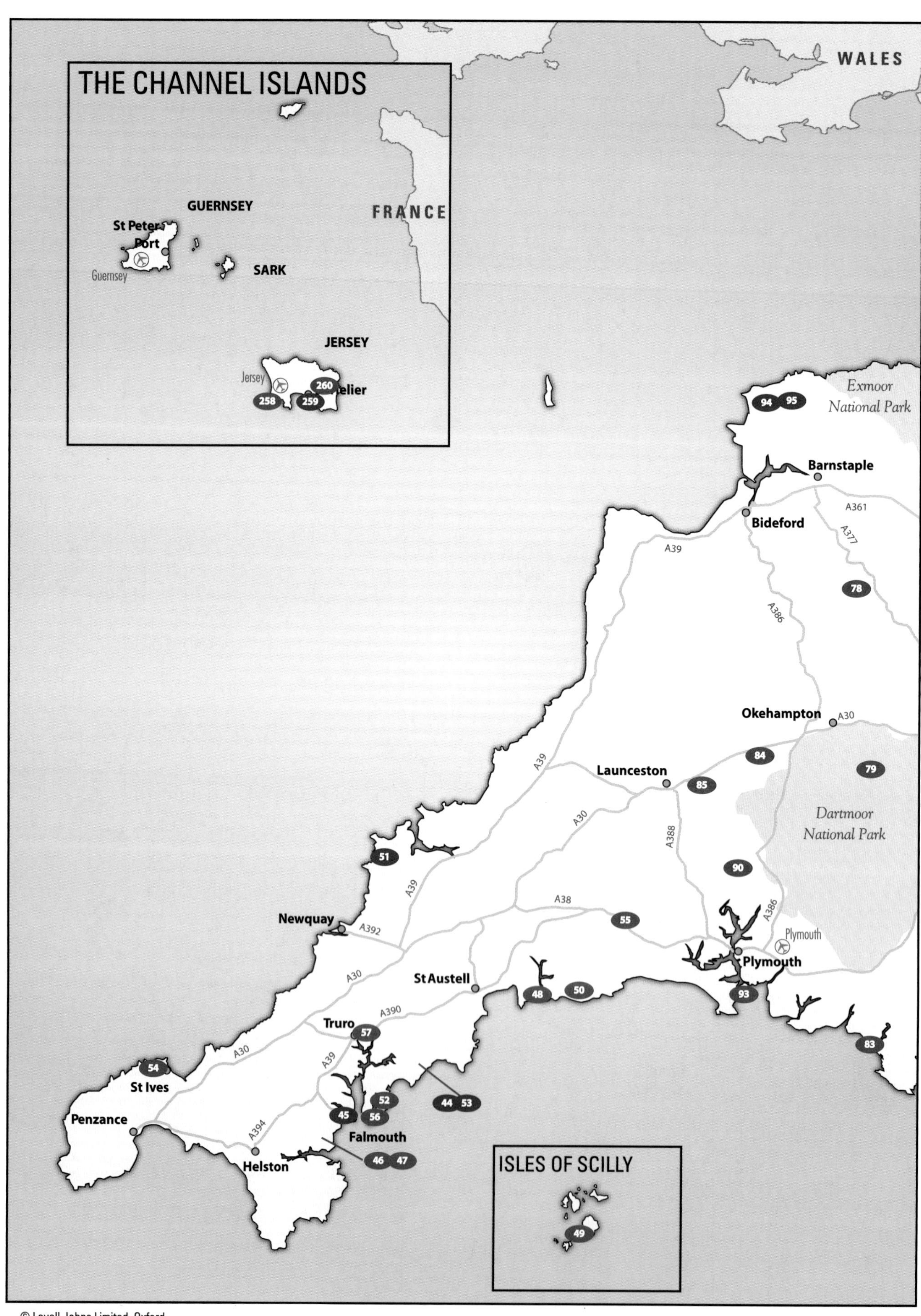

South West England

Hotel location shown in red (hotel) or purple (spa hotel) with page number

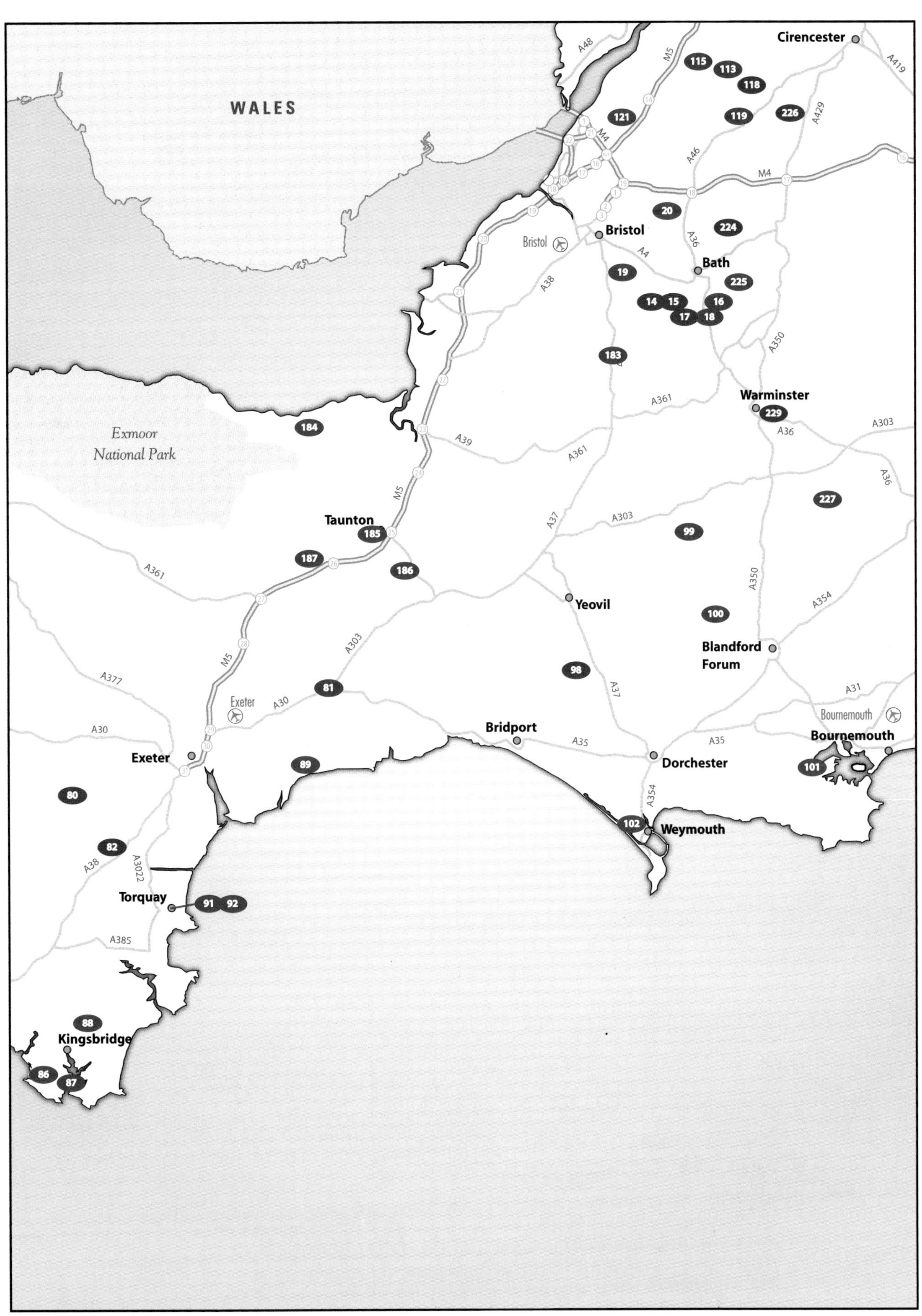

Southern England

Hotel location shown in red (hotel) or purple (spa hotel) with page number

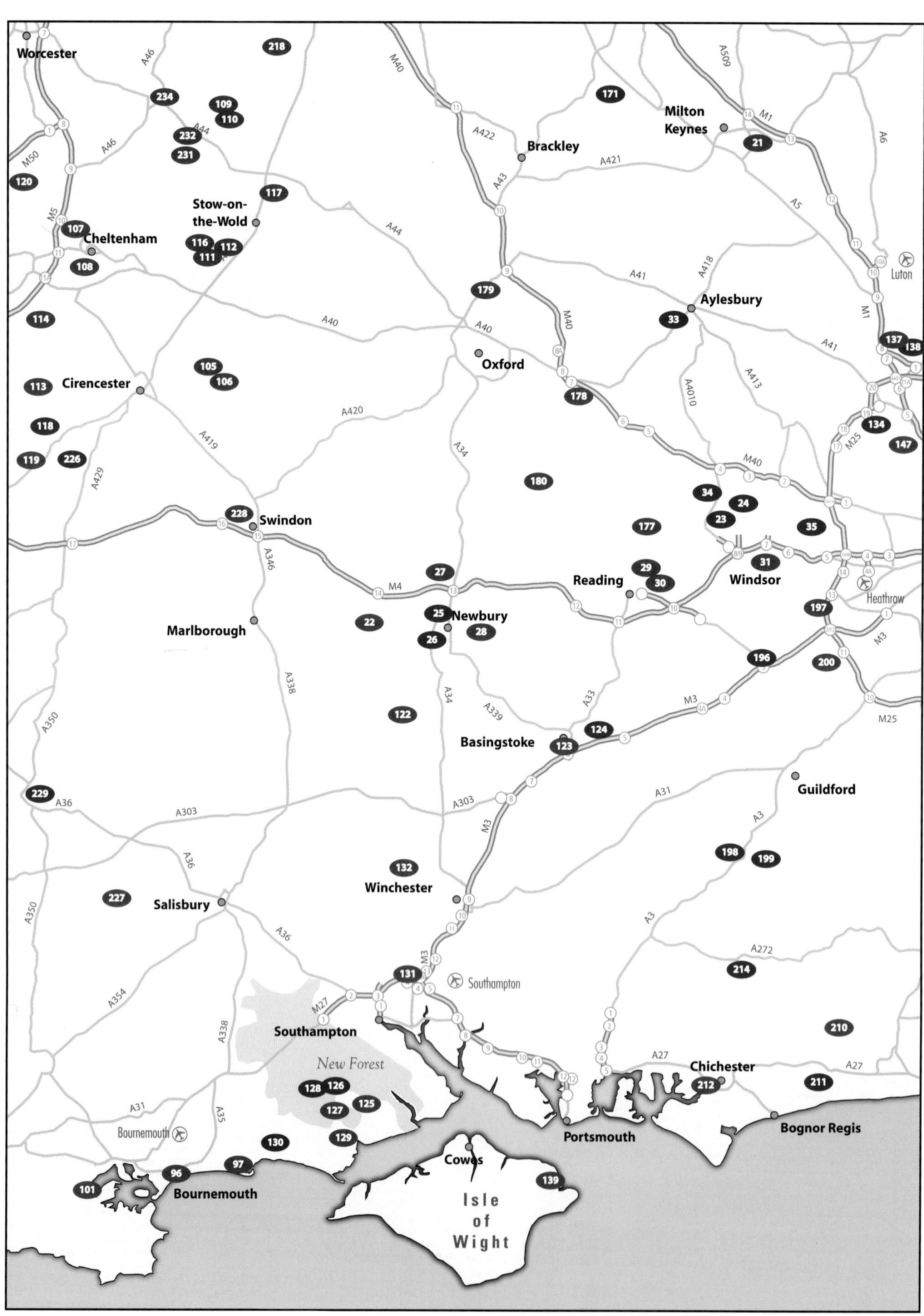

South East England

Hotel location shown in red (hotel) or purple (spa hotel) with page number

LONDON

Hotel location shown in red (hotel) or purple (spa hotel) with page number

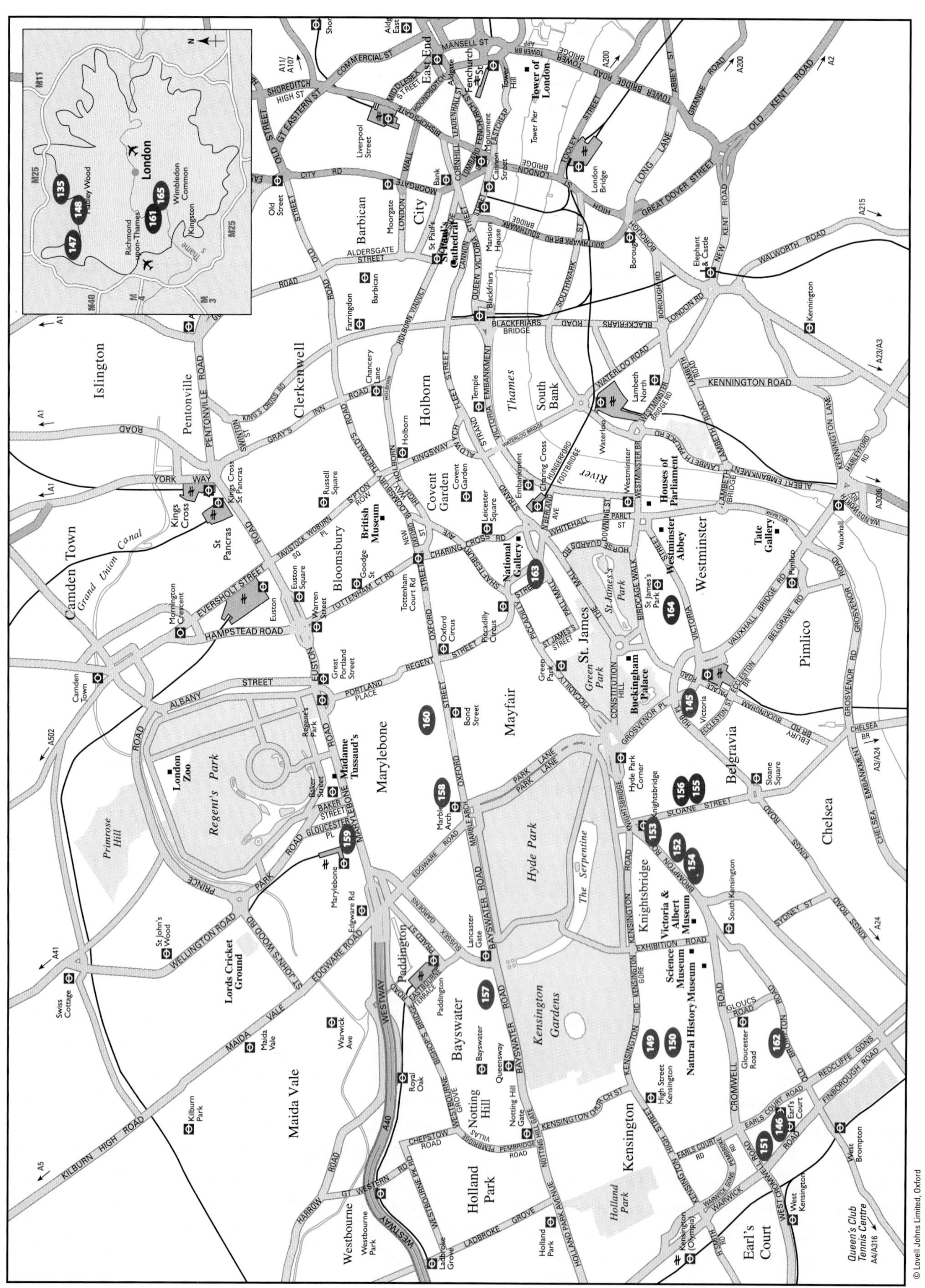

IRELAND

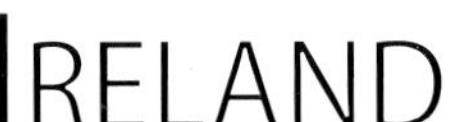

Hotel location shown in red (hotel) or purple (spa hotel) with page number

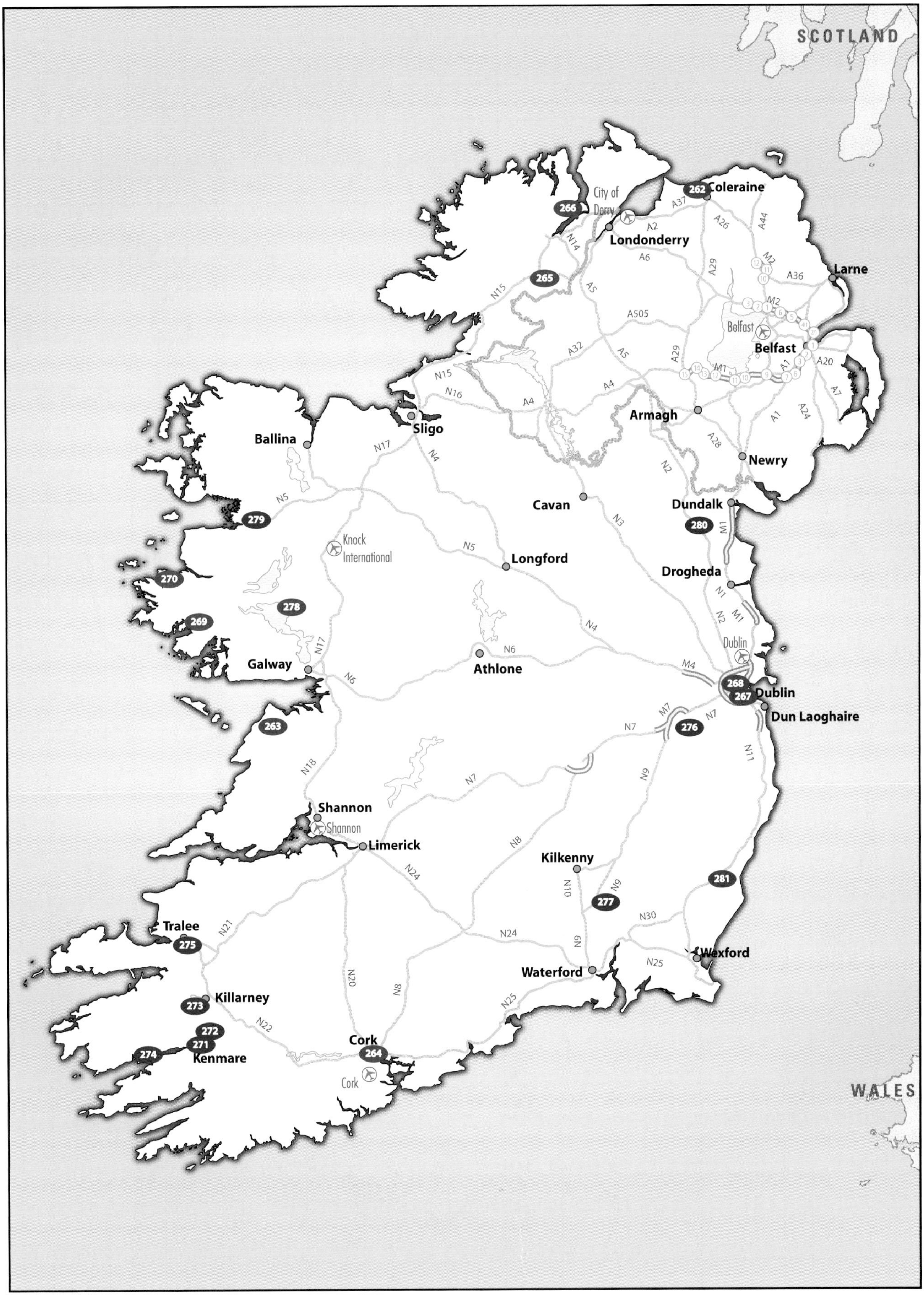

SCOTLAND
WALES
Coleraine
262
City of Derry
266
Londonderry
265
Larne
Belfast
Armagh
Newry
Ballina
Sligo
Cavan
Dundalk
280
279
Knock International
Longford
Drogheda
270
278
269
Dublin
Galway
Athlone
268
267
Dun Laoghaire
263
276
Shannon
Limerick
Kilkenny
281
277
Tralee
275
Wexford
Waterford
Killarney
273
272
271
274
Kenmare
Cork
264
N15
N16
N17
N4
N5
N6
N7
N8
N9
N10
N11
N14
N18
N20
N21
N22
N24
N25
N30
N1
N2
N3
M1
M2
M4
M7
A1
A2
A4
A5
A6
A7
A20
A24
A26
A28
A29
A32
A36
A37
A44
A505

SCOTLAND

Hotel location shown in red (hotel) or purple (spa hotel) with page number

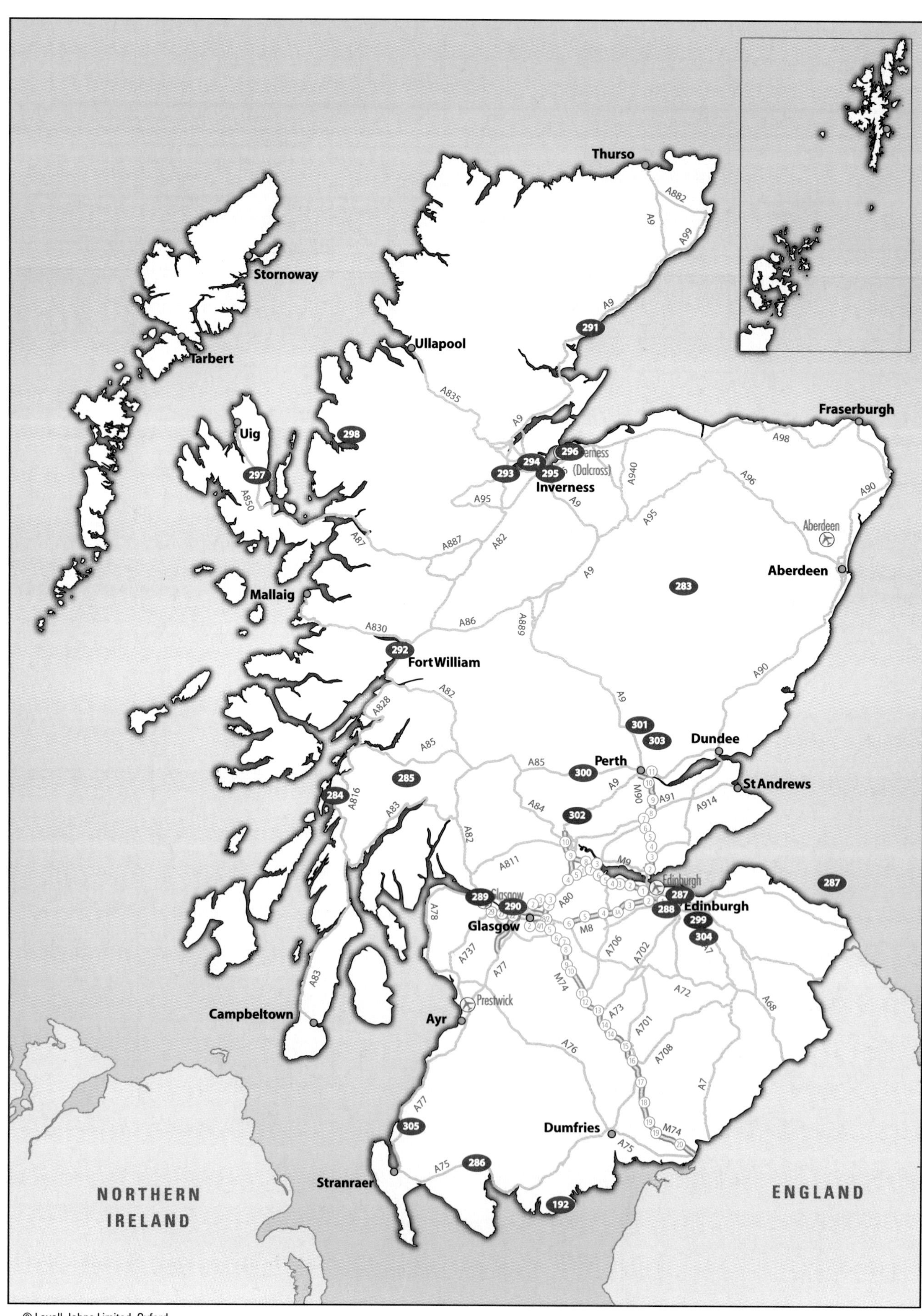

Wales

Hotel location shown in red (hotel) or purple (spa hotel) with page number

CHÂTEAU CHEVAL BLANC
1er Grand Cru Classé
1998
St Emilion Grand Cru
APPELLATION SAINT-ÉMILION GRAND CRU CONTRÔLÉE
Mis en bouteille au Château
St CIVILE DU CHEVAL BLANC
PROPRIETAIRE A ST-EMILION (GIRONDE) FRANCE
HILDON
NATURAL MINERAL WATER
ESTABLISHED
1989
HILDON
AN ENGLISH
NATURAL MINERAL WATER
OF EXCEPTIONAL TASTE
DELIGHTFULLY STILL
The King and I

GUIDE ORDER FORM

Up to £20 off when you order more than one Guide...

Order 4 Guides get £20 off, 3 Guides get £10 off, 2 Guides £5 off

Hotels & Spas
Great Britain & Ireland
£19.95

QUANTITY [ ] £ [ ]

Country Houses, Small Hotels
Inns & Restaurants, Great
Britain & Ireland - £16.95

QUANTITY [ ] £ [ ]

Hotels & Spas
Europe & Mediterranean
£19.95

QUANTITY [ ] £ [ ]

Hotels, Inns, Resorts & Spas
The Americas, Atlantic,
Caribbean, Pacific - £17.95

QUANTITY [ ] £ [ ]

Business Venues
(published Feb 2007)
£25.00

QUANTITY [ ] £ [ ]

Save over £44 when you order the **The International Collection...**

The International Collection
£75.00

QUANTITY [ ] £ [ ]

a boxed presentation set of the 4 leisure Guides,

PLUS the Business Venues Guide,

PLUS our exclusive silver-plated luggage tag.

A great offer for only £75 *(RRP £119.80)*

(silver-plated luggage tag RRP £15, presentation box RRP£5)

DISCOUNT - Discount does not apply to The International Collection 2 Guides = £5 off ☐ 3 Guides = £10 off ☐ 4 Guides = £20 off ☐

PACKING & DELIVERY - All UK Orders add £4.99 (Outside UK add £6 (per Guide) or £25 for The International Collection) £

GRAND TOTAL - Don't forget to deduct your discount £

☐ I enclose a cheque payable to Condé Nast Johansens

☐ Please charge my Visa/Mastercard/Amex/Switch/Maestro Card No.:

Card Security Code: Exp. Date: Issue No. (Switch/Maestro only): Start Date:

The **Card Security Code** is the last 3 digits of the number shown above the signature strip on the reverse side of the credit card.
For Amex, the 4 digit code is printed on the front of the card just above and to the right of your main credit card number.

Name: Signature:

Address:

Postcode: Tel: E-mail:

Please tick if you would like to receive information or offers from The Condé Nast Publications Ltd by telephone ☐ or SMS ☐ or E-mail ☐
Please tick if you would like to receive information or offers from other selected companies by telephone ☐ or SMS ☐ or E-mail ☐
Please tick this box if you prefer not to receive direct mail from The Condé Nast Publications Ltd ☐ and other reputable companies ☐

Mail to Condé Nast Johansens, FREEPOST (CB264), Eastbourne, BN23 6ZW (no stamp required)
or fax your order to 01323 649 350 or register online at www.cnjguides.co.uk quoting the reference below

CALL OUR HOTLINE NOW ON FREEPHONE 0800 269 397
OR ORDER ONLINE AT www.cnjguides.co.uk ref: K006

GUEST SURVEY REPORT

Evaluate your stay in a Condé Nast Johansens Recommendation

Following your stay in a Condé Nast Johansens Recommendation, please spare a moment to complete this Guest Survey Report. This is an important source of information for Condé Nast Johansens, in order to maintain the highest standards for our Recommendations and to support our team of Inspectors. It is also the prime source of nominations for Condé Nast Johansens Awards for Excellence, which are held annually and include properties from all over the world that represent the finest standards and best value for money in luxury, independent travel.

Your details

Name:

Address:

Postcode:

Telephone:

E-mail:

Hotel details

Name of hotel:

Location:

Date of visit:

Your rating of the hotel

	Excellent	Good	Disappointing	Poor
Bedrooms	❍	❍	❍	❍
Public Rooms	❍	❍	❍	❍
Food/Restaurant	❍	❍	❍	❍
Service	❍	❍	❍	❍
Welcome/Friendliness	❍	❍	❍	❍
Value For Money	❍	❍	❍	❍

Any other comments

If you wish to make additional comments, please write separately to the Publisher, Condé Nast Johansens, 6-8 Old Bond Street, London W1S 4PH

Please tick if you would like to receive information or offers from The Condé Nast Publications Ltd by telephone ☐ or SMS ☐ or E-mail ☐
Please tick if you would like to receive information or offers from other selected companies by telephone ☐ or SMS ☐ or E-mail ☐

Please fax your completed survey to 0207 152 3566
or go to www.johansens.com (E-Club login) where you can complete the survey online

GUEST SURVEY REPORT

Evaluate your stay in a Condé Nast Johansens Recommendation

Following your stay in a Condé Nast Johansens Recommendation, please spare a moment to complete this Guest Survey Report. This is an important source of information for Condé Nast Johansens, in order to maintain the highest standards for our Recommendations and to support our team of Inspectors. It is also the prime source of nominations for Condé Nast Johansens Awards for Excellence, which are held annually and include properties from all over the world that represent the finest standards and best value for money in luxury, independent travel.

Your details

Name:

Address:

Postcode:

Telephone:

E-mail:

Hotel details

Name of hotel:

Location:

Date of visit:

Your rating of the hotel

	Excellent	Good	Disappointing	Poor
Bedrooms	❍	❍	❍	❍
Public Rooms	❍	❍	❍	❍
Food/Restaurant	❍	❍	❍	❍
Service	❍	❍	❍	❍
Welcome/Friendliness	❍	❍	❍	❍
Value For Money	❍	❍	❍	❍

Any other comments

If you wish to make additional comments, please write separately to the Publisher, Condé Nast Johansens, 6-8 Old Bond Street, London W1S 4PH

Please tick if you would like to receive information or offers from The Condé Nast Publications Ltd by telephone ☐ or SMS ☐ or E-mail ☐
Please tick if you would like to receive information or offers from other selected companies by telephone ☐ or SMS ☐ or E-mail ☐

Please fax your completed survey to 0207 152 3566
or go to www.johansens.com (E-Club login) where you can complete the survey online

GUIDE ORDER FORM

Up to £20 off when you order more than one Guide...

Order 4 Guides get £20 off, 3 Guides get £10 off, 2 Guides £5 off

Hotels & Spas
Great Britain & Ireland
£19.95

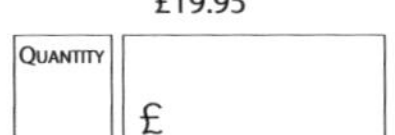

QUANTITY | £

Country Houses, Small Hotels
Inns & Restaurants, Great
Britain & Ireland - £16.95

QUANTITY | £

Hotels & Spas
Europe & Mediterranean
£19.95

QUANTITY | £

Hotels, Inns, Resorts & Spas
The Americas, Atlantic,
Caribbean, Pacific - £17.95

QUANTITY | £

Business Venues
(published Feb 2007)
£25.00

QUANTITY | £

Save over £44 when you order the **The International Collection...**

The International Collection
£75.00

QUANTITY | £

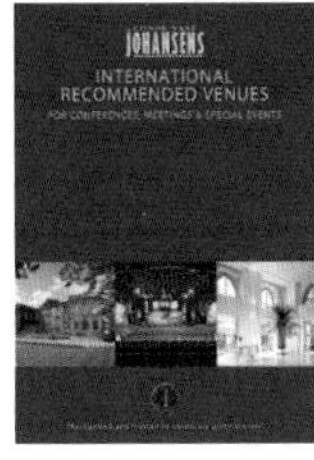

a boxed presentation set of the 4 leisure Guides,

PLUS the Business Venues Guide,

PLUS our exclusive silver-plated luggage tag.

A great offer for only £75 *(RRP £119.80)*

(silver-plated luggage tag RRP £15, presentation box RRP£5)

DISCOUNT - Discount does not apply to The International Collection 2 Guides = £5 off ☐ 3 Guides = £10 off ☐ 4 Guides = £20 off ☐

PACKING & DELIVERY - All UK Orders add £4.99 (Outside UK add £6 (per Guide) or £25 for The International Collection) £

GRAND TOTAL - Don't forget to deduct your discount £

☐ I enclose a cheque payable to Condé Nast Johansens

☐ Please charge my Visa/Mastercard/Amex/Switch/Maestro Card No.:

Card Security Code: Exp. Date: Issue No. (Switch/Maestro only): Start Date:

The **Card Security Code** is the last 3 digits of the number shown above the signature strip on the reverse side of the credit card.
For Amex, the 4 digit code is printed on the front of the card just above and to the right of your main credit card number.

Name: Signature:

Address:

Postcode: Tel: E-mail:

Please tick if you would like to receive information or offers from The Condé Nast Publications Ltd by telephone☐ or SMS☐ or E-mail☐
Please tick if you would like to receive information or offers from other selected companies by telephone☐ or SMS☐ or E-mail☐
Please tick this box if you prefer not to receive direct mail from The Condé Nast Publications Ltd ☐ and other reputable companies ☐

Mail to Condé Nast Johansens, FREEPOST (CB264), Eastbourne, BN23 6ZW (no stamp required)
or fax your order to 01323 649 350 or register online at www.cnjguides.co.uk quoting the reference below

CALL OUR HOTLINE NOW ON FREEPHONE 0800 269 397
OR ORDER ONLINE AT www.cnjguides.co.uk ref: K006

GUEST SURVEY REPORT

Evaluate your stay in a Condé Nast Johansens Recommendation

Following your stay in a Condé Nast Johansens Recommendation, please spare a moment to complete this Guest Survey Report. This is an important source of information for Condé Nast Johansens, in order to maintain the highest standards for our Recommendations and to support our team of Inspectors. It is also the prime source of nominations for Condé Nast Johansens Awards for Excellence, which are held annually and include properties from all over the world that represent the finest standards and best value for money in luxury, independent travel.

Your details

Name: __________

Address: __________

__________ Postcode: __________

Telephone: __________

E-mail: __________

Hotel details

Name of hotel: __________

Location: __________

Date of visit: __________

Your rating of the hotel

	Excellent	Good	Disappointing	Poor
Bedrooms	❍	❍	❍	❍
Public Rooms	❍	❍	❍	❍
Food/Restaurant	❍	❍	❍	❍
Service	❍	❍	❍	❍
Welcome/Friendliness	❍	❍	❍	❍
Value For Money	❍	❍	❍	❍

Any other comments

If you wish to make additional comments, please write separately to the Publisher, Condé Nast Johansens, 6-8 Old Bond Street, London W1S 4PH

____

____

Please tick if you would like to receive information or offers from The Condé Nast Publications Ltd by telephone ☐ or SMS ☐ or E-mail ☐
Please tick if you would like to receive information or offers from other selected companies by telephone ☐ or SMS ☐ or E-mail ☐

Please fax your completed survey to 0207 152 3566
or go to www.johansens.com (E-Club login) where you can complete the survey online

GUEST SURVEY REPORT

Evaluate your stay in a Condé Nast Johansens Recommendation

Following your stay in a Condé Nast Johansens Recommendation, please spare a moment to complete this Guest Survey Report. This is an important source of information for Condé Nast Johansens, in order to maintain the highest standards for our Recommendations and to support our team of Inspectors. It is also the prime source of nominations for Condé Nast Johansens Awards for Excellence, which are held annually and include properties from all over the world that represent the finest standards and best value for money in luxury, independent travel.

Your details

Name: __________

Address: __________

__________ Postcode: __________

Telephone: __________

E-mail: __________

Hotel details

Name of hotel: __________

Location: __________

Date of visit: __________

Your rating of the hotel

	Excellent	Good	Disappointing	Poor
Bedrooms	❍	❍	❍	❍
Public Rooms	❍	❍	❍	❍
Food/Restaurant	❍	❍	❍	❍
Service	❍	❍	❍	❍
Welcome/Friendliness	❍	❍	❍	❍
Value For Money	❍	❍	❍	❍

Any other comments

If you wish to make additional comments, please write separately to the Publisher, Condé Nast Johansens, 6-8 Old Bond Street, London W1S 4PH

____

____

Please tick if you would like to receive information or offers from The Condé Nast Publications Ltd by telephone ☐ or SMS ☐ or E-mail ☐
Please tick if you would like to receive information or offers from other selected companies by telephone ☐ or SMS ☐ or E-mail ☐

Please fax your completed survey to 0207 152 3566
or go to www.johansens.com (E-Club login) where you can complete the survey online